6. Outer frame first, but bottom line last.

country 冂 囩 国

sun 冂 月 日

moon 几 月 月

Note the order of ⊏ , with the left hand stroke joined to the bottom (e.g. 一 �₹ 匠).

7. Right-to-left diagonal stroke precedes left-to-right.

person 丿 人

father 丷 父

again 𠃌 又

8. Central vertical line last.

middle 口 中

vehicle 一 亘 車

thing 一 彐 事

9. Strokes which cut through come last.

woman 𡿨 女

child 了 子

boat 𦨖 舟

Note that the only exception is 世 (一 𠀋 世).

The following pointers should also be observed.

    a. squares are written with three strokes not four (丨 𠃌 口)
    b. vertical strokes should not slope (e.g. 中 not 𠁱)
    c. horizontal strokes may slope, but should be parallel (e.g. 羊)
    d. characters should be of uniform size.

A GUIDE TO REMEMBERING
JAPANESE CHARACTERS

A GUIDE TO REMEMBERING JAPANESE CHARACTERS

by Kenneth G. Henshall

CHARLES E. TUTTLE COMPANY
Rutland, Vermont & Tokyo, Japan

Published by the Charles E. Tuttle Company, Inc.
of Rutland, Vermont & Tokyo, Japan
with editorial offices at
Suido 1-chome, 2–6, Bunkyo-ku, Tokyo 112

Library of Congress Catalog Card No. 88–50325
International Standard Book No. 0–8048–1532–1

First edition, 1988
Sixth printing, 1992

Printed in Japan

CONTENTS

CONTENTS

ACKNOWLEDGEMENTS

I am greatly indebted to Tomoko Aoyama, of the Japanese Studies Unit of the University of Western Australia, for the calligraphy in this book. I am also greatly indebted to Professor Jim Everett, of the Department of Management, University of Western Australia, for his invaluable technical guidance in the computer-assisted preparation of camera-ready copy. In addition, my thanks are due to the Charles E. Tuttle Company for their guidance and support, and to my wife Carole for her many hours of proofreading.

In the research for this book I have been especially guided by the work of three of Japan's most highly regarded scholars in the field of kanji etymology, namely Tsunekata Kato, Katsumi Yamada, and Hideyuki Shindo. Those readers wishing to pursue further study of kanji are recommended to consult in particular their joint work <u>Jigen Jiten</u> (Etymological Dictionary of Kanji, Kadokawa, Tokyo, 2nd edition 1985), together with Katsumi Yamada's <u>Kanji no Gogen</u> (The Etymology of Kanji, Kadokawa, Tokyo, 1976).

With regard to stroke count, and in some cases arrangement of characters within a given grade, I have been guided by the reference work <u>Kanji Kakijun Jiten</u> (Dictionary of Kanji Stroke Order, edited by Hiroshi Fujiwara, Daiichi Hoki Publishing, Tokyo, revised edition 1982).

British spelling has been retained throughout.

PREFACE

The main aim of this book is to help students of the Japanese language overcome the obstacle presented by characters -- or kanji, to use the Japanese term. Without a sound knowledge of kanji it is impossible to acquire a proper command of the language, and yet so many students seem to spend years gaining merely a vague knowledge of no more than a few hundred of the two thousand kanji in general use. For every one student who feels confident in reading and writing kanji, there are dozens who seem daunted and full of despair.

For students accustomed to Western writing systems kanji can indeed be a daunting proposition. Mastering the twenty-six simple symbols in the English alphabet, even allowing for difficulties with their pronunciation, seems like child's play compared with tackling two thousand kanji of up to twenty or so strokes. It should be realised that there is no magic way to set about this task. Even Japanese nationals themselves often have problems learning and remembering kanji, despite the great advantage of constant exposure. There are, however, ways to make the task a lot easier.

I believe that for Western students the key to successful study of kanji lies not in rote learning, as favored by the Japanese themselves, but in breaking down the barrier of unfamiliarity. Once one can appreciate how a character is made up, how it acquired its shape and how and why it came into existence, then one is a long way towards achieving this end. Something that is understood and therefore familiar is far less daunting than something unknown, and far more easily remembered. A character that once seemed merely a lifeless and anonymous jumble of lines and dots becomes a 'character' in a different sense; that is, with a distinctive personality of its own.

Once a character is essentially understood, the proper use of mnemonics (memory aids) is a useful adjunct, though for the serious scholar it can be misleading to rely on mnemonics alone. That is, there is no harm in a student remembering the character used for 'east' (see # 184) by conveniently interpreting its elements as the sun rising behind a tree, provided the student also remembers that that is not the real meaning. Misunderstanding the origin of a character or element can in some cases lead to serious misconceptions regarding its connotations, its role in compounds, and its role as a window on the society of the day.

In this book I have explained the origin and subsequent evolution of each of the characters in general use, and where relevant have given the ancient forms. There are a few cases where the exact origin is obscure, and here, after clearly stating that the character is obscure, I have given the most authoritative theories and occasionally some thoughts of my own. I have also made frequent reference to Chinese character usage, since the kanji are -- with a handful of exceptions -- Chinese in origin (see Introduction). The elements forming each character are analysed and explained in detail, with cross-referencing to indicate where a recurring element is first introduced. Where relevant I have also added socio-historical comment to clarify the meaning and role of a character. Each character's usage is illustrated by three compound terms, alongside its modern readings and meanings. At the end of each explanation I have given a suggested mnemonic using the key elements in that character. Where possible I have tried in the mnemonic to use the elements in exactly the same way that they are used in the character itself, but since so many characters have changed their original meaning due to borrowing and/or miscopying this is usually not feasible. The suggested mnemonics are ones which I personally have found useful, but each reader may prefer to make up their own.

The characters are listed systematically in the order determined by the Japanese Ministry of Education (see Introduction). That is, the first 996 kanji, the so-called Educational Kanji which are prescribed for the six grades of elementary school, are set out in their respective grades (76 for Grade One, 145 for Grade Two, etc. etc.), followed by the remaining 949. Since these gradings approximately correspond to frequency of usage, the reader who wishes to learn only a few hundred kanji will be able to concentrate on the early grades confident in the knowledge that these will contain the most useful characters.

In the course of explaining the kanji in general use it has often been necessary to refer to characters outside the general use category, as well as to characters found in Chinese but to all intents and purposes no longer used in Japanese. For the reader's convenience I have listed these in an index under stroke count. The general use kanji are listed in both a stroke count index and a readings index. I have also added an appendix of the key elements found in kanji, and for the reader's interest an appendix showing the characters from which the two kana syllabaries have evolved. In the Introduction I have briefly outlined the history, structure, and types of kanji, together with a guide to general principles of stroke order. Following the Introduction there are Explanatory Notes which clarify the conventions and terms used in the text. The reader should consult both the Introduction and the Explanatory Notes before proceeding to the main text.

It is my hope and belief that the book will be of value not only to students tackling the entire corpus of the Japanese language, but also to those with more moderate aims, such as secondary students with a target of just two or three hundred kanji and private individuals wishing for an introduction to the Japanese writing system. In all cases, I will be happy if the book goes some way towards removing the mystique surrounding kanji.

K. G. Henshall,
Perth, Australia,
February 1988

INTRODUCTION

The History of Kanji

The characters from which kanji are ultimately derived originated between 2000 - 1500 B.C. in the Yellow River region of China. About 3000 characters have been discovered from this early period, mostly inscribed on bones and tortoise shells and often connected with divination. At the outset they were mostly simple pictographs, but with the passage of time became increasingly complex and abstract. Pictographs were combined to form ideographs, symbolic characters were also devised, and, as standardisation of form started to prevail, certain characters also acquired a more or less fixed phonetic role (see Types of Kanji below). A considerable degree of standardisation is evident in highly stylised characters from the third century B.C., while the square style forming the real prototype of today's characters (known in Japanese as kaisho 楷書) was established by about 200 A.D. By this stage the number of characters had grown to approximately 50,000.

Characters were first brought to Japan around the third or fourth century A.D. by migrating Chinese and Koreans, and became established during the following four centuries. (The word kanji 漢字 means literally 'symbols from Han China', the Han Period extending from 206 B.C. to 220 A.D.) At that stage the Japanese language existed only in spoken form, and Chinese characters were borrowed to enable it to be expressed in writing. For example, the Chinese character for mother, 母, pronounced BO (for the sake of illustration: its actual pronunciation at the time was different) was used to express the spoken Japanese word for mother, pronounced haha. Its own Chinese pronunciation also entered the Japanese language, and was generally favored in compounds. Thus many compounds using 母 take its Chinese reading of BO, such as BOSEI 母性(motherhood) and BOKOKU母国 (mother country). The Chinese reading is known as the on reading and the Japanese reading the kun reading. KOKU 国 of BOKOKU above is, as a further example, the on reading of the character for country, which has a kun reading of kuni. (Note that the convention usually followed is to romanise on readings in upper case and kun readings in lower case.)

As seen from the above examples, the adoption of the Chinese script presented no particular problems with simple lexical items and indeed contributed to the enrichment of the Japanese language, leading to the formation of many new terms (especially compounds) and in some cases new concepts and modes of expression. Its role has often been likened to that of Latin in the case of English. However, as a result of fundamental differences between the monosyllabic Chinese language and the polysyllabic, highly inflected Japanese language, the Chinese writing system proved decidedly unsuitable in the case of inflected items such as verbs. In practice a principal character was used for its meaning to represent the stem of a Japanese verb of similar meaning, while other characters were used for their sound to represent the variable ending of the verb. The potential for confusion was obviously considerable, even more so in view of the fact that a whole range of characters could be used to express a given sound, and it became necessary to use various methods to distinguish between the semantic characters and the phonetic characters. At one stage, for example, the latter were written smaller and/or to one side (script being vertical). Eventually, by about the ninth century, standardised characters used as phonetics were simplified into syllabaries known as kana (仮名 : literally 'assumed names'). There are two such syllabaries: hiragana, which generally derives from highly stylised cursive forms of full characters, and katakana, which generally uses just one part of a character (see Kana Appendix). Katakana symbols are now used primarily for expressing words borrowed from English or other Western languages, and hiragana used for inflections. For example, the Japanese verb meaning to go, iku, uses the Chinese character with that meaning, 行 (see # 118), to express its unchangeable stem i-. -ku is then expressed by means of hiragana, giving 行く. Not go, ikanai, is written with the kana symbols for ka, na, and i, giving 行かない. Thus i- is the principal <u>kun</u> reading of 行, while its <u>on</u> readings -- usually KŌ or GYŌ -- are generally used in compounds, e.g. ryokō 旅行 meaning travel.

Over the ensuing centuries the characters brought into Japan evolved in their own particular way, acquiring nuances and connotations not necessarily found in Chinese, and in most cases undergoing phonetic modification. Many characters were borrowed for their sound to express entirely different meanings, and in not a few cases miscopying also led to the acquisition of new meanings. Periods of renewed contact with China, such as around the ninth and thirteenth centuries, also tended to bring newly evolved Chinese readings and meanings, and thus the potential range of meanings and readings for any one character became quite considerable. The typical kanji now has two or three <u>on</u> readings and two or three <u>kun</u> readings, while some of the commoner kanji, such as life 生 42 and below 下 7, can have as many as ten fundamentally different readings. Not all readings are in common use, however. In a handful of cases new characters were created in Japan using Chinese elements, such as dry field 畑 369 and frame 枠 1943, and some of these have since been borrowed for use in Chinese (such as work 働 558). These 'made in Japan' characters usually -- but not necessarily -- have <u>kun</u> readings only.

Shortly after the end of World War Two the Japanese Ministry of Education attempted to rationalise the characters used in Japan by designating 1850 of them as the Tōyō Kanji 当用漢字(literally 'Temporary Use Kanji'), which were felt to represent the commonest and most important of the kanji. Of these 1850, 881 were designated as Kyōiku Kanji 教育漢字 (Educational Kanji), these being seen as particularly important and forming the basic requirement for the six years of elementary education. Accordingly the Kyōiku Kanji were divided into six grades to correspond to the elementary grades, with the grading also approximately corresponding to frequency of usage and/or degree of importance (though certain anomalies do appear to exist, such as in the omission of the characters for differ 違 1006 and sharp/ bitter 辛 1432). Readings were also prescribed, including the point in the syllabus at which a particular reading should be taught.

Theoretically no characters outside the Tōyō Kanji were supposed to be used except in proper nouns (for which there were an additional 92 approved characters in the case of personal names) and special circumstances such as the writing of literature. However, in practice these limitations were not infrequently ignored, and persons or companies involved in work related to printing and publishing sometimes appear to have followed their own guidelines. In this regard it might be of interest to the reader to note that a Japanese typewriter produced by a well known manufacturer as late as 1979 has, while containing several thousand characters, omitted no fewer than 35 of the Tōyō Kanji from its standard range (a fact which has caused considerable inconvenience in the preparation of the manuscript for this book!). The same typewriter also uses a number of old and variant forms, which is similarly not in keeping with the guidelines for the Tōyō Kanji.

In 1981 a revision of the Tōyō Kanji took place, resulting in the establishment of the Jōyō Kanji 常用漢字(which can be interpreted either as 'General Use Kanji' or 'Permanent Use Kanji'). The Jōyō Kanji comprise 1945 characters, of which 996 are designated as Kyōiku Kanji (the six grades containing 76, 145, 195, 195, 195, and 190 kanji respectively). However, the reader should still be prepared to encounter occasional characters outside the prescribed range.

<u>Types of Kanji</u>

Since as early as the second century A.D., when the first Chinese dictionary was produced, characters have traditionally been classified into six categories. However, in many cases the categorisation is open to difference of opinion, and similarly in many cases one character can legitimately belong to more than one category. Moreover, the categories are of questionable validity as classifications since they are based upon different criteria, the first four relating to character composition while the other two relate to character usage. In practice these traditional categories are unimportant to all but the specialist scholar, and may even be misleading. They are listed below for the reader's convenience, and do shed considerable light on the nature of kanji, but at the same time the reader should treat the the categories per se as no more than rough guides.

1. **The Pictograph** (象形文字 Shōkei Moji). Essentially a picture of a physical object, and usually quite simple. For example, tree 木 69 (from 米), or eye 目 72 (from ∅). Some of these have become highly stylised and to all intents and purposes unrecognisable as pictographs, such as horse 馬 191 (from 𤲰) or woman 女 35 (from 𡚼). Some have also been turned on their axis, such as moon 月 16 (from 𝒟).

2. **The Sign** or **Symbol** (指事文字 Shiji Moji). Essentially a symbol expressing an abstract concept, and usually quite simple. For example, above 上 37 (from 二) or rotational motion 回 86 (from ℮). There is some confusion as to whether certain characters are symbols or pictographs, with considerable evidence of miscategorisation. For example, one 一 1 is treated by many scholars as a symbol, but in fact it seems more appropriate to treat it as a pictograph, since it originally depicted a single finger.

3. **The Ideograph** (会意文字 Kaii Moji). Essentially a meaningful combination of two or more pictographs or symbols, and usually quite simple. For example, mountain pass 峠 1663, combining up 上 37, down 下 7, and mountain 山 24. See servant 僕 1820 for an unusually complex example, made more so by a high degree of stylisation. In many cases the ideograph category has a considerable overlap with the semasio-phonetic category (see 4 below).

4. **The Phonetic-Ideograph** or **Semasio-Phonetic** (形声文字 Keisei Moji). The largest of the categories, theoretically containing about 85% of all the characters, but at the same time a rather confused one. Essentially a combination of a semantic element with a phonetic element, the former usually indicating the general nature of the item to be represented and the latter usually giving more specific information by lending its sound to express the pronunciation of a descriptive word (which word typically has a character of its own too complex to be used easily in combination). For example, pour 注 344 has a semantic element water 氵 40, and a phonetic element 主 299 which expresses the sound of a word meaning continuous (specifically continue 続 536, both 536 and 299 having the same pronunciation at the time). Thus continuous (flow of) water, a reference to pouring. Since it could also be said that at the same time 主 necessarily acts phonetically to express the word pour itself, there is clearly an etymological link between pour and continui-

ty, and thus an analysis of semasio-phonetic characters sheds considerable light on the etymology of words and not just characters (cf. similar etymological/ phonetic links in English between birch, beech, bark, book etc.).

The element used as a phonetic was usually chosen from a range of similarly pronounced characters on the basis of its also lending relevant semantic connotations of its own. In the case of the example above it is almost certain that 主 was chosen as the phonetic because its original meaning was long stemmed lamp, thus suggesting connotations of column and hence column of water, thereby reinforcing the idea of continuous flow of water. Thus it is also possible to consider such semasio-phonetics as ideographs, and whether they are categorised as ideographs or semasio-phonetics then becomes a matter of degree, i.e. depending on whether the semantic role is felt to outweigh the phonetic or vice-versa. In the case of pour 注 it is clear that the sound is the more important and thus it is classified as a semasio-phonetic, but classification is not always so easy. The matter is made more complex since even in the case of seemingly obvious ideographs one of the elements also lends its sound, and could therefore be said to be a phonetic element expressing its own meaning through its own sound. For example, blind 盲 1852 combines die 亡 973 and eye 目 72, and is treated in this book as an ideograph meaning dead eyes. However, some scholars make out a case that it is technically a semasio-phonetic, with 亡 acting phonetically to express die and thus giving the same result of dead eyes.

This treatment of seemingly obvious ideographs as semasio-phonetics may seem unnecessarily complex, and in this book has been avoided where at all possible. However, the problem in attempting to attribute a semantic role to a phonetic element is that the present-day scholar is frequently reduced to speculation, since most of the principal ancient sources used in etymological research (such as the writings of the tenth century scholar Jokai 徐鍇) generally tend to state the phonetic role of an element but do not necessarily refer to any semantic role. The reason for this is not clear, since some of the characters treated as semasio-phonetics in Jokai's writings are treated as ideographs in still earlier writings. As a result of this relative wealth of information regarding phonetic roles the present-day scholar can be sure that, despite enormously convoluted changes in pronunciation over the centuries (for example en changing by degrees to soku and shi changing to ten), at a given point in time a particular element had a particular reading and served a particular phonetic role. With regard to semantic role, however, from today's perspective it is not at all easy to know with certainty what particular meaning an element had at a given point in time two thousand or more years ago (such as for instance at what precise point in time long stemmed lamp 主 in the example above ceased to mean long stemmed lamp and came to mean master). Thus in most cases comments regarding semantic roles must be expressed with varying degrees of tentativeness and qualification.

Some of the simpler elements do appear to have been used purely as phonetics in some cases, such as 工 113 in nape of neck 項 1262 (expressing rear/back, in place of 後 111), but in general one must reasonably assume that any element with more than a few strokes was chosen for its connotations as well as its sound. If this were not the case, one would surely see a more or less fixed pattern in which a given sound was expressed by the same (simple) element. One can however only ever say 'more or less fixed', since there is evidence to suggest that in some cases complex characters were chosen as a phonetic despite their complexity, or even because of it, in order to display erudition and/or to lend a degree of visual substance or elegance to a character. (See also borrowings in Category 5 below.)

A further type of semasio-phonetic which is treated by some scholars as a distinct category is the onomatopoeic character. For example, in the case of mosquito 蚊 1056 the element 文 68 is used purely for its sound BUN, combining with insect 虫 56 to give 'insect that makes a BUN sound'. There are only a few of these onomatopoeic characters, however.

5. **Characters of borrowed meaning and pronunciation** (轉注文字 Tenchū Moji). A rather vague category which has never been properly defined, but essentially kanji whose meanings and/or pronunciations have changed as a result of borrowing. Some scholars take the category to include extended and associated meanings, while others restrict it simply to pure borrowings. Since the majority of characters have undergone some change of meaning, now often displaying extended or associated meanings in addition to or in place of their original meanings (such as a sword meaning by association to cut -- see 181), and since a very large number have also experienced a change of pronunciation, any category based upon such changes is now in effect pointless, though it may have had some relevance in the second century.

The confusing vagueness of the category is perhaps typified by the fact that it is traditionally illustrated by the character for music and enjoyment 楽 218, which is popularly said to have pictographically depicted a drum and then to have acquired its present meanings by association and/or borrowing. This is a very poor example since in fact the character is not a pictograph at all, but essentially an ideograph which originally meant oak tree, and it is not really clear how it came by its present meanings. Nevertheless, it still serves as an example of how a character can acquire new meanings and pronunciations, though not for the reasons popularly cited. A better example is 占 1491, which originally meant divination but has now also acquired a major meaning of occupy as a result of its being used instead of a similarly pronounced but more complex character of that meaning (in very similar fashion to many of the phonetic elements in the semasio-phonetic characters of Category 4). See domination 覇 1683 for an example of a rare case where a more complex character was deliberately borrowed.

6. Phonetically borrowed characters (仮借文字 Kasha Moji or Kashaku Moji). Somewhat confused with the preceding category, but essentially characters borrowed phonetically in what is in effect a kanji alphabet (in that sense very similar to the origins of the kana syllabaries). For example, the four kanji used to express one syllable each of A-me-ri-ca, namely 亜米利加.

In addition to the above six categories, some scholars treat as a seventh category the dozen or so characters made in Japan, known as Kokuji (国字, literally National Characters). They are mostly ideographic, as for example mountain pass 峠 used to illustrate Category 3, but do include extremely unusual characters such as monme 匁 1858, which is a strange graphic amalgam devised for phonetic reasons and does not readily fit into any recognised category.

<u>The Structure of Kanji</u>

Though some of the simpler kanji, such as the pictographs and symbols seen in Categories 1 and 2 above, are essentially single element characters, most kanji comprise two or more elements. In almost all cases there is one key element, known as the radical, which indicates the general nature of the character . This radical combines with one or more other elements which give more specific information, either semantically or phonetically (see Categories 3 and 4 above). For example, earth 土 60 is often used as a radical, usually at the bottom of the composite character or in slightly stylised form 扌 on the left, and indicates that the character relates in some way to earth, or soil, or ground (though its present meanings may have changed through borrowing or extension). For example, 城 903 originally meant earthen ramparts and now means castle (成 primarily acting phonetically to express pile up), while 型 468 originally meant a clay mold and now usually means model in a broad sense (刑 primarily acting phonetically to express make). There are about two hundred of these radicals, most of which are listed in the Elements Appendix towards the end of this book. Most character dictionaries list their characters under radicals, but unfortunately such listings can be misleading from an etymological point of view as they sometimes use graphic similarity as an expedient. For example, leave 去 258 is listed in many dictionaries under the earth radical 土 due to the presence of the shape 土, but in fact 土 derives from a double lid 太 and has nothing to do with earth.

introduction

There are seven basic positions in which a radical can be used, as listed below.

1. On the left (hen or -ben). For example, person イ 39 in rank 位 421 (combining with standing person 立 73 to give person standing in position in a line), or tree/ wood 木 69 in timber 材 485 (in which 才 primarily acts phonetically to express cut down). Person on the left is known as ninben and tree/ wood on the left is known as kihen.

2. On the right (tsukuri or -zukuri). For example, sword/ cut 刂 181 in divide 割 823 (with 害 primarily acting phonetically to express dismember), or strike/ coerce 攵 101 in government 政 724 (combining with correct 正 41 to give an original meaning of enforce correctness/ make correct). Sword on the right is known by the special term rittō ('standing sword'), while strike/ force on the right is known as bokuzukuri (boku meaning strike).

3. On the top or crown (kanmuri). For example, bamboo 竹 170 in pipe/ tube 管 443 (in which 官 primarily acts phonetically to express pierce), or hole 穴 849 in sky/ space 空 15 (with 工 primarily acting phonetically to express open). Bamboo crown is known as take kanmuri and hole crown is known as ana kanmuri.

4. At the base or foot (ashi or shita-). For example, heart/ feelings 心 147 in endure 忍 1677 (in which blade 刃 1446 acts phonetically to express bear and also lends connotations of something painful), or fire 灬 8 in fierce/ intense 烈 1929 (in which 列 primarily acts phonetically to express destroy, to give an original meaning of destructive fire). Heart at the base is known as shitagokoro, while fire at the base is known by the special term rekka ('fire in a row').

5. The outside or frame (kamae or -gamae). For example, enclosure 囗 123 in country 国 123 (with 玉 being a simplification of delineated area 或 809), or gate 門 211 in space 間 92 (combining with sunlight 日 62), or container 匚 225 in craftsman 匠 1388 (combining with ax 斤 1176 to give an original meaning of tool box). Enclosure frame is known as kunigamae, gate frame is known as kadogamae, and container frame is known as kakushigamae ('hiding frame').

6. Hanging or trailing (tare or -dare). For example, building 广 114 in store 店 178 (in which 占 primarily acts phonetically to express display), or sickness 疒 381 in epidemic 疫 1019 (combining with strike 殳 153). Hanging building is known as madare (being named after the character hemp [pronounced ma] 麻 1829), while hanging sickness is known as yamaidare.

7. L-shaped (nyō). For example, movement 辶 129 in advance 進 326 (combining with bird 隹 216 to give move like a bird, i.e. forwards), or run 走 161 in proceed 赴 1751 (with ⼘ acting phonetically to express announce and giving an original meaning of run to announce something). L-shaped movement is known as shinnyō or shinnyū, while L-shaped run is known as sōnyō.

Of these seven basic positions, on the left (hen) is the most common.

<u>General Principles of Stroke Order</u>

Though there are inevitably a number of exceptions, most characters are written according to established principles of stroke order. A knowledge of these principles is important in order to achieve the proper shape and to write in the cursive style or semi-cursive style, in which normally separate strokes flow into one another. The basic principles listed below were issued by the Ministry of Education in 1958, and are considered the most authoritative. The guidelines apply either to individual strokes or to the arrangement of component elements as the case may be. The first two are especially important.

1. Top to bottom.

three 23

word 274

guest 252

2. Left to right.

province 304

faction 955

example 605

3. Horizontal strokes usually precede vertical strokes when crossing.

ten 33

earth 60 　一 十 土

till 673 　三 丰 耒 耒 耕

4. However, in a few cases vertical strokes precede horizontal ones.

king 5 　一 丁 干 王

field 59 　冂 冂 田 田

bend 261 　冂 曲 曲 曲

5. Center usually precedes right and left where latter do not exceed two strokes each.

small 36 　亅 小 小

water 40 　亅 刁 水 水

receive 713 　了 手 手 承 承

Note that the two exceptions are the heart radical 忄 (丶 忄) and fire 火 (丶 火).

6. Outer frame first, but bottom line last.

country 123 　冂 国 国

sun 62 　冂 円 日

moon 16 　几 月 月

Note the order of 匚 , with the left hand stroke joined to the bottom (e.g. 一 万 匠).

7. Right-to-left diagonal stroke precedes left-to-right.

person 39 　丿 人

father 197 　丷 父

again 1835 　ス 又

8. Central vertical line last.

middle 55 　口 中

vehicle 31 　一 亘 車

thing 293 　一 冒 事

9. Strokes which cut through come last.

woman 35 　く 女

child 25 　了 子

boat 1354 　门 舟

Note that the only exception is 世 (一 せ 世).

The following pointers should also be observed.

a. squares are written with three strokes not four (｜ 冂 口)

b. vertical strokes should not slope (e.g. 中 not 屮)

c. horizontal strokes may slope, but should be parallel (e.g. 羊)

d. characters should be of uniform size.

EXPLANATORY NOTES

Characters are set out according to the conventions established by the Ministry of Education, that is with the first 996 characters (the Kyōiku Kanji or Educational Kanji) divided into six grades corresponding to the six grades of elementary school, followed by the remaining 949. There is slight potential for confusion in that the latter are usually referred to as general use kanji, while General Use Kanji is also the generic term for the whole set of 1945 characters comprising the Jōyō Kanji.

Within each grade characters are arranged in the gojūonjun (a-i-u-e-o order) according to their principal reading, with a 'hard' sound following the unmodified sound (e.g. GA after KA, JI after SHI). Where two or more characters within a given grade share the same reading they are listed in ascending order according to their stroke count. Where characters in a given grade share both the same readings and the same stroke count there is no real convention regarding order, and this book has simply followed the order of printing in Ministry of Education lists. <u>On</u> readings take precedence over <u>kun</u> readings of the same sound. That is, the 15 stroke KA 樣 (1055) comes after the 14 stroke KA 箇 (1054) but before the 10 stroke ka 蚊 (1056) . Principal readings are usually <u>on</u>, but not necessarily so (e.g. ka 蚊 above, which is listed under its <u>kun</u> reading ka but also has an <u>on</u> reading BUN).

There are a few dozen characters which are the subject of difference of opinion as to which of their readings is the principal one, and accordingly kanji lists arranged by some scholars do not neccessarily follow the same order as the Ministry of Education lists (though gradings etc. are unaffected). After surveying a range of such lists I have made the following six alterations to the order given in the Ministry of Education lists: 樂 218 listed under RAKU not GAKU; 象 533 under ZŌ not SHŌ; 治 544 under CHI not JI; 興 652 under KYŌ not KŌ; 率 803 under RITSU not SOTSU; and 矢 981 under its <u>kun</u> reading ya not its <u>on</u> reading SHI. I have also made a number of alterations which do not affect order, such as listing 大 53 as TAI, DAI rather than DAI, TAI. The Ministry of Education recognises the right of scholars to make such alterations to arrangement within a given grade and in no way claims its own arrangement to be definitive. No alteration should be made to actual gradings themselves, however.

<u>On</u> readings are given in upper case, <u>kun</u> readings in lower case. Word stems are given in bold type, with italics being used to indicate variable endings (i.e. the part of the word which should be expressed in kana, known in this case as okurigana), such endings being

separated from one another by an oblique (/). The use of okurigana is very vague, and the reader should not be alarmed at the frequent discrepancy between the okurigana given in the readings block, which usually follows strict theory, and examples given in the compounds block, which usually follow actual practice. For example, jibiki (dictionary) can be written either as 字引き or 字引, though technically the former is correct. With regard to theory I have generally followed the conventions found in Ministry of Education publications, while with regard to practice I have been guided by such widely used dictionaries as Nelson's <u>Japanese-English Character Dictionary</u> (Tuttle, Tokyo, 1962) and Kenkyusha's <u>New Japanese-English Dictionary</u> (Kenkyusha, Tokyo, 4th edition 1974).

The reader should similarly expect minor graphic discrepancies between the form of the character given in brush and the typed form in the compounds block. The latter occasionally uses slightly old forms (e.g. 挾 for 挟 1165) or even variant forms (e.g. with upturned dish 西 instead of west 西 in the case of 覇 1683, though it should be noted that even the more usual west 西 is in any case a simplification/ variant of rain 雨). Since these were the forms supplied with a typewriter manufactured as late as 1979 it is clear that they are still widely used, and thus the reader should be prepared to recognise them. One should similarly be prepared to encounter any form of character described in the explanation as 'formerly written.....', which usually indicates a form that was standard until shortly after World War Two, whereas forms described as 'ancient', 'still earlier', 'once written....', or 'original' are almost without exception no longer found in Japanese (though they may be in Chinese).

Characters which lie outside the General Use/ Jōyō Kanji but are still found in Japanese (usually in the Nelson dictionary cited above, which lists 5446 characters in total) are referred to in this book as NGU characters, standing for Non General Use. Characters found in Chinese (in Mathews' <u>Chinese-English Dictionary</u> [Harvard U.P., Massachusetts, 1966], which lists 7773 characters) but not normally in Japanese are referred to as CO characters, standing for Chinese Only. It should however be noted that, with the possible exception of the very modern simplified forms, any Chinese character can theoretically be used in Japanese in an NGU capacity (some of the pre-war Japanese dictionaries listing as many as 50,000 characters). Some 400 NGU/CO characters occur incidentally in the course of the Jōyō Kanji explanations given in this book, and for the reader's convenience are listed under stroke count in a separate index. It should be appreciated, however, that there is no systematic explanation of them nor any listing of their readings.

As a general principle, when seeking characters in any stroke count index the reader should always be prepared to check one or two strokes either side of the estimated number. Some characters are legitimately permitted to be written in slightly different ways, which can affect the stroke count, and some variant forms also result in a slightly different stroke count. In some dictionaries, it seems that there are also occasional cases of honest miscounts!

Obliques have been used in the explanations with considerable frequency, partly as a stylistic expedient and partly in order to aid flexibility of conceptualisation. It is a serious error to assume that each word in Japanese corresponds exactly to a word in English, and the same applies to characters and their component elements. For example, 貝 90 means shell when used as an independent character, but as an element usually means money, and occasionally means valuable item or asset in a broad sense. Thus it is usually referred to as shell/ money rather than just shell. Similarly 示 695 is used as an independent character to mean show, but as an element sometimes has its literal meaning of altar and generally has its associated meaning of 'relating to the gods'. Thus it is usually referred to as altar/ show or altar/ of the gods etc.

The question of classification into nouns, verbs, adjectives etc. should similarly be treated with considerable conceptual flexibility. For this reason the readings and compounds blocks have omitted (o/ to) suru (and its variant jiru), meaning to do, on the grounds that so many nouns can be made into verbs (especially in their on readings) by adding suru/ jiru that it is in effect pointless to list each one (e.g. KAN feeling 感 246 giving kanjiru/ to feel, or BATSU punishment 罰 1709 giving bassuru/ to punish). Similarly almost any adjective can be made into a verb by adding suru to its adverbial form (e.g. TAI/ ō big 大 53 giving ōkiku suru/ to enlarge).

The main text is generally written in semi-note style. I have deliberately kept the explanations in the early grades relatively brief and simple, while those in the later grades go into greater detail in the expectation of a more specialised readership.

In one or two cases I have used the adjective 'authoritative' in front of the term 'scholars'. This is in no way intended to imply that scholars not so described lack authority, but in most cases is simply used to indicate that an explanation which may possibly seem unlikely to the general reader is in fact supported by scholars whose views are particularly highly respected in their field.

Examples used in the compounds block are chosen to illustrate a variety of readings and meanings. The vast majority of the terms can be found in the Nelson dictionary and/ or Kenkyusha dictionary mentioned above, but a few are reasonably rare and will only be found in large Japanese-Japanese dictionaries. Where such terms contain a character outside the Jōyō Kanji, kana has been used. Asterisks denote irregular readings.

Generally only principal readings and meanings have been given, particularly in the early grades, though specific minor meanings/ readings have been given where important to a proper understanding of the evolution of a particular character. It should be appreciated that where a character has multiple readings and multiple meanings, it does not necessarily follow that each reading can be used to express each meaning.

Finally, as a convenient reference I give below a simple summary explanation of key terms with which some readers may not be completely familiar:

CO character:	found in Chinese only
connotation(s):	suggested or implied meaning
etymology:	the history/ evolution of a word or character
ideograph:	combination of meaningful elements to express a new idea
lexical:	relating to vocabulary
mnemonic:	relating to memory; as a noun, memory aid
NGU character:	found in Japanese but not in general use
phonetic:	relating to sound/ pronunciation
pictograph:	picture-drawing
q.v.	quod vide/ which see (by way of cross reference)
semantic:	relating to meaning
semasio-phonetic:	combination of meaning-element and sound-element
syllabary:	form of alphabet

THE 76 FIRST GRADE CHARACTERS

1　　　　　**ICHI, ITSU, hito-**　　一月　ICHIGATSU　　January
　　　　　　　ONE　　　　　　　　均一　KINITSU　　　uniformity
　　　　　　　1 stroke　　　　　　　一人　HITORI　　　one person

The easiest character of all. A pictograph of a **single** extended finger 一.

Mnemonic: **ONE FINGER**

2　　　　　**U, YŪ, migi**　　　右派　UHA　　　rightist faction
　　　　　　　RIGHT　　　　　　　右岸　UGAN　　　right bank
　　　　　　　5 strokes　　　　　　　右手　MIGITE　　right hand

Originally 㕜, showing a **right hand** 又 over a **mouth** 口 20. The right hand symbolised **strength/support**, and the original meaning of 2 was **support verbally** (still occasionally found in Chinese). This meaning was later assumed by an NGU character 佑 that adds **person** 亻 39, while 2 itself came to mean simply **right hand.** The retention of mouth 口 may have been influenced by a popular interpretation of the elements as **hand favored for feeding.**

Mnemonic: **RIGHT HAND TO THE MOUTH**

3　　　　　**U, ame, ama-**　　　雨季　UKI　　　rainy season
　　　　　　　RAIN　　　　　　　大雨　ŌAME　　heavy rain
　　　　　　　8 strokes　　　　　　　雨雲　AMAGUMO　rain cloud

Ancient form 𠕲 or 𠕭. **Raindrops** ∴ falling from **clouds** ⌒ beneath a symbol of the **heavens** 一. Some scholars feel that ⌒ alone is cloud, and that | is a symbol of **falling.**

Mnemonic: **RAIN FROM HEAVENLY CLOUDS**

1

---

4 円

EN, maru*i*
ROUND, YEN
4 strokes

円形 ENKEI   circle
円高 ENDAKA   strong yen
百円 HYAKUEN   hundred yen

Formerly 圓 . 囗 indicates **roundness**, while 員 is **round kettle** 228 q.v., here emphasising roundness and also lending its sound to express **circle**. The meaning **coin** (**yen** in Japan) stems from an association of shape. A simpler if facetious mnemonic is to see the character as a **bank-teller's window**, from which **round coins** are issued.

Mnemonic: **ROUND COINS FROM BANK-TELLER'S WINDOW**

---

5 王

Ō
KING, RULER
4 strokes

王子 ŌJI   prince
女王 JOŌ   queen
王様 ŌSAMA   king

Usually explained as a symbol of the three orders of **heaven, earth,** and **man** 三 united by an **all-pervading force** 丨, to give a meaning of **great potentate** or **king**. A useful mnemonic, but incorrect. 王 was once written 玉 and 大, depicting the **blade of a large battle ax**. Over the years, rather like the English terms 'big gun' and 'big shot', it came to mean **powerful figure**, and eventually **king.**

Mnemonic: **KING WITH AX RULES HEAVEN, EARTH AND MAN**

---

6 音

ON, IN, oto, ne
SOUND
9 strokes

音楽 ONGAKU   music
子音 SHIIN   consonant
発音 HATSUON pronunciation

Once written 𤶸 . The old form of **speak** 言 274 q.v., 𧮫 , with the addition of **tongue** - inside the mouth 口 to show greater **vocalisation**, i.e. **shout/sing**. This led to just **sound**. Suggest taking 立 as **rise/stand** 73, and 日 as **sun** 62.

Mnemonic: **SOUND OF RISING SUN**

---

7 下 KA,GE,shita,shimo,moto, 低下 TEIKA decrease
kuda*saru/ru*, sa*garu*, o*riru* 下車 GESHA alighting
BASE, UNDER, LOWER 川下 KAWASHIMO
3 strokes downstream

Symbol indicating an area **below** a given line. Originally ⸗ , with a vertical line added later for emphasis. The downwards tilt of the short third stroke is also believed to be for emphasis.

Mnemonic: **T-BAR WITH DROOPY LOWER HANDLE**

---

8 火 KA, hi 火曜日 KAYŌBI Tuesday
FIRE 火山 KAZAN volcano
4 strokes 火花 HIBANA spark

Stylised derivative of pictograph of **fire** with **flames** and **sparks** ₩ . As a radical often occurs as ⺌⺌⺌ .

Mnemonic: **FLAMES OF FIRE**

---

9 花 KA, hana 花弁 KABEN petal
FLOWER, BLOSSOM 花火 HANABI fireworks
7 strokes 花見 HANAMI
blossom viewing

Grass/plant ⲛ (derived from a pictograph of growing plants ⲛⲛ to ⲛⲛ to ⁺⁺ to ⁺⁺) plus **change** 化 238 q.v., to give a meaning of **change in state of plants**, i.e. **blossoming**.

Mnemonic: **FLOWERS APPEAR WHEN PLANTS UNDERGO CHANGE**

3

10	学	GAKU, mana*bu* LEARNING 8 strokes	学校 GAKKŌ	school
			化学 KAGAKU	chemistry
			学者 GAKUSHA	scholar

Somewhat obscure. Formerly 學, and originally 學. 臼/曰 represents **hands**. 爻 is a CO character meaning **intertwine**, and shows interwoven sticks. Since the sticks had to be matched it has connotations of **match** and by extension **emulate**. Thus 學 means **emulate manually.** An old form 學 suggests that 冖 derives from a **roof/ building** 宀, but some scholars maintain that 宀 was originally merely a stylisation of 爻, and cite another old form 學. **Child** 子 25 is a later addition, presumably from a natural association of children with the idea of manual emulation (i.e. learning by imitation to use the hands, symbolic of **learning** in general). Suggest taking 𭥫 as an **ornate roof**.

Mnemonic: **CHILD LEARNING UNDER ORNATE ROOF**

11	気	KI, KE SPIRIT 6 strokes	気分 KIBUN	mood, feeling
			天気 TENKI	weather
			電気 DENKI	electricity

Formerly written 氣 . 米 is **rice** 201, while 气 is a representation of **vapors** 气. 11 originally meant **vapors rising from (cooked) rice,** and eventually came to mean **invisible movement/ unseen force/ spirit** etc. Suggest taking メ as **X.**

Mnemonic: **SPIRIT-LIKE VAPORS FROM SOURCE X**

12	九	KYŪ, KU, kokono- NINE 2 strokes	十九 JŪKYŪ	nineteen
			九日 KOKONOKA	ninth day
			九月 KUGATSU	September

Originally written 九, depicting a **bent elbow**. In ancient times a bent elbow was used to indicate the number **nine** when counting with only one arm. The commonly heard explanation that it is the character for **ten** 十 33 with a hook on the cross stroke to represent the concept of **subtraction** is incorrect, but is useful as a mnemonic.

Mnemonic: **LESS THAN PERFECT TEN: WORTH ONLY NINE**

13 休 KYŪ, yasu*mu* 休日 KYŪJITSU holiday
REST 休戦 KYŪSEN truce
6 strokes 夏休み NATSUYASUMI
summer vacation

イ is **person** 39 and 木 is **tree** 69. 木 is used partly phonetically to express **stop/stay**, and partly semantically as **tree**, i.e. a shady place where **people stop to rest**. Now means **stop** or **rest** in general.

Mnemonic: **PERSON RESTS AGAINST TREE**

---

14 金 KIN, KON, kane, kana- 金曜日 KINYŌBI Friday
GOLD,MONEY,METAL 金色 KONJIKI gold color
8 strokes 金持 KANEMOCHI
rich person

Once written . The four dots ∷ , now reduced to two, represent **nuggets** buried in the **ground** 土 60. There is a range of opinion regarding 스/仝 . Some scholars take it to show a **mound** ◠ , others an element indicating **covering** (see 87), which also lent its sound to express **shine**. The latter theory seems more likely.

Mnemonic: **TWO GOLD NUGGETS UNDER COVER OF EARTH**

---

15 空 KŪ, sora, kara, a*ku* 空気 KŪKI air
SKY, EMPTY 空色 SORAIRO sky-blue
8 strokes 空箱 KARABAKO empty box

Hole 穴 849 (literally **open space under roof**) and **work upon** 工 113. The latter is used for its sound to express **opening** as well as its meaning. Originally 15 meant to **work upon** the digging out of a **hole** that would then be covered with a **roof** to form a primitive dwelling. Since the roof was domed the idea of **(empty) space** within the dwelling naturally became particularly associated with the central vaulted area, and eventually the concept of **upper space** extended to the **sky** itself.

Mnemonic: **WORK TO OPEN HOLE IN ROOF TO SEE EMPTY SKY**

| 16 | GETSU, GATSU, tsuki
MOON, MONTH
4 strokes | 今月 KONGETSU　this month
月曜日 GETSUYŌBI　Monday
月見 TSUKIMI　moon viewing |

From a pictograph of a **crescent moon** with **pitted surface** gradually tilted on its axis in the course of stylisation (⧽ to 𐀼 to 月). Popularly interpreted as a **crescent moon behind wispy clouds**, but this appears incorrect. See also 44.

Mnemonic: **PITTED CRESCENT MOON SHINING DOWN**

| 17 | KEN, inu
DOG
4 strokes | 猟犬 RYŌKEN　hunting-dog
犬小屋 INUGOYA　kennel
小犬 KOINU　puppy |

Stylised derivative of a pictograph showing a **dog** with pointed ears standing on its hind legs barking 犮. As a radical found as 犭 (also symbolising **beast**). Suggest remembering by association with **big** 大 53, with 丶 as a **spot**.

Mnemonic: **BIG SPOTTED DOG REARING UP**

| 18 | KEN, miru/seru/eru
LOOK, SEE, SHOW
7 strokes | 発見 HAKKEN　discovery
見物 KENBUTSU　sightseeing
見物 MIMONO　spectacle |

Eye 目 72 and **bent legs** 儿, the latter deriving from a pictograph of **a person kneeling** 人 39 (to **stare** at something).

Mnemonic: **BENDING DOWN TO LOOK CLOSELY WITH SEEING EYE**

| 19 五 | GO, itsu-
FIVE
4 strokes | 五月 GOGATSU　May
五人 GONIN　five people
五日 ITSUKA　fifth day |

Five was once shown by **five fingers** 𝌆. However, from ancient times a **thread-reel** 𠄌 (𠄌 to 五) was used as a substitute, both for its sound and the fact that it replaced the **five fingers** when winding yarn.

Mnemonic: **A REEL IS BETTER THAN FIVE FINGERS**

20		KŌ, KU, kuchi MOUTH, OPENING 3 strokes	人口 JINKŌ	population
			口実 KŌJITSU	pretext
			出口 DEGUCHI	exit

A pictograph of an **open mouth**, originally written ⊔. Can also symbolise **speech**.

Mnemonic: **OPEN MOUTH**

21		KŌ SCHOOL, CHECK 10 strokes	校正 KŌSEI	proof reading
			高校 KŌKŌ	high school
			校長 KŌCHŌ	school principal

木 is **tree/wood** 69. 交 is **crossed legs** 115. 21 originally meant **wooden shackles** (i.e. wooden item to encumber the legs). However, owing to the similarity in both meaning and depiction to **crossed sticks** 爻 in Character 10 q.v., reinforced by a similarity in pronunciation at the time, it took on the latter's meanings of **collate/match/ emulate**. In fact, at one stage the two characters seem to have been virtually interchangeable. Eventually 10 came to mean **learning** while 21 became **checking** and also **place of learning**. Suggest taking 六 as **six** 76 and 乂 as a **cross**.

Mnemonic: **CHECK SIX WOODEN CROSSES FOR SCHOOL**

22		SA, hidari LEFT 5 strokes	左派 SAHA	leftist faction
			左側 HIDARIGAWA	left side
			左手 HIDARITE	left hand

Left hand 𠂇 and **work upon** 工 113 q.v. Rather like the right hand, the left hand also symbolised **support**, but with connotations of **reserve/auxiliary** as opposed to the strength of the right (see 2). Thus 22's original meaning was **assist someone at work** (still found in Chinese). Again like 2, its original meaning was later taken over by a character adding **person** 亻 39, giving **assist** 佐 1283, while 22 itself came to mean simply **left hand**, with 工 retained though redundant. Suggest taking 工 literally as **carpenter's square**.

Mnemonic: **LEFT HAND STEADIES CARPENTER'S SQUARE**

23 三	SAN, mi- **THREE** 3 strokes	三月 SANGATSU	March
		三日 MIKKA	third day
		三角 SANKAKU	triangle

Three extended fingers 三 .

Mnemonic: **THREE FINGERS**

---

24 山	SAN, yama **MOUNTAIN** 3 strokes	氷山 HYŌZAN	iceberg
		沢山 TAKUSAN	a lot
		山場 YAMABA	peak, climax

A range of **mountains** with a prominent central peak .

Mnemonic: **TRIPLE-PEAKED MOUNTAIN**

---

25 子	SHI, SU, ko **CHILD** 3 strokes	電子 DENSHI	electron
		子供 KODOMO	child
		様子 YŌSU	look, situation

An **infant** wrapped in swaddling clothes waving its arms .

Mnemonic: **LONG-ARMED CHILD IN SWADDLING CLOTHES**

---

26 四	SHI, yon, yo- **FOUR** 5 strokes	四月 SHIGATSU	April
		四日 YOKKA	fourth day
		四回 YONKAI	four times

Four was once shown by **four fingers** 亖 , while 四 originally meant **breath** (that which emerges 八 66 from a mouth 口 20). 四 was later used as a phonetic substitute for 亖 , but may also have been chosen since its shape was a rough approximation of the **four fingers** of a **fist** held palm side down .

Mnemonic: **FOUR FINGERS IN CLENCHED FIST**

27	**SHI, ito**	製糸	SEISHI	silk making
	THREAD	毛糸	KEITO	woolen yarn
	6 strokes	糸巻き	ITOMAKI	thread-reel

From a pictograph of a **skein of yarn** 💃, originally doubled 💃💃.

Mnemonic: **SKEINS OF TWISTED THREAD**

28	**JI**	字引き	JIBIKI	dictionary
	LETTER, SYMBOL	赤字	AKAJI	'the red', deficit
	6 strokes	数字	SŪJI	digit, number

Roof ⼧ (from ⼍), symbolising **house/home**, and **child** 子 25. It originally meant a **house where children are raised** (still found in Chinese in the minor meanings **suckle/nourish/bring forth**). This came to symbolise **proliferation** and, fanciful as it may seem, came to be figuratively applied to **written symbols**, which like children became increasingly numerous and complex.

Mnemonic: **CHILD AT HOME STUDYING LETTERS**

29	**JI, mimi**	耳科	JIKA	otology
	EAR	耳鳴り	MIMINARI	tinnitus
	6 strokes	耳飾り	MIMIKAZARI	earring

Stylised derivative of the pictograph of an **ear** 🂀.

Mnemonic: **POINTED EAR**

30	**SHICHI, nana-**	七月	SHICHIGATSU	July
	SEVEN	七日	NANOKA*	seventh day
	2 strokes	七晩	NANABAN	seven nights

Originally ╋ , with a longer lateral line than the character for **ten** ╋ 33, to represent and mean a line **cutting** another. It was one of several characters used phonetically to express **seven**, and was probably especially favored since it roughly resembled a **bent finger under a fist**, an old way of signaling **seven.**

Mnemonic: **BADLY WRITTEN TEN AGAIN: NOW WORTH ONLY SEVEN**

31

SHA, kuruma
VEHICLE, CHARIOT
7 strokes

電車 DENSHA train
発車 HASSHA departure
口車 KUCHIGURUMA cajolery

From a pictograph of a long-shafted **two-wheeled chariot**, viewed from above 車.

Mnemonic: **CHARIOT WITH TWO WHEELS**

32

SHU, te
HAND
4 strokes

手段 SHUDAN means
手本 TEHON model, standard
上手 JŌZU* skill

From a semi-stylised pictograph of a **hand** with **five fingers** (one bent), a **palm**, and **wrist** 手. As a radical usually found as 扌.

Mnemonic: **HAND WITH FINGERS SPREAD**

---

33 十

JŪ, tŏ
TEN
2 strokes

十月 JŪGATSU October
十日 TŌKA tenth day
十字 JŪJI a cross

Usually explained as **two lines crossing** to symbolise the **four main directions**, which in turn expressed the concept of **completeness** and by association **all the fingers**, i.e. **ten**. However, this seems a confused version of its actual origin. It derives from a depiction of a **sewing needle** ↑, and was used purely as a substitute for the more complex character **ten** 拾 305 q.v. (literally **hands together**).

Mnemonic: **ALL POINTS CONSIDERED, TEN OUT OF TEN**

34

SHUTSU, de*ru*, da*su*
EMERGE, PUT OUT
5 strokes

出発 SHUPPATSU departure
思い出 OMOIDE memory
引き出し HIKIDASHI drawer

Once written 出, with **foot** 止 129 q.v. and ∪. Some scholars take ∪ to indicate a **cover**, i.e. **shoe**, to symbolise **going out**, while others take it to be a **line of containment**, beyond which the foot has **emerged**. Another theory sees the character as derived from a pictograph of an **emerging plant** 出 (see 42), but this is not widely supported. Suggest taking it as two **mountains** 山 24.

Mnemonic: **MOUNTAIN EMERGING ATOP ANOTHER**

35		JO, NYŌ, NYO, onna, me WOMAN 3 strokes	女性 JOSEI	woman
			女房 NYŌBŌ	wife
			女の子 ONNA-NO-KO	girl

From a pictograph of a **kneeling woman** with outstretched arms 乙.

Mnemonic: **KNEELING WOMAN**

36		SHŌ, ko-, o-, chiisai SMALL 3 strokes	小人 SHŌJIN/KOBITO	dwarf
			小牛 KOUSHI	calf
			小川 OGAWA	brook, stream

Commonly but erroneously explained as a **person standing with their arms at their side**, i.e. **looking small**. The error is no doubt attributable to the pictographic origin of the opposite **big** 大 53 q.v. (literally a person with arms outstretched). 小 is actually a stylised representation of **three small points**, as is clear from the older version ⼩. Some scholars feel the lengthening of the middle stroke serves to express the concept of **one large** item being **divided** into **two small ones**.

Mnemonic: **A STROKE DIVIDED INTO TWO SMALL ONES**

37	上	JŌ, ue, kami, uwa-, noboru, agaru/geru UP, TOP, OVER, GO UP 3 strokes	以上 IJŌ	over, above
			川上 KAWAKAMI	upstream
			値上げ NEAGE	price rise

Symbol indicating an area **above** a line. Originally written ⼆ , with a vertical line added later for clarity.

Mnemonic: **BAR WITH HANDLE, STICKING UP OVER BASELINE**

38		SHIN, mori WOODS 12 strokes	森林 SHINRIN	forest
			森厳 SHINGEN na	solemn
			森閑 SHINKAN	silence

An ideograph showing **many trees** 木 69. See also **forest** 林 75.

Mnemonic: **THERE ARE MANY TREES IN THE WOODS**

39 人 JIN, NIN, hito
PERSON, PEOPLE
2 strokes

日本人 NIHONJIN　　Japanese
人間 NINGEN　　human being
人出 HITODE　crowd, turn-out

From a pictograph of a **standing person** viewed side-on 人 , though in compounds often a bending or stooping person 乀/儿 . As a radical usually found as 亻 , but occasionally 𠆢/𠂉 , or even 丄 . Better taken as **headless, armless person**.

Mnemonic: **HEADLESS, ARMLESS PERSON**

40 水 SUI, mizu
WATER
4 strokes

水曜日 SUIYŌBI　　Wednesday
水素 SUISO　　hydrogen
大水 ŌMIZU　　flood

From a pictograph of a **river** 氺, the central stroke showing **current** and the dots **ripples**. Since ancient times blurred with **river** 川 48. As a radical, usually found as 氵, best remembered as **falling droplets**. Suggest taking フく as **narrow banks**.

Mnemonic: **WATER SQUEEZES BETWEEN BANKS**

41 正 SEI,SHŌ,masa,tada*shii/su*
CORRECT, PROPER
5 strokes

正解 SEIKAI　　correct answer
正月 SHŌGATSU　New Year
正直 SHŌJIKI na　　honest

Often explained as **foot/stop** 止 129 q.v. and a **bar** 一, to indicate **stopping at the right place**, i.e. being **correct**. A useful mnemonic, especially in view of the English term **toe the line**, but in fact old forms such as 𧾷 show it to be a variant of **lower leg** 足 51, which was **straight** and by figurative extension **proper/correct**.

Mnemonic: **TO STOP AT THE LINE IS TO DO THE CORRECT THING**

42 生 SEI, SHŌ, nama,
ikiru, u*mu/mareru*, ha*eru*
LIFE, BIRTH, GROW
5 strokes

学生 GAKUSEI　　student
一生 ISSHŌ　one's whole life
生き物 IKIMONO　　living thing

From a pictograph of a **growing plant** 生, symbolising **vitality**. Note that there is a character-element 止, derived from a differently written **plant** 㞢, which confusingly is identical to **foot/stop** 止 129.

Mnemonic: **GROWING PLANT IS A SYMBOL OF LIFE**

43 青 SEI, SHŌ, ao*i* 青年 SEINEN a youth
BLUE, GREEN, YOUNG 青空 AOZORA blue sky
8 strokes 青物 AOMONO greens

Also written 靑 . 主 is a simplified version of **growing plant/life** 生 42. 円/月 is a simplified version of 丼 . Now an NGU character meaning **receptacle/bowl**, 丼 originally depicted a **well** 井 1470 with a mark to indicate **water** in it. Here it has that original meaning, and combines with 主 to express **growth around a full well**, which is **fresh** and **green**. Green overlaps conceptually with **blue**, and also has a figurative association with **immature** and **young** (as in English). Suggest taking 月 as **moon 16**.

Mnemonic: **YOUNG BLUE-GREEN PLANTS LIVE ON THE MOON**

44 SEKI, yū 今夕 KONSEKI this evening
EVENING 夕食 YŪSHOKU evening meal
3 strokes 夕日 YŪHI setting sun

To all intents and purposes derived from the same pictograph of a **crescent moon** as moon 月 16 q.v., but without the pitted surface. The **unpitted,** only semi-tilted **crescent moon** of 44 came to symbolise **evening**.

Mnemonic: **CLEAR MOON INDICATES EVENING**

45 石 SEKI, SHAKU, ishi 化石 KASEKI fossil
STONE, ROCK 小石 KOISHI pebble
5 strokes 石油 SEKIYU petroleum

A slightly modified **cliff** 厂 (to 丆) and a **boulder** 口 . Usually explained as a **boulder having rolled down a cliff**, but it is more likely a **boulder hewn from a cliff-face.**

Mnemonic: **ROUND STONE AT BASE OF CLIFF**

46 SEKI, SHAKU, aka*i* 赤道 SEKIDŌ equator
RED 赤面 SEKIMEN blush
7 strokes 赤ん坊 AKANBŌ infant

Usually explained as an ideograph combining **earth** 土 60 and **fire** 小(variant ⺌ 8), with a meaning of **fired earth/terracotta**. However, an old form 交 clearly shows that 土 is a variant of **big** 大 53, giving a meaning of **big blaze** with a **ruddy glow.**

Mnemonic: **BIG FIRE MAKES EARTH GLOW RED**

47	SEN, chi THOUSAND 3 strokes	千円 SENEN thousand yen 五千 GOSEN five thousand 千鳥 CHIDORI plover

A combination of **person** 亻 39 and **one** 一 1. Possibly partly for phonetic reasons, in ancient times the **body** symbolised a **thousand**, with one thousand being written 千, two thousand 千, and so on.

Mnemonic: **THAT ONE PERSON IS WORTH A THOUSAND OTHERS**

48	SEN, kawa RIVER 3 strokes	川口 KAWAGUCHI rivermouth 川端 KAWABATA riverside 江戸川 EDOGAWA Edo River

Once written 川, showing **water** flowing between **two banks** 川. See also 40.

Mnemonic: **RIVER FLOWING BETWEEN BANKS**

49 先	SEN, saki PREVIOUS, PRECEDE, TIP 6 strokes	先生 SENSEI teacher 先月 SENGETSU last month 指先 YUBISAKI fingertip

A combination of 屮 and 儿. As an old form 先 clearly reveals, 屮 derives from **foot/stop** 止 129 and 儿 derives from **person** 人 39. **Stop** came to mean by extension **cease to be/ die**, and the whole character meant **dead people/ancestors**. By association of ideas it later acquired meanings such as **precede, lead, tip**, and so on. Suggest taking 屮 as a variant of **life** 生 42.

Mnemonic: **THOSE DEAD PEOPLE PRECEDED US IN LIFE**

50	SŌ, hayai EARLY, PROMPT, FAST 6 strokes	早急 SŌKYŪ immediately 早口 HAYAKUCHI rapid speech 早死に HAYAJINI early death

Sun 日 62 and **cutting/opening** 十 (see 30), to give a meaning of the **sun breaking through** (the darkness). The popular theory that 十 represents a **plant**, to give a meaning of the **sun just rising through the plants**, is incorrect. **Fast** is an associated meaning with **early**. Suggest taking 十 as **ten** 33.

Mnemonic: **SUN SHOWS TEN BUT IT'S STILL EARLY**

51 足 SOKU, ashi, ta*riru*
LEG, FOOT, SUFFICIENT
7 strokes

不足 FUSOKU　　insufficiency
足首 ASHIKUBI　　　ankle
足音 ASHIOTO　　footsteps

Foot 止 (variant 止 129) and a **kneecap** 口, giving **(lower) leg**. Borrowed phonetically to express **suffice**, though it may also have lent an idea of **able** (i.e. not maimed).

Mnemonic: **ROUND KNEE AND FOOT SUFFICE TO SHOW LEG**

---

52 村 SON, mura
VILLAGE
7 strokes

村長 SONCHŌ　　village head
農村 NŌSON　　farming village
村人 MURABITO　　　villager

Surprisingly obscure. Of confused etymology, though its elements are clearly **tree** 木 69 and **hand/measure** 寸 909. According to one theory 村 is a simplification of 杶, a CO character comprising **tree** 木 and **encampment** 屯 1669 q.v. and meaning **lacquer tree**, with 屯 felt to be used partly for its original meaning of **shoot** and partly phonetically for the name of the tree (寸 had the same pronunciation). 杶 became confused with 阯, a CO character meaning **village** (composed of **encampment** 屯 and **village** 阝 355). Thus at one stage both 杶 and 阯 were used for **village**. 村 then replaced 杶 in this meaning, and 杶 went back to meaning **lacquer tree**.

Mnemonic: **MEASURE TREES IN VILLAGE**

---

53 大 TAI, DAI, ōkii
BIG
3 strokes

大会 TAIKAI　　　assembly
大学 DAIGAKU　　university
大声 ŌGOE　　loud voice

A **person standing with arms and legs spread out** to look as **large** as possible 大. Occasionally used to indicate **person**, as well as **big**.

Mnemonic: **PERSON LOOKING BIG AS POSSIBLE**

---

54 男 DAN, NAN, otoko
MAN, MALE
7 strokes

男子 DANSHI　　　　boy
長男 CHŌNAN　　eldest boy
男気 OTOKOGI　　gallantry

Usually explained as the **strength** 力 74 out in the **fields** 田 59, though there is also a theory that 田 was used purely phonetically to express a word **reliable**, to give a meaning of **reliable strength**.

Mnemonic: **MAN PROVIDES STRENGTH IN FIELD**

15

55 CHŪ, naka
MIDDLE, INSIDE, CHINA
4 strokes

中立 CHŪRITSU　neutrality
中国 CHŪGOKU　China
真ん中 MANNAKA　very middle

Once written 𠆢. Some scholars take this to be a stylised depiction of a **flagpole** reinforced by a **second pole** running through its **center**, while others take it to show an **arrow piercing the center of a target**. In Chinese it can still mean **hit center**, suggesting the latter theory is correct. Also refers to **China, the middle kingdom**. See also 496.

Mnemonic: **CHINESE ARROW PIERCES MIDDLE OF TARGET**

56 CHŪ, mushi
INSECT, WORM
6 strokes

寄生虫 KISEICHŪ　parasite
害虫 GAICHŪ　harmful insect
虫歯 MUSHIBA　decayed tooth

From a pictograph of a **partly coiled snake**. The earliest form 𠃊 suggests a **large-headed snake**, whereas a later form 𠁽 suggests a **hooded snake (cobra)**. In ancient times **snakes** and **insects** were treated much alike. Suggest taking 中 as **inside** 55.

Mnemonic: **COILED HOODED SNAKE: SIMILAR INSIDE TO INSECT**

57 CHŌ, machi
TOWN, BLOCK
7 strokes

町民 CHŌMIN　townspeople
町長 CHŌCHŌ　town mayor
下町 SHITAMACHI　downtown

Field 田 59 q.v. and **nail** 丁 346. The latter was used phonetically to express **walk**, and also lent its T-shape to suggest **junction of paths**. 57 originally meant **paths through the fields**, and by extension **place where fields join**, then **area/community**.

Mnemonic: **TOWN AT T-JUNCTION OF PATHS THROUGH FIELDS**

58 天 TEN, ama-
HEAVEN, SKY
4 strokes

天使 TENSHI　angel
天皇 TENNŌ　emperor
天下り AMAKUDARI
descent from heaven

Originally written 夨, showing person 大 53 with an **exaggerated head** symbolising **uppermost/ upper part**. By association it came to mean **that up above**.

Mnemonic: **PERSON'S HEAD IS CLOSEST PART TO HEAVEN**

59		DEN, ta RICE FIELD 5 strokes	田園 DENEN	rural district
			田植え TAUE	rice planting
			田舎 INAKA*	countryside

A pictograph of a **rice field** □ crossed by **ridges/paths** 十.

Mnemonic: **RICE FIELD CROSSED BY PATHS**

60		DO, TO, tsuchi EARTH, SOIL, GROUND 3 strokes	土曜日 DOYŌBI	Saturday
			土地 TOCHI	land
			土臭い TSUCHIKUSAI	cloddish

From a pictograph of a **clod of earth** on the ground ⊆. The popular theory that it shows a **plant** 十 growing in the **earth** — is incorrect but a useful mnemonic.

Mnemonic: **PLANT GROWS IN EARTH**

61		NI, futa- TWO 2 strokes	二月 NIGATSU	February
			二十 NIJŪ	twenty
			二人 FUTARI	two people

Two extended fingers ニ.

Mnemonic: **TWO FINGERS**

62		NICHI, JITSU, hi, -ka SUN, DAY 4 strokes	日曜日 NICHIYŌBI	Sunday
			本日 HONJITSU	today
			二日 FUTSUKA*	second day

A pictograph of the **sun with a sunspot** ⊙. Also indicates **day**, and **light**.

Mnemonic: **SUN WITH SPOT**

63	入	NYŪ, hairu, ireru/ru ENTER, PUT IN 2 strokes	輸入 YUNYŪ	import
			入り口 IRIGUCHI	entrance
			入れ物 IREMONO	container

Popularly said to show a person **bending down** ∧ to **enter** a primitive dwelling. However, old forms such as 人, ∧ and ∧ show it to be the **entrance** itself.

Mnemonic: **ENTER THROUGH INVERTED V OPENING**

64 NEN, toshi
YEAR
6 strokes

来年 RAINEN next year
五年生 GONENSEI fifth grader
年寄 TOSHIYORI old person

Stylised derivative of ideograph 秂, showing **rice-plant** 禾 81 q.v. and **bending person** 𠂉 39. Some scholars take it to show a **person bending to cut rice**, others as simply showing the relationship between **man** and **rice**, while yet others feel that 𠂉 was used phonetically to express **abundant**. The first view is the most likely, but all involve the **annual harvest**, which symbolised the **cycle of a year**. Suggest taking ⼂ as **person**, and 𫝀 as variant of **well** 井 1470.

Mnemonic: **PERSON VISITS WELL EVERY YEAR**

---

65 白 HAKU, shiroi
WHITE
5 strokes

白書 HAKUSHO White Paper
面白い OMOSHIROI interesting
白人 HAKUJIN Caucasian

From a **pointed thumbnail** ⽩ (some forms such as ⽩ show the exaggerated length in vogue in ancient China), used phonetically to express **white**, and also suggesting **paleness** (relative to the skin). However, there is also some evidence to support a popular belief that ⽩ shows an **acorn**, whose inside is **whitish** (see 218), suggesting that two pictographs may have coexisted at one stage. See also 67. Suggest taking 日 as **sun** 62, with ノ as a **stroke**.

Mnemonic: **SUNSTROKE LEAVES ONE WHITE?!**

---

66 HACHI, ya-
EIGHT
2 strokes

八月 HACHIGATSU August
八百屋 YAOYA* greengrocer
八つ当り YATSUATARI
outburst of anger

Once written)(, symbolising **splitting/dividing**. Some scholars feel it was later used for **eight** since it is a **readily divided number**, others that its shape was close to the old way of showing **eight** by bending down the three middle fingers and extending the **thumb** and **little finger**. In compounds, often found as ハ or ソ, with a meaning of **divide/ disperse/ away/ out**.

Mnemonic: **EIGHT CAN BE EASILY DIVIDED**

18

| 67 | | HYAKU
HUNDRED
6 strokes | 百倍 HYAKUBAI hundred-fold
百性 HYAKUSHŌ farmer
百貨店 HYAKKATEN
department store |

One 一 1 and white 白 65 q.v., here used for its meaning of **thumbnail**. In ancient times the **thumb** was used to indicate a **hundred**, and two hundred was written 百 , five hundred 百 (see 19), and so on.

Mnemonic: **SCORE ONE HUNDRED WITH ONE WHITE THUMBNAIL**

| 68 | | BUN, MON, fumi
WRITING, TEXT
4 strokes | 文学 BUNGAKU literature
文字 MO(N)JI character
文部省 MONBUSHŌ
Ministry of Education |

Originally written 文, depicting a **beautifully/ intricately patterned overlaid collar** (it can still mean stripe/pattern in Chinese). The core meaning of **intricate pattern** was eventually extended to **writing**. Suggest taking メ as **cross** and 亠 as a **top**.

Mnemonic: **CROSS IS BASIC FORM OF WRITING: TRY TO TOP IT**

| 69 | | BOKU, MOKU, ki, ko-
TREE, WOOD
4 strokes | 木曜日 MOKUYŌBI Thursday
木目 KIME grain, texture
木立ち KODACHI grove |

Pictograph of a **tree** with **sweeping branches** 木. Often indicates **wood(en)**.

Mnemonic: **TREE WITH SWEEPING BRANCHES**

| 70 | | HON, moto
ROOT,TRUE,BOOK,THIS,
CYLINDER-COUNTER
5 strokes | 日本 NIHON/NIPPON Japan
本屋 HONYA bookstore
本店 HONTEN
head office, this store |

Usually explained as an ideograph showing the **base** 一 of a **tree** 木 69, but an old form 本 shows it to be a pictograph of the **roots**. Numerous extended meanings have evolved from this concept, usually involving **essence/origin**. Also used for counting cylindrical objects.

Mnemonic: **TREE WITH ONE CENTRAL ROOT**

| 71 | 名 | MEI, MYŌ, na
NAME, FAME
6 strokes | 有名 YŪMEI
名人 MEIJIN
名前 NAMAE | famous
expert
name |

Mouth/say 口 20 and **evening** 夕 44. The latter also lends its sound to express **call**. That is, in the dim light of evening it was necessary to identify people verbally, calling their **names**.

Mnemonic: **MOUTH CALLS NAME AT NIGHT**

| 72 | 目 | MOKU, BOKU, me, ma-
EYE, ORDINAL SUFFIX
5 strokes | 一つ目 HITOTSUME
注目 CHŪMOKU
一目 HITOME de | first one
attention
at a glance |

Pictograph of an **eye**, originally written . Sometimes found as ⍟, but usually tilted on its axis to 目. Borrowed to express ordinals.

Mnemonic: **UPRIGHT EYE**

| 73 | 立 | RITSU, RYŪ, ta*tsu/teru*
STAND, RISE, LEAVE
5 strokes | 自立 JIRITSU
立場 TACHIBA
目立つ MEDATSU | independence
standpoint
stand out |

From a pictograph of a **person standing on the ground** 企. Originally it meant to **stand still**, then to **stand up**, and by extension came to mean **leave**.

Mnemonic: **PERSON STANDING**

| 74 | 力 | RYOKU, RIKI, chikara
STRENGTH, EFFORT
2 strokes | 能力 NŌRYOKU
人力車 JINRIKISHA
力試し CHIKARADAMESHI | ability
rickshaw
test of strength |

From a pictograph of an **arm with bulging biceps** , simplified to 九 and later 力, pushing down and symbolising **strength/ effort/ force.**

Mnemonic: **HAND PRESSING DOWN WITH STRENGTH**

75 林	RIN, hayashi	林学 RINGAKU	forestry
	FOREST	小林 KOBAYASHI	a surname
	8 strokes	密林 MITSURIN	dense forest

As with **woods** 森 38 q.v., an ideograph showing plural **trees** 木 69. In comparison to 38 the trees are fewer, but taller and more stately, which some may feel to be the difference between **forest** and **woods**.

Mnemonic: **FOREST CONTAINS TALL STATELY TREES**

76 六	ROKU, mu-	六月 ROKUGATSU	June
	SIX	六日 MUIKA*	sixth day
	4 strokes	六角 ROKKAKU	hexagon

One popular theory claims that an early form 𝓡 shows **two hands** of which the **thumbs** and **index fingers** are joined in a circle and the remaining **three fingers** are pointed downwards. However, 𝓡 is simply a stylistic variation of a still earlier form 𠕁. This was in fact a **roof**, and originally had that meaning before being used as a phonetic substitute for a complex character meaning **clenched fist**, which was an old way of showing **six**. Suggest taking 八 as **eight** 66 and 亠 as a **top**.

Mnemonic: **EIGHT TOPPED BY SIX?!**

END OF FIRST GRADE

21

THE 145 SECOND GRADE CHARACTERS

77   IN, hiku   引力 INRYOKU   gravitation
    PULL, DRAW   字引 JIBIKI   dictionary
    4 strokes   取り引き TORIHIKI dealings

Bow 弓 836 and a line |. Some scholars interpret the line as the bow string, i.e. **that which is pulled**, while others see it simply as an abstract symbol representing **stretching**.

Mnemonic: **BOW WITH STRING WAITING TO BE DRAWN**

78   UN, kumo   雲母 UNMO*   mica
    CLOUD   星雲 SEIUN   nebula
    12 strokes   浮き雲 UKIGUMO drifting cloud

Originally written 〓, later inverted to 〓 and eventually 云, representing **billowing vapors**. This was later used as an NGU character to mean **speak**, so **rain** 雨 3 was added to emphasise **cloud**. Suggest taking 云 as **two** = 61 **noses** 厶 134.

Mnemonic: **BILLOWING RAIN-CLOUDS LOOK LIKE TWO NOSES**

79 遠   EN, tōi   遠足 ENSOKU   excursion
    DISTANT   遠回り TŌMAWARI detour
    13 strokes   遠視 ENSHI   longsighted

Movement 辶 129 and 袁. The latter is a CO character meaning **long robe**, to all intents and purposes combining a variant of **clothing** 衣 420 with 口, meaning **encircling** and by extension **spacious** and **big**, leading by association to **long**. Here 袁 acts phonetically to express **long**, and also lends similar connotations of its own. Thus **long movement**, i.e. **distance/ distant**.

Mnemonic: **LOOSE CLOTHES FOR TRAVELING ANY DISTANCE**

22

80

KA, nani, nan
WHAT? HOW MANY?
7 strokes

何回 NANKAI   how often?
何者 NANIMONO   who?
何人 NANNIN
    how many people?

Person イ 39 and **can** 可 816 q.v., here acting phonetically to express **bear** and also lending its own connotations of **bending**. Thus **person bending bearing (heavy load)**, still retained as a minor meaning in Chinese. In Japanese this meaning has been entirely taken over by 荷 239 q.v., while 80 itself has come to be used purely phonetically to express **what?** Suggest taking 口 as **mouth/say** 20 and 丁 as a variant of **to a T/ exactly** 丁 346.

Mnemonic: **WHAT EXACTLY CAN A PERSON SAY?**

81

KA
COURSE, SECTION
9 strokes

科学 KAGAKU   science
学科 GAKKA   school subject
研究科 KENKYŪKA
    research section

Rice plant 禾 (from a pictograph 禾), symbolising **grain**, and **measure** 斗 1633, to give a meaning of **measure grain**. By extension this came to mean **sift/sort** and then **category**, which by further extension came to mean **section**. **Course** is an associated meaning. See also 599.

Mnemonic: **COURSE TO CATEGORIZE RICE MEASURES**

82

KA, GE, natsu
SUMMER
10 strokes

初夏 SHOKA   early summer
真夏 MANATSU   midsummer
夏祭 NATSUMATSURI
    summer festival

Originally written 夒, showing a person **dancing** (symbolised by stopping and starting 夂 438 q.v.) **holding** (symbolised by hands 臼彐) a **mask** (represented by head 頁 93 q.v.). How exactly it came to mean **summer** is not clear. Some scholars claim it was borrowed purely phonetically, but its complexity suggests otherwise. Presumably summer was associated with a particular dance or festival. Suggest remembering 夂 as the shape of **crossed legs**.

Mnemonic: **MASKED HEAD AND CROSSED LEGS IN SUMMER DANCE**

23

| 83 | | KA, KE, ie, ya HOUSE, SPECIALIST 10 strokes | 農家 NŌKA 武家 BUKE 作家 SAKKA | farmhouse warrior family writer |

Roof/building 宀 28 and pig 豕 1670. Long believed to refer to supposed ancient practice of keeping pigs in house. However, many scholars now take 豕 to be used phonetically to express **leisure/relax**, giving **building for relaxing**. The pig may also have been associated with **not working**, as opposed to a working animal such as a horse. Ironically, 83 has now also come to mean **(house of) a specialist**.

Mnemonic: **HOUSE LOOKING LIKE PIG-STY**

| 84 | | KA, uta, uta*u* SONG, SING 14 strokes | 歌手 KASHU 短歌 TANKA 数え歌 KAZOEUTA | singer short verse counting-rhyme |

Lack/**gaping mouth** 欠 471 q.v. and 哥. The latter is an NGU character that doubles **can** 可 816 q.v. It can mean elder brother (presumably associated with permission or potential), but here acts phonetically to express the sound KA doubled, i.e. KA-KA. This was the ancient Chinese equivalent of (TRA-)LA-LA, and indicated **singing**. From its literal meaning of **emerge from the mouth** 可 may also act to reinforce **gaping mouth** 欠. Thus **KA-KA from a wide open mouth**.

Mnemonic: **GAPING MOUTH SINGS THE CAN-CAN**

| 85 | | GA, KAKU PICTURE, STROKE 8 strokes | 映画 EIGA 画面 GAMEN 計画 KEIKAKU | movie screen plan |

Formerly 畫 or 畵 or 畵. 聿 shows a **hand** ⺕ applying a **brush** 大 142. 田 is **rice field** 59. ⊔/一 indicates **partitioning**. Thus to **partition fields with a brush**, i.e. on a map. By extension it also came to mean **strokes** or **diagram/picture**.

Mnemonic: **FIELD IN PICTURE PARTITIONED BY STROKES**

| 86 | | KAI, mawa*ru/su* TURN, ROTATE 6 strokes | 回転 KAITEN 回数 KAISŪ 言い回し IIMAWASHI | revolution frequency turn of phrase |

From a symbol of **rotational motion** ◉.

Mnemonic: **COAXIAL ROTATION**

24

87 会	KAI, E, *au*	会社	KAISHA	company
	MEET	会釈	ESHAKU	greeting
	6 strokes	国会	KOKKAI	the Diet

Formerly 會 , and in ancient times 會 . 曾 is a **pot** for steaming rice, and 𠆢 is its **lid**. Putting the lid on the pot came to mean **put together** in general, and eventually became the intransitive **come together/ meet**. The simplification using **speak** 云 78 may possibly stem from confusion with **put together** 合 121 (literally mouth/<u>say</u> and lid), compounded by confusion of the lower part of the pot 日 with an old NGU character meaning **say**, 曰 (see 688) . However, an intermediate form 㑹 suggests it may result merely from a graphic simplification. Suggest taking 云 as **two** ニ 61 **noses** ム 134, with 𠆢 as a **roof.**

Mnemonic: **TWO NOSES MEET UNDER ROOF**

88		KAI, umi	海軍	KAIGUN	navy
		SEA	日本海	NIHONKAI	Japan Sea
		9 strokes	海辺	UMIBE	seaside

Water 氵 40 and **every** 毎 206, which may also act phonetically to express **salty**. Thus **every (drop of) (salty?) water**. All waters finish in the **sea**.

Mnemonic: **EVERY DROP OF WATER GOES INTO SEA**

---

89 絵	KAI, E	絵画	KAIGA	picture,painting
	PICTURE	口絵	KUCHIE	frontispiece
	12 strokes	絵本	EHON	picture book

Formerly 繪 . **Thread** 糸 27 and **put together/meet** 會 / 会 87. Originally **embroidered picture**, now **picture** in general.

Mnemonic: **THREADS MEET IN EMBROIDERED PICTURE**

90		kai	帆立貝	HOTATEGAI	scallop
		SHELL, SHELLFISH	貝殻	KAIGARA	seashell
		7 strokes	貝類	KAIRUI	shellfish

Usually claimed to be derived from a pictograph of a **cone-shell** or similar with **feelers** protruding. A useful mnemonic, but old forms such as 𦨶/𤰞 show that it derives from an exaggeratedly pointed **bivalve**. Shells were once used as **money** and symbolised **valuable items** or **assets**. In compounds 90 is generally used in such an extended sense.

Mnemonic: **SHELLFISH WITH PROTRUDING FEELERS**

91		GAI,GE,soto,hoka,hazus*u*	外人	GAIJIN	foreigner
		OUTSIDE,OTHER,UNDO	外科	GEKA	surgery
		5 strokes	外側	SOTOGAWA	exterior

Crescent moon 夕 44 and ⼘. The latter shows a **crack** (in a turtle shell used in divination), and is in fact an NGU character meaning **divination** . 夕 is used phonetically to express **split open**, and also lends its crescent shape to suggest a **turtle shell**. Since the cracks generally appeared on the **outside** (convex) surface of the shell, 91 came to mean **outside/outer**. **Other** and **undo** are associated meanings.

Mnemonic: **CRESCENT MOON WITH CRACK ON OUTSIDE**

92		KAN, KEN, aida, ma	時間	JIKAN	hour, time
		SPACE, GAP	人間	NINGEN	human being
		12 strokes	間違い	MACHIGAI	mistake

Door/gate 門 211 with **sun(light)** 日 62 showing through, indicating a **gap** or **space**. In olden times **moon** 月 16 could be used instead of sun with no change of meaning.

Mnemonic: **GATE WITH SPACE TO LET SUN SHINE THROUGH**

93		GAN, kao	顔面	GANMEN	face
		FACE	顔色	KAOIRO	complexion
		18 strokes	顔付き	KAOTSUKI	features

頁 is an NGU character now used to mean **page**, but in Chinese can still be used in its original meaning of **head.** It derives from 𧵎, showing **person** へ39 with exaggerated head 囟. 彥 is an NGU character meaning **handsome**. 文 is a variant of intricate/ elegant **collar** 文 68, here meaning **attractive**, while 彡 is a CO character meaning **hair,** showing three delicate hairs and sometimes meaning **delicate** and by extension **attractive** . 厂 is cliff 45, here used largely phonetically to express **forehead** but probably also suggesting **brow** in itself. Thus 彥 means literally **attractive forehead**, with **head** 頁 reinforcing this. It then came to mean attractive face, then just **face**. Suggest taking 产 as a variant of **stand** 立 73.

Mnemonic: **ONLY THREE HAIRS STAND ON HEAD: GLUM FACE**

94		KI	汽車	KISHA	steam train
		STEAM, VAPOR	汽船	KISEN	steamship
		7 strokes	汽圧	KIATSU	steam pressure

Water 氵 40 and **vapor** 气 11.

Mnemonic: **STEAM COMPRISES WATERY VAPORS**

95		**KI**	記者 KISHA	journalist
		ACCOUNT, CHRONICLE	記事 KIJI	article
		10 strokes	日記 NIKKI	diary

Words 言 274 and **self/thread** 己 855 q.v., used both for its sound to express **account** and for its idea of **from end to end**. Thus **thorough verbal account**, now also of written accounts.

Mnemonic: **WORDY ACCOUNT OF ONESELF**

96	帰	**KI, kae*ru***	帰化 KIKA	naturalisation
		RETURN	帰省 KISEI	homecoming
		10 strokes	帰り道 KAERIMICHI	way back

Formerly 歸. is an NGU character meaning **broom** (from a hand ⺕ holding a broom 巾), and by extension meant (house-)**wife** (see also 779). 皀 is a variant of **follow** 追 350. Thus **wife following**. In ancient China it was the custom for a groom to spend some time at his new bride's home, before **returning** to his own home with his wife following. Suggest taking simplified 刂 as **sword** 181.

Mnemonic: **RETURN WITH WIFE CARRYING BROOM AND SWORD**

97	牛	**GYŪ, ushi**	牛肉 GYŪNIKU	beef
		COW, BULL	牛乳 GYŪNYŪ	milk
		4 strokes	牛飼い USHIKAI	cowherd

From a stylised pictograph of a **cow's head and horns** 半. Opinion is divided as to whether the lower cross-stroke depicts **ears** or represents the crown of the head.

Mnemonic: **COW WITH EARS AND BROKEN HORN**

98	魚	**GYO, uo, sakana**	金魚 KINGYO	goldfish
		FISH	魚つり UOTSURI	fishing
		11 strokes	魚屋 SAKANAYA	fishmonger

From a pictograph of a **fish** . Suggest remembering by association with **fire** 灬 8.

Mnemonic: **FISH WITH FIERY TAIL**

99 京	KYŌ, KEI CAPITAL 8 strokes	東京 TŌKYŌ	Tokyo
		上京 JŌKYŌ	going to capital
		京浜 KEIHIN	
			Tokyo-Yokohama

Often explained as deriving from a pictograph of a **stone lantern** at the gate of the emperor's palace in the **capital**. A useful mnemonic, but incorrect. It derives from a pictograph 朵 . Some scholars see this as a **tower** of the emperor's palace, others as a **house on a hill** . In ancient China nobles generally lived on hilltops, with commoners on the flatland. Since nobles also spent much of their time in the **capital** (to be near the emperor), the idea of the **place where nobles live** is felt to have eventually become associated with the capital. It can still mean **height** in Chinese.

Mnemonic: **STONE LANTERN AT EMPEROR'S PALACE IN CAPITAL**

100 強	KYŌ, GŌ, tsuyoi STRONG 11 strokes	勉強 BENKYŌ	study
		強化 KYŌKA	strengthening
		強味 TSUYOMI	strongpoint

Formerly 強 . 虫 is **insect** 56. 弘 (also 弘) is an NGU character meaning **big/strong**, and is technically a simplification of the NGU character 彊, also **big/strong**. This comprises **bow** 弓 836 and **big** 畺 (actually large area of delineated fields, similar to 85 q.v.), giving **big, strong bow.** In the case of 100 it acts phonetically to express **pierce**, and also lends an idea of **big** and **strong**. Thus **big, strong insect that pierces**, a reference to the **horsefly.** This came to represent **strength**, possibly via an intermediate meaning of **persistent.** Suggest taking ム as **nose** 134.

Mnemonic: **STRONG INSECT DRAWS BOW WITH ITS NOSE**

101 教	KYŌ, oshieru TEACH 11 strokes	教会 KYŌKAI	church
		教室 KYŌSHITSU	classroom
		教え子 OSHIEGO	pupil

Formerly 敎 and originally 敎, showing that 孝 is not **filial piety** 孝 860 q.v. 爻 (now ⺑) is the same **crossed sticks/ emulation** as in 10 q.v., while 𠃌/子 is **child** 25. 𠬝/攵 shows a **hand holding** a cane or stick, and means **strike/ coerce/ cause to do** (sometimes interchanged with 攴/攴 , showing a hand holding a **whip**). Thus **force a child to emulate**, i.e. **teach.** See also 197.

Mnemonic: **CANE IN HAND TEACHES CHILD STICK ARRANGING**

102 GYOKU, tama
JEWEL, BALL
5 strokes

玉杯 GYOKUHAI   jade cup
玉突き TAMATSUKI   billiards
目玉 MEDAMA   eyeball

From a pictograph of a **string of beads** 􏰀, probably originally jade discs. **Ball** is an extended meaning. The extra point ˋ was added to distinguish it from **king** 王 5, but is dropped in the radical 𤣩 .

Mnemonic: **STRING OF JEWELS FIT FOR KING**

103 KIN, chika*i*
NEAR
7 strokes

近所 KINJO   neighborhood
最近 SAIKIN   recently
近道 CHIKAMICHI   shortcut

Movement 辶 129 and **ax** 斤 1176, here used phonetically to express **short** and probably also lending an idea of **chop/make small**. Thus **short movement**, indicating **near**.

Mnemonic: **DISTANCE TO MOVE CHOPPED, MAKING IT NEAR**

104 KEI, GYŌ, kata, katachi
SHAPE, PATTERN
7 strokes

形式 KEISHIKI   form
人形 NINGYŌ   doll
形作る KATACHIZUKURU
    form

Once written 井彡 . 井 is not **well** 井 1470, but a **grille** or **lattice window**, here meaning **pattern** or **frame**. 彡 is **hairs** 93, here also suggesting **pattern** and reinforcing 井 . Thus **pattern/shape**. Some scholars feel 彡 indicates a **brush**, to give a meaning of **write down/copy a pattern**.

Mnemonic: **PUT HAIRS INTO PATTERN OF WELL-FRAME**

105 KEI, haka*ru*
MEASURE
9 strokes

合計 GŌKEI   total
計算 KEISAN   calculation
寒暖計 KANDANKEI
    thermometer

Words 言 274 and **ten** 十 33, meaning to **count in tens** and later just **count/measure**.

Mnemonic: **COUNTING IN TENS IS A WAY OF MEASURING**

106	GEN, GAN, moto ORIGIN, SOURCE 4 strokes	元気 GENKI good health 元来 GANRAI originally 元通り MOTODŌRI as before

Once written 兀, showing a **person** 人 39 with the **head** exaggerated. As in English, the head symbolised **upper part** or **prime part**, and by extension **origin**. An extra top stroke was added later for emphasis. Suggest taking ニ as **two** 61.

Mnemonic: **TWO PERSONS OF SAME ORIGIN**

107	GEN, hara PLAIN, ORIGIN 10 strokes	原子 GENSHI atom 原文 GENBUN original text 草原 KUSAHARA grassy plain

厂 is **cliff** 45. 泉 is a variant of **spring** 泉 915 q.v. Thus **cliffside spring**, and by extension **source** or **origin**, often with connotations of **primary/primitive/natural**. **Plain/moor** is felt by some scholars to be a borrowed meaning, and by others to stem from the idea of primitive and undeveloped land.

Mnemonic: **ORIGINALLY CLIFF WITH FUNNY SPRING, NOW A PLAIN**

108	KO, to DOOR 4 strokes	戸外 KOGAI outdoor 戸主 KOSHU head of house 戸口 TOGUCHI doorway

From a pictograph of a **door** 戸, being one half of **door/gate** 門 211.

Mnemonic: **ONE DOOR FORMS HALF A GATE**

109	KO, furui OLD 5 strokes	復古 FUKKO restoration 考古学 KŌKOGAKU archeology 古本 FURUHON secondhand book

Somewhat obscure. Commonly explained as mouth/**say** 口 20 and **ten** 十 33, with the latter meaning **many**, to give **something told many times** and therefore **old**. A useful mnemonic, but shown to be incorrect by old forms such as 古. Some scholars take this to indicate a **skull-like mask** (sometimes an actual skull) worn at festivals honoring **ancestor-gods**. Since the ancestor-gods were people of old, the mask itself came to symbolise **antiquity** and hence **old**.

Mnemonic: **AN OLD STORY, TOLD AT LEAST TEN TIMES**

| 110 | 午 | GO NOON 4 strokes | 午前 GOZEN a.m., morning
 午後 GOGO p.m., afternoon
 正午 SHŌGO noon |

From a pictograph of a **pestle** 𝙄. It was borrowed to express the **central zodiac/horary sign**, i.e. the **middle part of the day**, partly because a pestle was associated with striking the **center** of a mortar. Pestle itself is now represented by an NGU character adding wood 木 69, 杵. Distinguish **cow** 牛 97.

Mnemonic: **NOON STRIKES, KNOCKING TOP BIT OFF COW**

| 111 | 後 | GO, KŌ, ushiro, ato, nochi, okureru BEHIND, AFTER, DELAY 9 strokes | 以後 IGO after
 後半 KŌHAN second half
 後味 ATOAJI aftertaste |

Road/movement 彳 118 q.v., **inverted foot** 夂 438, and 幺, a CO character meaning **small** and to all intents and purposes a **short** version of **thread** 糸 27. 彳 normally combines with <u>uninverted</u> foot 止 to give **normal progress/movement** (see 129), but here, in combination with <u>inverted</u> foot, indicates **abnormal progress**. 幺 acts phonetically to express **go** but also lends its meaning of **little**. Thus to **make (abnormally) little progress**, indicating **delay** and by extension **coming after/behind**. Suggest taking 夂 as **sitting crosslegged**.

Mnemonic: **SIT CROSSLEGGED ON THREADING ROAD, FALL BEHIND**

| 112 | 語 | GO, kataru TELL, SPEAK, TALK 14 strokes | 語調 GOCHŌ tone
 物語 MONOGATARI saga
 日本語 NIHONGO Japanese language |

Words 言 274 and 吾. The latter is an NGU character meaning **I/me**, but in Chinese can also mean **resist**. It was originally written 𦤻, showing **two identical reels** 𠀎 19. This expressed the idea of **being equal** and **well matched**, leading both to **resist** and to its use as a first person pronoun: that is, **one who is a person just like anyone else**. Note that not all first person references were depreciatory (see also 817). 112 originally meant **match someone verbally**, i.e. in an argument or similar, but later came to mean **speak well** and later **tell/speak** in a broad sense. Suggest taking 五 as **five** 19 and 口 as **mouth** 20.

Mnemonic: **FIVE MOUTHS SPEAK MANY WORDS**

113		**KŌ, KU** **WORK** 3 strokes	工場 KŌJŌ 人工 JINKŌ 大工 DAIKU	factory manmade carpenter

A **carpenter's adze-cum-square**, originally written 工. Symbolises **work**.

Mnemonic: **WORK WITH CARPENTER'S SQUARE**

114		**KŌ, hiroi**/*geru* **WIDE, SPACIOUS** 5 strokes	広大 KŌDAI 広島 HIROSHIMA 広告 KŌKOKU	vast place name advertisement

Formerly 廣, and originally 黄. ∩/广 shows a **roof/building**. 黄/黄 is **yellow** 120 q.v., here used phonetically to express **space** but possibly also lending an idea of **big area** from its original meaning of flaming arrow, with its connotations of illuminating an area. 114 originally referred to a **spacious building**, and now means **spacious** in a broad sense. Suggest taking the modern 厶 as an **elbow**.

Mnemonic: **SPACIOUS BUILDING WITH ELBOW-ROOM**

115		**KŌ, majiru, kawasu** **MIX, EXCHANGE** 6 strokes	交通 KŌTSU 外交 GAIKŌ 交換 KŌKAN	traffic diplomacy exchange

From a pictograph of a **person sitting with crossed legs** 交. Crossing gave rise to various extended meanings such as **intermingle, mix, change, exchange**. Suggest taking 六 as **six** 76 and 乂 as a **cross**.

Mnemonic: **MIX SIX CROSSES**

116		**KŌ, hikaru, hikari** **LIGHT, SHINE** 6 strokes	日光 NIKKŌ 光年 KŌNEN 光学 KŌGAKU	sunlight light year optics

Old forms such as 光 show 业 to be a variant of **fire** 火 8, with 儿 being **bending person** 39. Some scholars feel 儿 is used purely phonetically to express **big**, giving **big fire** and by extension **light**. However, the positioning of the components suggests a fire carried overhead, i.e. a **torch**.

Mnemonic: **PERSON CARRIES FIRE THAT SHINES LIGHT**

117 考	KŌ, kangae*ru* CONSIDER 6 strokes	考案 KŌAN	idea
		参考 SANKŌ	reference
		考え事 KANGAEGOTO	concern

Once written 芳. 芳 (now 耂) is a rather awkward ideograph showing a **bent figure** 人 39 and **long hair** 𠂇 (the same form as hair 㠯/毛 210), both of which were associated with **old age**. 丁/丂 (also 丂) is **twisting waterweed** 281, emphasising the idea of **bending**. Thus an **old man bent with age**, a meaning still found in Chinese. Some scholars feel **consider** is a borrowed meaning, others see it as stemming from the wisdom associated with old age. Suggest remembering old man 耂 by association with **earth** 土 60, with / representing something **half-buried**, i.e. ready for grave.

Mnemonic: **BENT OLD MAN CONSIDERS BURIAL IN EARTH**

118 行	KŌ, GYŌ, AN, *iku*, *yuku*, okona*u* GO,CONDUCT,COLUMN 6 strokes	実行 JIKKŌ	carrying out
		行列 GYŌRETSU	procession
		行方 YUKUE *	whereabouts

From a pictograph of **crossroads** 𣎳. Has a range of extended meanings, such as **go, travel, column**, and **act**. As a radical, simplified to 彳. Often combined with **foot** 止 129 q.v. to produce 辶 or 辵, both indicating **movement**.

Mnemonic: **COLUMN GOES ALONG TO CROSSROADS**

119 高	KŌ, taka, takai TALL, HIGH, SUM 10 strokes	高原 KŌGEN	plateau
		最高 SAIKŌ	highest
		高値 TAKANE	high price

Also 高. From a pictograph of a **tall watchtower** 髙. **Sum** derives from the idea of **build up**.

Mnemonic: **TALL WATCHTOWER**

120 黄

KŌ, Ō, ki*iro*
YELLOW
11 strokes

黄葉 KŌYŌ yellow leaves
黄金 ŌGON gold
黄色 KIIRO yellow

Formerly 𦰩 , and in ancient times 𡩬 or 𦳕. 𡥜 shows an **arrow**, while ⊖ is **combustible material** bound to it (some scholars claim a **weight** to counterbalance combustible material at tip). The exact meaning of 廿 (earliest form 廿) is not clear, but it is known to be associated with **burning** and is possibly a stylised variant of an early form of fire 8. The original meaning of 120 was **flaming arrow**. **Yellow** was the color of the light given off, and came to prevail as a meaning. Suggest remembering flaming arrow by association with **grass** 艹 9 and **field** 田 59.

Mnemonic: **ARROW BURNS YELLOW WITH GRASS FROM FIELD**

121 合

GŌ, KATSU, a*u/waseru*
MEET, JOIN, FIT
6 strokes

合理 GŌRI rationality
合戦 KASSEN battle
話し合い HANASHIAI discussion

Originally 合 . 亼 is a **lid** or **cover**. Some scholars see 口 as a **container**, to give a similar meaning to that of 87, while others see it as **mouth /say** 20, to give a meaning similar to the English term **cap off a remark**, i.e. **reply fittingly**. The role of 121 in **reply** 答 185 q.v. supports the latter theory. It now means **fit** or **join** in a broad sense.

Mnemonic: **CAP FITS MOUTH**

122 谷

KOKU, tani, ya
VALLEY, GORGE
7 strokes

幽谷 YŪKOKU deep ravine
谷底 TANIZOKO valley bottom
長谷川 HASEGAWA* surname

Opening 口 20 and **splitting** 八 66, doubled for emphasis. Thus **deeply/ widely split opening**, i.e. **valley** or **gorge**.

Mnemonic: **VALLEY IS DOUBLY SPLIT OPENING**

123 国

KOKU, kuni
COUNTRY, REGION
8 strokes

外国 GAIKOKU overseas
四国 SHIKOKU Shikoku
国家 KOKKA state

Formerly 國 . 或 is **delineated area** 809 q.v., while 囗 indicates **enclosed**. The modern form uses **jewel** 玉 102, though king 王 5 might have been a more logical choice.

Mnemonic: **ONE'S COUNTRY IS AN ENCLOSED JEWEL**

124		KOKU, kuro*i*	黒人	KOKUJIN	negro
		BLACK	黒字	KUROJI	(in) 'the black'
		11 strokes	黒死病	KOKUSHIBYŌ	
					black death

Formerly 黑, and originally 熏. 炎 is **flame** 1024. ⊕ represents a **grille** or **window** ⊕ with marks ╌ on it resulting from its position over the flames, i.e. **soot**. Soot symbolises **black**. Suggest following the popular but incorrect theory that 田 is **field** 59 and 土 is **ground** 60, with 灬 as **fire** 8, giving the **color of the ground in a burnt field**.

Mnemonic: **GROUND IN BURNT FIELD IS BLACK**

125	今	KON, KIN, ima	今週	KONSHŪ	this week
		NOW	今度	KONDO	this time
		4 strokes	今年	KOTOSHI*	this year

Somewhat obscure. Once written 仐 and 仐. 亼 is **cover** 87. ㇅ is felt to mean **put in a corner /conceal** (variant ㇄ 349). Thus to **cover/hide**. Some scholars feel it was borrowed to express **sudden**, which came to mean **imminent** and finally **now**.

Mnemonic: **COVER THE CORNER, RIGHT NOW**

126	才	SAI	天才	TENSAI	genius
		TALENT, YEAR OF AGE	才能	SAINŌ	talent
		3 strokes	五才	GOSAI	five years old

Originally ㇌, later 才, depicting a **dam** ▽ across a **stream** ㇑. Its current meanings result from borrowing.

Mnemonic: **FUNNY DAM BUILT BY TALENTED ONE-YEAR-OLD**

127	作	SAKU, SA, tsuku*ru*	製作	SEISAKU	production
		MAKE	作品	SAKUHIN	a work
		7 strokes	動作	DŌSA	action

亻 is **person** 39. 乍 is an NGU character now borrowed phonetically to express **while** but it originally meant **make**. It derives from 㐌, with ㇄ being a type of **adze** and 木 being **wood** 69, giving **adze on wood** and thus **make/construct** something. Here it lends its early meaning of **make**, and also acts phonetically to express **deceive**. Thus a **made/ constructed person used to deceive**, i.e. a **dummy** or by extension **stand-in**. Over the years the elements became reinterpreted as **person who makes**, rather than **person who is made**, and finally came to mean just **make**. Suggest taking 乍 as a **saw**.

Mnemonic: **PERSON WITH SAW ABOUT TO MAKE SOMETHING**

128 SAN
RECKON, COUNT
14 strokes

計算	KEISAN	calculation
予算	YOSAN	budget
算数	SANSŪ	arithmetic

竹 is bamboo 170. 昇 derives from 貝, showing **two hands** 廾 holding what is felt to be an **abacus** 目. Thus **use a bamboo abacus**.

Mnemonic: **COUNT BY USING BAMBOO ABACUS WITH BOTH HANDS**

---

129 止 SHI, to*meru*/*maru*
STOP
4 strokes

中止	CHŪSHI	suspension
止め処	TOMEDO	end
止まり木	TOMARIGI	perch

From a pictograph of a (left) **footprint** , later 凵. Originally meant **foot**, but also came to mean **stop**, from the idea of **planting the foot**. Confusingly, it can also be used in compounds to mean **move**, from the idea of a **trail of footprints**, but when used in this sense it is almost always used in combination with **road** 彳 118 to give 辻 and hence 辶 / 辶 / 辶. Also confusingly, the shape 止 is virtually identical with 龷, a rarely encountered variant of **growing plant** 生 42. Suggest remembering by association with **above** 上 37.

Mnemonic: **FOOTPRINTS STOP ABOVE LINE**

---

130 市 SHI, ichi
CITY, MARKET
5 strokes

吹田市	SUITASHI	Suita City
市場	SHIJŌ	market
魚市	UOICHI	fishmarket

Originally 巿. 止 is **stop** 129.) 〡 indicates **confines** and by extension **delineated area**. 丁 is a variant of **waterweed** 丂 281, which normally indicates **bending** but confusingly can occasionally mean **flat** (from the idea of the weed twisting up to the surface and then spreading out flat). Thus **place where things flatten out and stop**. Fanciful as it may seem, this was a reference to the abstract idea of the leveling of opposed interests of buyer and seller, which took place in a **market**. Markets were usually held in **large towns**. Suggest taking 巾 as **cloth** 778 and 上 as a **top hat**.

Mnemonic: **GO TO CITY MARKET TO BUY CLOTH TOP HAT**

131	SHI, om*ou* THINK 9 strokes	思想 SHISŌ 思考 SHIKŌ 思い出す OMOIDASU	ideology thought recall

Usually explained as **heart/feelings** 心 147 q.v. and **field** 田 59, to the effect that people of old were constantly thinking of their fields and crops. A useful mnemonic, but incorrect. Old forms such as 𤔔 show that 田 is a **brain** (from a depiction of a brain with crenellations ⊕). Thus the **feelings in one's brain**, i.e. **thoughts**.

Mnemonic: **ALWAYS THINKING OF ONE'S FIELD IN ONE'S HEART**

132	SHI, kami PAPER 10 strokes	表紙 HYŌSHI 和紙 WASHI 手紙 TEGAMI	book-cover Japanese paper letter

糸 is **thread** 27, here meaning **silk thread**. 氏 is **spoon/ladle** 495 q.v., here used phonetically to express **smooth** and possibly also lending similar connotations (the surface of a spoon usually being smooth). 132 originally referred to **smooth silk**, and by extension **smooth cloth**. In ancient times cloth was used as writing material, and thus 132 came to mean **writing material** and hence **paper**.

Mnemonic: **POUND THREADS WITH SPOON TO MAKE PAPER**

133	JI, tera TEMPLE 6 strokes	竜安寺 RYŌANJI 寺院 JIIN 山寺 YAMADERA	Ryoan Temple Buddhist temple mountain temple

Once written 㞑 , leading to long-standing belief that 止 is **stop** 止 129. However, an earlier form 㞢 shows that it is in fact the confusingly similar variant of **growing plant** 生 42 q.v. It is used here to symbolise **activity** (an extended meaning from living growth as opposed to inanimate inertia), and combines with **measure/hand** 寸 909, which here means **regular and methodical use of the hands**, to give **active and methodical use of the hands** (rather than stationary work with hands when 止 is taken to mean stop). This was a reference to **clerical work** (the English use of the term manual labor to mean physical labor being somewhat misleading), and by extension **place of work/ government office**. It can still have this meaning in Chinese, but generally came to mean **temple** since temples were often associated with clerical work. Suggest taking 土 as **ground** 60.

Mnemonic: **TEMPLE HAS MEASURED GROUNDS**

134

自

JI, SHI, mizuka*ra*
SELF
6 strokes

自分 JIBUN   self
自然 SHIZEN   nature
自信 JISHIN   self-confidence

From a stylised depiction of the **nose** 𦣻, for some reason showing what appears to be a
ridge ＝. **Self** stems from the Oriental practice of pointing to the nose to refer to oneself,
as opposed to the chest as in the West. **Self** is sometimes expressed by 厶, an NGU character and a common element in compounds. Its early form is 𠮟, the same form as **plow**
419 q.v. Some scholars see these as one character, plow, with **self** stemming from a phonetic borrowing, while others see it as depicting a **nose** seen side-on and thus by association **self**. Suggest remembering by association with **eye** 目 72, taking ╱ as a **stroke.**

Mnemonic: **NOSE IS JUST A STROKE FROM EYE, SYMBOLISING SELF**

135

時

JI, toki
TIME, HOUR
10 strokes

時代 JIDAI   era, period
二時 NIJI   two o'clock
時時 TOKIDOKI   sometimes

Surprisingly obscure. Originally written 𣅉, showing **stop** 㞢/止 129 and **sun /day** 日
62, and possibly having a meaning such as **end of the day** and thus symbolising the
passage of time. However, at a very early stage **stop** 止 appears to have become confused with **growing plant** 㞢/生 42 q.v., giving 𣅉, which possibly meant **emergence
of the sun**. At a later stage 㞢 was replaced by **temple** 寺 133 q.v., used phonetically
to express **move** and probably also lending connotations of **regularity**. Thus **regular
movement of the sun**, i.e. **time**. **Hour** is an associated meaning.

Mnemonic: **TELL TIME BY SUN ON TEMPLE**

136

室

SHITSU, muro
ROOM, HOUSE
9 strokes

室内 SHITSUNAI   indoors
居室 KYOSHITSU living room
室津 MUROTSU   place-name

宀 is **roof** 28. 至 is **arrive** 875 q.v., here acting phonetically to express **stop** and also
lending a similar idea of **arrive and stop** (from an arrow sinking in). Thus **place under
roof where one can stop**, i.e. a **room**. By extension it is sometimes used to mean
house or **household**.

Mnemonic: **ARRIVE AT ROOFED ROOM**

137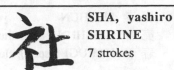

SHA, yashiro
SHRINE
7 strokes

社会 SHAKAI   society
神社 JINJA   shrine
社員 SHAIN
      company employee

Formerly 祉. 示/礻 is **altar** 695 q.v. 土 is **ground** 60. The ground around an altar was sacred, and thus a **shrine**.

Mnemonic: **ALTAR GROUND IS SHRINE**

---

138 弱

JAKU, yowai
WEAK
10 strokes

弱点 JAKUTEN   weak point
弱小 JAKUSHŌ   puniness
弱虫 YOWAMUSHI weakling

Formerly 弱 and earlier , showing a doubling of **bow** 弓 836, here meaning **bending**, and **delicate hairs** 彡 93. Thus **something bent easily as delicate hair**, i.e. **weak**.

Mnemonic: **WEAK HAIRS BEND LIKE BOWS**

---

139 首

SHU, kubi
HEAD, NECK, CHIEF
9 strokes

首領 SHURYŌ   leader
首輪 KUBIWA   necklace
首切り KUBIKIRI decapitation

Originally 𦣻, showing an **eye** with exaggerated eyebrow and indicating the eye area of the face. However, later forms such as 𦣻 show confusion with **head** 首/頁 93, with **hair** 川 added. Can also be used figuratively as **chief**. **Neck** is an associated meaning. Suggest taking 百 as a variant of 93, with ⸍ as **hair**.

Mnemonic: **CHIEF HAS HAIR ON HEAD**

140

SHŪ, aki
AUTUMN
9 strokes

晩秋 BANSHŪ   late autumn
秋分 SHŪBUN autumn equinox
秋空 AKIZORA   autumn sky

Rice plant 禾 81 and **fire** 火 8. Some scholars feel 火 is used purely phonetically to express **gather**, thus referring to the autumn harvest. However, it may also lend a meaning of **dry** (after the heat of summer) or refer literally to the **autumn crop-fires** caused by the Foehn Wind.

Mnemonic: **RICE PLANTS CAN GET BURNED IN AUTUMN**

141 春	SHUN, haru	青春	SEISHUN	youth
	SPRING	売春	BAISHUN	prostitution
	9 strokes	春着	HARUGI	spring clothes

Originally 萅, showing the **vigorous growth of a mulberry plant** 𣎴 (see 1518) in the **sunshine** 日 62. Vigorous growth symbolises **spring**. Suggest taking 夫 as **three** 三 23 **people** 人 39.

Mnemonic: **THREE PEOPLE ENJOY SPRING SUN**

---

142 書	SHO, ka*ku*	書記	SHOKI	secretary
	WRITE	教科書	KYŌKASHO	textbook
	10 strokes	葉書	HAGAKI	postcard

聿 shows a **hand** ⺕ holding a **brush** ⼅. 日 is a simplified form of **thing** 者 298, which also lends its sound to express **copy**. Thus **copy a thing by brush**, i.e. **write**. Suggest taking 日 as **day** 62.

Mnemonic: **TAKE BRUSH IN HAND DAILY AND WRITE**

---

143 少	SHŌ, suko*shi*, suku*nai*	少年	SHŌNEN	a youth
	FEW, A LITTLE	少数	SHŌSŪ	minority
	4 strokes	多少	TASHŌ	more or less

Originally ⼩. As **small** 小 36 but with four points instead of three, to suggest smaller size. It originally meant **tiny size** but is now generally applied to quantity rather than size.

Mnemonic: **SMALL WITH JUST A LITTLE EXTRA**

---

144 場	JŌ, ba	会場	KAIJŌ	meeting place
	PLACE	入場	NYŪJŌ	admission
	12 strokes	広場	HIROBA	open space

土 is **ground** 60. 昜 is a CO character now meaning **bright** and **open out**. Its early form 昜 shows the **sun** 日 62 rising high and shining down (represented by a symbol 勿 conveniently thought of as **rays**), and in compounds it often lends a meaning of **rise**. **Sun rising and shedding light** led by association to **bright** and to the idea of **opening something up to the light**. Here it lends a meaning of **open** and also lends its sound to express **clear**. Thus **clear open ground**, now used to mean **place**.

Mnemonic: **PLACE WHERE SUN SHINES DOWN ON GROUND**

145

SHOKU, SHIKI, iro
COLOR, SENSUALITY
6 strokes

好色 KŌSHOKU amorousness
色素 SHIKISO pigment
銀色 GINIRO silver color

Once written 产. ル/ケ shows a **person bending**. 己/巴 also shows a **person bending** (originally kneeling, but used to indicate bending body in general). Thus one person bending over another bending person, which was a reference to the **sex act**. It still retains strong sexual connotations, especially in Japanese. It is not completely clear how it came to mean **color**. However, many scholars feel that it was used to refer to **sexual partner**, especially from a male perspective, and that it then came to mean **sexually attractive**, leading in time to **attractive/ pretty** in a general sense and then by association to **colorful.**

Mnemonic: **COLORFUL TALE ABOUT BODIES BENT IN SEX ACT**

146

SHOKU, ta*beru*, ku*u*
FOOD, EAT
9 strokes

食事 SHOKUJI meal
食べ物 TABEMONO food
食い物 KUIMONO food, victim

Originally 畠, showing **food piled in a long-stemmed dish** and essentially the same prototype as vessel 豆 1640. At an early stage the piled food ∧ became a **lid** ∧ 87, giving **covered food in dish**. Thus **food** and by association **eat**. Suggest remembering by association with **good** 良 598. As a radical, usually 飠, 食, or 𩙿.

Mnemonic: **COVERED FOOD GOOD FOR EATING**

147

SHIN, kokoro
HEART, FEELINGS
4 strokes

中心 CHŪSHIN core
心臓 SHINZŌ heart
真心 MAGOKORO sincerity

From a pictograph of a **heart** 心. Also used figuratively as **feelings** or **mind**. As a radical usually 忄. Suggest remembering as a heart whose **strokes** have been **'damaged'** by stylisation.

Mnemonic: **HEART SHOWS STROKE DAMAGE**

148 新 SHIN, atara*shii*, ara*ta*   新年 SHINNEN   New Year
NEW   新品 SHINPIN   new article
13 strokes   新人 SHINJIN   newcomer

Originally 𢧌, showing **ax** 乍/斤 1176 and **needle/sharp** 𠂤/辛 1432. Thus **sharp ax**. At an early stage the barbs of the needle became merged or confused with **tree** 木 69 and its branches, giving 新 and a meaning of **chop down a tree**. The idea of cutting wood is retained in **firewood** 薪 1445, that adds plant 艹 9. (Note also that 亲 exists as a CO character meaning thorn-tree, but does not act in that capacity here.) How exactly 148 came to mean **new** is not clear. Some scholars feel it was borrowed phonetically, but its complexity suggests otherwise. More likely, the idea of chopping down trees was associated with building, i.e. **new** construction, or else **newly cut** wood requiring seasoning. Suggest taking 立 as **stand** 73.

Mnemonic: **STAND OF TREES NEWLY CUT DOWN BY SHARP AX**

149 親 SHIN, shita*shii*, o*ya*   両親 RYŌSHIN   parents
INTIMATE, PARENT   親類 SHINRUI   relatives
16 strokes   親子 OYAKO   parent and child

Somewhat obscure. Originally 𡩡, showing **see** 見 18 and **needle/sharp** 𠂤/辛 1432. The latter acted phonetically to express **kin**, giving **kin one sees** (all the time), i.e. one's **immediate family**. Possibly because of the similarity to 148 q.v., 149 similarly (but at a later stage) replaced needle 𠂤 with needle-tree 亲, though the sound value was unaffected. Suggest taking 立 as **stand** 73 and 木 as **tree** 69.

Mnemonic: **PARENT SEES ALL FROM STAND OF TREES**

150 ZU, TO, haka*ru*   地図 CHIZU   map
PLAN, DIAGRAM   図画 ZUGA   drawing
7 strokes   図書館 TOSHOKAN   library

Formerly 圖. 囗 is an **enclosure**. 啚 is to all intents and purposes a variant of the **fields and sections** seen in **picture** 画 85 q.v. In fact, 150 and 85 are very similar in their basic meaning of **partitioning fields on a map**. Suggest taking 乂 as **X** and 丶 as **two pointers**.

Mnemonic: **DIAGRAM WITH SPOT MARKED BY X AND TWO POINTERS**

151

S Ū, SU, kazu, kazo*eru*
NUMBER, COUNT
13 strokes

数学 SŪGAKU mathematics
数珠 JUZU* rosary
数数 KAZUKAZU many

Formerly 數. 攵 is **stick in hand** 101, usually meaning strike but here indicating a **hand holding counting sticks**. 婁 is a rare NGU character now meaning **tie** or **often** (also **wear** in Chinese), but its original meaning was **shamaness**. It comprises **woman** 女 35 and 婁, an obscure element that appears to mean **link items** (not unlike skewer 串 1101). A shamaness was a woman linked to the gods (kamigakari). Here 婁 lends its sound to express **chant**, and presumably lends similar connotations of its own from the chanting associated with a shamaness. Thus **chant while holding counting sticks**, giving **count** and **number**. The modern form uses **rice** 米 201, primarily as a graphic simplification but possibly also using rice grains to suggest quantity.

Mnemonic: **WOMAN COUNTS NUMBER OF RICE GRAINS BY HAND**

152

SEI, SAI, nishi
WEST
6 strokes

西洋 SEIYŌ the West
関西 KANSAI Kansai area
西日 NISHIBI afternoon sun

Originally 卤, showing a **basket**. The basket was used as a crude **wine press**, and later forms such as 卤 show the addition of a pressing device ┏. It was used phonetically to express **west**, but also lends a suggestion of **falling (sun)** from the idea of falling drops of wine. See also 399.

Mnemonic: **SUN FALLS IN WEST LIKE DROP FROM WINE PRESS**

153

SEI, SHŌ, koe
VOICE
7 strokes

声援 SEIEN vocal support
大音声 DAIONJŌ loud voice
泣き声 NAKIGOE sobbing voice

Formerly 聲. 耳 is **ear** 29. 殸 is a simplification of 磬, a CO character indicating a musical instrument using suspended stones. It comprises **stone** 石 45, **strike** 殳 (a hand 又 holding an ax 𠂇/几, now used rather like strike 攵 101), and 声, which derives from a pictograph of the **instrument** itself 㕦. Thus **that which enters the ear when a musical instrument is struck,** i.e. **sound**. It can still mean sound in Chinese, but in Japanese is found only in its extended meaning of **voice**. Suggest taking 士 as **samurai** 494 and 尸 as a variant of **door** 戸 108.

Mnemonic: **VOICE OF SAMURAI AT DOOR**

154	SEI, SHŌ, hoshi STAR 9 strokes	火星 KASEI Mars 明星 MYŌJŌ Venus 流れ星 NAGAREBOSHI shooting star

Formerly 曐, and originally simply 晶, showing a trebling of **sun** 日 62. 晶 is now **bright** 1403, but its original meaning was **many points of light**. **Birth/life** 生 42 was added primarily for its sound, to express **clear**, but may also lend an idea of **activity**, i.e. light that twinkles as opposed to inert light. Thus **many points of (twinkling?) light**, i.e. **stars**.

Mnemonic: **STARS BORN FROM SUN**

155	SEI, ha*reru* CLEAR, BRIGHT 12 strokes	晴天 SEITEN clear sky 晴晴 HAREBARE bright 晴着 HAREGI best clothes

Also 晴. 日 is **sun** 62. 靑/青 is **blue/ young** 43, here used phonetically to express **open/ clear** and possibly also lending an idea of **fresh** and **blue**. Thus **clear open sun**, i.e. **clear weather**.

Mnemonic: **SUN AGAINST BLUE MEANS CLEAR WEATHER**

156	SETSU, SAI, ki*ru* CUT 4 strokes	親切 SHINSETSU kindness 一切 ISSAI all 腹切り HARAKIRI harakiri

刀 is **sword/cut** 181. 七 is **seven** 30 q.v., with its literal meaning of **cutting**.

Mnemonic: **SEVEN SWORD CUTS**

157	SETSU, yuki SNOW 11 strokes	降雪 KŌSETSU snowfall 大雪 ŌYUKI heavy snow 除雪車 JOSETSUSHA snowplow

Also 雪, and earlier 雪. 雨 is **rain** 3, here meaning **that which falls from the heavens**. ヨ is **hand**, while 彗 is a **broom** doubled for emphasis and symbolising **clearing away**. (彗 exists as an NGU character now meaning comet, from the idea of a sweeping tail, but in Chinese still means **broom/sweep**.) Being able to clear away that which has fallen from the heavens indicates that it has some substance to it, i.e. **snow**.

Mnemonic: **RAIN THAT HAND SWEEPS AWAY IS SNOW**

158 船 SEN, fune, funa-
BOAT, SHIP
11 strokes

船長 SENCHŌ captain
こぎ船 KOGIBUNE rowboat
船便 FUNABIN sea-mail

舟 is **boat** 1354. 㕣 is a CO character now meaning water at base of hill, but it originally meant **hollowed out** (from split/out 八 66 and opening 口 20), and was virtually a lesser version of valley 谷 122. Thus a **hollowed out boat**. Opinion is divided as to whether this initially referred to a primitive dug-out or rather to the carrying capacity of a boat (cf. English **vessel**). Suggest taking 八 as **eight** and 口 as **hole**.

Mnemonic: **BOAT WITH EIGHT PORTHOLES IS SHIP**

---

159 前 ZEN, mae
BEFORE, FRONT
9 strokes

前者 ZENSHA the former
空前 KŪZEN unprecedented
前払い MAEBARAI prepayment

Formerly , and earlier 歬. 刂/刀 is **sword/cut** 181. 歬/𣥷 is a now defunct character meaning **advance**, comprising foot 止 129 (now 龰), here meaning **go**, and **boat** 舟/舟 1354, which from its connotations of **hollowed out (wood)** was occasionally used, as here, to refer to a primitive type of **clog**. Thus 歬 meant literally **put on one's shoes and go**, thus coming to mean **go ahead/ advance**. In combination with **cut** it lent its sound to express **trim/ arrange** and also lent an idea of **progress**, to mean **make progress in trimming with a cutting tool**. However, eventually 歬 reverted to the meaning of 歬, i.e. **advance** and by extension **front/ before**. The idea of trimming with a cutting tool is now conveyed by an NGU character **prune** 剪, that adds an extra **cut** 刀 181. (Note also that adding hand 扌 32 gives the NGU character **arrange** 揃.) Suggest taking 月 as **meat** 365, with 龰 as **horns**.

Mnemonic: **BEFORE CUTTING MEAT CUT HORNS**

---

160 SO, kumi, ku*mu*
GROUP, ASSEMBLE
11 strokes

組織 SOSHIKI organisation
組合 KUMIAI union
組み立て KUMITATE assembly

Thread 糸 27 and **furthermore/ cairn** 且 1091 q.v., here used in its early meaning of **build up**. **Build up threads** meant to **braid**, and by extension **assemble**. **Group** is an associated meaning.

Mnemonic: **FURTHERMORE, THREADS CAN BE ASSEMBLED IN GROUP**

| 161 | | SŌ, hashi*ru*
RUN
7 strokes | 競走 KYŌSŌ
走行 SŌKŌ
走り書き HASHIRIGAKI | race
traveling
scrawl |

Originally 𢪉, showing foot 匕/止 129, here meaning **move**, and a **man moving frantically** 夭. Thus **frantic movement with the feet**, i.e. **running**. Suggest taking 土 as **ground** 60.

Mnemonic: **FOOT RUNNING ALONG GROUND**

| 162 | | SŌ, kusa
GRASS, PLANT
9 strokes | 雑草 ZASSŌ
草書 SŌSHO
草地 KUSACHI | weed
cursive script
grassland |

Grass/plant 艹 9 and **early** 早 50 q.v. The latter is used phonetically to express **plant**, and possibly also lends an idea of a **seed splitting open** and thus being about to develop into a **plant** . (Though the 十 of 50 can conveniently be taken as the crossed lines/cut of seven 七 30, it also overlaps with the crossed cuts 十 of the early forms ⊕ and 十 of shell 甲 1243 q.v., depicting a seed splitting open. 50 and 1243 were in fact sometimes confused.) **Plant** and **grass** are less clearly differentiated than in English.

Mnemonic: **GRASS IS EARLY PLANT**

| 163 | | TA, ō*i*
MANY
6 strokes | 多数 TASŪ
多面 TAMEN
多過ぎる ŌSUGIRU | majority, mass
many sides
too many |

Evening 夕 44 doubled to indicate plurality. Thus **many evenings/ often**, finally just **many**.

Mnemonic: **MANY EVENINGS**

| 164 | 太 | TAI, TA, futo*i/ru*
FAT, BIG
4 strokes | 太子 TAISHI
太陽 TAIYŌ
太字 FUTOJI | prince
sun
bold type |

A simplification of 态, showing **two** 二 61 and **big** 大 53, which was in turn a simplification of 夳, being a doubling of 大 for emphasis. Thus **very big**, now often used for **fat**.

Mnemonic: **FAT IS A BIT MORE THAN JUST BIG**

---

165 体   TAI, TEI, karada   体格   TAIKAKU   physique
     BODY   風体   FŪTEI   appearance
     7 strokes   体付き   KARADATSUKI   figure

Formerly also 體, showing **bone** 骨 867 and **plentiful** 豊 790. Thus, **that in which bones are plentiful,** meaning the **entire body** as opposed to a limb. The form using **person** イ 39 and **root** 本 70, to give the **root of a person,** has been used for several centuries as a substitute, but is technically a separate character with an early meaning of crude (presumably **basic person** or similar).

Mnemonic: **ROOT OF A PERSON IS THE BODY**

---

166 台   DAI, TAI   土台   DODAI   base
     STAND, PLATFORM   台風   TAIFŪ   typhoon
     5 strokes   台所   DAIDOKORO   kitchen

In Japanese formerly also written 臺, but this is a separate character and is generally treated as such in Chinese. 臺 is the correct character for **platform**, and comprises **tall** 咼(variant 高 119), **earth** 士 (variant 土 60), and **peak/arrive** 至 875, which also acts phonetically to express stop/be stationed. Thus **mound of earth on the top of which one is stationed,** i.e. look-out rampart and hence **platform**. 台 is used in Chinese to mean **self** (confusingly both as I and you), and comprises **self** ム 134 and **mouth/say** 口 20, giving **name oneself** and finally just **self**. It was borrowed phonetically as a simple substitute for 臺.

Mnemonic: **I MOUNT STAND TO SAY SOMETHING**

---

167 地   CHI, JI   地方   CHIHŌ   region
     GROUND, LAND   地下   CHIKA   underground
     6 strokes   生地   KIJI*   cloth, texture

土 is **ground** 60. 也 is an NGU character now borrowed to express **to be,** but originally meant **twisting creature** (opinion is divided as to whether early forms such as 𧍙 and 𧌟 depict a scorpion, snake, or some type of insect, though snake seems most likely), and often lends an idea of **twisting**. Here it means **undulating,** giving **undulating ground** and eventually just **ground/land/region** with various extended usages. Unfortunately there is no easy mnemonic for 也.

Mnemonic: **LAND WITH ODD TWISTING CREATURES ON GROUND**

---

168 CHI, ike

POND, LAKE

6 strokes

用水池 YŌSUICHI reservoir
電池 DENCHI battery
古池 FURUIKE old pond

Water 氵 40 and **twisting creature** 也 167. The latter is used phonetically to express **bank**, and probably also lends an idea of **coiling** and thus joining with itself. Thus **water encircled by banks**.

Mnemonic: **WATERS OF POND CONTAIN TWISTING CREATURES**

---

169 CHI, shi*ru*

KNOW

8 strokes

知識 CHISHIKI knowledge
知性 CHISEI intellect
知り合い SHIRIAI acquaintance

Mouth/say 口 20 and **arrow** 矢 981, to give a meaning of **speak with speed of arrow** , thus indicating **thorough knowledge**. Suggest taking 口 as a **hole**.

Mnemonic: **KNOW ARROW HOLE**

---

170 CHIKU, take

BAMBOO

6 strokes

竹材 CHIKUZAI bamboo
竹田 TAKEDA a surname
竹やぶ TAKEYABU
bamboo grove

Often believed to show bamboo segments 𝌀, but in fact early forms such as ↑↑ depict **stems of dwarf bamboo with spiky leaves**. Now **bamboo** in general.

Mnemonic: **TWO BAMBOO STEMS**

---

171 CHA, SA

TEA, ANNOY

9 strokes

茶わん CHAWAN teabowl
茶茶 CHACHA interruption
茶菓 SAKA tea and cakes

Formerly also 茶, incorrectly showing tree 木 69. サ is **plant** 9, while 朶 is a simplification of **ample** 余 800. The latter is used phonetically to express **bitter**, but its semantic role is unclear. **Bitter plant** is a reference to **tea**. The very occasional use of 171 to mean **annoy** or similar may derive from **bitter**.

Mnemonic: **AMPLE TEA PLANTS**

---

172 昼

CHŪ, hir*u*
NOON, DAYTIME
9 strokes

昼食　CHŪSHOKU　　lunch
昼行性　CHŪKŌSEI　　diurnal
昼間　HIRUMA　　daytime

Formerly written 晝, and earlier as 𦘔. Very similar to early form of **picture** 画 85 q.v., 畫 (also earlier as 𦘕), except field 田 59 is replaced by **sun/day** 日 62. 𦘔/𦘕 still acts to indicate **section off/ partition**, and also lends its sound to express **bright**. Thus the **bright section of the day**, i.e. **daytime** or **noon**. Suggest taking ＿ as **horizon** and the modern simplification 尺 as **measure in feet** 尺 884 , of which it may in fact be a deliberate borrowing.

Mnemonic: **MEASURE IN FEET NOON SUN OVER HORIZON**

---

173 長

CHŌ, naga*i*
LONG, SENIOR
8 strokes

成長　SEICHŌ　　growth
会長　KAICHŌ　　chairperson
長生き　NAGAIKI　　long life

Also 镸 . From a depiction of an **old man with long flowing hair** (a sign of age), bent with age and leaning on a stick (see also old 老 609). This gave rise to **long, grow,** and **senior,** with associated meanings such as **excel** and **chief.**

Mnemonic: **LONG HAIRED OLD MAN WITH STICK IS VERY SENIOR**

---

174 鳥

CHŌ, tori
BIRD
11 strokes

白鳥　HAKUCHŌ　　swan
野鳥　YACHŌ　　wild bird
鳥居　TORII　　shrine gate

From a pictograph of a **bird** .

Mnemonic: **BIRD WITH WINGS AND TALONS**

---

175 朝

CHŌ, asa
MORNING, COURT
12 strokes

朝食　CHŌSHOKU　　breakfast
朝日　ASAHI　　morning sun
朝廷　CHŌTEI　　imperial court

Formerly 朝, and earlier as 𦥑川, showing that 月 is not **moon** 16 but a derivative of **river** 川 48. 𦥑/𠦝 shows the **sun** 日 62 **rising** through **plants** 十 9, lending a meaning of **rise** to give **rising river**. This is still found in **tide** 潮 941, which adds water ⺡ 40. In the case of 175 the rising sun element came to prevail in its own right, leading to **morning.** **Court** is felt to derive from figurative association with the idea of **source of light**. Suggest taking 月 as **moon.**

Mnemonic: **MORNING SUN RISES ON PLANTS, DISPLACING MOON**

176 **TSŪ, tō*ru*/*su*, kayo*u***
PASS, WAY, COMMUTE
10 strokes

通行 TSŪKŌ — passage
通勤 TSŪKIN — commuting
大通り ŌDŌRI — main road

辶 is **movement** 129. 甬 is a CO character meaning **raised**. It was originally written 甬, showing the **sun** ☉ / 日 62 rising above a **brushwood fence** 𦥑/用 215, and also has connotations of **break clear** or **emerge**. In combination with 辶 it gives a meaning of **uninterrupted movement**, giving **pass through**, a **road/way**, and **commute** (i.e. go directly). Suggest taking 用 in its modern sense of **use**, with マ as a **bent figure**.

Mnemonic: **BENT FIGURE USES EXTRA MOVEMENT TO PASS**

---

177 **TEI, DAI, DE, otōto**
YOUNGER BROTHER
7 strokes

子弟 SHITEI — sons
弟子 DESHI — pupil
兄弟 KYŌDAI — brothers

Once written 弟. 干 is a **stake**, still technically listed as an NGU character 弋 with that meaning but now usually found as an NGU character **stake** 杙 that adds wood 木 69. 乙 shows **binding**, which was necessary as a grip since stakes were used as weapons (弋 overlaps with 弐, the prototype of lance/halberd 493). There was a set **order** to the manner of binding, and hence 177 also came to mean **sequence** or **order**. It can still be used in this sense in Chinese, though it is generally replaced by **order** 第 339, that adds **bamboo** 竹 170. By association the idea of order was also applied to **sons** in a family, especially those other than the eldest, since **age-order** was an important factor in **ranking**.

Mnemonic: **YOUNG BROTHERS PUT IN ORDER AS BINDING ON STAKE**

---

178 **TEN, mise, tana**
STORE, PREMISES
8 strokes

店員 TENIN — store clerk
夜店 YOMISE — night stall
店立て TANADATE — eviction

广 is **building** 114. 占 is **divination** 1491 q.v., here acting phonetically to express **arrange/ display** and probably also lending its own idea of **arrange and announce**. Thus **building where goods are arranged on display (and announced?)**, i.e. a **store**. It is sometimes used of **premises** in general. Suggest taking 占 in its commoner meaning of **occupy**.

Mnemonic: **STORE OCCUPIES BUILDING**

179

TEN
POINT, MARK
9 strokes

点線 TENSEN   dotted line
得点 TOKUTEN   points
重点 JŪTEN   emphasis

Formerly 點 . 黒 is **black** 124. 占 is **divination** 1491 q.v., here acting phonetically to express **small** and also lending an idea of **meaningful sign**. Thus **small black sign**, i.e. **point/ mark**, also used as in English to mean **score**. Suggest taking 占 in its commoner meaning of **occupy**, and ⺀ as **fire** 8.

Mnemonic: **MARK LEFT AFTER OCCUPATION BY FIRE**

180

DEN
ELECTRICITY
13 strokes

電話 DENWA   telephone
電球 DENKYŪ   light bulb
電流 DENRYŪ electric current

Once written 電 , and earlier 霝 . 雨 is **rain** 3, here meaning **sent down from the heavens**. 甩/电/电 is the prototype of **lightning** 申 322 q.v. 180 can still occasionally mean **lightning**, but is usually used nowadays to refer to **electricity**. Suggest taking 电 as **field** 田 59 with **lightning bolt** ∟.

Mnemonic: **LIGHTNING STRIKES FIELD IN ELECTRIC RAIN STORM**

181

TŌ, katana
SWORD
2 strokes

大刀 DAITŌ   long sword
軍刀 GUNTŌ   military sword
小刀 KOGATANA pocket knife

From a pictograph of a **curved sword** ⼑ , broader than the typical Japanese katana. As a radical usually found as ⺉ . Often symbolises **cut**.

Mnemonic: **BROAD-BLADED SWORD**

182 冬

TŌ, fuyu
WINTER
5 strokes

冬眠 TŌMIN   hibernation
冬季 TŌKI   winter season
冬将軍 FUYUSHŌGUN

'Jack Frost'

Obscure. Formerly also 冬 , and earlier 夅 and 夂 . The exact meaning of 夂 is unclear, though it is known to have acted phonetically to express **gather together/become compact**. There is some evidence to support a view that it represents **hanging ropes tied together** (see 306), said by some scholars to be ropes from which cured meat was hung during **winter**. 仌/冫 is the prototype of **ice** 氷 378. Thus **when ice becomes compact**, i.e. **winter**. Suggest taking 夂 as **sitting crosslegged**.

Mnemonic: **SITTING CROSSLEGGED ON WINTER ICE**

183 TŌ, *ataru/teru*
APPLY, HIT MARK,
APPROPRIATE, THIS
6 strokes

相当 SŌTŌ appropriate
当人 TŌNIN person concerned
手当て TEATE allowance

Formerly 當 . 田 is **field** 59. 尚 is a variant of **furthermore** 尚 1392 q.v., used phonetically to express **in proportion** and possibly also lending its own connotations of **appropriate** (from its depiction of a house with window **appropriately** facing north to avoid the sun from the south). 183 originally referred to offering a field -- or by extension property -- as surety for a loan, the amount of land to be pledged being determined **in proportion** to the sum advanced and being therefore deemed **appropriate**. (More exactly, the surety was usually the right to farm the land, since private ownership was very limited.) It still retains **pledge** as a lesser meaning in Chinese. **Apply, this,** and **hit mark/ be accurate** are associated meanings. Suggest taking modern form as **small** ⺌ (variant 小 36) and **hand** 彐 (see 96).

Mnemonic: **SMALL HAND APPROPRIATELY HITS MARK**

184 東 TŌ, *higashi*
EAST
8 strokes

東洋 TŌYŌ Orient
中東 CHŪTŌ Middle East
東側 HIGASHIGAWA east side

Usually explained incorrectly as **sun** 日 62 **rising** behind **trees** 木 69 to indicate **dawn** and thus **east**, an error of many centuries' standing. Very old forms such as 東 reveal that it is a **tied sack** 東 with a **pole thrust through** to facilitate carrying, and in that regard it is in the same group as **bundle** 束 1535 and **select/ open bundle** 柬 608 (see also **ridge-pole** 棟 1653). The error appears to stem from a reasonably early form 東 in which the ends of the binding have become separated from the sack, thus suggesting the early form of tree/wood. It is not clear whether this is a simple copying error, an attempt to refer to the wooden nature of the pole, or a mistaken interpretation of the elements as sun and tree. In any event, from an early stage 184 was borrowed phonetically to express **east**. Some scholars feel that it also lent an idea of **thrusting through** (i.e. the pole through the binding) and thus by extension suggested the **sun thrusting up through the horizon**, giving **dawn** and hence **east**. The usual theory is useful as a mnemonic.

Mnemonic: **SUN RISING THROUGH TREES IN EAST**

---

185 TŌ, kota*eru*
ANSWER
12 strokes

解答 KAITŌ — solution
答案 TŌAN — answer paper
口答え KUCHIGOTAE — retort

Fit 合 121 q.v. and **bamboo** 竹 170. If 121 is taken to mean **lid on container** then this would give **bamboo lid**, but no such meaning has been discovered. It is thus assumed that 121 is **cap off a remark**, i.e. **reply fittingly**, and that, most unusually for a radical, 竹 is used phonetically, to express **firm**. Thus **fitting, firm answer**.

Mnemonic: **BAMBOO GIVES FITTING ANSWER**

---

186 TŌ, ZU, atama, kashira
HEAD, TOP, START
16 strokes

頭骨 TŌKOTSU — skull
頭痛 ZUTSŪ — headache
頭打ち ATAMAUCHI — top

Head 頁 93 and **bean/ vessel** 豆 1640, giving **vessel which is the head**. Also used figuratively as **brain**, **chief**, **top** or **start**.

Mnemonic: **HEAD IS A BEAN-LIKE VESSEL**

---

187 同 DŌ, ona*ji*
SAME
6 strokes

同様 DŌYŌ — similar
同時 DŌJI — same time
同意 DŌI — agreement

Somewhat obscure. Once written 凡. Taken by some scholars to indicate a **round hole** ㅂ in a **board** 片, a round hole having the **same** diameter from all angles. However, 片 is more likely to be a variant of **boat** 舟/舟 1354, used phonetically to express **together** and also lending an idea of **convey**, with ㅂ being **mouth/say** 20. Thus **convey verbally together**, meaning **say the same thing**, and hence **same**. Suggest taking 冂 as a **hoop**, 口 as an **opening**, and 一 as **single** 1.

Mnemonic: **ALL HOOPS HAVE SAME SINGLE OPENING**

---

188 DŌ, TŌ, michi
WAY, ROAD
12 strokes

鉄道 TETSUDŌ — railway
神道 SHINTŌ — Shinto
道端 MICHIBATA — roadside

辶 is **movement** 129. 首 is **head/chief** 139, here acting phonetically to express **direct** and also lending an idea of **chief/main**. Thus **chief means of direct movement**, meaning a **main road**. Also used figuratively as an abstract **way** (to enlightenment etc.).

Mnemonic: **HEAD MOVES, SHOWING WAY ALONG ROAD**

189 DOKU, TOKU, *yomu* 読者 DOKUSHA reader
READ 読本 TOKUHON reading-book
14 strokes 読み方 YOMIKATA reading

Formerly 讀. 言 is **words** 274. 賣 is to all intents and purposes a variant of the old form of **sell** 賣 / 売 192, which had connotations of **calling out** (one's wares). Thus **call out words**, i.e. **read**.

Mnemonic: **SELL WORDS TO READ**

---

190 NAN, minami 東南 TŌNAN south-east
SOUTH 南極 NANKYOKU South Pole
9 strokes 南側 MINAMIGAWA
south side

Somewhat obscure. Originally 峀, later 峀 and 峀 Some scholars feel 乂 depicts a primitive tepee-like **tent**, and take 出 to be the prototype of **red** 丹 1563 used phonetically to express **warm**. Thus, the **warm side of a tent**, i.e. the **south** side. Suggest taking 十 as **ten** 33, 冂 as a **hoop**, and ¥ as the sign for **yen**.

Mnemonic: **GET A HOOP FOR TEN YEN DOWN SOUTH**

---

191 BA, uma, ma 馬術 BAJUTSU equitation
HORSE 馬車 BASHA horse carriage
10 strokes 馬乗り UMANORI riding

From a pictograph of a **horse** 馬, stylised to 馬.

Mnemonic: **REARING HORSE**

---

192 BAI, *uru/reru* 売買 BAIBAI dealing
SELL 売店 BAITEN stall
7 strokes 売り物 URIMONO item for sale

Formerly 賣. 買 is **buy** 193 q.v. 士 is a simplification of **put out** 出 34. Thus **put out for buying**, i.e. **sell**. Suggest taking 士 as **samurai** 494, with 冗 as **legs behind a counter**.

Mnemonic: **SAMURAI STANDS BEHIND COUNTER SELLING**

193	買	BAI, ka*u* BUY 12 strokes	買収	BAISHŪ	purchase
			買い物	KAIMONO	shopping
			買い手	KAITE	buyer

Once written 圝. 㒵/貝 is **shell/money** 90. 㓁/罒 is a **net**, though there is disagreement over its role. Some scholars see it as acting phonetically to express **exchange**, giving **exchange money (for goods)**. Others see it as indicating a **bagful** of money, suggesting someone about to **buy**. It may serve both roles.

Mnemonic: **NET FULL OF SHELL-MONEY CAN BUY A LOT**

194		BAKU, mugi BARLEY, WHEAT 7 strokes	麦芽	BAKUGA	malt
			麦茶	MUGICHA	barley tea
			小麦	KOMUGI	wheat

Formerly 麥. 夾 derives from a pictograph of a **wheat plant** 夾. 夊 is **inverted foot** 438 q.v., acting phonetically to express **sharp/spiky** and possibly also lending an idea of **slow progress**. Thus **(slow growing?) wheat plant with spiky ears**. Suggest taking 夊 as **sitting crosslegged**, with 㞢 as a variant of **growing plant/life** 生 42.

Mnemonic: **SITTING CROSSLEGGED WATCHING WHEAT PLANT GROW**

195	半	HAN, naka*ba* HALF, MIDDLE 5 strokes	半分	HANBUN	half
			半島	HANTŌ	peninsula
			半年	HANTOSHI	half-year

Formerly 半, and earlier 𢆉. 八 is **split** 66, while 牛 is a variant of **cow** 牛 97. 195 originally referred to butchering a cow by splitting it in **half**, i.e. down the **middle**. Now used in a broader sense.

Mnemonic: **HALF A HORNLESS COW, SPLIT DOWN MIDDLE**

196		BAN TURN,NUMBER,GUARD 12 strokes	順番	JUNBAN	order, turn
			番人	BANNIN	watchman
			一番	ICHIBAN	number one

Once written 畨, showing **field** 田 59 and **rice** 米 201. At some stage 米 became 釆, apparently a confusion with **rice plant** 禾 81. The planting of rice in the fields followed a **set order** and also involved working by **roster**, i.e. in **turn**. **Roster** also led by association to **guard** (duty).

Mnemonic: **RICE SOWN IN FIELDS BY NUMBER, IN TURNS**

---

197   FU, chichi 父母 FUBO parents
FATHER お父様 OTŌSAMA Father
4 strokes 父親 CHICHIOYA father

Once written , showing a **hand holding a stick** (as strike 夂 101), indicating a **stern figure**.

Mnemonic: **FATHER HAS CANE IN HAND**

---

198 FŪ, kaze 風船 FŪSEN balloon
WIND, STYLE 神風 KAMIKAZE divine wind
9 strokes 和風 WAFŪ Japanese style

Somewhat obscure. Felt to be a simpler form of 鳳, an NGU character meaning **phoenix**. This comprises **bird** 鳥 174 and 凡, a variant of **common** 凡 1827. The latter is thought to be used phonetically to express **big**, but may also be used in a sense of **common** since the phoenix was a very common motif. The phoenix was believed by the ancients to **ride the wind** and hence came to symbolise it. **Wind** itself represented abstract concepts such as **invisible force** and **spirit**, with **manner** and **style** being extended meanings from **spirit**. **Insect** 虫 56 appears to have been used as a simple substitute for bird 鳥. The popular explanation using **sail** 帆 1711 q.v., giving **insect blown by wind against sail**, is incorrect but a useful mnemonic.

Mnemonic: **INSECT BLOWN AGAINST SAIL BY WIND**

---

199   BUN,FUN,BU,wa*karu/keru* 分子 BUNSHI molecule
DIVIDE, MINUTE, 一分 IPPUN one minute
UNDERSTAND 一分 ICHIBU one tenth
4 strokes

Split 八 66 and **sword/cut** 刀 181, giving **cut and split**, and hence **divide**. This has led to numerous extended meanings, such as **fraction, minute** (now of time, but originally meaning small portion, in similar fashion to the English term), and **understand** (i.e. something which is able to be divided/broken down).

Mnemonic: **UNDERSTAND ONE DIVIDES BY SPLITTING WITH SWORD**

200		BUN, MON, ki*ku*/*koeru*	新聞 SHINBUN	newspaper
		HEAR, ASK, LISTEN	聴聞 CHŌMON	listening
		14 strokes	聞き取る KIKITORU	catch, hear

Usually taken as an **ear** 耳 29 **listening** at a **gate** 門 211, though some scholars feel 門 also lends its sound to express **distinguish**. Thus **distinguish through ear (at gate)**. **Ask** is an associated meaning.

Mnemonic: **EAR LISTENING AT GATE HEARS A LOT**

201		BEI, MAI, kome	米価 BEIKA	price of rice
		RICE, AMERICA	米国 BEIKOKU	America
		6 strokes	白米 HAKUMAI	polished rice

From a **grain-laden ear of rice** ⍦. Later appears to have become confused with rice plant 禾 / 禾 81, resulting in central grains becoming joined as if a stalk, and in the variant 米. In Japanese also borrowed phonetically to refer to **AME**rica (from old reading ME).

Mnemonic: **GRAIN-LADEN EAR OF AMERICAN RICE**

202		HO, aru*ku*, ayu*mu*	進歩 SHINPO	progress
		WALK	歩行者 HOKŌSHA	pedestrian
		8 strokes	歩き出す ARUKIDASU	
				start walking

Formerly also 步, and earlier 㐄, showing a doubling of **foot** 止 129 q.v. (the lower one being a right foot, the upper a left) to indicate **putting one foot in front of the other**. Suggest taking stylised 少 as **few** 143.

Mnemonic: **FEW FEET WALK NOWADAYS**

203		BO, haha	母性 BOSEI	maternity
		MOTHER	お母様 OKĀSAMA	Mother
		5 strokes	母親 HAHAOYA	mother

Variant 母 of **woman** 女 35 with **nipples** ⠆ exaggerated to suggest **suckling** and **motherhood**. In compounds usually 毋.

Mnemonic: **MOTHER IS WOMAN WITH PROMINENT NIPPLES**

---

204 **HŌ, kata**
SIDE, WAY, SQUARE,
DIRECTION, PERSON
4 strokes

方角 HŌGAKU   direction
親方 OYAKATA   boss
見方 MIKATA   way of looking

Surprisingly obscure. Popularly felt to derive from a pictograph of a **tethered boat** 方 swinging in the **direction** of the current. There is evidence to support the view that it shows a boat (see 1815), though technically it is probably two boats tethered together to form a **square** (square being the main meaning of 204 in Chinese). However, many scholars feel that 204 in fact derives from a **plow**, and cite an old form 𠂤 as well as the similarity to sword/blade 刀/刀 181. **Direction** can then be taken as an associated idea, from the line of the plowed furrow. **Side** and **way** can be taken as extended meanings from **direction** (from the idea of **over that way**), as also **person** (originally an indirect and usually polite reference). No one interpretation seems to satisfy all meanings, though some of these may have been borrowed. The most likely explanation is that there were two separate pictographs in existence, one being boats tethered to form a square, the other a plow.

Mnemonic: **BOTH BOAT AND PLOW CAN POINT THE WAY**

---

205 **HOKU, BOKU, kita**
NORTH, FLEE
5 strokes

東北 TŌHOKU   north-east
敗北 HAIBOKU   defeat
北風 KITAKAZE   north wind

Originally 北, showing **two persons sitting back to back**. Turning one's back expressed the idea both of **fleeing** and of the **north**, the coldest direction and hence shunned.

Mnemonic: **PEOPLE FLEE, TURNING THEIR BACKS ON THE NORTH**

---

206 毎 **MAI, -goto**
EACH, EVERY
6 strokes

毎日 MAINICHI   daily
毎度 MAIDO   each time
日毎 HIGOTO   daily

Formerly 每. Usually interpreted as **every person** 𠂉/亻 39 has a **mother** 母 203, which is a useful mnemonic. However, old forms such as 𡙅 show that the upper part is not person but a **plant** 屮 9. **Mother** symbolised **fertility**, and the original meaning of 206 was **richly growing plant**. It is not clear how exactly it came to mean **every**. Some scholars feel it was borrowed, others that the idea of fertile growth led to **reproduction** and hence **repetition/ cycle**, with **every** being an associated idea.

Mnemonic: **EVERY PERSON HAS A MOTHER**

| 207 | MAI, imōto
YOUNGER SISTER
8 strokes | 姉妹 SHIMAI
妹分 IMŌTOBUN
令妹 REIMAI | sisters
'sister'
your sister |

Woman 女 35 and **immature** 未 794 q.v.

Mnemonic: **YOUNGER SISTER IS IMMATURE WOMAN**

| 208 | MEI, MYŌ, aka*rui*, a*keru*
CLEAR,OPEN,BRIGHT
8 strokes | 明白 MEIHAKU
明日 MYŌNICHI
明け方 AKEGATA | clarity
tomorrow
dawn |

Sun 日 62 and **moon** 月 16, both symbolising **light**. Thus **very light/bright**. **Open** is an associated idea.

Mnemonic: **BRIGHT SUN AND MOON GIVE CLARITY**

| 209 | MEI, na*ku/ru*
NON-HUMAN CRY
14 strokes | 鳴動 MEIDŌ
鳴き声 NAKIGOE
鳴り物 NARIMONO | rumbling
animal cry
music |

Mouth 口 20 and **bird** 鳥 174. Originally **bird-call**, later sound from a range of non-human sources including insects and inanimate objects.

Mnemonic: **BIRD'S MOUTH PRODUCES NON-HUMAN CRY**

| 210 | MŌ, ke
HAIR
4 strokes | 羊毛 YŌMO
毛皮 KEGAWA
毛虫 KEMUSHI | wool
fur
caterpillar |

From a pictograph of a **tuft of hair** 𭀢.

Mnemonic: **TUFT OF HAIR**

| 211 門 | MON, kado
GATE, DOOR
8 strokes | 正門 SEIMON
門番 MONBAN
門出 KADODE | main gate
doorman
departure |

From a pictograph of a **double-doored gate** 門.

Mnemonic: **DOUBLE-DOORED GATE**

212 **YA, yo, yoru**
NIGHT
8 strokes

本夜	HONYA	tonight
夜明け	YOAKE	dawn
夜顔	YORUGAO	moonflower

Once written 夾. 夕 is the old form of **moon** 月 16 (ancient forms show **moon/evening** 夕 44). 亦 is a variant of 大, the old form of the NGU character **again** 亦 (literally both sides ハ of a person 大 53). 亦 is used phonetically to express **clear**, but its semantic role is not known. Thus **when the moon is clear**, i.e. **night**. Suggest taking イ as **person** 39, ⊥ as a **top hat,** and 夂 simply as a variant of **moon**.

Mnemonic: **AT NIGHT, PERSON PUTS ON TOP HAT TO VIEW MOON**

---

213 **YA, no**
MOOR, WILD
11 strokes

野性	YASEI	wild
野球	YAKYŪ	baseball
野原	NOHARA	moor, field

里 is **village** 219. 予 is **already** 403 q.v., here with its early meaning of **ample space**. Thus **ample space around a village**, meaning the outer parts still not fully developed. Hence **moor** and **wild**.

Mnemonic: **VILLAGE ALREADY BUILT ON WILD MOOR**

---

214 **YŪ, tomo**
FRIEND
4 strokes

友人	YŪJIN	friend
友情	YŪJŌ	friendship
友達	TOMODACHI	friend

Often thought to be a **left hand** ナ 22 reaching out to grasp a **right hand** 又 2 in **friendship**. A useful mnemonic, but in fact old forms such as 𢎨 show **two right hands**, indicating **togetherness** and also both lending their sound to express **support** (i.e. **mutual support**).

Mnemonic: **HANDS REACHING OUT IN FRIENDSHIP**

---

215 **YŌ, mochiiru**
USE
5 strokes

用事	YŌJI	business
用意	YŌI	preparation
悪用	AKUYŌ	abuse

Once written 用 and 甩, showing crude **fencing**. It was borrowed to express **use**, but, since fencing was **used** to enclose pasture land, it may also have suggested something **useful** in its own right.

Mnemonic: **USE FENCE**

60

216 曜

YŌ
DAY OF WEEK
18 strokes

曜日 YŌBI   day of week
火曜 KAYŌ   Tuesday
七曜 SHICHIYŌ days of week

日 is **sun** 62. 羽 is **wings** 812. 隹 is **bird**, from a pictograph 𨾚. 翟 is a CO character meaning **bird's plumage**, and in combination with 日 means **dazzling** (i.e. plumage of the sun). This is still 216's meaning in Chinese. In Japanese it can very occasionally mean dazzling, but has generally had its elements reinterpreted as **sun winging like a bird**, giving the **passing of a day**.

Mnemonic: **SUN WINGS ITS WAY LIKE A BIRD, AND SO DAY PASSES**

---

217 来

RAI, ku*ru*
COME
7 strokes

来月 RAIGETSU   next month
新来者 SHINRAISHA   newcomer
出来る DEKIRU   be possible

Formerly 來, from a pictograph of a **wheat plant** 朵 (see 194). It still retains **wheat** as a minor meaning in Chinese. It is used to express **come** instead of **come** 徠, listed in Japanese as an old form of 217 but in Chinese as a separate character. 徠 comprises **road/movement** 彳 118 and **wheat** 來 217, which is used for its sound to express **move towards** but also lends its own connotations of **emerge** or **come out** (from the idea of a plant growing). Suggest taking as **ten** 十 33 **grains of rice** 米 201.

Mnemonic: **WHEAT COMES TO BE TEN GRAINS OF RICE?!**

---

218 楽

RAKU, GAKU,
tano*shii/shimu*
PLEASURE, MUSIC
13 strokes

気楽 KIRAKU   comfort
楽しみ TANOSHIMI pleasure
楽器 GAKKI
               musical instrument

Popularly said to be one of the easiest characters to explain but in fact one of the most difficult. The common explanation that it derives from a pictograph of a **tasseled drum-like musical instrument on a stand**, with **music** coming to mean **pleasure**, is incorrect, though a useful mnemonic. The earlier form 樂 shows **threads** 絲 111, **white** 白 65 q.v., and **tree/wood** 木 69, while the earliest form 𣏟 shows only threads and tree. It originally referred to a type of **oak**, whose leaves were eaten by silk worms (symbolised by thread 絲). The role of the later addition 白 is not clear. No phonetic use has been

61

identified. On the other hand, neither its early meaning of **thumb nail** nor its later meanings of **hundred** or **white** seem obviously relevant, unless white reinforced the idea of silk. It is also possible that thumb lent an idea of **principal** (as in 1694), to mean principal type from among a variety of oaks. However, it seems more likely that there existed a second prototype for white, the pictograph of an **acorn**. In any event, the original meaning of 218 was **oak tree**, now conveyed by an NGU character 櫟 that adds an extra tree. How it came to mean **pleasure** and **music** is not clear. Its complexity suggests it was not merely borrowed for its sound. It may possibly have symbolised the joy of a silk worm breeder upon finding such a type of oak, with music being an associated meaning of joy, or its shape may indeed have suggested a musical instrument, with pleasure being the associated meaning.

Mnemonic: **TASSELED DRUM ON STAND MAKES PLEASING MUSIC**

219	里	RI, sato	一 里	ICHIRI	one league
		VILLAGE, LEAGUE	里 人	SATOBITO	rustic
		7 strokes	古 里	FURUSATO	home town

Field 田 59 and **earth/ground** 土 60. The latter lent its sound to express **path**, and also lent an idea of the raised earthen ridges separating the fields. Thus **ground with fields and dividing paths**, indicating a **settlement**. Also used as a unit of distance (2.44 miles), i.e. **league**.

Mnemonic: **GROUND TILLED INTO FIELDS, INDICATING VILLAGE**

220	理	RI	理 性	RISEI	reason
		REASON, RATIONAL	無 理	MURI	unreasonable
		11 strokes	心 理 学	SHINRIGAKU	
					psychology

王 is **jewel** 102. 里 is **village** 219 q.v., here acting phonetically to express **split** and also lending its own loose connotations of **divide** (from paths dividing the fields). 220 originally meant to **split a jewel** (still retained as a minor meaning in Chinese). This involved splitting along the natural line of cleavage, which required considerable **attention**. Thus 220 came to mean **act carefully/ handle/ manage** (also still retained in Chinese), and also came to indicate **concentration**, leading to the idea of **using the mind** and hence the associated meaning **reason(ing)**.

Mnemonic: **KEEPING JEWELS IN VILLAGE IS REASONABLE**

| 221 話 | WA, hanashi, hanasu SPEECH, TALK 13 strokes | 会話 KAIWA conversation 話題 WADAI talking point 小話 KOBANASHI tale |

Usually explained as **words** 言 274 and **tongue** 舌 732 q.v., giving **articulated words** and hence **speak**. A useful mnemonic, but incorrect. Old forms such as 𧧺 show that 舌 is not tongue but the early form of **hollowed out space** 𠯑 244 q.v. Here it lends its sound to express **good**, and may also lend an idea of **booming/echoing**, or else **coming out from the space that is the mouth**. Thus **good words**, giving **speech**.

Mnemonic: **TONGUE CONTROLS WORDS WHEN TALKING**

END OF SECOND GRADE

THE 195 THIRD GRADE CHARACTERS

222 AKU, O, warui   悪意 AKUI   malice
BAD, HATE   悪寒 OKAN   chill
11 strokes   悪者 WARUMONO   rascal

Formerly 惡. 心 is **heart/feelings** 147. 亞/亜 is **sub-** 997 q.v., here acting phonetically to express **ugly** and also lending its own connotations of **ugly and twisted**. Thus **ugly, twisted feelings**. 222 originally referred to someone twisted with hatred, and can still occasionally be used in this sense, but in general it has come to mean **bad** in a broad sense.

Mnemonic: **SUB-HUMAN, UGLY, TWISTED FEELINGS ARE BAD**

---

223 AN, yasui/maru   不安 FUAN   unease
RESTFUL, EASE, CHEAP   安心 ANSHIN   relief
6 strokes   安物 YASUMONO   cheap item

Woman 女 35 q.v. and **building/home** 宀 28. Usually explained as a woman at home representing the idea of **peaceful normality**. However, old forms such as 全 reveal that 女 does not derive from the normal <u>kneeling</u> woman 乊, but a woman <u>sitting</u> on a thin, flat item 厹. It referred to a woman using a **napkin** during **menstruation**. At such times a woman was left alone to **rest quietly** in a corner of the house, and did no work. That is, she was **at her ease**. **Cheap** is an associated meaning, related to the idea of giving no cause for concern.

Mnemonic: **WOMAN AT HOME, RESTING AT EASE**

---

224 AN, kurai   明暗 MEIAN   light and dark
DARK, GLOOMY   暗殺 ANSATSU   assassination
13 strokes   真暗 MAKKURA   pitch dark

日 is **sun** 62. 音 is **sound** 6 q.v., here acting phonetically to express **shade** and possibly also lending connotations of **indistinctness** (from its stress on volume of sound rather than articulateness or clarity). Thus **shaded sun**, i.e. **darkness** and **gloom**.

Mnemonic: **SUN GOES DARK, ACCOMPANIED BY SOUND**

225 I , iyas*u*
HEAL, MEDICAL
7 strokes

医者 ISHA	doctor
外科医 GEKAI	surgeon
医学 IGAKU	medical science

Formerly 醫 . 殳 is **striking hand** 153, while 矢 is an **arrow** 981 in its **quiver** 匸, giving a now defunct character 殹 meaning to **attack**. 酉 is a **wine jar** 302, here indicating **alcohol**. Thus to **attack with alcohol**, which refers to the ancient practice of using alcohol as a medicine and possibly also anesthetic. By extension this came to refer to **healing** and **medical practice**.

Mnemonic: **DOCTOR'S BAG CONTAINS ARROW, USED FOR HEALING**

226 I
MIND, THOUGHT, WILL
13 strokes

注意 CHŪI	attention, care
決意 KETSUI	resolution
意見 IKEN	opinion

心 is **heart/feelings** 147. 音 is **sound** 6. Some scholars feel the latter is used to mean **state aloud**, to give **voicing one's feelings** and hence **opinion** or similar. Others feel it is used phonetically to express **full**, to give **that of which the heart is full**, i.e. **concerns** or **thoughts**. Some feel it may also lend an idea of sound but in a figurative sense, i.e. 'the sound of the heart'. A combination of the last two theories seems the most likely, i.e. **a heart full of thoughts which are its 'sounds'**. **Will** and **mind** are extended meanings.

Mnemonic: **A THOUGHT IS A SOUND FROM THE HEART**

227 IKU, soda*tsu/teru*
RAISE, EDUCATE
8 strokes

教育 KYŌIKU	education
育児 IKUJI	childcare
育て親 SODATEOYA	
	foster parent

Originally 㐬, showing a **woman** ㄊ / 女 35 q.v. (but sitting rather than kneeling) and inverted **child** 𠫓 / 子 25. The inversion indicates a **newborn infant**, emphasised by the **amniotic fluid** ' ' (see also 409). In a later form 㐬 the drops of fluid became stylised as 巛, and in a still later form 𠫓 became replaced by 肉/月. Some scholars see this as **meat** 365 used purely phonetically to express **birth** (replacing woman 女, which similarly represented birth), but it may just be a stylisation of 巛. 227 can still mean birth in Chinese, but it is generally used to mean **raise children** in a broad sense.

Mnemonic: **EDUCATE CHILD UPSIDE-DOWN LIKE PIECE OF MEAT**

228		IN	会員 KAIIN	group member
		MEMBER, OFFICIAL	全員 ZENIN	all members
		10 strokes	動員 DŌIN	mobilisation

Old forms such as show that 貝 is not shell 90 but a simplification of **round three legged kettle** 鼎 (now an NGU character with that meaning), which in itself symbolised **roundness** but is here reinforced by a **circle** 口. Thus the original meaning was **round kettle**. This led to **round** (still found in Chinese). **Member** and **official** are felt to derive from the idea of a group of persons gathered **around** (a superior) in a meeting. Suggest taking 貝 as shell-**money** and 口 as mouth/**say** 20.

Mnemonic: **OFFICIAL MEMBERS ALWAYS TALK OF MONEY**

229		IN	病院 BYŌIN	hospital
		INSTITUTE	寺院 JIIN	temple
		10 strokes	議院 GIIN	the House

β is from a pictograph of a **terraced slope** 阝, and often means **hill, mound,** or **embankment** (as here). It is the forerunner of the NGU character **hill** 阜. 完 is **complete** 440 q.v., which originally meant **building with surrounding fence/wall** and as such is the prototype of 229. The addition of embankment 阝 suggests an important building with solid surrounding walls. It can still mean **large building,** but generally indicates an **institute** or similar. Suggest remembering 阝 in its commonest sense of **hill**.

Mnemonic: **INSTITUTE COMPLETE WITH SURROUNDING HILLS**

230		IN, nomu	飲用水 INYŌSUI	drinking water
		DRINK, SWALLOW	飲み物 NOMIMONO	drinks
		12 strokes	飲み屋 NOMIYA	tavern

Though nowadays written with the **food/eat** radical 食 146, old forms such as 酓 show clearly that this is a substitute for **wine jar /alcohol** 酉 302. 欠 is **lack** 471, used here in its early sense of **gaping mouth**. Thus to **quaff alcohol with gaping mouth,** now to **drink** in general, as well as **swallow** (without chewing).

Mnemonic: **LACK FOOD, SO SWALLOW DRINK**

231 UN, hako*bu*
TRANSPORT, LUCK, MOVE
12 strokes

運動 UNDŌ   movement
不運 FUUN   misfortune
運送 UNSŌ   transportation

辶 is **movement** 129. 軍 is **army** 466 q.v. Some scholars take the latter in a literal sense, giving **army on the move** and by association **transportation** and the **fortunes** of war. Others take it to act phonetically to express **round**, as well as lending its own connotations both of **circle** and **vehicle** (from a circle of vehicles), thus giving a meaning of **vehicles rolling along**, and hence **transport**. **Luck** is then felt to stem from an association between fortune and circular/cyclic movement.

Mnemonic: **ARMY ON MOVE NEEDS LUCK AND TRANSPORT**

232 EI, oyo*gu*
SWIM
8 strokes

水泳 SUIEI   swimming
背泳 HAIEI   backstroke
平泳ぎ HIRAOYOGI breaststroke

氵 is **water** 40. 永 is **long** 615 q.v., here used phonetically to express **float** and also lending its original connotations of **flowing water**. 232 originally meant to **float with the current**, but has now broadened to mean **swim**.

Mnemonic: **LONG SWIM IN WATER**

233 駅 EKI
STATION
14 strokes

駅長 EKICHŌ   stationmaster
駅弁 EKIBEN   station lunch
東京駅 TŌKYŌEKI Tokyo Station

Formerly 驛. 馬 is **horse** 191. 睪 is a CO character meaning **spy on** and **lead**. It was once written 睪, showing an **eye** 罒 72 and 幸 (also 圶), a type of shackle used on **prisoners** and hence symbolising them. Thus 睪 is an ideograph meaning to **keep watch over prisoners**. Since the prisoners were chained together in a line it often also has connotations of **line** or **succession**, as here. Thus 233 means literally a **succession of horses**, and referred to the **relay stations** at which imperial messengers changed their horses. It now means **station** in a broader sense. Suggest taking the simplified form 尺 as a **person** 人 39 with a **pack** ヨ on their back.

Mnemonic: **LADEN PERSON MOUNTS HORSE AT RELAY STATION**

234 EN, sono   公園 KŌEN   park
GARDEN, PARK   動物園 DŌBUTSUEN   zoo
13 strokes   花園 HANAZONO
      flower garden

Enclosure 口 123 and spacious 袁 79. The latter also lends its sound to express
fence. Thus spacious fenced enclosure. Suggest remembering 袁 by association
with distant 遠 79.

Mnemonic: SPACIOUS PARK ENCLOSES CONSIDERABLE DISTANCE

---

235 横 Ō, yoko   横断 ŌDAN   crossing
SIDE, CROSSWAYS   横行 ŌKŌ   strutting
15 strokes   横顔 YOKOGAO   profile

Wood 木 69 and yellow 黄 120. The latter acts phonetically to express bar/block,
and may also lend connotations of wooden shaft from its original meaning of flaming arrow. 235 originally referred to a piece of wood laid across a gate to prevent its being
opened, leading to crossways and by extension on its side and side. It also occasionally has connotations of defiance (from prevent) and perversity (a figurative extension from
not upright).

Mnemonic: YELLOW PIECE OF WOOD LAID ON ITS SIDE

---

236 OKU, ya   屋上 OKUJŌ   roof
STORE, BUILDING   小屋 KOYA   hut
9 strokes   パン屋 PANYA   baker(y)

尸 is an NGU character meaning corpse, derived from a slumped figure 尸. In compounds it can also mean buttocks or, as here, slump in the sense of relax. 至 is arrive
(and stop) 875, which also acts phonetically to express room (in fact, some scholars feel
it is used as a simplified form of room 室 136). Thus a room where, having arrived, one can relax. This came by extension to mean house or building, and in Japanese is also used of store and by extension storekeeper.

Mnemonic: ARRIVE AND FIND CORPSE IN STORE BUILDING

237

ON, atatakai/meru
WARM
12 strokes

温泉 ONSEN   spa
温情 ONJŌ   kindness
温室 ONSHITSU   hothouse

Formerly 溫 . There is some difference of opinion as to its origins. Some scholars take it to refer to an act of **kindness** in giving a **prisoner** 囚 1353 a **bowl** 皿 1307 of **water** 氵 40, with the figurative sense of **warm** unusually preceding the physical one. Other scholars interpret 囚 as a variant of **vapors** 囚 26, with **watery vapors from a bowl** indicating steam and thus **heat.** Though the latter theory seems the more logical, 昷 is listed (though without examples) as a CO character meaning **feed a prisoner**, suggesting that the former theory is in fact accurate. For the modern form, suggest taking 日 as **sun** 62.

Mnemonic: **SUN WARMS WATER IN A BOWL**

238

KA, KE, bakeru
CHANGE, BEWITCH
4 strokes

変化 HENKA   change
化粧 KESHŌ   make-up
化け者 BAKEMONO   'spook'

亻 shows a <u>standing</u> person 39, while ヒ shows a <u>fallen</u> person, thus indicating a **change of state**. Some scholars feel that ヒ also acts phonetically to express **deceive**, leading to deceitful change and hence **bewitch,** while others see bewitch simply as an associated meaning of change.

Mnemonic: **BEWITCHED PERSON CHANGES AND FALLS**

239

KA, ni
LOAD, BURDEN
10 strokes

出荷 SHUKKA   consignment
船荷 FUNANI   ship's cargo
荷物 NIMOTSU   baggage

艹 is **plant** 9. 何 is **what?** 80 q.v. The latter is almost certainly used in its early sense of **bear a heavy load,** though its precise role is unclear. The original meaning of 239 was **lotus** (still retained in Chinese as a significant meaning). The idea of bearing a heavy load may possibly have been used to refer to the large head of the lotus. In any event, **bearing a load** came to prevail as the main meaning in Chinese and the sole meaning in Japanese.

Mnemonic: **WHAT A BURDEN THE LOTUS PLANT CAN BE!**

| 240 | | KAI
AREA, BOUNDARY
9 strokes | 世界 SEKAI world
境界 KYŌKAI boundary
政界 SEIKAI political world |

Field 田 59 and **come between** 介 1059. Thus **division of land**, leading to both **boundary** and **area**.

Mnemonic: **BOUNDARY BETWEEN FIELDS MARKS AREAS**

| 241 | | KAI, hira*ku*, a*keru*
OPEN
12 strokes | 開発 KAIHATSU development
開始 KAISHI inception
開き綱 HIRAKIZUNA rip-cord |

Once written 閞, showing a **gate** 門 211 and two **hands** 𠀉 reaching out to remove the **bar** — that is keeping it closed, thereby **opening** it.

Mnemonic: **HANDS REMOVE BAR AND OPEN GATE**

| 242 | | KAI
STORY, GRADE, STEP
12 strokes | 階段 KAIDAN stairs
二階 NIKAI upstairs
階級 KAIKYŪ class, grade |

阝 is **terraced hill** 229. 皆 is **all** 1064, here acting phonetically to express **row** and also lending similar connotations from its literal meaning of **row** (of people talking). Thus **row of terraces on a hillside**, now used to mean **step** or **graduation** in a broad sense.

Mnemonic: **ALL THE STEPS OF A TERRACED HILL**

| 243 | | KAKU, tsuno, kado
HORN, ANGLE, CORNER
7 strokes | 角度 KAKUDO angle
角笛 TSUNOBUE horn, bugle
町角 MACHIKADO
street corner |

From a pictograph of a **horn** 𩠐. Now has a range of extended meanings such as **corner**, **angle**.

Mnemonic: **ANGULAR HORN**

244		**KATSU**	生活 SEIKATSU	life
		ACTIVITY, LIFE	活気 KAKKI	liveliness
		9 strokes	活動 KATSUDŌ	activity

Usually explained as a **moist** 氵 (water 40) **tongue** 舌 732, which is a sign of **life**. A useful mnemonic, but old forms such as 湝 show that 舌 is in fact a derivative of 昏, an element combining opening 口 20 and scoop 乇 495 and meaning **hollowed out space**. 244 originally referred to **water rushing** into such a space. By extension it came to mean **activity** and, perhaps because of the life-giving property of water, **life**. Note that in Chinese it still retains a minor meaning of **sound of (rushing) water**.

Mnemonic: **WET TONGUE IS SIGN OF LIFE**

245		**KAN, samui**	寒波 KANPA	cold wave
		COLD	寒気 SAMUKE	chill
		12 strokes	寒暖計 KANDANKEI	
				thermometer

Somewhat obscure. Formerly 寠, and in ancient times 𡙇. 𠆢/宀 is **roof/building** 28. 人/丷 is **ice** 378, possibly symbolising winter. 𦰩 (also 茻) appears to be **plants** 9. 245 thus appears to be a reference to the custom of binding straw or rushes to the outside of a house to insulate it against the **cold** of winter. Suggest taking 井 as **well** 1470 and 𣎳 as a variant of **six** 六 76.

Mnemonic: **BUILDING'S SIX WELLS ICE OVER IN COLD**

246	感	**KAN**	感心 KANSHIN	admiration
		FEELING	感覚 KANKAKU	sense
		13 strokes	感情 KANJŌ	feeling

Heart/feeling 心 147 and 咸. The latter is a CO character meaning **unison**. It comprises **trimming tool/ sharp weapon** 戌 (variant 戊 515 q.v.), which symbolised trimming and making correct and by extension **harmonising**, and **mouth/say** 口 20, thus giving harmony of expression and unison. Here it acts phonetically to express **sway**, and probably also lends an idea of **all together**. Thus **all hearts swayed together**, indicating intense **emotion** or **feeling**. Suggest taking 戌 as a variant of **halberd** 戈 493, with 一 as **one** 1.

Mnemonic: **ONE HALBERD IN MOUTH CAUSES FEELING IN HEART**

247 **KAN**
LARGE BUILDING, HALL
16 strokes

会館 KAIKAN   hall
旅館 RYOKAN   inn
美術館 BIJUTSUKAN art gallery

Eat 食 146 and **official** 官 441 q.v., here with its original meaning of **official in a building**. 247 originally referred to a building where traveling officials could eat, i.e. an **inn**, but then came to mean **building** in a broader sense, usually with connotations of size and quality.

Mnemonic: **OFFICIAL EATS IN HALL**

248 **GAN, kishi**
BANK, SHORE
8 strokes

海岸 KAIGAN   coast
対岸 TAIGAN   far bank
川岸 KAWAGISHI riverbank

山 is **mountain** 24, here meaning **high ground**. 厂 is **cliff** 45. 干 is **dry** 825 q.v., here acting phonetically to express **high** and also lending an idea of **thrusting** from its original meaning of **thrusting weapon**. Thus **tall thrusting cliffs**, and by extension **shore** or **bank**.

Mnemonic: **MOUNTAINOUS CLIFF FORMS DRY SHORE**

249 **GAN, iwa**
ROCK, CRAG
8 strokes

岩石 GANSEKI   rock
岩屋 IWAYA   cave
火成岩 KASEIGAN igneous rock

Mountain 山 24 and **stone/rock** 石 45.

Mnemonic: **STONY MOUNTAIN SHOWS ROCKY CRAGS**

250 **KI, okiru/koru/kosu**
ARISE, CAUSE
10 strokes

起原 KIGEN   origin
早起き HAYAOKI   early rising
起動力 KIDŌRYOKU
            motive power

Formerly 起. 走 is **run** 161. 巳 is an NGU character meaning **serpent**, and derives from a pictograph 𛀸. Here it acts phonetically to express **stop**, and also lends an idea of **rearing up**. Thus to **stop running and rear up**, such as an animal at bay. The idea of rearing came to prevail, leading to associated meanings such as **rise, arise, occur**, and **cause**. Suggest taking 己 as **thread/ self** 855.

Mnemonic: **CAUSE ONESELF TO RUN**

251		KI, GO	学期 GAKKI	school term
		PERIOD, EXPECT	期待 KITAI	expectation
		12 strokes	最期 SAIGO	end

Once written 萁. **Sun/day** 日 62 has now been replaced by **moon /month** 月 16, both indicating **time**. 其 is an NGU character borrowed to express **that**, but it derives from a pictograph of a **winnowing device** 冀. Like the harvest itself (see 64) winnowing came to symbolise a **cycle of time**. This led to the idea of **regular** and **predictable**, i.e. something one can **expect**.

Mnemonic: **EXPECT PERIOD OF MONTHS BETWEEN WINNOWINGS**

252		KYAKU, KAKU	来客 RAIKYAKU	visitor
		GUEST, VISITOR	乗客 JŌKYAKU	passenger
		9 strokes	客員 KAKUIN	guest member

Roof/building 宀 28, and **each** 各 438 q.v., here with its literal meaning of **visit and stay**. Thus **person who visits building**(especially house). Suggest taking 各 as **sitting crosslegged**, and 口 as **mouth** 20.

Mnemonic: **EACH HOUSE GUEST SITS CROSSLEGGED,OPEN MOUTHED**

253		KYŪ, kiwa*meru*	研究 KENKYŪ	research
		INVESTIGATE, EXTREME	究明 KYŪMEI	investigation
		7 strokes	探究 TANKYŪ	inquiry

Hole 穴 849 and **nine** 九 12 q.v., here with its literal meaning of **bent elbow**. Though its exact etymology is somewhat disputed, many scholars feel that 253 originally referred to thrusting the arm into a hole in order to **'ferret' something out**, thus indicating going to **extreme** lengths.

Mnemonic: **EXTREME INVESTIGATION OF NINE HOLES**

254		KYŪ, iso*gu*	急死 KYŪSHI	sudden death
		HURRY, SUDDEN	急速 KYŪSOKU	rapidity
		9 strokes	大急ぎ ŌISOGI	great haste

Once written 悥. 刍/彐 is the prototype of **reach** 及 1148 q.v. 心 is **heart/feelings** 147. 254 originally indicated the feelings of someone trying to reach something, i.e. a sense of **urgency** or **haste**. **Sudden** is an associated meaning. Suggest taking 彐 literally as **bending person** 勹 and **hand** 彐.

Mnemonic: **HURRYING PERSON SUDDENLY BENDS, HAND TO HEART**

255		KYŪ RANK, GRADE 9 strokes	進級 SHINKYŪ	promotion
			同級生 DŌKYŪSEI	classmate
			上級 JŌKYŪ	upper grade

糸 is **thread** 27. 及 is **reach** 1148, which acts phonetically to express **order** and also lends its own connotations of **making contact**. Thus to **join threads in a set order**, i.e. weave. This gave rise to the idea of **relative position**, and eventually **rank** and **grade**.

Mnemonic: **REACH OUT AND GRADE THREADS**

256		KYŪ, GŪ, KU, miya PALACE, SHRINE, PRINCE 10 strokes	神宮 JINGŪ	shrine
			宮中 KYŪCHŪ	Court
			宮様 MIYASAMA	prince

宀 is **roof/building** 28. 呂 is an NGU character meaning vertebrae, though it is often used simply to mean **joined blocks**. Here it means **joined rooms**, suggesting a building of considerable size. It became particularly associated with **temples** and **palaces**, and in Japanese is also used to refer to **nobles** associated in turn with palaces.

Mnemonic: **PALACE IS BUILDING WITH JOINED ROOMS**

257		KYŪ, tama SPHERE, BALL 11 strokes	球戯 KYŪGI	ball game
			地球 CHIKYŪ	Earth
			球拾い TAMAHIROI	caddie

王 is **jewel** 102. 求 is **seek** 455 q.v., used partly phonetically to express **beautiful**, and partly for its connotations of **desirable object**. Thus **beautiful, desirable jewel**. It became particularly associated with **well formed round jewels** rather than faceted ones, partly because its sound could also express **curved**, and hence came to mean **perfectly round/ spherical**.

Mnemonic: **SEEK SPHERICAL JEWEL**

| 258 去 | KYO, KO, sa*ru*
GO, LEAVE, PAST
5 strokes | 去年 KYONEN
過去 KAKO
立ち去る TACHISARU | last year
the past
depart |

Once written 合, showing a **double-lid on a rice container**. The double-lid indicated security, indicating in turn the importance of rice. Though a lidded container might logically be expected to suggest fullness, as indeed it does in the case of joy 吉 1142 q.v., in the case of 258 it seems that since the rice was looked upon as vital rations its rate of **consumption** was of paramount importance. Consumption led to **used up** and **gone**, with **past** being a figurative extension. Suggest taking ム as **nose** 134 and 土 as **ground** 60.

Mnemonic: **NOSE TO GROUND SUGGESTS ONE'S GONE TOO FAR**

| 259 | KYŌ, hashi
BRIDGE
16 strokes | 鉄橋 TEKKYŌ
陸橋 RIKKYŌ
石橋 ISHIBASHI | steel bridge
overpass
stone bridge |

木 is **wood** 69. 喬 is an NGU character meaning **tall**. In effect it is a variant of tall 高 119 q.v., showing a watchtower 髙/冋 but surmounted by a person with bent neck 夭 279, symbolising **bent at the tip/top**. Thus **tall arched wooden structure**, now used of **bridges** in general.

Mnemonic: **TALL ARCHED WOODEN STRUCTURE IS BRIDGE**

| 260 業 | GYŌ, GŌ, waza
PROFESSION, DEED,
KARMA
13 strokes | 産業 SANGYŌ
罪業 ZAIGŌ
仕業 SHIWAZA | industry
sin
act, deed |

Once written 業, depicting a base and notched board of a **musical instrument**. Crosspieces were slotted into the notches and bells hung from them. Opinion differs as to how this pictograph of a musical instrument came to acquire its present meanings. Some scholars feel that there was a similar device from which wooden tablets inscribed with characters were hung, these tablets apparently being used as teaching aids. Thus the pictograph became associated with **learning**, leading to **profession** and hence to **work**, with work giving rise to **deed/act**, which in turn became associated with **karma** (the effect of a person's actions on the sum of their existence). Other scholars see the instrument as symbolising **intricacy** and **complexity**, and by extension something demanding much **study** in order to master. From **study**, the evolution of meaning is seen as similar to that of the first theory. Suggest remembering partly by association with **wood** 木 69.

Mnemonic: **STUDY COMPLEX WOODEN INSTRUMENT AS PROFESSION**

261 曲   KYOKU, ma*garu*/*geru*   曲線 KYOKUSEN   curve
BEND, MELODY   作曲 SAKKYOKU songwriting
6 strokes   曲げ物 MAGEMONO   round box

Somewhat obscure. Originally 凵 , and later 𠚓 and 𦥑. Some scholars see this as a **carpenter's tool** used in cutting **curves** and **angles**, while others see it as a crude **receptacle** made by **bending** softened wood. There is in fact evidence to support both views. **Melody** is an associated meaning, from the idea of **convoluted**. Suggest taking as a 'multi-pathed' variant of **field** 田 59.

Mnemonic: **FIELD HAS MANY BENDING PATHS**

262 局   KYOKU   局面 KYOKUMEN   situation
OFFICE, SECTION, END,   結局 KEKKYOKU   finally
CIRCUMSTANCES   郵便局 YŪBINKYOKU
7 strokes   post office

Obscure. Once written 局 and 局. Some scholars see 尺 as the prototype of **measure** 尺 884 q.v. and 口 as an **area**, giving **measured area** and by extension **prescribed section**, leading on the one hand to **division** and by figurative extension interruption and thence **termination/end**, and on the other to appropriate **part** of a larger unit, such as a specialised branch/office of a government ministry. However, such a theory does not easily explain the meaning **circumstances**. Other scholars see 尸/尸 as a slumped figure symbolising **bending** (essentially **corpse** 尸 236), plus the prototype 句 of **phrase** 句 655 q.v., used for its idea of **interlocking**, thus giving a meaning of interlocking and bending, i.e. **convoluted**. **Circumstances** is an associated meaning from convolutions. **Office** is seen as stemming from 262's replacement of a now defunct character of which it was an element in combination with building 宀 28, 宮 , which meant **complicated building** such as one housing many government offices. The **office** was a **section** of the maze-like building, which one **finally** found. (Similarly a **court lady's chamber**, which is a further minor meaning of 262.) A further theory is that 厂 is merely a variant of large building 广 114. The later use of corpse 尸 236 is consistent with the occasional use of 尸 as a simplification of building 屋 236. This gives **interlocking** (i.e. **complicated**) **building**, and then follows the second theory, but does not account for **circumstances**. It seems possible that 262 may in fact be a confusion of several characters. Suggest taking it as **corpse** and a variant of **phrase**.

Mnemonic: **OFFICE CORPSE USES ODD PHRASE IN CIRCUMSTANCES**

263 銀 GIN, shirogane
SILVER
14 strokes

銀行 GINKŌ — bank
銀河 GINGA — Milky Way
銀貨 GINKA — silver coin

金 is **metal** 14. 艮 is an NGU character meaning **stop**. It was once written 艮, showing an **eye** on **twisted legs** (as opposed to eye on bent legs in look 見 18), and indicated a **person turning round and staring**. Here it is used primarily for its sound, to express **white**, but also lends an idea of **take a second look**, i.e. **scrutinise**. That is, it required a careful examination to distinguish **silver** from similar but less precious metals. Thus **white, carefully examined metal**. Suggest remembering 艮 as **stop and stare**, distinguishing it from good 良 598. Note that shirogane means literally 'white metal'. See also 353.

Mnemonic: **STOP AND STARE AT SILVERY METAL**

---

264 苦 KU, kuru*shii*/*shimu*, nigai
PAINFUL, BITTER
8 strokes

苦心 KUSHIN — pains, trouble
苦痛 KUTSŪ — pain, agony
苦味 NIGAMI — bitterness

Plant 艹 9 and **old** 古 109, here used phonetically to express **bitter** but possibly also lending an extended idea of **lingering**. Thus **plant with (lingering?) bitter taste**. **Bitter** is also used figuratively.

Mnemonic: **OLD PLANT LEAVES BITTER TASTE**

---

265 具 GU, sona*eru*
EQUIP(MENT), MEANS
8 strokes

具合 GUAI — condition
用具 YŌGU — appliance
道具 DŌGU — tool

Formerly 具, and in ancient times 具, showing **hands** 八 holding up a **kettle** 鼎 228. Kettle symbolised **utensil**. Thus **offer a utensil**, meaning to **equip with the wherewithal**. Some later forms such as 具 suggest that kettle became confused with shell/money 貝 90, but the core meaning (provide wherewithal) remained unchanged. Suggest taking 目 as **eye** 72 and 八 as a **table**.

Mnemonic: **KEEP AN EYE ON TABLE: IT'S VALUABLE EQUIPMENT**

266 KUN, kimi
LORD, YOU, MR
7 strokes

暴君 BŌKUN   tyrant
細君 SAIKUN   wife
山田君 YAMADAKUN
(Mr) Yamada

口 is **mouth/say** 20. 尹 is a CO character meaning **govern**, deriving from **hand holding a stick** 尹 (see also 101). Thus to **govern by mouth**, i.e. command and by extension **commander/lord**. Also used as what was originally a very polite form of address (now informal).

Mnemonic: **LORD HOLDS STICK NEXT TO MOUTH**

267 KEI, KYŌ, ani
ELDER BROTHER
5 strokes

父兄 FUKEI   guardians
兄様 NIISAMA * Elder Brother
兄弟愛 KYŌDAIAI brotherly love

Once written 兄, showing a **person crouching** ∩ 39 and a **mouth** 口 20, indicating **speaking**. There is some disagreement over the role of crouching figure. Many scholars claim that it was used phonetically to express **big** and also lent similar connotations of its own (i.e. a big person bending to be on a level with other persons), and that 267 originally meant **big words/ exaggeration** before coming to mean **big** in general and finally **big brother**. However, there is little obvious evidence to support this claimed early meaning, and no explanation as to why big (person) 大 53 was not used. It seems equally if not more likely that the ideograph indicated a **person associated with speaking**, namely an **elder brother** whose role was to advise and represent his younger siblings. The occasional use of 267 to indicate big can then be seen as deriving from big brother, rather than vice-versa.

Mnemonic: **ELDER BROTHER IS ALL MOUTH AND LEGS**

268 KEI, kakari
INVOLVEMENT
9 strokes

関係 KANKEI   relationship
係争 KEISŌ   contention
係員 KAKARIIN
clerk in charge

Person 亻 39 and **joined threads** 糸 844 q.v., here meaning simply **connected**. Thus **person connected**, i.e. **involved** or **concerned**. Also used nowadays of **connection** in general.

Mnemonic: **PERSON INVOLVED WITH JOINING THREADS**

269  **KEI, karu*i***
LIGHT, FLIPPANT
12 strokes

軽食 KEISHOKU   snack
軽薄 KEIHAKU   flippancy
軽石 KARUISHI   pumice

Formerly 輕. 車 is **vehicle** 31. 巠 derives from 巠, showing the lengthwise (**warp**) threads of a loom. Since these have not yet had the crosswise (weft) threads woven in, they represent **incompleteness** and **bareness**. Thus 269 originally meant **bare vehicle**, i.e. one unladen and **light**. Light is now also used figuratively, such as **flippant** or **thoughtless**. Suggest taking 巠 as **hand** 又 and **ground** 土 60.

Mnemonic: **LIGHT VEHICLE PUSHED ALONG GROUND BY HAND**

---

270 **KETSU, chi**
BLOOD
6 strokes

血液 KETSUEKI   blood
鼻血 HANAJI   nosebleed
血統 KETTŌ   lineage

Once written 血, showing **vessel** 凵/皿 1307 and its **contents** ─ / '. The vessel in this case was a **sacrificial vessel**, and the contents **blood**.

Mnemonic: **VESSEL CONTAINS BLOOD**

---

271 **KETSU, ki*maru/meru***
DECIDE, SETTLE,
COLLAPSE
7 strokes

解決 KAIKETSU   solution
決心 KESSHIN   resolution
決裂 KETSURETSU
   breakdown

Once written 決. 氵 is **water** 40. 夬/夬 is a CO character meaning **part** or **fork**, and derives from a hand 又 drawing a bowstring | 77 while wearing an archer's glove ⇒. Thus to **pull apart/ open**. Note that the addition of a further hand 扌 32 gives the NGU character pull out by hand or gouge 抉, while the same character still retains draw a bow as a minor meaning in Chinese. Thus 271 means literally **pulled apart by water**, initially referring to **water breaking through** a bank or levee. On the one hand this led to **collapse** (now a minor meaning omitted from many dictionaries) and on the other, by similar figurative extension to the English term **breakthrough**, to the idea of **opening up a deadlock** and hence **deciding** upon a **solution**. Suggest taking 夬 as a variant of **person with pack on back** 尺 (see 233).

Mnemonic: **PERSON DECIDES TO CARRY WATER-PACK ON BACK**

272 KEN, *togu*　　　研修 KENSHŪ　　　　training
　　　HONE, REFINE　　　研ぎ革 TOGIKAWA　　　strop
　　　9 strokes　　　　　研究者 KENKYŪSHA researcher

Formerly 研 . 石 is **stone** 45. 幵 is felt to represent two stakes of **similar** size, indicating **regularity** and **uniformity**. Thus to **make a stone uniform**, i.e. to **hone** and by extension **refine**. Suggest remembering 幵 as **two forked sticks** 千 825.

Mnemonic: **HONE STONE WITH TWO FORKED STICKS**

273 KEN　　　　　　三重県 MIEKEN　Mie Prefecture
　　　PREFECTURE　　　県立 KENRITSU　　prefectural
　　　9 strokes　　　　　県庁 KENCHŌ

　　　　　　　　　　　　　　　　　　　prefectural office

Formerly 縣 , and in earlier times 櫐糸 . 木 is **tree** 69. 糸 is **joined threads** 844, indicating **attach**. 県 derives from 臬 , which is an inverted variant of **head** 首 139 q.v. and indicates a **severed head hung upside down**. 273 originally referred to the practice of hanging the decapitated head of a criminal in a tree, not unlike the European use of the gibbet. Some scholars have assumed that this was a display of the **power of the authorities**, leading by association to **regional/ prefectural authorities**. There may be some truth to this, but it is not quite such simple symbolism. Historical usage shows -- perhaps surprisingly -- that the core meaning of 273 is **attach**, i.e. the attaching of the head to the tree. It still retains a minor meaning of attach/hang in Chinese, and is also the key element in attach/worry 懸 1225 q.v.(literally hanging on the heart). It is known to have come to mean **prefecture/ administrative district** through an intermediate meaning of **that attached to the central government**, but how exactly this association of ideas was made is not clear, since there is no element indicating government in the original character. Thus it is possible that the decapitated head did indeed later become a symbol of the authorities, with attach 糸 coming to be used in a different role. It is ironic that in the simplified modern Japanese form the etymologically most important element has been omitted. Suggest taking 県 as **eye** 目 72 and a **stand** 小 .

Mnemonic: **KEEP AN EYE ON STAND AT PREFECTURAL SHOW**

274		GEN, GON, koto, i*u* WORD, SAY, SPEAK 7 strokes	発言 HATSUGEN	statement
			無言 MUGON	silence
			言葉 KOTOBA	word

Formerly 𡆠 and originally 𠱾 . 口 is **mouth/say** 20. ▽ / ᅮ is **needle/sharp** 辛 1432. Some scholars see the latter as acting purely phonetically to express **heart/ feelings**, to give **oral expression of feelings**, but this does not explain why the character for heart itself (147) was not used. Other scholars see sharp as lending an extended meaning of **articulate**, to give **articulate use of the mouth**. Still others see needle as representing **teeth**, which were considered necessary for good enunciation. The second theory seems the most likely, with ᅮ possibly also having a secondary phonetic role of expressing **feelings**. Suggest taking the modern form 𦥑 as **three** 三 23 and a **bit** ヽ.

Mnemonic: **MOUTH SPEAKS THREE AND A BIT WORDS**

275		KO STOREHOUSE 10 strokes	車庫 SHAKO	garage, depot
			倉庫 SŌKO	warehouse
			冷蔵庫 REIZŌKO	refrigerator

Large building 广 114 and **vehicle** 車 31. Some scholars feel that 275 once meant literally **large building for housing vehicles** (especially war-chariots), while others feel that by extension vehicle indicated the **goods** carried on a cart, giving **large building for cart-load of goods**, i.e. **storehouse**.

Mnemonic: **STOREHOUSE IS BUILDING CONTAINING VEHICLES**

276		KO, mizuumi LAKE 12 strokes	十和田湖 TŌWADAKO LakeTowada
			湖岸 KOGAN	lakeshore
			湖水 KOSUI	lake

Somewhat obscure. 氵 is **water** 40. 胡 is an NGU character now borrowed to express a range of meanings such as barbarian, but its original meaning was **beard** and by extension **old person** (both meanings still retained in Chinese). It comprises **old** 古 109 q.v., possibly used in an assumed early sense of skull but more likely in an extended sense of old person, and 月 (once 𠛟), which is felt to derive from a pictograph of a beard (a symbol of an old person). Here 胡 is used phonetically to express **big**. It may also have lent some meaning, possibly **long time** or similar, though this is not clear. Thus **big body of water** (taking a long time to cross?). Suggest taking 月 as **moon** 16.

Mnemonic: **OLD MOON SEEN IN WATERS OF LAKE**

277 KŌ, ōyake   公共 KŌKYŌ   public
PUBLIC, FAIR, LORD   公平 KŌHEI   fairness
4 strokes   紀州公 KISHŪKŌ   Lord Kishu

Once written 凸. 口 is an **enclosure**, indicating **private property**.)ᛁ is **split/away** 66, indicating **dissolution**. Thus the **dissolution of private property**, giving **public property**. It also led to the idea of belonging to the **state/government** as opposed to private individuals. Government conceptually overlapped with **royal household**, leading by association to **member of royal household** such as **prince** and eventually **lord**. **Fair** is an associated meaning of public and open. It is not clear whether 厶 is merely a graphic simplification of 口 or a deliberate use of **self** 厶 134. Suggest taking 厶 as **nose** 134 and 八 in its meaning of **eight**.

Mnemonic: **EIGHT LORDS SHOW NOSE IN PUBLIC**

278 KŌ, muku/keru/kō/kau   向上 KŌJŌ   improvement
FACE TOWARDS,   意向 IKŌ   intention
BEYOND   前向き MAEMUKI
6 strokes   forward looking

From a pictograph of a **house with a window** 向. The **direction** the window **faced** was considered important (usually north, since the southern sun was generally too hot). As in English, **facing** could also mean being **opposite**, leading to **other side** and by further extension to **beyond**.

Mnemonic: **HOUSE WINDOW FACES ONE**

279 KŌ, saiwai, shiawase, sachi   幸運 KŌUN   good fortune
HAPPINESS, LUCK   不幸 FUKŌ   misery, bad luck
8 strokes   幸い SAIWAI ni   fortunately

Once written 㚔. 夭 is an NGU character meaning **death** or **calamity**, and derives from a figure 大 53 with a slumped head ノ. 㚔 is an inverted stylisation 夭 of figure 53, the inversion indicating the **reversal** of the calamity. A reversal of calamity means **happiness** and **good fortune**. See also 646. Suggest remembering by association with needle/sharp 辛 1432, 279 having an extra stroke.

Mnemonic: **EXTRA SHARP STROKE BRINGS HAPPINESS**

280 **KŌ, minato**
HARBOR, PORT
12 strokes

空港 KŪKŌ   airport
入港 NYŪKŌ   port entry
港町 MINATOMACHI
             port town

Also written 港. 氵 is **water** 40. 巷 is an NGU character meaning **streets of a settlement**. It was once written 巷, showing the early forms of **village** 邑/阝 355 and **together** 戉/共 460, and referred to the coming together of roads near a village. Confusingly, though it usually means point of <u>convergence</u> of roads and hence **settlement**, from a different perspective it can also mean point of <u>divergence</u> and hence **forking road**. Some scholars take 巷 to mean settlement and thus assume 280 means simply **waterside settlement**, but usage in Chinese, where 280 can also mean **creek**, suggests that 氵 represented **river**, that 巷 meant **forking road**, and that 280 originally meant **forking river**. That is, it presumably then came to refer to a **delta** (characterised by branching) and hence **rivermouth**, the site of most **ports**. Suggest taking 共 as **together** and 己 as **self** 855.

Mnemonic: **FIND ONESELF TOGETHER WITH WATER IN PORT**

---

281 号 **GŌ**
NUMBER, CALL, SIGN
5 strokes

番号 BANGŌ   number
号令 GŌREI   command
号泣 GŌKYŪ   wailing

Formerly 號. 虎 is an NGU character meaning **tiger**. Though it looks like a variant of skin 皮 374 it is in fact derived from an extremely stylised pictograph of a tiger that appears to have accentuated the fangs 号 (to 虓 to 虎), and to all intents and purposes represents a mass of claw and fang. 人/ハ is felt to be legs 39 used ideographically, and is dropped in most cases in compounds. 口 is **mouth/say** 20. 丂 is a CO character meaning **seeking an exit**, and shows a **waterweed twisting** up to the surface before spreading out flat. Thus 号 indicates a call that is loud and/or drawn out, i.e. that is preceded by a certain build-up such as the gathering of breath. 281 originally referred to a **tiger's call**, then came to mean **loud call** in general. **Number** is an extended meaning from calling out a person's name or number, as in the army, and **sign** is a similar extension from designation.

Mnemonic: **MOUTH CALLS NUMBER OF TWISTING WEED**

| 282 | | KON, ne
ROOT, BASE
10 strokes | 根本 KONPON
大根 DAIKON
屋根 YANE | basis
giant radish
roof |

Tree 木 69 and **stopping and staring** 艮 263. The latter acts phonetically to express **root/base** and also lends an idea of **'rooted'** to the spot. Thus **root which fixes tree in place**, now also **root/base** in a figurative sense.

Mnemonic: **STOP AND STARE AT TREE ROOT**

| 283 | | SAI, matsuru, matsuri
FESTIVAL, WORSHIP
11 strokes | 祭日 SAIJITSU
祭壇 SAIDAN
雪祭 YUKIMATSURI | holiday
altar
snow festival |

Once written 祭, clearly showing a **hand** 彡 placing **meat** 肉 365 on an **altar** 示 695, thus indicating a sacrifice during a religious **ceremony**. **Festival** and **worship** are associated meanings.

Mnemonic: **HAND PUTS MEAT ON ALTAR IN FESTIVAL OF WORSHIP**

| 284 | | SAI, hosoi, komakai
SLENDER, FINE
11 strokes | 細工 SAIKU
細長い HOSONAGAI
細か KOMAKA ni | craftsmanship
slender
minutely |

Once written 絈, showing **thread** 糸/糸 27 and **brain** 囟/田 131. 田 acts phonetically to express **thin**, and also lends an idea of **fine** crenellations. Thus **fine, thin thread(s)**. Suggest taking 田 as **field** 59.

Mnemonic: **SLENDER PATH THREADS THROUGH FIELD**

| 285 | 仕 | SHI, JI, tsukaeru
SERVE, WORK, DO
5 strokes | 仕事 SHIGOTO
仕方 SHIKATA
仕組み SHIKUMI | work
way, means
arrangement |

Person イ 39 and **samurai** 士 494. A samurai was a person who **served** his master. **Do** and **work** are associated meanings.

Mnemonic: **SAMURAI IS PERSON WHO WORKS AND SERVES**

286		SHI, shin*u* DEATH 6 strokes	死体 SHITAI	corpse
			死去 SHIKYO	death
			若死に WAKAJINI	early death

Once written 屍. 冎 (now 歹) is a variant of **bone** 骨 867 q.v., its 'meatlessness' indicating **bare bone(s)** and hence **skeleton/ death**. 人 is **person** 39, now replaced by **fallen person** ヒ 238 which reinforces the idea of death. Thus **death of a person**, now **death** in general.

Mnemonic: **PERSON FALLS IN DEATH, SOON BARE BONES**

287		SHI, tsuka*u* USE, SERVANT 8 strokes	使用 SHIYŌ	use
			大使 TAISHI	ambassador
			小使 KOZUKAI	servant

Once written 使. イ is **person** 39. 叟 is the early form of **thing** 事 293 q.v., here with its original meaning of **work**. Thus 287 originally meant **working person**. In time it also acquired a causative meaning, i.e. to **make a person work**, and **employ/use** eventually became extended to inanimate objects also. See also **official** 吏 1894, and suggest taking 吏 as this.

Mnemonic: **OFFICIAL PERSON USES SERVANT**

288	始	SHI, haji*meru/maru* BEGIN, FIRST 8 strokes	始終 SHIJŪ	throughout
			始動機 SHIDŌKI	starter
			仕始める SHIHAJIMERU	
				start to do

Somewhat obscure. Once written 姤 and earlier as 姒. The later forms clearly show **name oneself** 台 166 q.v. The early form appears to use just **self/nose** ㄥ/ㄙ 134 without the **mouth/say** element 口 20. 女 is **woman** 35. ㄙ/台 is known to have acted phonetically to express **start**, giving **start of females** and by extension **first-born daughter**. Opinion differs, however, over its semantic role. Some scholars take ㄥ/ㄙ to be **plow** 419 q.v., used in its meaning of **starting point** and thus reinforcing the phonetic **start**, and take 台 to be a miscopying. However, it seems questionable whether plow had acquired this meaning at the time of the form 姒. Other scholars take ㄥ to be **self** 134, with an associated meaning of **first person**, and take 台 to be a later deliberate use of 166 in its meaning of **announce oneself**, since the first born daughter would have spoken on behalf of all the daughters of a family. In any event, from **beginning of female line** 288 came to mean **first** and **beginning** in a broad sense. Suggest taking 台 in its modern meaning of **platform**.

Mnemonic: **FIRST WOMAN BEGINS TO MOUNT PLATFORM**

289 指 SHI, yubi, sasu FINGER, POINT 9 strokes

指示 SHIJI indication
親指 OYAYUBI thumb
指図 SASHIZU directions

扌 is hand 32. 旨 is good 1312, here used phonetically to express branch and possibly also lending an idea of good in the sense of skilful or useful. Thus (useful?) branches of the hand, i.e. fingers. Point is an associated meaning. Suggest taking 旨 as person sitting ヒ 238 and sun 日 62.

Mnemonic: PERSON SITS POINTING AT SUN WITH FINGER

290 歯 SHI, ha TOOTH 12 strokes

歯根 SHIKON dental root
歯医者 HAISHA dentist
歯車 HAGURUMA gear

Formerly 齒, and earlier 齒. The earliest form ▨ is a pictograph of teeth in a mouth 口 20. Stop 止 129 was added later largely for its sound, to express row, but may also have lent an extended meaning of clamp. Its bottom stroke became fused with the upper stroke of mouth. Suggest taking the modern form as rice 米 201.

Mnemonic: TEETH ENSURE RICE STOPS IN MOUTH

291 詩 SHI POETRY 13 strokes

詩人 SHIJIN poet
詩的 SHITEKI poetic
詩情 SHIJŌ poetic feeling

言 is word 274. 寺 is temple 133 q.v., here used largely phonetically to express feeling but probably also lending connotations of regular, i.e. in this case rhythmic. Thus rhythmic words of feeling.

Mnemonic: WORDS FROM TEMPLE ARE PURE POETRY

292 次 JI, SHI, tsugi, tsugu NEXT, FOLLOW 6 strokes

三次 SANJI tertiary
次第 SHIDAI ni gradually
相次いで AITSUIDE in succession

Once written , showing that 冫 derives from two 二 61. 欠 is lack/ gaping mouth 471 q.v., here meaning yawn. When one person yawns, a second invariably follows suit. Thus sequence. Suggest taking 冫 as ice 378.

Mnemonic: LACK OF ICE FOLLOWS NEXT

293 事 **JI, ZU, koto**
THING, MATTER, ACT
8 strokes

大事 DAIJI importance
好事 KŌZU curiosity
出来事 DEKIGOTO event

Once written [illegible], and earlier as [illegible]. 又 is a **hand**, but the precise meaning of [illegible] is unclear. It appears to show a **flag on a pole** [illegible] (see 333), with some scholars taking 口 to be an outer support for the flagpole (see 55) and others taking it to be a placard or **signboard**. In any event it seems likely that 293 originally showed a hand holding aloft some form of identification, taken to indicate a guild or similar engaged in a particular type of **work** (not unlike the distinctive pole once seen outside a barber's shop in the West). Certainly its early meaning was **work** and by extension **worker/servant**, and in Chinese it still retains servant as a reasonably major meaning. It is also the prototype of servant 使 287 q.v. (and see also official 吏 1894). Its present meanings are all felt to be extensions of **work**. Suggest taking the modern form as a mix of **ten** 十 33, **box** 口, and **hand** 彐.

Mnemonic: **HANDLING TEN BOXES IS NO SMALL THING**

294 持 **JI, mo*tsu***
HOLD,HAVE,MAINTAIN
9 strokes

持参 JISAN bringing
持ち主 MOCHINUSHI owner
長持ち NAGAMOCHI durability

扌 is **hand** 32. 寺 is **temple** 133 q.v., here acting phonetically to express **use** and also lending its early meaning of **use of the hands**. Thus to **use the hands**. Though somewhat vague, this appears to have originally meant to **hold** something up, leading to the present meanings of **support/ maintain** and **hold/ have**. Hold is also found in the extended sense of hold out, i.e. **last/ endure.**

Mnemonic: **HOLD HANDS AT TEMPLE**

295 式 **SHIKI**
CEREMONY, FORM
6 strokes

新式 SHINSHIKI new style
方式 HŌSHIKI formula
開会式 KAIKAISHIKI opening ceremony

工 is carpenter's square 113, here meaning **measure**. 弋 is a **stake** 177. 295 originally referred to stakes planted in the ground at measured intervals, giving **scale**. Scale then came to mean **set format or order**, leading to **pattern, style** etc. In Japanese it also refers by association to a **formal ceremony**.

Mnemonic: **CARPENTER'S SQUARE IS A FORM OF STAKE**

---

296 **実**

JITSU, mi, minor*u*
(BEAR) FRUIT, TRUTH,
REALITY
8 strokes

実行 JIKKŌ   carrying out
事実 JIJITSU   fact
実入り MIIRI   crop, gains

Formerly 實 and originally 實 . 田 is **field full of ripe crops** 504, with **shell/ money** 貝 90 emphasising the value of the crop. 宀 is **building** 28. 296 originally referred to a house made prosperous through bumper crops. The idea of house has now disappeared, leaving such meanings as **crop, fullness, substance, ripen**, and by extension **bear fruit** and **reality**. Unusually, the semi-abstract idea of bumper crop was also extended to the physical crop, giving **fruit, nut**, etc. The use of **threaded money** 貫 1102 is a longstanding miscopying, though it still gives a meaning of prosperous house. Suggest taking 夫 as a **big man** 大 53 with **six arms**.

Mnemonic: **IN REALITY, A BIG SIX-ARMED MAN IS IN THE HOUSE!**

---

297 **写**

SHA, utsu*su/ru*
COPY, TRANSCRIBE
5 strokes

写真 SHASHIN   photograph
写実 SHAJITSU   realism
複写機 FUKUSHAKI   copier

Somewhat obscure. Formerly 寫 . 宀 is **building** 28. 舄 is a CO character now used in a number of rather unhelpful meanings such as **shoe** and **large**. It comprises 臼, which is a simplified form of **bird** 鳥 174, and **mortar** 臼 648, and this appears to be a variant of a similar combination of bird and mortar (with the latter used purely phonetically) found in **owl** 舊 648 q.v. Thus presumably 舄 also originally meant owl, which is a <u>large</u> bird (though how it came to mean shoe is not clear). In the case of 297 it is known to have acted phonetically to express **transfer**, to give a meaning of **transfer from one building to another**. Its semantic role is not clear, though some scholars feel it could also mean **magpie**, a bird associated with removing items. It is also possible that 舄 suggested talons, and by extension seizing and **removing**. Transfer from one building to another came to mean **transfer** in a broader sense, and for some unclear reason later became particularly associated with transferring written items, i.e. **transcribing** or **copying**. The modern form uses **convey** 与 1873, partly as a graphic simplification and partly for its meaning.

Mnemonic: **CONVEY COPY OF BUILDING**

298		SHA, mono **PERSON** 8 strokes	作者 SAKUSHA author 後者 KŌSHA the latter 若者 WAKAMONO young people

Formerly 者 and earlier 耆. 日 is a **storage box** (container 凵 plus contents -), while 米 is **kindling** (felt to be a combination of fire ⺍/火 8 and wood 木 69). Thus **box for storing kindling**. This became **box for storing odds and ends**, and eventually just **odds and ends** or **various things**. Thing later became used as a somewhat unflattering reference to certain **persons**, and later became **person** in a general sense. Suggest taking 耂 as **buried in the ground** 117, with 日 as **day** 62. Note that in compounds 298 often lends an idea of **many** (from **various things**).

Mnemonic: **PERSON WILL BE BURIED IN GROUND ONE DAY**

299		SHU, nushi, omo **MASTER, OWNER, MAIN** 5 strokes	主人 SHUJIN master, husband 地主 JINUSHI landowner 主要 SHUYŌ principal

From a pictograph of an **ornately stemmed burning oil lamp** 主. It became a symbol of the **master** of the house, who issued the command for the lamp to be lit. Master led to extended meanings such as **lord, owner, chief/main** etc. Suggest taking as **king** 王 5 and a **bit** ヽ.

Mnemonic: **KING WITH BIT EXTRA IS REAL MASTER**

300	守	SHU, SU, mamoru **PROTECT, KEEP** 6 strokes	保守 HOSHU conservatism 留守番 RUSUBAN caretaker 子守 KOMORI * nursemaid

Building/house 宀 28 and **hand/measure** 寸 909, here meaning **regulate** or **administer**. Thus **looking after a house**, later to **keep** or **protect** in general.

Mnemonic: **TAKE MEASURES TO PROTECT HOUSE**

301

SHU, to*ru*
TAKE, CONTROL
8 strokes

取得 SHUTOKU   acquisition
取り出す TORIDASU   take out
牛取る GYŪJIRU*   control

A **hand** 又 **taking hold** of an **ear** 耳 29. Usually explained as seizing a person by the ear, with the explanation often extended to ripping off the ear of a prisoner of war as a symbol of capture. Ripping off an ear by hand would be no easy matter, but it should be noted that there is a CO character 刵, using ear and cut 刂 181, which means cutting off a prisoner's ear. This was actually a punishment rather than a symbol of capture, but it may account for the popular misinterpretation of 301. It seems more likely that the ear actually represented an animal's ear. When **seizing** an animal that may bite or gore the ear is the safest part to **take hold** of. It is also a tender part, both for animals and humans, and thus an important part when attempting to **control** or subdue these. Thus **hand holding ear** represented both **seize/take** and **control**, though the latter is now a minor meaning.

Mnemonic: **HAND TAKES CONTROL OF EAR**

302

SHU, sake, saka-
ALCOHOL, SAKE
10 strokes

飲酒 INSHU   drinking
酒場 SAKABA   tavern
酒飲み SAKENOMI   hard drinker

酉 is a pictograph of a **wine jar**, and symbolises **alcohol** in general. (It now exists as a minor NGU character indicating a zodiac sign, deriving from the fact that a particular type of spirit was brewed [actually from millet] at a fixed point [the eighth month] of the year.) 氵 is **water** 40, here indicating **liquid**. Thus **liquid in wine jar**, i.e. **alcohol**. In Japanese it also refers to **sake**.

Mnemonic: **WATERY ALCOHOL IN WINE JAR**

303

JU, u*keru*
RECEIVE
8 strokes

受験者 JUKENSHA   examinee
受取 UKETORI   receipt
受付 UKETSUKE   reception

Once written 受, showing a **hand reaching down** 爫 (now an NGU character meaning claws/ talons), a **hand reaching up** 又, and 冖, the prototype of boat 舟 1354 q.v. which was often used as a symbol of **conveyance**. Thus to **convey from one hand to another**. 303 came to indicate the **receiving** hand, whereas the **giving** hand is now expressed by 授 702, which adds a further hand 扌 32. Suggest taking 冖 as a **baton**.

Mnemonic: **ONE HAND RECEIVES BATON FROM ANOTHER HAND**

| 304 | 州 | SHŪ, su PROVINCE, SANDBANK 6 strokes | 本州 HONSHŪ Honshu 砂州 SASU sandbank 州議会 SHŪGIKAI state parliament |

Once written 州 and earlier as ⦅⦆, showing a **sandbank** ○ in a **river** 川48. The idea of small amount of land surrounded by water gave rise to **separate area**, i.e. a **state** or **province**.

Mnemonic: **SANDBANK IN RIVER IS SEPARATE PROVINCE**

| 305 | | SHŪ, JŪ, hirou PICK UP, GATHER, TEN 9 strokes | 収拾 SHŪSHŪ control 拾い物 HIROIMONO bargain 拾壱 JŪICHI eleven |

Hand 扌32 and **join** 合 121, to give the idea of **using both hands** to **gather** or **pick up**. It also came to express **ten**, i.e. the **fingers of two hands**, and was in fact the precursor of ten 十 33.

Mnemonic: **JOINED HANDS CAN GATHER OR COUNT TO TEN**

| 306 | | SHŪ, owaru/eru FINISH 11 strokes | 終点 SHŪTEN end, terminus 終止 SHŪSHI termination 終わり OWARI ni finally |

Formerly 終, and once 夂 and 纟. 纟 is felt to be a pictograph of **ropes** with a **knot** in each **end** (to prevent fraying), and 夂 to be **ropes tied together**. Ropes tied together also led to **knot**, which by association meant **tying off** and thus **finishing**. **Thread** 糸 27 was added later for clarity. Suggest taking 冬 as **winter** 182.

Mnemonic: **THREADS FINISH IN WINTER**

307 SHŪ, nara*u* 練習 RENSHŪ practice
LEARN, TRAIN 習字 SHŪJI penmanship
11 strokes 見習い MINARAI apprentice

Somewhat obscure. Once written 習, and originally 習. The upper part is **wings** 羽 812. The meaning of the lower part is unclear, but it is known to have acted phonetically to express **repeat**, giving **repeated (flapping of the) wings**. This was a reference to a **fledgling learning** to fly. Some scholars take 臼 / 白 to be a simplification of **self** 自 134 q.v., used to symbolise **proper being** and thus giving an idea of the fledgling learning to become a proper (i.e. mature) bird. However, the earlier form ○ does not support this view. It may be **mouth** 口 20 (later **say** 曰 688 or a variant of it?), thus suggesting a fledgling learning to become a bird through using its wings and mouth. Suggest taking 白 as **white** 65, which may even have been used deliberately at a later point since it has connotations of innocence, youth, and **amateurishness** (cf. shirōto, though technically this uses a different character for shiro).

Mnemonic: **WHITE WINGS LEARNING TO FLY**

308 SHŪ 先週 SENSHŪ last week
WEEK 週間 SHŪKAN week
11 strokes 二週目 NISHŪME second week

Movement 辶 129 and **around** 周 504. It originally meant to **go around**, giving both **cycle/ circuit** and **walk around** (both still retained in Chinese). Cycle eventually came to mean **cycle of time** and was used to mean **week**, especially in Japanese where it is now the sole meaning of 308.

Mnemonic: **ANOTHER WEEK ROLLS AROUND**

309 SHŪ, atsu*meru/maru* 集団 SHŪDAN group
GATHER, COLLECT 編集 HENSHŪ editing
12 strokes 集中 SHŪCHŪ concentration

Formerly 雧, showing **birds** 隹 216 **gathered** in a **tree** 木 69. Now **gather** or **assemble** in general, including transitively.

Mnemonic: **BIRDS GATHER IN TREE**

310 JŪ, sum*u*
RESIDE, LIVE
7 strokes

住所 JŪSHO   address
住宅 JŪTAKU   dwelling
住み手 SUMITE   occupant

亻 is **person** 39. 主 is **master** 299 q.v., here used for its literal meaning of oil **lamp** lit by master of house. Thus **where a person is master of the lamp**, i.e. the **house** where he **lives**.

Mnemonic: **WHERE PERSON LIVES IS WHERE HE IS MASTER**

311 JŪ, CHŌ, kasa*neru/naru*,
omo*i, e*
HEAVY, PILE, -FOLD
9 strokes

重大 JŪDAI   seriousness
重さ OMOSA   weight
三重 MIE   threefold

Once written 𡕢, showing **person** 人 39, **ground** 土 60, and **east** 東/東 184 q.v., here used for its literal meaning of **(heavy) sack**. Thus **person standing on ground carrying heavy sack**, leading to **heavy** in general including figuratively as **grave**. **Pile (up)** and **-fold** are felt to derive from the idea of adding to the weight being carried. 311 is unusual in that, although it is an ideograph and not a pictograph, it shows three elements arranged vertically, whereas one might have expected 俥 or similar in the interests of balanced appearance (see also 363). Suggest taking it as a **'double wheeled' vehicle** 車 31.

Mnemonic: **HEAVY VEHICLE HAS DOUBLE WHEELS**

312 所 SHO, tokoro
PLACE, SITUATION
8 strokes

場所 BASHO   place
所有 SHOYŪ   possession
居所 IDOKORO   address

Door 戸 108 and **ax/chop** 斤 1176. Usually explained as the doorway being the **place** where wood was chopped, which is a useful mnemonic but almost certainly incorrect. 戸 was used purely for its sound, which was originally KO (cf. English CUt) before changing to CHO (cf. English CHOp) and finally SHO (cf. English SHEar/SHOre/SHOrn). Thus the **KO (CHO/SHO) sound of something being chopped**. It is not fully clear how it came to mean **place**. Some scholars feel it was borrowed phonetically as a substitute for SHO place 處 896, but it may also have derived from a particular place associated with chopping (wood). Thus there may be some slight support for the 'chopping in a doorway' theory. **Place** has also come to be used figuratively to mean **situation** or **circumstances**.

Mnemonic: **CHOP DOWN DOOR WITH AX TO GET INTO PLACE**

313

SHO, atsu*i*
HOT (WEATHER)
12 strokes

酷暑 KOKUSHO　　intense heat
避暑地 HISHOCHI　　cool resort
暑さ ATSUSA　　　　　　heat

Formerly 暑. 日 is **sun** 62. 者 / 者 is **person** 298 q.v., here acting phonetically to express **burn** and possibly also lending loose connotations of **much** (much/many being an occasional connotation lent by 298, felt to derive from its idea of various bits and pieces). Thus (**much?**) **burning sun**, i.e. **heat**.

Mnemonic: **PERSON UNDER HOT SUN**

314

JO, tasu*keru*/*karu*
ASSIST, HELP
7 strokes

助手 JOSHU　　　　　assistant
助力 JORYOKU　help, support
助け合い TASUKEAI　　mutual aid

Strength 力 74 and **furthermore**/ **cairn** 且 1091 q.v., here used for its original meaning of **build up**/ **add**. Thus **added strength**, i.e. **help**.

Mnemonic: **FURTHERMORE, HELP BY ADDING STRENGTH**

315

SHŌ
BRIGHT, LIGHT
9 strokes

昭和 SHŌWA　　Showa Period
昭昭 SHŌSHŌ　　　brightness
昭代 SHŌDAI　enlightened era

日 is **sun** 62, here indicating **brightness**. 召 is **summon** 1387, here acting phonetically to express **clear** and probably also lending an idea of **muster**. Thus (a mustering of?) **clarity** and **brightness**.

Mnemonic: **SUMMON SUN, AND LET THERE BE LIGHT**

316

SHŌ, ke*su*, ki*eru*
EXTINGUISH,
VANISH, CONSUME
10 strokes

消費 SHŌHI　　　　consumption
消しゴム KESHIGOMU　　　eraser
消火器 SHŌKAKI
　　　　　　fire extinguisher

Formerly 消. 氵 is **water** 40. 肖/ 肖 is **be like** 1391 q.v., here acting phonetically to express **few**/ **little** and also lending an idea of **reduced** from its original meaning of **miniature version**. The original meaning appears to have been **reduced to little water**, leading to the idea of **consuming** and hence **vanishing**. Suggest taking ⺌ as a variant of **little** 小 36 and 月 as **moon** 16.

Mnemonic: **WATER HAS VANISHED FROM OUR LITTLE MOON**

---

317 SHŌ, akina*u* 商業 SHŌGYŌ commerce
TRADE, DEAL, SELL, 商人 SHŌNIN merchant
SHANG CHINA 商売 SHŌBAI business
11 strokes

Obscure. Owing to its similarity in meaning and shape to **sell** 売 192 q.v. it is often felt
to be a variant of the latter, with **mouth/say** ☐ 20 indicating **hawking**. However, the
old forms of both characters show clearly that there is no connection. The oldest forms of
317 are 裛 and 禼. 內 is almost certainly **spread thighs** (see also 1103), the plump-
ness indicating female thighs, with **opening** ☐ 20 added to indicate **vagina**. 平 is the
early form of needle 辛 1432, which was often used to symbolise **pierce/ penetrate**.
Thus 317 appears to have originally meant **vaginal penetration**, i.e. copulation. From
this point the link with **trade** seems clear, i.e. the world's oldest trade of **prostitution**. A
number of authoritative Japanese scholars, however, while accepting that 內 is vagina,
take 平 to be used purely phonetically to express **birth**, giving **opening in female
thighs that gives birth** and thus reinforcing the meaning **vagina**. That is, they feel that
317 meant simply vagina and not copulation, and that it was then borrowed purely phonetically as a substitute for a complex character meaning to **peddle**. This does not seem especially convincing. Even less convincing is the obviously incorrect but often heard explanation that 317 is a variant of tall/high 高 119, to the effect that it meant high plateau and that
this name was given to dwellers of the high plains who were noted traders and who also
became the ancient **Shang** dynasty. Certainly, however, the Shang period was associated
with trade (and not prostitution or vaginas, though the apparent contemporaneity of the
Shang period [c.1500-c.1000 B.C.according to some sources, and 1766-1122 B.C. according to others] and the early forms given above [c.1500 B.C.] might be felt to leave
some room for doubt). Suggest taking ▽ as a variant of **stand** 立 73, ⌐ as a **counter**,
ﾉﾚas **legs** 39, and ☐ as **mouth** 20.

Mnemonic: **USE MOUTH AND LEGS TO TRADE, STANDING AT COUNTER**

318 SHŌ 記章 KISHŌ medal, badge
BADGE, CHAPTER 文章 BUNSHŌ writing, prose
11 strokes 章句 SHŌKU chapter, passage

Once written 垔. 平 is **needle** 辛 1432. The exact meaning of ⊖ is not clear, but it is
felt to be a stylisation influenced by needle 十 33 q.v., which was originally written ＋
with • indicating the eye. Whereas 33 was a sewing needle, 1432 was a **tattooist's
needle**, and was used in particular for tattooing slaves (usually on the forehead). The **tat-
too** was an **identifying mark**. This gave rise to the meaning **sign** or **badge**. It also
came to mean **pattern**, and even ornamental and beautiful (still retained in Chinese), which
was then applied to a **piece of writing** (not unlike pattern/text 文 68). Suggest taking
as **stand** 立 73 and **quickly** 早 50. See also 340.

Mnemonic: **BADGE QUICKLY STANDS OUT**

319 勝

SHŌ, ka*tsu*, masa*ru*
WIN, SURPASS
12 strokes

勝利 SHŌRI — victory
勝負 SHŌBU — outcome
勝ち気 KACHIKI — spiritedness

Formerly 勝 . 力 is **strength/effort** 74. 朕 / 朕 is a variant of **royal we** 朕 1603 q.v., here lending its sound to express **raise** and also lending similar connotations of its own. 319 originally referred to **exerting oneself in order to raise something.** This came to mean **succeed**, leading to **win** and **surpass**. Suggest taking 月 as **moon** 16, and 关 as **two** 二 61 **fires** 火 8.

Mnemonic: **WITH EFFORT, TWO FIRES CAN SURPASS MOON**

320 乗

JŌ, no*ru*/*seru*
RIDE, MOUNT, LOAD
9 strokes

乗船 JŌSEN — embarkation
乗数 JŌSŪ — multiplier
乗り物 NORIMONO — vehicle

Formerly 乘 and earlier 槳 , while the oldest form is 東 , showing a **person** 大 53 on top of a **tree** 木 69. Thus to **climb a tree**, with climb giving **mount** and thus **ride**, and **load** being the transitive form. The intermediate form 槳 shows person 人 39, tree 木 , and **opposed feet** 舛 422, indicating a firm position in the treetop. Suggest remembering by association with **come** 来 217, taking ㇛ as a variant of **two** 二 61.

Mnemonic: **TWO COME RIDING**

321 植

SHOKU, u*eru*
PLANT
12 strokes

植物 SHOKUBUTSU — flora
田植え TAUE — rice planting
植民地 SHOKUMINCHI — colony

Tree 木 69 and **straight** 直 349 q.v., meaning to **make a tree straight**, i.e. **plant.**

Mnemonic: **STRAIGHT TREE IS PROPERLY PLANTED**

322 申

SHIN, mō*su*
SAY, EXPOUND
5 strokes

申告 SHINKOKU — report
申し込む MŌSHIKOMU — apply
申し訳 MŌSHIWAKE — excuse

Once written 甶 and 㠯 , showing a jagged bolt of **forked lightning.** It is in fact the prototype of lightning/ electricity 電 180 q.v. How exactly it came to mean **say/ expound** is not clear. Some scholars feel it was borrowed purely phonetically, others feel that it (also) lent a meaning of **speaking with the impact of lightning**, i.e. a forceful or dramatic speech, while still others feel that lightning was considered the **voice** of the gods (see also 324). It usually means speak in detail. Suggest taking as a pierced | **sun** 日 62.

Mnemonic: **SUN IS PIERCED: WHAT CAN ONE SAY?!**

323		SHIN, mi **BODY** 7 strokes	身体 SHINTAI	body
			自身 JISHIN	oneself
			身分 MIBUN	status

Once written 㐆, showing a side-on view of the **body of a pregnant woman**. It originally meant pregnant body, but later came to mean **body** in a broad sense.

Mnemonic: **PREGNANT WOMAN HAS CONSPICUOUS BODY**

324		SHIN, JIN, kami **GOD, SPIRIT** 9 strokes	精神 SEISHIN	spirit
			神父 SHINPU	priest
			女神 MEGAMI*	goddess

Formerly 神. 示/礻 is **altar** 695, here in its extended sense of **related to the gods**. 申 is **say** 322 q.v., here in its literal sense of **lightning**. Lightning was thought to be a manifestation of the **gods** (some scholars feel **voice of the gods**). **Spirit** is an associated meaning.

Mnemonic: **GODS SAY SOMETHING SPIRITED AT ALTAR**

325		SHIN, fukai/meru **DEEP, DEEPEN** 11 strokes	深遠 SHINEN	profundity
			深海 SHINKAI	deep sea
			深入り FUKAIRI	going deeply

Once written 㵉. 川/氵 is **water** 40. 罙 is an element showing **hole** 穴 849, **hand** 㐅, and **fire** 火 8. It originally referred to a hand reaching into a chimney to remove the soot, then came to mean **chimney-like hole**. Thus **hole in water**, indicating a **deep** part of a river or similar. The modern form has mistakenly used **tree** 木 69, with 𠆢 being a variant of hole 穴.

Mnemonic: **FIND DEEP WATERHOLE NEAR TREE**

326		SHIN, susumu/meru **ADVANCE** 11 strokes	前進 ZENSHIN	advance
			進化 SHINKA	evolution
			進言 SHINGEN	proposition

Movement 辵 129 and **bird** 隹 216, giving **move like a bird**, i.e. **forwards**.

Mnemonic: **ADVANCE LIKE MOVING BIRD**

327 SEI, SE, yo   世紀 SEIKI   century
WORLD, GENERATION   世話 SEWA   care
5 strokes   世の中 YONONAKA   the world

Once written 卋 and 𠀡, both being stylised versions of **three tens** 十 **33. Thirty years** was the norm for a **generation**, and this later came to mean **the times** and **the world at large.** See also 405.

Mnemonic: **ODD WORLD OF THE THIRTIES' GENERATION**

328 SEI, totono*u/eru*   整理 SEIRI   arrangement
ARRANGE   整備 SEIBI   maintenance
16 strokes   微調整 BICHŌSEI   fine tuning

正 is **proper/ correct** 41. 攵 is **edict** 1600 q.v., here with its literal meaning of **enforcing correct action.** Thus to **make someone act correctly,** giving **bring order** and thus **arrange.** Suggest taking 攵 literally as **bundle** 束 1535 and **stick in hand/ force** 攵 101.

Mnemonic: **FORCE CORRECT ARRANGEMENT OF BUNDLES**

329 SEN   脱線 DASSEN   derailment
LINE   光線 KŌSEN   light ray
15 strokes   直線 CHOKUSEN   straight line

糸 is **thread** 27. 泉 is **source/ spring** 915, here acting phonetically to express **slender** and also lending a similar idea (from a **thin** stream of water). Thus **slender thread,** eventually giving **line.**

Mnemonic: **TRACE THREAD-LIKE LINE TO SOURCE**

330 ZEN, matta*ku*   全部 ZENBU   all
WHOLE, COMPLETE(LY)   全身 ZENSHIN   whole body
6 strokes   安全 ANZEN   safety

人 is a **cover** 87. 王 is **jewel** 102. Thus **jewel under cover,** indicating a protected and therefore precious jewel. A precious jewel was a **perfect,** unblemished one, and the idea of perfect eventually came to mean **whole** or **complete.** Suggest taking 王 as **king** 5.

Mnemonic: **KING COMPLETELY UNDER COVER**

331 送 | SŌ, oku*ru* | 放送 HŌSŌ | broadcast
SEND | 送金 SŌKIN | remittance
9 strokes | 見送る MIOKURU | see off

辶 is **movement** 129. ⺺ is the right hand part of **royal we** 朕 1603 q.v., with its meaning of **raise repeatedly**. Here it lends an extended idea of **following on** (from repeat), and also lends its sound to express **follow**. Thus **move and follow**. This originally referred to a **servant following** his master. Then, in very similar fashion to servant following/ send 遣 1220 q.v., it came to mean **servant sent on errands** and then just **send**. Suggest taking 关 as **heaven** 58 and ⸜ as **away** 66.

Mnemonic: **SENT AWAY FROM HEAVEN**

---

332 息 | SOKU, iki | 休息 KYŪSOKU | rest
BREATH,REST,CHILD | ため息 TAMEIKI | sigh
10 strokes | 息子 MUSUKO* | son

自 is **self** 134 q.v., here with its literal meaning of **nose**. 心 is **heart** 147, here meaning **essence of life**. The essence of life associated with the nose is **air that one breathes**. It is not fully clear how this also came to mean **rest** and **child**, but it is possible that rest is an associated meaning of breath (cf. English [take a] breather).

Mnemonic: **HEART BREATHES THROUGH NOSE**

---

333 族 | ZOKU | 家族 KAZOKU | family
CLAN, FAMILY | 民族 MINZOKU | race
11 strokes | 種族 SHUZOKU | tribe

Once written 㫃, showing an **arrow** 夨 / 矢 981 under a **streaming banner** ⌒ tied to a crude **pole** Ψ. There is some disagreement over the exact role of these elements, but many scholars take them to indicate a mustering or rallying of arms under a banner, with the idea of **people forming a group** eventually leading to **clan** and **family**. It can also occasionally mean **gather**. The modern form of streaming banner, 𭤫, derives from a rather confusing stylisation 㫃. Suggest taking it as **side** 方 204 and **person** 𠂉 39.

Mnemonic: **PERSON WITH ARROW IN SIDE IS ONE OF THE CLAN**

| 334 他 | TA, hoka
OTHER
5 strokes | 他人 TANIN
他国 TAKOKU
他所 YOSO* | stranger
foreign land
elsewhere |

Person イ 39 and **twisting creature** 也 167. Some scholars take the latter to mean **twisting**, which could sometimes mean by extension **unusual** (see also 1041), thus giving **unusual person** and hence **stranger** or **person from other parts**. Other scholars take twisting creature (either snake or scorpion) as a symbol of something dangerous, giving **dangerous person**, which was also a reference to an **unusual person** and hence person from other parts. Person from other parts came to mean **other** in general.

Mnemonic: **OTHER PERSON IS LIKE TWISTING CREATURE**

| 335 打 | DA, *utsu*
HIT, STRIKE
5 strokes | 打者 DASHA
打撃 DAGEKI
打ち返す UCHIKAESU | batter
blow
hit back |

扌 is **hand** 32. 丁 is **nail** 346, acting phonetically to express **strike** and possibly also lending an idea of **something to be struck**. Thus to **strike with the hand**, now **strike** in a broader sense.

Mnemonic: **HAND HITS NAIL**

| 336 対 | TAI, TSUI
OPPOSE, AGAINST,
PAIR
7 strokes | 反対 HANTAI
対象 TAISHŌ
対句 TSUIKU | opposition
object
couplet |

Formerly 對 . 丵 is the same complex **musical instrument** seen in profession 業 260 q.v. 寸 is **measure/hand** 909, here with its meaning of **regulate**. Thus 336 originally referred to adjusting the complex instrument. This involved balancing the crosspieces from which the bells were hung, leading to an idea of **counterbalance**. This eventually came to mean **be set in an opposed position**, usually of items in a **pair**. Suggest taking 文 as a variant of **text** 文 68.

Mnemonic: **MEASURE OPPOSITION TO TEXT**

337	待	TAI, ma*tsu* WAIT 9 strokes	待機 TAIKI	awaiting chance
			招待 SHŌTAI	invitation
			待ち伏せ MACHIBUSE	ambush

Movement along a road 彳 118 and temple 寺 133 q.v. The latter acts phonetically to express **stop**, to give **stop moving** and hence **wait**. It is not clear why 寺 was used instead of the simpler stop 止 129, but it may possibly lend an idea of **being active** (with the hands), thus suggesting **occupying oneself** while **waiting**.

Mnemonic: **WAIT AT TEMPLE BESIDE ROAD**

338	代	DAI, TAI, ka*waru/eru*, yo REPLACE, WORLD, GENERATION, FEE 5 strokes	世代 SEDAI	generation
			交代 KŌTAI	alternation
			部屋代 HEYADAI	room rent

彳 is **person** 39. 弋 is **stake** 177, here acting phonetically to express **replace** and possibly loosely lending similar connotations since stakes were generally of a set size and thus **interchangeable**. Thus **replacement person**, meaning a representative or stand-in. This gradually broadened to mean **generation**, i.e. people who replace others, and by extension **the times/world**, and also to mean **exchange** in a general sense. **Fee** is an associated idea, being exchanged for goods or services.

Mnemonic: **PERSON REPLACED BY STAKE**

339	第	DAI GRADE, ORDER 11 strokes	第二課 DAINIKA	Chapter Two
			次第書 SHIDAISHO	program
			及第 KYŪDAI	making grade

竹 is **bamboo** 170, here meaning **bamboo tablets** used for keeping records. 弔 is a variant of **younger brother** 弟 177 q.v., here with its literal meaning of **order/ sequence**. Thus to put **bamboo tablets in order**, leading to **order/ sequence** in general. See also 361.

Mnemonic: **BAMBOO TOPS YOUNG BROTHER IN ORDER OF THINGS**

340	題	DAI SUBJECT, TITLE 18 strokes	問題 MONDAI	problem, issue
			題名 DAIMEI	title
			話題 WADAI	topic

頁 is **head** 93. 是 is **proper** 910, here used phonetically to express **hairless** and possibly also loosely lending an idea of **straight** and by extension **flat**. The (flat?) hairless part of the head is the **forehead**, the original meaning of 340 (a meaning still listed in some Chinese dictionaries). Some scholars make a direct link between **forehead** and **title** in the same way as the English term **heading**. This is a useful mnemonic, but it seems more likely the evolution was somewhat similar to badge/chapter 章 318 q.v. That is, slaves were tattooed on the forehead with identifying marks, with **identifying mark** coming to mean **title** or **subject**. Suggest taking 是 as **day** 日 62 and **correct** 正 41.

Mnemonic: **GET SUBJECT HEADING CORRECT ON THE DAY**

341	炭	TAN, sumi CHARCOAL, COAL 9 strokes	石炭 SEKITAN	coal
			炭素 TANSO	carbon
			炭火 SUMIBI	charcoal fire

Somewhat obscure. Popularly explained as **combustible material** (from fire 火 8) taken from the **side** (from cliff 厂 45) of a **hill (mountain)** 山 24. This is a useful mnemonic for the modern form, but the older form 炭 shows that 厂 is not cliff, but a simplification of 屵 . This appears to be **hand**, with 灰/灰 seeming to be **ash** 818 q.v. Thus **ash and hill**, presumably a reference to **charcoal burning** that was normally carried out in the hills. However, some scholars maintain that 屵 is used as a purely phonetic element meaning **return**, giving **fire that returns (to fire)**, i.e. **charcoal**. Coal and charcoal are associated in meaning.

Mnemonic: **FIERY MATERIAL FROM MOUNTAIN CLIFF IS COAL**

342	短	TAN, mijikai SHORT 12 strokes	短所 TANSHO	shortcoming
			短気 TANKI	short temper
			手短か TEMIJIKA	brief

Arrow 矢 981 and **food vessel** 豆 1640. Arrows were generally of a fixed length and were occasionally used as crude **measures** (cf. English measures rod, perch, pole etc., and note that the addition of big/ carpenter's square 巨 1153 gives the NGU character rule/ measuring square 矩). 豆 acts phonetically to express **small**, and almost certainly lends a similar idea of generally **fixed dimensions**. (Though in many cases 豆 is used in characters in a rather vague sense to mean food vessel in general, technically it refers to a small one-legged table for one person [takatsuki], of a more or less fixed height.) Thus **small measurement** (comparable to arrow and food vessel), i.e. **short**.

Mnemonic: **BOTH ARROW AND FOOD VESSEL ARE SHORT**

343	CHAKU, tsu*ku*, ki*ru*	到着	TŌCHAKU	arrival
	ARRIVE, WEAR	着物	KIMONO	clothing
	12 strokes	船着き	FUNATSUKI	anchorage

A variant of remarkable/show/**wear/arrive** 著 937, q.v. Suggest taking 主 as **sheep** 986, 目 as **eye** 72, and ／ as **a line**.

Mnemonic: **SHEEP ARRIVES WEARING EYE-LINER!**

344	CHŪ, soso*gu*	注目	CHŪMOKU	attention
	POUR, NOTE	注射	CHŪSHA	injection
	8 strokes	注釈	CHŪSHAKU	notes

氵 is **water** 40. 主 is **master** 299 q.v., acting phonetically to express **continuous** and almost certainly also lending an idea of **column** from its literal meaning of long stemmed lamp (see also 345). Thus **continuous column of water**, giving **pour**. Also used figuratively as pour one's thoughts, i.e. **pay attention**.

Mnemonic: **MASTER POURS WATER**

345	CHŪ, hashira	柱石	CHŪSEKI	pillar
	COLUMN, PILLAR	電柱	DENCHŪ	telegraph pole
	9 strokes	氷柱	TSURARA*	icicle

木 is **wood** 69. 主 is **master** 299 q.v., acting phonetically to express **firm** and also lending an idea of **column** from its original meaning of long stemmed lamp. Thus **firm wooden column**, now **column** or **pillar** in a broader sense including the figurative.

Mnemonic: **MASTER WOODEN PILLAR**

346	CHŌ, TEI	丁度	CHŌDO	exactly
	BLOCK, EXACT	丁寧	TEINEI	civility
	2 strokes	丁目	CHŌME	city block

Once written 丁, depicting a **nail**. This meaning has now been taken over by an NGU character that adds metal 金 14, 釘, while 346 itself has come to be borrowed widely, both for its sound and its shape. **Block** comes from the idea of intersecting paths/ lines suggested by the shape (see also town/ block 町 57), while **exact** may, like the English term **to a T**, come from a suggestion of a carpentry joint.

Mnemonic: **BLOCK IS EXACT TO A T**

347		CHŌ REGISTER, DRAPE 11 strokes	手帳 TECHŌ 帳場 CHŌBA 蚊帳 KAYA*	notebook counter, desk mosquito net

巾 is **cloth** 778. 長 is **long** 173, here also acting phonetically to express **spread**. Thus **long spread cloth**, giving **drape**. It is not fully clear how it came to mean **register**, but it seems likely that records were kept on (rolls of) cloth before (scrolls of) paper became common.

Mnemonic: **LONG CLOTH DRAPE USED AS REGISTER**

348		CHŌ, shira*beru,* totono*eru* ADJUST, INVESTIGATE, TONE, TUNE 15 strokes	調整 CHŌSEI 調査 CHŌSA 調子 CHŌSHI	adjustment investigation tone, condition

Words/speak 言 274 and **around** 周 504. The original meaning was **discuss comprehensively** (i.e. talk all around a topic). From this it acquired meanings such as **examine, adjust** (one's views), and **overall situation** (leading to **condition**). Adjustment and condition were also applied to music, giving **tone** and **melody** (cf. English tune, etymologically the same word as tone).

Mnemonic: **INVESTIGATE BY TALKING AROUND**

349		CHOKU, JIKI, nao*ru/su,* su*gu,* tada*chi* DIRECT,UPRIGHT,FIX 8 strokes	直接 CHOKUSETSU 正直 SHŌJIKI 直立 CHOKURITSU	direct honesty erect

Once written 直, and earlier as 直. 𡆥/目 is **eye** 72, here meaning **look**. |/十 is **needle** 33, here acting phonetically to express **direct** as well as lending an idea of **pierce**. Thus **direct, piercing stare**. The later addition ∟ is a **corner**, felt by some scholars to indicate the object of the stare being **fixed in place**, and by others to indicate (attempted) **concealment**, giving **stare at something supposed to be hidden**. In very similar fashion to the English term **fix**, which can mean fix with a stare or make straight and/or firm, the meaning of 349 broadened from **fix with direct stare** to fix in the sense of **mend**, while **direct** also came to mean **straight** and **proper** and by extension **upright/ honest**. Suggest taking 十 in its modern sense of **ten**.

Mnemonic: **TEN EYES FIXED DIRECTLY ON CORNER**

| 350 | 追 | TSUI, *ou*
CHASE, PURSUE
9 strokes | 追究 TSUIKYŪ
追放 TSUIHŌ
追い払う OIHARAU | inquiry
banishment
drive off |

辶 is **movement** 129. 㠯 has long been confused with **terraced hill** 㠯 / ⻏ 229, and even exists as a CO character meaning pile or heap, but the oldest forms such as ⻏ show that it is in fact a pair of **buttocks**. Here it acts phonetically to express **chase**, and almost certainly lends an idea of **person's rear**. Thus to **move in pursuit of a person**. Though it originally meant chase in the sense of pursue, it can now also mean **chase off**. Pursue can also be used in the sense of **conduct** (investigations etc.).

Mnemonic: **PURSUE MOVING BUTTOCKS**

| 351 | 定 | TEI, JŌ, sada*meru*
FIX, ESTABLISH
8 strokes | 定期 TEIKI
不定 FUTEI
決定 KETTEI | fixed term
indefinite
decision |

Roof/building 宀 28 and **correct** 㝵 / 正 41. 351 originally referred to the correct erection of the framework of a building, then came to mean **establish** or **fix** in a broader sense.

Mnemonic: **FIX ROOF CORRECTLY**

| 352 | 庭 | TEI, niwa
GARDEN, COURTYARD
10 strokes | 家庭 KATEI
庭園 TEIEN
庭師 NIWASHI | household
garden
master gardener |

广 is **large building** 114, here meaning **palace**. 廷 is **court** 1610 q.v., here with its literal meaning of **people standing around at court**. People generally did their waiting at the palace/ court in the **courtyard** or **garden**.

Mnemonic: **PALACE COURTYARD IS FINE GARDEN**

353 **TETSU, kurogane**
IRON, STEEL
13 strokes

鉄板 TEPPAN   steel plate
地下鉄 CHIKATETSU   subway
国鉄 KOKUTETSU
        (former) National Railway

Formerly 鐵 . 金 is **metal** 14. 戴 (also 戓 ˋ) is an element known to have meant **big**, though for unclear reasons it is listed in some Chinese dictionaries (without illustration) as a character meaning scrape or advantageous. It was once written 戴 , showing that 弋 is not the usual cut 找 872, which is to all intents and purposes a variant of cut/ halberd 戈 493, but 493 plus big 大 53. 呈 is offer 1611. Thus 戴 presumably originally meant **cut up a big offering**. In the case of 353 it acts phonetically to express **black**, and presumably also lends an idea of **big** (i.e. **massive**). Thus **massive black metal**, a reference to **iron** and by extension **steel**. Note that kurogane literally means **black metal**. Suggest taking the modern simplification 失 as **lose** 501. See also 263.

Mnemonic: **LOST METAL PROVES TO BE IRON**

354 **TEN, koro***geru/garu/gasu/bu*
ROTATE, ROLL, TUMBLE
11 strokes

転送 TENSŌ   forwarding
運転 UNTEN   driving
自転車 JITENSHA   bicycle

Formerly 轉 . 車 is **vehicle** 31. 專 is the old form of exclusive 専 914 q.v., here acting phonetically to express **move** and also lending an idea of **rotating** from its literal meaning of spinning weight. Thus **rotational movement of vehicle**, i.e. **roll**. It is also used to mean **rotate** and **tumble**. Suggest taking 云 as **two** 二 61 **noses** 厶 134.

Mnemonic: **VEHICLE ROLLS OVER TWO NOSES**

355 **TO, TSU, miyako**
CAPITAL, METROPOLIS
11 strokes

都市 TOSHI   city
首都 SHUTO   capital
都合 TSUGŌ   circumstances

阝 is not hill 229 but an element meaning **village**, deriving from the NGU character village 邑 (once 㕔 , felt to show an enclosure 口 and a sitting person 己 , indicating at ease). 者 is **person** 298 q.v., acting phonetically to express **gather** and also lending its connotations of **many** and **various** in addition to **person**. Thus **village where many and various persons are gathered**, i.e. a **big town**.

Mnemonic: **METROPOLIS IS VILLAGE OF MANY PERSONS**

| 356 | 度 | DO, TAKU, tabi
DEGREE, TIMES
9 strokes | 程度 TEIDO
温度 ONDO
一度 ICHIDO | degree
temperature
once |

庐 is an abbreviation of **various** 庶, 1381, and also acts phonetically to express **measure**. 又 is **hand**, which was often used for **measuring** things. Thus to **measure various things with the hand**, finally giving **measurement** in a range of senses. It is not clear why measure/hand 寸 909 was not used instead of just hand. Suggest taking 广 as **building** 114, with 廿 as **two tens** 十 33 and **one** 一 1, i.e. **twenty-one**.

Mnemonic: **HAND MEASURES TWENTY-ONE DEGREES IN BUILDING**

| 357 | 投 | TŌ, nageru
THROW, CAST
7 strokes | 投手 TŌSHU
投票 TŌHYŌ
投げ出す NAGEDASU | pitcher
vote
abandon |

Hand 扌 32 and **strike with ax** 殳 153. The latter also acts phonetically to mean **throw**. Thus **throw a weapon**, then just **throw**.

Mnemonic: **HAND STRIKES BY THROWING AX**

| 358 | 島 | TŌ, shima
ISLAND
10 strokes | 列島 RETTŌ
島民 TŌMIN
島国 SHIMAGUNI | archipelago
islanders
island nation |

Formerly and 鳥, clearly showing **bird** 鳥 174 and **mountain** 山 24. **Mountains where birds alight** is a reference to **islands in the sea**. Some scholars feel that 鳥 also acts phonetically to express **tide** and by extension **sea**, thus clarifying the interpretation of the character.

Mnemonic: **BIRD ALIGHTS ON MOUNTAINOUS ISLAND**

| 359 | 湯 | TŌ, yu
HOT WATER
12 strokes | 銭湯 SENTŌ
湯気 YUGE
茶の湯 CHANOYU | public bath
steam
tea ceremony |

氵 is **water** 40. is **rising sun** 144, indicating **becoming hot**. Thus **heated water**.

Mnemonic: **RISING SUN HEATS WATER**

360

TŌ, TO, nobor*u*
CLIMB
12 strokes

登場　TŌJŌ　　　　appearance
登山　TOZAN　　　mountaineering
木登り　KINOBORI　tree climbing

Somewhat obscure. Once written 登, showing **two feet** 129, **hands**, and **food vessel** 豆 1640 q.v. It is not fully clear how these elements combined. Some scholars see them as as a virtual pictograph depicting a child or similar clambering onto the food vessel (this being taken in its literal meaning of a single legged table that could be several feet high). Others take 豆 to be used purely phonetically to express **climb**, giving **climbing feet (and hands)**. Still others take the hands to be **offering** up the food vessel (here meaning just dish of food), and take the element 登 to be used phonetically to express **climb** as well as lending connotations of **raise/ rise**, thus giving **climbing (and rising) feet**. The last theory seems the most likely, though the first is perhaps the simplest to remember.

Mnemonic: **TWO FUNNY FEET CLIMB FOOD VESSEL**

361

TŌ, hito*shii*, na*do*
CLASS, EQUAL,
ETCETERA
12 strokes

一等　ITTŌ　　　　　first class
上等　JŌTŌ　　　　high class
等圧線　TŌATSUSEN　isobar

Bamboo 竹 170, here meaning **bamboo tablets** used for keeping records, and **temple** 寺 133 q.v., which acts phonetically to express **arrange** and also lends its idea of **work with the hands**. Thus to **arrange bamboo tablets** (with the hands). This is very similar to order/ arrange bamboo tablets 第 339, but whereas 339 means putting in <u>sequential</u> order, 361 means putting in <u>equal</u> <u>groups</u>. Group of equal or similar items led to **class, equal**, and by extension **etcetera**.

Mnemonic: **BAMBOO TABLETS AT TEMPLE ARE ALL EQUAL**

362

DŌ, ugo*ku/kasu*
MOVE
11 strokes

動物　DŌBUTSU　　animal
自動車　JIDŌSHA　　vehicle
動き出す　UGOKIDASU　move off

力 is **strength** 74. 重 is **heavy** 311, which also acts phonetically to express **sway**. Thus to **apply strength and cause something heavy to sway**, leading to **move**.

Mnemonic: **STRENGTH MOVES HEAVY OBJECT**

363		DŌ, warabe	童話 DŌWA	nursery tale
		CHILD	児童 JIDŌ	children
		12 strokes	童心 DŌSHIN	child's mind

Somewhat obscure. Once written 童 , possibly the most esthetically unbalanced of all the characters in that it combines four elements vertically. The elements are, in descending order, **needle** 辛 / 辛 1432, **eye** ∅ / 目 72, **east/ sack** 東 /東 184, and **ground** 土 60. The original meaning is known to have been **slave**, and it seems likely that it is the early form of **heavy** 重 /重 311 q.v., namely **person standing on the ground carrying heavy sack**, with person 人 replaced by the combination of eye and (tattooist's) needle. (This substitution would partly explain the awkward vertical alignment.) Slaves had an identification mark tattooed on the forehead (see 340), i.e. above the eye, and it therefore seems probable that 辛 indicates slave. Thus <u>slave</u> **standing on ground carrying heavy sack**. How this came to mean **child** is not clear. Child slaves were far from uncommon so it may have been an associated meaning, though this is unlikely. Some scholars feel it was used instead of a CO character meaning **child**, 僮 , comprising person 亻 39 and slave 童 363, in which 童 is believed to lend a meaning to the effect of **person not having full rights as a citizen** as well as lending its sound to express **growing up**. Suggest taking the modern form of 363 as **stand** 立 73 and **village** 里 219.

Mnemonic: **CHILD STANDS IN VILLAGE**

364		NAI, DAI, uchi	内部 NAIBU	inner part
		INSIDE	家内 KANAI	wife
		4 strokes	内気 UCHIKI	shyness

Formerly 内 , and earlier 内, showing **enter** 入 / 入 63 q.v. and a **dwelling** ∩/冂. Once entered, one is **inside**. Suggest taking 人 as **person** 39 and 冂 as a **hoop**.

Mnemonic: **PERSON TRIES TO GET INSIDE HOOP**

365		NIKU	馬肉 BANIKU	horsemeat
		MEAT, FLESH	肉屋 NIKUYA	butcher
		6 strokes	肉眼 NIKUGAN	naked eye

From a pictograph of a **fillet of meat** showing the graining of the flesh 肉. As a radical usually 月 , and often having a meaning of **relating to the body**. Suggest remembering as **inside** 内 364 q.v. and **person** 人 39.

Mnemonic: **INSIDE PERSON THERE IS MEAT**

| 366 | 農 | NŌ
FARMING
13 strokes | 農場 NŌJŌ
農民 NŌMIN
農業 NŌGYŌ | farm
farmers
agriculture |

辰 is now an NGU character used for dragon, but its original meaning was **clam** (now conveyed by an NGU character 蜃, that adds insect 虫 56). It derives from a pictograph of a clam with fleshy feelers protruding . The clam shell was used as a crude cutting tool, and so 辰 occasionally symbolises **cutting**, as here. 曲 is not **bend** 曲 261, though it may be helpful to remember it as such. One early form of 366 shows it as , which clearly reveals hands ヒ ヨ held to a brain/head 厶 131. This has been interpreted by some scholars as **racking one's brains**, and has resulted in some intriguing theories attempting to link clam, racking one's brains, and farming. However, still older forms such as 𧂒 and 𣝀 show that 曲 is a miscopying of **field** 田 59 and either **plants/grass** 艹 9 or **trees** 木 69. Thus the original meaning of 366 was **cutting grass/trees to clear fields**, giving **working on the land** and hence **farming**.

Mnemonic: **FARMING UNEARTHS BENT CLAM SHELL**

| 367 | 波 | HA, nami
WAVE
8 strokes | 周波 SHŪHA
音波 ONPA
波乗り NAMINORI | frequency
sound wave
surfing |

氵 is **water** 40. 皮 is **skin** 374 q.v., here acting phonetically to express **rise and fall** and probably also lending an idea of **peeling off**. Thus **water which rises and falls** (and peels off?), i.e. **wave**.

Mnemonic: **WAVES FORM SKIN OF WATER**

| 368 | 配 | HAI, kubaru
DISTRIBUTE
10 strokes | 心配 SHINPAI
配達 HAITATSU
配り手 KUBARITE | worry
delivery
(card) dealer |

Somewhat obscure. Once written 𨤃, showing **wine jar** 酉 302 and a **kneeling person** 卩 39, but the role of these elements is not clear as there is almost no example of historical usage. In the absence of evidence to the contrary it is assumed to indicate a person pouring -- i.e. **distributing** -- wine. Suggest taking 己 as **self** 855.

Mnemonic: **DISTRIBUTE WINE TO ONESELF**

| 369 | hata, hatake (DRY-)FIELD 9 strokes | 茶畑 CHABATAKE tea field 田畑 TAHATA field, estate 麦畑 MUGIBATAKE wheat field |

A 'made in Japan' character comprising **field** 田 59 and **fire** 火 8, giving **field that is burned off** (as opposed to a paddy field).

Mnemonic: **BURNED FIELD IS A DRY FIELD**

| 370 | HATSU, HOTSU DISCHARGE, START, LEAVE 9 strokes | 発表 HAPPYŌ announcement 発足 HOSSOKU inauguration 発電機 HATSUDENKI generator |

Formerly 發 . 癶 is **two (planted) feet** 360, here indicating **standing firm**. 弓 is **bow** 836. 殳 is **strike/ hand holding weapon** 153. Thus to **take up firm stance and shoot arrow from bow**. This has led to a range of derived meanings such as **discharge, leave**, and by extension **start**. Suggest taking 龹 as **two** 二 61 **bent legs** 儿 39.

Mnemonic: **DISCHARGED WITH TWO BENT LEGS AND FUNNY FEET**

| 371 | HAN, TAN, soru/rasu OPPOSE,ANTI,REVERSE, BEND,CLOTH,MEASURE 4 strokes | 反応 HANNŌ* reaction 反核 HANKAKU anti-nuclear 反物 TANMONO textiles |

又 is a **hand**. 厂 is **cliff** 45, acting phonetically to express **turn over**, and probably also lending an idea of **abrupt** (an occasional connotation of cliff, from the idea of abrupt rise). 371 originally meant **suddenly turn the hand over**. This led to a range of derived meanings, such as **go against** or **oppose, reverse**, and **twist** or **bend**. In Japanese it is also used of **cloth**, from the idea of a draper flicking out a roll of cloth, and can mean a **measure** of cloth (a roll of some 10m), as well as a measure of area.

Mnemonic: **CLIFF OPPOSES HAND**

372		**HAN, saka** **SLOPE** 7 strokes	急坂 KYŪHAN	steep slope
			坂道 SAKAMICHI	slope
			下り坂 KUDARIZAKA	downhill

Ground 土 60 and **oppose** 反 371. The latter is used primarily for its sound, to express **slanting**, but may also lend an idea of **reverse** (i.e. a slope can be either an upgrade or a downgrade) or of **opposition/ resistance** (i.e. an upgrade). Thus **slanting ground**.

Mnemonic: **SLOPE IS OPPOSED GROUND**

373		**HAN, BAN, ita** **BOARD, PLATE** 8 strokes	黒板 KOKUBAN	blackboard
			板紙 ITAGAMI	cardboard
			板前 ITAMAE	chef

Wood 木 69 and **oppose** 反 371. The latter is used primarily for its sound, to express **thin (and flat)**, but may also lend an idea of **reverse** (i.e. a board is reversible). Thus **thin, flat piece of wood**, i.e. **board**, now also used of non-wooden **sheets** or **plates**.

Mnemonic: **OPPOSED TO WOODEN BOARDS**

374		**HI, kawa** **SKIN, LEATHER** 5 strokes	皮膚 HIFU	skin
			皮肉 HINIKU	sarcasm
			木の皮 KINOKAWA	bark

From a pictograph 𡰪, showing a hand 又 pulling the **hide** off an animal with its head still attached ㄅ. Suggest remembering by association with **oppose** 反 371, with ⼁ as **one stroke**.

Mnemonic: **OPPOSED TO SKINNING WITH ONE STROKE**

375		**HI, kana***shii/shimu* **SAD** 12 strokes	悲劇 HIGEKI	tragedy
			悲鳴 HIMEI	shriek, wail
			悲しさ KANASHISA	sadness

心 is **heart/feelings** 147. 非 is **not** 773 q.v., acting phonetically to express **sad** and also lending connotations of **splitting open** (from its literal meaning of wings opening in opposite directions). Thus **sad feelings which rend the heart**.

Mnemonic: **BROKEN HEART DOES NOT WANT TO BE SAD**

| 376 | | BI, utsuku*shii*
BEAUTIFUL, FINE
9 strokes | 美人 BIJIN   a beauty, belle
美術 BIJUTSU   fine arts
美学 BIGAKU   esthetics |

Sheep 羊 986 and **big** 大 53. A **big** (i.e. fat) **sheep** was highly prized and **desirable**. **Desirable appearance** eventually led to **beautiful** in a broad sense.

Mnemonic: **BEAUTIFUL BIG SHEEP**

| 377 | | BI, hana
NOSE
14 strokes | 鼻音 BION   nasal sound
鼻先 HANASAKI   tip of nose
鼻薬 HANAGUSURI   bribe |

Formerly 鼻 . 自 is **self/nose** 134. 畀 is a CO character meaning **give**, but is also known to lend a meaning here of **prominent**. (Its old form 畀 suggests that 廾 is not derived from hands offering ㄨㄨ [the usual origin], but represents a table. ⊕ presumably represents an item, giving a meaning of item intended as gift <u>prominently</u> displayed on table.) Thus **prominent nose**, now just **nose**. Suggest taking 田 as **field** 59 and 廾 as **two tens** 十 33, i.e. **twenty**.

Mnemonic: **OWN NOSE FOLLOWS TRAIL THROUGH TWENTY FIELDS**

| 378 | | HYŌ, kŏri
ICE
5 strokes | 氷原 HYŌGEN   ice floe
氷点 HYŌTEN   freezing point
氷水 KŌRIMIZU   ice water |

Formerly 冰 , and originally 氼. 川/水 is **water** 40, while 仌 (now 冫) represents the **cracks in ice**.

Mnemonic: **ICE IS FROZEN WATER**

| 379 | 表 | HYŌ, arawa*su*, omote
SHOW, SURFACE, LIST
8 strokes | 表面 HYŌMEN   surface
表現 HYŌGEN   expression
時刻表 JIKOKUHYŌ   timetable |

Once written 裘 , combining the early form 仌 of **clothing** 衣 420 and **hair/fur** 毛 210. **Fur clothing** was worn on the outside, thus giving **outer surface** and by association **manifest/ show** and **list** (cf. English term ship's manifest). Suggest remembering by association with **long** 長 173.

Mnemonic: **SHOWN LONG-LOOKING LIST**

380 BYŌ
SECOND (OF TIME)
9 strokes

二秒 NIBYŌ　two seconds
秒針 BYŌSHIN　second hand
秒速 BYŌSOKU
speed per second

禾 is **rice plant** 81, here meaning **grain plant**. 少 is **few/little** 143 q.v., here with its original meaning of **miniscule**. 380 originally referred to the **tip of the ear of a grain plant,** but then came to mean **tiny bit** and eventually something even smaller than minute, i.e. **second**.

Mnemonic: **LITTLE RICE, EATEN IN A MERE SECOND**

381 BYŌ, HEI, ya*mu*, ya*mai*
ILLNESS
10 strokes

病気 BYŌKI　illness
病人 BYŌNIN　sick person
らい病 RAIBYŌ　leprosy

疒 is an element indicating **sickness**. It was once written 疒人, showing **bed** 爿 1389 and **person** 人 39 and indicating someone **'laid up'**. 丙 is **third rate** 1773 q.v., here acting phonetically to express **increase**, giving **illness that increases (in severity)**. There is some disagreement as to the semantic role of 丙. Its original meaning was **big altar**, leading some scholars to assume that it lends an idea of **big**, giving **major illness**. Others take it to suggest **rigidity** and **immobility**, since the altar was sturdy and rigid, giving **crippling illness**. Still others take it to symbolise **about to die**, from the idea of sacrifice associated with the altar, giving **fatal illness**. In any event, 381 originally meant **serious illness**, but is now used of **illness** in general. Suggest taking 丙 in its modern sense of **third rate**.

Mnemonic: **THIRD RATE HEALTH LEADS TO ILLNESS**

382 HIN, shina
GOODS,QUALITY,KIND
9 strokes

商品 SHŌHIN　commodity
品質 HINSHITSU　quality
品物 SHINAMONO　goods

Three **mouths** 口 20, indicating a **group of people**. This came to mean **assemblage**, and eventually specifically **group of things** rather than people. **Quality** and **kind** are associated ideas. Note that 382 has switched from meaning person to thing, while 者 298 has switched from thing to person. Suggest taking as three **boxes**.

Mnemonic: **QUALITY GOODS COME IN BOXES**

114

383 負 FU, ma*keru*/*kasu*, *ou*　　　負傷　FUSHŌ　　　wound
　　　DEFEAT, BEAR　　　　　　負担　FUTAN　　　burden
　　　9 strokes　　　　　　　　　負け嫌い　MAKEGIRAI　unyielding

Somewhat obscure. Once written 負, showing a **bending person** 人 39 and **shell/money** 貝 90. (The variant form 負 using sword/cut 刀 181 is a miscopying.) There is some disagreement as to the role of these elements. Some scholars take 貝 to be used phonetically to express **back** (as well as having its own loose idea of back as an extension of shell), giving **(on)** a **bending person's back** and hence **bear**, leading to ideas such as **suffer an imposition** and hence **defeat**. Other scholars take 貝 to be used in its sense of **valuables**, as well as possibly also acting phonetically to express **back**, to give an idea of a **person bent under a load of valuables** (on their back). This later came to symbolise being **defeated** or routed, i.e. fleeing with one's valuables. Note that 383 can also occasionally be used causatively, giving **to defeat**.

Mnemonic: **DEFEATED PERSON FLEES BEARING MONEY**

384 BU, BE　　　　　　　　　　部分　BUBUN　　part
　　　PART, SECTION, CLAN　　部族　BUZOKU　　tribe
　　　11 strokes　　　　　　　　　部屋　HEYA*　　room

Obscure. Once written 咅邑. 邑/阝 is **village** 355. 咅/音 is not **say** 音/言 274 but a CO character meaning **spit**. Its etymology is unclear, though 口 is presumably **mouth** 20. There is some support for a view that 㐬 is a variant of 又, the old form of **not** 不 (read FU) 572 q.v. The latter originally indicated a bud **emerging** from a whorl of leaves, and may thus indicate **coming out**, giving 咅 a meaning of **that coming out of the mouth**. It should be noted that in compounds 咅 often seems to be associated both with **dividing** and **growing**, both of which can be interpreted as derived meanings of 又 though not, strictly speaking, of 咅 itself. It should also be noted that a combination of **not** and **mouth** definitely exists as the character **deny** 否 962 q.v., which literally means **make the negating sound 'fu' with the mouth**. Thus, if the 立 part of 咅 is a variant of 不, this would mean that 咅 is ipso facto a variant of 否, raising the possibility that **spit** similarly derives from **making the sound 'fu' with the mouth**. Unfortunately not only is the etymology of 咅 unclear, its role here (both semantic and/or phonetic) is also unclear. Some scholars claim that it lends a meaning of **division**, giving **division or part of a village** and hence **clan**. However, 384 is known to have once referred to a specific clan in ancient China, thus suggesting that the clan was associated with a **village called FU**. From this point opinion is further divided, some scholars claiming that the meaning **division** and hence **section /part** is the result purely of borrowing or miscopying (involving **divide** 剖 1813), while others take the village in question to be a division or part of a larger administrative district. Still others see it as a village of outcasts (from spit out/ reject). Suggest taking 立 as **stand** 73 and 口 as **(open) mouth**.

Mnemonic: **CLAN STANDS OPEN MOUTHED IN PART OF VILLAGE**

385 服 FUKU
CLOTHES, YIELD, SERVE
8 strokes

服装 FUKUSŌ — clothing
服従 FUKUJŪ — submission
服部 HATTORI* — a surname

Somewhat obscure. Once written 舟攵, showing a **boat** 月/舟 1354 q.v., a **person bending** 亻 39, and a **hand** 又. Still older forms such as 月攴 show boat and a hand holding a **weapon** or **tool**, suggesting that the hand is **working**, and also suggesting that the later bending person may be a miscopying. The early meaning of 385 is known to have been **work**, and some scholars feel that it meant literally bend down in order to work on (building or repairing) a boat. **Yield/ serve** is felt to derive from a combined idea of bending down and performing work. How exactly it came to mean **clothes**, however, is not clear. It is assumed to be a borrowed meaning, though it is also possible that 385 once came by extension to indicate a **servant's livery**. Suggest taking 月 as **moon**, 又 as a **hand**, and 卩 as a **clothes hoist**.

Mnemonic: **SERVILE HAND PUTS CLOTHES ON HOIST UNDER MOON**

386 福 FUKU
GOOD FORTUNE
13 strokes

幸福 KŌFUKU — happiness
福引き FUKUBIKI — lottery
福音書 FUKUINSHO — Gospels

Formerly 福. 示/礻 is **altar/ of the gods** 695. 畐 is a CO character meaning **full**, and derives from a pictograph of a **(full) wine jar** 畐. 386 originally referred to wine blessed by the gods and used in religious ceremonies. The idea of **blessed by the gods** then came to mean **blessed** or **fortunate** in general. Suggest taking 畐 as **single** 一 1 **entrance** 口 20 to **field** 田 59.

Mnemonic: **ALTAR AT SINGLE ENTRANCE TO FIELD -- GOOD FORTUNE**

387 物 BUTSU, MOTSU, mono
THING
8 strokes

人物 JINBUTSU — person
食物 SHOKUMOTSU — food
食べ物 TABEMONO — food

牜 is **cow** 97. 勿 is an NGU character now used to mean **not**, but it originally depicted a **variety of streamers** ⋐ (still listed as a minor meaning in Chinese). Here it lends a meaning of **variety**, thus giving **variegated cow**, a reference to a type of cow with a mottled hide. 387 then came to mean **creature**, and then **thing** in a broad (but usually tangible) sense. Suggest taking 勿 as a **'thing' with four legs**.

Mnemonic: **COW IS A THING WITH FOUR LEGS**

388 平 **HEI, BYŌ, tai*ra*, hira*tai***
FLAT, EVEN, CALM
5 strokes

平気	HEIKI	calmness
平等	BYŌDŌ	equality
平手	HIRATE	palm of hand

Possibly because 388 can mean **set of scales or balance** in Chinese it is often explained as deriving from a supposed pictograph of scales, and some scholars even refer to a mysterious 'pictograph' 丣. However, old forms such as 𠂱 in fact appear to show a combination of **twisting water weed** 丁 / 丂 281 and **small** 小 36. 丁 usually has a meaning of bending but can occasionally, as here, mean **flat**, since the weed **flattens** out across the surface of the water (see also 130). 小 is felt to be added for clarity, to distinguish the water weed in question from a larger type less suited to symbolising flatness. Similarly a lateral stroke 一 was added to later forms to emphasise **flatness**, giving 乎 and hence the modern form. **Scales** is felt to derive from **flatness**, not vice-versa. Note that scales is conveyed in Japanese by an NGU character that adds rice (plant) 禾 81, 秤 (i.e. an even measure of rice). Note also that waterweed is now conveyed by a CO character that adds plant 艹 9, 苹, and by an NGU character that adds plant and water 氵 40, 萍. In view of the symmetrical shape of 388, suggest using the scales theory as a mnemonic.

Mnemonic: **BALANCED SCALES ARE FLAT AND EVEN**

389 返 **HEN, kae*su/ru***
RETURN
7 strokes

返事	HENJI	reply
返済	HENSAI	repayment
仕返し	SHIKAESHI	retaliation

⻌ is **movement** 129. 反 is **oppose** 371, here meaning **reverse**. Thus **reverse movement,** i.e. **return**. Now often used in the transitive sense, i.e. **give back.**

Mnemonic: **REVERSE MOVEMENT AND RETURN**

390 勉 **BEN**
STRIVE
10 strokes

勉強	BENKYŌ	study
勤勉	KINBEN	diligence
勉学	BENGAKU	study

力 is **effort** 74. 免 is **avoid** 1849 q.v., here used in its literal meaning of **woman striving to give birth**. Thus **woman striving with great effort to give birth,** now just **strive/ try hard** in general. Give birth is now conveyed by an NGU character 娩 that uses woman 女 35 instead of effort 力, and a CO character 挽 that uses child 子 25.

Mnemonic: **STRIVE TO AVOID EFFORT?!**

391

放

HŌ, hana*su/tsu*
RELEASE, EMIT
8 strokes

解放 KAIHŌ   liberation
放射 HŌSHA   radiation
手放す TEBANASU   let go

Usually explained as **direction** 方 204 and **stick in hand/ strike** 攵 101, giving **driving off in all directions** and thus **radiate** and hence **release**. A useful mnemonic, but not quite correct. Old forms such as 𠦚 show 方 to be a miscopying of **person** 人 39. Thus **drive off a person**, leading to **discharge** and then **release** and **emit**.

Mnemonic: **STRIKING IN ALL DIRECTIONS IS A FORM OF RELEASE**

392

万

MAN, BAN
TEN THOUSAND,
MYRIAD
3 strokes

五万 GOMAN   fifty thousand
万事 BANJI   everything
万年筆 MANNENHITSU
     fountain pen

Often thought to be a simplification of 萬, which tended to be used until recently to express **ten thousand**, but in fact they are separate characters. 万 was once written 𠂕, and is felt by some scholars to be a variant of **twisting waterweed** 丂 281 borrowed for its sound. Other scholars feel it is a simplification of the ancient **swastika** symbol 卐 or 卍 (both NGU characters), which has connotations of **all encompassing** and by association **myriad**. 萬 derives from a pictograph of a **scorpion** 𧊒 with the addition of nine/**bent elbow** 九 12 q.v. to emphasise the curling tail, and originally meant (striking) **scorpion**. It is not clear how it came to represent ten thousand. Certainly it was used partly for its sound, but its complexity suggests some additional significance. It may have been that scorpions were **extremely numerous**. Suggest remembering 万 by association with **direction** 方 204, taking it to be a 'wrong' version of this.

Mnemonic: **TEN THOUSAND MARCH IN WRONG DIRECTION**

393

味

MI, aji, aji*wau*
TASTE, RELISH
8 strokes

意味 IMI   meaning
興味 KYŌMI   interest
味見 AJIMI   tasting

口 is **mouth** 20. 未 is **unfinished** 794, here acting phonetically to express **good** and also lending an idea of **lingering**. Thus **something good lingering in the mouth**, i.e. **nice taste**. It can now be used of **taste** in general, but at times still retains connotations of **appreciation**. It is also sometimes used of an **attribute** or **quality**.

Mnemonic: **TASTE LINGERS UNFINISHED IN THE MOUTH**

394 MEI, MYŌ, inochi   命令 MEIREI   order
LIFE, ORDER   生命 SEIMEI   life
8 strokes   命取り INOCHITORI   fatal

Order 令 603 with a **mouth /say** 口 20 added to emphasise the **issuing** of the order. The issuing of an order came to symbolise the expression of will of those superiors who govern one's life, including the gods, and thus 394 also came to mean **one's lot** or **fate**, and eventually **life**.

Mnemonic: **LIFE CAN HINGE ON A SPOKEN ORDER**

395 MEN, omote, omo, tsura   外面 GAIMEN   exterior
FACE, ASPECT, MASK   仮面 KAMEN   mask
9 strokes   鼻面 HANAZURA   muzzle

Once written 圙 . 面 is **face** 93, while 口 indicates **enclosing** or **covering**. Thus **that which encloses the face**, i.e. a **mask**. This led to the idea of **external appearance**, giving **aspect**. 395 is also used for the **face** itself. Suggest remembering by partial association with **eye** 目 72.

Mnemonic: **MASK ENCLOSES FUNNY FACE WITH BIG EYE**

396 MON, to*u*   質問 SHITSUMON   question
ASK   学問 GAKUMON   scholarship
11 strokes   問屋 TOIYA/TONYA*   dealer

Usually explained simply as a **mouth** 口 20 asking at a **door/gate** 門 211, but some scholars feel that 門 acts largely phonetically to express **question**.

Mnemonic: **MOUTH ASKING AT GATE**

397 YAKU, EKI   役人 YAKUNIN   functionary
ROLE, SERVICE, DUTY   役者 YAKUSHA   actor
7 strokes   兵役 HEIEKI   military service

Movement along road 彳 118 and **weapon in hand** 殳 153. 397 originally referred to soldiers **going off to fight** (still occasionally used in this meaning), then came to mean **service, duty**, and by extension **role**.

Mnemonic: **MOVE OFF WITH WEAPON IN HAND TO DO ONE'S DUTY**

398		**YAKU, kusuri**	薬局	YAKKYOKU pharmacy
		MEDICINE, DRUG	火薬	KAYAKU gunpowder
		16 strokes	薬指	KUSURIYUBI
				ring finger

サ is **plant** 9. 楽 is **pleasure** 218, acting phonetically to express **cure** and also lending an idea of **soothing**. Thus **curative, soothing plant**, i.e. a **medicinal herb**.

Mnemonic: **MEDICINAL PLANT GIVES PLEASURE**

399		**YU, YŪ, yoshi**	由来	YURAI derivation
		REASON, MEANS, WAY	理由	RIYŪ reason
		5 strokes	自由	JIYŪ freedom

From the same pictograph of a **basket /wine press** 田 as west 152 q.v. Whereas 152 focussed on the <u>falling drops</u>, 399 focussed on the abstract idea of the drops falling <u>**from**</u> the basket. **From** came by association to mean **cause**, i.e. **reason**, and by extension also came to mean **significance**, **means**, and **way**. Suggest remembering by association with **field** 田 59, taking Ⅰ as a **derrick** (and see oil 油 400).

Mnemonic: **THERE'S A REASON FOR DERRICK IN FIELD**

400		**YU, abura**	油田	YUDEN oil field
		OIL	灯油	TŌYU/TŌYŪ kerosene
		8 strokes	油絵	ABURAE oil painting

Basket/ wine press 由 399 q.v. and **water/liquid** ; 40. Originally the **liquid from the press**, later **viscous fluid**, eventually **oil**. Suggest taking 田 as a **field** 田 59 with a **derrick** Ⅰ.

Mnemonic: **LIQUID FROM FIELD WITH DERRICK IS OIL**

401	有	**YŪ, U, aru**	所有者	SHOYŪSHA owner
		HAVE, EXIST	有無	UMU existence
		6 strokes	有り難う	ARIGATŌ* thank you

Once written 㞢, showing a (right) **hand** ナ 2 holding a piece of **meat** 月 365. This symbolised **possession** or **having**, which also came by association to mean **existing**.

Mnemonic: **HAVE MEAT IN YOUR HAND**

120

402	YŪ, YU, asob*u*	遊覧	YŪRAN	sightseeing
---	PLAY, RELAX	遊山	YUSAN	excursion
遊	12 strokes	遊び場	ASOBIBA	playground

Often explained as **children** 子 25 **gathering** under a **flag** 㫃 333 (symbolising **gathering**) and **moving about** 辶 129, i.e. **playing**, with **relax** being an extension of **play**. A useful mnemonic, but incorrect. 斿 is a CO character meaning the **billowing shape of a waving flag** (from fluttering flag 㫃, with child 子 used to mean small part, and originally referring to the small scalloped parts formed as the flag waves). In combination with movement (along a road) 辶 it meant **moving in a wave-like and hence indirect fashion**, giving saunter and the idea of **acting in an unhurried fashion**. Thus **relax** (or more exactly, **not work**) is the earlier meaning, with **play** being the extension. Suggest taking 㫃 as **person** 亻 39 and **side** 方 204.

Mnemonic: **CHILDREN PLAY AT MOVING PERSON'S SIDE**

403	YO, kane*te*	予約	YOYAKU	booking
---	ALREADY, PRIOR, I	予想	YOSŌ	expectation
予	4 strokes	予定	YOTEI	schedule

Formerly also 豫, though technically this is a separate character. Old forms such as 㐒 show a combination of symbol and pictograph, namely a **weaving shuttle** 𠃌 (from 𠄑) being **pushed** | **to one side** 㐒. This came to represent the idea of doing one action as part of a sequence, i.e. **prior** to doing the next action. The idea of **doing something in advance** also came to mean leaving a **margin**. Elephant 象 533 was added to give an idea of **big** margin, though it is not clear why such a complex character was chosen. Thus at one stage 403 had a secondary meaning similar to ample/margin 余 800, and it is interesting that both 403 and 800 have been borrowed to express **I/me**. This has always been assumed to be for purely phonetic reasons, but the coincidence of meaning may suggest some additional but now unclear semantic connection. Margin has now faded as a major meaning, leaving the earlier idea of **acting in advance** and hence **already**.

Mnemonic: **I'VE ALREADY PUSHED THE SHUTTLE**

404 YŌ
OCEAN, WESTERN
9 strokes

西洋人 SEIYŌJIN Westerner
大西洋 TAISEIYŌ Atlantic
洋食 YŌSHOKU Western food

Water 氵 40 and **sheep** 羊 986. Usually explained to the effect that a sheep indicates **white**, giving **whitecaps** and hence suggesting a **large body of water** (i.e. an ovine version of the English term white horses). Some scholars feel that 羊 was used in an unknown phonetic role and that 404 once referred to a specific river in ancient China (details unclear) before coming to be applied by extension to the ocean. The former theory seems the more helpful. **Ocean** came to symbolise **from across the ocean**, i.e. **foreign** and especially **Western**.

Mnemonic: **OCEAN OF WHITE SHEEP, NOT WHITE HORSES**

405 YŌ, ha
LEAF
12 strokes

針葉樹 SHINYŌJU conifer
葉巻き HAMAKI cigar
葉書 HAGAKI postcard

Somewhat obscure. Often assumed to be **generation** 世 327 q.v. of **plant-life** 艹 9 on a **tree** 木 69, which is an excellent mnemonic. Since it is also possible that, through early forms such as 世, 327 may have become somewhat confused graphically with a growing plant and hence life and generation (see also 42), as opposed to its literal origin of three tens (thirty years) and hence generation, it would seem quite reasonable to assume that 葉 means **generation/ plant growth on a tree** and that 艹 is used merely to reinforce this. This is especially so in view of the fact that 某 does indeed exist as a CO character meaning **leaf**. However, 某 also means **flat piece of wood/ writing tablet**, and some scholars feel that this is its main meaning (from wood 木, with 世 suggesting grouping together, as of wooden tablets bound together) and that its meaning of leaf results from its later being used as a simple version of 葉. Thus, according to the latter view, 405 means **plant-life resembling a group of flat wooden tablets**, i.e. **leaves**.

Mnemonic: **LEAVES ARE GENERATION OF PLANTS ON TREE**

406 YŌ, hi
SUNNY, MALE, POSITIVE
12 strokes

陽極 YŌKYOKU anode
陽気 YŌKI gaiety, season
太陽系 TAIYŌKEI solar system

Hill 阝 229 and **sun shining down** 昜 144, to give **sunny (side of) hill**. This has led to various extended meanings, primarily the concept of **yang** (as opposed to yin 陰 1013).

Mnemonic: **SIDE OF HILL IS POSITIVELY SUNNY**

407 様

YŌ, sama, zama
SITUATION, APPEARANCE,
WAY, POLITE SUFFIX
14 strokes

仕様 SHIYŌ　way, means
有様 ARISAMA　situation
皆様 MINASAMA　everyone

Somewhat obscure. Formerly 樣, and incorrectly as 橢. 木 is **tree** 69. 羕 is a now defunct character meaning **tributary**, comprising tributary/ long 永 615 and **sheep** 羊 986 (the latter presumably used for its literal meaning of branching horns). It acts here phonetically to express **resemble**, giving **tree that resembles**. This was a reference to the **horse chestnut**, which resembles the edible chestnut. The reason for such a complex character occurring as a phonetic is possibly that it was initially confused with elephant / **resemble** 象 533, which had the same pronunciation at the time (SHŌ) and which is also combined with tree 木 to give the NGU character horse chestnut 橡. It is not clear how 407 came to acquire its present meanings. Some scholars feel they are purely borrowed meanings, while others feel 407 was confused with **image** 像 740, from which many of the present meanings can be taken to have derived. In Japanese 407 can also be used as a **polite suffix**, though again the process of acquisition of this meaning is unclear. Suggest taking 羕 as a combination of **sheep** 羋 / 羊 and **water** 水 40.

Mnemonic: **SHEEP APPEARS TO WATER TREE -- AWKWARD SITUATION**

408

RAKU, ochiru/tosu
FALL, DROP
12 strokes

落下 RAKKA　fall, descent
落ち葉 OCHIBA　fallen leaf
落とし物 OTOSHIMONO
dropped item

艹 is **plant** 9. 洛 is an NGU character now used to refer to the **old capital** (Kyoto), but in Chinese it refers to a certain river and originally meant **falling water**. It comprises **water** 氵 40 and **each** 各 438 q.v., here with its early meaning of **descend** (and stop). Thus **plants falling like water**, which was a reference to **falling leaves**. It now means **fall** in a broad sense.

Mnemonic: **FROM EACH PLANT, LEAF FALLS LIKE DROP OF WATER**

---

409 流 **RYŪ, RU, naga*reru/su***　　流行 RYŪKŌ　　　　fashion
　　　　FLOW, STREAM　　　　　流布 RUFU　　　　　　spread
　　　　10 strokes　　　　　　　　流れ木 NAGAREGI　　driftwood

Once written 氺熹. 熹 is an inverted (indicating **newborn**) **infant** 子 25 in **amniotic fluid** ''', to all intents and purposes the same element as birth/ raise children 育 227 q.v. 氵 is **water** 40, emphasising the fluid. Thus the **flow of fluid at birth**, later **flow** in a broad sense. There is also a theory that 川レ represents the dangling **hair** of the infant, and that this serves to emphasise the idea of flowing (down). This is a useful mnemonic, but in view of the clear use of amniotic fluid in 227 almost certainly incorrect. The element 㐬 often lends an idea of **dangle** in compounds, but this is felt to be an extended meaning from flow and not hair. It also exists as a minor CO character confusingly listed in some dictionaries (but without illustration) as meaning **cap with pendants**. This appears to be a popular mnemonic interpretation with no academic basis.

Mnemonic: **HAIR AND WATER FLOW AS CHILD IS BORN**

---

410 旅 **RYO, tabi**　　　　旅行 RYOKŌ　　　　　trip
　　　　JOURNEY　　　　　　旅人 TABIBITO　　　traveler
　　　　10 strokes　　　　　　　旅費 RYOHI　　travel expenses

Once written 旅, showing **two (i.e. plural) persons** 亻 39 gathered under a **streaming banner** 𠂉 333. It originally referred to warriors rallying under a banner prior to **setting out** on a campaign. On the one hand this came to mean simply **set out** or **make a journey**, and on the other came to mean a group of warriors (specifically five hundred). The latter meaning is retained in Chinese but has disappeared in Japanese. Suggest taking 方 as **side** 方 204, and 𠂊 as an 'odd' variant of **clothes** 衣 420.

Mnemonic: **PUT ODD CLOTHES ON ONE SIDE FOR JOURNEY**

---

411 両 **RYŌ**　　　　　　　両方 RYŌHŌ　　　　both sides
　　　　BOTH, PAIR, COIN　　両手 RYŌTE　　　　both hands
　　　　6 strokes　　　　　　　両替え RYŌGAE　money change

Formerly 兩 , and earlier 冊. Popularly taken to be a set of **scales** symbolising **equality**, which is a useful mnemonic but almost certainly incorrect. It seems more likely to be a **gourd** (with a wrinkled membraneous inside) split into **two equal halves**. The role of the later addition ‾ is not clear, but it may symbolise unity, i.e. the **equality** between the two halves. 411 was also used for a **measure of silver** (in Japan the old ryo coin), which probably did derive from association with weighing on scales and may account for the popular theory mentioned above.

Mnemonic: **SCALES WEIGH BOTH PARTS OF A PAIR**

412
RYOKU, ROKU, midori   常緑樹   JŌRYOKUJU   evergreen
GREEN   緑青   ROKUSHŌ   verdigris
14 strokes   緑色   MIDORIIRO   green

Formerly 綠 . 糸 is **thread** 27. 彔 is an element depicting **liquid** 氺 (originally drops
∴ and a symbol of falling |, but probably stylised under the influence of **water** 水 40)
falling from a basket used as a crude wine press 冃 (inverted version of 甶 399). That
is, it is very similar to oil 油 400. It came to mean **ooze** or **exude** (a meaning it still retains in some compounds), and was used with metal 金 14 to give 録 611 q.v., now
meaning inscription or record but originally meaning **verdigris** (the **green** rust which
'oozes' out of copper). 彔 itself thus became associated with **green**, and usually lends
such a meaning in compounds, as indeed here. Thus **green threads**, and now **green** in
general. Note that 彔 exists as a minor CO character, confusingly listed in some Chinese
dictionaries (but without illustration) as meaning to carve wood. This is presumably a
meaning ascribed or assumed under the influence of 611's later meaning of inscription.
Suggest taking 糸 as **strand**.

Mnemonic: **WATERY GREEN LIQUID OOZES IN THREAD-LIKE STRANDS**

413
REI   失礼   SHITSUREI   rudeness
PROPRIETY, BOW   礼服   REIFUKU   full dress
5 strokes   敬礼   KEIREI   bow

Formerly also written 礼 and 禮, though technically the two are separate characters. 示/
ネ is **altar** 695. L is a **kneeling figure**, not a simplification of 豊. Thus **kneeling at
the altar**, meaning to pray and thus **act with propriety**. 豊 is plentiful 790 q.v., literally meaning full vessel, giving 禮 a meaning of offer a full vessel (of sacred wine) at the
altar and thus similarly **act with propriety**.

Mnemonic: **PRAYING AT ALTAR IS ACT OF PROPRIETY**

414
RETSU   列車   RESSHA   train
ROW, LINE   列次   RETSUJI   sequence
6 strokes   前列   ZENRETSU   front row

Denuded bone 歹 286 and **cut** 刂 181. Thus **cut to the very bone**, which was
originally a reference to **butchery**. The meaning of **row** is felt to stem from the fact that
there was a set **sequence** for dismembering a carcass (sequence/ order is still a strong
meaning in Chinese).

Mnemonic: **CUT UP BONES LINED UP IN A ROW**

| 415 | | RO, ji
ROAD, ROUTE
13 strokes | 道路 DŌRO
線路 SENRO
旅路 TABIJI | road
rail track
journey |

足 is **foot** 51. 各 is **each** 438 q.v., here used in its early meaning of **stop and start** and by extension **move slowly**. 415 originally referred to moving slowly forward, testing the ground with one's foot. This came to mean **path**, and eventually **route** or **road** in a broader sense.

Mnemonic: **EACH FOOT FOLLOWS SAME ROUTE**

| 416 | | WA,O,yawaragu,nagoyaka
PEACE, SOFT, JAPAN
8 strokes | 平和 HEIWA
大和 YAMATO*
和食 WASHOKU | peace
Japan
Japanese food |

Formerly also sometimes written 咊. **Rice plant** 禾 81 and **mouth/say** 口 20. The rice plant was often a symbol of **pliancy** and **softness**, and lends such connotations here to mean **pliant in speech**, i.e. accommodating and **harmonious**. This eventually came to mean **peaceful**. It is also used to refer to **Japan**.

Mnemonic: **RICE SOFTENED IN THE MOUTH IN PEACEFUL JAPAN**

END OF THIRD GRADE

THE 195 FOURTH GRADE CHARACTERS

417 AI
LOVE
13 strokes

愛情 AIJŌ   love
母性愛 BOSEIAI   maternal love
愛国者 AIKOKUSHA   patriot

Obscure. Often explained as a hand reaching down/ **convey** 〈/ 303, a **cover** ⌐, **heart** 心 147, and **stop and start** 又 438 q.v., to give a meaning of **convey something to the heart and (hesitantly) keep it hidden there**, i.e. a **secret love** that one frequently almost reveals. A useful mnemonic, but an old form 愛 shows that 〈/ is not in fact a hand. Some scholars take 愛 to be the prototype of a now defunct character 忎 meaning a **charitable feeling** of wishing to give food and hence **kindness** and **warm feelings**. It comprises heart/**feelings** 心 and **satiated person** 旡 688, the latter also acting phonetically to express **give**. Thus feeling of giving food to a person till they become satiated. In the case of 417 愛 is felt to have acted phonetically to express **hidden**, though its semantic role (if any) is unclear. Stop and start 又 is felt to have been used in a sense of **move hesitantly**. Thus the original meaning is believed to have been **move forward hesitantly and furtively,** with the idea of **warm kind feelings** contained in 愛 eventually prevailing and replacing move furtively. Still others see 愛 as encircled/ **enveloped heart** (see 655), and 夊 as opposed feet 422 q.v., the latter lending its meaning of **all around**. Thus **that which completely envelops the heart**. The last theory seems the most likely, but suggest taking the modern form as **hand** 〈/ **covering** ⌐ **heart** 心, with 夊 as **sitting crosslegged**.

Mnemonic: **SIT CROSSLEGGED, HAND ON HEART, IN LOVE**

418 AN
PLAN,CONCERN,TABLE
10 strokes

提案 TEIAN   proposal
案外 ANGAI   unexpectedly
案上 ANJŌ   on the table

Wood 木 69, here indicating item made of wood, and **restful** 安 223 q.v. The latter acts phonetically to express **put down and leave**, and may possibly also lend similar connotations of **being left** from its original meaning of a woman being left to rest quietly. 418 originally referred to a **wooden table on which eating utensils were set out and left**, i.e. by way of preparation. It is still occasionally used to mean **table**, especially in Chinese. However, rather like the English term **table a proposal**, it also came to mean something put carefully on a table, and by extension a **proposal** or **plan**. **Concern** is an associated idea, i.e. something obliging consideration.

Mnemonic: **CONSIDER PLAN AROUND RESTFUL WOODEN TABLE**

419

I, motte
STARTING POINT, MEANS,
USE, THROUGH, BECAUSE
5 strokes

以下 IKA   below
以内 INAI   within
以外 IGAI   outside, except

Once written 㐆, also ㇛ or ㇙, depicting a **person** 人 39 behind a **plow** ㇛. It is not clear how it came to acquire its present meanings. Some scholars assume them to be borrowed, but it seems possible that **plow** came to symbolise **utensil** and hence something **used** as a **means through** which an end is achieved. **Starting point** is possibly an associated idea with **through**, both overlapping with the concept of **from**. **Because** is an extension of through. See also 134.

Mnemonic: **PERSON USES PLOW AS STARTING POINT**

420

I, koromo
CLOTHING
6 strokes

衣服 IFUKU   clothing
衣類 IRUI   clothing
衣替え KOROMOGAE
          change of clothes

Originally 衣, showing a **collar** 𠆢 and **sleeves** 𠆢 and thus ideographically expressing **clothing**. As a radical usually found as 衤, and sometimes split as 衣 or 衣.

Mnemonic: **COLLAR AND SLEEVES SYMBOLISE CLOTHING**

421

I, kurai
RANK, EXTENT
7 strokes

地位 CHII   position, rank
学位 GAKUI   academic degree
十二位 JŪNIGURAI about twelve

Person 人 39 **standing** 立 73. This referred to a person standing in a row, their **position** determined by order of precedence, i.e. **rank**. By association position came to mean **extent**, which as in English also became used of **approximation**.

Mnemonic: **PERSON STANDS ACCORDING TO RANK**

422 I, kako*mu/u*
SURROUND
7 strokes

周囲 SHŪI   perimeter
範囲 HANI   range
囲い込む KAKOIKOMU   enclose

Formerly 圍. □ is an **enclosure** (see 123). 韋 is a CO character now confusingly used to mean leather/ hide (probably through graphic confusion with leather/hide 革 821), but its original meaning was essentially **patrol**. Once written 𩹄, it shows **opposed feet** 刄 /㐃 (variants of feet 㞢 /止 129) **around a central point** o (abstract symbol), and can mean **be opposed, move all around, guard all quarters** and so on. Here it acts phonetically to express **surround**, and also lends an idea of **moving all around**. Thus an **enclosure that emphatically surrounds**. Suggest taking 井 as **well** 1470.

Mnemonic: **ENCLOSURE SURROUNDS WELL**

423 I, yuda*neru*
ENTRUST
8 strokes

委員会 IINKAI   committee
委任 ININ   entrustment
委託金 ITAKUKIN   trust money

禾 is **rice plant** 81, here symbolising **softness** and **pliancy**. 女 is **woman** 35, also a symbol of softness and pliancy. Thus to **be soft and pliant,** which came by extension to mean be pliant in one's affairs and then leave decisions to others, eventually leading to **entrust**. The popular explanation that gathering the rice crop was entrusted to women is incorrect but a useful mnemonic. See also 416.

Mnemonic: **ENTRUST RICE PLANTS TO WOMAN**

424 I
STOMACH
9 strokes

胃液 IEKI   gastric juice
胃袋 IBUKURO   stomach
胃弱 IJAKU   dyspepsia

From a pictograph of the **stomach** ⊗ (showing folds and possibly hairs), reinforced by **flesh/ of the body** 月 365. Suggest taking 田 as **field** 59.

Mnemonic: **FLESHY STOMACH SEEN IN FIELD**

425 IN, shirushi
SEAL, SIGN, SYMBOL
6 strokes

印刷 INSATSU   printing
印判 INBAN   seal
目印 MEJIRUSHI guiding mark

Originally ⿰爫卩, showing a **hand pressing down** ⿰ on a **bending person** 卩 39. The original meaning of **press down** then came to be used of pressing down on a **seal**, with seal giving rise to **sign** or **symbol**. 425 is also borrowed for the IN of **India** (Indo).

Mnemonic: **HAND PRESSES DOWN ON PERSON AS ON SEAL**

426 英	EI SUPERIOR, ENGLAND 8 strokes	英才 EISAI	talent
		英国 EIKOKU	England
		英語 EIGO	English language

艹 is **plant** 9. 央 is **center** 429 q.v., here acting phonetically to express **bloom** and possibly also lending an idea of **blocked off at the head** from its assumed original meaning of person yoked at the neck. 426 originally meant a **flower that blossomed but lacked seed**, such a flower being **exceptionally beautiful**. It can still mean beautiful flower in Chinese. Exceptionally beautiful came to mean **superior**, with extended meanings such as **talented** or **brave**. It is also used for the first syllable of **England**, largely under the influence of Chinese in which 426 is pronounced YING and is a closer approximation to ENG.

Mnemonic: **ENGLAND HAS SUPERIOR PLANTS IN ITS CENTER**

427 栄	EI, saka*eru*, ha*eru* GLORY,FLOURISH,SHINE 9 strokes	光栄 KŌEI	glory, honor
		栄養 EIYŌ	nutrition
		繁栄 HANEI	prosperity

Formerly 榮. It originally indicated a **tree** 木 69 **covered** 冖 with flowers as dazzling as **flame** 火 8, specifically a type of paulownia. Eventually the idea of **blossoming into something dazzling** came to prevail, being used in a range of extended senses such as **flourish** and **shine**. Suggest taking 𣤄 as **ornate cover**.

Mnemonic: **TREE FLOURISHES GLORIOUSLY UNDER ORNATE COVER**

428 塩	EN, shio SALT 13 strokes	食塩 SHOKUEN	table salt
		塩水 SHIOMIZU	saltwater
		製塩所 SEIENSHO	saltworks

Formerly 塩 or 鹽. The latter is a modified combination of supervise/ **look carefully** 監 1111 and 卤, an NGU character meaning **salt** (from a pictograph of a basket 卤 [essentially the same as an early form of basket/west 西 152 q.v.] used as a primitive salt shaker). The exact role of 監 is not clear, but it is felt to have acted phonetically to express **salty taste** and possibly also to have lent an idea of **careful** (salt being a precious commodity in certain areas, and thus something used carefully). The shaker 卤 was also used for things other than salt, thus necessitating the clarification given by 監. The later use of **ground** 土 60 may be a simplification of 臣, but may also be a deliberate reference to a principal source of salt, the **salt pan**. Suggest taking 盍 as **person** ⼓ 39, **mouth** 口 20, and **dish** 皿 1307.

Mnemonic: **PERSON THROWS SALTY DISH FROM MOUTH TO GROUND**

| 429 央 | Ō CENTER 5 strokes | 中央 CHŪŌ center
中央部 CHŪŌBU central part
中央口 CHŪŌGUCHI central exit |

Somewhat obscure. Once written 𠮟, showing a **person** 大 53 with what many scholars take to be a **yoke** 𠃌 on the **neck**. It is felt to have originally meant **restrained at the neck**, with the idea that the neck represented the **central line of the body** later coming to prevail. Other scholars feel that 𠃌 is not a yoke but an abstract symbol indicating **confines** and thus focusing on what lies (centrally) within the confines, i.e. in this case the **neck/ central line**. (Some scholars take ㅣㅣ as the confines and 大 as man 573.) The use of 央 in 426 q.v. seems to support the yoke theory. Suggest taking 大 in its usual sense of **big**, and 央 as a combination of 大 and **opening** 口 20.

Mnemonic: **BIG OPENING IN CENTER**

| 430 億 | OKU HUNDRED MILLION 15 strokes | 二億 NIOKU 200 million
十億 JŪOKU billion
億万長者 OKUMANCHŌJA
billionaire |

亻 is **person** 39. 意 is **thought** 226 q.v., here lending its literal meaning of **heart full of thoughts and feelings**. 430 originally referred to a person brimming over with thoughts and feelings, then came to mean **brimming over** in general. This eventually came to mean **too numerous to contain**, giving the idea of a **very large number**. It became particularly associated with a hundred thousand, and still represents this number in Chinese, but in Japanese, from the medieval period on, it gradually came to mean a **hundred million** (i.e. a squaring of ten thousand 万 392).

Mnemonic: **PERSON WITH HUNDRED MILLION THOUGHTS**

| 431 加 | KA, kuwae*ru*/*waru* ADD, JOIN 5 strokes | 増加 ZŌKA increase
参加 SANKA participation
加え算 KUWAEZAN addition |

Mouth/say 口 20 and **strength** 力 74. It originally meant **add strength to an argument by adding one's own words**, then came to mean **add** or **join** in general.

Mnemonic: **STRENGTHENED BY ADDED MOUTH**

131

432 貨

KA
GOODS, MONEY
11 strokes

貨物船	KAMOTSUSEN	freighter
硬貨	KŌKA	currency
雑貨	ZAKKA	sundry goods

Shell/**money** 貝 90 and **change** 化 238, giving **that which can be exchanged for money**, i.e. **goods**. It then came to mean **assets** and later also **money**.

Mnemonic: **CHANGE GOODS FOR MONEY AND VICE-VERSA**

433 課

KA
SECTION,LESSON,LEVY
15 strokes

課税	KAZEI	taxation
課長	KACHŌ	section head
第二課	DAINIKA	Lesson Two

言 is **word** 274. 果 is **fruit/perform** 627 q.v., here acting phonetically to express **consider** and probably also lending a meaning of **carry out**. 433 originally meant to consider a person's words, and by extension **carry out an investigation** (still a major meaning in Chinese). It became particularly associated with investigating with a view to levying a tax or amount of work, and hence eventually came to mean **levy**. It also came to acquire connotations of order and ranking, and some scholars feel that **lesson and section** both derive from the idea of being part of a sequence, but it seems more likely that they stem from the idea of **that which is levied**, i.e. a **task** or **section** of a task or by extension **lesson** to be worked on.

Mnemonic: **SECTION OF LESSON CONTAINS FRUITFUL WORDS**

434 芽

GA, me
BUD, SPROUT, SHOOT
8 strokes

発芽	HATSUGA	sprouting
新芽	SHINME	bud, sprout
芽生える	MEBAERU	bud, sprout

艹 is **plant** 9. 牙 is an NGU character meaning **fang** (from a pictograph of interlocking fangs 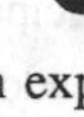). Thus **fang-like plant**, i.e. a **shoot**.

Mnemonic: **PLANT WITH FANG-LIKE SHOOTS**

435 改

KAI, arata*meru/maru*
REFORM
7 strokes

改革	KAIKAKU	reform
改正	KAISEI	amendment
改めて	ARATAMETE	once again

Often explained as **strike/force** 攵 101 and **twisting thread/self** 己 855, to give **enforce (the straightening of) something twisted** and hence **reform**. A useful mnemonic, but incorrect. Old forms such as  show that 己 is actually the same variant of **serpent** 巳 as in arise 起 250 q.v. 435 originally meant **drive off serpents** (a symbol of undesirable things), and thus **clear an area** and hence by extension **reform**. Suggest taking 己 as **self**.

Mnemonic: **FORCE ONESELF TO REFORM**

436	械	KAI DEVICE 11 strokes	器械 KIKAI	apparatus
			機械 KIKAI	machine
			機械化 KIKAIKA	mechanisation

木 is **wood** 69. 戒 is **admonish** 1060. Thus **wooden item for admonishing**, a reference to **shackles**. This meaning is still very occasionally encountered in Japanese, and with more frequency in Chinese. Wooden shackles came to mean **wooden device** and then **device** in general.

Mnemonic: **WOODEN DEVICE FOR ADMONISHING**

437	害	GAI HARM, DAMAGE 10 strokes	損害 SONGAI	damage, loss
			殺害 SATSUGAI	murder
			妨害 BŌGAI	obstruction

Once written 𡧱, showing **old** 古 109 q.v., here felt to be used for its assumed literal meaning of **skull** and by extension **head**, and an inverted **basket** 冉 399. Thus to **cover a head with a basket**. It is not clear how this came to mean **harm**. Some scholars feel it meant cover, and that harm is a purely borrowed meaning that replaced cover. Others feel it meant **smother a person**, then **kill** or **cause harm** in general. Suggest taking 口 as **mouth** 20, 宀 as a roof and by extension **cover** (see 28), and 主 as a variant of **life** 生 42.

Mnemonic: **COVERING LIVE MOUTH CAN CAUSE HARM**

438	各	KAKU, ono-ono EACH 6 strokes	各駅 KAKUEKI	each station
			各国 KAKKOKU	each country
			各自 KAKUJI	each

Originally 𠂤, showing a **mouth** 口 20 and an **inverted foot** 夂 / 止 129 q.v. Just as 止 can mean either stop or go, the inverted form can have a similar range of often confusing meanings, but usually indicates <u>abnormal</u> progress in the sense of **stopping and starting**. It is listed as a CO character meaning **follow**, and can also mean **go somewhere and then stop**, or **fall over**, or **come down from above**. Here it is felt to mean **come down from above and stop**, with 口 acting phonetically to express the reinforcing meaning of **descend**. This referred to visits by high ranking dignitaries, who would visit one place, stop for a while, then move to another place. Thus **stop at each place**, eventually giving just **each**. Other scholars feel that **each** is a purely borrowed meaning (that replaced descend). Suggest taking 夂 as **sitting crosslegged**.

Mnemonic: **EACH PERSON SITS CROSSLEGGED AND OPEN MOUTHED**

439

KAKU,obo*eru*, sa*meru*/*masu*   自覚 JIKAKU self-awareness
REMEMBER, WAKE   目覚め MEZAME awakening
12 strokes   覚え書き OBOEGAKI memorandum

Formerly 覺. 𦥯 is **emulate manually** 10, here meaning **emulate/learn**. 見 is **look** 18. Thus **learn by looking**, giving **remember** on the one hand and **be alert** and hence **wide awake** on the other. Suggest remembering by association with **learning** 学 10.

Mnemonic: **REMEMBER TO BE AWAKE WHEN LEARNING BY LOOKING**

440

KAN   完成 KANSEI completion
COMPLETE   未完 MIKAN incomplete
7 strokes   完全 KANZEN perfection

宀 is **roof/building** 28. 元 is **origin** 106 q.v., here acting phonetically to express **fence/wall** and probably also lending connotations of **round** (from its depiction of an exaggerated head, which occasionally symbolised roundness). Thus **building with fence/wall around**. Some scholars feel that **complete** comes from the idea of the fence **completely** surrounding the building, others from the idea that the building is truly **completed** when the fence is erected.

Mnemonic: **COMPLETELY ORIGINAL BUILDING**

441

KAN   警官 KEIKAN policeman
GOVERNMENT,OFFICIAL   官僚 KANRYŌ bureaucracy
8 strokes   官庁 KANCHŌ

                   government office

宀 is **roof/building** 28. 𠂤 is **buttocks** 350, here acting phonetically to express **work** and almost certainly also lending an idea of **sedentary**. Thus **person doing sedentary (i.e. clerical) work in a building**, which came to have particular associations with an **official** doing work for the **government**.

Mnemonic: **GOVERNMENT OFFICIAL IN BUILDING SITS ON BACKSIDE**

---

442 漢 KAN 漢字 KANJI character
HAN CHINA, MAN 悪漢 AKKAN rogue
13 strokes 漢詩 KANSHI Chinese poetry

Ironically one of the most obscure of the kanji. Formerly 漢 , and earlier 漢 and 漢. ; is **water** 40, here meaning **river**. 堇 is known to have acted phonetically to express the name of a river, specifically the **Han River** from which the Han Dynasty took its name. However, as an element it is obscure. It shows strong similarities to the early forms of **flaming arrow/ yellow** 黄 120 q.v. (unconnected with the Yellow River), possibly suggesting **Han River gleaming (in the sunset) like a flaming arrow**. However, some scholars have interpreted it as a **beast being roasted** (see 949 and then 842, 1281 and 821), though what connotations such a meaning might lend here are not clear. It also shows strong similarities to **rare/few/violet** 堇 (see 842), which is itself of obscure origin and is indeed taken by some scholars to be a variant of 堇. However, variant or not, it is still not clear what meaning it might have lent. Han China became a reference to **China** in general, and by association **belonging to China** and hence **Chinese man** and finally just **man** (a lesser meaning). Suggest remembering by association with **man** 夫 573, **grass** 艹 9, and **mouth** 口 20.

Mnemonic: **MAN FROM MOUTH OF HAN RIVER IN GRASSY HAN CHINA**

443 管 KAN, kuda 管理 KANRI control
PIPE, CONTROL 気管 KIKAN wind pipe
14 strokes 管楽器 KANGAKKI
wind instrument

竹 is **bamboo** 170. 官 is **official** 441, here acting phonetically to express **pierce** and probably also lending an idea of **control**. 443 originally referred to **pierced bamboo which controlled sound**, i.e. a **wind instrument**. It then came to mean on the one hand any type of **pipe** and on the other **control**.

Mnemonic: **BAMBOO PIPE UNDER CONTROL**

| 444 | | KAN, seki
BARRIER, CONNECTION
14 strokes | 関東 KANTŌ Kanto area
関心 KANSHIN interest
関の山 SEKINOYAMA utmost |

Formerly 關. 門 is **gate** 211. 絲 is a CO character now meaning **thread/ weave**, but it originally referred specifically to a **treadle on a loom**, and derives from (short) threads 幺 111 and crossed pieces of wood 丱 (once ↔). Here 絲 acts phonetically to express **bar** and also lends its idea of **crossed pieces of wood**. Thus **crossed pieces of wood barring a gate**, i.e. **barrier**. **Connection** is an associated idea, since a barrier also represents the point of contact between the areas either side of it. Suggest taking 关 as **heaven** 天 58 and **away** ✓ 66 (and see **send** 送 331).

Mnemonic: **HEAVEN'S GATES ARE IMPASSABLE BARRIER: SENT AWAY**

| 445 | | KAN
WATCH, OBSERVE
18 strokes | 観光 KANKŌ sightseeing
観察 KANSATSU observation
観客 KANKYAKU spectator |

Formerly 觀. 見 is **look** 18. 雚 is a CO character meaning **heron**, comprising **bird** 隹 216 and a **crest** 祏 (once 氺冋). (Note that in Japanese the addition of an extra bird 鳥 174 gives the NGU character **stork** 鸛.) Here it acts phonetically to express **turn**, giving **turn and look (around)**, and may possibly also lend an idea of a heron's habit of looking around as it wades. The idea of turning as such has now disappeared, but the connotations of **observing widely** are retained. Suggest remembering 隺 as **crested bird**.

Mnemonic: **LOOK AND OBSERVE CRESTED BIRD**

| 446 | | GAN, negau
REQUEST, WISH
19 strokes | 志願者 SHIGANSHA applicant
願望的 GANBŌTEKI wishful
願い事 NEGAIGOTO prayer |

頁 is **head** 93. 原 is **spring/origin** 107, here acting phonetically to express **big**. Thus **big head**. It is not clear why such a complex character was chosen for the phonetic. Some scholars feel that a big head was seen as a **source** of **intellectual ability**, and that 446 originally meant therefore **big ideas (from a big head)**. This may serve to explain how it later came to mean **wish**. Others see wish as a pure borrowing.

Mnemonic: **WISH SPRINGS FROM HEAD NOT HEART**

447 希 **KI, KE**
DESIRE, SCANTY, RARE
7 strokes

希望 KIBŌ hope
希求 KIKYŪ desire
希薄 KIHAKU thinness

Once written 希, showing **interweave** 爻 10 and **cloth/ threads** 巾 778. 447 originally meant **weaving threads**, i.e. **embroidery**, and its current meanings all result from borrowings.

Mnemonic: **INTERWOVEN CLOTH THREADS DESIRABLE BUT RARE**

448 **KI**
SEASON, YOUNG
8 strokes

季節 KISETSU season
四季 SHIKI four seasons
季女 KIJO youngest daughter

Rice plant 禾 81 and **child** 子 25, and originally meaning **young rice plant**. This came to mean **young** in a broader sense, and is especially applied to the **youngest of a line** (and hence very occasionally has an associated meaning of **end**). Some scholars feel that **season** is a borrowed meaning, others that it stems from association between young rice and a particular time of the year.

Mnemonic: **RICE PLANTS IN SEASON GROW LIKE YOUNG CHILDREN**

449 紀 **KI**
CHRONICLE, START
9 strokes

紀元 KIGEN epoch, era
紀行 KIKŌ travelogue
二十世紀 NIJŪSEIKI 20th century

Thread 糸 27 and **self/ twisting thread** 己 855, meaning **thread from end to end**. On the one hand this gave rise to **end/start,** and on the other to the idea of an **account** or **chronicle** (which threads from one end of an episode to the other).

Mnemonic: **CHRONICLE OF SELF THREADS FROM BEGINNING TO END**

450 **KI, yorokob**u
REJOICE, HAPPY
12 strokes

喜劇 KIGEKI comedy
歓喜 KANKI delight
大喜び ŌYOROKOBI great joy

口 is **mouth** 20. 壴 was once written 𣌭 and 𣌭, showing a **plant** 屮 / 屮 (9 and variant 42) and a **food vessel** 豆 / 豆 1640, and essentially means **edible plant**. Here it also acts phonetically to express **soft**. 450 originally meant **putting soft plants in the mouth**, i.e. **eat cooked vegetables**. This came to mean simply **eat**, which in turn symbolised **pleasure**. Suggest taking 士 as **samurai** 494.

Mnemonic: **FOOD POT AT MOUTH MAKES SAMURAI HAPPY**

451

KI, hata
FLAG
14 strokes

国旗　KOKKI　　　national flag
旗持ち　HATAMOCHI　flag bearer
旗魚　KAJIKI*　　　billfish

Somewhat obscure, though its elements are clearly **fluttering flag** 方 333 and **winnowing device/ that** 其 251 q.v. The latter is felt by some scholars to act phonetically to express **gather**, giving **flag under which one gathers** (i.e. warriors rallying). Since winnowing symbolised the arrival of a specific time of year it may also lend an idea of **the time having arrived** (to assemble and go off to fight). Suggest taking 方 as **person** 亻 39 and **side** 方 204.

Mnemonic: **PERSON AT SIDE OF WINNOWING DEVICE HOLDS FLAG**

452

KI, utsuwa
VESSEL,UTENSIL,SKILL
15 strokes

器具　KIGU　　　utensil
食器　SHOKKI　　tableware
器用　KIYŌ　　　adroitness

Somewhat obscure. Formerly 器 and earlier 器, showing **dog** 犬 17 and what appears to be **four mouths** 口 20. The exact role of these elements is not clear. The positioning of the mouths suggests a **dog wheeling with open mouth (i.e. barking?) to face all quarters** (see also 1522), though some scholars feel 452 originally had a meaning of a dog panting (i.e. open mouthed). It is believed that the **four mouths** eventually dominated the original meaning and came to suggest a **collection of openings/ receptacles**, leading to **vessel** and thus **utensil**. **Skill** is felt to be an associated meaning with utensil, both sharing an idea of enabling a function to be carried out. Suggest taking 犬 as **big** 53, and 品 as **four boxes**. Note that a sometimes encountered simplified form 器 is unconnected with **work** 工 113.

Mnemonic: **FOUR BIG BOX-LIKE VESSELS ARE USEFUL UTENSILS**

453

KI, hata
LOOM, DEVICE,
OCCASION
16 strokes

機能　KINŌ　　　function
機会　KIKAI　　opportunity
機織り　HATAORI　weaving

木 is **wood** 69. 幾 is **how many** 1129 q.v., here used in its original meaning of **loom**. Thus **wooden loom**, now also **device** in general. This gave rise to the idea of the **wherewithal/ means** to perform a function, leading to associated ideas such as **opportunity** and **occasion**.

Mnemonic: **ON HOW MANY OCCASIONS IS WOODEN LOOM USED?**

454		GI	議論	GIRON	discussion
		DISCUSSION	会議	KAIGI	conference
		20 strokes	議会	GIKAI	the Diet

言 is **words/speak** 274. 義 is **righteousness** 645, acting phonetically to express **mutual (exchange)** and also lending an idea of **propriety**. Thus **proper mutual exchange of words**.

Mnemonic: **DISCUSSION INVOLVES RIGHTEOUS USE OF WORDS**

455		KYŪ, moto*meru*	要求	YŌKYŪ	demand
		REQUEST, SEEK	追求	TSUIKYŪ	pursuit
		7 strokes	求職	KYŪSHOKU	
					seeking work

Once written 求, known to represent the **skin/fur of a fanged creature**, though it is not clear whether it is a pictograph of the body with legs attached or an ideograph combining the head and body ψ with bristles 朮, possibly under the influence of fur/hair 毛 210 q.v. 455 originally meant **fur coat**, which was a highly **desirable** object. Some scholars feel its present meanings stem from such an object being much **sought after**, while others feel they result from borrowings. Suggest remembering by association with **water** 水 40, taking ー as a **cross** (stroke) and 丶 as a **spot**.

Mnemonic: **CROSS WATER TO SEEK SPOTTED FUR COAT**

456		KYŪ, suku*u*	救命ブイ	KYŪMEIBUI	lifebuoy
		RESCUE, REDEEM	救援	KYŪEN	relief, rescue
		11 strokes	救い出す	SUKUIDASU	extricate

求 is **seek/ request** 455. 攵 is **threaten/ coerce** 101. 456 originally meant to **request threateningly**, i.e. **demand**. Some scholars feel 求 also acts phonetically to express **cease**, giving **demand a cessation**. It is not fully clear how it came to mean **rescue**. Some scholars see it as a borrowed meaning, others as an extended meaning from the idea of demanding the release of a prisoner or similar.

Mnemonic: **RESCUE BY COERCIVE REQUEST**

457

KYŪ, tama*u*
SUPPLY, BESTOW
12 strokes

供給 KYŌKYŪ — supply
月給 GEKKYŪ — monthly pay
来給え KITAMAE — Come!

Thread 糸 27 and **join** 合 121, giving **join threads**. The idea of joining threads to achieve a desired length came to mean **furnish by whatever means**, later **supply/ bestow** in a broad sense. It is also used as a verbal suffix (originally polite).

Mnemonic: **SUPPLY JOINED THREADS**

458

KYO, a*geru*, kozo*tte*
OFFER, RAISE, ACT,
PERFORM, TOGETHER
10 strokes

挙手 KYOSHU — raising hands
選挙 SENKYO — election
一挙 IKKYO ni — at a stroke

Formerly 擧. 與 is the old form of **give** 与 1873 q.v., here used both in its early sense of **(hands) working together to perform a task** and in its later sense of **give/ raise/offer**. The additional **hand** 手 32 emphasises the idea of doing something with the hands. Suggest taking 兴 as a **laden table**.

Mnemonic: **RAISE LADEN TABLE BY HAND: SOME ACT!**

459

GYO, RYŌ
FISHING
14 strokes

漁船 GYOSEN — fishing boat
漁師 RYŌSHI — fisherman
漁業 GYOGYŌ — fishery

Fish 魚 98 with **water** 氵 40 added to indicate **fish in water**, i.e. in the natural state and not yet caught. This came to mean **fish waiting to be caught** and eventually (professional) **fishing**.

Mnemonic: **FISHING REQUIRES BOTH FISH AND WATER**

460

KYŌ, tomo
TOGETHER
6 strokes

共通 KYŌTSU — commonality
共食い TOMOGUI — cannibalism
共産主義 KYŌSANSHUGI
— communism

Originally 㖾 and later 苂, showing **two hands** 㐅 offering a jewel 〇 /廿. The idea of **offering** was later conveyed by a character adding person 亻 39, i.e. offer 供 839, while 460 came to focus on the idea of doing something with **both** hands and by extension **jointly/ together**. Suggest taking 艹 as **plant** 9 and 六 as a **table**.

Mnemonic: **PLANT AND TABLE GO TOGETHER**

---

461 協 KYŌ 協定 KYŌTEI agreement
COOPERATE 協力 KYŌRYOKU cooperation
8 strokes 協会 KYŌKAI association

劦 is a trebling of **strength** 74. 十 is **ten** 33, here acting phonetically to express **gather** and also lending an idea of **many**. Thus **many persons' strength**, i.e. **cooperation**.

Mnemonic: **THIRTEEN STRONG ARMS COOPERATING**

462 鏡 KYŌ, kagami 望遠鏡 BŌENKYŌ telescope
MIRROR 鏡台 KYŌDAI dresser
19 strokes 手鏡 TEKAGAMI hand mirror

金 is **metal** 14. 竟 is an NGU character meaning **finish**, comprising **sound** 音 6 q.v. and a **bent figure** 儿 39 and originally indicating the conclusion of a musical recital (some scholars taking the bent figure to indicate the performer bowing, others taking it to be used phonetically to express **finish**). Here 竟 is used phonetically to express **scene**. Its semantic role is unclear, though it may possibly suggest **transitoriness** (i.e. soon finished). Thus **metal which shows (transitory?) scene**, i.e. a **bronze mirror**, later **mirror** in general. Suggest taking 音 literally as **shout aloud**, and 儿 as **bent legs**.

Mnemonic: **SHOUT ALOUD AT BENT LEGS IN METAL MIRROR**

463 競 KYŌ, KEI, kiso*u*, se*ru* 競争 KYŌSŌ competition
COMPETE, BID 競馬 KEIBA horse race
20 strokes 競り売り SERIURI auction

Formerly written 競, showing that 誩 derives from 誩, the old form of a CO character 誩 meaning **argue/ wrangle** (comprising **words** 言 274 q.v. set against each other). 从 shows **two persons** 亻 39, emphasising the adversaries in the dispute. (Note that 从 is a CO character now used largely to mean follow, but its original meaning is simply two persons.) Thus **two persons vying against each other**. Suggest taking as a doubling of **elder brother** 兄 267 and **stand** 立 73.

Mnemonic: **TWO ELDER BROTHERS COMPETE IN STAND-OFF**

464		KYOKU,GOKU,kiwa*meru* EXTREME, POLE 12 strokes	北極 至極 消極	HOKKYOKU North Pole SHIGOKU extremely SHŌKYOKU negative pole

木 is **wood** 69. 亟 is a CO character meaning **urgency**. Its exact etymology is unclear, but an early form shows a **hand** 又 appearing to **push a person** 人 39 between **two lines** 二 (indicating **constraint** or **pressure**) into an **opening** 口 20. Here it acts phonetically to express **extreme**, and almost certainly lends similar connotations of its own. 464 originally meant **wood in an extreme position**, and was a reference to the **ridgepole** (the highest beam of a house), but later came to mean **extreme** in general. Suggest taking 二 as **poles**, with a play on the word pole.

Mnemonic: **PERSON PUSHED INTO OPENING BETWEEN WOODEN POLES**

465		KU WARD, SECTION 4 strokes	区別 地区 北区	KUBETSU distinction CHIKU district KITAKU Kita Ward

Formerly 區. 匸 is an **enclosure**. 品 is now clearly associated with **three mouths** 口 20 (see 1034), but probably originally meant three smaller **enclosures**, indicating **partitioning within partitioning** and thus **section**. A **ward** is a section of a city.

Mnemonic: **ENCLOSED SECTION X IS A WARD**

466	軍	GUN ARMY, MILITARY 9 strokes	空軍 軍人 米国軍	KŪGUN airforce GUNJIN military man BEIKOKUGUN US Forces

Popularly explained as a **covered** 冖 **vehicle** 車 31, namely a **supply wagon** symbolising an **army** on the move. A useful mnemonic, but incorrect. Old forms such as 軍 and 軍 show a vehicle with a protective encircling arm ㇇ or womb ♀ (see 655). 466 actually referred to **carts drawn into a circle** to form a protected encampment, an ancient military practice long before the days of the Wild West. The circle of carts symbolised the **army**.

Mnemonic: **COVERED WAGONS ENCIRCLE ARMY CAMP**

467	GUN, kŏri	郡部 GUNBU	rural district

467   **GUN, kŏri**   郡部 GUNBU   rural district
COUNTY, DISTRICT   郡山 KŌRIYAMA a placename
10 strokes   和気郡 WAKEGUN

Wake County

阝 is **village** 355. 君 is **governor/ lord** 266. Usually explained as **villages under the same governership** and thus forming an **administrative district**. Some scholars feel that 君 also acts phonetically to express **gather**, giving a **gathering/ grouping of villages**.

Mnemonic: **VILLAGE BELONGS TO LORD OF COUNTY DISTRICT**

468   **KEI, kata**   元型 GENKEI   prototype
TYPE, MODEL, MOLD   大型 ŌGATA   large size
9 strokes   典型的 TENKEITEKI   typical

土 is **earth** 60. 刑 is **punish** 1193 q.v., here acting phonetically to express **make** and also lending its idea of **frame**. Thus to **make an earthen frame**, i.e. a **clay mold**. This later came to mean **pattern**, **type**, **model**, and so forth.

Mnemonic: **MODEL PUNISHMENT FOR EARTHY TYPES**

469   **KEI, KE**   光景 KŌKEI   scene
SCENE, VIEW, BRIGHT   景気 KEIKI liveliness, business
12 strokes   景色 KESHIKI   scenery

日 is **sun** 62. 京 is **capital** 99 q.v., here acting phonetically to express **clear and open** and almost certainly lending connotations of **exposed** from its literal meaning of **building on a hill**. Thus **open to the sun** (as a hilltop), i.e. **bright**. In Chinese this is still a major meaning, whereas in Japanese it is usually found in the figurative sense of **lively**. **Scene/ view** is an extension of **open to the light**.

Mnemonic: **SUNNY CAPITAL IS A BRIGHT SCENE**

470	芸	GEI ART, SKILL, PLANT 7 strokes	芸術 GEIJUTSU	art
			種芸 SHUGEI	planting
			芸者 GEISHA	geisha

Formerly 藝. 埶 derives from 坴 of which 木 is **tree** 69, 土 is **earth** 60, and 丸 is a **person kneeling** 乚 413 with **arms outstretched** 𠂇. Thus 埶 depicts a person kneeling to **plant** a tree in the ground. It was later enforced by the addition of **plant** 艹 9. Both 埶 and 蓺 still exist as CO characters interchangeable with 藝. Speak/ **vapors** 云 78 was added later in a phonetic capacity to express **cultivate**, but it should be noted that 芸, the de facto simplified form of 藝, is not a mere graphic simplification. It still exists in Chinese as a separate character from 藝, with a meaning of **fragrant plant** (i.e. plant giving off fragrant vapors). Thus 云 may have been chosen partly with this in mind, i.e. to link up with the other addition 艹 and lend an elegant connotation of **plant a fragrant tree**. The idea of planting a tree properly came to mean **horticultural skill** and then **skill** in a broader sense, usually in relation to **artistic accomplishment.** Suggest taking 云 as **two** 二 61 **noses** 厶 134.

Mnemonic: **TWO NOSEY PEOPLE EXAMINE ART OF PLANTING**

471	欠	KETSU, ka*ku/keru* LACK 4 strokes	欠席者 KESSEKISHA	absentee
			欠点 KETTEN	fault
			欠け目 KAKEME	break

From a pictograph of a **person yawning** 𠂢 (person 人 39 with gaping mouth 𠂋). **Gaping mouth** came to mean **be wide open**, then **be vacant**, then **be lacking.** The character 缺 is often assumed to be an old form of 471 of which 欠 is assumed to be a simplification, but in fact it is a separate character of similar meaning. It comprises container /bottle 缶 1095 and open 夬 271, and originally meant open container.

Mnemonic: **PERSON WITH GAPING MOUTH LACKS DIGNITY**

472	結	KETSU, musu*bu*, yu*u* BIND, JOIN, END 12 strokes	結婚 KEKKON	marriage
			結果 KEKKA	result
			結び目 MUSUBIME	knot

糸 is **thread** 27. 吉 is good luck 1142 q.v. Some scholars take the latter to act phonetically to express **entwine**, giving **entwine threads** and thus **join** them. Others take it to lend its early meaning of **lidded container**, giving **bind lid on container.** It may in fact combine both phonetic and semantic roles, giving **bind lid on container by entwining it with thread. End/ conclusion** is an associated meaning, as in the English term **tie up.** Suggest taking 吉 as **samurai** 士 494 and **mouth** 口 20.

Mnemonic: **BIND SAMURAI'S MOUTH WITH THREAD**

473		KEN, KON, ta*tsu*/*teru* **BUILD, ERECT** 9 strokes	建設 KENSETSU 建立 KONRYŪ 建物 TATEMONO	building erection building

Movement 廴 129 and **hand holding brush** 聿 142. 473 originally referred to the **movement of a brush** when writing. The brush was held **erect**, leading to **make erect** and then, as in English, to **build**.

Mnemonic: **HAND HOLDS PEN ERECT**

474		KEN, suko*yaka* **HEALTHY** 11 strokes	健康 KENKŌ 健全 KENZEN 健筆家 KENPITSUKA	health soundness prolific writer

Person イ 39 and **erect** 建 473. A **person standing erect** is a sign that they are **healthy**. Some scholars feel that 建 also lends its sound to express **strong**.

Mnemonic: **HEALTHY PERSON STANDS ERECT**

475		KEN **EXAMINE** 18 strokes	試験 SHIKEN 実験 JIKKEN 経験 KEIKEN	examination experiment experience

Formerly 驗 . 馬 is **horse** 191. 僉 is a CO character meaning whole/all. It derives from 僉, showing **two talking persons** 兄兄 267, here representing **plurality of opinion**, and **cover** 亼 87, here meaning **bringing together**. Thus **synthesis of opinions**, leading to unity and hence its modern meanings. In compounds it often lends connotations such as overview, arbitrate, combine, discuss, examine, and so forth. In the case of 475 it essentially means **examine**, giving **examine horses** and eventually **examine** in a broad sense, including **try out**. Suggest taking 兄 in its more common meaning of **elder brother**.

Mnemonic: **ELDER BROTHER EXAMINES HORSE COVER**

476		KO, kata*i*/*meru*/*maru* **HARD, FIRM, SOLID** 8 strokes	固体 KOTAI 強固 KYŌKO 固まり KATAMARI	solid state solidity lump, mass

口 is **enclosure** 123. 古 is **old** 109, here acting phonetically to express **solid** and probably also lending an extended idea of **long in place** and thus **firmly established**. 476 originally referred to **solid walls surrounding a castle**, then came to mean **solid** in a general sense.

Mnemonic: **SOLID OLD ENCLOSURE**

477 功 **KŌ, KU**
MERIT, SERVICE
5 strokes

成功	SEIKŌ	success
功罪	KŌZAI	pros and cons
功労	KŌRŌ	distinguished service

Strength/ effort 力 74 and **work** 工 113, giving **dedicated work.**

Mnemonic: **MERITORIOUS SERVICE ENTAILS EFFORTFUL WORK**

478 候 **KŌ, sōrō**
WEATHER, SIGN, ASK, POLITE SUFFIX, SERVE
10 strokes

気候	KIKŌ	climate
候補	KŌHO	candidacy
候文	SŌRŌBUN	polite style

Somewhat obscure, having become etymologically confused with marquis 侯 1256 q.v. 亻 is **person** 39. 㑅 is a variant of 矦, a now defunct character meaning **meet/ greet**. It derives from **bending person** ク (originally ル) and 矦. The latter is a now defunct character meaning **target range** (矢 being arrow 981 and 厂 being a leather curtain hung down to protect the judges, though some scholars feel it indicated the target itself) and by extension **target**. Thus 矦 is **target person**, meaning a **person one wishes to meet/ greet**. In the case of 478 a further **person** 亻 was added for clarity, while the bent person ク/ㇷ, which originally seems to have applied to the person being met, came through its bent posture (apparently actually just a stylisation) to be taken as the person instigating the meeting, whose bent posture was taken as a symbol of **humility**. Thus at this stage 478 meant **humbly await/request a meeting or visit**. It can still mean **request** or **greet** (or **await** in Chinese), which all stem from this early meaning. In Japanese its use as a **polite suffix** and its meaning of **serve** also stem from its early connotations of humility. **Sign** is an associated meaning, from the idea of having an audience with a superior, stating one's business, and watching for **signs** indicating the superior's response. In Japanese **sign** has extended to **weather**. Unfortunately there is no easy mnemonic for the entire character, but suggest remembering by partial association with **arrow** 矢 and **person** 亻, perhaps taking 丨 as a pointer symbolising **point**.

Mnemonic: **PERSON POINTS TO WEATHER SIGNS WITH ARROW**

479 KŌ

SAIL, VOYAGE

10 strokes

航空 KŌKŪ — flight
航海 KŌKAI — sea voyage
航路 KŌRO — route

舟 is **boat** 1354. 亢 is an NGU character now meaning **high**, but in Chinese it can mean **neck** and does in fact derive from 亣, showing a person 人 39 and an exaggerated neck held erect 几. In Chinese it can also mean stiff, prim and proper, erect, straight, and haughty, and often lends such meanings in compounds. Here it acts phonetically to express **side** (by side), and also lends a meaning of **straight**. 479 originally referred to **lashing boats together (side-on) in a straight line** to form a pontoon bridge. This came to mean **cross water**, and eventually **voyage**. Suggest taking ⊥ as a **top** and 几 as a **desk** 832.

Mnemonic: **DESKTOP BOAT VOYAGE**

---

480 KŌ

PEACE, HEALTH

11 strokes

小康 SHŌKŌ — respite
不健康 FUKENKŌ — ill health
健康体 KENKŌTAI healthy body

Originally written 𠭥, showing **hands** ⺍ holding a **pestle** 干 110 pounding cereals/rice, with **bran** ⼆ being produced. 480 originally meant **rice-bran**. This meaning is now conveyed by an NGU character 糠 that adds rice 米 201, while 480 itself has become used as a substitute for a complex character meaning **peace**. **Health** is an associated meaning from the idea of nothing to cause concern. Suggest remembering 肀 as hand holding pestle, i.e. **pound**, with 广 as **building** 114.

Mnemonic: **HAND POUNDS HEALTHY BRAN FLAKES IN BUILDING**

---

481 KOKU, tsu*geru*

PROCLAIM, INFORM

7 strokes

抗告 KŌKOKU — complaint
公告 KŌKOKU — public notice
広告 KŌKOKU — advertisement

Formerly written 𠮷, leading to the popular explanation that it is **cow/bull** 牛 97 and **mouth/say** 口 20 to give **roar like a bull**, i.e. **proclaim**. A useful mnemonic, that may in fact have been believed for many centuries, but incorrect. Very ancient forms such as 告 and 告 show that 屮 derives from a variant of **growing plant** 生 42, which acts phonetically to express **advance/ proffer** and may also lend an idea of **emerge** (a growing plant emerging from the ground). Thus to **proffer from the mouth, i.e. verbally**, meaning to **make a statement** and hence **proclaim** or **inform**.

Mnemonic: **PROCLAIM WITH BULL-LIKE ROAR FROM MOUTH**

| 482 | | SA, sas*u* **DIFFERENCE, THRUST** 10 strokes | 時差 JISA time lag 差別 SABETSU discrimination 差し込む SASHIKOMU insert |

Once written 㢠 . 㣇 is a **plant with new side-shoots/ leaves hanging down** (see 907). 㞊 is **left hand** 22, acting phonetically to express **uneven/ unequal**. Some scholars feel that it also lends a similar connotation of unequal by implied comparison with the right hand, to which it was considered inferior in terms of strength. Thus 482 originally appears to have referred to the **uneven lengths of the new shoots on a plant**, though some scholars feel rather that it indicated the **uneven length of fingers on a hand**, before coming to mean **unevenness** and thus **difference** in general. It is not fully clear how it came to mean **thrust**, but it is assumed to be an extended meaning from the idea of the new shoots (or fingers) thrusting out. Suggest taking as a modified combination of **sheep** 羊 986 and **left** 左 22 .

Mnemonic: **SHEEP ON LEFT IS DIFFERENT**

| 483 | | SAI, na **VEGETABLE, RAPE** 11 strokes | 野菜 YASAI vegetables 菜種 NATANE rape-seed 菜食主義 SAISHOKUSHUGI vegetarianism |

采 is an NGU character meaning **take/gather/pluck**, and shows a **reaching hand** 爫 303 and **tree/shrub** 木 69. Some scholars take it to be a hand plucking a shrub, others a hand plucking fruit from a tree or bush. ⺾ is **plant** 9, giving **gather/pluck plants**. 483 means **edible plants** in general, i.e. **vegetables**, but has particular associations with the **rape plant**.

Mnemonic: **HAND PLUCKS VEGETABLES NEAR TREE**

| 484 | 最 | SAI, motto*mo* **MOST, -EST** 12 strokes | 最大 SAIDAI biggest 最後 SAIGO last 最新式 SAISHINSHIKI latest style |

Once written 𦣻, showing that 日 is not sun 日 62 but a variant of warrior's helmet 冃 1812 q.v., here symbolising **attack** (and to all intents and purposes a simplification of attack 冒 1812). 取 is **take** 301. Thus to **attack and take**, i.e. **seize by force**. This meaning is now conveyed by seize 撮 1305, that adds hand 扌 32, although in Chinese 484 itself still has the related minor meaning of gather. How exactly 484 came to mean **most** is not clear. Some scholars assume it to be a borrowed meaning, others see it as an associated meaning from the idea of **extreme** force/behavior. Suggest taking 日 as **sun**.

Mnemonic: **TAKE MOST SUN WHEN IT'S AT ITS HIGHEST POINT**

485	**ZAI** **TIMBER, RESOURCE** 7 strokes	材木 材料 人材	ZAIMOKU ZAIRYŌ JINZAI	timber material, data talented person

木 is **tree** 69. 才 is **dam** 126, acting phonetically to express **cut down** (some scholars feel **use**) and probably also lending an idea of **fallen trees**. Thus **felled trees** (i.e. **trees cut for use/ timber**). It later came to mean **material** or **resource** in a wider sense, including the figurative idea of **resourcefulness**.

Mnemonic: **LOTS OF TIMBER IN DAM OF FELLED TREES**

486	**SAKU** **YESTERDAY, PAST** 9 strokes	昨日 昨夜 昨年	SAKUJITSU SAKUYA SAKUNEN	yesterday last night last year

日 is **day** 62. 乍 is **make** 127, here acting phonetically to express **accumulate** and probably also lending an idea of **build up**. Thus **accumulated days**, indicating the **passage of time** and by extension the **past**. It became particularly associated with **yesterday**, according to some scholars because its sound could also express **removed one unit of distance**.

Mnemonic: **PAST MADE UP OF YESTERDAY AND OTHER DAYS**

487 刷	**SATSU, su*ru*** **PRINT, RUB** 8 strokes	印刷所 刷新 校正刷り	INSATSUSHO SASSHIN KŌSEIZURI	printery reform proofs

Etymologically somewhat indelicate. Originally the idea of rubbing was conveyed by a character 㕞, which in Chinese is interchangeable with 487. It shows **buttocks** 尸 236, **cloth** 巾 778, and a **hand** ㄆ , and first meant **wipe the buttocks with a cloth**. It then came to mean **rub/wipe** in a broader sense, including the idea of rubbing in order to **print** (an early technique). As the association with printing became stronger, hand ㄆ was replaced by **cut** 刂 181, to refer to **printing by engraving**. However, it still retains the idea of **rubbing**, though as a minor meaning.

Mnemonic: **'BUTTOCK CLOTH' HAS FINELY CUT PRINT**

| 488 | | SATSU, SETSU, koro*su* KILL 10 strokes | 殺人 SATSUJIN murder
自殺 JISATSU suicide
殺し屋 KOROSHIYA killer |

Once written 殺, showing that 米 is a corruption of **pig** 豕 1670. 殳 is **strike/ weapon in hand** 153. Thus 488 originally meant **kill a pig**, then **kill** in general. Suggest taking 米 as a **wooden** 木 69 **cross** ×.

Mnemonic: **KILL BY STRIKING WITH WOODEN CROSS**

| 489 | | SATSU JUDGE, SURMISE, REALISE 14 strokes | 警察 KEISATSU police
察知 SATCHI inference
観察 KANSATSU observation |

Somewhat obscure, though its elements are clearly **roof/ building** 宀 28 and **worship** 祭 283 q.v. Most scholars feel that from its literal meaning of **sacrifice** 祭 had strong connotations of **purify**, i.e. **make clean**, which came by association to mean **open up**. 宀 is taken here to mean **cover**. Thus **open up that which is covered**. By figurative extension this came to mean **realise**, leading to **surmise** and **judge**.

Mnemonic: **SURMISE WHY ONE WORSHIPS UNDER ROOF**

| 490 | | SAN, mai*ru* ATTEND,GO,BE IN LOVE, BE AT A LOSS, THREE 8 strokes | 参加 SANKA participation
参考 SANKŌ reference
参議 SANGI Councilor |

Formerly 參, and in ancient times 㚓, showing a kneeling **woman** 㔾 (see 35) wearing either a tiara or, more likely, **three ornamental hairpins**. The original meaning was **attractive woman. Three hairs** 彡 93 was added later for its reinforcing meaning of **delicate** and **attractive**, giving 㕘. At an early stage the character was used to express **three**, both for its sound and for its **trios** of pins and hairs. How it came to acquire its other meanings is not fully clear. Some scholars take them to be borrowed, others to be extended meanings from the idea of suitors **flocking around** an attractive woman, **falling in love**, and **losing their sense of reason**. Still others feel that it acquired an idea of **cluster** from the three hairpins, that **cluster** came to mean on the one hand **gather** and thence **attend** and on the other **too many to choose from** and thus **confusion**, and that **falling in love** is an associated idea with confusion. Suggest taking 大 as **big** 53 and ム as **nose** 134.

Mnemonic: **GO TO GET BIG NOSE WITH THREE HAIRS ATTENDED TO**

491 SAN, u*m*u 生産 SEISAN production
BIRTH, PRODUCE 産物 SANBUTSU product
11 strokes 出産 SHUSSAN birth

Somewhat obscure. 生 is **birth/life** 42. 产 appears to be a simplification of handsome/ attractive (forehead) 彦 93. 产 is known to have acted here phonetically to express **birth/ growth**, thus reinforcing 生 , but any semantic role is unclear. **Produce** is an extended meaning from **bear**. Suggest taking 产 as a combination of **stand** 立 73 and **cliff** 厂 45.

Mnemonic: **LIVE BIRTH STANDING ON CLIFF**

---

492 SAN, chiru/rasu 散歩 SANPO stroll
SCATTER 散文 SANBUN prose
12 strokes 散らし CHIRASHI leaflet

Once written 枝攵 and earlier just 枇攵, showing that 龶 is derived from a doubling of **wood/shrub** 木 69, in fact indicating **hemp** (see 1829). 攵 is **strike with stick** 101. 492 originally meant **beat hemp with sticks** (to make cloth). This led to **pulverise** and hence **break into little pieces** and **scatter**. **Meat** 夕 / 月 365 was added later, to give a meaning of **shred meat**, but has now become redundant. Suggest remembering 龶 as **two tens** 十 33 and **one** 一 1, i.e. **twenty-one**.

Mnemonic: **HAND STRIKES MEAT, SCATTERING TWENTY-ONE PIECES**

---

493 残 ZAN, nokoru/su 残金 ZANKIN balance
LEAVE, CRUEL, HARM 残念 ZANNEN regret
10 strokes 残忍 ZANNIN brutality

Formerly 殘 . 歹 is **bare bone/ death** 286. 戋 is an NGU character meaning **lance/ halberd**, deriving from a pictograph 戈 (essentially an elaboration of stake 弋 177), here doubled for emphasis. 戋 often means **cut, pierce, kill, menace**, or similar. Here it means **cut and kill**, giving **kill someone cruelly by cutting them to the bone**. Thus the meanings of **cruel, harm,** etc., which are still 493's main meanings in Chinese. **Remain/ leave** is felt by some scholars to be a borrowed meaning, by others to derive from the idea of hacking a person till only the bare bones **remain**. Suggest taking 戋 as **halberd** 弋 and **two** 二 61.

Mnemonic: **TWO CRUEL HALBERDS LEAVE ONLY BARE BONE**

494 士 **SHI, samurai**
WARRIOR, SCHOLAR, MAN
3 strokes

武士	BUSHI	samurai, warrior
士官	SHIKAN	military officer
修士	SHŪSHI	Master (degree)

Often explained as a stylised simplification of **man standing** 立 73, but this is incorrect. Very old forms such as ⊥ show a symbol indicating **being erect**, a reference to the **erect male organ.** The later cross-stroke is seen by some scholars as an esthetic embellishment to give balance to the character, by others as a stylised indication of the glans. The erect male organ symbolises **masculinity**, and hence **man**. **Samurai/ warrior** is felt by some scholars to be a borrowed meaning from serving man 仕 285 q.v., but this is something of a circular argument and unconvincing. It is more likely that the warrior was seen as the epitome of masculinity. **Scholar** is an associated meaning.

Mnemonic: **SAMURAI STANDS ERECT**

495 氏 **SHI, uji**
CLAN, FAMILY, MR
4 strokes

氏名	SHIMEI	full name
氏族	SHIZOKU	clan
加とう氏	KATŌSHI	Mr Kato

Once written [illegible], showing a utensil that was essentially a **ladle** with a cutting edge. **Clan/ family** stems from 495's becoming confused with (or deliberately being substituted for) **hill** 𠂤 (now 阝) 229. Since noble families invariably lived on hilltops 氏 then became used as a reference to a **particular noble family.** It is now used of **family** regardless of social rank. **Mr** similarly relates to reference to a family.

Mnemonic: **MR HILL BORROWS FAMILY LADLE**

496 史 **SHI**
HISTORY, CHRONICLER
5 strokes

歴史	REKISHI	history
女史	JOSHI	Miss, Mrs
史上	SHIJŌ	in history

Often thought to be associated with official 吏 1894, but old forms such as 史 reveal a **hand** 又 holding 中. The latter is thought to be a combination of a **counting-stick** | and **mouth/say** 口 20, to give a meaning of **person counting out loud** or **tallying** and by extension **recording things.** 中 is confusingly the same shape as middle 中 55 q.v., and indeed some scholars feel that the graphic evolution of the latter was influenced by the 中 of 496. Suggest taking 中 as a variant of **middle/ center**.

Mnemonic: **HAND OF MAN CENTRAL TO HISTORY**

497 SHI, tsukasado*ru* 司法 SHIHŌ judicature
ADMINISTER, OFFICIAL 司令部 SHIREIBU headquarters
5 strokes 司会者 SHIKAISHA
master of ceremonies

Once written ㄱ, being a mirror image of **anus** 占 858 q.v., i.e. an **opening** 口 20 under **buttocks** 厂/尸 236. (Just as the elements of characters were sometimes repositioned [e.g. 416], so also mirror images were not unknown, though it is not clear whether they had any particular significance.) It is not clear how 497 came to mean **administer/ official**. Some scholars feel it results from borrowing or confusion with chronicler 史 496, but in view of the fact that buttocks in a building 官 441 q.v. came to mean sedentary work and hence government/ official, it is not impossible that anus/ posterior similarly came to symbolise **sedentary work** and hence **official**. Suggest taking 口 as **entrance**, 一 as **one** 1, and ㄱ as a **corner**.

Mnemonic: ONE OFFICIAL ADMINISTERS CORNER ENTRANCE

498 SHI, ane 姉さん NEESAN* elder sister
ELDER SISTER 姉上 ANEUE Elder Sister
8 strokes 姉妹都市 SHIMAITOSHI sister city

Formerly 姉. 女 is **woman** 35. 朿 is confusingly similar to binding on a stake/ order/ younger brother 弟 177 q.v., but is taken to be a **vine winding round a stake** to symbolise **growth** and by association **starting point**. It also acts phonetically to express **start**. Thus **female starting point**, meaning the first born daughter and hence **elder sister** (see also 288). 朿 later became confused with **city** 市 130, which lends no meaning but still acts phonetically to express **start**.

Mnemonic: ELDER SISTER WORKS IN CITY

499 SHI, kokoro*miru*, tame*su* 試合 SHIAI match
TRIAL, TEST 試験官 SHIKENKAN examiner
13 strokes 試み KOKOROMI trial, test

言 is **words** 274. 式 is **form** 295, which also acts phonetically to express **observe**. 499 originally referred to **observing which form of words was most effective**, leading to **test**.

Mnemonic: TEST FORMS OF WORDS

500 辞	JI, ya*meru* **WORD, DECLINE, LEAVE** 13 strokes	辞書 JISHO dictionary 辞職 JISHOKU resignation 修辞学 SHŪJIGAKU rhetoric

Somewhat obscure. Formerly written 屬庠. 屬 derives from 屬 , showing **hands** 屬 **untying a knot** 屬 , and came by extension to mean **unravel, solve, perceive, judge** and so forth. 辛 is **(tattooist's) needle/ sharp** 1432. Some scholars take the latter to symbolise a **prisoner** (who, like a slave, was tattooed [see 318]), and take 500 to have originally meant **judge a prisoner**. All its modern meanings are taken to be essentially borrowed. However, **words** may possibly have evolved from the idea of a judge's **pronouncement**, or else simply from confusion between the simplified form 舌 and **tongue** 舌 732, i.e. giving **sharp tongue/ incisive words**. Other scholars in fact feel that from the outset 辛 meant **sharp**, giving 屬庠 a meaning of **sharp insight**. This is felt to have come to mean **be to the point**, then **speak to the point**, with 舌 thus being a later deliberate use of tongue (symbolising **speak**) and not a mere graphic simplification. In view of the fact that the words in 500 came to have a particular association with **refusal** (which might be considered a form of speaking to the point), the latter theory seems the more helpful. **Leave** is an associated meaning of refuse.

Mnemonic: **DECLINE WITH WORDS FROM SHARP TONGUE**

501 失	SHITSU, ushina*u* **LOSE** 5 strokes	失敗 SHIPPAI failure 失敬 SHIKKEI rudeness 失業 SHITSUGYŌ unemployment

Once written . 屮 is **hand** 32. 乚 is a variant of **odd** 乙 1041, here acting phonetically to express **lose** but also felt by many scholars to suggest the idea of **slipping** by its shape. Thus to **lose by slipping from the hand**. Suggest taking 夫 as **man** 573 and ノ as a **baton**.

Mnemonic: **MAN ABOUT TO LOSE BATON**

502 借	SHAKU, ka*riru* **BORROW, RENT** 10 strokes	借金 SHAKKIN debt 借家 SHAKUYA rented house 借り主 KARINUSHI borrower

亻 is **person** 39. 昔 is **past** 1481 q.v., here acting phonetically to express **imitate** and probably also lending an idea of **duplicate** from its original meaning of succession of days. 502 originally meant **imitate a person**, the idea of deception still being found in its minor Chinese meaning of **make a pretext of**. From this it came to mean **not the real thing**, which by association came to mean something **not really one's own**, i.e. something **borrowed** or **rented**.

Mnemonic: **PERSON WHO HAS BORROWED IN THE PAST**

154

503

SHU, tane
SEED, KIND
14 strokes

一種 ISSHU   a kind, sort
人種 JINSHU   humankind
種無し TANENASHI   seedless

禾 is **rice plant** 81. 重 is **heavy** 311, here acting phonetically to express **slow** and probably also lending an idea of **ponderous**. 503 originally referred to a **particular type** of late ripening rice, then came to mean **type/ kind** in general. **Seed** is felt to derive from a reinterpretation of 503's elements as **heavy part of the rice (or grain) plant**, namely the **seed**-bearing head.

Mnemonic: **KIND OF RICE PLANT HEAVY WITH SEED**

504

SHŪ, mawari
CIRCUMFERENCE,
AROUND
8 strokes

周辺 SHŪHEN   perimeter
周到 SHŪTŌ   circumspect
一周 ISSHŪ   a lap, circuit

Formerly 周 and once 囲 or 甾, showing a **field** 田 59 **completely full of crops** ∴ (i.e. in all corners). This gave rise to the idea of **complete**, leading by association to completion of a **cycle** and hence **around**. The later element 口 appears to be a **circle**, reinforcing the idea of **round** (as 228). However, some scholars feel that 口 is actually **mouth** 20, giving what was originally **full mouth** (or, according to one view, a completely closed mouth, with 甾 acting essentially phonetically to express **close**) before it was borrowed to express **around**. Suggest taking 口 as **mouth**, 土 as **earth** 60, and 冂 as a **hoop**.

Mnemonic: **EARTH AROUND MOUTH OF HOOP**

505

SHUKU, yado, yadoru
LODGE, SHELTER,
HOUSE
11 strokes

宿題 SHUKUDAI   homework
宿屋 YADOYA   inn
下宿人 GESHUKUNIN   boarder

Once written 倜, showing **building** ∩/宀 28, **person** 亻/イ 39, and a **rush mat** (bedding, symbolising **resting**) 囙. Thus **building in which a person can rest**, i.e. **house** or **inn**. The use of **hundred** 百 67 results from a long-standing miscopying.

Mnemonic: **HUNDRED PEOPLE LODGING IN ONE HOUSE**

155

| 506 | | JUN
SEQUENCE, COMPLIANCE
12 strokes | 順序 JUNJO
従順 JŪJUN
順調 JUNCHŌ ni | sequence
obedience
favorably |

頁 is **head** 93. 川 is **river** 48, here acting phonetically to express **comply** and also lending an idea of **flowing down** and by association not being upright (i.e. **bowing**). 506 originally referred to a **person bowing their head in compliance**. This gave rise to **follow** and hence **order** or **sequence**, the latter meanings probably also influenced by the strong presence of river/ **flow**. Note that the English word **order** similarly has associations both with sequence and compliance (but the latter from the causative rather than passive perspective).

Mnemonic: **COMPLIANT HEADS IN SEQUENCE LIKE FLOWING RIVER**

| 507 | | SHO, hatsu-, haji*me*
BEGINNING, FIRST
7 strokes | 最初 SAISHO
初めて HAJIMETE
初恋 HATSUKOI | first
first time
first love |

衤 is **clothing** 420. 刀 is **cut** 181. Thus **to cut cloth to make clothes**. This came to mean **set about doing something**, as well as **new** and therefore **for the first time**.

Mnemonic: **CLOTHES MUST FIRST BE CUT**

| 508 | | SHŌ, tona*eru*
RECITE, PREACH
11 strokes | 提唱 TEISHŌ
合唱 GASSHŌ
唱え値 TONAENE | advocacy
chorus
asking price |

口 is **mouth/say** 20. 昌 is an NGU character meaning **bright** or **intense**, comprising two **suns** 日 62, which also acts phonetically to express **raised**. (Some scholars feel that originally 昌 was actually a symbol showing the position of the sun higher than its earlier position, and that it therefore meant **high/ raised**, though it soon became interpreted as double sun in the sense of bright/ intense.) Thus **to speak in a raised and intense voice**, as when **reciting** or **preaching**. Suggest taking 日 in its meaning of **day**.

Mnemonic: **PREACHER'S MOUTH RECITES FOR TWO DAYS**

509 SHŌ, *yaku/keru* 　　　燃焼 NENSHŌ　　combustion
BURN, ROAST 　　　　　焼け跡 YAKEATO　burnt remains
12 strokes 　　　　　　　焼き立て YAKITATE　fresh baked

Formerly 燒． 火 is **flames/fire 8**. 堯 is a CO character meaning **high** (literally raised earth, from a trebling of **earth** 土 60 and 兀, an NGU character meaning **high** that is to all intents and purposes a variant of **upper part** 元 106). Thus **high flames**, indicating **burning**. Suggest taking 垚 as **three tens** 十 33 and **one** — 1, and 儿 as **legs**.

Mnemonic: **ROAST THIRTY-ONE LEGS ON FIRE**

510 SHŌ, *teru/rasu* 　　　参照 SANSHŌ　　　reference
ILLUMINATE, SHINE 　　対照 TAISHŌ　　　contrast
13 strokes 　　　　　　　照明 SHŌMEI　　illustration

Bright light 昭 315 with **fire** 灬 8 emphasising **brightness**. Thus **shine/ illuminate**.

Mnemonic: **ILLUMINATE BY BRIGHT LIGHT OF FIRE**

511 SHŌ 　　　　　　　賞品 SHŌHIN　　　　prize
PRIZE, PRAISE 　　　　賞讃 SHŌSAN　　　praise
15 strokes 　　　　　　　一等賞 ITTŌSHŌ　first prize

貝 is **shell 90**, here meaning **money** or **valuable item**. 𫩏 is a variant of **furthermore** 尚 1392 q.v., here acting phonetically to express **bestow** and also lending connotations of **esteem**. Thus **bestow valuable item as token of esteem**, leading to **prize** and **praise** (note that the English terms are etymologically the same word).

Mnemonic: **MOREOVER, SHELLS ARE PRIZES**

512 臣 SHIN, JIN 　　　　　臣下 SHINKA　　　vassal
RETAINER, SUBJECT 　臣民 SHINMIN　　subjects
7 or 6 strokes 　　　　　大臣 DAIJIN　　　minister

Once written 𦣞 , showing an **eye** with deliberate exaggeration of the pupil to symbolise **wide eyed alertness** (cf. English keep an eye out). This came to mean **guard**, and by extension **retainer, servant, public servant**, and **subject**. Distinguish huge 巨 1153.

Mnemonic: **RETAINER KEEPS WATCHFUL EYE OUT**

---

513 信 | SHIN
TRUST, BELIEVE
9 strokes | 信用 SHINYŌ — trust
迷信 MEISHIN — superstition
確信 KAKUSHIN — conviction

Word 言 274 and **person** 亻 39. A person's word is something which can be **believed** and **trusted**.

Mnemonic: **PERSON'S WORD IS BELIEVED AND TRUSTED**

---

514 真 | SHIN, ma
TRUE, QUINTESSENCE
10 strokes | 真実 SHINJITSU — truth
写真機 SHASHINKI — camera
真っ白 MASSHIRO* — pure white

Formerly 眞 and earlier 貞. 匕 is **fallen person** 238. 臭／眞 derives from an **inverted head** 首 139 (see also 273). 514 originally meant **person upside-down** and then **upside-down** or **overturn** in a broader sense. This meaning is now conveyed by an NGU character 顚 that adds a further **head** 頁 93. It is not clear how it came to mean **truth/ essence**. It is generally assumed to result from borrowing, but it is probable that upside-down person meant **dead** person, and therefore possible that this led to the idea of **soul** or **spirit**, giving in turn **essence** and eventually **truth**. It should be noted that in Chinese 514 has strong connotations of the human soul or spirit. Suggest taking as **equipment** 具 265 and **ten** 十 33.

Mnemonic: **IT'S TRUE THAT EQUIPMENT IS IN TEN PIECES**

---

515 成 | SEI, JŌ, naru/su
BECOME, MAKE,
CONSIST
6 strokes | 成分 SEIBUN — component
成人 SEIJIN — adult
成り立ち NARITACHI — formation

Once written , showing **exact** 丁 346 and 戉. The latter derives from 戈, showing **halberd** 戈／戉 493 with an exaggerated **blade** ▷/⊢. The large blade was also used for shaving wood and fine trimming, and in compounds often lends an idea of **making just so**. It lends such a meaning in 515, reinforced by 丁. It meant **exactly right**, giving **make right** or **be right**. **Consist** is an associated meaning from the idea of **being properly formed**. Note that there is a range of half a dozen or so CO and NGU characters based upon 戈, chiefly being used either for zodiac signs or for concepts involving cutting or weapons. They appear to have become somewhat confused etymologically. For example, 戉 is a CO character meaning halberd or battle ax, while 戌 is listed as a zodiac sign, but they are clearly essentially the same character. Suggest treating them all as variants of **halberd** 戈.

Mnemonic: **BECOME EXACT AFTER TRIMMING WITH HALBERD BLADE**

516

SEI,SHŌ,habuku,kaerimiru 　反省 HANSEI 　　　　reflection
MINISTRY, OMIT, 　　　　省略 SHŌRYAKU 　　omission
EXAMINE 　　　　　　　　厚生省 KŌSEISHO
9 strokes 　　　　　　　　　　　　　　　Welfare Ministry

Somewhat obscure, though its elements are clearly **eye** 目 72 and **few/ little** 少 143. Some scholars take the latter to act phonetically to express **obstructed**, as well as lending a meaning of **small**, to give **reduced vision**, and take all the modern meanings to be borrowings. However, most scholars take the elements to be used ideographically to give a meaning of **narrowing one's eyes** in order to **scrutinise**. Scrutinise led to **examine**, and became particularly associated with the idea of scrutinising in order to **trim to an optimum**, i.e. by **removing** unnecessary elements. This led to **omit**. Examining also appears to have become associated with **government**, leading by association to **government ministry** (and **administrative district** in Chinese). Note that a different positioning of the same elements gives the NGU character 眇, which means both minute and squint.

Mnemonic: **FEW EYES EXAMINE MINISTRY: AN OMISSION**

517

SEI, SHŌ, kiyoi/meru 　　清潔 SEIKETSU 　　cleanliness
PURE, CLEAN 　　　　　清浄 SEIJŌ/SHŌJŌ 　　purity
11 strokes 　　　　　　　清水 SHIMIZU* 　spring water

氵 is **water** 40. 青 is **blue/ green** 43 q.v., here acting phonetically to express **clear/ clean** and also lending an idea of **fresh**. **Fresh clear water** came to mean **pure** in general.

Mnemonic: **BLUE WATER IS PURE AND CLEAN**

518

SEI, ikioi 　　　　　　勢力 SEIRYOKU 　　　　power
POWER, FORCE 　　　大勢 ŌZEI 　　　　　multitude
13 strokes 　　　　　　勢いよく IKIOIYOKU 　vigorously

力 is **strength** 74. 埶 is **kneeling to plant a tree** 470, here meaning **plant** in general. Planting requires great strength, thus the **strength required for planting** indicates considerable **power**. Suggest taking 埶 as **round** 丸 830 and **mounds of earth** 坴 597.

Mnemonic: **STRONG POWER FORCES UP ROUND EARTHEN MOUNDS**

159

519		SEI, JŌ, shizu*ka*/*maru* QUIET, CALM 14 strokes	静止 SEISHI	stillness
			静けさ SHIZUKESA*	quietude
			静脈 JŌMYAKU	vein

Formerly 靜 . Somewhat obscure, though its elements are clearly **green** 青/青 43 q.v. and **conflict** 爭/争 529 q.v. Some scholars take the latter to act phonetically to express **beautiful**, giving **beautiful green color**, and take **quiet/ calm** to be a borrowed meaning. However, if 519 did indeed originally mean **beautiful green**, then it might be felt that quiet/ calm is an associated meaning (from the apparently universal interpretation of green as a **restful color**). Other scholars take 青 to indicate **clear** (partly phonetically, partly from its own idea of fresh [and clean]), and take 争 in its meaning of **conflict,** to give **clear of conflict.** Still others take 青 to mean **fresh/ pure** and take 争 to mean **stop/ stay** (from its assumed literal meaning of one arm stopping another), to give **staying pure.** Quiet/ calm is then taken to be an associated meaning from the idea of **desirable lack of movement.** It should be noted that 519 has a lesser meaning of **pure** in Chinese, and that it also has connotations of **lack of movement,** suggesting that the last theory is the most likely.

Mnemonic: **CONFLICT QUIETENED BY SIGHT OF CALMING GREEN**

520		SEKI SEAT, PLACE 10 strokes	出席 SHUSSEKI	attendance
			欠席 KESSEKI	absence
			空席 KŪSEKI	empty seat

A much changed character. Originally written 𠩄, showing a **rush mat** (see 505) used as crude **seating** or bedding. Cliff 厂 45 was added as a phonetic to express **spread,** giving 𢋀, later being replaced by 庶. The latter is an abbreviation of **various** 庶 1381, used in a similar phonetic role to 厂 and presumably also used to lend an idea of **plurality.** Finally rush mat 囚 was replaced by **cloth** 巾 778, presumably indicating an improvement in the quality of the seating. Suggest taking 广 as **building** 114 and 廿 as **two tens** 十 33 and **one** 一 1, i.e. **twenty-one.**

Mnemonic: **BUILDING WITH TWENTY-ONE CLOTH SEATS**

521		SEKI, tsu*mu*/*moru* PRODUCT, PILE 16 strokes	面積 MENSEKI	dimensions
			積雪 SEKISETSU	snow depth
			積もり TSUMORI	intention

禾 is **rice plant** 81. 責 is **blame** 728 q.v., here acting phonetically to express **gather/ accumulate** and possibly also lending its own similar connotations of **accumulate.** 521 originally referred to the **rice crop being gathered and heaped in a pile. Product** is an extended idea from **pile/ total.**

Mnemonic: **TAKE BLAME FOR PILE UP OF RICE PLANTS**

522
SETSU, ori, *oru/reru*
BEND, BREAK,
OCCASION
7 strokes

屈折 KUSSETSU   refraction
折り目 ORIME   fold, crease
折り紙 ORIGAMI   origami

扌 is **hand** 32. 斤 is **ax/chop** 1176. Usually explained as **'chopping'** with the hand, i.e. **bending** or **breaking**. In fact, while an old form 㪿 shows hand 屮, the earliest forms such as 㘇 show **two plants** 屮 9. Plant 屮 was occasionally used to mean **tree**, instead of the normal 木 69, and in fact 522 originally meant to **chop down trees**. However, the miscopying is of very long standing, and the original meaning has long since disappeared. It is not clear how 522 also came to mean **occasion** (Japanese only).

Mnemonic: **HAND-AX CAN BREAK OR BEND**

523
SETSU, SECHI, fushi
SECTION,JOINT,PERIOD,
POINT,TUNE,RESTRAIN
13 strokes

調節 CHŌSETSU   adjustment
関節 KANSETSU   joint
節穴 FUSHIANA   knothole

⺮ is **bamboo** 170. 即 is **namely** 1534 q.v., here acting phonetically to express **division** and also lending an idea of **order** (from seating order at a table). Thus **ordered division of bamboo**, a reference to (the **ordered arrangement of**) its **nodes and sections**. This gave rise to a wide range of extended meanings, including a **section of time** (**period**), a section of a song (originally a **stanza** or **verse**, now **tune**), and even the idea of keeping oneself in order (giving **restraint** and **integrity**).

Mnemonic: **BAMBOO HAS JOINTS, NAMELY SECTIONS**

524
SETSU, *toku*
PREACH, EXPLAIN
14 strokes

説明 SETSUMEI   explanation
小説 SHŌSETSU   novel
学説 GAKUSETSU   theory

言 is **words/speak** 274. 兑 is an NGU character meaning **exchange** or **barter** (or **issue** in Chinese), comprising **speaking person** 兄 267 and **away/out/disperse** 丷 66 and literally meaning a **person dispersing words**. Here 兑 means **issuing words**, and also acts phonetically to express **construct**. Thus **speak while issuing constructive words**, i.e. **preach** or **explain**. Suggest taking 兄 in its modern meaning of **elder brother**.

Mnemonic: **ELDER BROTHER DISPERSES WORDS, PREACHING AWAY**

525 SEN, asa*i*
SHALLOW, LIGHT
9 strokes

浅薄 SENPAKU shallowness
浅瀬 ASASE shallows
浅黄 ASAGI light yellow

Formerly 淺. 氵 is **water** 40. 戔 is **two halberds** 493, here acting phonetically to express **small (amount)** and also lending an idea of **cut away** and thereby **reduce**. Thus **water reduced to a small amount**, giving **shallow**. **Light** is an associated meaning.

Mnemonic: **WATER SHALLOW: DEPTH OF TWO HALBERDS**

526 SEN, tataka*u*, ikusa
FIGHT, WAR
13 strokes

大戦 TAISEN major war
戦場 SENJŌ battleground
作戦 SAKUSEN strategy

Formerly 戰, and originally just 戔, namely **two halberds** 493. In later times the halberds were reduced to one, while **simple** 單/单 542 q.v. was added in its literal sense of **forked thrusting weapon**. Thus **two (i.e. many) weapons**, indicating **fighting** and **war**.

Mnemonic: **FIGHT WAR WITH SIMPLE HALBERD**

527 SEN, era*bu*, yo*ru*
CHOOSE
15 strokes

当選 TŌSEN election
選手 SENSHU player
選び出す ERABIDASU pick out

Formerly 選. 辶 is **movement (along a road)** 129. 巽/巽 is somewhat obscure. It exists as a CO character with a current meaning of bland, while its core meaning appears to be **arrange in sequence**, giving rise to extended meanings such as follow and comply (hence bland). It appears to comprise **twisting threads** 乙 855 (or twisting serpents 巳 250), indicating a **line or sequence**, and **together** 共 460. Here it acts phonetically to express **follow** (after someone), and almost certainly lends similar connotations of its own. Thus 527 originally meant **follow someone along a road**. Some scholars see **choose** as being an extension of this, i.e. choosing a leader, while others see it as a borrowed meaning.

Mnemonic: **CHOOSE TO MOVE TOGETHER LIKE TWISTING THREADS**

528 然	ZEN, NEN, shikaru/shi DULY, THUS, SO, BUT 12 strokes	当然 TŌZEN 天然 TENNEN 然るべく SHIKARUBEKU	rightly nature duly

Fire ⺣ 8, meat 月 365, and dog 犬 17. 528 originally meant to **roast dog meat**, then came to mean **roast** or **burn** in a broad sense. It can still occasionally mean roast or burn in Chinese, but in Japanese this meaning has been entirely assumed by 燃 765, that adds an extra fire 火 8. It was later borrowed phonetically to express **thus/ duly/ as things should be** (**but** derives from an inflexion of this term [shikaru to shikashi], to the effect of **be that as it may**). It is not clear why such a complex character was chosen as a phonetic, but it is possible that 528 had connotations of **contentment**, and was thus considered appropriate to express **as things should be**.

Mnemonic: **DULY EAT ROAST DOG MEAT, BUT...**

529 争	SŌ, arasou CONFLICT, VIE 6 strokes	戦争 SENSŌ 言い争い IIARASOI 競争者 KYŌSŌSHA	war quarrel competitor

Formerly 爭, and earlier . This clearly shows a **hand reaching down** ⺥ 303 and another **hand** ⺕ holding an **item** /, for possession of which the hands are presumably vying. However, still older forms such as 𠬞 reveal that ⺤ is a miscopying of a **hand** ⺕ **seizing an arm** with bulging biceps 𠂆 (the prototype of strength 力 74). 529 originally meant to **take hold of someone** and **restrain** them, indicating a **conflict**. **Vie** is an associated meaning. Suggest taking 勹 as **bent person** 145, and 尹 as **hand holding stick**.

Mnemonic: **VIE WITH BENT OLD MAN, STICK IN HAND**

530 相	SŌ, SHŌ, ai- MUTUAL, MINISTER, ASPECT 9 strokes	相談 SŌDAN 相手 AITE 首相 SHUSHŌ	discussion other party Prime Minister

Somewhat obscure, though its elements are clearly **tree** 木 69 and **eye** 目 72. Most scholars assume it to refer to an eye watching from behind a tree, symbolising **cautious observation**. It still means **observe carefully** in Chinese. **Mutual** is taken by some scholars to be an associated meaning, since the observer might himself be under observation (as in two adversaries carefully weighing each other up). Others take it to be a borrowing. Similarly some scholars take **minister** to be an associated meaning from the idea of **examining** or **keeping alert**, as in the case of examine/ ministry 省 516 or keep alert/ public servant 臣 512, while others take it to be a borrowing. **Aspect**, in the sense of the **appearance of a situation**, appears to stem from **careful observation**.

Mnemonic: **MINISTERS EYE EACH OTHER FROM TREES**

163

531

SŌ, kura
WAREHOUSE, SUDDEN
10 strokes

船倉 SENSŌ   ship's hold
倉皇 SŌKŌ   bustle
倉荷 KURANI

warehouse goods

Formed from a **cover** 人 87, here indicating **preserving**, and 㐭. The latter is a now defunct character meaning **door** (comprising opening/ **entrance** 口 20 and a variant 尸 of **door** 戸 108). Thus **that which is covered and behind a door**, a reference to **goods in a storehouse**. Some scholars feel that 㐭 also lent its sound to express **smell**, being a reference to the smell of stored grain. The minor meaning **sudden** is assumed to be a borrowing, but may possibly relate to the idea of hurrying to put crops in storage.

Mnemonic: **WAREHOUSE HAS COVER AND DOORED ENTRANCE**

532

SŌ, SO
IDEA, THOUGHT
13 strokes

着想 CHAKUSŌ   concept
理想 RISŌ   ideal
愛想 AISO/AISŌ   affability

心 is **heart/ feelings** 147. 相 is **mutual** 530 q.v., here used for its literal meaning of **observe carefully** and by extension **examine**. Thus **examine carefully in one's heart**, i.e. **cogitate**.

Mnemonic: **THOUGHTS CAN BE MUTUAL FEELINGS**

533

ZŌ, SHŌ
ELEPHANT, IMAGE
12 strokes

象げ ZŌGE   ivory
印象 INSHŌ   impression
象徴的 SHŌCHŌTEKI symbolic

From a pictograph of an **elephant** 𧰨. The elephant has a dramatic **form**, and thus 533 also acquired connotations of **form, shape**, and **image**. By association it can also occasionally mean **resemble**. Suggest remembering by association with **pig** 豕 1670, perhaps taking 囝 as **two big ears** and 勹 as a curled **trunk**.

Mnemonic: **ELEPHANT RESEMBLES PIG WITH BIG EARS AND TRUNK**

164

534

SOKU, hayai, sumiyaka
SPEED, FAST
10 strokes

速記 SOKKI　　　　shorthand
時速 JISOKU　　speed per hour
高速道路 KŌSOKUDŌRO freeway

辶 is **movement** (along a road) 129. 束 is bundle/ **manage** 1535, acting phonetically to express **hurry** and also probably lending an idea of **control**. Thus **(controlled?) hurrying movement**.

Mnemonic: **MANAGE FAST MOVEMENT**

535

SOKU, kawa, gawa, soba
SIDE
11 strokes

側面 SOKUMEN　　side, flank
右側 MIGIGAWA　　right side
側仕え SOBAZUKAE　　valet

亻 is **person** 39. 則 is rule/ **model** 742. The role of the latter is disputed. Some scholars feel it acts phonetically to express **lean** and that 742 meant **leaning person**, i.e. a cripple, before coming to mean **leaning to one side** in general and hence **side**. Other scholars feel that 則 did express **lean**, but that this was used in the figurative sense of **tend /incline**, and that it also lent its own meaning of **model**. Thus a **person whom one looks upon as a model and towards whom one inclines**. One is always at the **side** of such a person.

Mnemonic: **BE AT SIDE OF MODEL PERSON**

---

536 続

ZOKU, tsuzuku/keru
CONTINUE, SERIES
13 strokes

続続 ZOKUZOKU successively
連続 RENZOKU　　continuity
手続き TETSUZUKI　　procedure

Formerly 續. 糸 is **thread** 27. 賣 / 売 is **sell** 192, here acting phonetically to express **join** and also lending an idea of **equivalence** (from the idea of exchanging goods for an equivalent amount of money). Thus to **join threads of equal length**, giving the idea of **continuity** and **succession**.

Mnemonic: **CONTINUE TO SELL THREADS**

537		SOTSU	卒業 SOTSUGYŌ	graduation
		SOLDIER, END	兵卒 HEISOTSU	soldier
		8 strokes	卒去 SOKKYO	death

Once written . 仒 is the early form of **clothing** 衣 420 q.v., with the lower stroke lengthened in order to accommodate ╱, a CO character meaning **dash** or **mark**. 537 originally referred to **marked clothing**, indicating a slave or, later, a **soldier**. The lesser meaning of **end** is borrowed. Suggest taking 亠 as a **top hat**, 从 as persons/ **men** 39, and 十 as **ten** 33.

Mnemonic: **TEN SOLDIER-MEN IN TOP HATS**

538		SON, mago	子孫 SHISON	descendants
		DESCENDANTS,	孫引き MAGOBIKI	requotation
		GRANDCHILDREN	孫娘 MAGOMUSUME	
		10 strokes		granddaughter

Originally 孖8, showing **child** 孑/子 25 and **short thread** 8/糸 111. The latter symbolised **very small**, giving **very small child**, a reference to **grandchildren**. **Descendants** is an associated meaning. The modern form uses **joined threads/ lineage** 系 844.

Mnemonic: **DESCENDANTS ARE CHILDREN IN THREAD-LIKE LINEAGE**

539	帯	TAI, obi, *obiru*	地帯 CHITAI	zone
		BELT, OBI, WEAR,	帯地 OBIJI	obi material
		ZONE	熱帯魚 NETTAIGYO	tropical fish
		10 strokes		

Formerly 帶, combining **cloth** 巾 778 and a pictograph of a **belt/ obi** with items attached to it 芈. Also used figuratively as a belt/ **zone** of land. Suggest remembering by association with **mountain** 山 24.

Mnemonic: **FIND CLOTH BELT IN MOUNTAIN ZONE**

---

540 **TAI**   兵隊 HEITAI   soldier
CORPS, UNIT   軍隊 GUNTAI   army
12 strokes   部隊 BUTAI   troop

Hill β 229 and (group of) **pigs moving** 㒸 1458 q.v. The latter acts phonetically to express **come down** and almost certainly also lends an idea of **moving in an ungainly fashion**. 540 originally meant **fall down a hill** (still retained as a minor meaning in Chinese). It is not fully clear how it came to acquire its present meaning. Some scholars feel it is purely the result of borrowing, but since hills were often associated with **troop encampments** there may be some loose semantic connection such as **commotion on a hillside** or similar.

Mnemonic: **UNIT OF PIG-LIKE SOLDIERS ON HILL**

---

541 **TATSU, -tachi**   発達 HATTATSU development
ATTAIN, PLURAL SUFFIX   達人 TATSUJIN   expert
12 strokes   人達 HITOTACHI   people

辶 is **movement** 129. 羍 was once written 羍, comprising **sheep** 羊 986 and **big** 大 53, and refers to the **ease** with which sheep are born and grow big (note that a different arrangement of the same elements big and sheep gives beautiful 美 376). Here 羍 acts phonetically to express **pass**, and also lends connotations of **ease**. Thus **easy movement**, indicating the **attainment of a goal** without difficulty. In Japanese it was later borrowed as a **plural suffix**, though the exact reason for this is not clear. In Chinese 541 can also be used to mean lamb. Suggest taking 土 as **ground** 60.

Mnemonic: **SHEEP MOVE ON GROUND TO ATTAIN GOAL**

---

542 **TAN**   単位 TANI   unit
SIMPLE, SINGLE, UNIT   単純 TANJUN na   simple
9 strokes   単独 TANDOKU   solo

Formerly 單 and in ancient times 單, showing a **forked thrusting weapon** Ψ (see also 825) with guard — and exaggerated binding ⊖. It was borrowed essentially phonetically to express **simple** -- with **single** and **unit** being associated meanings of this -- but as a primitive weapon may also have had its own connotations of simple. Suggest remembering by association with **ten** 十 33 and **field** 田 59.

Mnemonic: **SIMPLE UNIT OF TEN FIELDS**

167

| 543 | DAN
CONVERSATION, TALK
15 strokes | 相談役 SŌDANYAKU adviser
会談 KAIDAN conference
談話 DANWA conversation |

Words 言 274 and **leaping flames** 炎 1024, indicating a **spirited discussion**.

Mnemonic: **CONVERSATION OF FIERY WORDS**

| 544 | CHI, JI, osa*meru*, nao*su*
GOVERN, RULE, CURE
8 strokes | 政治 SEIJI politics
治安 CHIAN public order
治療 CHIRYŌ remedy |

Somewhat obscure. 氵 is **water** 40, while 台 is **platform/ self** 166. Some scholars feel that 544 originally referred to a certain river in ancient China and that its present meanings result from borrowing. Others feel that it meant to **bring water to oneself**, i.e. by irrigation, and that this symbolised **control** over the environment, with its present meanings being extensions of control.

Mnemonic: **GOVERN FROM A WATERY PLATFORM**

| 545 | CHI, o*ku*
PUT, PLACE
13 strokes | 放置 HŌCHI leaving as is
置き物 OKIMONO ornament
置き場 OKIBA repository |

罒 is **net** 193. 直 is **direct** 349, here acting phonetically to express erect/ **set up** and also lending connotations of **directly**. Thus to **set up a net directly** (in something's path), leading to **put in place**.

Mnemonic: **PUT NET DIRECTLY IN PATH**

| 546 | CHO, takuwa*eru*
STORE, SAVE
12 strokes | 貯金 CHOKIN savings
貯蔵 CHOZŌ storage
貯水池 CHOSUICHI reservoir |

Once written 宁, showing a frame for **storing** yarn (now simplified to 宁). Shell/ **money** 貝 90 was added later to give the idea of **storing assets/ wealth**. Suggest taking 宀 as **roof** 28 and 丁 as **exactly** 346.

Mnemonic: **STORED WEALTH FITS EXACTLY UNDER ROOF**

| 547 | | CHŌ, harawata
INTESTINE(S)
13 strokes | 腸線 CHŌSEN
腸炎 CHŌEN
大腸 DAICHŌ | (cat) gut
enteritis
large intestine |

月 is **flesh/ of the body** 365. 昜 is **rising sun** 144, here acting phonetically to express **long** and probably also lending an extended idea of path/ **passage** (i.e. the course of the sun). Thus **long passage in the body**. Note that long itself, 長 173, combines with 昜 to give distend 脹 1593.

Mnemonic: **FLESHY INTESTINES EXPOSED TO RISING SUN**

| 548 | | TEI, hikui
LOW
7 strokes | 最低 SAITEI
低利 TEIRI
低落 TEIRAKU | lowest
low interest
decline |

亻 is **person** 39. 氐 is **bottom of a hill**, comprising **scoop/ hill** 氏 495 q.v. and a **base line** —. Thus **people at bottom of hill**, i.e. **lowly** commoners as opposed to the nobles who lived on top of the hill (see 99). Lowly person later came to mean **low position** and then **low** in general.

Mnemonic: **PERSON SCOOPS LOW, DOWN TO BASE LINE**

| 549 | | TEI, soko
BOTTOM, BASE
8 strokes | 海底 KAITEI
奥底 OKUSOKO
底流 TEIRYŪ | seabed
depths
undercurrent |

广 is **building** 114, and 氐 is **bottom of hill** 548. Thus **building at bottom of hill**, later **bottom** or **base** in general. Suggest taking 氐 literally as hill/ **scoop** 氏 495 and a **base** —.

Mnemonic: **SCOOP OUT BASE OF BUILDING**

| 550 | | TEI
STOP
11 strokes | 停止 TEISHI
停車所 TEISHAJO
停電 TEIDEN | stoppage
station
power cut |

Person 亻 39 and **inn** 亭 1614, giving **inn where person stays** and eventually **stay/ stop** in general.

Mnemonic: **PERSON STOPS AT INN**

551

TEKI, mato
TARGET, -LIKE,
ADJECTIVAL SUFFIX
8 strokes

目的 MOKUTEKI　　　purpose
理想的 RISŌTEKI　　　ideal
的外れ MATOHAZURE
　　　　　　　　off the mark

White 白 65, here meaning **conspicuous**, and **ladle/ scoop** 勺 1342, here meaning **select** and by extension **set apart**. Thus **something conspicuous and set apart**, i.e. a **target**. (Some old forms such as 日勺 show sun/bright 日 62 instead of white 白, but the meaning of conspicuous is unaffected.) Setting something apart also gave rise to the idea of **classification**, which in turn gave rise to **likeness**. The idea of **-like** became a common way of forming adjectives.

Mnemonic: **WHITE LADLE MAKES GOOD TARGET**

552

TEN, nori
CODE, RULE,
PRECEDENT
8 strokes

辞典 JITEN　　　　dictionary
典拠 TENKYO　　　authority
典型 TENKEI　　type, model

Originally 興. 卌 is the prototype of **books** 冊 874 q.v., namely a collection of writing tablets bound together, while 丌 is a table/ **desk**. Thus **collection of written material on a desk**, i.e. reference material, leading to **codex, code, law** etc. Suggest remembering by association with **bend** 曲 261 and **six** 六 76.

Mnemonic: **BEND SIX RULES**

553

DEN, tsutaeru/waru
CONVEY, TRANSMIT
6 strokes

伝説 DENSETSU　　　legend
伝記 DENKI　　　biography
伝染病 DENSENBYŌ
　　　　　contagious disease

Formerly 傳. 亻 is **person** 39. 專 is the old form of **exclusive** 専 914 q.v., here used for its literal meaning of spinning weight to give an idea of **rotating**. Thus **to rotate amongst people**, i.e. **convey** or **transmit**. Suggest taking 云 as **two** 二 61 and **nose** 厶 134.

Mnemonic: **TWO PEOPLE NOSE TO NOSE CONVEYING SOMETHING**

554		TO, ada, itazura FOLLOWER, FUTILITY 10 strokes	生徒 SEITO	pupil
			徒歩者 TOHOSHA	pedestrian
			徒花 ADABANA	wasted effort

Usually explained as **movement along a road** 彳 118 and **run** 走 161 q.v., giving **run along a road** and by extension **pursue** and **follow**. A useful mnemonic, but old forms such as ⻌走 show that 走 is not run but literally **foot** 止 129 and **ground** 土 60. 554 originally meant **someone who went on foot**, especially foot soldiers (still a meaning in Chinese) but also crowds and **followers**. Follower later came to prevail as the main meaning. It is not clear how 554 also came to mean **futility**, though it may be an idea associated with the difficulty of traveling on foot (as opposed to horseback).

Mnemonic: **FOLLOWER RUNS FUTILELY ALONG ROAD**

555		DO, tsutomeru ENDEAVOR, TRY 7 strokes	努力 DORYOKU	effort
			努力家 DORYOKUKA	'worker'
			努めて TSUTOMETE	
				to best of one's ability

Strength/ **effort** 力 74 and **slave** 奴 1638, giving **work like a slave**, i.e. **try hard**.

Mnemonic: **TRY WITH SLAVE-LIKE EFFORT**

556		TŌ, hi LIGHT, LAMP 6 strokes	灯台 TŌDAI	lighthouse
			電灯 DENTŌ	electric light
			灯船 TŌSEN	lightship

Formerly 燈. 火 is **fire** 8. 登 is **climb** 360 q.v., here with its literal meaning of **atop a pedestal**. Thus fire atop a pedestal, i.e. a **beacon** or **lamp**. **Exactly** 丁 346 was used partly as a graphic simplification and partly for its stand-like shape.

Mnemonic: **LAMP'S FLAME IS EXACT**

557	堂	DŌ HALL, TEMPLE 11 strokes	講堂 KŌDŌ	auditorium
			食堂 SHOKUDŌ	dining hall
			堂堂 DŌDŌ	grandly, fairly

Furthermore 尚 1392 q.v., here with its original meaning of **tall building** (with window), and **ground** 土 60, here meaning **mound**. Thus **tall building on raised ground**, indicating an important and stately building.

Mnemonic: **FURTHERMORE, HALL IS ON RAISED GROUND**

558 　　DŌ, hata*raku*　　労働　RŌDŌ　　　　　labor
WORK　　　　　働き手　HATARAKITE　worker
13 strokes　　　働き者　HATARAKIMONO
　　　　　　　　　　　　　　　　　hard worker

A 'made in Japan' character, though it is now also used in Chinese, ideographically combining **person** 亻 39 and **move** 動 362 to express the idea of **being busy** and **working**.

Mnemonic: **WORKING PEOPLE ON THE MOVE**

559 　　DOKU　　　　　有毒　YŪDOKU na　　poisonous
POISON　　　　気の毒　KINODOKU　　　sorry
8 strokes　　食中毒　SHOKUCHŪDOKU
　　　　　　　　　　　　　　　　food poisoning

Somewhat obscure. 主 is generally seen as a simplification of **growing plant/ life** 生 42, and 毋 as **mother** 203. It is not fully clear how these elements differ from the similar elements of **every** 毎 206 q.v. Some scholars feel that 毋 acts phonetically to express **harm**, giving either **harmful to life** or **harmful plant** depending on the semantic role ascribed to 主. However, it would seem unlikely that the character for mother, with such benign and life-giving connotations, would be borrowed for such a negative phonetic role, and perhaps more likely that 559 originally meant **life-giving plant**, then **powerful herb/drug**, then somehow acquired the sinister connotations of **drug able to control/ take away life**.

Mnemonic: **MOTHER LIVES ON, DESPITE POISON**

560 　　NETSU, *atsui*　　熱心　NESSHIN　　　　fervor
HEAT　　　　　　熱帯　NETTAI　　　　tropics
15 strokes　　　熱力学　NETSURIKIGAKU
　　　　　　　　　　　　　　　　thermodynamics

.... is **fire** 8. 埶 is person bending to plant tree 470 q.v., here meaning by association **person kneeling holding a stick**, as in early methods of making fire. According to some scholars 埶 also acts phonetically to express **rising heat**. Suggest remembering by association with **round** 丸 830 and **mound of earth** 坴 597.

Mnemonic: **EARTHEN MOUNDS ROUND FIRE BECOME HOT**

172

561		NEN	念力 NENRIKI	will
		THOUGHT, CONCERN	念入り NENIRI na	careful
		8 strokes	念仏 NENBUTSU	
				Buddhist prayer

心 is **heart/ feelings** 147. 今 is **now** 125 q.v., here used in its early sense of **cover/ hide** and also acting phonetically to express **firmly possess**. Thus **something firmly possessed and hidden in the heart**, such as a religious conviction or similar. It has now broadened to mean **profound thought**, and in Chinese can also mean remember.

Mnemonic: **HAVE THOUGHTS IN HEART EVEN NOW**

562		HAI, yabu*reru*	敗戦 HAISEN	lost fight
		DEFEAT	敗走 HAISŌ	rout
		11 strokes	敗北主義 HAIBOKUSHUGI	
				defeatism

貝 is **shell/money** 90, here meaning **asset** or property. 攵 is **striking hand** 101, here meaning **attack and damage**. Thus to **attack and damage someone's assets**, meaning to **defeat/ destroy**. It has now generally come to be used in the passive sense of **be defeated.**

Mnemonic: **SHELL 'DEFEATED' BY STRIKING HAND**

563		BAI	五倍 GOBAI	five-fold
		DOUBLE, -FOLD	倍加 BAIKA	doubling
		10 strokes	倍数 BAISŪ	multiple

亻 is **person** 39. 音 is the obscure element **spit** 384 q.v., here acting phonetically to express **turn against** and probably also lending an idea of **division** and/or **rejection**. 563 originally referred to two persons turning their back on each other. This came to symbolise **division into two**, and by extension the idea of a mathematical **multiple**. Suggest taking 音 as **stand** 立 73 and **open mouth** 口 20.

Mnemonic: **PERSON STANDS OPEN MOUTHED WITH DOUBLE**

564

HAKU, BAKU
EXTENSIVE, SPREAD,
GAIN, GAMBLE
12 strokes

博士 HAKASE*   Ph.D.
博徒 BAKUTO   gambler
博物館 HAKUBUTSUKAN
                 museum

Though confusingly similar to **exclusive** 専 914, 尃 is a different element. It can also be written 尃, and as such is a CO character meaning **spread** (interchangeable with spread 敷/敷 1756). It comprises (**crude**) **start** 甫 970 q.v. and **measure/hand** 寸 909, a crude start to measuring being to **spread** the fingers of the hand. 尃 also acts phonetically to express **big/ extensive**. 十 is **ten** 33, here used to mean **numerous** and also lending connotations of **acquire** from its associations with the fingers of both hands and thus to **pick up** (see ten/ gather 拾 305). Thus the overall idea of **spreading and making numerous/ extensive gains**, with **gamble** being an associated meaning. Suggest using **exclusive** 専 as a mnemonic, taking the extra stroke ﹀ as a **point**.

Mnemonic: **GAIN TEN EXCLUSIVE POINTS BY EXTENSIVE GAMBLING**

565

HAN, meshi
COOKED RICE, FOOD
12 strokes

御飯 GOHAN   rice, food
昼飯 HIRUMESHI   lunch
飯田 IIDA*   a surname

食 is **food/ eat** 146. 反 is **oppose** 371 q.v., here acting phonetically to express **eat** and almost certainly also lending its literal meaning of **turn the hand over**. Thus to **eat food** (turning the hand over in so doing). It can still mean eat in Chinese, but has generally come to refer to the **food** being eaten (especially **rice**) rather than the act of eating.

Mnemonic: **OPPOSED TO EATING COOKED RICE**

566

HI, tobu
FLY
9 strokes

飛行機 HIKŌKI   airplane
飛語 HIGO   wild rumor
飛び出す TOBIDASU   jump out

Once written 飛, showing a **long-necked crane with spread wings**, soaring upwards in **flight**. Suggest taking as **two 'streamlined' cranes** with particularly slim bodies and **long beaks** 飞 skimming low through tall **reeds** 刂.

Mnemonic: **TWO LONG BEAKED CRANES FLY THROUGH TALL REEDS**

567		**HI, tsui***yasu* **SPEND** 12 strokes	費用 HIYŌ costs 消費者 SHŌHISHA consumer 生活費 SEIKATSUHI cost of living

貝 is shell/ **money** 90. 弗 is a CO character meaning **not**. It shows **binding** 弓 (see 177) being **undone** ノ乀 (see 66), and originally meant undo/ remove/ **disperse**. Thus to **disperse money until none is left**, i.e. **spend** (heavily).

Mnemonic: **UNWIND AND SPEND MONEY**

568		**HITSU, kanara***zu* **NECESSARILY** 5 strokes	必要 HITSUYŌ need 必死 HISSHI no desperate 必然 HITSUZEN no inevitable

Once written 戍, showing a **halberd/ lance** 戈 493 between **two poles**)|. The poles were strapped to the lance to prevent the possibility of the latter's breakage while not in use. It is not fully clear how this came to mean **necessarily**, but some scholars feel that the idea of keeping something **safe and secure** led to the idea of **sureness**, with this eventually leading to **surely** and hence by association **necessarily**. Suggest remembering by association with **heart** 心 147, taking ノ as a **bent lance**.

Mnemonic: **LANCE THROUGH HEART IS NECESSARILY BENT**

569		**HITSU, fude** **WRITING BRUSH** 12 strokes	鉛筆 ENPITSU pencil 筆者 HISSHA writer 筆使い FUDEZUKAI penmanship

Bamboo 竹 170 and **brush in hand** 聿 142. Originally bamboo writing brush.

Mnemonic: **TAKE BAMBOO WRITING BRUSH IN HAND**

570		**HYŌ** **VOTE, LABEL, SIGN** 11 strokes	票決 HYŌKETSU vote 投票 TŌHYŌ voting 伝票 DENPYŌ chit, slip

Once written 燹. 火 is **flames/ fire** 8. 囟 is often taken to be a variant of waist 腰 593 (literally hands 乚⺕ 'gathering in' a backbone 夂), but it seems more likely that 囟 is brain/ head 131 and that 囟 therefore means **neck** rather than waist. Here it acts phonetically to express **leap** and probably also lends an idea of **upper tapered part**. Thus **leaping (tongues of?) flame**. 570 was later used as a simpler substitute for **mark/ sign** 標 571 q.v., and by association also came to acquire connotations of **vote**. Suggest taking as **west** 西 152 and **show** 示 695.

Mnemonic: **VOTE SHOWS WEST IS BEST**

| 571 | | HYŌ, shirushi
SIGN(POST), MARK
15 strokes | 標準 HYŌJUN
里程標 RITEIHYŌ
標識 HYŌSHIKI | standard
milestone
signal |

木 is **tree** 69. 票 is **sign** 570 q.v., here acting phonetically to express **tip** and almost certainly lending an idea of **upper tapered part**. Thus the **tip of a (particularly tall) tree**, which by extension came to mean **landmark** and then **mark** or **sign** in general. Suggest taking 票 as **west** 西 152 and **show** 示 695.

Mnemonic: **TREE IS A SIGNPOST SHOWING WEST**

| 572 | | FU, BU
NOT, UN-, DIS-
4 strokes | 不明 FUMEI na
不平 FUHEI
不気味 BUKIMI na | unclear
complaint
weird |

Originally 夭 (later 朩), showing a **calyx** (**bud** ▽ surrounded by a **whorl of leaves** 朩). It was later borrowed purely for its sound FU, this being a sound of **denial** and **negation** (cf. English Huh, Phooey etc.). Suggest remembering as **one** 一 1 and **three down**-strokes 朩.

Mnemonic: **PUT DOWN ONCE, THEN THRICE, FOR EMPHATIC 'NOT SO'**

| 573 | | FU, FŪ, otto
HUSBAND, MAN
4 strokes | 人夫 NINPU
夫人 FUJIN
夫婦 FŪFU | laborer
wife, Mrs -
married couple |

Originally 夫 , showing a **big (i.e. adult) male** 大 53 with an ornamental **hairpin** 一 through his hair (a sign of **adulthood** in ancient China).

Mnemonic: **BIG MAN WITH PIN THROUGH HEAD IS GOOD HUSBAND**

| 574 | 付 | FU, tsuku/keru
ATTACH, APPLY
5 strokes | 付着 FUCHAKU
付き合う TSUKIAU
名付ける NAZUKERU | adhesion
associate
name, call |

Originally 仅, showing **person** 亻 39 and a **hand** reaching out holding something 又. The original meaning was to **reach out and give something to someone**. The idea of **give to** later came by association to mean **add to** or **attach**. Later forms use **hand/measure** 寸 909, which appears to be a miscopying.

Mnemonic: **HAND ATTACHES MEASURE TO PERSON**

575

FU
GOVERNMENT CENTER,
URBAN PREFECTURE
8 strokes

政府 SEIFU   government
府県 FUKEN   prefectures
京都府 KYŌTOFU
         Kyoto Prefecture

广 is **large building** 114. 付 is **attach** 574 q.v. The original meaning of 575 was **storehouse** (still retained in Chinese). Some scholars argue that this meaning stems from **that attached to a large building**, i.e. an annex and by extension storehouse, others that it stems from **large building for that attached to one**, i.e. one's belongings. Some also feel that 付 acts phonetically to express **accumulate**. The present meanings are felt to derive from the extended idea of **large building belonging to the government** (though there is no specific element referring to government: see also 273), and hence eventually just **attached/ belonging to the government** (including an **administrative district**).

Mnemonic: **LARGE BUILDING ATTACHED TO GOVERNMENT CENTER**

---

576 副

FUKU
DEPUTY, VICE-, SUB-
11 strokes

副業 FUKUGYŌ   side-job
副詞 FUKUSHI   adverb
副領事 FUKURYŌJI vice-consul

刂 is **sword/ cut** 181. 畐 is **full** 386, used phonetically to express **cut open** and probably also lending an idea of **wide open** from its original meaning of wide-lipped jar. Thus to **cut wide open/ split**. Splitting led to the idea of **duplicating** (i.e. making one large item into two smaller parts similar to each other), which by association led to **substituting** and hence the present meanings. Suggest taking 畐 as **single** 一 1 **entrance** 口 20 to **field** 田 59.

Mnemonic: **DEPUTY CUT DOWN AT SINGLE ENTRANCE TO FIELD**

577

FUN, kona, ko
POWDER
10 strokes

花粉 KAFUN   pollen
粉粉 KONAGONA fragments
麦粉 MUGIKO   wheat flour

Rice 米 201 and **divide/ cut into minute pieces** 分 199. Originally **reduce rice to powder**, now **powder** in a wider sense. Still occasionally used to mean **fragments**.

Mnemonic: **MINUTELY DIVIDED RICE BECOMES POWDER**

578		**HEI, HYŌ**	兵士	HEISHI	soldier
		SOLDIER	歩兵	HOHEI	infantry
		7 strokes	兵器	HEIKI	weapon

Originally 𠬛, showing an **ax** ⼍ / 斤 1176 being held with **both hands** 𠂇 and indicating a **fighting man**. Suggest taking 丌 as a **table**.

Mnemonic: **SOLDIER PUTS AX ON TABLE**

579		**BETSU, waka*reru***	別名	BETSUMEI	alias
		DIVERGE, SPLIT,	特別	TOKUBETSU	special
		DIFFER, SPECIAL	別れ	WAKARE	parting
		7 strokes			

Once written 㕕. 刀/刂 is sword/ **cut** 181. 冎/咼 is a variant of **bone** 冎 867. Thus to **cut through a bone**, leading to **chop up** and **divide** in a broad sense. **Differ** and **diverge** are extended meanings, while **special** is an associated meaning (i.e. something set apart). Suggest taking 号 as **mouth** 口 20 with 勹 as a variant of **cut** 刀 181.

Mnemonic: **TWO CUTS TO THE MOUTH MEAN SPLIT LIP**

580		**HEN, ata*ri*, be**	辺境	HENKYŌ	frontier
		VICINITY, BOUNDARY	近辺	KINPEN	vicinity
		5 strokes	川辺	KAWABE	riverside

Formerly 邊. ⻌ is **movement** 129. 臱 is an element meaning **blind** (of unclear etymology, but apparently comprising nose/self 自 134, hole 穴 849, and direction 方 204, and presumably having a meaning such as heading blindly into a trap/hole). 臱 is used here phonetically to express edge/ **boundary**, and almost certainly lends an idea of **with uncertainty**. Thus to **move with uncertainty along a boundary**, i.e. reach the limits of known territory. Boundary came by association to mean **that included within**, i.e. **general area**. This in turn came to mean **vicinity**, which, like the English term, can also be used of approximation. Suggest taking the modern form 刀 as sword/ **cut** 181.

Mnemonic: **MOVEMENT CUTS THROUGH BOUNDARY**

581 変 **HEN, ka*eru*/*waru*** 変成 HENSEI metamorphosis
CHANGE, STRANGE 大変 TAIHEN very
9 strokes 変わり者 KAWARIMONO eccentric

Formerly 變, showing that 夂 is not stop and start 夂 438 but a variant of **striking hand/ coerce** 攵 101. 䜌 is a CO character meaning **tied together** (threads 糸 27 put together like words 言 274), and acts phonetically to express **reverse** as well as lending an idea of **complicated**. Thus to **coerce someone into reversing something complicated**. This became **cause to change** in a wider sense, and eventually the causative aspect faded to leave just **change**. Suggest taking 亦 as a 'sort of' variant of **red** 赤 46. Suggest taking 夂 as **sitting crosslegged**.

Mnemonic: **CHANGE TO A SORT OF RED AS ONE SITS CROSSLEGGED**

582 便 **BEN, BIN, tayo*ri*** 便利 BENRI na convenient
CONVENIENCE, 便所 BENJO toilet
SERVICE, MAIL 郵便 YŪBIN mail
9 strokes

亻 is **person/man** 39. 更 is **change** 1248, here acting phonetically to express **servant** and also lending an idea of **bring about a result.** 582 originally meant **efficient servant**, but later came to mean **service** and hence **convenience**. As with the English term convenience, it also has euphemistic associations with bodily waste. **Mail** is an associated idea from service/ servant.

Mnemonic: **CHANGE OF MAIL MAN LEADS TO CONVENIENT SERVICE**

583 包 **HŌ, tsutsu*mu*** 小包み KOZUTSUMI parcel
WRAP, ENVELOP 包囲 HŌI encircle
5 strokes 包み紙 TSUTSUMIGAMI wrapping paper

Formerly 包, and originally 㔾. 勹 is a **womb** 655, while 巳, though having the same shape as **serpent** 巳 / 巳 250, is a human **embryo**. The idea of carrying a child in the womb broadened to **envelop** in a general sense.

Mnemonic: **SERPENT-LIKE EMBRYO ENVELOPED IN WOMB**

584 HŌ, HATSU
LAW
8 strokes

法学 HŌGAKU jurisprudence
文法 BUNPŌ grammar
不法 FUHŌ illegal

シ is **water** 40. 去 is **leave** 258 q.v., here used in its early sense of **tight-lidded container** and also acting phonetically to express **envelop/ hold securely**. Thus a **tight-lidded leak-proof container holding water**. This was later applied figuratively to the **law**, which similarly **contains/ constrains** human behavior.

Mnemonic: **CONSTRAINED BY LAW TO LEAVE WATER**

585 BŌ, MŌ, nozom*u*
WISH, HOPE, GAZE
11 strokes

失望 SHITSUBŌ despair
願望 GANMŌ/GANBŌ wish
望見 BŌKEN watch from afar

Once written 望 , showing a **person** ⼈ 39 standing on the **ground** 土 60 **gazing with wide open eyes** 臣 512 at the **moon** 夕 / 月 16. Rather like the English terms staring into space or wishing on a star this symbolised **wishful thinking**, though it can also be used literally as **gaze**. Suggest taking 亡 as **death** 973 and 王 as **king** 5.

Mnemonic: **KING GAZES AT MOON, WISHING FOR DEATH**

586 BOKU, maki
PASTURE
8 strokes

牧場 BOKUJŌ pasture
放牧 HŌBOKU grazing
牧場鳥 MAKIBATORI meadowlark

Cow 牛 97 and **strike with stick** 攵 101, a reference to **herding cattle** and by association **grazing ground/ pasture**.

Mnemonic: **HAND WITH STICK MAKES COW GO INTO PASTURE**

587 MATSU, BATSU, sue
END, TIP
5 strokes

週末 SHŪMATSU weekend
末つ子 SUEKKO* youngest child
世紀末 SEIKIMATSU fin de siecle

Originally the same character as **immature** 未 794 q.v., with both deriving from a pictograph showing the **top of a tree** 末 (**tree** 木 69 with an additional cross-stroke 一 indicating the **topmost branches**). Whereas the short cross-stroke in 794 came to indicate fresh/young growth, the fuller cross-stroke of 587 came to indicate the **treetop** proper, and by extension **extremity** or **tip**. There is still some overlap between the two characters.

Mnemonic: **TIP OF TREE**

588 MAN, michiru/tasu
FULL, FILL
12 strokes

満月 MANGETSU full moon
満足 MANZOKU satisfaction
満潮 MANCHŌ/ MICHISHIO
full tide

Formerly 滿 . シ is **water** 40. 㒼 is known to have meant **join both halves of a gourd**, with 兩/両 clearly being **both** (halves of a gourd) 両 411 and 卝 assumed to be a symbol of **joining** (though the latter is somewhat unclear). 㒼 also acts phonetically to express **full/ overflowing**. Thus a **gourd full of water to the point of overflowing**. Suggest taking 卝 as **grass** 9.

Mnemonic: **BOTH GRASS AND WATER CAN BE FILLING**

589 MYAKU
VEIN, PULSE
10 strokes

脈管 MYAKKAN blood vessel
鉱脈 KŌMYAKU ore-vein
山脈 SANMYAKU
mountain range

Formerly also 脉 . 月 is **flesh/ of the body** 365. 永/ 𠂢 derives from a depiction of a **tributary** 𣲘 (see also 955 and 615). Thus **tributaries of the body**, i.e. **veins**. **Pulse** is an associated meaning. As in English, vein is also used figuratively to mean branch or line.

Mnemonic: **VEINS ARE TRIBUTARIES OF THE BODY**

590 MIN, tami
PEOPLE, POPULACE
5 strokes

国民 KOKUMIN nation
民間 MINKAN no private
民主主義 MINSHUSHUGI
democracy

Somewhat obscure. Once written 𠃉 . 十/七 is **needle** 十 33, but there is some difference of opinion as to whether 𠃋 is a **handle**, making 𠃉 a pictograph of a **gimlet** (i.e. needle with handle), or a variant of **eye** 𠕋 / 目 72, making 𠃉 an ideograph meaning **blind** (i.e. needle in the eye). Scholars of the latter view feel that blinded person symbolised **slave** (blinding being a common punishment), which later came to mean **lowly people** or **commoners** in general. Scholars of the former view feel that 590 was borrowed as a simple substitute for a more complex character meaning **outcast**, with outcast then coming to mean lowly people or commoners. 590 is unconnected with the graphically similar **clan** 氏 495 q.v. (though it is remotely possible that there was some mutual influence in the graphic evolution of the modern forms, especially of 495 upon 590), but it may be useful to take 590 as a more 'substantial' version of 495.

Mnemonic: **POPULACE IS MORE SUBSTANTIAL THAN CLAN**

591

YAKU 約束 YAKUSOKU promise
PROMISE, SUMMARIZE, 節約 SETSUYAKU economise
APPROXIMATELY 約五十人 YAKUGOJŪNIN
9 strokes about fifty people

Formerly also 約 . 糸 is **thread** 27. 勺/勹 is **ladle/** measure 1342, here used phonetically to express **tie tightly**. Thus to **tie threads tightly (into a knot)**. On the one hand this came by figurative association to be applied to **binding agreements**, and on the other to mean **tighten up** in the sense of remove non-essential elements, i.e. **summarize**. By further association summary/ gist led to **approximation**.

Mnemonic: **KNOTTED THREAD REMINDS OF PROMISE ABOUT LADLE**

592

YŪ, isa*mu/mashii* 勇者 YŪSHA hero
BRAVE, SPIRITED 勇気 YŪKI courage
9 strokes 勇み足 ISAMIASHI rashness

Once written 勈, showing **break through/ emerge** 甬/甬 176 and **strength** 勿/力 74, and expressing the idea of having enough determination to succeed. The modern form, which uses 甬 instead of 甬, may have been influenced by **man** 男 54. Suggest using this as a mnemonic, taking マ as a **bent figure** (see 176), i.e. bent with age.

Mnemonic: **OLD MAN BENT WITH AGE BUT STILL BRAVE**

593

YŌ, *iru*, kaname 不必要 FUHITSUYŌ unnecessary
NEED, VITAL, PIVOT 要点 YŌTEN gist
9 strokes 重要 JŪYŌ important

Originally 要, showing **hands** 臼 holding in a **waist** 8 (some scholars see this as a waist itself, others as a backbone), with 八 being **legs**. **Woman** 女 35 later replaced legs to emphasise the focus on the **waist**, which was the original meaning of 593. Waist then came by association to mean **middle part**, leading to **pivot** and the idea of **being essential**. Waist itself is now conveyed by 腰 1879, a character that adds flesh/ of the body 月 365. Suggest taking 西 as **west** 152.

Mnemonic: **EVERY WESTERN HAS VITAL NEED FOR WOMAN IN IT**

594

YŌ, yashinau
REAR, SUPPORT
15 strokes

養成 YŌSEI — training
栄養士 EIYŌSHI — dietitian
教養 KYŌYŌ — culture

Sheep 芏 986 and food/ eat 食 146. Originally to **rear sheep for food**, now **rear** in a broader sense.

Mnemonic: **REAR SHEEP FOR FOOD**

595

YOKU, abiru
BATHE
10 strokes

浴室 YOKUSHITSU bathroom
日光浴 NIKKŌYOKU sunbathing
水浴び MIZUABI — bathing

氵 is **water** 40. 谷 is **valley** 122 q.v., here acting phonetically to express **spray** and also lending an idea of **cleave open**. Thus to **cleave open water and send up spray**, as in plunging into a river in order to **bathe**.

Mnemonic: **VALLEY WATER IS GOOD FOR BATHING**

596

RI, kiku
PROFIT, GAIN, EFFECT
7 strokes

利益 RIEKI — profit, gain
利用 RIYŌ — utilisation
利き目 KIKIME — efficacy

Rice plant 禾 81 and sword/ cut 刂 181. The idea of **reaping the harvest** led to **profit** and **gain** on the one hand, and on the other to the idea of cutting the plants with the sharpest and thus most **effective** tool possible (presumably to maximise gain).

Mnemonic: **EFFECTIVE SHARP TOOL CUTS RICE FOR PROFIT**

597

RIKU
LAND
11 strokes

陸軍 RIKUGUN — army
上陸 JŌRIKU — landing
大陸 TAIRIKU — continent

阝 is **hill** 229. 坴 is a CO character meaning **mound(s) of earth/ hill(s)**. It was originally written 坴, showing **earth** 土 60 piled up like **houses** 夼 (see 76), and later 坴 and finally 坴. Thus 597 means **numerous hills**, i.e. **land** as opposed to sea.

Mnemonic: **HILLS AND EARTHEN MOUNDS INDICATE LAND**

---

598 良 **RYŌ, yo*i***
GOOD
7 strokes

良心	RYŌSHIN	conscience
改良	KAIRYŌ	improvement
良さ	YOSA	worth, quality

Once written , showing a **sieve** into which material was **poured** and from which **sifted** material **flowed** . Sifting led by association to **selecting the good.** Suggest remembering the modern form as **eat/ food** 食 146 without the **lid** 亼.

Mnemonic: **TAKE LID OFF FOOD -- LOOKS GOOD**

---

599 料 **RYŌ**
MATERIALS, MEASURE, CHARGE
10 strokes

原料	GENRYŌ	raw material
料金	RYŌKIN	charge, fee
料理	RYŌRI	cooking

Rice 米 201 and **measure** 斗 1633, and originally meaning **measure rice.** In that regard it is similar to measure 科 81 q.v., but whereas 81 came to connote sorting, 599 generally came to connote rather the **substance** itself, as well as the **quantity**. **Charge** is felt to be an associated meaning, from the idea of apportionment.

Mnemonic: **MEASURE OF RICE HAS FIXED CHARGE**

---

600 量 **RYŌ, haka*ru***
MEASURE, QUANTITY
12 strokes

重量	JŪRYŌ	weight
分量	BUNRYŌ	quantity
大量生産	TAIRYŌSEISAN	mass production

Once written . is the prototype of heavy /重 311 q.v., but minus person 人 to leave just **heavy sack on the ground** . is a vessel full of something 一, reinforcing . Thus a **heavy (i.e. full) sack of something left on the ground,** indicating a **completed measure** or **quantity**. Suggest taking as **village** 里 219, **one** 一 1, and **day** 日 62.

Mnemonic: **VILLAGE GETS MEASURED QUANTITY, FOR ONE DAY**

---

601 輪 **RIN, wa**
WHEEL, HOOP
15 strokes

車輪	SHARIN	vehicle wheel
三輪車	SANRINSHA	tricycle
輪投げ	WANAGE	quoits

車 is **vehicle** 31. 侖 is a CO character meaning **arrange/ align neatly,** and derives from a bundle of bamboo tablets bound together and stacked on end 冊 874, **capped** with a lid 亼 121 to indicate being neatly finished off. It also acts here phonetically to express **roll.** Thus **aligned rolling parts of a vehicle,** i.e. the **wheels.**

Mnemonic: **VEHICLE HAS ALIGNED AND CAPPED WHEELS**

602 RUI
RESEMBLE, VARIETY,
SORT
18 strokes

種類 SHURUI   sort, kind
分類 BUNRUI   classification
類似 RUIJI   resemblance

Formerly 類, clearly showing **rice** 米 201, **dog** 犬 17, and **head** 頁 93. Rice and head once formed a now defunct character 頪, meaning **close resemblance** (i.e. as heads of rice). This was then borrowed -- largely for its sound but also for its meaning of resemble -- and combined with dog 犬 to give 類, which originally referred to a mythical raccoon-like creature (a meaning still occasionally found in Chinese). Somewhat unusually, 類 replaced the simpler character 頪, acquiring the latter's meaning of **resemble**. **Variety** and **sort** are associated meanings. The modern form uses **big** 大 53 as a simplification of dog 犬.

Mnemonic: **VARIETY OF RICE WITH BIG HEAD**

---

603 REI, RYŌ
ORDER, RULE
5 strokes

令状 REIJŌ   warrant
命令法 MEIREIHŌ   imperative
司令官 SHIREIKAN commander

Also 令, and originally 亼. 𠆢 is a **kneeling person** 39 (see also 425). 亼 is cover/ **cap** 87/121, here acting phonetically to express **summon** and probably also lending an idea of **imposing from above**. 603 originally referred to people summoned to hear the orders of their lord, but now means **order** or **rule**.

Mnemonic: **KNEELING PERSON ORDERED TO DON CAP**

---

604 冷 REI, tsume*tai*, hi*eru*/*yasu*,
sameru/*masu*
FREEZE, COLD
7 strokes

冷蔵 REIZŌ   refrigeration
冷静 REISEI na   cool-headed
冷え性 HIESHŌ sensitivity to cold

Also 泠. 冫 is **ice** 378. 令/令 is order/ **rule** 603, here acting phonetically to express **tremble** and also lending an idea of **prevail**/ dominate. Thus **tremble as a result of prevailing ice**, now **freeze** or **ice-cold**.

Mnemonic: **ICE RULES IN FREEZING COLD**

185

605 **REI, tato*eru***
EXAMPLE, LIKEN,
PRECEDENT
8 strokes

例外 REIGAI exception
例年 REINEN normal year
例えば TATOEBA for example

Person 亻 39 and **line/ row** 列 414. 605 originally referred to **people lined up in proper order**, but gradually changed to a meaning of **comparison** (cf. **compare** 比 771). This led in turn to its present associated meanings.

Mnemonic: **PEOPLE IN LINE SHOW EXAMPLE OF PRECEDENT**

606 **REKI**
HISTORY, PATH
14 strokes

歴史家 REKISHIKA historian
経歴 KEIREKI past career
遍歴 HENREKI travels

Formerly written 歴, in ancient times 𣥆, and nowadays sometimes simply as 厂. 凵/ 止 is **footprint** 129 q.v., here used in the sense of **trail**. 秝 is a doubling of **rice plant** 81, meaning plural rice plants. Thus 秝 meant a **trail of rice plants**, a reference to rice plants in an ordered, **regularly spaced row**. The role of the later addition 厂 is not clear. It appears to be cliff 45, possibly used in some unclear phonetic role, but may possibly be an abbreviation of **large building** 广 114, indicating a building in which rice seedlings were planted. In any event, **regular row of rice plants** came to mean **regular row** or **path** in a wider sense, and was eventually applied figuratively to **history** and to a **career path** or similar. Suggest taking 止 in its usual sense of **stop**.

Mnemonic: **HISTORY STOPS WITH INDOOR RICE PLANTS?!**

607 **REN, tsu*reru*, tsura*neru***
ACCOMPANY, ROW
10 strokes

連絡船 RENRAKUSEN ferry
連中 RENCHŪ/ RENJŪ party
連想 RENSŌ
thought association

Movement 辶 129 and **vehicle** 車 31, giving **(succession of) moving vehicles**. This came to mean **row** on the one hand, and **be part of a group/ accompany** on the other.

Mnemonic: **ACCOMPANIED BY ROW OF MOVING VEHICLES**

608 **REN,** ne*ru*
REFINE, KNEAD, TRAIN
14 strokes

訓練 KUNREN　　training
洗練 SENREN　　refinement
練り粉 NERIKO　　dough

Formerly 練. 糸 is **thread** 27. 柬 is a CO character now meaning **select**, and is felt to derive from a combination of bundle 束 1535 and disperse/ away 丶 ノ 66 (i.e. remove selected items from a bundle). 柬 also lends its sound to express **soften by boiling**. Thus to **soften selected threads by boiling**, which was a reference to the glossing of raw silk. This led to associated ideas such as **kneading, improving,** and by extension **training.**. Suggest taking 束 as **east** 184.

Mnemonic: **REFINED THREADS FROM THE EAST**

---

609 **RŌ,** oiru, fu*keru*
OLD, AGED
6 strokes

老人 RŌJIN　　old person
老練 RŌREN na　　veteran
老齢年金 RŌREINENKIN
　　　　　old age pension

Originally 耂, showing an **old man** 人 / 耂 117 q.v. leaning on a **stick** ├ / ヒ. As with 117, suggest taking 耂 as **half buried** / **in ground** 土 60, with ヒ as **fallen person** 238.

Mnemonic: **OLD MAN FALLS, READY FOR BURYING IN GROUND**

---

610 **RŌ**
LABOR, TOIL
7 strokes

労働者 RŌDŌSHA　　laborer
苦労 KURŌ　　pains, trouble
労働関係 RŌDŌKANKEI
　　　　　labor relations

Formerly 勞. 炏 is **covered in flame** 427 while 力 is **strength/ effort** 74. The original meaning was to **do physical work under torchlight**, which came to mean **work hard and long** in a general sense. Suggest taking ⺌ as an **ornate roof**.

Mnemonic: **LABOR WITH EFFORT UNDER ORNATE ROOF**

187

611		**ROKU**	記録	KIROKU	record
		RECORD, INSCRIBE	実録	JITSUROKU	true record
		16 strokes	録音	ROKUON	
					sound recording

Formerly 録．金 is **metal** 14, while 录 is **exude** 412 q.v. 611 originally referred to the 'green rust' or verdigris which is 'exuded' from copper. Having largely had this meaning taken over by 412, 611 came to mean **marks on metal** in a broad sense, and later became particularly associated with **inscriptions**. A metal inscription is an enduring **record**. Suggest remembering by association with **green** 緑 412.

Mnemonic: **RECORD ON GREEN METAL**

END OF FOURTH GRADE

THE 195 FIFTH GRADE CHARACTERS

612 ATSU PRESSURE 5 strokes

圧力 ATSURYOKU　pressure
電圧 DENATSU　voltage
圧倒的 ATTŌTEKI　overwhelming

Formerly 壓 . 土 is ground/ **earth** 60. 厭 is an NGU character meaning **satiated/ weary**. It derives from **roof** 厂 (variant 广 114), here meaning cover and by figurative extension smother, **dog** 犬 17, **meat** 月 365, and 日 , a simplification of **sweet** 甘 1093, and its original meaning was be smothered in sweet dog meat (i.e. have a surfeit of/ **be satiated with sweet dog meat**). This came to mean be bloated, with connotations of **ready to burst** and therefore **pressure**. In the case of 612 厭 also acts phonetically to express **push/ press**. Some scholars feel 612 originally meant **earth pressing as if to burst**, as in a cave-in, while others feel it meant **push with earth**, as in attempting to reinforce defensive earthworks. The idea of earth gradually faded, leaving **press/ pressure** in general.

Mnemonic: **ROOF UNDER PRESSURE FROM EARTH**

613 I, utsu*ru*/*su* TRANSFER, MOVE 11 strokes

移住 IJŪ　migration
移民 IMIN　migrant
移動 IDŌ　move

Rice plant 禾 81 and **much/ many** 多 163, with the latter also lending its sound to express **sway**. 613 originally referred to a field full of (i.e. many) rice plants swaying (in the breeze), but later became confused with 迻 , a CO character interchanged with 613 and clearly meaning **much movement** (see movement 辶 129).

Mnemonic: **TRANSFER MANY RICE PLANTS**

614

IN, yor*u*
CAUSE, BE BASED ON,
DEPEND ON
6 strokes

原因 GENIN cause
死因 SHIIN cause of death
因果関係 INGAKANKEI
cause-and-effect

Of disputed etymology, though its elements are clearly (**big**) **man** 大 53 and **enclosure** 囗 123. Some scholars take it to be an **enclosed man**, i.e. a prisoner, which by association raises the question of the **cause** of his imprisonment, with **based on/ depend on** being extensions of cause. Other scholars see 囗 as symbolising a **territory** (or even house), and take 大 to act phonetically as well as semantically, lending its sound to express **visit/ stay**. Thus a man visiting and staying in a certain territory/ house, meaning that he is **based** there and is also **dependent upon** the goodwill of the host. **Cause** is seen as an extension from dependent. A combination of the two theories seems possible, in that enclosed man might suggest protected man, who is **dependent** upon his protector, with **based upon** and **cause** being associated meanings.

Mnemonic: **ENCLOSED MAN HAS CAUSE TO DEPEND ON OTHERS**

615

EI, naga*i*
LONG, LASTING
5 strokes

永遠 EIEN eternity
永続 EIZOKU perpetuity
永住者 EIJŪSHA
permanent resident

From a pictograph of the **confluence of a tributary and main river** 𣲖 (see also 589 and 955). 615 originally meant **long distance** (presumably from the idea of an extensive river-system), but eventually came rather to mean **long** in the sense of **enduring** (possibly because a confluence of rivers was a lasting source of water). Suggest remembering by association with **water** 水 40 and **ice** 氷 378, from which distinguish.

Mnemonic: **WATER LOOKS ICY FOR A LONG TIME**

616

EI, itonam*u*
CONDUCT, BARRACKS
12 strokes

経営 KEIEI management
営業 EIGYŌ business
営所 EISHO barracks

Formerly 營. 𤇭 is covered in flame/ light 427, here meaning **surrounded by torches**. 呂 is **joined rooms** 256, here indicating a **large building/ encampment**. Thus **large building/ encampment surrounded by torches**, a reference to **military barracks**. It was later also used to express **conduct,** partly through confusion with conduct 為 1003. Suggest taking ⺍ as an **ornate roof**.

Mnemonic: **ORNATELY ROOFED BARRACKS WITH JOINED ROOMS**

617   EI
GUARD, PROTECT
16 strokes

衛生 EISEI hygiene
守衛 SHUEI guard
自衛 JIEI self-defense

A combination of **guard all directions** 韋 422 and **go** 行 118, giving **patrol/ guard thoroughly**. Suggest taking 乩 as 'almost' **five** 五 19, 圭 as 'almost' **year** 年 64, and 口 as **opening** 20.

Mnemonic: **OPENING TO GO ON GUARD FOR ALMOST FIVE YEARS**

---

618   EKI, I, yasu*i*, yasa*shii*
EASY, CHANGE,
DIVINATION
8 strokes

貿易 BŌEKI trade
易者 EKISHA fortuneteller
安易 ANI na easy-going

Once written 昜, showing a **big-eyed lizard** 昜 and **rays of the sun** ⸜. 618 originally referred to the sun's rays reflecting off a lizard's (iridescent) skin. This led to the idea of **readily changing**, giving both **change** and **readily/ easy**. **Divination** is an associated meaning, from the idea of interpreting changes. The graphic evolution of the character may have been influenced by sun shining down 昜 144, though some scholars feel that the sunrays ⸜ became misinterpreted as the lizard's legs. Suggest taking 日 as **sun** 62, and 勿 as **legs**.

Mnemonic: **SUN BOUNCES EASILY OFF LIZARD'S CHANGING LEGS**

---

619 益   EKI, YAKU, masu
GAIN, PROFIT,
BENEFIT
10 strokes

有益 YŪEKI profitable
益益 MASUMASU increasingly
利益配当 RIEKIHAITŌ dividend

Formerly 盆. 皿 is **dish** 1307. 𠔼 derives from 㲼, a variant of **water** 氵/水 40. Thus **dish full of water**, leading to **overflowing** and by association **profit** and **gain**. Suggest taking ⸜ as a variant of **eight** 八 66, and 大 as a **table**.

Mnemonic: **MAKE PROFIT ON EIGHT SETS OF TABLEWARE**

191

620 **EKI**
LIQUID
11 strokes

液体 EKITAI   liquid
液化 EKIKA   liquefaction
血液型 KETSUEKIGATA
                       blood type

氵 is **water** 40, here meaning **liquid**. 夜 is **night** 212, here acting phonetically to express **immerse** and possibly also lending a loose idea of **engulfing**. Thus **liquid in which things are immersed (and engulfed?)**, eventually **liquid** in general.

Mnemonic: **NEED FOR LIQUID, EVEN WATER AT NIGHT**

---

621 **EN**
ACT, PERFORM
14 strokes

演出 ENSHUTSU   production
出演 SHUTSUEN performance
演説 ENZETSU   speech

氵 is **water** 40, here meaning **river**. 寅 is an NGU character now borrowed to refer to a zodiac sign. However, it was originally written 𡩟, showing two hands 𦥑 straightening an arrow 矢 120/981, and meant **straighten an arrow**. This came by association to mean **lengthen/ extend**, and when combined with 氵 meant **long/ extensive river**. The river element eventually faded, leaving just **extensive**. This is still one of 621's meanings in Chinese, but in Japanese it has given way entirely to derived meanings such as **extended performance**, and even simply **performance** and **act**. Suggest taking 宀 as roof / **building** 28, and 更 as a variant of **yellow** 黄 120 q.v.

Mnemonic: **PERFORM IN BUILDING BY YELLOW RIVER**

---

622 **Ō**
RESPOND, REACT
7 strokes

応答 ŌTŌ   response
反応 HANNŌ*   reaction
応用 ŌYŌ   application

Formerly 應. 心 is **heart/ feelings** 147. 雁 is the prototype of the NGU character hawk 鷹 (which adds an additional bird 鳥 174). It now comprises roof 广 114, here meaning by extension shelter (formerly illness 疒 381, suggesting care for), person 亻 39, and bird 隹 216, to give **bird sheltered by person,** i.e. taken in hand. In the case of 622 雁 lends its sound to express **respond**, and possibly also lends an idea of **taking in**. Thus to **(take in a situation and?) respond with one's heart**, now simply **react/ respond**.

Mnemonic: **REACT WITH FEELING TO BUILDING**

623 往 Ō
GO, GONE, PAST
8 strokes

往復 ŌFUKU round trip
往事 ŌJI things past
往来 ŌRAI coming and going

Once written 徃, and earlier as 坓, showing **king** 太 / 王 5 and **foot** Ш / 止 129. The latter is used in its sense of **move**, while 王 is used both for its sound, to express **go**, and for its idea of **leading person**. 坓 meant **person going in front**, with **go/ movement** 彳 118 added later for emphasis. Rather like precede 先 49 q.v., this idea eventually led to that of **things past**. It is not clear whether the later use of **master** 主 299 is a purely graphic simplification or one that purposely keeps an idea of leading person.

Mnemonic: **MASTER GOES OFF**

624 恩 ON
FAVOR, KINDNESS
10 strokes

恩人 ONJIN benefactor
恩知らず ONSHIRAZU ingrate
恩返し ONGAESHI return favor

心 is **heart/ feelings** 147. 因 is **cause** 614 q.v., which acts phonetically to express **pity**. The exact semantic role of the latter is unclear due to its unclear origins, but it would presumably lend either supporting connotations of **pity** (for an imprisoned man) or **charity** (for a man needing protection and/or lodgings). Thus **feelings of pity**, leading to its present meanings.

Mnemonic: **FEELINGS ARE CAUSE OF KIND FAVOR**

625 仮 KA, KE, kari
TEMPORARY, FALSE
6 strokes

仮説 KASETSU hypothesis
仮に KARI ni provisionally
仮病 KEBYŌ feigned illness

Formerly 假, and earlier 叚. The latter, which is still found as a CO character meaning **false**, was still earlier written 叚. This reveals **two hands** ψ ╕ and ⻌, a variant of **cliff** 厂 45 (possibly showing terracing or steps ∶). The two hands are felt to show **manual dexterity** and by extension **emulation** (see 10), while ⻌ acts phonetically to express **false/ deceive**. Thus 叚/ 叚 (the latter apparently a graphic confusion) means literally to **emulate skillfully and deceitfully**. **Person** 亻 39 was added to give the idea of a **skilled impersonator**, leading by extension to the present meanings of **temporary** and **false**. The modern form replaces 叚 with **oppose** 反 371 q.v., partly for its idea of **change** and partly for the fact that it uses essentially the same components of cliff and hand but in simpler form.

Mnemonic: **PERSON OPPOSED TO EVEN TEMPORARY FALSEHOOD**

626

KA, atai
PRICE, VALUE, WORTH
8 strokes

価値　KACHI　　　　value
価格　KAKAKU　　　price
物価　BUKKA　　price of goods

Formerly 價. 賈 is an NGU character technically meaning **trader** (perhaps best thought of as a variant of the old form 賣 of sell 売 192), though it appears from an early stage to have developed strong connotations of the **act of buying and selling** and of the **items being traded** and their **value** rather than the person doing the trading. It retained these connotations despite the later addition of **person** イ 39, and in particular became associated with **value** and **price**. Suggest taking 西 as **west** 152.

Mnemonic: **PERSON FROM WEST HAS PRICE ON HEAD**

627

KA, ha*te*, ha*tasu*
FRUIT, RESULT,
CARRY OUT
8 strokes

成果　SEIKA　　　　result
果物　KUDAMONO*　　fruit
果たして　HATASHITE　as expected

Originally 菓, showing **fruit** 𢆥 on a **tree** 木 69. From an early stage 𢆥 was replaced by full rice field 圖 504 to give the idea of **abundant crop**, and later this was simplified to just **field** 田 59. As in English, fruit was used figuratively to mean **outcome/ result**, and by extension also came to mean **bring about an outcome**, i.e. **carry out/ perform**.

Mnemonic: **TREE, LIKE FIELD, PRODUCES FRUITFUL RESULTS**

628

KA, kawa
RIVER
8 strokes

河口　KAKŌ　　　rivermouth
河豚　FUGU*　　　globefish
河馬　KABA　　　hippopotamus

氵 is **water** 40, here meaning **river**. 可 is **can** 816 q.v., here with its literal meaning of **coil (slowly) to a mouth** and also lending its sound to express **twist/ meander**. Thus **river meandering to the sea**, now used of **rivers** in general.

Mnemonic: **WATER CAN FORM RIVER**

629 KA, su*giru*/*gosu*, ayama*chi* 通過 TSŪKA passage
PASS,EXCEED,ERROR 過去形 KAKOKEI past tense
12 strokes 言い過ぎ IISUGI exaggeration

辶 is **movement** 129. 咼 is **bone**/ **vertebrae** 867, here lending an idea of flexibility and suppleness and by extension **ease of movement**. Opinion is divided as to whether 口 represents another vertebra (see 256) or mouth 20 (thus giving twisted mouth or similar). In any event, 咼 is known to have acted phonetically to express much/ **substantial**. Thus 629 originally referred to **making easy and substantial movement/ progress**. As well as leading to the idea of **slip by** and **pass**, it also led by extension to the idea of **going too far**, including in the sense of **making an error**. Suggest taking 口 as **mouth**.

Mnemonic: **EXCESSIVE MOVEMENT MAKES BACKBONE PASS MOUTH!**

630 GA 賀詞 GASHI congratulations
CONGRATULATIONS 年賀状 NENGAJŌ New Year Card
12 strokes 祝賀会 SHUKUGAKAI celebration

加 is **add** 431. 貝 is **shell**/ **money** 90, here used to mean **valuable item**. To **add valuable items** was a reference to adding one's gift to a number of other gifts, indicating an occasion for **congratulations**.

Mnemonic: **CONGRATULATIONS ON ADDING TO ONE'S MONEY**

631 KAI, kokoroyo*i* 不愉快 FUYUKAI unpleasant
PLEASANT, CHEERFUL 快楽 KAIRAKU pleasure
7 strokes 快活 KAIKATSU cheerful

Heart/ **feelings** 忄 147 and **open up** 夬 271, giving to be in an **expansive mood** and hence **cheerful**. **Pleasant** is an associated meaning. Suggest remembering 夬 by association with a 'waterless' (see water 氵 40) **decide** 決 271.

Mnemonic: **NO WATER, BUT DECIDEDLY CHEERFUL FEELINGS**

632

KAI, GE, to*ku*	解説 KAISETSU commentary
UNRAVEL, EXPLAIN,	理解 RIKAI understanding
SOLVE	分解 BUNKAI break-up
13 strokes	

刀 is sword/ **cut** 181, 牛 is **cow** 97, and 角 is **horn** 243. Some scholars feel that 刀 and 牛 combine to give **cut up/ butcher a cow**, with 角 acting purely phonetically by way of emphasis to express **dissect**, while others feel that the three elements combine ideographically to convey the idea of **cutting off a cow's horn to disentangle it**. The present meanings are extensions of either cut up or disentangle.

Mnemonic: **SOLVE PROBLEM BY CUTTING OFF COW'S HORN**

633

KAKU, KŌ	資格 SHIKAKU qualification
STANDARD, STATUS	性格 SEIKAKU character
10 strokes	所有格 SHOYŪKAKU genitive

木 is **tree** 69. 各 is **each** 438 q.v., here acting phonetically to express **tall** and possibly also lending its own connotations of **descending from a height**. 633 originally meant **tall tree**, leading to various extended and associated meanings such as **reach a height** (still a meaning in Chinese) and therefore **achieve status** as well as **set a standard**. It can also mean **case** (in grammar).

Mnemonic: **EACH TREE SETS A STANDARD**

634

KAKU, tashi*ka*/*kameru*	正確 SEIKAKU precise
ASCERTAIN, FIRM	確認 KAKUNIN confirmation
15 strokes	確実 KAKUJITSU reliable

Once written 石𮥝. 石 is **rock** 45. 𮥝/寉 is a crested 冖 bird 隹 216, specifically a **crane** (now conveyed by an NGU character 鶴 that adds an extra bird 鳥 174: distinguish heron 雚/雈 445). Here 寉 acts phonetically to express **hard**, and is also felt by some scholars to lend an associated idea of **white** (cranes being predominantly white). Thus **hard (white?) rock**, a reference to **granite**. This came to mean **hard** or **firm** and by association **reliable**. Note that the occasionally encountered variant form 碻 is a miscopying. However, it may be usful to remember 冖 as a variant of **roof** 宀 28, with a pun on **rock** and **roc** (a mythical bird).

Mnemonic: **ASCERTAIN THAT BIRD UNDER ROOF IS A ROC**

---

635 GAKU, hitai
SUM, PLAQUE,
FRAME, FOREHEAD
18 strokes

金額 KINGAKU sum of money
額面 GAKUMEN face value
額際 HITAIGIWA hairline

Formerly also written 頟 (still found in Chinese). 頁 is **head** 93. 各 is **each** 438 q.v., while 客 is **visitor** 252 q.v. Both 各 and 客 act phonetically to express **shave**, and both may also lend extended connotations of **attend** from their original meaning of **visit and stay**. Thus **shaven part of the head (to which one attends?)**. This was a reference to the **forehead**, which in ancient China was often exaggerated by shaving back the hairline. **Frame** (of picture etc.) and **plaque** are felt to be associated meanings, from the idea of **clear, angular area** (though it is not impossible that there might be some connection with the ancient practice of tattooing/ identifying slaves on the forehead -- see 340). It is not clear how 635 also came to mean **sum**, though some scholars feel it may stem from the idea of **high point** (cf. taka 高 119, meaning both height and sum).

Mnemonic: **VISITOR'S FOREHEAD LOOKS LIKE PLAQUE**

636 KAN
PUBLISH, ENGRAVE
5 strokes

刊行 KANKŌ publication
日刊 NIKKAN daily issue
発刊 HAKKAN launching

刂 is **sword/ cut** 181. 干 is **dry** 825 q.v., here acting phonetically to express **carve/ engrave** and also lending an idea of **cut** from its original meaning of **thrusting weapon**. The original meaning was simply **engrave**, but it then came to be associated with engraving as part of the **printing** process. It now means **publish** in a broad sense.

Mnemonic: **PUBLISH BOOK ON HOW TO KEEP SWORD DRY**

637 KAN, miki
TRUNK, MAIN
13 strokes

幹線 KANSEN trunk line
幹部 KANBU leaders
幹事 KANJI manager

Once written 榦. 木 is **tree** 69. 𣘻 is a variant of 倝, a CO character meaning **sunrise** (comprising **rising sun** 𠦝 175 and a **person** 人 39 presumably watching it, though the exact role of 人 is unclear). 𣘻 acts phonetically to express **base/ support**, and almost certainly also lends an extended idea of **rising straight up**. Thus the **base of a tree that rises straight up**, i.e. the **trunk**. **Main** is an associated meaning. The modern form uses **dry** 干 825 q.v., which is generally assumed to be a miscopying but may in fact make deliberate use of 825's literal meaning of **thrusting wooden item**. Suggest taking 𠦝 literally as **sun** 日 62 rising through **grass** 十 9.

Mnemonic: **PERSON DRIES TRUNK AS SUN RISES THROUGH GRASS**

| 638 | | KAN, na*reru*
BECOME USED TO
14 strokes | 習慣 SHŪKAN habit, custom
慣例 KANREI convention
世慣れた YONARETA worldly-wise |

忄 is **heart/ feelings** 147. 貫 is **pierce** 1102 q.v., here acting phonetically to express **accumulate** and also lending similar connotations from its literal meaning of threaded amount of money. Thus **accumulate feelings**, a reference to **increasing familiarity**.

Mnemonic: **BECOME USED TO HAVING HEART PIERCED**

| 639 | | KAN, yoroko*bu*
REJOICE, MERRY
15 strokes | 歓迎 KANGEI welcome
歓楽 KANRAKU pleasure
交歓 KŌKAN fraternisation |

Formerly 歡. 藋/雚 is **crested bird/ heron** 445 q.v., acting phonetically to express **banquet** and possibly also loosely lending similar connotations since the heron was a delicacy at banquets. 欠 is **lack** 471 q.v., here with its literal meaning of **gaping mouth**. Thus to **gorge oneself at a banquet**, symbolising **making merry**.

Mnemonic: **MERRIMENT IS GAPING MOUTH FULL OF CRESTED BIRD**

| 640 | | GAN, manako
EYE
11 strokes | 双眼鏡 SŌGANKYŌ binoculars
肉眼 NIKUGAN naked eye
血眼 CHIMANAKO
bloodshot eyes |

目 is **eye** 72. 艮 is **stop and stare** 263, here also acting phonetically to express **round**. Thus to **stop and stare with round eyes**, i.e. **wide eyed**. Wide eyed eventually led to just **eye**.

Mnemonic: **STOP AND STARE WITH WIDE EYES**

| 641 | | KI, moto, moto*zuku*
BASE
11 strokes | 基本 KIHON basis, standard
基金 KIKIN foundation
基地 KICHI base (army etc.) |

Formed from **winnowing device** 其 251 q.v., which is itself set on a **base/ stand** 六 and here lends such connotations, and **earth/ ground** 土 60. Thus **earthen base/ foundation**, now **base** in a broad sense.

Mnemonic: **WINNOWING DEVICE BASED ON FIRM GROUND**

642		KI, *yoru/seru* DRAW NEAR, SEND, VISIT 11 strokes	寄与 KIYO	contribution

			寄与 KIYO	contribution
			寄せ波 YOSENAMI	surf
			立ち寄る TACHIYORU	visit, call

宀 is **roof/ house** 28. 奇 is **strange/ unfamiliar** 1123, which also acts phonetically to express **seek protection**. 642 originally referred to **seeking protection in a stranger's house**. This gave rise to a range of extended and associated meanings, particularly **visit** and by association **draw near**. **Send** is the causative form of visit.

Mnemonic: **DRAW NEAR TO STRANGE HOUSE**

643	規	KI STANDARD, MEASURE 11 strokes	規則 KISOKU	rule
			定規 JŌGI	rule(r)
			大規模 DAIKIBO	large scale

夫 is (person becoming) **adult male** 573 q.v., used here to indicate attainment of a certain **standard** and thus something to be **measured** against, while 見 is **look** 18 q.v. Some scholars see the two elements as combining ideographically to give **adult male looked upon as a standard**. Others see 見 as being used essentially phonetically to express **round**, though it would almost certainly also lend an idea of **observe carefully** (from its literal meaning of person kneeling to stare). Thus a **round measure (which is observed)**, i.e. a **compass**. The fact that 643 can mean compass in Chinese suggests strongly that the latter theory is correct, though the former may be more helpful as a mnemonic.

Mnemonic: **ADULT MALE LOOKED UPON AS STANDARD**

644	技	GI, waza CRAFT, SKILL 7 strokes	技術 GIJUTSU	technique
			技師 GISHI	engineer
			演技 ENGI	acting

支 is **support** 691 q.v., here lending both its literal meaning of **hold in hand** and its sound to express **work**. 扌 is **hand** 32, the additional hand giving **both hands**. Thus to **work with both hands**, suggesting an **intricate task**. By association this came to mean **skill** and **craft**.

Mnemonic: **SUPPORT FROM SKILLED HANDS FACILITATES CRAFT**

645 **GI**
RIGHTEOUSNESS
13 strokes

主義 SHUGI principle, ism
義理 GIRI justice
意義 IGI significance

Somewhat obscure, though its elements are clearly **sheep** 羊 986 q.v. and **I/ self** 我 817 q.v. Some scholars feel that sheep is used in its extended sense of **praiseworthy**, to give the idea of **being able to consider oneself praiseworthy** (i.e. through one's **righteousness**). Others see 我 as being used purely phonetically to express **ceremony**, giving **praiseworthy ceremony**, i.e. one that is performed **properly** (with righteousness being an extension of proper). Still others agree that it meant proper and praiseworthy ceremony, but arrive at this through interpreting the elements ideographically as **slaughter** (i.e. **sacrifice**) **a sheep** (我 literally meaning to **kill with a lance/ halberd**). The first theory is perhaps the most helpful.

Mnemonic: **I AM LIKE A SHEEP, FULL OF RIGHTEOUSNESS**

---

646 **GYAKU, saka**rau
REVERSE, OPPOSE
9 strokes

逆行 GYAKKŌ retrogression
逆説 GYAKUSETSU paradox
反逆 HANGYAKU treason

辶 is **movement** 129. 屰 derives from 屰, a stylised and inverted variant of (**big**) **man** 大 53, the inversion indicating **opposite to normal**. Thus a **man going backwards**, leading to **reverse** and by association **oppose**.

Mnemonic: **BIG UPSIDE-DOWN MAN MOVES IN REVERSE**

---

647 久 **KYŪ, KU, hisa**shii
LONG TIME, LASTING
3 strokes

永久 EIKYŪ permanence
久遠 KUON* eternity
久し振り HISASHIBURI
for the first time in ages

Somewhat obscure. Early forms such as 入 have been interpreted as a **person** 𠂉 39 **held in place** (indicated by the abstract sign ＼), with this leading by extension to **stay in place** and hence **last a long time**. Suggest taking ク as a **stooping person** and ＼ as a **prop**.

Mnemonic: **STOOPING PERSON PROPPED UP FOR A LONG TIME**

200

648

旧

KYŪ
OLD, PAST
5 strokes

旧友 KYŪYŪ   old friend
旧派 KYŪHA   old school
旧式 KYŪSHIKI   old style

Formerly 舊 and 舊. 萑 is not the CO character reed 萑 (literally bird-grass, from bird 隹 216 and grass 艹 9). Old forms such as 萑 show that it is a **crested bird**, though different from crested bird/ heron 鷺/雚 445 and crested bird/ crane 寉 634. It is in fact a white-horned owl (see below). 臼 is an NGU character meaning **mortar**, taken by some scholars to show a bowl with bits in it (from a stylised old form 臼) but more likely originally a mouth with grinding teeth (old form 臼). Here 臼 is used purely for its sound **KYŪ**, to give 舊 a meaning of **crested bird with a cry of KYŪ**, which was a reference to the (**white-horned**) **owl**. (Note that 舊 was once interchanged with 鵂, a CO character which combines bird 鳥 174 with KYŪ rest 休 13 and which similarly means white-horned owl/ bird that cries KYŪ.) 舊 was then drastically simplified to 旧 and used as a phonetic alternative to **KYŪ long time** 久 647, eventually acquiring its own particular connotations of **old** and **past**. It is not clear why any need was felt for an alternative to the already simple 久, but it is possible that 日 was seen as **day** 62 and | as **draw** (bowstring 77), giving the **drawing out of days** or similar. Suggest taking 日 as **day** and | as **one**.

Mnemonic: **ONLY ONE DAY OLD, BUT OLD NONETHELESS**

649

居

KYO, *iru*, *oru*
BE, RESIDE
8 strokes

居住 KYOJŪ   dwelling
住居 JŪKYO   dwelling
居所 IDOKORO   whereabouts

尸 is **person sitting slumped** 236. 古 is **old** 109, here acting phonetically to express **crouch** and possibly also lending an idea of **the passing of time**. 649 originally referred to a **person staying in a crouched position**. This came to mean **be immobile** and **stay in one place**, leading to the idea of **residing** and by extension **being/existing**.

Mnemonic: **OLD PERSON SITTING SLUMPED IS AT HOME**

201

650		KYO, yuru*su*, moto PERMIT, FORGIVE, PLACE, HOME 11 strokes	許可 KYOKA	permission
			特許 TOKKYO	patent
			手許 TEMOTO	at hand

言 is **word/ speak** 274. 午 is **noon** 110 q.v., here acting phonetically to express **approve/ forgive** and according to some scholars also possibly lending an idea of **pounding** (a table or similar) as a sign of **hearty endorsement** (from its literal meaning of pestle, which could symbolise pounding). Thus to **approve/ forgive someone's words**. It is not clear how it acquired the meaning of **place/ home**, but it may possibly have been used as a phonetic alternative to **reside** (and by extension residence) KYO 居 649.

Mnemonic: **PERMIT SPEECH AT NOON**

651		KYŌ, KEI, sakai BOUNDARY, BORDER 14 strokes	国境 KOKKYŌ	frontier
			境内 KEIDAI	precinct
			境界線 KYŌKAISEN	boundary line

土 is **ground** 60. 竟 is **finish** 462. Thus **finish of a piece of ground**, i.e. a **boundary**. Suggest taking 立 as **stand** 73, 日 as **sun** 62, and 儿 as **legs**.

Mnemonic: **STAND ON SUNNY GROUND, LEGS ASTRIDE BOUNDARY**

652		KYŌ, KŌ, okosu/ru RISE, RAISE, INTEREST 16 strokes	興奮 KŌFUN	excitement
			復興 FUKKŌ	revival
			興味深い KYŌMIBUKAI	very interesting

Once written 𦥛, showing **raise/ hands working together** 臼 458/1873 and **same** 同 187, here also meaning **together/ in unison**. Thus to **raise up together**, giving **raise** and **rise**. **Interest/ excitement** is an associated meaning, from the idea of raised feelings. Suggest taking ㇒ヨ as **hands** and 八 as **table**.

Mnemonic: **SAME HANDS RAISED AT TABLE -- HOW INTERESTING**

653

KIN, hito*shii*
AVERAGE, LEVEL,
ALIKE
7 strokes

平均 HEIKIN average
均等 KINTŌ uniformity
不均衡 FUKINKŌ imbalance

Somewhat obscure. 土 is **ground** 60. 勹 is often thought to be a variant of **ladle**/ measure 勹/ 勺 1342, but in fact old forms such as 𠣧 and 圴 show **coiling** (some scholars take the latter form to derive from a pictograph of a snake coiled on the ground, but it is safer to think of both forms simply as symbols of coiling -- see 655). 勹 is known to have acted phonetically to express **flat**, and presumably it also lent similar connotations from the idea of coiling (coils lying flat). Thus **flat ground**, leading to **level** and by figurative extension **average**. **Alike** is an associated meaning, from the idea of **norm**. Suggest taking 勹 as a combination of **ladle** 勹 and **one** 一 1.

Mnemonic: **LEVEL GROUND WITH ONE LADLE?!**

654

KIN
BAN, FORBID
13 strokes

禁止 KINSHI prohibition
禁煙 KINEN 'No Smoking'
厳禁 GENKIN
strictly prohibited

示 is **show**/ **altar** 695 q.v., here with its connotations of **religious**/ **of the gods**. 林 is **forest** 75, used purely phonetically to express **abstain**. Thus **abstain for religious reasons**, leading to **abstain**/ **taboo**/ **ban**/ **forbid** etc. in a wider sense.

Mnemonic: **ALTAR IN FORBIDDEN FOREST**

655

KU
PHRASE, CLAUSE
5 strokes

字句 JIKU phraseology
句切り KUGIRI punctuation
文句 MONKU words, complaint

口 is **mouth/say** 20, here meaning **word**. 勹 is an element generally meaning **cover**/ **wrap**/ **encircle**. Strictly speaking, in the case of 655 its old form is 𠃍, showing interlocking strokes to convey the idea of **intertwining**/ **wrapping around**. However, the graphic evolution of 𠃍 into 勹 seems to have been influenced by a number of other forms of similar meaning, such as encircling arm 勹/ 勹, womb 勹/ 勹, and possibly also coiled snake 勹/ 勹. **Intertwining words** led to **phrase**, **clause**, etc.

Mnemonic: **MOUTH WRAPS ITSELF AROUND PHRASE**

203

656		KUN LESSON, RULE, KUN READING 10 strokes	訓読み KUNYOMI kun reading 訓練士 KUNRENSHI trainer 教訓的 KYŌKUNTEKI edifying

言 is **words/** speak 274. 川 is **river** 48, here acting phonetically to express **order** and also lending an idea of **flowing in a given way**. 656 originally meant **logical argument**, then came to mean **teaching** and by association **lesson, standard** or **rule**. It is also used for the **kun reading** of a character (i.e. the Japanese as opposed to Chinese).

Mnemonic: **WORDS FLOW LIKE RIVER IN LESSON**

657		GUN, mura, mure/reru GROUP, FLOCK 13 strokes	群集 GUNSHŪ crowd 魚群 GYOGUN school of fish 群居 GUNKYO gregarious

羊 is **sheep** 986. 尹 is **lord** 266 q.v., here acting phonetically to express **assemble** and also lending its literal connotations of **command (with a stick)**. 657 originally referred to **herding sheep**, but then came to focus rather on the **group of animals**. Now also used of humans.

Mnemonic: **LORD OF SHEEP FLOCK**

658		KEI, KYŌ, heru, tatsu PASS, SUTRA, LONGITUDE 11 strokes	経済 KEIZAI economy 経線 KEISEN meridian 経過 KEIKA passage

Formerly 經 . 巠 is **lengthwise threads on a loom (warp)** 269, reinforced by **thread** 糸 27. **Pass (through)** and **longitude** are associated meanings. Since the warp threads act as **guides** for the crosswise weft threads, 658 also came to represent **guiding principles**, including the **sutras**. Suggest taking 巠 as **ground** 土 60 and **hand** 又.

Mnemonic: **GUIDING HAND PASSES THREADS TO GROUND**

659 KETSU, isagiyo*i*
CLEAN, PURE
15 strokes

潔白 KEPPAKU na immaculate
潔癖 KEPPEKI na fastidious
潔く ISAGIYOKU valiantly

Formerly 潔 . 丯 is a **tally**, namely a piece of wood with serrations that was interlocked with another serrated piece (i.e. the matching other half) upon the proper fulfilment of a contract or similar. Sword/ **cut** 刀 181 emphasises the idea of cutting notches. As with the English term, **tally** also has connotations of making things **right and proper**. When combined with **thread** 糸 27, giving the CO character 絜 , it originally meant to **adjust threads and make them right**, though it presently came to mean simply to **correct**. The addition of **water** 氵 40 gave to **correct with water**, i.e. to **purify by ablution**. This came to mean **clean** or **pure**, including in the figurative sense of honorable. See also 1195. Suggest taking 圭 as a variant of **master** 主 299.

Mnemonic: **MASTER CUTS THREADS, WASHES CLEAN IN WATER**

---

660 KEN
ITEM, MATTER
6 strokes

事件 JIKEN incident
用件 YŌKEN business
条件 JŌKEN condition, term

Person 亻 39 and **cow** 牛 97. 660 originally referred to a **person leading a cow away** from a herd, having **selected** and **purchased** it. It was later used of sorting out items for business in a general sense (including slaves, an early meaning of 660), and thus came to mean **something to be attended to**. Note that in Chinese it can still mean to separate.

Mnemonic: **PERSON LEADING AWAY COW IS A SERIOUS MATTER**

---

661 KEN
TICKET, PASS, BOND
8 strokes

旅券 RYOKEN passport
証券 SHŌKEN bond
定期券 TEIKIKEN commuter pass

刀 is sword/ **cut** 181. 关 is an element once written 关 , showing **rice** (plant) 禾/朱 81, and **two hands** 丷. It originally meant to roll rice. It acts here phonetically to express **notched pledge/ tally** (see 659), but it is not clear whether it also lends any meaning. Thus **cut/ notched tally**, which in addition to being a symbol of a contract or pledge was also used as a symbol of official business or authority, and hence a **guarantee of safe conduct**, i.e. **pass** or **ticket** (cf. English term tally). Suggest taking 关 as **two** 二 61 **fires** 火 8.

Mnemonic: **START TWO FIRES WITH CUT UP TICKETS**

662

KEN, kewa*shii*
STEEP, SEVERE,
PERILOUS
11 strokes

険悪 KENAKU na   dangerous
保険 HOKEN   insurance
険そ KENSO na   precipitous

Formerly 險. 阝 is **hill** 229. 僉/僉 is synthesised **opinion** 475 q.v., here acting phonetically to express **combine** and also lending similar connotations of its own. Thus **combined hills**, a reference to **particularly hilly terrain** and hence the present meanings. Suggest taking 僉 as a modified combination of **cover/ cap** 스 87/121 and **elder brother** 兄 267.

Mnemonic: **ELDER BROTHER DONS CAP TO CLIMB STEEP HILL**

663

KEN
INVESTIGATE
12 strokes

検討 KENTŌ   enquiry
探検 TANKEN   exploration
検査員 KENSAIN   inspector

Formerly 檢. 僉/僉 is synthesised **opinion** 475 q.v., here acting phonetically to express **store safely** and also lending its meaning of **examine**. 木 is **wood** 69, here meaning wooden tablet upon which records were kept. Thus to **examine wooden records**, now **investigate** in a broad sense. Suggest taking 僉 as a modified combination of **cover/ cap** 스 87/121 and **elder brother** 兄 267.

Mnemonic: **ELDER BROTHER INVESTIGATES WOODEN COVER**

664

KEN, kinu
SILK
13 strokes

絹布 KENPU   silk cloth
人絹 JINKEN   rayon
絹物 KINUMONO   silk goods

糸 is **thread** 27. 肙 is a CO character meaning **small worm** or **coil** (coil/ circle/ **round** ㅁ and **flesh** 月 365), here acting phonetically to express the color **cream** and almost certainly also lending connotations of **silkworm**. Thus **cream colored thread (from a worm)**, i.e. **silk**.

Mnemonic: **SILK THREADS FROM ROUND FLESHY WORM**

665 限

GEN, kagi*ru*
LIMIT
9 strokes

限度 GENDO   limit
限界 GENKAI   boundary
無限 MUGEN   infinity

阝 is **hill** 229. 艮 is **stop and stare** 263 q.v., acting phonetically to express **difficult** and almost certainly also lending an idea of **turning round**. Thus to reach a difficult hill, stop, and turn to look back, suggesting that one has reached the **limits** of familiar territory.

Mnemonic: **STOP AND STARE FROM HILL, HAVING REACHED LIMITS**

666

現

GEN, arawa*reru*/*su*
APPEAR, EXIST, NOW
11 strokes

発現 HATSUGEN　revelation
現象 GENSHŌ　phenomenon
現実 GENJITSU　reality

Jewel 王 102 and **see** 見 18. Thus to **see a jewel**. On the one hand this came to refer to its luster (still listed as a minor meaning in Chinese), and on the other to the idea of **being visible/ appear**. **Exist** and **now** are associated meanings, from the idea of being before one's very eyes.

Mnemonic: **SEE JEWEL THAT NOW APPEARS**

667

GEN, he*ru*/*rasu*
DECREASE
12 strokes

減少 GENSHŌ　decrease
加減 KAGEN　extent, state
目減り MEBERI　weight loss

氵 is **water** 40. 咸 is unison 246 q.v., here acting phonetically to express **small amount**. In view of its complexity 咸 must presumably also have lent some meaning, possibly the idea of cutting away/ **reducing** from its trimming/ halberd element 戌 515. Thus a **small amount of water**, symbolising **reduction** and **decrease**. Suggest remembering by association with **feeling** 感 246, taking 咸 as a **'heartless'** version (see heart 心 147).

Mnemonic: **DECREASED WATER BRINGS ON HEARTLESS FEELING**

668

故

KO, yue
PAST, REASON
9 strokes

事故 JIKO　accident
故事 KOJI　history
故山田氏 KOYAMADASHI
the late Mr Yamada

Stick in hand/ coerce 攵 101, here acting as a causative element, and **old** 古 109, here indicating **the past**. Thus to **make something a thing of the past**. This led on the one hand to **past/ deceased**, and on the other to the idea of **causality/ reason**, i.e. with past events influencing the present/ future.

Mnemonic: **OLD STICK IN HAND A THING OF THE PAST**

669

KO
INDIVIDUAL, COUNTER
10 strokes

個人 KOJIN　individual
個性 KOSEI　individuality
一個 IKKO　one item

Person 亻 39 and **hard** 固 476. 669 originally referred to a person wearing armor (i.e. made hard), but from an early stage became confused with 箇 1054 q.v., which was a **counter** for bamboo slats. Probably because of the presence of person 亻, 669 has strong associations with the idea of **individuality**.

Mnemonic: **THAT INDIVIDUAL IS A HARD PERSON**

670		**GO** **DEFEND, PROTECT** 20 strokes	弁護士 BENGOSHI	lawyer
			保護 HOGO	protection
			護衛 GOEI	guard, escort

言 is **words** 274. 蒦 is crested bird 隹 648 in hand 又, here lending a meaning of **seize/ snare** and according to some scholars also acting phonetically to express spin/ **make dizzy**. Thus to **snare with words** (making the other party dizzy?), a reference to **proving an argument**. This came to have particular associations with **defence** against an accusation. Eventually the idea of words faded, leaving just **defend/ protect**. Suggest taking 隹 as **bird** 隹 216 and **grass** 艹 9.

Mnemonic: **WORDILY DEFEND HAND SEIZING BIRD IN GRASS**

671		**KŌ, ki**ku **EFFECT, EFFICACY** 8 strokes	効果 KŌKA	effect
			有効 YŪKŌ na	valid
			効き目 KIKIME	effect

Formerly 效. 交 is **exchange** 115, here meaning **interchange** and by extension match/ **emulate** (see also 21). 攵 is strike/ **coerce** 101, here acting as a causative element. Thus to **make someone emulate**, i.e. **make them learn to perform** a given task. Eventually the causative aspect faded, leaving just **ability to perform** a given task, i.e. **efficacy**. In modern popular usage coerce 攵 has been replaced by **strength** 力 74. Note that in Chinese both forms now exist as separate characters, with 效 meaning emulate/ effect and 効 meaning toil/ effect.

Mnemonic: **EXCHANGE OF STRENGTH PROVES MOST EFFECTIVE**

672		**KŌ, atsu**i **THICK, KIND** 9 strokes	部厚 BUATSU na	bulky, thick
			厚生 KŌSEI	welfare
			厚情 KŌJŌ	courtesy

Once written 厚 and later 厚. 厂 is **cliff** 45. 旲/旱/厚 is an inversion of 㐬/畗, a tall watchtower that is the prototype of **tall** 高 119. 672 originally meant **tall cliff**. The reason for the inversion is not clear, though it is possible that the original meaning had specific connotations of <u>descending</u> a tall cliff. Tall cliff eventually came to mean simply **substantial**, leading to **thick**. **Kind** is an associated meaning, from the idea of depth of feeling. Suggest taking 旱 as **day** 日 62 and **child** 子 25.

Mnemonic: **KIND BUT 'THICK' CHILD PLAYS DAILY BY CLIFF**

673 耕 KŌ, tagaya*su*
TILL, PLOW
10 strokes

耕地 KŌCHI — arable land
耕作 KŌSAKU — farming
耕うん機 KŌUNKI — cultivator

Formerly 耕. 耒 is a CO character meaning **plow** (of unclear etymology, but once written 耒, suggesting tree/shrub 米 69 and possibly serrated wood 丰 659, here representing a saw or similar cutting device, to give an idea of cutting away shrubs and thus preparing ground). 井 is **well** 1470, acting phonetically to express **conquer** and possibly also lending an associated idea of **fertile**. Thus to **conquer with a plow (and make fertile?)**, i.e. **till**. Suggest remembering 耒 as a **many branched tree** 木 69.

Mnemonic: **TILL AROUND WELL AND MANY BRANCHED TREE**

674 鉱 KŌ
MINERAL, ORE
13 strokes

鉱物 KŌBUTSU — mineral
鉱石 KŌSEKI — ore
炭鉱 TANKŌ — colliery

Formerly 鑛, and earlier 磺. The early form shows **rock** 石 45 and **yellow** 黄/黃 120, giving **yellow rock** and hence **mineral/ ore**. Yellow 黄 was later replaced by **wide/ extensive** 廣 / 広 114, possibly as a result of a miscopying influenced by the cliff part 厂 of 石 but possibly also for semantic reasons, and rock itself was replaced by **metal** 金 14.

Mnemonic: **EXTENSIVE METAL ORE**

675 構 KŌ, kama*u/eru*
BUILD, MIND
14 strokes

構成 KŌSEI — construction
結構 KEKKŌ — structure, fine
心構え KOKOROGAMAE — mental readiness

木 is **wood** 69. 冓 is a CO character meaning **large amount** or **accumulation**. It was originally written 冓, showing two bamboo (storage) **baskets piled up** (one inverted). Here 冓 acts phonetically to express **interweave** and also lends a meaning of **accumulate/ build up**. Thus to **build up by interweaving wood**, a reference to erecting the timber frame of a building. This came to mean **build** in a broader sense. **Mind/ care** is an associated meaning, from the idea of building up thoughts/ worries. Suggest remembering 冓 as **build with baskets**.

Mnemonic: **DO YOU MIND IF IT'S BUILT WITH WOODEN BASKETS?**

676		KŌ	講義	KŌGI	lecture
		LECTURE	講演	KŌEN	address
		17 strokes	講師	KŌSHI	lecturer

言 is **words** 274. 冓 is accumulation 675 q.v., here meaning **build up** and according to some scholars also acting phonetically to express **clarify**. Thus **something built of (clarifying?) words**, i.e. an **argument, speech, lecture**, or similar. Suggest taking 冓 literally as **build with baskets**.

Mnemonic: **LECTURE BUILT WITH 'BASKETS' OF WORDS**

677		KON, ma*jiru/zeru*	混血	KONKETSU mixed blood
		MIX, CONFUSION	混乱	KONRAN confusion
		11 strokes	混ぜ物	MAZEMONO mixture

氵 is **water**. 昆 is multitude 1276 q.v., here acting phonetically to express **spin/ swirl** and also lending its own idea of **confusion** (from people milling around). 677 originally referred to **water rushing and swirling** with no fixed course, as in a flood (still a meaning in Chinese). **Confused waters** then came to mean **confused** in a broader sense. **Mix** is an associated meaning, from the idea that in a state of confusion sundry impure elements can become mixed in. Suggest taking 昆 as **sun** 日 62 and **compare** 比 771.

Mnemonic: **COMPARE SUN AND WATER -- A CONFUSING MIX**

678	査	SA	検査	KENSA	inspection
		INVESTIGATE	審査	SHINSA	investigation
		9 strokes	査問	SAMON	inquiry

Wood 木 69, here meaning **timber**, and **furthermore** 且 1091 q.v., here with its literal meaning of **build up** and according to some scholars also acting phonetically to express **crosswise**. Thus to **build something with timber (laid crosswise?)**. In Chinese it can still be used in associated meanings, such as raft, but in Japanese it has come to be used purely in the borrowed meaning of **investigate**.

Mnemonic: **FURTHERMORE, WOOD SHOULD BE INVESTIGATED**

210

679 　SAI, SA, futata*bi*　　再生　SAISEI　　　　regeneration
　　　　　AGAIN, TWICE, RE-　再刊　SAIKAN　　　　　reprint
　　　　　6 strokes　　　　　再来年 SARAINEN year after next

舟 is the lower part of accumulate/ **build with baskets** 冓 675, namely an inverted **basket. One** 一 1 was added to indicate **one further basket** being added to the pile. The idea of **one more** led to the present meanings.

Mnemonic: **ADD ONE BASKET AGAIN**

680 　SAI, wazawa*i*　　　災難　SAINAN　　　　calamity
　　　　　CALAMITY　　　　　災害　SAIGAI　　　　　disaster
　　　　　7 strokes　　　　　火災　KASAI　　　conflagration

Once written 𡿧, showing **river** 川 48, here meaning **flood**, and **fire** 火 8. **Fire** and **flood** were symbols of **calamity**.

Mnemonic: **FIRE AND FLOODING RIVER ARE POTENTIAL CALAMITIES**

681 　SAI, tsuma　　　　後妻　GOSAI　　　　second wife
　　　　　WIFE　　　　　　　夫妻　FUSAI　husband and wife
　　　　　8 strokes　　　　　人妻　HITOZUMA
　　　　　　　　　　　　　　　　　　　　married woman

女 is **woman** 35. 彗 derives from 㞷, showing a **hand** ⇒ **holding a broom** ψ (to all intents and purposes a variant of hand holding broom 帚 96). See also 779.

Mnemonic: **WIFE HOLDS BROOM IN HAND**

682 　SAI, to*ru*　　　　採用　SAIYŌ　　　　adoption
　　　　　TAKE, GATHER　　採集　SAISHŪ　　　collection
　　　　　11 strokes　　　　採取　SAISHU　　　harvesting

Hand plucking (fruit) from a tree 采 483, with an extra **hand** 扌 32. Suggest taking 采 literally as (reaching) **hand** 爪 303 and **tree** 木 69.

Mnemonic: **GATHER FRUIT FROM TREE WITH TWO HANDS**

211

683 SAI, kiwa
OCCASION, EDGE,
CONTACT
14 strokes

実際 JISSAI　　　　actuality
国際 KOKUSAI　　international
窓際 MADOGIWA
　　　　　　　beside window

β is **hill** 229 q.v., here meaning **earthen rampart**. 祭 is **festival** 283, acting phonetically to express **meet/ come into contact** and possibly also loosely lending similar connotations of its own (from the idea of meeting associated with a festival). Thus **earthen ramparts meeting**, i.e. the junction of walls. This later came to mean **meet/ come into contact** in general. **Edge** is an associated meaning from that which comes into contact. **Occasion** is also felt to be an associated meaning, i.e. when one can come into contact with others.

Mnemonic: **FESTIVAL AT EDGE OF HILL IS QUITE AN OCCASION**

684 ZAI, aru
BE LOCATED, DWELL,
COUNTRYSIDE, BE
6 strokes

存在 SONZAI　　　　existence
在留 ZAIRYŪ　　　residence
在所 ZAISHO　　country home

才 is a variant of **talent** 才 126 q.v., here used in its literal meaning of **dam** and by extension **barrier**. 土 is **earth** 60. Thus **earthen dam/ barrier**. The idea of substantial/ solid barrier led to the idea of **being firmly in place**, eventually giving **be located** and simply **be**. **Dwell/ reside** is an extension of be located. It is not fully clear how 684 also came to mean **countryside**, but it is assumed to be an associated meaning of dwell, i.e. one's **country home**.

Mnemonic: **FUNNY DAM IS LOCATED NEAR COUNTRYSIDE DWELLING**

685 ZAI, SAI
WEALTH, ASSETS
10 strokes

財産 ZAISAN　　wealth, assets
財団 ZAIDAN　　　foundation
財政的 ZAISEITEKI　　financial

貝 is **shell/ money** 90, here meaning **wealth/ assets**. 才 is **talent** 126 q.v., here acting phonetically to express **accumulate** and also lending a similar idea from its literal meaning of **dam** (i.e. that which causes a build-up). Thus **accumulated wealth/ assets**.

Mnemonic: **DAM FULL OF MONEY MEANS GREAT WEALTH**

686 罪	ZAI, tsumi CRIME, SIN 13 strokes	犯罪 HANZAI	crime
		罪悪 ZAIAKU	vice
		罪深い TSUMIBUKAI	sinful

Somewhat obscure. 罒 is **net** 193, here with connotations of **catching**. 非 is **not** 773 q.v. Some scholars feel the latter acts purely phonetically to express **catch**, giving **catch in a net**, while others feel that it lends its literal meaning of **going in opposite directions** to refer by extension to **rebels**, thus giving **catch rebels in a net**. It is also not clear whether **crime/ sin** is a borrowed meaning or an associated meaning from the idea of that which results in one being caught, though the latter seems more likely.

Mnemonic: **NOT A NETWORK, BUT STILL CRIMINAL**

687 雑	ZATSU, ZŌ MISCELLANY 14 strokes	雑談 ZATSUDAN	chitchat
		雑音 ZATSUON	noise, static
		雑兵 ZŌHYŌ	rank and file

Formerly 襍. 杂 is **cloth** 420 q.v. 椎 is a variant of 集, an element showing **tree** 木 69 and **bird** 隹 216 and meaning **birds gathering in a tree**. Here 椎 acts phonetically to express **gather** and also lends a similar meaning. 687 originally referred to **gathering bits of cloth** and making up a **patchwork** garment from them. Rather like the English term patchwork, it came to mean **miscellany** in a broad sense. Cloth 杂 was later replaced with **nine** 九 12, presumably to indicate plurality/ **many** (i.e. gather many bits). It is somewhat surprising that the cloth radical 衤 was never used, to give 襍.

Mnemonic: **NINE MISCELLANEOUS BIRDS GATHERED IN TREE**

688	SAN, kaiko SILKWORM 10 strokes	蚕業 SANGYŌ	sericulture
		養蚕 YŌSAN	sericulture
		蚕豆 SORAMAME*	broad bean

Formerly 蠶. 蝨 is **insect** 虫 56 doubled for emphasis. 朁 is a CO character meaning **if/ supposing**. It comprises the CO character **not/ without** 旡 (of unclear etymology, but derived from 旡, felt to show a person kneeling [at a table] with head turned, indicating that they are **unable** to eat any more), and the NGU character **say** 曰 (often written as 日 and confused with sun/day 日 62, but in fact the cross-stroke is only threequarter size and indicates a tongue — inside a mouth 口 20, not unlike the lower element of sound 音 6), thus giving a meaning of **not actually stated** and by extension **(but) if/ supposing (that)**. In the case of 688 朁 acts phonetically to express **swollen**, to give **swollen insect**, a reference to a **silkworm full of silk threads**. In view of its complexity 朁 probably also lent some meaning, but this is unclear. It may have lent connotations of swollen/ bloated from the satiated person element 旡, or may have lent some idea of hypotheticality, as in a silkworm which <u>should</u> produce silk. Suggest taking 天 as **heaven** 58.

Mnemonic: **SILKWORM IS A HEAVENLY INSECT**

689

SAN, sui/*ppai*
ACID, BITTER
14 strokes

酸素 SANSO oxygen
酸性 SANSEI acidity
塩酸 ENSAN hydrochloric acid

酉 is wine jar/ **alcohol** 302, here meaning **alcohol-like liquid**. 夋 is a CO character meaning **linger/ dawdle** (of unclear etymology, but showing stop and start 夂 438 q.v, meaning slow progress, and 允, which appears to be self 厶 134 and legs 儿). Here 夋 acts phonetically to express **sharp**, and almost certainly also lends its meaning of **linger**. Thus **sharp alcohol-like liquid (that lingers in the mouth?)**, leading to **bitter taste** and eventually also **acid**. Suggest remembering 夋 as **linger**.

Mnemonic: **ALCOHOL HAS LINGERING BITTER ACID TASTE**

690 賛

SAN
PRAISE
15 strokes

賛成 SANSEI approval
賛美歌 SANBIKA hymn
賛辞 SANJI eulogy

Formerly 贊. 貝 is shell/ **money** 90, here meaning **valuable object**. 兟 is precede/ **advance** 先 49 doubled for emphasis. The latter lends its sound to express **offer**, and may also lend an associated transitive meaning of **advance/ proffer**. 690 originally meant to **offer someone a valuable object**, leading to the idea of **reward** and **praise**. Suggest taking 夫 as **male** 573.

Mnemonic: **TWO MALES PRAISED AND GIVEN MONEY**

691

SHI, sasa*eru*
BRANCH, SUPPORT
4 strokes

支店 SHITEN branch office
支持 SHIJI support
支点 SHITEN fulcrum

Once written 支, showing a **hand** ⇁ holding up a **branch/** section of bamboo 个 (see 170). It originally meant **break off a branch/** small section/ offshoot. The physical branch is now represented by 枝 1315, that adds wood/tree 木 69, whereas 691 has come to refer to **branch** in the figurative sense (as in branch office etc.) **Support** derives from the idea of holding up.

Mnemonic: **HAND SUPPORTS CROSS-SHAPED BRANCH**

692 SHI,kokoroza*su*,kokorozashi 意志 ISHI   will
WILL, INTENT   志望 SHIBŌ   aspiration
7 strokes   有志 YŪSHI   voluntary

Usually explained as the **heart** 心 147 of a **warrior** 士 494. A useful mnemonic, but incorrect. Old forms such as 㞢 and 㞢 show that 士 derives from **emerging plant** 㞢/生 42, here acting phonetically to express **move** and also lending similar connotations of its own (from growth/ emerge). Thus **movement of the heart**, indicating **intent** or **will**.

Mnemonic: **WARRIOR'S HEART SHOWS WILL**

693 SHI   教師 KYŌSHI   teacher
TEACHER, MODEL, ARMY   師表 SHIHYŌ   paragon
10 strokes   師団 SHIDAN   army division

Somewhat obscure. 𠂤 is shown in some early forms to be **hill** 229 q.v. and in others to be **buttocks** 350 q.v., though in both cases the meaning is known to be **swelling/ rising**. 帀 is an inverted form of 㞢, itself a variant of **growing plant** 生 42 q.v., which acts phonetically to express **hill** and also lends a similar meaning of **rising** (from the idea of growing up from the ground). Thus **prominent hill**. Hills were often associated with **troop encampments** (see 540), and 693 eventually came to acquire such associations itself, leading to the present meaning of **army**. **Teacher** results from confusion with **commander/ leader** 帥 1454 q.v., of which it is an extended meaning, while **model** is an associated meaning with teacher. Suggest taking 𠂤 as **buttocks**, and 帀 as **cloth** 巾 778 and **one** 一 1.

Mnemonic: **MODEL TEACHER HAS ONE BIT OF CLOTH OVER BUTTOCKS**

694 SHI   資本 SHIHON   capital
CAPITAL, RESOURCES   資料 SHIRYŌ   raw materials
13 strokes   資金 SHIKIN   funds

貝 is shell/ **money** 90. 次 is **next** 292 q.v., here acting phonetically to express **possess** and almost certainly also lending an idea of **continuity**. Thus to **possess** (a **continuity of?**) **money**, i.e. **capital/ resources**.

Mnemonic: **NEXT SUM OF MONEY PROVIDES CAPITAL**

695

JI, SHI, shimes*u*
SHOW
5 strokes

暗示 ANJI　　　　　hint
展示 TENJI　　　　display
示教 SHIKYŌ　　　guidance

Once written 示 or 示 . 丁 is a primitive **altar**. ' ' / ' ' is **drops** of blood (or possibly sacrificial wine). A top stroke ¯ was added later to indicate a **sacrifice**/ item placed on the altar. Though as an independent character 695 is no longer used to mean altar, as a radical (usually 礻) it frequently has a meaning of **related to the gods**. **Show** is an extended meaning, from the idea of the outcome of a sacrifice showing the will of the gods.

Mnemonic: **DROPS FROM ALTAR SACRIFICE SHOW WILL OF GODS**

696

JI, ni*ru*
RESEMBLE
7 strokes

類似品 RUIJIHIN　　imitation
似非 ESE-*　　false, sham
似合う NIAU　　　be suited

亻 is **person** 39. 以 is **starting point**/ means 419, acting phonetically to express **resemble** and possibly also lending an idea of **starting point**. Thus to **resemble a person** (whom one takes as a starting point?). Now used of **resemble** in a broad sense.

Mnemonic: **STARTING POINT FOR PERSON IS TO RESEMBLE ONE**

697

JI, NI, ko
CHILD
7 strokes

孤児 KOJI　　　　orphan
小児 SHŌNI　　　infant
児童文学 JIDŌBUNGAKU
　　　　　juvenile literature

Formerly 兒 , and earlier as 兒 ハ/ハ shows a **person kneeling** (i.e. **not standing**) 39, while 臼 is mortar 648. Some scholars feel the latter is used purely phonetically to express **weak**/ **helpless**, giving **helpless person (unable to stand)**, that could originally apply to a very aged or sick person as well as a very young one. Others feel that 臼 is used in its literal sense of **grinding teeth**, referring to **young children during the teething stage**, and take ハ to refer to **crawling**. Thus **crawling, teeth-grinding person**. The latter theory seems the more likely. (Note also similar English slang terms for a teething, crawling infant, such as anklebiter.) Suggest taking 旧 as **old** 648.

Mnemonic: **OLD PERSON IS REALLY A CHILD**

698 **SHIKI** 常識 JŌSHIKI common sense
KNOWLEDGE 意識 ISHIKI awareness
19 strokes 知識人 CHISHIKIJIN intellectual

言 is **words** 274, 音 is **sound** 6, and 戈 is **lance/ halberd** 493, though there is some disagreement as to how these elements are grouped. 戈 is known to have acted to mean **marker** or **sign**. (A lance was sometimes thrust into the ground -- in some cases with a banner attached -- as a crude marker or pointer [note also the graphic and semantic overlap with stake 戈 177].) Some scholars take 識 as the NGU character **memorise**, ascribing a meaning to 698 of **memorise signs** and therefore **possess knowledge**. Others take 識 as meaning **marker**. (It is in fact a CO character with a range of borrowed meanings, but its original meaning is felt to have been lance that produces 'sound', i.e. conveys a message. This was a reference to the fact that messages as well as banners were sometimes attached to marker lances.) Thus **marker that produces words**, i.e. with words 言 reinforcing the message-conveying role discussed above. Conveying information then came by association to mean **intelligence/ knowledge**. Since 音 and 戈 have become combined to 識, suggesting that they are treated as one element, and since the element occurs with some frequency in compound characters, the latter theory seems the more likely.

Mnemonic: **HAVE KNOWLEDGE OF A WORD SOUNDING LIKE LANCE**

---

699 **SHITSU, SHICHI, CHI** 品質 HINSHITSU quality
QUALITY, PAWN 質屋 SHICHIYA pawnshop
15 strokes 人質 HITOJICHI hostage

貝 is **shell/ money** 90. 斦 is **ax** 1176 doubled for emphasis, acting phonetically to express **equivalence** and almost certainly lending an idea of **chop up** (figuratively) and hence **analyse/understand** (see 199). Thus **something whose monetary equivalence is understood**, leading on the one hand to **quality** and on the other to **pawn/ pledge**.

Mnemonic: **TWO AXES CHOP PAWNED SHELL TO ASCERTAIN QUALITY**

---

700 **SHA** 宿舎 SHUKUSHA lodgings
HOUSE, QUARTERS 舎営 SHAEI billet
8 strokes 田舎者 INAKAMONO* yokel

Formerly 舍, and earlier 舍. 口 is **mouth** 20, here meaning by extension **breathe**. 余/ 舍/ 全 is margin 余 800 q.v., here lending its connotations of **easily**. Thus **breathe easily/ relax**. Possibly because of the **roof/ building** element 人 in 全, 700 presently came (like 800) to mean **building where one can relax**, i.e. one's **house** or **quarters**. Suggest taking 人 as **roof**, 土 as **ground** 60, and 口 as **opening/ entrance**.

Mnemonic: **QUARTERS WITH ROOF AND ENTRANCE BELOW GROUND**

217

| 701 | | SHA, ayama*ru*
APOLOGIZE, THANK
17 strokes | 謝罪 SHAZAI
謝礼 SHAREI
感謝 KANSHA | apology
honorarium
gratitude |

言 is **words** 274. 射 is **shoot** 882 q.v., here acting phonetically to express **leave** and almost certainly lending similar connotations (from an arrow leaving the bow, and cf. English slang 'shoot off' meaning leave). Thus **words said upon leaving**.

Mnemonic: **WORDS OF APOLOGY AND THANKS AS ONE SHOOTS OFF**

| 702 | | JU, sazu*keru*
CONFER, TEACH
11 strokes | 授業 JUGYŌ
授与 JUYO
教授 KYŌJU | tuition
conferment

teaching, professor |

Receive 受 303 q.v., here in its literal sense of **convey**, with an extra **hand** 扌 32. Whereas 303 came to mean receive, 702 came rather to mean **confer/ bestow**, including in the sense of confer knowledge / **teach**.

Mnemonic: **TEACHER'S HAND CONFERS RECEIPT**

| 703 | | SH Ū, osa*meru/maru*
OBTAIN, STORE,
SUPPLY
4 strokes | 収入 SHŪNYŪ
収益 SHŪEKI
収容力 SHŪYŌRYOKU | income
gains
capacity |

Formerly 收. 攵 is **striking hand/ coerce** 101, here used as a **causative** element. 丩 derives from 𠃑, showing **intertwined threads** and meaning put together/ **assemble**, and by extension **gather**. Some scholars feel 丩 also acts phonetically to express **seek out**. Thus to **cause threads to be (sought out and?) gathered together**. This came to mean simply **gather** and by extension **obtain**, with **store** being an associated meaning. **Supply** is felt to be in turn an associated meaning with store. The modern form uses **hand** 又 instead of striking hand 攵. Suggest taking 丩 as a **pitchfork**.

Mnemonic: **HAND OBTAINS PITCHFORK FROM SUPPLY STORE**

704

SHŪ, SHU, osa*meru*/*maru*
PRACTICE, MASTER
10 strokes

修理 SHŪRI　　　　　repair
修正 SHŪSEI　　　amendment
修業 SHUGYŌ /SHŪGYŌ
　　　　　　　　　　study

彡 is **delicate hairs** 93 q.v., here lending an idea both of **elegant** and of **brush**. 攸 comprises **stick in hand/ strike** 攵 101, a further **stick** | , and **person** 亻 39, and means to **strike a person with a stick**. 704 originally referred to 'striking' a person with a brush in order to make them appear elegant, i.e. brushing specks of dust/ dirt off their clothes. It then came to mean **make something just so**, leading by association to **practice** and **master**.

Mnemonic: **PERSON PRACTICES TO MASTER STRIKING WITH BRUSH**

705

SHŪ, SHU
MULTITUDE, MASS
12 strokes

公衆 KŌSHŪ　　　　　public
大衆 TAISHŪ　　　the masses
合衆国 GASSHŪKOKU　USA

Formerly 眾. An early form 𥇡 shows that 血 derives from **eye** 𥃭/目 72 tilted on a horizontal axis, while the oldest form 𠂤 shows that it is in fact a miscopying of **sun** ☉/ 日 62. 乑 shows **person** 亻 39 trebled to indicate a **large number**. Thus a **large number of people gathered (working?) under the sun**, later presumably misinterpreted as a large number of people gathered under a **watchful eye**. The reason for the later addition of ⟋ over the eye is not clear, but suggest taking it as an **eyelash**, with a play on the word **lash**.

Mnemonic: **MASS OF ODD PEOPLE UNDER WATCHFUL EYE WITH LASH**

706

SHUKU, SHŪ, iwa*u*
CELEBRATE
9 strokes

祝賀 SHUKUGA　　celebration
祝辞 SHUKUJI congratulations
祝い事 IWAIGOTO　happy event

Formerly 祝. 示/ネ is **altar** 695. 兄 is **elder brother** 267 q.v., here used in its literal sense of **person speaking (and crouching/ bending?)**. Thus **person (kneeling?) at altar**, i.e. **giving thanks**.

Mnemonic: **ELDER BROTHER CELEBRATES AT ALTAR**

219

707		JUTSU, noberu	前述 ZENJUTSU no	the said
		STATE, RELATE	述語 JUTSUGO	predicate
		8 strokes	叙述 JOJUTSU	description

Originally 術, showing **movement** 彳/辶 129 and a **hand** ⇒ with **bits** (of glutinous rice)丶 **sticking** to it. 朮/朮 thus has a meaning of **stick/ adhere**, and 707 originally referred to 'sticking' to a person as they moved, i.e. **following** them. This came to mean 'shadow' a person in a broad sense, including **repetition** of their words. Repeat then came to mean simply **relate** or **state**. Suggest taking 朮 as a **'funny' tree** 木 69.

Mnemonic: **STATE HOW ONE MOVED AROUND FUNNY TREE**

708		JUTSU, sube	技術的 GIJUTSUTEKI technical	
		MEANS, TECHNIQUE	芸術的 GEIJUTSUTEKI artistic	
		11 strokes	手術 SHUJUTSU operation	

彳 is **go** 118, here also lending its literal connotations of **roads**. 朮 is **adhere** 707 q.v., here acting phonetically to express **twisting** and almost certainly lending its meaning of adhere/ follow. Thus **twisting road/ path to which one adheres**, a reference to the **means/ technique** to be followed in order to achieve one's goal. Suggest taking 朮 as a **'funny' tree** 木 69.

Mnemonic: **GO AROUND FUNNY TREE WITH CERTAIN TECHNIQUE**

709		JUN	準備 JUNBI	preparation
		LEVEL, CONFORM,	水準 SUIJUN	standard
		QUASI-	準決勝 JUNKESSHŌ	semifinals
		13 strokes		

Formerly also 準, with **ice** 冫 378 replacing **water** 氵 40. 隼 is a CO character meaning hawk, deriving from **bird** 隹 216 and either talons or a branch 十. 隼 is used here phonetically to express **level**, and possibly also lends connotations of **settled** from the idea of a hawk settled on a branch. Thus 709 meant **water (settled?) at a level**. **Quasi-** and **conform** both stem from the idea of more or less attaining a level. Suggest taking 十 as **ten** 33. See also 1376.

Mnemonic: **TEN BIRDS ON WATER, ALL AT SAME LEVEL**

710 JO, tsuide
BEGINNING, ORDER
7 strokes

序文 JOBUN   preface
序列 JORETSU   order
序数 JOSŪ   ordinal number

广 is **building** 114. 予 is **already/ in advance** 403. Thus **that which one does in advance of (erecting) a building**, namely lay the foundations. Thus the **beginning** of something, and by extension (proper) **order**.

Mnemonic: **BUILDING ALREADY BEGINNING TO SHOW ORDER**

---

711 JO, JI, nozo*ku*
EXCLUDE, REMOVE
10 strokes

除去 JOKYO   removal
免除 MENJO   exemption
掃除 SŌJI   cleaning

阝 is **mound/ hill** 229 q.v. 余 is **margin/ surplus** 800 q.v. Some scholars feel the latter lends its literal meaning of **open up** to give **open up hilly ground**, i.e. by **removing** obstacles. Others feel that 阝 is used in its sense of **terracing/ steps** with 余 acting purely phonetically to express **order/ sequence**, giving **sequence of steps**, and that the present meanings are borrowed. The fact that in Chinese 711 has a lesser meaning of **steps** suggests that the latter theory is correct, though the former may be a useful mnemonic.

Mnemonic: **SURPLUS HILLS MUST BE REMOVED**

---

712 SHŌ, mane*ku*
INVITE, SUMMON
8 strokes

招待 SHŌTAI   invitation
招集 SHŌSHŪ   convocation
手招く TEMANEKU   beckon

Hand 扌 32 and **summon** 召 1387 q.v., giving **summon with the hand/ beckon**. Now **invite** in a broad sense.

Mnemonic: **INVITE BY SUMMONING WITH HAND**

221

713 承

SHŌ, uketamawaru
RECEIVE, HEAR, KNOW
8 strokes

承知 SHŌCHI   consent
承認 SHŌNIN   recognition
継承者 KEISHŌSHA   successor

Originally 承, showing a **hand** 𠂇/手 32 and **two hands holding up an object** 𠬻. The latter is to all intents and purposes the prototype of **together** 共 460 q.v., but confusingly, the same pictograph can also indicate (as here) **receiving**, since the formal manner of receiving is to hold the item up level with the forehead. The extra hand 𠂇 is theoretically for clarity, though it might be argued that it would have been better added to 460 than to 713. Possibly because the object ○ was misinterpreted as **mouth/ say** 20, 713 also came to acquire connotations of **receiving spoken information**, leading to **hear** and **know**. Suggest taking 承 as a **baby** 子 25 with **bristles** ≡, and ⌄< as a variant of **water** 水 40.

Mnemonic: **HEAR ABOUT A BRISTLY WATER-BABY**

---

714 称

SHŌ
PRAISE, NAME, CHANT
10 strokes

称号 SHŌGŌ   title
称賛 SHŌSAN   praise
名称 MEISHŌ   name

Formerly 稱. 禾 is **rice plant** 81. ⩘ is **hand reaching down** 303. 冉 is **basket** 675. Thus **hand reaching down to (pluck) rice plants and put same in basket**. This work was invariably accompanied by singing and **chanting**, and thus 714 later came to mean **chant**. **Name** is an associated meaning. **Praise** is also felt by some scholars to be an associated meaning, and by others to be a borrowing. Suggest remembering 尓 by partial association with **bamboo** 竹 170 and **eight** 八 66.

Mnemonic: **PRAISE EIGHT BAMBOO-LIKE RICE PLANTS**

---

715 証

SHŌ
PROOF
12 strokes

証人 SHŌNIN   witness
論証 RONSHŌ   demonstration
証明 SHŌMEI   proof

Formerly also 證, though technically they are separate characters. 言 is **words** 274. 登 is **climb** 360, acting phonetically to express **clear/ clarify** and possibly also lending an idea of **offer up**. Thus (to offer up?) **clarifying words**, i.e. **prove/ proof**. 登 has now been replaced with **correct** 正 41, though 証 is actually a character of long standing that originally meant **remonstrate/ counsel against**.

Mnemonic: **CORRECT WORDS ARE PROOF**

716 JŌ
CLAUSE, ITEM, LINE
7 strokes

無条件 MUJŌKEN unconditional
条約 JŌYAKU treaty
条鉄 JŌTETSU bar-iron

Formerly 條, showing **wood/tree** 木 69 and **hand striking person with stick** 攵 704. Thus **wooden stick/ branch for striking**. On the one hand **stick** led to the idea of something straight and thus **line**, including in the figurative sense of a line of argument, and on the other **branch** led to the idea of something small broken off from the main part, and thus acquired connotations of **small part** and hence **item/ detail**. The two meanings overlapped to give a detailed line of argument, leading to **clause**. Suggest taking 夂 as **sitting crosslegged**.

Mnemonic: **ITEM ABOUT SITTING CROSSLEGGED IN TREE**

717 JŌ
CONDITION, LETTER
7 strokes

状態 JŌTAI situation
現状 GENJŌ status quo
招待状 SHŌTAIJŌ
letter of invitation

Formerly 狀. 犬 is **dog** 17. 爿 is bed 1389, here used purely phonetically to express **appearance**. Thus **appearance/ condition of a dog**. This later came to mean **condition/ situation** in a broad sense, and also extended to the idea of writing a **report** about a situation, hence **letter**. Suggest taking 丬 as a **bar** | of ice 冫 378.

Mnemonic: **DOG EATS BAR OF ICE, NOW IN BAD CONDITION**

718 JŌ, tsune
USUAL, ALWAYS
11 strokes

非常 HIJŌ emergency
常例 JŌREI convention
日常 NICHIJŌ daily

巾 is **cloth/ threads** 778. 尚 is **furthermore** 1392 q.v., here acting phonetically to express **long** and probably also lending an idea of **trailing** from its original meaning of smoke trailing upwards from a window. Thus **long trailing threads**, later used figuratively to describe something **ongoing** and hence **usual/ always**.

Mnemonic: **FURTHERMORE, THE USUAL CLOTH, AS ALWAYS**

223

719				
	JŌ, SEI, nasake	同情	DŌJŌ	sympathy
	FEELING, PITY, FACT	情勢	JŌSEI	situation
	11 strokes	情け無い	NASAKENAI	wretched

忄 is **heart/ feeling** 147. 青 is **blue/ green** 43 q.v., here lending its connotations of **fresh** and **pure**. Thus **pure heart**, leading by association to **compassion** (cf. English 'heart'). **Fact/ situation** stems from the idea of a heart with nothing to hide, i.e. exposing the truth.

Mnemonic: **HEART MADE BLUE WITH FEELING OF PITY**

720				
	SHOKU, SHIKI, oru	織機	SHOKKI	loom
	WEAVE	組織的	SOSHIKITEKI	systematic
	18 strokes	織り物	ORIMONO	textiles

糸 is **thread** 27. 戠 is **marker-lance** 698. Some scholars see 720 as an ideographic combination of these elements to give **marker threads**, used at a certain stage in **weaving**. Others feel that 戠 acts phonetically to express **straight/ upright**, as well as lending similar connotations of its own (from a lance thrust upright in the ground), to give **upright threads**, a reference to the warp threads that symbolise the start of **weaving**. Suggest taking 戠 literally as **lance** 戈 493 and **noise** 音 6.

Mnemonic: **WEAVE THREADS WITH NOISE LIKE A LANCE**

721				
職	SHOKU	職人	SHOKUNIN	artisan
	EMPLOYMENT, JOB	職業	SHOKUGYŌ	profession
	18 strokes	職員	SHOKUIN	staff

耳 is **ear** 29, here used figuratively to mean **flap/ attached item**. 戠 is **marker-lance** 698 q.v., here used in its literal sense of pole stuck in ground to indicate something. Thus 721 originally meant **marker-pole with something (flag or similar) attached to it**. This was a reference to tradesmen's practice of erecting outside their premises a flagpole bearing a flag which indicated the nature of their business. Hence 721 came to refer to **employment**. Suggest taking 戠 literally as **lance** 戈 493 and **noise** 音 6.

Mnemonic: **JOB AS LANCER LEAVES NOISE IN EARS**

722

SEI
SYSTEM, CONTROL
8 strokes

制度 **SEIDO** — system
制止 **SEISHI** — restraint
強制 **KYŌSEI** — compulsion

Once written 㓞, showing sword/ **cut** 刀/刂 181 and a **many branched tree** 朱 (variant **tree** 木 69). 722 originally meant **prune a tree**, leading by extension to **put in order** and thence **control**, with **system** being an associated meaning. Suggest remembering 制 by partial association with **cow** 牛 97.

Mnemonic: **TREE CUT IN SHAPE OF COW SHOWS SYSTEM OF SORTS**

723

SEI, SHŌ
NATURE, SEX
8 strokes

男性 **DANSEI** — male
性的 **SEITEKI** — sexual
性分 **SHŌBUN** — disposition

Heart/ **feeling** 忄 147 and **birth** 生 42, giving the **heart one is born with**, i.e. one's **nature**. **Gender**/ **sex** is an associated meaning.

Mnemonic: **ONE'S NATURE IS THE HEART ONE IS BORN WITH**

724

政

SEI, SHŌ, matsurigoto
GOVERNMENT
9 strokes

行政 **GYŌSEI** — administration
政治家 **SEIJIKA** — politician
中央政府 **CHŪŌSEIFU** — central government

正 is **correct** 41. 攵 is **strike**/ **force** 101, here acting as a causative element. Thus to **make something correct**, leading to **govern** and **government**.

Mnemonic: **GOVERNMENT FORCES CORRECTNESS**

725

SEI, SHŌ
SPIRIT, VITALITY,
REFINE, DETAIL
14 strokes

精力 **SEIRYOKU** — vitality
精密 **SEIMITSU** — precision
不精 **BUSHŌ** — indolence

米 is **rice** 201. 青 is **blue**/ **green** 43 q.v., here lending its connotations of **fresh** and **pure**. Thus **pure rice**. This led by extension to **refine**, with **detail** being an associated meaning (i.e. going into detail by removing even the tiniest impurity). **Spirit** is an associated meaning with purity (cf. English quintessence), leading by extension to **vitality** (cf. English spirit).

Mnemonic: **REFINED GREEN RICE FILLS ONE WITH SPIRIT**

225

726 　SEI
MANUFACTURE
14 strokes

製造　SEIZŌ　manufacture
精製　SEISEI　refining
日本製　NIHONSEI made in Japan

衣 is **clothing** 420. 㓞 is **system**/ control 722 q.v., here lending its meaning of **cut to shape**. Thus **cut clothes to shape**, i.e. **make clothes**, later **make**/ **manufacture** in a broad sense.

Mnemonic: **SYSTEM FOR MANUFACTURING CLOTHING**

727 　ZEI
TAX, TITHE
12 strokes

税金　ZEIKIN　tax
税務所　ZEIMUSHO　tax office
所得税　SHOTOKUZEI income tax

禾 is **rice (plant)** 81. 兌 is exchange 524 q.v., here acting phonetically to express **divide** and also lending connotations of disperse/ **give away**. Thus to **divide up rice and give (part of) it away**, a reference to paying a **tithe**/ **tax**. Suggest taking 兌 literally as **elder brother** 兄 267 and **away** ⸜ 66.

Mnemonic: **ELDER BROTHER GIVES AWAY RICE-TAX**

---

728 責　SEKI, se*meru*
LIABILITY, BLAME
11 strokes

責任　SEKININ　responsibility
自責　JISEKI　self-reproach
責務　SEKIMU　duty

Popularly explained to the effect that 貝 is shell/ **money** 90 and 主 is a variant of **growth** 生 42, giving a meaning of **growing**/ **accumulating money** and by association growing **responsibilities / liabilities**. A useful mnemonic, but old forms such as 寋 show that 主 is in fact a variant of **taper** 朿 873. Here it acts phonetically to express **demand**, and may possibly also lend connotations of **sharp**. Thus **money which can be demanded** (sharply/ promptly?), i.e. a **loan**/ **debt** (still retained in Chinese, and see also debt/ loan 債 1292). A debt necessarily involves the idea of **liability**. **Blame** is felt to stem from an associated idea of culpability. Since 728 often seems to lend a meaning of accumulate in compounds (e.g. 521and 729) it is possible that the 'growing money' interpretation is of long standing, though it is also possible that accumulation is a concept associated with debt/ liability.

Mnemonic: **GROWING MONEY DEBTS MEAN GROWING LIABILITY**

---

729 績 **SEKI**   成績 SEISEKI   result
ACHIEVEMENT, SPIN   業績 GYŌSEKI   achievement
17 strokes   紡績 BŌSEKI   spinning

糸 is **thread** 27. 責 is **blame/ liability** 728 q.v., here used phonetically to express **join** and possibly also lending an idea of **accumulate**. 729 originally referred to **joining threads by spinning**, and also had strong connotations of the **amount** of thread spun. Amount led to the figurative **achievement**.

Mnemonic: **BLAME THREADS FOR POOR ACHIEVEMENTS IN SPINNING**

---

730 接 **SETSU, tsugu**   面接 MENSETSU   interview
CONTACT, JOIN   接続 SETSUZOKU connection
11 strokes   接ぎ目 TSUGIME   joint

扌 is **hand** 32. 妾 is an NGU character meaning concubine. It was once written 妾, showing that 立 is a variant of (tattooist's) **needle** 辛 1432, while 女 is **woman** 35. Some scholars interpret needle 立 as symbolising tattooed **slave** (see 340), giving **slave woman**, but as it could also symbolise penetration and by extension **copulation** 妾 may simply mean **woman with whom one copulates**. In fact, in view of its strong connotations of **join** (e.g. with tree 木 69 it gives the CO character graft 楼) the latter explanation seems the more likely. In the case of 730 妾 acts phonetically to express **take** and almost certainly also lends a meaning of **join**, giving **take someone by the hand/ join hands** and hence eventually **join/ contact** in a broad sense. Suggest taking 立 as **stand** 73.

Mnemonic: **JOIN HANDS WITH WOMAN STANDING ALONE**

---

731 設 **SETSU, mōkeru**   設置 SETCHI   founding
ESTABLISH, BUILD   設計 SEKKEI   design
11 strokes   設立 SETSURITSU founding

Once written 設, but earlier still as 𣪊, showing that **words** 音/言 is in fact a miscopying of ▽, which is assumed to be a wedge or **stake**. 夂/殳 is a **striking hand holding a utensil** (see 153), in this case a mallet or **hammer**. 731 originally meant to **set about laying foundations by driving in stakes**, and hence came to mean **build, found**, and so forth.

Mnemonic: **BUILD WITH WORDS, DESPITE HAMMER IN HAND**

732		ZETSU, shita TONGUE 6 strokes	舌戦 ZESSEN war of words 舌足らず SHITATARAZU lisping 弁舌 BENZETSU eloquence

Once written 舌, showing **mouth** 口 20 and **dry/ forked thrusting weapon** ㄑ /千 825 q.v. The latter acts phonetically to express **emerge**, and also lends its own connotations of **thrusting out**. It may also be felt to lend an idea of **fork**, a forked tongue being a distinctive symbol of a tongue in general. Thus **that (forked item?) which thrusts forth from the mouth**, i.e. the **tongue**.

Mnemonic: **TONGUE SHOWS DRY MOUTH**

733		ZETSU, ta*eru*, ta*tsu* CEASE, SEVER, END 12 strokes	絶望 ZETSUBŌ despair 絶対的 ZETTAITEKI absolute 絶えず TAEZU unceasingly

Formerly 絕 and earlier 𢆡, showing that 色 is not color 色 145 but a miscopying of **bending body** ク / 巴 145 and **sword/ cut** ㇉ /刀 181. 糸 is **thread** 27. 色 acts phonetically to express **bend/ break** and almost certainly lends similar bending connotations of its own (bend and break conceptually overlapping). Thus to **cut and break threads**, leading to **sever** and **cease** in a broad sense. However, suggest taking 色 as **color**.

Mnemonic: **SEVER COLORFUL THREADS**

734		SEN, zeni SEN, COIN, MONEY 14 strokes	小銭 KOZENI small change 金銭 KINSEN money さい銭 SAISEN offertory

Formerly 錢, showing **gold/ metal/ money** 金 14 and two **halberds** 戔 493 q.v. Since the latter often has connotations of **cutting away / reducing** and by extension **small amount** it is often assumed that 734 simply means **small amount of money**. This is a useful mnemonic, but not quite correct. 戔 also has connotations of **sharp**, and in the case of 734 not only lends such a meaning but also acts phonetically to express **taper**. 金 is used in the sense of **metal** rather than money. The character originally meant **sharp tapered piece of metal**, and referred to a **plowshare**. Note that it still retains this meaning in Chinese. Since one of the ancient Chinese **coins** (of small value) resembled the shape of the plow 734 came by association to be applied to this coin, though it is possible that this process may also have been influenced to some extent by a popular reinterpretation of the elements of the character (or at least of 金 as money). In Japanese it is applied by further association to the sen coin, equivalent to one hundredth of a yen. Suggest taking 戔 as **two** = 61 **halberds** 戈 493.

Mnemonic: **TWO GOLD HALBERDS REDUCED TO MERE COIN**

735		ZEN, *yoi*	善意	ZENI	good faith
		GOOD, VIRTUOUS	親善	SHINZEN	friendship
		12 strokes	善後策	ZENGOSAKU	remedy

Once written 羨 , and earlier as 譱. 羊 is **sheep** 986 q.v., here lending its connotations of **fine** and **praiseworthy**. 譱 is the old form of **argue** 諳 463 (literally words 言 274 set against each other). Thus a **praiseworthy argument**, i.e. a **fine debate**. This later came to mean **fine** or **praiseworthy** in a broad sense. Suggest taking as a combination of **sheep** 羊 , **one** 一 1, **small** 小 36, and **mouth** 口 20.

Mnemonic: **SHEEP HAS ONE SMALL BUT GOOD MOUTH**

736	祖	SO	祖先	SOSEN	ancestors
		ANCESTOR	先祖	SENZO	ancestors
		9 strokes	祖父母	SOFUBO	grandparents

Formerly 祖 . 示/ネ is **altar** 695, here indicating **(worship) gods**. 且 is **furthermore/ cairn** 1091, here indicating **accumulation** and also felt by some scholars to act phonetically to express **beginning**. Thus **(worship) an accumulation of gods (going back to the beginning?)**. **Gods** conceptually overlapped with **ancestors**.

Mnemonic: **FURTHERMORE, AT ALTAR ONE WORSHIPS ANCESTORS**

737	素	SO, SU, *moto*	元素	GENSO	element
		ELEMENT, BASE, BARE	要素	YŌSO	factor
		10 strokes	素足	SUASHI	bare feet

Once written 𧃍 , showing **thread** 糸/糸 27 and the prototype 屮 of **droop** 垂 907. The latter acts phonetically to express **white** and almost certainly also lends connotations of **soft**. Thus **soft white threads** (i.e. **silk**), leading to **white silkcloth**. White silkcloth came to represent something **unpatterned** and therefore **undeveloped/ pristine** in a broad sense, giving **elemental, basic, bare**, etc. Suggest taking 主 as a variant of life/ **raw** 生 42.

Mnemonic: **RAW THREADS ARE BARE AND BASIC ELEMENTS**

229

738

SŌ, subete
WHOLE, TOTAL
14 strokes

総額 SŌGAKU   total amount
総合 SŌGŌ   synthesis
総理大臣 SŌRIDAIJIN
    prime minister

Formerly 總. 糸 is **thread** 27. 恖 is an old variant of **window** 窓 919, here acting phonetically to express **gather** and possibly also lending an idea of **widely** (wide/ sweeping being an associated concept with window). Thus to **gather threads (widely?)**, eventually leading to the idea of **assembling every item** in a category and hence **whole/ total**. Suggest taking 公 as **public** 277 and 心 as heart/ **feeling** 147.

Mnemonic: **THREAD RUNS THROUGH PUBLIC FEELING**

739

ZŌ, tsukuru
MAKE, BUILD
10 strokes

造船 ZŌSEN   shipbuilding
木造 MOKUZŌ   wooden
人造 JINZŌ   manmade

Once written 艁, showing **boat** 月/舟 1354 and **proclaim** 告/告 481 q.v. The latter acts phonetically to express **reach** and may also lend its own loose connotations of reach (from the idea of reaching a point where words emerge from the mouth). Thus to **reach somewhere by boat**, with boat 月 later being replaced by **movement** 辶 129 to give just **reach/ arrive** and by extension **attain**. Note that 739 still retains these meanings in Chinese. It is not clear how it came to mean **make/ build**. Some scholars assume it to be a borrowing, while others see it as an associated idea with traveling by boat, i.e. building a boat in order to reach the other side of a body of water, leading to the general idea of making something in order to attain a goal. The fact that in Chinese 739 has strong connotations of acting with haste and expediency suggests the latter theory is correct.

Mnemonic: **PROCLAIM THAT ONE HAS MADE A MOVE**

740

ZŌ
IMAGE
14 strokes

想像 SŌZŌ   imagination
木像 MOKUZŌ   wooden statue
現像 GENZŌ   developing (film)

Person/ man イ 39 and **elephant/ image** 象 533. 740 originally referred to the **image of a person**, but is now used of **image** in a broad sense.

Mnemonic: **IMAGE OF ELEPHANT MAN**

741

ZŌ, ma*su*, fu*eru*/*yasu*
INCREASE, BUILD UP
14 strokes

増大 ZŌDAI　　　increase
増税 ZŌZEI　　tax increase
増幅 ZŌFUKU　amplification

Formerly 增 . 土 is **earth** 60. 曾/曽 is an NGU character now used to express **formerly**, but it originally meant **build up** (symbolically expressed as steam issuing forth 八 66 from a rice cooker 曾 87, indicating a build up of steam/ pressure). Thus 741 originally meant a **build up/ accumulation of earth**, as in a rampart or dam, but now means **build up** or **increase** in general. Suggest taking 曽 as **eight** 八 / 66, **field** 田 59, and **day** 日 62.

Mnemonic: **BUILD UP EARTH IN FIELD OVER EIGHT DAYS**

742

SOKU, nori, notto*ru*
RULE, MODEL,
STANDARD
9 strokes

規則的 KISOKUTEKI　　regular
法則 HŌSOKU　　　　law
原則 GENSOKU　　principle

Once written 䢎, showing that 貝 is not shell/ **money** 貝 90 but a simplification of **kettle** 鼎 228. 刀 / 刂 is sword/ **cut** 181. 貝 acts phonetically to express **mark/ cut** (notches), and may also lend similar connotations (i.e. the kettle may have been marked with a series of notches as a scale of capacity). Thus **cut marks**, a reference to a **scale** or **measure**, leading to the present meanings. Suggest taking 貝 as **money**.

Mnemonic: **RULES REGARDING THE CUTTING OF MONEY**

743

SOKU, haka*ru*
MEASURE, FATHOM
12 strokes

測定 SOKUTEI　measurement
測知 SOKUCHI　　inference
測り難い HAKARIGATAI
　　　　　　hard to fathom

氵 is **water** 40. 則 is **rule** 742 q.v., here used in its sense of **measure**. Thus **measure (the depth of) water**, i.e. **fathom**. Like the English term, fathom is now used in a broad sense.

Mnemonic: **MEASURE WATER WITH FATHOM-RULE**

744 **ZOKU**
BELONG, GENUS
12 strokes

金属 KINZOKU   metal
付属 FUZOKU   attached
属名 ZOKUMEI generic name

Somewhat obscure. Formerly written 屬. 尸 is a variant of **tail** 尾 1734 q.v., while 蜀 is an NGU character meaning **caterpillar** (specifically, a large eyed 皿 72 coiled 勹 655 insect 虫 56). Beyond this point opinions diverge. Some scholars take tail 尸 in its euphemistic role of **genitals**, specifically **vagina** (though it should be noted that it is more commonly used of testicles), and take 蜀 to act phonetically to express **continually emerge**. Thus **that which continually emerges from a vagina**, namely a **succession of children**. The children all **belong** to the same mother, and thus form a **category** (the latter leading to **genus**). Others take **tail** literally, and take 蜀 similarly to act literally as **caterpillar** as well as acting phonetically to express **immovable**. The character is then seen as a reference to the habit of the caterpillar of coiling itself head to tail in what is in effect an immovable position. **Belong** is seen as deriving from the idea of the tail being **firmly joined** to the head in such a position, and **genus** is seen as an associated meaning from the idea of belonging (together). Suggest taking 尸 as **buttocks** 236, and 禹 as **insect** 虫 56 with long **legs** 冂 and **head** ノ.

Mnemonic: **INSECT WITH BUTTOCKS, LEGS, AND HEAD BELONGS TO WHICH GENUS?**

745 **SON, soko**nau
LOSS, SPOIL, MISS
13 strokes

損失 SONSHITSU   loss
損害高 SONGAIDAKA damages
言い損い IISOKONAI
slip of the tongue

扌 is **hand** 32. 員 is **member** 228 q.v., here acting phonetically to express **remove** and also lending its literal connotations of **round vessel**. Thus to **remove with a round (i.e. cupped) hand**. Removing some part led to the idea of being **less than complete/ full**, i.e. having **something missing**, hence **loss** and **spoil**.

Mnemonic: **MEMBER HAS HAND MISSING -- SERIOUS LOSS**

232

746

TAI, shirizoku/keru 後退 KŌTAI　　　　retreat
RETREAT, WITHDRAW 退職 TAISHOKU　retirement
9 strokes 退位 TAII　　　　abdication

Often explained as **movement** 辶 129 and **stop and stare** 艮 263, the latter with its connotations of **turning back**, to give **move back**. A useful mnemonic, but incorrect. Old forms such as 𢓜 reveal that 艮 is actually derived from **sun** 日 62 and **inverted foot** 夂 438 q.v., the latter lending its idea of **coming down from above**. Thus 746 originally referred to the **movement of the setting sun**, i.e. **declination** and by extension **withdrawal** and **retreat**. The graphic evolution of 昮 into 艮 (as opposed to 早 or 夏) suggests a longstanding confusion with stop and stare 艮.

Mnemonic: **STOP AND STARE, THEN MOVE BACK IN RETREAT**

747

TAI, kasu 貸費 TAIHI　　　loan
LEND, LOAN 貸し金 KASHIKIN　　loan
12 strokes 貸し家 KASHIYA　house to let

Shell/ **money** 貝 90 and **replace** 代 338, to express the idea of **providing money against a surety**.

Mnemonic: **LOAN IS REPLACEMENT MONEY**

748

TAI, waza, zama 態度 TAIDO　　　attitude
APPEARANCE, INTENT 態勢 TAISEI　　　position
14 strokes 態態 WAZAWAZA　purposely

Somewhat obscure, though its elements are clearly **heart/ feelings** 心 147 and **ability** 能 766 q.v. Some scholars take the latter to lend connotations of **speed**, giving **quickly changing feelings** and by extension **feelings/ attitude/ intent/ appearance of the moment**. Of the moment is then assumed to have faded with time, leaving just **appearance** and **intent**. Others take 能 to be used primarily phonetically to express **praiseworthy**, as well as lending an extended idea of **dependable**, thus giving **praiseworthy dependable heart/ spirit**. **Appearance** and **intent** are then assumed to be borrowed meanings.

Mnemonic: **HAVE APPEARANCE OF ABLE HEART**

233

749

DAN, TON
GROUP, BODY, MASS,
BALL, ROUND
6 strokes

団体 DANTAI   group
布団 FUTON   bedding
団結 DANKETSU   solidarity

Formerly 團 . 囗 is a **circle** and/or a symbol of **rotation** (see rotate 回 86). 叀 is the old form of exclusive 専 914 q.v., here lending connotations both of **round** and **force** from its literal sense of **spinning weight** and also felt by some scholars to lend its sound to express **round**. 749 originally referred to **something made round**, i.e. a **ball**. By extension this came to mean **lump, mass, body,** etc. **Group** is also generally seen as an extension of the idea of compressing, though some scholars see it rather as deriving from **circle** (of people). The modern form uses just the **measure/ hand** element 寸 909 of 専 .

Mnemonic: **MEASURED CIRCLE PRODUCES WELL ROUNDED GROUP**

750

DAN, kotowa*ru*, ta*tsu*
CUT, DECLINE, WARN,
JUDGE, BE DECISIVE
11 strokes

切断 SETSUDAN   amputation
断言 DANGEN   affirmation
断り書 KOTOWARIGAKI

                 proviso

Formerly 斷 . 斤 is **ax** 1176, here indicating **cutting cleanly**. 㡭 is an element indicating **cut threads** (truncated threads 幺 111 and a symbol of cutting/ compartmenting 匚). Thus to **cut threads cleanly**, later **cut cleanly** in general. This gave rise to a range of extended and associated meanings, such as to **be decisive** and hence **judge, decline,** etc. (cf. the cutting connotations of the English de<u>cis</u>ive). Suggest taking the modern form 米 as **rice** 米 201 in a **corner** 匚 .

Mnemonic: **DECISIVELY DECLINE RICE CUT WITH AX IN CORNER**

751

CHIKU, kizu*ku*
BUILD
16 strokes

建築 KENCHIKU   building
建築家 KENCHIKUKA architect
築き直す KIZUKINAOSU rebuild

木 is **tree/ wood** 69. 筑 is an NGU character meaning **percussion instrument**. It comprises **bamboo** 竹 170 and 㧬, which was originally written 𢒰. This shows a hand holding a plectrum/ stick or similar 又 and the instrument itself 工 (possibly a string), and referred to a stringed instrument struck with bamboo. Here 筑 acts phonetically to express **pound** and lends similar connotations of **striking**. 751 originally referred to a **wooden stamper** used for tamping down ground prior to building, and later came to refer to the act of **building** itself. Suggest taking 工 as **work** 113 and 凡 as **mediocre** 1827.

Mnemonic: **MEDIOCRE WORK WITH WOOD AND BAMBOO IN BUILDING**

| 752 | | CHŌ, har*u*
STRETCH
11 strokes | 主張 SHUCHŌ assertion
拡張 KAKUCHŌ extension
見張る MIHARU guard |

弓 is **bow** 836. 長 is **long** 173, here acting phonetically to express **swell/ curve outwards** and also lending its connotations of **drawn out**. Thus to **draw out bow till it curves**, i.e. **stretch**.

Mnemonic: **DRAW LONGBOW TO FULL STRETCH**

| 753 | | TEI, CHŌ, sa*geru*
HOLD, CARRY, OFFER
12 strokes | 提出 TEISHUTSU presentation
前提 ZENTEI premise
提灯 CHŌCHIN* lantern |

扌 is **hand** 32. 是 is **proper** 910 q.v. The latter acts phonetically to express **hold**, but its semantic role is not clear. It is possible that it lends its later meaning of **proper**, to give **hold properly in the hands** (as when formally **offering/ presenting** something), but also possible that from its literal meaning of **spoon** it lends an extended meaning of **scoop up**, giving **scoop up with the hands**. **Offer/ present** can then be taken as an extended meaning of **hold/ carry**. Somewhat confusingly, 753 is now also used for dangling something from the hands, such as a bucket or similar (see also sageru 下 7).

Mnemonic: **HOLD PROPERLY IN HAND**

| 754 | | TEI, hodo
EXTENT, ABOUT,
ORDER
12 strokes | 程度 TEIDO degree
過程 KATEI process
程近い HODOCHIKAI near |

Somewhat obscure. 禾 is **rice plant** 81. 呈 is **present (verbal report)** 1611. Some scholars feel that 754 originally meant **present a verbal report concerning the rice crop**, and that this involved **estimation/ approximation**, thus leading to the present meanings (cf. English **in the order of**). Others feel that 呈 acts purely phonetically to express **arrange in order**, giving **pile up harvested rice in an orderly fashion**. **Order** is then felt to have given rise to the associated meaning of **degree/ extent**. Suggest taking 呈 as **mouth** 口 20 and **king** 王 5.

Mnemonic: **TO AN EXTENT, RICE ENDS UP IN KING'S MOUTH**

755

TEKI
SUITABLE, FIT, GO
14 strokes

適当 TEKITŌ na　　suitable
適性 TEKISEI　　aptitude
適帰 TEKKI leading, following

辶 is **movement** 129. 啇 is a CO character meaning **base/ starting point**. The latter is of somewhat unclear etymology, though it is known that 啇 is a variant of **emperor/ altar** 帝 1616 q.v. Some scholars take this in its early sense of **altar** and take 口 as a **block** at the **base** of same. Others take 帝 as **emperor** and take 口 to be **mouth/ say** 20, giving **emperor's words**, which were seen as the **basis/ starting point** of all actions. In compounds 啇 often lends a meaning of **appropriate**, suggesting that the latter theory is correct. Here it lends such a meaning, and also acts phonetically to express **proceed**. Thus to **proceed in an appropriate fashion**, leading to **go about one's business** and eventually **go** in a broad sense (now a minor meaning in Japanese, but reasonably major in Chinese). **Suitable** is felt by some scholars to result from confusion with **match** 敵 756 q.v., and by others to be an extension from proceeding in an appropriate fashion. 755 also occasionally has a meaning of **by chance**, which is felt to stem from the idea of things happening by chance to be suitable. Suggest taking 啇 as a combination of **emperor** 帝 and **old** 古 109.

Mnemonic: **MOVE IN MANNER BEFITTING OLD EMPEROR**

756

TEKI, kataki
MATCH, ENEMY
15 strokes

敵意 TEKII　　hostility
無敵 MUTEKI no　　matchless
敵討ち KATAKIUCHI　　vendetta

攵 is **strike** 101, here meaning **attack/ fight**. 啇 is **base/ starting point** 755 q.v., here acting phonetically to express **equivalence** as well as lending its connotations of **appropriate**. Thus to **fight with someone appropriately matched**, leading to both **enemy** and **match**. Suggest taking 啇 as a combination of **emperor** 帝 1616 and **old** 古 109, as well as remembering by association with **suitable** 適 755.

Mnemonic: **OLD EMPEROR STRIKES SUITABLY MATCHED ENEMY**

757

TŌ, suberu
SUPERVISE, LINEAGE
12 strokes

伝統 DENTŌ　　tradition
統計 TŌKEI　　statistics
大統領 DAITŌRYŌ　　president

糸 is **thread** 27. 充 is **full** 1362 q.v., here acting phonetically to express **beginning** and also lending similar connotations from its literal meaning of **newborn babe** (i.e. at the beginning of its life). Thus the **beginning of a thread**. Since this is also the same as its **end** 757 came to mean **thread from end to end**, and by extension **lineage**. The idea of following a thread from end to end led to **overview** and **supervise**.

Mnemonic: **SUPERVISE LINEAGE FULL OF THREADS**

| 758 銅 | DŌ, akagane
COPPER
14 strokes | 銅像 DŌZŌ
銅貨 DŌKA
青銅 SEIDŌ | bronze statue
copper coin
bronze |

金 is **metal** 14. 同 is **same** 187, used phonetically to express **red** and possibly also being chosen as a phonetic due to its similarity to **red** 丹 1563. **Red metal** is a reference to **copper** (akagane meaning literally red metal).

Mnemonic: **COPPER IS SAME METAL AS RED METAL**

| 759 導 | DŌ, michibiku
GUIDE, LEAD
15 strokes | 指導 SHIDŌ
主導権 SHUDŌKEN
伝導 DENDŌ | guidance
initiative
conduction |

Hand/ measure 寸 909, here meaning **careful use of the hand**, and **road/ way** 道 188. Thus to **lead someone carefully along the road by hand**, now **lead/ guide** in a broader sense.

Mnemonic: **MEASURED GUIDING HAND LEADS ALONG WAY**

| 760 特 | TOKU
SPECIAL
10 strokes | 特長 TOKUCHŌ
特有 TOKUYŪ no
特色 TOKUSHOKU | forte
peculiar
characteristic |

Somewhat obscure, though its elements are clearly **cow/bull** 牛 97 and **temple** 寺 133. Some scholars take the elements to be used ideographically, giving **cow/bull in temple grounds**. Such a creature, which was kept for sacrifice, was usually a **bull**, moreover a bull of outstanding and thus **special** quality (see also sacrifice 犠 1140). Others take 寺 to be used purely phonetically to express **male** (as an alternative to male/warrior 士 494, both characters having the same pronunciation SHI at the time), thus giving **male cow**, i.e. **bull**. **Special** is then taken to be a borrowed meaning. However, this theory does not account for the difference between 特 and the NGU character bull/male 牡, which does use male 土, nor is it clear why there should be any need to replace the three stroke character 士 with the six stroke 寺, especially since the latter has no intrinsic semantic relevance to the concept of male. Note that in Chinese 760 can still mean bull and male (the latter presumably being an associated meaning of bull if the former theory is followed).

Mnemonic: **SPECIAL BULL SENT TO TEMPLE**

---

761   TOKU, e*ru*, u*ru* 得点 TOKUTEN marks, score
GAIN, POTENTIAL 所得 SHOTOKU income
11 strokes 有り得る ARIURU possible

Originally 㝵, showing shell/money/**valuable item** 㝵/貝 90 and a **hand** 又, and indicating **obtaining something valuable**. Hand 又 was later replaced by **measure/ hand** 寸 909, presumably lending an idea of **handle carefully**. **Go/ move** 彳 118 was added at a still later stage to give a meaning of **go somewhere to obtain something valuable**. This led to **do something (potentially) to one's gain**. Suggest taking 㝵 as **day** 日 62, **one** — 1, and **measure** 寸.

Mnemonic:**MEASURE POTENTIAL GAINS IN MOVEMENT OVER ONE DAY**

---

762 德 TOKU 道徳 DŌTOKU morality
VIRTUE 徳義 TOKUGI integrity
14 strokes 徳利 TOKKURI* sake bottle

Formerly 德 and earlier 悳. 心 is **heart/feeling** 147. 直 is a variant of direct/**upright** 直 349. Thus **upright heart**, meaning **virtue**. **Go/ move** 彳 118 was added later, with 直 being used phonetically to express **lofty** and also lending connotations of **steep**, to give **go to a steep and lofty place**, but eventually the meaning reverted to that of 悳, i.e. **virtue**. Suggest taking 十 as **ten** 33 and 皿 as **eye** 72.

Mnemonic: **MOVE THAT VIRTUOUS HEART IS WORTH TEN EYES**

---

763   DOKU, hito*ri* 独英 DOKUEI Anglo-German
ALONE, GERMANY 独り言 HITORIGOTO soliloquy
9 strokes 独立 DOKURITSU
independence

Formerly 獨. 犭 is **dog** 17. 蜀 is caterpillar 744 q.v., here acting phonetically to express **fight** and probably also lending a meaning of **join firmly together**. 763 originally referred to **dogs locked together in a fight** so tightly that they are **inseparable** and **as if one body**. This later came to mean **as if one** in a broad sense, leading to **alone**. 763 is also used to refer to **Germany** (Deutschland/ <u>Doitsu</u>). The modern form uses **insect** 虫 56.

Mnemonic: **INSECT-RIDDEN GERMAN SHEPHERD DOG IS LEFT ALONE**

238

764		NIN, maka*seru*	任命 NINMEI	appointment

NIN, maka*seru*
DUTY, ENTRUST
6 strokes

任命 NINMEI appointment
任意 NINI no optional
責任者 SEKININSHA
person in charge

亻 is **person** 39. 壬 derives from 𡈼, a spindle on which thread is wound. The latter acts phonetically to express **burden** and also lends similar connotations of carrying/ **bearing**. Thus the **burden borne by a person**, leading to **duty** and by association **giving/ entrusting** a duty to a person. Suggest taking 壬 as a variant of **jewel** 王 102.

Mnemonic: **ENTRUST JEWELS TO PERSON ON DUTY**

765

NEN, mo*eru/yasu*
BURN
16 strokes

燃料 NENRYŌ fuel
燃焼 NENSHŌ combustion
燃え付く MOETSUKU ignite

Originally the same as **duly/ roast dog meat** 然 528 q.v.(literally **fire** 灬 8, **dog** 犬 17, and **meat** 月 365), but with an extra **fire** 火 8 added when 然 underwent a change in meaning.

Mnemonic: **DOG MEAT DULY BURNS WITH EXTRA FIRE**

766

NŌ, atou
ABILITY, CAN, NOH
10 strokes

可能性 KANŌSEI possibility
能力 NŌRYOKU ability
能面 NŌMEN Noh mask

Originally 㠯, showing **claws and chest** 比, **head** or **body** ム, and **flesh/ of the body** 月/ 月 365. Later forms such as 能 show **nose** 乙/ ㄥ 134 instead of body/ head ム. Thus **creature with fleshy body, claws, and prominent head/ nose**, a reference to the **bear**. (Some scholars feel that 肖 also acts phonetically to give **black**, i.e. **black bear**.) Bear is now conveyed in practice by the NGU character 熊, that adds **fire** 灬 8, but it should be noted that 能 technically means raging fire (literally a fire as strong and fierce as a bear), a meaning still found by association in the lesser meaning of **bright/ glare** that 熊 has in Chinese. **Ability/ can** is assumed by some scholars to be a borrowed meaning, and by others to be an associated meaning stemming from the attributes of a bear (strength, agility, etc.). In Japanese 766 also refers to **Noh drama**, which appears to be an extension from ability.

Mnemonic:**FLESHY BEAR WITH CLAWS AND NOSE CAN PERFORM NOH**

767

HA, yabu*ru/reru*
BREAK, TEAR
10 strokes

破産 HASAN bankruptcy
破損 HASON damage
破れ目 YABUREME tear

石 is **rock** 45. 皮 is **skin** 374 q.v., here acting phonetically to express **small piece** and also lending an idea of **pulling/breaking apart**. Thus to **break a rock into small pieces**, later **break** in a general sense. Possibly because of the presence of skin, which may be felt to suggest clothing or material, it has also acquired particular connotations of **tearing**.

Mnemonic: **SKIN A ROCK!? MUST MEAN BREAK IT**

768

HAN, oka*su*
CRIME, VIOLATE,
COMMIT, ASSAULT
5 strokes

犯人 HANNIN criminal
犯意 HANI malice
犯罪学 HANZAIGAKU criminology

犭 is **dog** 17. 㔾 is a **slumped/prone figure** (to all intents and purpose a variant of slumped figure ヒ 238), which is felt by some scholars to lend its sound to express **injure** as well as lending its own idea of **injured person**. Thus **person injured by dog**, leading to **assault** and a number of associated and derived meanings such as **crime** and **commit**.

Mnemonic: **DOG COMMITS CRIME OF ASSAULTING PRONE PERSON**

769

HAN, BAN
JUDGE, SEAL, SIZE
7 strokes

判断 HANDAN judgment
判事 HANJI judge
判子 HANKO personal seal

刂 is **sword/ cut** 181. 半 is **half** 195 q.v., here used in its literal sense of **cut in two** and by extension **dissect**. Not unlike divide/ understand 分 199, this came by association to mean **analyse**, **judge**, etc. The idea of cutting finely also led to **engraving** and hence **seal**. It is not clear how it also came to mean **size** (in printing), but this is assumed to stem from the idea of cutting to size.

Mnemonic: **CUT IN HALF -- A JUDGMENT WITH SOLOMON'S SEAL**

770   HAN   出版者   SHUPPANSHA publisher
        PRINT, BOARD   版画   HANGA   woodcut print
        8 strokes   版権   HANKEN   copyright

片 is **thin piece of wood** 969. 反 is **oppose** 371 q.v., here acting phonetically to express **cut thinly** and possibly also lending an idea of **reversible** (a board being reversible). Thus **thin wooden board**. 770 is very similar to board 板 373, but has come to acquire particular connotations of an **engraved plate** or block used in printing, and by extension **printing** and **print**.

Mnemonic: **OPPOSED WOODEN BOARD MAKES PRINT**

---

771   HI, kura*beru*   比例   HIREI   proportion
        COMPARE, RATIO   比較   HIKAKU   comparison
        4 strokes   比べ物   KURABEMONO
                                         comparison

Once written 𠤎, showing **two figures sitting next to each other**. This led to the idea of **comparison**, while **ratio** is an associated meaning with compare.

Mnemonic: **COMPARE TWO PERSONS SITTING SIDE BY SIDE**

---

772   HI, ko*eru*/*yasu*   肥料   HIRYŌ   fertiliser
        FATTEN, ENRICH   肥満   HIMAN   corpulence
        8 strokes   肥え土   KOETSUCHI   rich soil

月 is **flesh/of the body** 365. 巴 is **bending body** (i.e. **person not standing**) 145. Some scholars take the elements to be used ideographically, to convey the idea of a **person too fleshy (i.e. fat) to stand up properly**. Others take 巴 to be used phonetically to express **increase/ add**, to give **added flesh** (or possibly **that added to the body**), i.e. **layer of fat**. A combination of both theories seems possible. **Enrich** is an associated meaning with fat/ fatten.

Mnemonic: **FLESHY BENDING BODY HAS BEEN FATTENED**

773

非

HI
NOT, UN-, FAULT
8 strokes

非人	HININ	'non-person'
非合理的	HIGŌRITEKI	irrational
非行	HIKŌ	misdemeanor

Originally 羽, depicting the **wings of a bird spreading apart** as it flies off. 773 originally meant to **move in opposite directions**, then, not unlike oppose 反 371 q.v., came to mean **anti-** and by extension **un-** and **not**. Going in opposition to something led by association to **misdemeanor** or **fault**, i.e. going against the rules.

Mnemonic: **WINGS UNFOLD -- NOT A FAULT**

774

備

BI, sona*eru*/*waru*
EQUIP, PREPARE
12 strokes

設備	SETSUBI	facilities
準備中	JUNBICHŪ	in preparation
備え付け	SONAETSUKE	
		equipment

Somewhat obscure. 亻 is **person** 39. 蒲 is felt by many scholars to derive from , a **quiver with arrows in it**. Thus a **person equipped with arrows**, i.e. **prepared** to fight. Later forms such as 𪲔 and 𦯖 appear to show confusion with **use** 甩/用 215, presumably because of the similarity both graphically and semantically. Suggest taking 蒲 as **use** 用, **grass** 艹 9 and **roof** 广 (variant 广 114).

Mnemonic: **PERSON EQUIPPED WITH GRASS USES IT FOR ROOF**

775

俵

HYŌ, tawara
SACK, BAG
10 strokes

一俵	IPPYŌ	one bag
米俵	KOMEDAWARA	ricesack
土俵	DOHYŌ	
		sandbag, sumo ring

A somewhat obscure character of relatively late origin, comprising **person** 亻 39 and **list/ show** 表 379. Some scholars feel the latter acts purely phonetically to express **light/ nimble**, giving **light and nimble person**, and that its present meanings (including **distribute** in Chinese) are borrowed. However, the Chinese meaning of distribute (its sole meaning) suggests the possibility that persons to whom distributions were made were recorded on a list, i.e. that the elements acted ideographically to give **listed persons**. Distributions might also have been made in **sacks** and **bags**, though it is not clear why these meanings are not also found in Chinese.

Mnemonic: **LISTED PERSONS RECEIVE SACKS**

776	HYŌ CRITICISM, COMMENT 12 strokes	評価 HYŌKA	appraisal
		評判 HYŌBAN	reputation
		悪評 AKUHYŌ	notoriety

Words 言 274 and flat/ even 平 388, giving **even/ balanced words**, i.e. **fair appraisal/ comment**.

Mnemonic: **EVEN WORDS ARE FAIR COMMENT**

777	HIN, BIN, mazushii POOR, MEAGER 11 strokes	貧血 HINKETSU	anemia
		貧困 HINKON	poverty
		貧乏人 BINBŌJIN	pauper

貝 is shell/ **money** 90, here meaning **wealth**. 分 is cut up/ **divide** 199 q.v., here meaning **reduce to miniscule pieces**. Thus **wealth reduced to a miniscule amount**, giving both **poor** and by association **meager**.

Mnemonic: **MONEY DIVIDED, SO NOW POOR**

778	FU, nuno CLOTH, SPREAD 5 strokes	配布 HAIFU	distribution
		毛布 MŌFU	blanket
		布地 NUNOJI	cloth

Once written 朱. 朮/ 巾 is an NGU character now meaning towel but clearly showing **threads** and generally having a meaning of **cloth** in compounds, as here. 又 is **hand holding stick/ strike** 101, simplified in the modern form to just **hand** 𠂇 2. Thus **hand beating cloth**, i.e. hemp or similar, now **cloth** in general. **Spread/ stretch** is an associated meaning.

Mnemonic: **HAND WORKS ON SPREAD OF CLOTH THREADS**

779	FU WOMAN, WIFE 11 strokes	婦人 FUJIN	woman
		主婦 SHUFU	housewife
		婦長 FUCHŌ	chief nurse

Woman 女 35 and **hand holding broom** 帚 96 q.v. See also wife/ woman holding broom 妻 681. Some scholars feel that 帚 acts purely phonetically to express **elegant**, giving **elegant woman**, but this is not convincing in view of 96 and 681.

Mnemonic: **WOMAN HOLDING BROOM MAY BE WIFE**

780

FU, FŪ, tomi, to*mu*
WEALTH, RICHES
12 strokes

富裕　FUYŪ　　　wealth
富くじ　TOMIKUJI　　lottery
富士山　FUJISAN　Mount Fuji

Roof/ **house** 宀 28 and **full** 畐 386. The latter acts phonetically to express **rich** and also lends its own connotations of full. Thus **house full of riches**, later just **riches/ wealth**. Suggest taking 畐 as **single** 一 1 **entrance** 口 20 to **field** 田 59.

Mnemonic: **HOUSE AT SINGLE ENTRANCE TO FIELD GROWS WEALTHY**

781

BU, MU
MILITARY, WARRIOR
8 strokes

武士道　BUSHIDŌ　warrior code
武器　BUKI　　　　weapon
武者　MUSHA　　　warrior

Once written 珷. 止 is **foot** 129, here meaning **advance (on foot)**. 戈 is **halberd** 493. Thus **advance on foot with a halberd**, a reference to a **warrior** and by extension **things military**. The reason for the change of stroke arrangement in the modern form (戈 going to 弋) is not clear, but it is assumed to be a stylistic variation.

Mnemonic: **WARRIOR ADVANCES ON FOOT WITH HALBERD**

782

FUKU
AGAIN, REPEAT
12 strokes

復活　FUKKATSU　　revival
回復　KAIFUKU　　recovery
復習　FUKUSHŪ　　revision

复 is a CO character meaning **go back**. It derives from a food container of **reversible** shape 畐 (now 白), indicating **reverse**, and inverted foot 夂 438 q.v., here in its sense of **go somewhere and stop**. Thus to **go somewhere and then reverse** (one's steps), an idea reinforced in the case of 782 by the addition of **go** 彳 118. It is still occasionally found in the sense of **return**, but in general has come to mean **redo/ repeat** in a broad sense. Suggest taking 复 as **person** 𠂉 39, **sun** 日 62, and **sitting crosslegged** 夂.

Mnemonic: **PERSON GOES REPEATEDLY TO SIT CROSSLEGGED IN SUN**

783		

783

FUKU
DOUBLE, AGAIN
14 strokes

重複 CHŌFUKU　　repetition
複製 FUKUSEI　　reproduction
複雑 FUKUZATSU complexity

Clothing ネ 420 and go back 复 782 q.v., here with connotations of **duplicate**. Thus to **duplicate clothing**, i.e. wear **double** layers. Clothing gradually faded to leave just **duplicate/ do something again/ double**. Suggest taking 复 as **person** ⊢ 39, **sun** 日 62, and **sitting crosslegged** 夊.

Mnemonic: PERSON CROSSLEGGED IN SUN WITH DOUBLE CLOTHING!

784

BUTSU, FUTSU, hotoke
BUDDHA, FRANCE
4 strokes

仏教 BUKKYŌ　　Buddhism
成仏 JŌBUTSU　　　　death
のど仏 NODOBOTOKE
　　　　　　　Adam's apple

Formerly 佛. イ is **person** 39, while 弗 is unwind/ disperse/ **not** 567 q.v. The latter acts phonetically to express **resemble**, and may also lend an idea of **not**. Thus 784 originally meant **resemble a person (but not really a person?)**. It was then borrowed to express the BU of **Buddha** (possibly also being considered to have an appropriate sense of **he who resembles a [normal] person but is not**), and also to express the FU of Furansu/ **France**. Suggest taking ム as **nose** 134.

Mnemonic: BUDDHA HAS PROMINENT NOSE

785

HEN, a*mu*
EDIT, KNIT, BOOK
15 strokes

編集者 HENSHŪSHA　editor
編成 HENSEI　　compilation
編み物 AMIMONO　　knitting

糸 is **thread** 27. 扁 is an NGU character now meaning level or small, but its original meaning was **doorplate** (still retained in Chinese). It comprises **door** 戸 108 and **book/ bundle of bound writing tablets** 冊 / 冊 874 q.v., the latter indicating **writing tablet**. Thus writing tablet at the door. Its present meanings are presumably extensions, since the tablet was flat -- giving level -- and small. It should also be noted that in compounds 扁 occasionally appears to lend an idea of to one side, presumably because the doorplate was to one side of the door. In the case of 785 扁 seems to be misused, lending a meaning of **bind together** that is properly conveyed by 冊 rather than 扁, and also acts phonetically to express **arrange in order**. Thus to **bind together in ordered arrangement using threads**, leading to **knit** on the one hand and **edit/ compilation** on the other.

Mnemonic: BOOKS BOUND WITH THREAD LEFT AT EDITOR'S DOOR

786

BEN
SPEECH, KNOW, VALVE,
PETAL, BRAID
5 strokes

弁当 BENTŌ　　packed lunch
弁論 BENRON　　argument
弁膜 BENMAKU　　valve

An awkward character in that it is actually four separate characters, being the modern form of **speech** 辯, **knowledge** 辨, **valve/petal** 瓣, and **braid** 辮. In all cases the key element is 辡, which is a doubling of **needle/ sharp** 辛 1432 and basically means **great sharpness** or **penetration**. In the case of speech 辯 it combines with **words/ speak** 言 274 q.v. (itself formed from needle and mouth), to give **very penetrative/ articulate words**. In the case of knowledge 辨 it combines with sword/ **cut** 刂 181, here used in the sense of **incisiveness/ analysis** (see also 199 and 769), to give **penetrative analysis**. In the case of valve/ petal 瓣 it combines with **melon** 瓜 1229 to give **cut open a melon cleanly**, leading by extension to **that which opens cleanly**, such as a **petal** and **valve**. In the case of braid 辮 it almost certainly acts in the literal sense of **needle** and by extension **sew**, combining with **thread** 糸 27 to give **sew threads**. 弁 itself derives from 𠔁, showing **two hands** ㅆ offering up a **cap (of office)** 人, and originally indicated someone being **raised to a certain rank or position** (a meaning still retained in Chinese). It was then borrowed as a simple phonetic substitute for the above four characters. Suggest taking 厶 as **nose** 134 and 廾 as **two tens** 十 33, i.e. **twenty**.

Mnemonic: **SPEECH ABOUT TWENTY NOSES!?**

787

HO, HŌ, tamo*tsu*
PRESERVE, MAINTAIN
9 strokes

確保 KAKUHO　　security
保存 HOZON　　preservation
生命保険 SEIMEIHOKEN
　　　　　　life insurance

Once written 伃 and later 保. 亻 is **person** 39 (here **mother** or **nursemaid**) and 孚 / 子 is **child** 25. ﾉ indicates a **carrying blanket** by which the child was strapped to the mother's back. The reason for the later stroke ﾉ is unclear, but it is assumed to represent the idea of the blanket **thoroughly** wrapping the child (i.e. **on all sides**). A mother with a child strapped to her back came to symbolise **care** and **protection**, with **maintain** being an extended meaning. Wrapped child 呆 later became graphically confused with tree/ **wood** 木 69. Suggest taking 呆 as **wood** 木 and **box** 口.

Mnemonic: **PERSON PRESERVED IN WOODEN BOX**

788 **BO, haka** 墓地 BOCHI graveyard
GRAVE 墓標 BOHYŌ grave marker
13 strokes 墓参り HAKAMAIRI grave visit

土 is **earth** 60. 莫 is an NGU character now mostly used to express **not**. It derives from 茣, showing **sun** 日 62 and **grass/plants** ㄓㄓ 9. Confusingly, whereas sun among plants 専 / 車 175 means sun rising, this **sun among (many) plants** 茣 / 莫 means **sun setting** (a meaning seen most clearly in sunset 暮 1789, that adds an extra sun 日). As a result it often lends a meaning in compounds of **sinking out of sight, disappearing, hidden, ceasing to exist** (from which it takes its present meaning of **not**), and occasionally extended meanings from hidden of **obscure** and **vague**, leading by further extension to **undefined** and even **unlimited** and **vast**. Here it acts phonetically to express **cover** and also lends such connotations as **covered, out of sight**, and **ceasing to exist**. Thus to **cover with earth that which has ceased to exist**, i.e. **bury the dead**, leading to **grave**. Suggest taking ㄓ as **grass**, 日 as **sun**, and 大 as a variant of **big** 大 53.

Mnemonic: **SUN SHINES ON BIG, GRASS COVERED, EARTHEN GRAVE**

---

789 **HŌ, muku**iru 報告 HŌKOKU report
REPORT, REWARD 電報 DENPŌ telegram
12 strokes 報酬 HŌSHŪ compensation

幸 is not **good fortune** 幸 279, though it may be useful to remember it as such, but **prisoner/ criminal** 233 q.v. 及 derives from 戾, showing a **hand** 丈 **seizing** a person 卩 (actually bending person/ buttocks 236, indicating being seized from behind). 789 originally referred to **seizing a criminal**, leading by extension to pronouncing judgment and **meting out justice**. Thus to **give someone that which they deserve**, i.e. **reward** in the full (not just positive) sense. **Report** is felt by some scholars to be a borrowed meaning, and by others to be an associated meaning connected with the judicial process.

Mnemonic: **BY GOOD FORTUNE SEIZE PERSON, REPORT FOR REWARD**

790		**HŌ, yutaka**	豊作	HŌSAKU	good harvest
		ABUNDANT, RICH	豊富	HŌFU na	rich
		13 strokes	豊満	HŌMAN na	corpulent

Formerly 豐, and earlier 豐 and 豐. 豐 shows **food vessel plus edible plant** 豆 450, with additional **plants** 艸 (variant growing plant 生 42). Thus **food vessel full of edible plants**, indicating **abundance** and **plenty**. Later forms appear to have confused plant 屮 with a further vessel 凵/凵, and to have used **food vessel** 豆 1640 in its modern form (i.e. with the extra top stroke ˉ, giving 豆 as opposed to 豆). 丰 is also a variant of plant 生. Suggest taking 曲 as **bend** 261.

Mnemonic: **FOOD VESSEL BENDS UNDER WEIGHT OF RICH CONTENT**

791		**BŌ, fusegu**	予防	YOBŌ	prevention
		PREVENT, DEFEND	防水	BŌSUI	waterproof
		7 strokes	防衛	BŌEI	defense

Hill/ embankment 阝 229 and **side** 方 204. Thus a **hill/ embankment to one side**, which came to symbolise **defense** and by extension **prevention**.

Mnemonic: **DEFENSIVE HILL TO ONE SIDE PREVENTS ATTACK**

792		**BŌ**	貿易業	BŌEKIGYŌ	trading
		TRADE, EXCHANGE	貿易風	BŌEKIFŪ	trade wind
		12 strokes	貿易者	BŌEKISHA	trader

貝 is **shell/ money/ valuable item** 90. 卯 derives from 卯, showing a **horse's bit**. Here it acts phonetically to express **exchange**, and almost certainly also lends its own idea of **controlled change** (from the role of the bit). Thus **controlled exchange of items for money (or other valuable items)**, i.e. **trade**. Suggest taking 刀 as **sword** 181 and 𠂉 as a symbol of **bending**.

Mnemonic: **EXCHANGE BENT SWORD FOR MONEY IN TRADE DEAL**

793

BŌ, BAKU, aba*reru*/*ku*
VIOLENCE, EXPOSE
15 strokes

暴力　BŌRYOKU　　violence
暴露　BAKURO　　exposure
暴れ者　ABAREMONO roughneck

Once written 㬥, showing **rice** 米 201, **sun** 日 62, and 卄, the prototype of **offer** 奉 1793 comprising two hands 𦥑 offering up a thickly growing plant 丰 (variant **growing plant** 生 42). 793 originally meant **expose rice to the sun** (to dry it), then came to mean **expose** in general. **Violence** is popularly believed to be an associated meaning related to torture by exposure to the sun. Though useful as a mnemonic, this is almost certainly incorrect. The word abaku can mean both **divulge** and **violate a grave**, suggesting strongly that violence stems from violate, which in turn stems from **laying bare/ open** (disturbing privacy/ sanctity). Suggest taking 共 as **together** 460, and 氺 as an **'insufficient'** variant of **water** 水 40.

Mnemonic:**EXPOSED TO VIOLENT SUN TOGETHER WITH INSUFFICIENT WATER**

794

MI, mada
IMMATURE, NOT YET
5 strokes

未来　MIRAI　　future
未知　MICHI　　unknown
未未　MADAMADA　　still

Tree 木 69 with additional **branches** 一 at the top. Originally the same as **end/tip** 末 587 q.v., but in time the shorter tip of 794 came to indicate **still growing/ immature/ not yet complete**.

Mnemonic: **GROWTH OF IMMATURE TREE NOT YET FINISHED**

795

MU, tsuto*meru*
(PERFORM) DUTY
11 strokes

義務　GIMU　　duty
事務所　JIMUSHO　　office
職務　SHOKUMU　　job duties

敄 is a CO character now meaning **perform a task/ work**. It comprises **lance/halberd** 矛 1843 q.v. and **strike/ force** 攵 101, and originally meant **force someone at lance-point to do something**. In time both lance-point and the causative faded to leave just **do something/ perform a task**. Here it is reinforced by strength/ **effort** 力 74, giving **perform a task/ duty with effort**.

Mnemonic: **LANCE FORCES EFFORT IN PERFORMING DUTY**

796

MU, BU, nai/*shi*
NOT, NONE,
CEASE TO BE
12 strokes

無料 MURYŌ   free of charge
無事 BUJI na   safe
無くなる NAKUNARU   vanish

Of somewhat confused and obscure etymology. 無 derives from 炊, later stylised to 㷊, showing a **dancer** 大 (person 53) with exaggeratedly **tasseled sleeves** 㸚/㠭. The original meaning was **dance** (with flapping sleeves), a meaning now conveyed by **dance** 舞 1761 q.v. 無 was then borrowed phonetically to express **not/ cease to be**, though it is not clear why such a complex character should have been chosen. **Cease to be/ die** 亡 973 was added later for clarity, though confusingly its modern much abbreviated form 灬 is identical to **fire** 灬 8. Further confusion is caused by an intermediate form 㷊, in which the tasseled sleeves look very similar to **trees** 㸚/林 69. In fact, 舞 does exist in Chinese as a corrupt variant of 無, causing some scholars to evolve convoluted theories linking trees, dance, and cease to exist. Suggest taking 灬 as **fire/ burn** and 無 as a **sheaf of wheat**.

Mnemonic: WHEATSHEAF BURNED, NOW NONE LEFT

797

MEI, mayo*u*
BE LOST, PERPLEXED
9 strokes

迷路 MEIRO   maze
迷夢 MEIMU   illusion
迷い子 MAYOIGO   lost child

辶 is **movement** 129. 米 is **rice** 201, acting here phonetically to express **uncertain**. Thus **uncertain movement**, as when one is **lost** or **perplexed**. It is not clear why 米 was chosen as a phonetic, but it is possible that it was at one stage confused with **not yet** (finished) 未 794 q.v., giving movement unable to be completed (due to uncertainty). 未 may in turn have been intended as a simpler version of 眛 or 眯, NGU characters meaning **dark/ obscure** and hence uncertain (combining **not yet** 未 with **sun/light** 日 62 and **eye/see** 目 72 respectively).

Mnemonic: RICE IS MOVED AND LOST -- HOW PERPLEXING

798

MEN, wata
COTTON, COTTON WOOL
14 strokes

木綿 MOMEN*   cotton
綿毛 WATAGE   down, fluff
綿菓子 WATAGASHI candy floss

Formerly 緜. 帛 is **white** 白 65 and **threads** 巾 778, indicating **cotton** (though some scholars feel that it originally indicated silk), while 糸 is **joined threads** 844. Thus **many joined white threads**. The modern form simply uses **thread** 糸 27.

Mnemonic: MANY WHITE THREADS OF COTTON MAKE COTTON WOOL

799
YU
TRANSPORT, SEND
16 strokes

輸 出	YUSHUTSU	export
輸 送	YUSŌ	transportation
運 輸	UNYU	transportation

Formerly also written 輸, though 《 is merely a misleading variant of sword/ **cut** 刂 181. 俞 is a CO character now used to express affirmation, but it originally meant **convey**. It comprises **cut** 刂, **boat** 舟/舟/月 1354, and **cap** 亼 121 q.v., here used in the sense of **cap off** or **finish** and by extension **succeed**, and originally referred to **succeeding in cutting timber in order to make a boat to convey goods** (note that boat and convey conceptually overlapped, as seen in 303 etc.). In the case of 799 俞 also acts phonetically to express **transfer** as well as lending its meaning of **convey**. **Vehicle** 車 31 was added to give a meaning of **convey (goods) by vehicle**, i.e. **transport**. **Send** is an associated meaning. Suggest taking 月 as **meat** 365 and 人 as **cover** (see 87).

Mnemonic: **TRANSPORT CUT MEAT UNDER COVER IN VEHICLE**

800
YO, amari/ru/su
EXCESS, AMPLE, I
7 strokes

余 分	YOBUN	surplus
余 計	YOKEI	superfluity
五 十 余 り	GOJŪAMARI	fifty plus

Formerly also 餘, and in ancient times 余. 亼 is **cover** 87, here meaning **roof**, while 朿 is a **wooden crossframe** supporting it. The spread of the upper beams indicated that the building was large, leading to **'roomy'** and **ample**, with **excess** being an associated meaning. 800 was also borrowed to express **I/me**. The reasons for this are not clear, but it should be noted that **already** 予 403, which also had a secondary meaning of **margin/ ample**, was similarly borrowed to express I/me, suggesting the possibility of some now unknown semantic connection. **Food** 倉 146 was added at one stage, giving an idea of **ample food**. This has now disappeared in Japanese, but in Chinese 餘 is used to express ample and 余 to express I. Suggest taking 禾 as **dry** 干 825 and **eight** 八 66.

Mnemonic: **EIGHT EXCESSIVELY DRY BEAMS UNDER AMPLE ROOF**

801
YO, azukaru/keru
DEPOSIT,
LOOK AFTER
13 strokes

預金	YOKIN	deposit
預かり人	AZUKARININ	trustee
預かり証	AZUKARISHŌ	receipt

頁 is **face** 93. 予 is **already** 403 q.v., here acting phonetically to express **relax** and probably lending similar connotations from its early meaning of ample/ margin (i.e. lack of pressure/ constraint). 801 originally referred to a **facial expression of relaxation and comfort**, and it can still mean comfort in Chinese. Its present meanings are borrowed.

Mnemonic: **ALREADY FACED WITH HAVING TO LOOK AFTER DEPOSITS**

| 802 | | YŌ, *ireru*
CONTAIN, LOOKS
10 strokes | 美容院 BIYŌIN
内容 NAIYŌ
形容詞 KEIYŌSHI | beauty parlor
contents
adjective |

宀 is **roof/ building** 28. 谷 is **valley** 122 q.v., here acting phonetically to express **ample** and also lending its own connotations of **ample capacity**. Thus **building of ample capacity**, i.e. which can **contain** many things or people. **Looks/ appearance** is essentially a borrowed meaning, but it may be felt that **contain** led to **content** and that **looks** is an associated meaning with this.

Mnemonic: **ROOFED VALLEY LOOKS ABLE TO CONTAIN A LOT**

| 803 | | RITSU, SOTSU, hiki*iru*
RATE, COMMAND
11 strokes | 能率 NŌRITSU
統率 TŌSOTSU
税率 ZEIRITSU | efficiency
command
tax rate |

Once written ⁑8⁑, showing **short thread** 8 / 幺 111 and **bits** ∷ and originally meaning **bits of thread**. 十 was added later, representing two **devices used to twist threads into rope**. Twisting bits of thread into rope led to the idea of **put in order** and hence **control/ command**. Some scholars take **rate** to be a borrowed meaning, while others see it as an associated meaning with order. Suggest taking 亠 as a symbol of **top**, and 十 as **ten** 33.

Mnemonic: **TEN BITS OF THREAD COMMAND TOP RATE**

| 804 | | RYAKU
ABBREVIATE, OUTLINE
11 strokes | 略語 RYAKUGO
略説 RYAKUSETSU
略図 RYAKUZU | abbreviation
summary
sketch |

Formerly also 畧. 田 is **field** 59. 各 is **each** 438, here acting phonetically to express **separate/ divide** and also lending its own idea of **separateness**. Thus **that which divides and separates fields**, namely a **boundary**. Boundary led to **outline**, with **summarise/ abbreviate** being a figurative extension of this.

Mnemonic: **ABBREVIATED OUTLINE OF EACH FIELD**

805	RYŪ, RU, to*maru*/*meru* STOP, FASTEN 10 strokes	留守番 RUSUBAN caretaker 留め金 TOMEGANE clasp 留学生 RYŪGAKUSEI overseas student

Formerly 雷 . 卯/㐅刀 derives from **horse's bit** 卯 792. 田 is a simplification of **reason/ means** 由 399 q.v., here acting phonetically to express the word for the **linkage between the bit and the reins**, and possibly also lending an idea of **connection** or **means**. **Fasten to the bit** came to mean **fasten/ stop** in a very broad sense. Suggest taking 刀 as **sword** 181, 㐅 as a symbol of **bending**, and 田 as **field** 59.

Mnemonic: **STOP IN FIELD TO FASTEN ON BENT SWORD**

806	RYŌ CONTROL, POSSESS, CHIEF, TERRITORY 14 strokes	領事 RYŌJI consul 領土 RYŌDO territory 要領 YŌRYŌ gist

Also 領 . 頁 is **head** 93. 令/令 is **order/ rule** 603, here felt by many scholars to act phonetically to express **neck** though it almost certainly also lends a meaning of **rule**. Thus the **head and neck**. As with **head/ neck/ chief** 首 139 q.v., 806 came from an early stage (in the view of some scholars, from the outset) to mean **chief** and by extension **that which** (or **he who**) **rules**, with **possess** and **territory** being associated meanings.

Mnemonic: **HEAD RULES, CONTROLLING POSSESSED TERRITORY**

END OF FIFTH GRADE

THE 190 SIXTH GRADE CHARACTERS

807 **I, koto*naru***
DIFFER, STRANGE
11 strokes

異様 IYŌ na   strange
異常 IJŌ   abnormality
異人 IJIN   foreigner, alien

A misleading early form 異 has led to the popular explanation that hands 〵〳 are placing something special (i.e. **different** from usual) ⊕ on a table or altar 八 . However, still earlier forms such as 異 show this to be incorrect, and show a **person** 大 53 **putting on** 〵〳 a **mask** ⊕ (see also 1128). This led to associated meanings such as **being different from normal** and of **strange appearance**, eventually giving just **differ** and **strange**. Suggest taking 田 as **field** 59 and 共 as **together** 460.

Mnemonic: **TOGETHER AGAIN IN DIFFERENT FIELD -- HOW STRANGE**

808 **I, YUI**
LEAVE, BEQUEATH, LOSE
15 strokes

遺伝 IDEN   heredity
遺失 ISHITSU   loss
遺言 YUIGON/ IGON   will

辶 is **movement** 129. 貴 is **precious** 834, here acting phonetically to express **lose** and probably also lending its meaning of **precious item**. Thus to **lose something (precious) while on the move**. It then also came to mean **leave behind**, which, like the English term, included the idea of **bequeath**.

Mnemonic: **MOVE ON AND LEAVE BEHIND SOMETHING PRECIOUS**

809 域 **IKI**
AREA, LIMITS
11 strokes

領域 RYŌIKI   domain
地域 CHIIKI   region
区域 KUIKI   limits, zone

土 is **ground** 60. 或 is an NGU character meaning **a certain** -. It comprises **lance/halberd** 戈 493, here used in its sense of **marker** (see 698), and 〻, which is to all intents and purposes a simplification of 畺 depicting the **boundaries** 二 of a **field** 田 59 (see also 85). 809 thus referred to **ground in a field delineated by markers**, leading to **area** and **limits** in a broad sense. Suggest taking 口 as **entrance** 20 and 一 as **one/ sole** 1.

Mnemonic: **LANCE IN GROUND AT SOLE ENTRANCE -- OFF LIMIT AREA**

| 810 | 壱 | ICHI
ONE
7 strokes | 壱万円 ICHIMANEN 10,000 yen
壱千 ISSEN one thousand
弐拾壱 NIJŪICHI twenty-one |

Formerly 壹 and earlier 壼, showing a **double-lidded** 亼 258 **food vessel** 豆 1640, which had connotations of **fullness**. Its use as the formal character for **one** is the result of phonetic borrowing, though it is remotely possible that its choice as a phonetic was influenced by the fact that full vessel suggested completeness and by association being whole/ one. Suggest taking 士 as **samurai** 494, ⌐ as **cover**, and ヒ as a **prone figure** 238.

Mnemonic: **ONE SAMURAI STANDS COVERING PRONE FIGURE**

| 811 | 宇 | U
EAVES, ROOF, HEAVEN
6 strokes | 宇宙 UCHŪ universe
堂宇 DŌU hall
宇頂天 UCHŌTEN ecstasy |

⌐ is **roof** 28. 于 is an NGU character meaning **from/ emerge/ go**. It was originally written 丂, showing twisting waterweed/seek an exit 丂 281 q.v. and a symbol ⌐ of unclear meaning, and it also has connotations of twisting. Here it acts phonetically to express **complete cover**, and may possibly also lend a loose idea of **extensive** from the lengthy and convoluted waterweed element 丂. Thus 811 originally meant **roof that completely covers**, leading to **eaves** and by extension **firmament/ heaven**. Suggest facetiously taking 于 as a **'stiff' (i.e. dead) child** 子 25.

Mnemonic: **CHILD LIES STIFF UNDER ROOF, SET TO GO TO HEAVEN**

| 812 | | U, ha, hane
WING, FEATHER,
BIRD COUNTER
6 strokes | 羽毛 UMŌ plumage
羽織 HAORI haori coat
一羽 ICHIWA one bird |

Formerly 羽. A pictograph of a **bird's wings**.

Mnemonic: **FEATHERED WINGS**

| 813 | | EI, utsuru/su, haeru
REFLECT, SHINE
9 strokes | 映画館 EIGAKAN cinema
反映 HANEI reflection
夕映え YŪBAE sunset glow |

日 is **sun** 62. 央 is **center** 429, here acting essentially phonetically to express **bright** but probably also lending its meaning. Thus **bright (center of?) sun**, giving **shine** and by association **reflect**.

Mnemonic: **CENTER OF SUN SHINES BRIGHTLY**

814

EN, no*biru*/*beru*/*basu*
EXTEND, POSTPONE
8 strokes

延長 ENCHŌ   extension
延期 ENKI   postponement
延び延び NOBINOBI   delay

Somewhat confused. Once written 㢟, showing **foot/ movement** 止/止 129 q.v. and **go/ move** 彳/彳 118 q.v. 㢟 is in fact the prototype of 廴 itself, showing that a further foot 止 has been added in the case of the modern form. The extra stroke ノ is felt by some scholars to symbolise **dragging** and thus **lengthening** and **protraction** , while others see it as the CO character mark ノ 537, used purely phonetically to express **lengthen. Lengthy, protracted movement** led to **extend** and **postpone**.

Mnemonic: **DRAG FEET IN EXTENDED MOVEMENT**

815

EN, so*u*
GO ALONGSIDE
8 strokes

沿岸 ENGAN   coast
沿道 ENDŌ   roadside
沿線 ENSEN   railside

氵 is **water** 40, here meaning **river**. 㕣 is hollowed out 158, here acting phonetically to express **follow** and probably also lending an idea of **from a source** (from a different interpretation of its literal elements from/away 八 66 and source/opening 口 20). Thus **follow a river (from its source?)**, leading to **follow/ go alongside** in a broader sense. Suggest taking 口 as **opening** and 八 in its commoner meaning of **eight**.

Mnemonic: **GO ALONGSIDE OF WATER, THROUGH EIGHT OPENINGS**

816

KA, -be*ki*/*shi*/*ku*
APPROVE,CAN,SHOULD
5 strokes

可能 KANŌ na   possible
可決 KAKETSU   approval
言う可き IUBEKI   should say

Once written 叮, showing **mouth/say** 口/口 20 and **twisting waterweed/ seek an exit** 丂/丂/丁 281. That is, the components are the same as drawn out **call** 号 281 q.v., but in this case they refer rather to a statement that is finally made after considerable hesitation (symbolised by the waterweed twisting its way to the surface), such as **grudging approval**. Some scholars feel that 丂/丁 also acts here phonetically to express **approve**. Approval led to the idea of **that which can be done**, and by extension **that which should be done**. Suggest taking 丁 as a variant of **exact** 丁 346.

Mnemonic: **SAY EXACTLY WHAT CAN AND SHOULD BE APPROVED**

817

GA, ware, wag*a*
I, SELF, MY
7 strokes

自我 JIGA   self
我まま WAGAMAMA selfishness
我我 WAREWARE   we

Once written 弎 and 弐, showing a **broadbladed halberd** 戈/戊 515 q.v. and **tassels** ⺊. The tassels were hung on weapons to indicate a **killing**, rather like notches being scored on a gun handle in the West. Thus 817 originally meant to **kill with a halberd**. It was later borrowed phonetically to express **I/me/my** and by extension **self**. Why a character with such an unpleasantly aggressive meaning should be chosen as a phonetic is a matter of some conjecture, but it is in line with the 'being as good as anyone else' first person pronoun 吾 112 q.v. It may indeed be appropriate to draw again a parallel with the gun in the West, which was seen as the great equaliser.

Mnemonic: **I HAVE A TASSELED HALBERD, A SYMBOL OF ME MYSELF**

818

KAI, hai
ASHES
6 strokes

石灰 SEKKAI   lime
灰色 HAIRO   gray
火山灰 KAZANBAI volcanic ash

Formerly 灰 and earlier 灰, showing a **hand** ⺕/ナ and **fire** 火 8. Some scholars take ナ to be used phonetically to express **use up**, giving **used up fire**, while others take the elements to be used ideographically to give **fire that one can hold in the hand**. The latter theory seems more convincing. Suggest taking the simplified 厂 as cliff/ **hillside** 45.

Mnemonic: **HILLSIDE ABLAZE -- REDUCED TO ASHES**

---

819 街

GAI, KAI, machi
ROAD, TOWN, AREA
12 strokes

市街 SHIGAI   town, city
街道 KAIDŌ   highway
商店街 SHŌTENGAI
           shopping street

A combination of **go** 行 118 q.v., here with its literal meaning of **crossroads**, and 圭. The latter is an NGU character meaning **edge/ angle/ jewel**. It comprises **earth** 土 60 doubled to indicate **raised earth**, and originally referred to the **raised earthen paths** that formed edges/ boundaries between fields (a meaning now conveyed by the NGU character 畦, that adds field 田 59). The idea of raised edges/ ridges also led by association to facets on a jewel (now conveyed by the NGU character 珪, that adds jewel 王 102), and to angle. In the case of 819 圭 is used phonetically to express **diverge**, and also lends an idea of **multiple paths**. Thus **many diverging roads**, which by association also necessarily meant **many converging roads** (see also 280), leading to such meanings as **town, road**, and **area/ hub of activity**.

Mnemonic: **ROAD-TOWN IS JUST CROSSROADS OF RAISED EARTH**

820

KAKU
SPREAD
8 strokes

拡大 KAKUDAI magnification
拡散 KAKUSAN dissemination
拡声器 KAKUSEIKI loudspeaker

Formerly 擴 · 扌 is **hand** 32, while 廣/広 is **wide** 114. Thus **make the hands wide**, i.e. **spread**.

Mnemonic: **SPREAD HANDS WIDE**

821

KAKU, kawa
LEATHER, REFORM
9 strokes

革命 KAKUMEI revolution
革新 KAKUSHIN reform
革工場 KAWAKŌBA tannery

Once written 革, apparently showing **hands** ㇇ ㇈ pulling the **skin** off a **horned creature** 丫 in similar fashion to skin/ leather 皮 374 q.v. However, still earlier forms such as 革 and 革 show that the later 'hands' are a miscopying of **flaps of skin** ㇔㇒. Unlike 374, 821 came to be used only of **hairless hide** (usually **tanned leather**), and its connotations of **processing** eventually led to **change/ reform**. Suggest taking 半 as a combination of **middle** 中 55 and **ten** 十 33, with 艹 as a **horned head**.

Mnemonic:**GET LEATHER FROM MIDDLE OF TEN HORNED CREATURES**

822

KAKU
CABINET, CHAMBER
14 strokes

閣下 KAKKA Your Excellency
内閣 NAIKAKU Cabinet
閣僚 KAKURYŌ
Cabinet member

門 is **door/ gate** 211, here meaning by extension a **place with a door/ gate** and by further extension a **place sealed off for privacy**. 各 is **each** 438 q.v., here used in its sense of **visit by a dignitary**. Thus a **private place which dignitaries visit**, such as a **council chamber** or Cabinet.

Mnemonic: **EACH GATE LEADS TO CABINET**

823

KATSU, wari, waru
DIVIDE, RATE
12 strokes

分割 BUNKATSU division
割引 WARIBIKI discount
割合 WARIAI rate

刂 is **sword/ cut** 181. 害 is **harm** 437, acting phonetically to express **dismember** and probably also lending an idea of damage/ destroy. 823 originally meant **cut up/ dismember**, leading by extension to **divide**. **Rate** is an associated meaning (cf. English pro rata).

Mnemonic: **SWORD HARMS BY DIVIDING**

824

kabu

STOCK, SHARE, STUMP

10 strokes

切り株 KIRIKABU   stump
株式 KABUSHIKI   stocks
株主 KABUNUSHI stockholder

木 is **tree** 69. 朱 is **red** 1346 q.v., here acting phonetically to express **firm** and also lending its literal meaning of **central part of a tree**. Thus **that central part of a tree which stands firm**. This originally referred to its **base** but later came to mean **stump/ stock**, i.e. the part left standing firm after the tree proper is cut down. In Japanese, but not Chinese, the idea of firm base extended to include **stocks/ shares** in a company (cf. English stock).

Mnemonic: **RED TREE STUMP PROVIDES FIRM STOCK**

---

825 干

KAN, ho*su*, hi*ru*

DRY, DEFENSE

3 strokes

干潮 KANCHŌ   ebb/ low tide
干城 KANJŌ   bulwark
干し肉 HOSHINIKU dried meat

Originally ¥, depicting a primitive **forked thrusting weapon** Y with either a large **hand-guard** — or, to judge from some almost contemporaneous forms such as ¥, **sturdy binding** ●. The weapon was used both for defense and attack. It thus acquired a large range of extended meanings, such as **attack**, **defend**, **thrust**, and **fork**, and was also borrowed widely as a phonetic due its simplicity. It was borrowed for its sound to express **dry**, although some scholars feel that technically it is an abbreviation of the NGU character drought 旱, which has the same pronunciation and which uses 干 both for its sound to express dry and for its connotations of attack, combining it with sun 日 62 to give attack from the sun that causes dryness.

Mnemonic: **FLATTENED FORKED POLE FOR DRYING WASHING**

826

KAN, maki, ma*ku*

ROLL, REEL, VOLUME

9 strokes

第一巻 DAIIKKAN Volume One
巻き物 MAKIMONO   scroll
糸巻き ITOMAKI   bobbin

Formerly 卷 and occasionally 卷, though the latter appears to be a confusion with settlement 巷 280. 关 is **hands rolling rice** 661, with the idea of **rolling** emphasised by **curled body** ㄹ 768 or **bent body** 己 (from ㄹ 145). Thus **roll and curl**, giving **roll** and **reel** and leading by extension to **scroll** and hence **volume**. Suggest taking 己 as **self** 855 and 关 as **two** 二 61 **fires** 火 8.

Mnemonic: **LIGHT TWO FIRES BY ONESELF WITH ROLLED VOLUMES**

827		**KAN**	看護婦	KANGOFU	nurse
		WATCH	看板	KANBAN	signboard
		9 strokes	看守	KANSHU	warder

Hand 手 32 above eye 目 72, to give a meaning of **place hand above eye**. This was a reference to shading the eyes in order to **gaze intently**.

Mnemonic: **PUT HAND ABOVE EYE TO WATCH BETTER**

828		**KAN, susu*meru***	勧告	KANKOKU	advice
		ENCOURAGE, ADVISE	勧奨	KANSHŌ	encouragement
		13 strokes	勧誘	KANYŪ	persuasion

Formerly 勸 . 力 is **strength/ effort** 74. 藿 / 雚 is **crested bird/ heron** 445, acting phonetically to express **strong** and possibly also lending its own loose idea of **persistence** (from a heron persistently searching for food). 828 originally meant to **make great and determined efforts** to achieve something. This later came to include the idea of **exhorting others** to make similar efforts, leading to **encourage**. **Advise** is an associated meaning with encourage.

Mnemonic: **ENCOURAGED BY EFFORTS OF CRESTED BIRD**

829		**KAN**	簡単	KANTAN na	simple
		SIMPLE, BRIEF, LETTER	書簡	SHOKAN	letter
		18 strokes	簡略	KANRYAKU	
					conciseness, simplicity

Formerly also 簡 . 竹 is **bamboo** 170, here indicating **bamboo tablet used for records**. 閒 / 間 is **space** 92. Thus **bamboo record with space (left)**, indicating that the record is a **simple** and **brief** one. Brief text later came to include **letter** (cf. English brief), while **simple** and **brief** came to be used in a general sense.

Mnemonic: **SPACE LEFT ON BRIEF AND SIMPLE BAMBOO LETTER**

830		GAN, maru, marui	丸薬 GANYAKU	pill
		ROUND, CIRCLE, BALL,	丸味 MARUMI	roundness
		SHIP'S MARK	日本丸 NIPPONMARU	
		3 strokes		Vessel Nippon

Originally 夰. 𠂉 is a **bending/ hunched person** (mirror image of 人 39). 乀 is a **cliff/ hillside** (mirror image of 厂 45), acting phonetically to express **roll** as well as lending its meaning of **slope**. Thus a **person hunched as they roll down a slope**, leading to **ball** and by association **round** and **circle**. 830 is also used of a **ship's mark**, said to derive from the ancient practice of licensing vessels with a round seal. It is not clear why the elements in 830 are in mirror image form. Suggest taking as **nine** 九 12 with an **extra stroke** 丶.

Mnemonic: **NINE ROUNDED OFF WITH EXTRA STROKE**

831		KI, abunai, ayaui	危機 KIKI	crisis
		DANGEROUS	危険 KIKEN	danger
		6 strokes	危害 KIGAI	harm

Once written 夗, showing a **person crouching** 𠂊 145 on the edge of a **cliff** 厂 45, fearful of the **danger**. This came to symbolise a **dangerous** situation. A further **bending figure** 2 145 was added later for emphasis, giving 危, but in time this apparently became confused with **prone/ fallen figure** ᄃ 768, leading to the popular interpretation of the modern form as a person kneeling on the edge of a dangerous cliff looking down at his companion who has fallen over the edge. This explanation is technically incorrect but is a useful mnemonic. See also **misfortune** 厄 1859.

Mnemonic: **CROUCH ON EDGE OF DANGEROUS CLIFF -- MATE FALLEN**

832		KI, tsukue	机上 KIJŌ no	theoretical
		DESK, TABLE	机辺 KIHEN	around table
		6 strokes	事務机 JIMUTSUKUE	office desk

几 is an NGU character pictographically representing a **small table** or armrest (or occasionally stool), while 木 is tree/ **wood** 69. Thus **small wooden table**. Now used for **table/ desk** in a broader sense.

Mnemonic: **USE WOODEN TABLE FOR DESK**

833 揮 **KI**
WIELD, SHAKE, COMMAND
12 strokes

発揮 HAKKI display
指揮 SHIKI command
揮発性 KIHATSUSEI volatility

扌 is **hand** 32. 軍 is **army** 466, here acting phonetically to express **agitate** and possibly also lending loose connotations of agitation/ commotion. 833 originally meant to **shake the hands wildly**, leading to **brandish/ wield** and by extension **command.**

Mnemonic: **ARMY HAND WIELDS COMMAND**

834 貴 **KI, tattoi/bu, tōtoi**
PRECIOUS, REVERED
12 strokes

貴族 KIZOKU aristocrat
貴重 KICHŌ na precious
貴方 KIHŌ/ ANATA* you

貝 is **shell/ money/ valuable item** 90. 虫 is a simplification of 臾, the prototype of the NGU character 臾. The latter is now used to mean urge, but has a core meaning of **gather**, and in Chinese can mean **basket**. It is not clear whether 臾 derives from a pictograph of a **basket** (symbolising gathering) or an ideograph of **hands gathering** something in. In the case of 834 虫 acts phonetically to express **accumulate** and also lends a meaning of **gather**. Thus **gather and accumulate valuable items**, leading to **something of great value** and hence **precious**. **Revered** is an associated meaning. Suggest taking 虫 as **middle** 中 55 and **one** 一 1, with 貝 literally as **shell**.

Mnemonic: **ONE PRECIOUS SHELL IN MIDDLE OF COLLECTION**

835 疑 **GI, utagau**
DOUBT, SUSPECT
14 strokes

質疑 SHITSUGI question
疑問 GIMON doubt
疑似 GIJI false

Etymologically and graphically somewhat confused. Once written 𠤕. As very early forms such as 矣 show, 匕 is not sitting person 匕 238 but a confusing stylisation of an **(old) man's stick** ト (see 609). 矢 is similarly an extreme and confusing stylisation (through an intermediate form 夫) of a pictograph of an **(old) man** 夫, whose long hair (a symbol of age) is trailing as his head moves from side to side 牛. The fact that his head is moving indicates that he is **in doubt**, and looking about him wondering where to turn. At a later stage two further elements were added, **child** 子/子 25 and foot/ **stop** 止/止 129, and in fact in some versions replaced stick ト/匕, thus giving 疑 and hence the modern 疑. This originally referred to a child becoming lost, standing still and looking about him not knowing which way to turn. Both 疑 and 𠤕 became blurred, and resulted in a meaning of **not knowing what to do**, which eventually led by association to **doubt** and **suspicion**. Suggest taking 匕 as **sitting person**, マ as a **bending person** (thus giving **two 'felled' persons**), 矢 as **arrow** 981, and 疋 as **correct** 41.

Mnemonic: **TWO PEOPLE FELLED BY ONE ARROW? DOUBT IF CORRECT**

| 836 | KYŪ, yumi
BOW, ARCHERY
3 strokes | 弓道 KYŪDŌ
弓状 KYŪJŌ
弓取り YUMITORI | archery
arch
archer |

From a pictograph of **bow** ß / ß , **minus the string**. Note that 836 can also be used of an **arc** or **bend** (cf. English bow, and etymological connection between arc, arch, archery).

Mnemonic: **STRINGLESS BOW**

| 837 | KYŪ, su*u*
SUCK, INHALE
6 strokes | 吸収 KYŪSHŪ
吸血鬼 KYŪKETSUKI
吸い取る SUITORU | absorption
vampire
soak up |

口 is **mouth** 20. 及 is **reach** 1148 q.v., here acting phonetically to express **pull** and probably also lending connotations of **draw towards oneself**. Thus to **pull/ draw with the mouth**, i.e. **suck/ inhale**.

Mnemonic: **IF IT REACHES MOUTH, THEN SUCK IT IN**

| 838 | KYŪ, na*ku*
WEEP, CRY
8 strokes | 泣訴 KYŪSO
泣き虫 NAKIMUSHI
泣き出す NAKIDASU | imploring
crybaby

burst into tears |

シ is **water** 40. 立 is **stand** 73, here acting phonetically to express **tear** and almost certainly also lending an idea of **verticality** and by association **falling** (see also pour 注 344). Thus **falling drops of 'tear-water'**.

Mnemonic: **PERSON STANDS WEEPING WATERY TEARS**

| 839 | KYŌ, KU, tomo, sona*eru*
OFFER, ATTENDANT
8 strokes | 提供 TEIKYŌ
供回り TOMOMAWARI
供養 KUYŌ | offer
retinue
memorial service |

亻 is **person** 39. 共 is **together** 460 q.v., here with its literal meaning of **offer**. Thus **offer something to a person**, later just **offer**. It is not fully clear how the meaning of **attendant** evolved. Some scholars take it to be an extension of offer to a person, i.e. a **person who offers** something to another person, while others take it to stem from a reinterpretation of the elements as **together with a person**, i.e. **companion** and hence **attendant**.

Mnemonic: **ATTENDANT OFFERS TOGETHERNESS TO PERSON**

840 KYŌ, mune, muna-
CHEST, BREAST, HEART
10 strokes

胸部 KYŌBU — thorax
胸毛 MUNAGE — chest hair
度胸 DOKYŌ — heart, courage

Once written simply as 匈, and earlier as 匃. 勹/勹 is womb 655, here indicating **container**, while 凶 is **empty container** 1159. Some scholars feel that 凶 also acts phonetically to express **air**. Thus **empty container (associated with air?)**, a reference to the **lungs**. 匈 does in fact exist as an NGU character that once meant lung (and still has this meaning in Chinese), but is now used largely as a phonetic to represent Hungary (easily remembered by a facetious association with 'hungry', i.e. referring to an empty container of a different kind). **Lungs** led by extension to the **chest area** in general. **Flesh/ of the body** 月 365 was added later for clarity. Suggest taking 勹 as **encircle**, and 凶 as a **scarred** ✕ **container** 凵.

Mnemonic: FLESH ENCIRCLING SCARRED 'CONTAINER' IS THE CHEST

841 KYŌ, GŌ
VILLAGE, RURAL
11 strokes

望郷 BŌKYŌ — homesickness
郷士 GŌSHI — squire
郷土 KYŌDO — local

Of somewhat confused graphic origin. Formerly written 鄉 or 鄉, and in ancient times as 𨞠 and 鄉. 皀/皀/皀/皀 are **food** 食 146 q.v., while ヒク clearly shows **two persons** sitting either side of the food. On the one hand this led to the idea of **meeting over dinner**, which just as in the modern West often indicated meeting with a **superior** to discuss something. This meaning is still retained in the NGU character 卿/卿, which means lord, minister, or you, and is etymologically the same character as 841. On the other hand it led to the idea of **feasting** and holding a **get-together**, indicating a **community event** and by extension the **community/ village** itself. This in turn led to the replacement of ヒク with 㚱, being the prototype 邑 of **village** 阝 355 q.v. and its mirror image. It is not clear whether this substitution was done deliberately or in error. Suggest taking 幺 as a variant of short thread 幺 111, taking this by extension as **string**.

Mnemonic: ODD STRINGY FOOD SERVED IN VILLAGE

842

KIN, tsuto*meru*
WORK, DUTIES
12 strokes

出勤　SHUKKIN　　　　attendance
勤勉性　KINBENSEI　　diligence
勤め先　TSUTOMESAKI
　　　　　　　　　place of work

Somewhat obscure due to the obscure nature of 堇, which was formerly written 堇 and earlier 菫. 堇 is an NGU character with the unhelpful meaning of **violet** (the flower). In Chinese it can mean **yellow loam** or **season** as well as **rare** and **few**, the last two meanings of which are also found in a number of compounds in Japanese (such as few words/ circumspect 謹 1180 q.v. [言 being word 274] and the NGU character few 僅 [亻 being person 39]). Some scholars take the early form 菫 to show **earth** 土 60 plus a combination 英 of **horned beast** 苹 (see 821) and **fire** 火 8, to give a meaning of **roast a beast in an earthen firepit**, but it is not clear how any of the present meanings came about. In any event, in the case of 842 堇 is known to have acted phonetically to express **muscle**, combining with **strength/effort** 力 74 to convey the idea of **making a great physical effort**. It is also possible that 堇 lends an idea of **rare**, to give **make a rare (i.e. outstanding) physical effort**. Make a physical effort eventually came to mean **do one's work/ duties** in a broad sense. Suggest taking 堇 as a combination of **plants** 艹 9, **grow** 主 (variant 生 42), and **(seed-)box** 口.

Mnemonic: **WORK WITH EFFORT TO GROW PLANTS FROM SEED-BOX**

843

KIN, suji
MUSCLE, SINEW, THREAD
12 strokes

筋肉　KINNIKU　　　　muscle
筋道　SUJIMICHI　　　logic
筋書き　SUJIGAKI　　synopsis

竹 is **bamboo** 170. 肋 is an NGU character meaning **rib**, namely that which gives **strength** 力 74 to the **flesh** 月 365. The ribs of a bamboo plant are its **fibers**, the original meaning of 843. In time this came to mean **thread**, with **sinew** and **muscle** being associated meanings (probably also influenced by the presence of flesh 月).

Mnemonic: **BAMBOO HAS STRONG FLESHY SINEWS**

844

KEI
LINEAGE, CONNECTION
7 strokes

家系　KAKEI　　　　lineage
系統　KEITŌ　　system, line
系列　KEIRETSU　succession

Once written 爲, showing a **hand** 爪 holding **two threads** 夊/糸 27. This indicated **twisting/ intertwining** them, with intertwined threads being used figuratively to describe a **lineage** or **connection**. Suggest taking ／ as a symbol of **twisting**.

Mnemonic: **LINEAGE COMPOSED OF TWISTED CONNECTED THREADS**

845 **KEI**
PATH, DIRECT
8 strokes

直径 CHOKKEI diameter
しょう径 SHŌKEI shortcut
直情径行 CHOKUJŌKEIKŌ
impulsiveness

Formerly 徑 . 彳 is **go/ road** 118. 巠 is **lengthwise threads on a loom** 269 q.v., here acting phonetically to express **small** and also lending an idea of **direct** (from going in a straight line, though confusingly the stylised 巜 shows unstraight threads). Thus **small, direct road**, leading both to **path** and **direct**. Suggest taking 巠 as **hand** 又 and **ground** 土 60.

Mnemonic: **DIRECT PATH ENTAILS MOVING WITH HANDS ON GROUND**

846 **KEI, uyama***u*
RESPECT
12 strokes

尊敬 SONKEI respect
敬語 KEIGO polite language
い敬 IKEI awe

攵 is **strike/ force** 101, here acting as a causative element. 苟 is an NGU character now used to convey insignificance, but a very early form 口犭 shows a **person bending** (in a position of **humility**) 𠆢 39 and **speaking** 口 (mouth/say 20), and it originally meant **speak respectfully**. The exact meaning of 乂 / 卄 is not clear, but other early forms such as 𠔉 and 𣪊 support the theory that it shows a minor chieftain's headdress (of sheep's horns), to give a specific meaning of minor chieftain speaking respectfully to his lord. The addition of force 攵 gave **force someone to speak respectfully**, but this has now faded to leave just **show respect** in a broad sense. The graphic evolution of the character may have been influenced by **phrase** 句 655, which may be useful as a mnemonic. Suggest taking 卄 as **plants** 9.

Mnemonic: **FORCE PERSON TO USE RESPECTFUL PHRASES OF PLANTS**

847 **KEI**
WARN, REPROACH
19 strokes

警官 KEIKAN police officer
警告 KEIKOKU warning
警報 KEIHŌ warning, alarm

言 is **words/ speak** 274. 敬 is **respect** 846, here lending connotations of acting **cautiously** as well as **respectfully**. 847 originally meant **speak cautiously and respectfully**, but later came to mean **be cautious** as well as **counsel caution**, i.e. **warn**. As with the English term, warn later came to be used in the sense of **reproach** as well as counsel.

Mnemonic: **WARN WITH RESPECTFUL WORDS**

848		GEKI DRAMA, INTENSE 15 strokes	劇場 GEKIJŌ	theater
			劇的 GEKITEKI	dramatic
			劇痛 GEKITSŪ	intense pain

刂 is **sword/ cut** 181, 虍 is **tiger** 281, and 豕 is **pig** 1670. Though there is some disagreement over the interpretation of these elements, the character is generally seen as an ideograph meaning **attack with a sword in the manner of a tiger attacking a pig**, i.e. **fiercely**, with **intense** being an extended meaning. Some scholars take **drama/ dramatic** to be a borrowed meaning, while others take it to stem from the idea of **exciting** and **intense** (cf. English drama/ dramatic).

Mnemonic: **TIGER ATTACKS PIG WITH SWORD?! -- WHAT DRAMA!**

849		KETSU, ana HOLE 5 strokes	穴居人 KEKKYOJIN	troglodyte
			穴子 ANAGO	conger eel
			穴埋め ANAUME	stopgap

宀 is **roof/ cover** 28. 八 is **disperse/ away** 66, here meaning **open up** and according to some scholars also acting phonetically to express **dig**. 849 originally referred to a **space being opened up (in the ground) and covered**, a primitive method of forming a dwelling (see also 15). It later came to mean **hole** in general.

Mnemonic: **TAKE COVER AWAY AND EXPOSE HOLE**

850		KEN, ka*neru* COMBINE, UNABLE 10 strokes	兼業 KENGYŌ	side business
			兼用 KENYŌ	dual purpose
			為兼ねる SHIKANERU	cannot do

Once written 兼, showing a **hand** ⺕ holding **two rice plants** 禾 81 and symbolising **doing two things at once**. Its use as a verbal suffix to express being **unable** to do something is felt to stem from the idea that in trying to do two things at once one is unable to do either thing properly. Suggest remembering 秝 as **combined rice plants**.

Mnemonic: **HAND REALLY UNABLE TO HOLD COMBINED RICE PLANTS**

---

851 **KEN, GON**
RIGHT, AUTHORITY,
BALANCE
15 strokes

権利 KENRI　　　right, claim
権衡 KENKŌ　　　balance
権化 GONGE　　embodiment

Formerly 權 . 木 is **tree/ wood** 69. 蘿/雀 is **crested bird/** heron 445, here acting phonetically to express **cream** (color) but of unknown semantic role. 851 originally referred to a certain **tree whose flowers were cream.** As a result of miscopying it was later used instead of a now defunct character 攉 . This comprised heron 蘿 , used phonetically to express **stone** but of unknown semantic role, and **hand** 扌 32, and referred to stones of a more or less given size -- just able to be held in one hand-- which were used as **weights** in a primitive **set of scales/ balance. Right** and **authority** are felt to be associated meanings, from the fact that the person doing the weighing had the right to provide his own weighing-stones and thereby possibly gain some slight advantage. **Balance** is now a very minor meaning.

Mnemonic: **CRESTED BIRD HAS RIGHT TO BALANCE IN TREE**

---

852 憲 **KEN**
LAW, CONSTITUTION
16 strokes

憲法 KENPŌ　　constitution
憲章 KENSHŌ　　　charter
憲兵 KENPEI　military police

Somewhat obscure. Once written 寯, showing an **inverted basket** 冉/由 399 and an **eye** ⼼/目 72. Some scholars feel that inverted basket 冉/宙 acted purely phonetically to express **quick/ sharp**, to give a meaning of **sharp eyed.** When **heart/ feelings** 心 147 was added later the meaning changed to **quick with feelings**, i.e. **emotional/ sensitive.** Its present meaning of **legal authority** is then assumed to be borrowed. Other scholars feel that inverted basket symbolised **covering**, giving **covered eye** and by extension **acting blindly.** The later addition of heart/ feeling 心 is then felt to extend the meaning to **acting blindly and without emotion**, in other words **doing something without question.** The **law/ constitution** is something that should be obeyed in this fashion. The fact that in Chinese 852 can also mean **ruler** and **complacent** supports the latter theory, since both meanings can be interpreted as stemming from a core concept of **acting or obeying without question.** Suggest taking 宀 as **cover**, and 主 as a variant of **life** 生 42.

Mnemonic: **CONSTITUTIONAL LAW COVERS ALL ONE SEES AND FEELS IN LIFE**

853		GEN, minamoto SOURCE, ORIGIN 13 strokes	資源 SHIGEN resources 源泉 GENSEN source 源氏 GENJI Minamoto Clan

原 is **plain/ origin** 107 q.v., here in its early sense of **spring**. **Water** ⺡ 40 was added after 107 started to lose its original meaning. 853 is now often used in the figurative sense of **origin**, though it can still mean specifically a **water source**.

Mnemonic: **WATER SOURCE IS IN ORIGINAL SPRING ON PLAIN**

854		GEN,GON,kibi*shii*, ogoso*ka* SEVERE, STRICT, SOLEMN 17 strokes	厳格 GENKAKU strictness 厳秘 GENPI strictly secret 壮厳 SŌGON solemnity

Formerly 嚴, and earlier 嚴. 厂 is **cliff** 45. 敢 is **daring** 1106 q.v., here acting phonetically to express **gape** and possibly also lending connotations of **remove** and by extension **be missing**. 厰 originally referred to **holes in a cliffside**, i.e. **fissures** or **caves**, but gradually came to mean just **cliff**. In an attempt to shift the focus back to the holes in the cliff the element ⼛⼛ was added. It technically shows a doubling of mouth/ say 口 20 and means noisy, but was used here for its idea of **two openings** (also 20) as well as for its sound, which like 敢 expressed **gape**. However, once again **cliff** came to prevail. Ironically, cliff is now conveyed by the NGU character 巌, which adds **mountain** 山 24, while 854 became used to express **severe/ strict/ solemn** instead of the NGU character 儼. This adds **person** 亻 39 and means literally **person as firm as a cliff/ rock**. Suggest taking 厂 as an **ornate building** (see 10 and 114).

Mnemonic: **DARINGLY ORNATE BUILDING IS STRICTLY SOLEMN!**

855		KO, KI, onore I, ME, YOU, SELF 3 strokes	自己 JIKO self 知己 CHIKI friend 利己 RIKO selfishness

From a pictograph of a **twisting thread** 己, which was its original meaning. Its use as a **first person pronoun** is felt by some scholars to be a purely phonetic borrowing, but it seems highly likely that it became graphically confused with the early form 㠯 of **I/ self** 厶 134. Confusingly, 855 is also occasionally used as a **second person pronoun**, a usage that is felt to stem from generalisations involving the concept of **self** (cf. English use of **you** instead of **oneself**).

Mnemonic: **I MYSELF FOLLOW THE THREAD -- WHAT ABOUT YOU?**

269

856 呼	**KO,** ***yobu***	呼吸	KOKYŪ	breathing
	CALL, BREATHE	点呼	TENKO	roll call
	8 strokes	呼び物	YOBIMONO	drawcard

口 is **mouth/ say** 20. 乎 is an NGU character now used to indicate a question or exclamation, but was originally a symbol of **exhalation**, being written 乎. This shows **seeking an exit** 丂 281, **away** 八 66, and a further symbol of **expulsion** ノ. Rather like call 号 281 q.v. (and see also 816), 856 originally referred to something **emerging from the mouth**, and was applied both to **breathing** (especially exhaling) and **vocalising.** Suggest taking 乎 as an **'odd' hand** 手 32.

Mnemonic: **ODD HAND BY MOUTH STOPS BREATHING OR CALLING**

857 誤	**GO,** ***ayamaru***	誤解	GOKAI	misunderstanding
	MISTAKE, MIS-	誤判	GOHAN	mistrial
	14 strokes	誤訳	GOYAKU	mistranslation

Formerly 誤. 呉/呉 is **give** 1237 q.v., here used in its literal sense of brag/ **deviate from the truth,** with **words/ speak** 言 274 added after 1237's meaning became vague. Words which deviate from the truth led to **mistake** and the idea of **not saying/doing something properly.**

Mnemonic: **MISTAKEN WORDS GIVEN**

858 后	**KŌ, GO,** ***kisaki***	皇后	KŌGŌ	empress
	EMPRESS, BEHIND,	后妃	KŌHI	queen
	LATER	午后	GOGO	afternoon
	6 strokes			

⺁ is a variant of **buttocks** 尸/尸 236, while 口 is **opening** 20. **Opening in the buttocks** was a reference to the **anus,** the original meaning of 858. Not unlike the English term **behind,** this later also came to be used in the prepositional sense, including of time. **Empress** is felt by some scholars to be a borrowed meaning, but it seems far more likely to stem from a practice of referring to the empress indirectly as the **one who follows behind** (the emperor). Suggest remembering ⺁ by partial association with **ax** 斤 1176. See also 497.

Mnemonic: **EMPRESS COMES BEHIND, CUTTING OPENING WITH AX**

859

KŌ, su*ku*, kono*mu*/*mashii*
LIKE, GOOD, FINE
6 strokes

好意 KŌI goodwill
好き SUKI na nice, liked
好男子 KŌDANSHI
handsome man

Popularly explained as the **liking a woman** 女 35 has for a **child** 子 25, symbolising a **fine** and **loving** relationship. However, some authoritative Japanese scholars feel that child 子 is used essentially phonetically to express **beautiful**, as well as probably lending connotations of **that which one wishes to embrace** and/or **that towards which one feels tender**, to give a meaning of **beautiful woman (to whom one feels tender?)**. Beautiful/ attractive then came to mean **fine** and **good** in a broader sense, with **like** being seen as an associated meaning. It is possible, however, that the evolution of the meaning **like** was influenced by the above popular interpretation of the elements as **woman liking child**, which is a useful mnemonic.

Mnemonic: **WOMAN LIKES CHILD -- WHAT A FINE THING**

860

KŌ
FILIAL PIETY
7 strokes

孝子 KŌSHI dutiful child
孝行 KŌKŌ filial piety
不孝 FUKŌ filial impiety

Popularly explained as an **old man** 耂 117 q.v. and **child** 子 25 symbolising the **relationship between the generations**, with **filial piety** being an associated meaning. However, some authoritative Japanese scholars feel that child 子 is used essentially phonetically to express **care for**, as well as probably lending a meaning of **offspring**, to give a meaning of **(offspring?) caring for an old person**. The fact that at one stage child 子 was interchanged with food 食 146, as seen in an early form 𩙿, supports this theory (i.e. with food 食 playing a similar phonetic role and also semantically suggesting look after/ provide for). However, suggest using the popular explanation as a mnemonic, and rembering 耂 as **old man** by partial association with **earth** 土 60.

Mnemonic: **FILIAL PIETY IS CHILD CARING FOR EARTHY OLD MAN**

861

KŌ, Ō
EMPEROR
9 strokes

皇太子 KŌTAISHI crown prince
法皇 HŌŌ monk-emperor
明治天皇 MEIJI TENNŌ*
Emperor Meiji

Once written 𝟺, showing **king** 王 5 and a **crown** 𦥑. 861 originally referred to a **king's crown** or **ceremonial headpiece** (still a meaning in Chinese), but later came to refer to the person wearing such an item, i.e. the **ruler/ emperor**. Suggest taking 白 as **white** 65.

Mnemonic: **EMPEROR IS WHITE KING**

862	**KŌ, KU, kurenai, beni**	紅葉 KŌYŌ	red leaves
	RED, CRIMSON, ROUGE	真紅 SHINKU	crimson
	9 strokes	紅茶 KŌCHA	brown tea

糸 is **thread** 27. 工 is **work** 113, here acting phonetically to express **pink** and possibly also lending an idea of **process**. Thus **(processed?) pink threads**. This later came to mean pink in general, then **red/ crimson/ rouge**. As with the English term rouge, it is also used to refer to cosmetics, including lipstick.

Mnemonic: **WORK WITH CRIMSON THREADS**

863	**KŌ, furu, oriru/rosu**	降雨 KŌU	rainfall
	FALL, ALIGHT,	降伏 KŌFUKU	surrender
	DESCEND	乗り降り NORIORI	
	10 strokes		getting on and off

阝 is **hill** 229. 夅 was once written 𨸏, showing **two inverted feet** 夅 (又 438 and 丬 422). Inverted feet is used in its sense of **come down from above** (see 438), giving **come down a hill** and hence the present meanings. Suggest taking 又 as **sitting crosslegged** and 丬 as a variant of **well** 井 1470.

Mnemonic: **DESCEND HILL AND SIT CROSSLEGGED BY WELL**

864	**KŌ, hagane**	鋼鉄 KŌTETSU	steel
	STEEL	製鋼所 SEIKŌJO	steelworks
	16 strokes	鋼色 HAGANEIRO	steel blue

岡 is an NGU character meaning **hill**. It was once written 𡶡, showing **hill** 屮/山 24 and net 冂/冈 193, the latter lending a meaning of **draw in/up**. Thus **hill that is drawn up**, i.e. one that is **towering** and **formidable**. Here it lends an idea of **formidable** as well as acting phonetically to express **strong**, combining with **metal** 金 14 to give **strong/ formidable metal**. It is now used particularly of **steel**.

Mnemonic: **METAL IN HILLS PROVES TO BE STEEL**

865 KOKU, kiza*mu*   時刻 JIKOKU   time, hour

CHOP, MINCE,   刻印 KOKUIN   engraved seal

ENGRAVE   刻み目 KIZAMIME   notch

8 strokes

刂 is sword/ **cut** 181. 亥 is an NGU character used as the zodiac sign **hog**, and is to all intents and purposes a variant of **pig** 豕 1670. Here it acts phonetically to express **carve**, and possibly also lends similar connotations of **cutting/ carving** from the idea of butchering (e.g. see 195). Thus to **cut and carve**, leading both to **engrave** and to the idea of **cutting twice over**, i.e. **mince**. Suggest taking 亠 as a symbol of **top** and 久 as a variant of (short) **thread** 幺 111.

Mnemonic: **MINCE THREADS BY CUTTING TOPS OFF**

866 KOKU   穀物 KOKUMOTSU   cereals

GRAIN, CEREALS   穀類 KOKURUI   cereals

14 strokes   穀倉 KOKUSŌ   granary

Formerly 穀 . 禾 is **rice plant** 81, here meaning **food plant**. 殻 is a variant of shell/ **husk** 殻 1075. Thus **husked food plant**, i.e. **grain/ cereal**. Suggest taking 殳 as **beat/ strike** 153, 士 as **samurai** 494, and 冖 as **cover**.

Mnemonic: **SAMURAI BEATS RICE UNDER COVER TO MAKE CEREALS**

867 KOTSU, hone   骨折 KOSSETSU   fracture

BONE, FRAME   老骨 RŌKOTSU   old person

10 strokes   骨折る HONEORU   strive

冎 derives from 咼 , showing **skull and vertebrae** and meaning **bone(s)**. **Flesh/ of the body** 月 365 was added later, to give **bones in the body/ skeleton**. This is still seen occasionally in the lesser meaning of **frame**, but generally 867 has come to mean simply **bone(s)** in a broad sense. Suggest remembering by partial association with **cover** 冖 .

Mnemonic: **FLESH COVERED BONES**

273

868

KON, koma*ru*
BE IN DIFFICULTY
7 strokes

困難 KONNAN trouble
困苦 KONKU hardship
困らせる KOMARASERU annoy

Widely interpreted as a **tree** 木 69 in a **confined area** or **box** 囗 (see 123), to symbolise being **constrained** or **in difficulty**. However, some scholars feel that 木 acts rather in its meaning of **wood**, as well as lending its sound to express **barrier**, and that 囗 is **opening/ entrance** 20. Thus **wooden barrier barring entrance**, leading by association to the idea of a place that is **difficult to enter** and eventually just **difficult/ difficulty**. Suggest following the former theory.

Mnemonic: **TREE IN DIFFICULTY, TRAPPED IN BOX**

869

SA, SHA, suna
SAND, GRAVEL, GRAIN
9 strokes

砂金 SAKIN gold dust
砂利 JARI* gravel
砂浜 SUNAHAMA sandy beach

石 is **stone** 45, while 少 is **little/ few** 143 q.v., here used in its literal sense of **tiny points**. Thus **tiny stones**, leading to the present meanings. Note that 869 is to all intents and purposes interchangeable with the NGU character SA/SHA sand 沙, which uses **water/ river** 氵 40 instead of stone 石 to give tiny items in a river.

Mnemonic: **SAND COMPRISES LITTLE STONES**

870

ZA, suwa*ru*
SEAT, SIT, GATHER
10 strokes

座席 ZASEKI seat
座談会 ZADANKAI symposium
銀座 GINZA the Ginza

Formerly also written 坐, showing **two persons** 人 39 on the **ground** 土 60. Though the use of <u>standing</u> persons as opposed to <u>sitting</u> persons (e.g. 尸 236 or ヒ 238) is somewhat confusing, 870 does in fact refer to **persons sitting on the ground**. **Building / roof** 广 114 was added later, giving persons **sitting on the ground under a roof**, suggesting a **gathering**.

Mnemonic: **PERSONS SIT ON GROUND UNDER ROOF AT GATHERING**

871 SAI, SEI, su*mu/masu*　　経済学　KEIZAIGAKU economics
SETTLE, FINISH　　　返済　HENSAI　　　repayment
11 strokes　　　　　　済まない SUMANAI　be improper

Formerly 濟. 氵 is **water** 40. 斉/斉 is alike 1473 q.v., here acting phonetically to express **clear** and probably also lending its own connotations of **pure** (from items prepared for offering to the gods). Thus **clear pure water**, which by extension is **settled** water. This meaning is now conveyed by 澄 1597, while 871 has come to mean settled in the sense of **concluded** and **put in order** (note the various meanings of the verb sumu). Suggest taking 斉 as writing/ **text** 文 68 and an **'odd' moon** 月 16.

Mnemonic: **TEXT ABOUT ODD MOON SEEN IN SETTLED WATER**

---

872 SAI, saba*ku*, ta*tsu*　　　裁判　SAIBAN　　　　trial
JUDGE, DECIDE, CUT 裁ちくず TACHIKUZU　　shreds
12 strokes　　　　　　裁ち方 TACHIKATA　　cut, fit

衣 is **clothing/ cloth** 420. 𢦏 is a CO character meaning **wound/ cut,** and is to all intents and purposes a **'fancy'** variant of **lance/ halberd/ cut** 㦮 493. (Some scholars see 𢦏 as a variant of trim/ broad bladed halberd 戌 515, but old forms such as 𢦏 suggest rather that it is technically a variant of tasseled lance/ halberd 我 817.) Thus to **cut cloth** (**into clothing**). As with judge/ cut 断 750, cutting came to represent **being decisive** and hence **judging**.

Mnemonic: **JUDGE DECIDES TO CUT CLOTH WITH FANCY HALBERD**

---

873 策 SAKU　　　　　　　政策　SEISAKU　　　　policy
POLICY, PLAN, WHIP 対策　TAISAKU　　counterplan
12 strokes　　　　　策動家 SAKUDŌKA　　schemer

竹 is **bamboo** 170, here meaning **thin stem of wood**. 朿 is an NGU character meaning **thorn** (see also thorn 刺 1314). It derives from a combination of **tree/ wood** 木 69 and a symbol of **tapering** △, giving 本 and later 朿 and hence 朿. Here it acts phonetically to express **beat** and also lends its meaning of **sharply tapered piece of wood**. Thus 873 originally meant **sharply tapered thin piece of wood for beating**, and referred to a **horsewhip**. It is still occasionally used in this sense, especially in Chinese. **Policy/ plan** is felt to stem from confusion with **book/ bamboo records** 冊 874 q.v., which has the same pronunciation and shares common semantic ground of thin piece of bamboo/wood. Keeping a written record of something led by association to the idea of formulating a detailed policy/ plan. Suggest taking 朿 as a **tree with droopy branches**.

Mnemonic: **PLAN TO FIX DROOPY TREE BRANCHES WITH BAMBOO**

874

SATSU
BOOK, VOLUME
5 strokes

冊子 SASSHI   booklet
二冊 NISATSU   two volumes
短冊 TANZAKU

paper strip for poem

Formerly 丗丗 and earlier 丗丗丗, depicting a **bundle of thin bamboo tablets (used for records) bound together.** Hence **collection of written material.**

Mnemonic: **STACKED BOUND TABLETS RESEMBLE VOLUMES OF BOOKS**

875

SHI, itaru/ri
GO, REACH, PEAK
6 strokes

至急 SHIKYŪ   emergency
夏至 GESHI   summer solstice
至らない ITARANAI   imperfect

From a pictograph ⚐ , showing an **arrow** ⚐ (probably with something bound to its stem) **falling to the ground** _ . While this occasionally lends connotations of upside-down, it usually connotes **reaching a point (and stopping)**, that point being the **maximum** edge of its range. You may prefer to see the arrow the other way up, i.e. ⚐ , or else take 至 as **ground** 土 60, **nose** 厶 134, and a symbol of **flatness** ‾ .

Mnemonic: **NOSE FLAT TO GROUND AS ONE REACHES ONE'S PEAK**

876

SHI, wata[ku]shi
I, PRIVATE, PERSONAL
7 strokes

私立 SHIRITSU   private
私達 WATASHITACHI   we
私事 SHIJI   personal affairs

Rice plant 禾 81 and **self** 厶 134, to give **one's own rice** and by extension **private, personal**, and **things pertaining to oneself** (i.e. **I/ me/ my**).

Mnemonic: **RICE IS PRIVATE AND BELONGS TO ME MYSELF**

877

SHI, sugata
FORM, FIGURE
9 strokes

姿勢 SHISEI   posture
容姿 YŌSHI   form
姿見 SUGATAMI   full mirror

女 is **woman** 35. 次 is **next** 292 q.v., acting phonetically to express **voluptuous** and probably also lending a literal idea of **people standing open mouthed.** 877 originally referred to a **woman of stunning attractiveness**, and later came to mean **fine figure** and eventually just **figure/ form** in a broad sense.

Mnemonic: **NEXT WOMAN HAS A GOOD FIGURE**

878		SHI, mi*ru* SEE, LOOK, REGARD 11 strokes	視力 SHIRYOKU	eyesight
			視覚 SHIKAKU	vision
			無視 MUSHI	disregard

Formerly 視. 示/ネ is show 695. 見 is look 16. Some scholars feel 見 also lends its sound to express **stop/ fix in place**. Thus **look at something on show (and fix one's gaze on it?)**, later **look/ regard** in a broader sense.

Mnemonic: **LOOK AND SEE WHAT'S ON SHOW**

879		SHI, kotoba WORD, PART OF SPEECH 12 strokes	動詞 DŌSHI	verb
			歌詞 KASHI	lyrics
			詞書 KOTOBAGAKI	foreword

言 is **word** 274. 司 is **administer/ official** 497 q.v., acting phonetically to express **join** and almost certainly also lending a meaning of **control**. Thus words **which join (other words) (and control them?)**, a reference to **parts of speech** and by extension **words** in a broader sense.

Mnemonic: **PARTS OF SPEECH ARE OFFICIAL WORDS**

880		SHI RECORD, JOURNAL 14 strokes	本誌 HONSHI	this journal
			雑誌 ZASSHI	magazine
			週間誌 SHŪKANSHI	a weekly

言 is **word** 274. 志 is **will/ intent** 692, acting phonetically to express **record** and almost certainly also lending an idea of **intent**. Thus to **record words (with intent?)**, giving **record** and by extension **journal**. Suggest taking 志 as **samurai** 士 494 and **heart/ feeling** 心 147.

Mnemonic: **SAMURAI'S HEARTFELT WORDS RECORDED IN JOURNAL**

881	磁	JI MAGNET, PORCELAIN 14 strokes	磁石 JISHAKU	magnet
			磁器 JIKI	porcelain
			磁力 JIRYOKU	magnetism

Formerly 磁. 石 is **stone** 45. 兹 is an NGU character now used to convey **this/ here**. Its semantic evolution is somewhat unclear, but it is a doubling of **twisted thread/ occult/ invisible** 玄 1227 q.v. It acts here phonetically to express **draw/ pull**, and probably also lends similar connotations from its literal meaning of threads drawn together by a twisting device, and/or connotations of invisibility/ mystery. Thus **stone that draws/ pulls (mysteriously/ invisibly?)**, i.e. a **magnet**. **Porcelain** is a borrowed meaning.

Mnemonic: **ROCK HAS INVISIBLE MAGNETIC THREADS**

882   **SHA,** *iru* 注射器 CHŪSHAKI   syringe
SHOOT 射倒す ITAOSU   shoot down
10 strokes 射撃場 SHAGEKIJŌ   rifle range

Originally 𝔅, a pictograph showing a **bow** 𝔅 836 and **arrow** ↤ 981. A **hand** 𝔁 was added later to draw attention to the **shooting** of the arrow, giving 𝔅𝔁, and this was then replaced with **measure/ hand** 寸 909 q.v., with its connotations of **careful use of the hand**. The use of **body** 身 323 (early form 𝔞) instead of bow and arrow 𝔅 results from a miscopying.

Mnemonic: **HAND SHOOTS MEASURED ARROW INTO BODY**

---

883   **SHA,** *suteru* 喜捨 KISHA   charity
ABANDON 捨て子 SUTEGO   foundling
11 strokes 捨て置く SUTEOKU   leave alone

扌 is **hand** 32. 舍 is house/ **quarters** 700 q.v., here acting phonetically to express **put down (and leave)** and possibly also lending its literal meaning of **relax/ not worry**. Thus to **put something down with the hand and leave it (without worrying?)**, leading to **abandon**.

Mnemonic: **FIND ABANDONED HAND IN ONE'S QUARTERS!**

---

884   **SHAKU, SEKI** 尺度 SHAKUDO   scale, gauge
MEASURE, FOOT 尺八 SHAKUHACHI   flute
4 strokes 尺地 SEKICHI   strip of land

Once written 𝔁. 𝔂 depicts the **elbow** and **lower arm** down to an **extended finger tip**, while ⌐ depicts a **spread hand**. 884 thus referred to the **span of a hand**, which became a measuring unit roughly equivalent to one **foot** (actually 30.3 cms, as opposed to 30.48 for the Western foot). It also came to represent **measure** in a broad sense. See also 1415. Suggest taking 尸 as a **'topless' variant of door** 戸 108 and ヽ as a **prop**, with a pun on 'foot'.

Mnemonic: **MEASURE PROP FOR FOOT OF TOPLESS DOOR**

885

SHAKU, to*ku*
EXPLAIN, RELEASE
11 strokes

解釈 KAISHAKU interpretation
釈放 SHAKUHŌ release
釈明 SHAKUMEI explanation

Formerly 釋. 釆 is the same apparent confusion of **rice** 米 201 and **rice plant** 禾 81 seen in 196 q.v., and similarly has connotations of **planting**. 睪 is **keep watch over prisoners** 233 q.v., here acting phonetically to express **scatter** and probably also lending an idea of **succession**. Thus to **scatter rice (seeds) (in succession?)**. This came to mean **scatter/ disperse** in a broad sense, including such ideas as **release** and **undo,** and eventually acquired connotations of **undoing/ solving** a problem, i.e. **explaining**. Suggest taking the modern form 尺 as **person** 人 39 with a **pack** ⺄ on their back.

Mnemonic: **PERSON EXPLAINS, IS RELEASED AND GIVEN RICE PACK**

886

JAKU, waka*i*, mo*shi*
YOUNG, IF
8 strokes

若年 JAKUNEN youth
若しくは MOSHIKUWA or
若者 WAKAMONO youth

Very old forms such as 𦰩 show a **person kneeling** attending to their **long flowing hair**. Ironically, long hair is generally a symbol of old age (e.g. see 173), but here it symbolised **wavy/ pliant**. It combined with mouth/ **say** 口 20 to give a meaning of **pliant words**, i.e. **agreement**. This meaning is now conveyed by agree 諾 1557, which added words 言 274 after the meaning of 886 became vague. Softness and pliancy also symbolised **weakness** (e.g. see 138), and eventually 886 itself acquired this meaning. **Young** is an associated meaning with weak. **If** is a borrowed meaning. The present form results from an early miscopying of 𦰩 (variant 𦰩) as 𦰩, i.e. showing a hand ⺕/ナ 2 and plants 屮屮 9. Suggest taking 右 as **right** 2 and 艹 as **plants** 9.

Mnemonic: **PLANTS ON RIGHT ARE YOUNG**

---

887 需

JU
NEED, DEMAND
14 strokes

需要 JUYŌ demand
必需品 HITSUJUHIN necessities
需給 JUKYŪ supply and demand

雨 is **rain** 3. 而 is an NGU character now used to convey **however**, but it derives from a stylised pictograph of a **beard** 𣬛 and originally had that meaning (still in fact a minor meaning in Chinese). Here it acts phonetically to express **wet**, to give a **beard soaked by the rain**. (Note that **become soaked** is now expressed by the NGU character 濡 , which adds water 氵 40.) Some scholars feel that **need/ demand** is a purely borrowed meaning, while others see it as convolutedly deriving from the idea of waiting to avoid becoming soaked and hence waiting for something better, leading to **desire** and hence **need/ demand**. Suggest taking 而 as a **rake**.

Mnemonic: **RAIN FALLS ON RAKE -- NEED NEW ONE**

| 888 | | JU, ki
TREE, STAND
16 strokes | 樹脂 JUSHI
樹立 JURITSU
樹皮 JUHI | resin
founding
bark |

Once written 尌 . 壴 is **edible plant** 450, while 寸 is **hand/ measure** 909 q.v., here meaning **careful use of the hands**. The food vessel element 豆 1640 q.v. of 壴 also acts phonetically to express **stand/ erect**, as well as lending similar connotations of its own (from the fact that the vessel had a long upright stem). Thus to **erect an edible (i.e. food-bearing) plant with care**, i.e. **carefully plant it upright**. **Tree** 木 69 was added later to enforce the idea of upright flora, and presently 888's meaning changed to **plant a tree**, and eventually **tree** itself. It is however still occasionally used in the sense of **erect/ stand**. Suggest taking 壴 as **food pot** 昱 / 豆 1640 and **samurai** 士 494.

Mnemonic: **SAMURAI'S HAND STANDS FOOD POT NEXT TO TREE**

| 889 | | SHŪ, SŌ
RELIGION, MAIN
8 strokes | 宗教 SHŪKYŌ
宗家 SŌKE
宗派 SHŪHA | religion
main family
sect |

Roof/ building 宀 28 and **altar** 示 695, to give **building with altar**, i.e. shrine or in some cases mausoleum. By association this also came to symbolise **religion**. **Main** is felt to stem from the fact that such a building was the main building in a community.

Mnemonic: **BUILDING WITH ALTAR IS MAIN CENTER OF RELIGION**

| 890 | 就 | SHŪ, JU, tsuku
TAKE UP,
BE INVOLVED
12 strokes | 成就 JŌJU
に就いて NITSUITE
就職 SHŪSHOKU | accomplishment
concerning
finding employment |

京 is **capital** 99 q.v., here in its literal sense of **(aristocrat's) house on a hill**. 尤 is an NGU character meaning **outstanding**. Its origin is somewhat unclear, but old forms such as 尤 suggest a person with long hair, which was usually associated with old age and by association sometimes with excellence (see 173). Here 尤 lends connotations of **prominence**, and also acts phonetically to express **arrive**. 890 originally meant **prominent person arriving at a prominent house on a hill**, a reference to a dignitary arriving at a town to **take up a new post**. Taking up a post led to the idea of **becoming involved**. Suggest taking 尤 as a **dog** 犬 17 with a **crooked leg**.

Mnemonic: **TAKE UP ISSUE OF CRIPPLED DOGS IN CAPITAL**

891 從 JŪ, shitaga*u* 従業員 JŪGYŌIN employee
FOLLOW, COMPLY 従者 JŪSHA follower
10 strokes 従って SHITAGATTE
accordingly

Formerly 從. 彳 is **road/ move** 118 q.v. and 止 is **foot/ move** 止 129 q.v., with the combination in fact being the prototype of **move** 辶 129. 从 is **follow** 463 (literally **two persons** 人 39). Thus **two persons moving along (a road)**, with one **following** the other. Follow also came to be used in the figurative sense of **comply**. Suggest taking 㐬 as **correct** 疋/正 41 and **eight** ソ/八 66.

Mnemonic: **FOLLOW EIGHT ROADS CORRECTLY**

892 縦 JŪ, tate 縦線 JŪSEN vertical line
VERTICAL, SELFISH 放縦 HŌJŪ self-indulgence
16 strokes 縦書き TATEGAKI vertical script

Formerly 縱. 糸 is **thread** 27, here meaning **cord/ binding**. 從/従 is **follow** 891 q.v., here acting phonetically to express **slacken** and possibly also lending an idea of **movement** from its literal meaning of one person moving along after another. 892 originally meant **slacken binding (thus permitting movement?)**. It is still very occasionally used in this sense, but more often in the associated sense of **selfish** (i.e. from **lax** and **unconstrained** behavior). Its most common meaning of **vertical**, in which it often replaces lengthwise/ warp threads 経 658, is felt to stem from a popular reinterpretation of its elements as **threads to follow**, i.e. the generally **vertical** warp.

Mnemonic: **THREADS TO FOLLOW ARE THE VERTICAL ONES**

893 縮 SHUKU, chiji*mu/meru* 縮小 SHUKUSHŌ reduction
SHRINK, REDUCE 短縮 TANSHUKU contraction
17 strokes 縮み止め CHIJIMIDOME
shrinkproof

糸 is **thread** 27. 宿 is **lodge** 505 q.v., here acting phonetically to express **arrange** and possibly also lending an idea of **gather** from its connotations of a gathering place for travelers. Thus to **arrange threads (by gathering them in?)**. Some scholars see its present meaning as borrowed, others as an extension of drawing together loose/ slack threads and thus making them **tight** and **compact**.

Mnemonic: **REDUCED TO THREADBARE LODGINGS**

894 熟 **JUKU**
RIPE, MATURE, COOKED
15 strokes

成熟	SEIJUKU	maturity
半熟	HANJUKU	half-boiled
熟練	JUKUREN	mastery

Somewhat obscure. Formerly 孰. This now exists as an NGU character used to convey who/ where, but it was originally written 𦏧, showing a **person bending and holding something** 丮, **woman** 女/女 35, and what appears to be a **lidded cooking pot** 亯 (possibly variant 會 87), and its original meaning was **cook by boiling**. 亯 appears to have become confused with **receive** 亯/享 1162, while 丮 has become confused with **round** 丸 830 (see also 470). **Fire** 灬 8 was added later for clarity, when 孰 itself started to become semantically vague, and it should be noted that 𤋳 also exists as an NGU character meaning boil. Something that is boiled is ready for eating, leading by association to **ripe**, with **mature** being a figurative extension. Suggest taking 享 as **lid** 亠, **child** 子 25, and **mouth** 口 20.

Mnemonic:**MATURE CHILD PUTS ROUND LID OVER MOUTH OF FIREPIT**

895 純 **JUN**
PURE
10 strokes

純粋	JUNSUI	purity
純毛	JUNMŌ	pure wool
純益	JUNEKI	net profit

糸 is **thread** 27. 屯 is encampment 1669 q.v., here acting phonetically to express **superior** and also lending connotations of **fresh/ pure** from its literal meaning of **sprout** (i.e. fresh growth). 895 originally meant **superior pure (silk) threads**, but now means **pure** in a broad sense. Suggest remembering 屯 by association with **hair** 毛 210.

Mnemonic: **PURE THREADS LOOK LIKE HAIR**

896 処 **SHO**
DEAL WITH, PLACE
5 strokes

処理	SHORI	management
処置	SHOCHI	measure
処処	SHOSHO	here and there

Once written 処, showing **table/ rest/ stool** 几 832 and **inverted foot** 夂/夂/夂 438 q.v., here in its sense of **visit and stop**. Thus to **visit somewhere and stop, sitting on a stool**. This came to mean **be settled down**, leading on the one hand to **place** (where one is settled) and on the other to settle in a broader figurative sense, i.e. **conclude** or **deal with**. 896 was formerly also written 處, though technically this is a separate character of somewhat obscure etymology. It is generally interpreted as 処 with the addition of tiger 虍 281, which is felt to act phonetically to express sit casually. However, old forms such as 處 and 處 suggest strongly that it was in fact a highly stylised pictograph showing a person 虎 sitting down on a stool 几 before becoming confused with early forms of tiger such as 虎 and 虎. Suggest taking 夂 as **sit crosslegged**.

Mnemonic: **SIT CROSSLEGGED ON STOOL TO DEAL WITH SITUATION**

897 SHO 署名 SHOMEI signature
GOVERNMENT OFFICE, 署員 SHOIN official
SIGN 警察署 KEISATSUSHO
13 strokes police station

Formerly 署 . 网 is **net** 193. 者 / 者 is **person** 298, here also acting phonetically to express **put**. 897 originally referred to **persons given the task of putting the net in place** during a hunt. It then came to mean **employed person**, then **official**, then **place where officials work**. **Sign** is generally assumed to be a borrowed meaning, but it is possible that it is an idea associated with government office.

Mnemonic: **PERSON NETTED, SIGNS UP FOR GOVERNMENT OFFICE**

---

898 SHO, moro 諸島 SHOTŌ island group
VARIOUS, MANY 諸君 SHOKUN 'my friends'
15 strokes 諸手 MOROTE both hands

Formerly 諸 . 言 is **words** 274. 者 / 者 is **person** 298 q.v., here acting phonetically to express **many** and also lending similar connotations of its own from its early meaning of **many various things**. 898 originally meant **many/ various words**, but then came to mean **many/ various** in general.

Mnemonic: **PERSON'S WORDS ARE MANY AND VARIOUS**

---

899 SHŌ, masa 将来 SHŌRAI future
COMMAND, ABOUT TO 将軍 SHŌGUN generalissimo
10 strokes 将に MASA ni on the point of

Formerly 將 and earlier 牆, showing that **measure/ hand** 寸 909 is a miscopying of/ substitution for **two hands** 𦥑 (indicating **offering**) and that **hand reaching down** 爫 303 is a miscopying of/ substitution for **meat** 夕 / 月 365. 爿 / 丬 / 冫 is **bed** 1389, here acting phonetically to express **offer up** and possibly also lending a meaning of **litter**. 899 originally meant **offer meat to a superior** (the latter reclining on a litter?). Some scholars feel that its present meaning of **command** is borrowed, while others see it as stemming from the idea of the superior rank of the person being offered meat, i.e. that person being a commander or a person who has commanded that meat be brought. It is not clear how it also came to mean **be about to**, although it is possible that this may also have evolved from the idea of offering meat, i.e. with the person being offered the meat **being about to** receive/ eat it. Suggest taking 丬 as a **bar** 丨 of **ice** 冫 378.

Mnemonic: **COMMANDER'S HAND ABOUT TO REACH FOR BAR OF ICE**

900

SHŌ, warau, emu
LAUGH, SMILE
10 strokes

苦笑 KUSHŌ   wry smile
笑い声 WARAIGOE   laughter
笑顔 EGAO*   smiling face

Of confused etymology. ⺮ is **bamboo** 170, though this is a longstanding miscopying of **plant** ⁺ 9. 夭 is **person with bowed head** 279. 笑/芺 originally referred to a type of **thistle** (presumably associated with a drooping head). It then became further confused with **smile/ laugh** 哭/咲 1303 q.v., in which 笑/关 acts phonetically to express **crease** and also lends its own connotations of **thin** (from the stem of the thistle), combining with **mouth** 口 20 to give **thin creases around the mouth**, i.e. **smile** and hence **laugh**. Suggest taking 夭 literally as **big person** 大 53 with **head bent** ノ, and following the common but incorrect explanation that the character shows a person bent over (like bamboo bends) laughing.

Mnemonic: **BIG PERSON BENT OVER LIKE BAMBOO, LAUGHING**

901

SHŌ, kizu, itami/mu/meru 死傷者 SHISHŌSHA casualties
WOUND, INJURY   傷害 SHŌGAI   injury
13 strokes   傷付ける KIZUTSUKERU wound

亻 is **person** 39. 昜 is to all intents and purposes a variant of **rising sun** 昜 144, technically showing a **person** ⼂ 39 watching the sun rise (see also 637). Here 昜 acts phonetically to express **wound**, and may also lend connotations of (becoming) **intense** from its idea of rising. Thus a **(badly?) wounded person**, now **wound** in a broad sense.

Mnemonic: **WOUNDED PERSONS LEFT EXPOSED TO RISING SUN**

902

SHŌ, sawaru
HINDER, BLOCK
14 strokes

障害 SHŌGAI   impediment
障子 SHŌJI   shoji screen
差し障る SASHISAWARU hinder

阝 is **hill** 229, while 章 is **badge** 318 q.v. The latter acts phonetically to express **barrier**, but any semantic role is unclear. However, since it can also symbolise **slave** it is remotely possible that it also lends connotations of **impeded/ impediment** (i.e. not free). Thus **hill(s) forming barrier**, leading to **block** and **hinder**.

Mnemonic: **GET BADGE FOR OVERCOMING HINDERING HILL**

903

城

JŌ, shiro
CASTLE
9 strokes

城下町 JŌKAMACHI castle town
姫路城 HIMEJIJŌ Himeji Castle
城跡 SHIROATO castle ruins

土 is **earth** 60. 成 is **become/ consist/ make** 515 q.v., here acting phonetically to express **pile up** and also lending its connotations of **being properly finished**. 903 originally referred to **properly (i.e. soundly) constructed earthen ramparts**, then came by extension to mean **castle**.

Mnemonic: **CASTLE CONSISTS OF EARTHEN RAMPARTS**

904

蒸

JŌ, mu*su/reru*
STEAM
13 strokes

蒸気 JŌKI steam
蒸留 JŌRYŪ distillation
蒸し暑い MUSHIATSUI humid

Once written 祩, showing **plants/ grass** 屮屮/屮 9, **two fires** 屮/火 8, **two hands** 屮屮, and **smoke/ heat rising** ⺗. This was a depiction of **hands throwing brushwood on a fire**, and the original meaning was **brushwood** (still found in Chinese). However, it was then used instead of the simpler 丞, a CO character meaning **heat rising from a fire** (i.e. 904 minus the plants/ brushwood 屮, with hands 屮屮/八 retained in error or else in the sense of hands being warmed at a fire). For some unclear reason 904 later came to be used particularly of (rising) **steam**, though it has no element connected with water. It is possible however that 氺 became confused with **water** 水 40. Suggest taking 氺 as a combination of **water** and **baby/ child** 子 25, with 一 as a **hotplate**.

Mnemonic: **GRASS COVERED WATERBABY STEAMS ON FIERY HOT-PLATE**

905

針

SHIN, hari
NEEDLE, POINTER
10 strokes

方針 HŌSHIN policy, line
針路 SHINRO course
針金 HARIGANE wire

金 is **metal** 14. 十 is **ten** 33 q.v., here in its literal meaning of **needle**. Thus **metal needle**.

Mnemonic: **TEN METAL NEEDLES**

906

JIN, NI
BENEVOLENT,
HUMANITY
4 strokes

仁愛 JINAI   benevolence
仁者 JINSHA   humanitarian
仁王 NIŌ   Deva king

Popularly explained as an ideographic combination of **two** 二 61 and **person** イ 39 to indicate the **relationship between two people,** which ideally should be one of **humanity** and **benevolence.** A useful mnemonic, but possibly incorrect since early forms such as 冫二 show a <u>bending</u> person. Some scholars feel that 二 acts phonetically to express **burden,** to give a meaning of **person bent under a burden.** This is then felt to have come by extension to a **person bearing someone else's burden** (possibly under the influence of two 二, suggesting two [persons'] burdens), leading eventually to the present meanings.

Mnemonic: **TWO PEOPLE SHOW BENEVOLENT RELATIONSHIP**

907

SUI, *tareru/rasu*
SUSPEND, HANG DOWN
8 strokes

垂直 SUICHOKU   verticality
雨垂れ AMADARE   raindrops
垂れ飾り TAREKAZARI   pendant

Once written 坐, showing a combination of **ground** 土 60 and 屮, a **plant with drooping leaves.** Thus **plant with leaves hanging down to the ground,** now **hang** in a broader sense. Suggest remembering by association with **ride** 乗 320, from which distinguish.

Mnemonic: **LOOK LIKE RIDING HANGING DOWN TO GROUND!**

908

SUI, *osu*
INFER, PUSH AHEAD
11 strokes

推理 SUIRI   reasoning
推薦者 SUISENSHA   referee
推進機 SUISHINKI   propeller

扌 is **hand** 32. 隹 is **bird** 216, here acting phonetically to express **thrust/ push** and almost certainly also lending an idea of **forward motion** (birds being unable to go backwards). Thus to **push forward with the hand,** now also used in the figurative sense of **promote. Infer** is a borrowed meaning.

Mnemonic: **PUSH BIRD AHEAD WITH HAND**

286

909

寸

SUN
MEASURE, INCH
3 strokes

寸法 SUNPŌ   size, plan
一寸 ISSUN   tiny bit, one inch
寸分 SUNBUN   a little

Originally written 剥, though some later forms such as ⧧ replace the **dot** · with **one** — 1. 剥 is a **hand**. 909 originally referred to the **pulse**, as loosely indicated by the position of the dot relative to the hand. This was conveniently taken to be one SUN from the base of the palm, a SUN being the rough equivalent of the width of a finger (commonly taken as **one inch**, but now specifically standardised as 3.03 cms, which is a somewhat thick finger). Now also used to refer to **measure** in a broad sense, as well as **small amount**. In compounds sometimes confused with a simple hand, but often combining the ideas of both hand and measure to lend a meaning equivalent to **measured/ careful use of the hand**.

Mnemonic: **PULSE MEASURED AS ONE INCH FROM HAND**

910

是

ZE, kore
PROPER, THIS
9 strokes

是正 ZESEI   correction
是ら KORERA   these
是非 ZEHI   right and wrong,
                  at any cost

Of confused etymology. Very early forms such as 𦻌 show a **spoon/ ladle** 𠃌 and a **triple hook** ⩊, which was used for hanging appliances on. The original meaning was thus **spoon kept on (proper) hook**. From an early stage hook ⩊ became confused with **foot/ stop** Ɫ / 止 129, with stop being taken transitively to mean **keep in place**, and the character became reinterpreted but without significant change of meaning as **spoon kept in proper place**. Spoon itself is now conveyed by the NGU character 匙, which adds 匕 (itself a CO character pictographically depicting a scoop/ ladle), while 910 came to convey the idea of **being in the proper place**, and hence **proper** in a broad sense. (However, some scholars maintain that proper is technically a borrowed meaning, not an extended one.) The modern form erroneously uses **correct/ proper** 正 / 正 41, while spoon 𠃌 has become abbreviated to a form equivalent to **sun/ day** 日 62. **This** is a borrowed meaning.

Mnemonic: **SUN IS CORRECT -- THIS IS ONLY PROPER**

911

SEI, hijiri
SAINT, SAGE, SACRED
13 strokes

聖書 SEISHO — bible
聖人 SEIJIN — saint
神聖 SHINSEI — sanctity

Formerly 聖 . 耳 is **ear** 29, 口 is **opening/ hole** 20, and 壬 is **person standing still** 1610, here acting phonetically to express **clear** and possibly also lending a suggestion of **standing alertly**. 911 originally referred to a **person whose hearing** (literally **ear-hole**) **was excellent (clear)**, and who could hear things not heard by other people. This was in turn a reference to a **holy man**, who could hear the words of the gods. Thus **saint** and **sage**, with **sacred** being an extended meaning. 911 is also sometimes used as a term of respect to a ruler, which may have influenced the graphic evolution of 壬 into a form equivalent to **king** 王 5.

Mnemonic: **SAINTLY KING'S EARHOLE IS SACRED**

912

SEI, makoto
SINCERITY
13 strokes

誠意 SEII — sincerity
誠実 SEIJITSU — honesty
誠に MAKOTO ni — truly

言 is **words** 274. 成 is **consist/ become/ make** 515 q.v., here acting phonetically to express **pile up** and by extension **duplicate** and also lending its connotations of being **properly formed**. Though confusingly 912 contains no element specifically indicating **heart/ feelings** (e.g. 心 147), it originally referred to **words which properly duplicated one's heart/ feelings**, i.e. which contained **sincerity**. It now means sincerity in general.

Mnemonic: **WORDS BECOME SINCERE**

913

SEN
PROMULGATE, STATE
9 strokes

宣伝 SENDEN — propaganda
宣告 SENKOKU — verdict
宣教師 SENKYŌSHI — missionary

宀 is **roof/ building** 28. 亘 is an NGU character now used to express request, but it was originally written 𠄢 , showing a **vortex** @ 86 within **two boundaries** 二 , and meant **go around** in a broad sense (still found in Chinese). Thus **that which goes around a building**, namely a **fence/ wall**. (Some scholars feel that 亘 also acts phonetically to express fence/ wall.) A building with a wall around it was an **important building**, and this was the original meaning of 913 (not unlike institute 院 229 q.v.). Its present meanings result from borrowing. Suggest taking 亘 as **two** 二 61 **days** 日 62.

Mnemonic: **STATE THAT ROOF WILL BE FINISHED IN TWO DAYS**

288

914 専 SEN, moppara 専門 SENMON specialty
EXCLUSIVE, SOLE 専用 SENYŌ exclusive use
9 strokes 専制 SENSEI despotism

Somewhat obscure. Formerly 專 and earlier 叀, showing a **hand** 又 and a **round weighted device used in spinning** 叀. The latter is taken by some scholars to have been largely used as a **child's toy**. Hand 又 was later replaced by **hand/ measure** 寸 909 q.v., which with its connotations of **careful use of the hands** tends to contradict the toy theory. However, adherents of the theory feel that 寸 simply meant hand, and that the character originally referred to a **child holding the toy**. Since a child is generally reluctant to release a toy it then came to symbolise **keeping possession for oneself**, leading to the present meanings. Other scholars feel that the character originally depicted a hand **dedicatedly performing the task of spinning**, with **dedication** leading to **exclusive devotion** and hence by extension the present meanings. The third and possibly most likely theory is that, not unlike a modern gyroscope, the spinning weight tended through its inertia to remain **fixed in place**, symbolising **unswerving devotion/ dedication** and hence the present meanings. Suggest taking 甫 as **ten** 十 33 **fields** 田 59.

Mnemonic: **EXCLUSIVE POSSESSION OF TEN MEASURED FIELDS**

915 SEN, izumi 温泉場 ONSENJŌ spa resort
SPRING 泉水 SENSUI fountain
9 strokes 飛泉 HISEN waterfall

From a pictograph of **water emerging from a hole in a rock/ hillside** 㒼. Suggest taking 水 as **water** 40 and 白 as **white** 65. In fact, the modern form may have deliberately used 白, since it has connotations of **purity**.

Mnemonic: **SPRING PRODUCES WHITE WATER**

916 洗 SEN, arau 洗礼 SENREI baptism
WASH, INVESTIGATE 洗濯 SENTAKU (the) washing
9 strokes 手洗い TEARAI washroom

氵 is **water**. 先 is **precede/ tip** 49 q.v., here acting phonetically to express **feet** and almost certainly lending a similar meaning through its elements of **person** 儿 39 and **foot** 㐅 / 止 129. 916 originally referred to a **person washing their feet**, and then came to mean **wash** in general. The minor meaning of **investigate** is a figurative extension, from the idea of making something clean.

Mnemonic: **WASH TIP IN WATER**

917 SEN, so*maru/meru*, shi*miru* 染色 SENSHOKU   dyeing
DYE, SOAK, PERMEATE 染め物 SOMEMONO dyed goods
9 strokes   染み込む SHIMIKOMU   soak into

Once written 𣲥, showing that 九 is not **nine** 九 12, though it may be useful to remember it as such, but a **person bending** 𠃌 39. 木 is **tree** 69, here meaning **shrub/ plant**. 氺 / 氵 is **water** 40. 917 thus depicts a **person bending to soak a plant in water**, a reference to **dyeing** using the indigo plant or similar. Thus **dye** and **soak**, with **permeate** being an extended meaning.

Mnemonic: **SOAK NINE SHRUBS IN WATER TO MAKE DYE**

918 SŌ, kana*deru*   伴奏 BANSŌ   accompaniment
PLAY, REPORT   奏楽堂 SŌGAKUDŌ concert hall
9 strokes   奏上 SŌJŌ   report to emperor

Somewhat obscure, largely since its old forms vary considerably. An old form 𡛥 shows **hands offering** 廾 what appears to be a **plant** 屮 (thus making it very similar to **offer** 奉 1793 q.v.), though some scholars interpret 屮 as a variant of **cow** 牛 97. 夅 has been interpreted as **ten** 十 33 (indicating **many**) and (**big**) **person** 大 53, to give a meaning of **many persons offering things up** (to a ruler). However, those who take 屮 to be cow take 夅 to be a highly stylised version of **sheep** 𦍌 / 羊 986 q.v., a view supported by another old form 𡘾, and conclude that the character originally referred to **offering animal sacrifices** (to the gods). In any event, **offer to a high authority** came in time to mean **report to a ruler**, though it is not clear why that which was offered became narrowed to information. **Play an instrument** is felt by some scholars to be a borrowed meaning, by others to derive from the idea of a musical presentation for the benefit of a ruler, and by still others to be an associated meaning, from the fact that the offering of tribute was generally accompanied by a fanfare of musical instruments. Suggest taking 天 as **heaven** 58 and 夫 as **two** 二 61 **big men** 大 53.

Mnemonic: **TWO BIG MEN PLAY HEAVENLY MUSIC**

919 SŌ, mado   窓口 MADOGUCHI   window
WINDOW   出窓 DEMADO   bow window
11 strokes   同窓会 DŌSŌKAI
                alumni association

Somewhat obscure. Formerly 窻. 囪 derives from a pictograph of a **window with grille** 囱 (the short upper stroke ✓ being felt to be a stylistic embellishment), and **hole** 穴 849 was added later for emphasis. At a still later stage **heart/ feeling** 心 147 was added, giving 窻 (also 窗), though its role is unclear. (Some scholars interpret it as 'window of the heart', enforcing the idea of opening up.) Suggest taking 厶 as **nose** 134.

Mnemonic: **NOSE MAKES HOLE IN WINDOW, LEFT FEELING DOWN**

920

創

SŌ, haji*meru*
START, WOUND
12 strokes

創造 SŌZŌ　　　　creation
創立者 SŌRITSUSHA　founder
創い SŌI　　　　　wound

刂 is **sword/ cut** 181. 倉 is **warehouse** 531 q.v., acting phonetically to express **wound**. It is not clear if 倉 also lends any meaning. (It is unlikely to lend its lesser meaning of **sudden**, since this is a later borrowed meaning, but by association with storehouse 蔵 923 q.v. [note shared reading of kura] it may possibly lend loose connotations of **wounded person requiring harboring**.) Thus **wounded with a sword. Start** is a borrowed meaning.

Mnemonic: **FOR A START, PUT SWORD IN WAREHOUSE**

921

層

SŌ
STRATUM, LAYER
14 strokes

下層 KASŌ　　　　lower classes
層雲 SŌUN　　　　stratus cloud
高層ビル KŌSŌBIRU　skyscraper

Formerly 層. 尸 is technically **corpse** 236, but acts here as a simplification of **building** 屋 236 (see also 262). 曾/曽 is **build up** 741. Thus **built up building**, indicating a **building of more than one story**. It then came by association to mean **story, layer, stratum,** and so forth. Suggest taking 曽 as **eight** ヾ 66, **field** 田 59, and **day** 日 62.

Mnemonic: **LAYERS OF CORPSES BUILD UP IN FIELD OVER EIGHT DAYS**

922

操

SŌ, misao, ayatsu*ru*
HANDLE, CHASTITY
16 strokes

操縦士 SŌJŪSHI　　　pilot
節操 SESSŌ　　　　　integrity
操り人形 AYATSURININGYŌ
　　　　　　　　　　　puppet

扌 is **hand** 32. 喿 is a CO character meaning **birds chirping**, and shows **three mouths** 口 20 in a **tree** 木 69. Here 喿 acts phonetically to express **take**, and may possibly also lend a loose suggestion of **intensity**. Thus to **take with the hand (firmly?)**. Just like the English term **handle**, this also came to mean **manage/ operate/ control**. **Chastity** is an associated meaning with control, from the idea of restraint. Suggest taking 品 as **three boxes**, and 木 in its meaning of **wooden**.

Mnemonic: **THREE WOODEN BOXES TAKE SOME HANDLING**

---

923 ZŌ, kura
STORE(HOUSE), HARBOR
15 strokes

蔵書 ZŌSHO — one's library
蔵匿 ZŌTOKU — harboring
酒蔵 SAKAGURA — wine cellar

Formerly 藏 . ⺾ is **grass** 9. ⼢ is a variant of **sickness** 疒 / 疒 381, here indicating **incapacitated**. 臣 is **eye/ guard** 512, here in an extended sense of **protect**, and 戈 is **halberd/ weapon**, here symbolising **wound**. 923 originally referred to **concealing a wounded and incapacitated person with grass**, thereby **protecting** them (from their pursuers). This later extended to mean **put away and look after** in a broad sense, and hence **store** and **harbor**. Suggest taking 厂 as **cliff** 45.

Mnemonic: **STORE AND GUARD HALBERDS UNDER GRASSY CLIFF**

---

924 ZŌ, harawata
ENTRAILS, VISCERA
19 strokes

臓器 ZŌKI — intestines
内臓 NAIZŌ — viscera
心臓学 SHINZŌGAKU — cardiology

Flesh/ of the body 月 365 and **store/ harbor** 蔵 923, giving **that stored/ harbored in the body**, i.e. the **viscera/ entrails**.

Mnemonic: **ENTRAILS ARE HARBORED IN BODY**

---

925 ZOKU
WORLDLY, VULGAR,
CUSTOM
9 strokes

俗語 ZOKUGO — slang
俗化 ZOKKA — vulgarisation
風俗 FŪZOKU — customs

亻 is **person** 39. 谷 is **valley** 122 q.v., here acting phonetically to express **transmit (orally)** and possibly also lending connotations of **out of mouths** from its literal elements of a doubling of **out of** 八 66 and **mouth/ opening** 口 20. Thus **that transmitted orally from person to person**, a reference to **common rumors**. This led on the one hand to **worldly** and **vulgar**, and on the other by association to **custom** (i.e. that which is common).

Mnemonic: **VALLEY PEOPLE HAVE VULGAR CUSTOMS**

926 SON, ZON   生存 SEIZON   existence
EXIST, KNOW, THINK 存じ寄り ZONJIYORI   opinion
6 strokes   存在者 SONZAISHA   a being

Very similar in meaning and etymology to **dam firmly in place/ exist** 在 684 q.v. イ is the same variant of **dam** 才 126, with **child** 子 25 acting phonetically to express **pile up** to give **piled up dam**, i.e. a dam **firmly in place** and hence the extended meaning of **exist**. Whereas 684 developed connotations of existence in a location 926 came to mean exist in a broader sense. It is not clear how in Japanese it also came to mean **know/ think**.

Mnemonic: **CHILD KNOWS OF EXISTENCE OF FUNNY DAM**

927 SON, tattoi/bu, tōtoi   尊重 SONCHŌ   respect
VALUE, ESTEEM, YOUR 尊王家 SONNŌKA*   royalist
12 strokes   尊慮 SONRYO   your will

Formerly 酋 and earlier 尊, clearly showing **hands** ㄚㄟ **offering up** (indicating doing something **for a superior**) a **wine jar** 酉 /西 302. Out of ㇄ノ 66 was added later to convey the idea of **pouring**, and hands ㄚㄟ were replaced by **hand/ measure** 寸 909 q.v., to lend an idea of careful use of the hands. (According to some scholars, 寸 also acts phonetically to express offer.) Thus to **offer and pour wine (for a superior)**. Some scholars feel that the present meanings are borrowed, but it seems more likely that they are all extended or associated meanings (i.e. pouring wine being a symbol of **respect**, with the use of the character as a **second person honorific** being an associated idea). Note that in Chinese 927 still retains a minor meaning of wine vessel, while in Japanese the addition of wood 木 69 gives the NGU character **barrel** 樽. Note also that 酋 exists as an NGU character meaning superior or chief, while in Chinese it means fermented liquor.

Mnemonic: **POUR OUT MEASURE OF WINE FOR ESTEEMED GUEST**

928 TAKU   自宅 JITAKU one's own house
HOUSE, HOME   宅地 TAKUCHI   housing land
6 strokes   お宅 OTAKU   you, your home

Once written 向. ∩/宀 is **roof/ house/ building** 28. ㄗ /乇 is a depiction of a plant whose head and roots are both growing, indicating that it has **taken root**. Some scholars take these elements to act ideographically to express the **building in which one takes root/ settles**, i.e. one's **house/ home**, while others take 乇 to act essentially phonetically to express **open up** (also possibly lending similar connotations from a seed opening up into a growing plant), giving **open up a house**, which was a reference to digging out a hole that was then roofed to provide a primitive troglodytic dwelling (see 15). Suggest taking 乇 as **seven** 七 30 and a **top** ノ.

Mnemonic: **SEVEN ROOMED HOUSE WITH ROOF ON TOP**

929

担

TAN, katsug*u*, nina*u*
CARRY, BEAR
8 strokes

担当　TANTŌ　responsibility
担い商人　NINAIAKINDO* peddler
学習負担　GAKUSHŪFUTAN
study load

Of somewhat confused and obscure etymology. Formerly 擔 and earlier 儋. Both of these now exist as CO characters with similar meanings of **carry a burden**, though 儋 is also used to express a small jar. 儋 is the older character. 扌 is **hand** 32 and 亻 is **person** 39. 詹 is a CO character with a confusing range of meanings, such as verbosity, reach, oversee, suffice, and excellent, and it is also used with some frequency in compounds, though it lends no obvious or consistent meaning. It is of unclear etymology, but an old form 詹 reveals words 㕣/言 274, bending person 八/亻 39, and an unknown element 厃/厃. Here it is known to act phonetically to express **bear/ carry**, thus giving 儋 a meaning of **person carrying something** and 擔 a meaning of **carry something in the hand** (suggesting a smaller load). The modern Japanese form uses the NGU character **dawn** 旦 (literally **sun** 日 62 over the **horizon** 一) as a simple phonetic substitute for 詹, but it should be noted that in Chinese 擔 is still used to mean bear, and that 担 exists as a separate character meaning to dust off (etymology unclear). Suggest taking 日 in its meaning of **day** and 一 as **one** 1.

Mnemonic: **CARRY BURDEN IN HAND FOR ONE WHOLE DAY**

930

探

TAN, sagur*u*, sagas*u*
SEARCH, PROBE
11 strokes

探知　TANCHI　detection
探究者　TANKYŪSHA researcher
探り出す SAGURIDASU
search out

Hand 扌 32 and **hand reaching into a hole** 罙 325 q.v., ideographically expressing the idea of **groping about** for something. Hence **search/ probe**. Suggest taking 木 as **tree** 69 and 灬 as a variant of hole 穴 849.

Mnemonic: **HAND PROBES HOLE IN TREE**

931		DAN	段階	DANKAI	step, grade
		STEP, GRADE	段段	DANDAN	gradually
		9 strokes	回り階段	MAWARIKAIDAN	
					spiral stairs

Of disputed etymology. 殳 is **strike with weapon/tool** 153. As a result of an old form 𠬝, 𠂤 is interpreted by some scholars as deriving from a variant 𠂤 of **cliff** 厂 45 that shows **steps** or terracing = (see also 625), but as a result of a later form 段 it is interpreted by others as deriving from a variant 𠂤 of the prototype 𣫍 of **bushy plant** 㠯 1567 q.v., which is itself of somewhat unclear etymology. Adherents of the cliff theory see 931 as an ideograph meaning to **cut steps in a cliff/ hillside** and hence **step/ grade**. Adherents of the bushy plant theory take 𠂤 to act phonetically to express **beat** as well as lending a meaning of **grain plant**, to give **beat/ thresh grain**. The present meaning of **grade/ step** is then seen as a borrowing. The cliff theory seems the more likely.

Mnemonic: **CUT STEPS BY STRIKING CLIFF**

932		DAN, atata*kai/maru/meru*	暖房	DANBŌ	heater
		WARM	暖流	DANRYŪ	warm current
		13 strokes	暖冬	DANTŌ	mild winter

日 is **sun** 62. 爰 is an NGU character now meaning **at this point**, but it originally meant **draw up/ draw to oneself**. It comprises **hand reaching down** 爫 303, **hand reaching up** 又, and a **knotted rope** 𠂇 (once 𠂻), and indicated one person **hauling up** another by means of the knotted rope. Here 爰 acts phonetically to express **warmth**, and almost certainly also lends its meaning of **drawing to oneself**. Thus **(to draw) the warmth of the sun (to oneself)**, later **warm** in a broader sense but usually of ambient temperature rather than warm to the touch. 932 is in fact a later version of the NGU character warm 煖, which uses fire 火 8 rather than sun. Suggest taking 𠂇 as a variant of another **hand** 手 32.

Mnemonic: **THREE HANDS WARMING IN THE SUN**

933		CHI, atai, ne	価値観	KACHIKAN	values
		PRICE, VALUE	値段	NEDAN	price
		10 strokes	値引き	NEBIKI	discount

亻 is **person** 39. 直 is **fix/ direct** 349, which acts phonetically to express **equivalent** and probably also lends its meaning of **direct**. Thus a **person (directly?) equivalent (to another)**, conveying the idea that a person is **worth** as much as any other person, and hence **value** and **price**.

Mnemonic: **PERSON HAS FIXED PRICE**

934		CHŪ, naka	仲裁 CHŪSAI	mediation
		RELATIONSHIP	仲人 NAKŌDO*	go-between
		6 strokes	仲良く NAKAYOKU	cordially

Person イ 39 and middle 中 55, giving **person in the middle** and by extension a **relationship** (involving those parties on either side).

Mnemonic: **PERSON IN MIDDLE MAKES FOR GOOD RELATIONSHIP**

935		CHŪ	宇宙船 UCHŪSEN	spaceship
		SPACE, SKY	宙返り CHŪGAERI	somersault
		8 strokes	宙乗り CHŪNORI	aerial stunt

宀 is **roof** 28. 由 is **reason** 399 q.v., here used in its literal sense of **basket** and by extension conveying the idea of **contain**. Thus **that contained under a roof**, namely the **eaves** and the **space** directly under them. Like eaves/ heaven 宇 811, this came to be applied figuratively to the **firmament/ heaven** and by extension **space/ sky**, but unlike 811 it is now no longer used in its original sense.

Mnemonic: **REASON FOR SPACE UNDER ROOF IS TO LET IN SKY**

936		CHŪ	忠実 CHŪJITSU na	loyal
		LOYALTY, DEVOTION	忠誠 CHŪSEI	fidelity
		8 strokes	忠告 CHŪKOKU	advice

Heart/ feelings 心 147 and **middle/ center** 中 55. Some scholars take these elements to be used ideographically to convey the idea of **that which should be at the center/ core of one's heart**, namely **loyalty/ devotion**. Others take 中 to be used purely phonetically to express **void**, to convey the idea of **making one's heart a void**, i.e. **becoming selfless**, leading by extension to concerning oneself only with others and hence **devotion/ loyalty**. Suggest following the former theory.

Mnemonic: **LOYALTY AND DEVOTION AT CENTER OF ONE'S HEART**

937 CHO, ichijiru*shii,* arawa*su*   著者 CHOSHA   author
NOTABLE, WRITE BOOK   著名 CHOMEI   eminence
11 strokes   名著 MEICHO   masterpiece

Of disputed etymology. Formerly 著 . ⺿ is plants 9, while 者/者 is person 298
q.v., here with its connotations of **many and various.** Some scholars feel that 937 is a
miscopying of the NGU character chopsticks 箸 , with plants/ grass ⺿ being used instead
of the latter's bamboo 竹 170. 者 is felt to be used phonetically to express pluck, as well
as lending its literal connotations of bits of wood, to give bits of bamboo used for plucking.
All the present meanings (including wear and arrive -- see below) are then seen as borrowings. Other scholars feel that 937 meant from the outset **variety of plants** and hence
profusion of flowers, and that this in turn gave rise to a range of extended and associated meanings. To **reach a peak of growth** came to mean just **reach**, while **flowers in
full bloom** came to mean **bedecked with color** and hence by association **adorn/ put
on/ wear. Reach** and **wear** are now conveyed by 着 343 q.v., which is a variant of
937. Other meanings included **colorful** and **showy**, giving **prominent** and **notable.**
Some scholars take **write a book** to be a borrowed meaning resulting from confusion
with SHO write 書 142 and/or SHO sign 署 897 (the latter itself possibly being a borrowed meaning). However, in Chinese 937 can also mean **show/ display/ manifest,**
and it should be noted that in Japanese arawasu (write a book) can mean show/ display/
manifest if a different character is used (379). Thus it seems likely that **write a book** is
an extended meaning of **display**, i.e. displaying one's talent and/or views.

Mnemonic: **PERSON WRITES NOTABLE BOOK ABOUT PLANTS**

938 庁 CHŌ   官庁 KANCHŌ   authorities
GOVERNMENT OFFICE,   庁令 CHŌREI   ordinance
AGENCY   環境庁 KANKYŌCHŌ
5 strokes   Environment Agency

Formerly 廳 . 广 is **(large) building** 114, while 聽 is the old form of **listen care-
fully/ inquire** 聴 1598. Thus **large building associated with careful inquiry,**
i.e. a **government office.** The modern form uses **exact** 丁 346.

Mnemonic: **GOVERNMENT OFFICE IS BUILDING OF EXACTITUDE**

939

CHŌ, kiza*shi/su*
SIGN, OMEN, TRILLION
6 strokes

兆候 CHŌKŌ — sign
前兆 ZENCHŌ — omen
億兆 OKUCHŌ — zillion

Once written 狀, showing the **cracks** 外 appearing on a heated **turtle shell** (, the cracks being **signs** used in divination (see 91). Some scholars take (to be a sign of sep- arating/ analysing rather than the shell itself. The shell/ sign of separation (was later doubled to)(, though this appears unconnected with eight/ away 八 ノ ハ 66. **Trillion** is a borrowed meaning.

Mnemonic: TWO CRACKED TURTLE SHELLS SHOW TRILLION SIGNS

940

CHŌ, itadaki, itada*ku*
RECEIVE, CROWN, TOP
11 strokes

頂点 CHŌTEN — apex
頂上 CHŌJŌ — summit
頂だい CHŌDAI receiving, please

頁 is **head** 93. 丁 is **exact/ nail** 346 q.v., here acting phonetically to express **top** and possibly also lending similar connotations through its depiction of a **nail** with a prominent **head/ top**. 940 originally referred to the **top/ crown of the head**, then came to mean **top/ peak** in general. The verb itadaku originally meant to **be crowned** with something, with **receive** being an extended meaning.

Mnemonic: RECEIVE NAIL EXACTLY THROUGH TOP OF HEAD

941

CHŌ, shio
TIDE, SEAWATER
15 strokes

潮流 CHŌRYŪ — tide, current
潮水 SHIOMIZU — seawater
潮時 SHIODOKI — good chance

朝 is **morning** 175 q.v., used in its literal sense of **rising waters**. Water 氵 40 was added after 175 lost its original meaning. 175 technically referred to a rising river, whereas 941 is generally applied to **tide** and by association **seawater**.

Mnemonic: SEAWATER RISES WITH MORNING TIDE

---

942 賃

CHIN
WAGES, FEE
13 strokes

賃金 CHINGIN — wages
運賃 UNCHIN — fare, freight
家賃 YACHIN — house rent

貝 is **shell/ money** 90. 任 is **entrust** 764 q.v., here used in its literal sense of **person carrying a load**. 942 originally meant **money paid to person for carrying load**, i.e. porterage, and then came to mean **fee/ wages** in a general sense.

Mnemonic: ENTRUST WITH WAGES MONEY

298

943

TSŪ, itai/mu/meru
PAIN, PAINFUL
12 strokes

頭痛 ZUTSŪ headache
痛手 ITADE bad wound
痛切 TSŪSETSU na poignant

疒 is **sickness** 381, here indicating **affliction**. 甬 is **burst through** 176, acting phonetically to express **penetrate/ pass through** and also lending similar connotations of **pierce**. Thus a **piercing pain that afflicts one, passing through (the body)**. Now **pain** in general. Suggest remembering 甬 by association with **pass through** 通 176.

Mnemonic: **PAIN PASSES THROUGH SICK BODY**

944

TEN
EXPAND, SPREAD,
DISPLAY
10 strokes

発展 HATTEN development
展覧会 TENRANKAI exhibition
展望 TENBŌ outlook

Once written 𡲀 , showing **slumped figure/ buttocks** コ/尸 236, here indicating **sitting, clothes** 𧘇/衣 420, here meaning **cloth**, and **four tiles/ bricks** 㧪, here indicating **weight(s)**. 944 originally referred to **sitting heavily on a piece of cloth as it is being spread out**, and later came to mean **spread** and **display** in a broad sense. Suggest taking 艹 as **grass** 9 and 衣 as a 'short' version of **clothes** 衣 , i.e. **shorts**.

Mnemonic: **SLUMPED FIGURE IN SHORTS SPREAD OUT ON GRASS**

945

TŌ, utsu
ATTACK, (TO) DEFEAT
10 strokes

討議 TŌGI debate
討ち入る UCHIIRU raid
討伐軍 TŌBATSUGUN punitive force

言 is **words** 274. 寸 is **hand/ measure** 909 q.v., here acting phonetically to express **censure** and probably also lending connotations of **acting carefully**. 945 originally meant to **make a (careful?) verbal attack** on someone, and then came to mean **attack** in general, usually with connotations of **defeating**.

Mnemonic: **ATTACK AND DEFEAT WITH MEASURED WORDS**

299

946		**TŌ**	政党 SEITŌ	political party
		PARTY, FACTION	労働党 RŌDŌTŌ	Labor Party
		10 strokes	党派 TŌHA	faction

Formerly 黨 . 黑 is the early form of **black** 黒、124 q.v., probably used here in its literal sense of **blackened window.** 尚 is furthermore 1392 q.v., here acting phonetically to express **cover** and probably also lending an idea of **window in a building** from its element 向 . Thus to **cover something with blackness** (literally **building with blackened windows?**), a reference to **doing things in a clandestine fashion.** **Faction/ party** is an associated meaning. Suggest taking 党 as **elder brother** 兄 267 and **fancy roof** 丷 (see 28 and 10).

Mnemonic: **ELDER BROTHER'S FACTION MEETS UNDER FANCY ROOF**

947		**TŌ**	砂糖 SATŌ	sugar
		SUGAR	糖衣 TŌI	sugar coating
		16 strokes	糖分 TŌBUN	sugar content

米 is **rice** 201. 唐 is **Tang China** 1645 q.v., here acting phonetically to express **dry/ heat** and probably also lending its literal connotations of **pound**. Thus **heated (and pounded?) rice**, a reference to a form of **sweet confectionery**. It later came to be used of **sugar**.

Mnemonic: **RICE FROM TANG CHINA LOOKS LIKE SUGAR**

948	届	*todoku/keru*	届け書 TODOKESHO	report
		DELIVER, REPORT	届け出る TODOKEDERU	notify
		8 strokes	行き届く YUKITODOKU	
				be attentive

Formerly 屆 . 尸 is **slumped person/ corpse** 236, here indicating a **sick/ injured person.** 凷 is formed from **earth** 土 (variant 士 60, and not samurai 士 494) in a **container** 凵 , indicating a **dead and inert weight.** 凷 also acts phonetically to express **move slowly.** 948 originally referred to a **sick/ injured person moving along slowly.** Some scholars take its present meanings to be borrowed, others see them as deriving from move slowly, namely move slowly but surely and eventually **reach**, with **deliver** being a transitive form of reach and **report** being an associated meaning. Suggest taking 由 as **reason** 399.

Mnemonic: **DELIVER CORPSE AND REPORT REASON**

949 難	NAN, muzukashii, katai	難民 NANMIN	refugees
	DIFFICULT, TROUBLE	難儀 NANGI	trouble
	18 strokes	見難い MIGATAI	hard to see

Obscure. Formerly 難. 隹 is **bird** 216. 堇/堇 is the obscure element seen in 漢 442 q.v., and has been interpreted variously as a variant of 堇, which is itself an obscure element that has been interpreted by some scholars as a **beast being roasted** (see 勤 842), and as a variant of **yellow/ flaming arrow** 黄 / 黄 120. In view of the fact that in Chinese 949 is still listed as having a meaning of **bird with golden plumage**, which is known to have been its original meaning (though the exact name of the bird is unclear), the latter interpretation seems more likely. It is also not clear how it came to mean **difficult/ trouble**, but these are assumed to be borrowed meanings. Suggest remembering by association with a **'waterless' Han China** 漢 442 (氵 being water 40).

Mnemonic: **BIRD IN TROUBLE IN WATERLESS HAN CHINA**

950 弐	NI	弐万円 NIMANEN	20,000 yen
	TWO	弐拾 NIJŪ	twenty
	6 strokes	弐千 NISEN	two thousand

Formerly also 貳, though this is technically a separate character. 弐 derives from 弍, showing an ideographic combination of **two** 二 61 and **stake** 弋 177 q.v., the latter being used as a simplification of **halberd** 戈 493, to give **two stakes/ halberds** and hence just **two**. 貳 adds shell/ money 貝 90 as a phonetic element to express **double**, thereby reinforcing the concept of **two**. Note in passing that an early form of 貳, 戜, shows broad-bladed halberd 戊 /戉 515 and clearly illustrates the overlap between stake and the various forms of halberd.

Mnemonic: **TWO STAKE-LIKE HALBERDS**

951	NYŪ, chichi, chi	牛乳 GYŪNYŪ	(cow's) milk
	BREASTS, MILK	乳酸 NYŪSAN	lactic acid
	8 strokes	乳房 NYŪBŌ/ CHIBUSA	
			breasts

Popularly explained as a **child** 子 25 **reaching** 爫 303 for a **breast** し. A useful mnemonic, but incorrect. While 爫 is indeed **reaching hand**, 孔 is **hole** 1241 q.v., here in its literal sense of **child-producing hole/ vagina**. 951 originally meant **manually assist in removing a child from the vagina**. Its present meanings are felt by some scholars to be borrowed, but it seems more likely that they derive from a core concept of **looking after an infant**, and it is possible that the semantic evolution was also influenced by a longstanding misinterpretation of し as a pictograph of a breast (giving the popular interpretation outlined above).

Mnemonic: **CHILD REACHES FOR BREAST SWOLLEN WITH MILK**

301

952

NIN, mito*meru*
RECOGNISE, APPRECIATE
14 strokes

認識 NINSHIKI   cognition
認可 NINKA   approval
認め印 MITOMEIN   signet

Formerly 認 . 言 is **words** 274. 忍/忍 is **endure** 1677. To **endure someone's words** leads by extension to the idea of **recognition** and **appreciation** of what they are saying. Some scholars feel that 忍 also acts phonetically to express **approve**. Suggest taking 忍 literally as **blade** 刃 1446 and **heart** 心 147.

Mnemonic: **WORDS OF APPRECIATION AS BLADE REACHES HEART!?**

953 納

NŌ, NA, NATSU, TŌ, osa*meru*
OBTAIN, STORE, SUPPLY
10 strokes

納税 NŌZEI   tax payment
納屋 NAYA   shed, barn
出納簿 SUITŌBO*   account book

Formerly 納 . 糸 is **thread** 27, here meaning **cloth**. 内/内 is **inside** 364 q.v., here in its literal sense of **enter a building**. A building which cloth enters was a reference to a **store(house)**, with **obtain** and **supply** being associated meanings. See also 703. There is an alternative theory to the effect that 内 acts purely phonetically to express **wet**, giving **wet threads**, with the present meanings being borrowed. This does not seem especially convincing.

Mnemonic: **STORE OBTAINED THREADS INSIDE, READY TO RESUPPLY**

954 脳

NŌ
BRAIN
11 strokes

頭脳 ZUNŌ   brain
主脳 SHUNŌ   leader
脳障害 NŌSHŌGAI   brain injury

Formerly 腦 and earlier 𦜝. 甶 is **brain** 131. 巛 is **hair**, combining with 甶 to give a meaning to 甾 of **head**. ヒ is **spoon/ scoop** 910. Some scholars feel that this acts phonetically to express **flesh/ fat**, to give **fleshy/ fatty part of the head** and thus **brain** (with the later **flesh/ of the body** 月 365 then being taken as **flesh**). However, it is by no means convincing that fleshy/ fatty part of the head connotes brain, and it seems far more likely that ヒ acts literally to give **that part of the head which is scooped out**, i.e. the **brain(s)**. Brains have long been a delicacy in China, and were traditionally eaten 'in situ', i.e. by being scooped out from a skull at the table. The later 月 would then act in its meaning of **of the body**, to focus on the brain within the body as opposed to as a food dish. Suggest taking ⩔ as **hair**, ✕ as a **cross**, and 凵 as a **box** (cf. English slang brain-box).

Mnemonic: **BODY'S BRAIN-BOX MARKED BY CROSS AND HAIRS**

302

| 955 | HA
FACTION, SEND
9 strokes | 派遣 HAKEN
立派 RIPPA na
田中派 TANAKAHA | despatch
splendid

Tanaka faction |

Tributary 沠 589 reinforced by **water/ river** 氵 40. Though tributaries flow <u>into</u> a larger body, the idea of convergence merged with that of divergence, leading to the idea of **branching/ splitting** and thus **faction. Send** is an associated meaning.

Mnemonic: **FACTION IS LIKE TRIBUTARY RELATIVE TO RIVER**

| 956 | HAI, oga*mu*
WORSHIP, RESPECTFUL
8 strokes | 礼拝 REIHAI
拝見 HAIKEN
拝具 HAIGU | worship
looking
Yours faithfully |

Somewhat obscure. Early forms such as 𥩟 show **hand** 龵 / 扌 32 and what appears to be a **thickly growing rice plant/ grain plant** 㭆 (variant 米 / 禾 81). Thus a **hand offering a token from the harvest** (as part of a **religious act**), with **worship** and **respectful** being derived meanings. Some scholars interpret 㭆 as intestines ⌒ hanging from a tree 木 69, though this also was part of a religious ceremony and thus results in the same semantic evolution. There is also a theory that 㭆 is used phonetically to express **line up**, giving **line up hands**, which is taken as a reference to **praying**. The first theory seems the most helpful. Suggest remembering 丰 as an **eight-leaved plant**.

Mnemonic: **HAND OFFERS EIGHT-LEAVED PLANT IN WORSHIP**

| 957 背 | HAI, se, sei, somu*ku*/*keru*
BACK, STATURE, DEFY
9 strokes | 背後 HAIGO
背中 SENAKA
背信 HAISHIN | background
back
betrayal |

Meat/ of the body 月 365 and **north** 北 205, the latter acting in its literal sense of persons sitting **back to back**. Thus **back of the body**. Now also used of **stature**, and in the sense of **turn one's back/ defy**.

Mnemonic: **TURN BACK DEFIANTLY ON MEAT FROM THE NORTH**

---

958 HAI
LUNG(S)
9 or 8 strokes

肺病 HAIBYŌ　　lung disease
肺炎 HAIEN　　pneumonia
肺臓 HAIZŌ　　lungs

Once written 殊. 夕/月 is flesh/ **of the body** 365. 朮 depicts a **growing plant** (to all intents and purposes a 'droopy-leaved' variant of growing plant 屮/生 42), and acts here phonetically to express **expel** as well as lending its own connotations of **emerge**. Thus **that which is expelled from the body**, a reference to **breath**. By association it later came to refer to **that part of the body from which breath is expelled**, i.e. the **lungs**. Suggest taking 市 as **city** 130.

Mnemonic: **BODIES IN CITIES HAVE BAD LUNGS**

---

959 HAI
AMUSEMENT, ACTOR
10 strokes

俳優 HAIYŪ　　actor
俳句 HAIKU　　haiku poetry
俳人 HAIJIN　　haiku poet

Person イ 39 and **not/ spread wings** 非 773 q.v. Numerous theories exist as to the interpretation of these elements, of which two related theories seem particularly plausible. The first is that 959 originally meant **'non-person'/ outcast** (note that when used as individual characters the same elements give HININ non-person 非人), and that, as in Europe (until recently), outcasts were associated with **acting** and other forms of **entertainment/ amusement**. The second agrees that the original meaning was **non-person**, but takes this rather in the sense of **deformed person**, largely because 非 is also felt to act phonetically to express **ugly**. As in medieval Europe, deformed persons were often employed as **jesters**, leading to both **amusement** and **actor**.

Mnemonic: **NON-PERSON IS AN AMUSING ACTOR**

---

960 班 HAN
SQUAD, GROUP, ALLOT
10 strokes

班長 HANCHŌ　group leader
救護班 KYŪGOHAN relief squad
班田 HANDEN
　　　　farmland allotment

玨 is a doubling of **jewel** 102, thus indicating **many/ various jewels**. 刂 is **sword/ cut** 181, here in the sense of **divide**. 960 originally referred to a ruler **dividing up jewels** (tribute) and **allotting** them to various nobles. This came to mean **allot** on the one hand and **division** on the other, with **section/ group** being an associated meaning.

Mnemonic: **SQUAD RECEIVES A CUT OF THE JEWELS**

| 961 | BAN
EVENING, LATE
12 strokes | 晩飯 BANMESHI evening meal
晩夏 BANKA late summer
今晩 KONBAN this evening |

日 is **sun/ day** 62, here in an extended sense of **light**. 免 is **escape** 1849 q.v., here acting phonetically to express **obscure(d)** and also lending connotations of **striving with difficulty** to do something (from its literal meaning of a woman striving to give birth). Thus **striving with difficulty (to see) when the sun/ light is obscure**, a reference to **evening**. **Late** is an associated meaning.

Mnemonic: **SUN ESCAPES EVERY EVENING**

| 962 | HI, ina, ina*mu*
NO, DECLINE, DENY
7 strokes | 否認 HININ denial
否定語 HITEIGO negative
否めない INAMENAI undeniable |

口 is **mouth/say** 20. 不 is **not** 572 q.v., which also lends its sound **FU** (the original reading of 962) as a sound of **denial/ negation**. Thus to **say the negative sound FU**.

Mnemonic: **DENY, SAYING NOT SO**

| 963 | HI
CRITICISE,STRIKE,PASS
7 strokes | 批判 HIHAN criticism
批評 HIHYŌ commentary
批准 HIJUN ratification |

扌 is **hand** 32. 比 is **compare** 771 q.v., acting phonetically to express **strike** and possibly also lending an idea of **both together**. Thus to **strike with (both?) hand(s)**. This is now a very minor meaning in Japanese, though somewhat more common in Chinese. Strike came to mean **attack**, leading by figurative extension to **criticise**. **Pass/ endorse** (a very minor meaning in Japanese, but reasonably major in Chinese) is seen as a further extension, from the idea of critically examining something.

Mnemonic: **CRITICISM CAN INVOLVE A HANDY COMPARISON**

| 964 | HI, hi*meru*
(KEEP) SECRET
10 strokes | 秘密 HIMITSU secret
極秘 GOKUHI top secret
秘書 HISHO secretary |

Formerly 祕 . 示 is **altar/ of the gods** 695. 必 is **necessarily** 568 q.v., here acting phonetically to express **hide** and probably lending similar connotations of **concealment** from its literal meaning of encased halberd. Thus **hidden things of the gods**, i.e. **mystical secrets**, and now **secret** in a broad sense. The modern use of **rice plant** 禾 81 is almost certainly the result of miscopying.

Mnemonic: **RICE PLANT NECESSARILY KEPT SECRET**

965

FUKU, hara
BELLY, GUTS
13 strokes

腹部 FUKUBU   abdomen
腹立ち HARADACHI   anger
中腹 CHŪFUKU   mid-slope

月 is **flesh/ of the body** 365. 复 is go back/ **reverse** 782 q.v., here used phonetically to express **bulge** and also felt by some scholars to lend connotations of a **central container with limbs either side** (from its literal meaning of reversible food container of that shape). Thus the **bulging central container of the body**, i.e. the **belly**. As with the English slang term **guts**, it is also used to indicate courage and resolve. Suggest taking 复 as **person** ⼂ 39, **sun** 日 62, and **sitting crosslegged** 夂.

Mnemonic: **PERSON SITS CROSSLEGGED, FLESHY BELLY IN SUN**

966

FUN, furuu
BE EXCITED, STIR
16 strokes

奮起 FUNKI   stirring
奮闘 FUNTŌ   hard fight
奮い立つ FURUITATSU   be stirred

田 is **field** 59. 奞 is a CO character meaning big stride, but technically **big** 大 53 is a miscopying of **clothing** 衣 420. This combined with **bird** 隹 216 to give a meaning of **clothing flapping like a bird in flight**, hence a person walking quickly. Here, however, it lends an idea rather of **birds flapping in flight**, and also acts phonetically to express **fly**. 966 originally referred to **birds taking off from a field with much flapping**, indicating that they have been frightened/ **roused**, and hence the present meanings.

Mnemonic: **BIG BIRD STIRS, FLYING EXCITEDLY FROM FIELD**

967

陛

HEI
MAJESTY, THRONE
10 strokes

陛下 HEIKA   Majesty
陛見 HEIKEN   audience
天皇陛下 TENNŌ HEIKA *
His Majesty the Emperor

阝 is **terraced hill** 229, here indicating **steps**. 坒 is a CO character now meaning **compare**, but it originally referred to a succession of hillocks/ terraces, comprising **compare/ in a row** 比 771 and **earth/ ground** 土 60. Here it lends a meaning of **in a row**, giving a **row of terraces/ steps**. By association this was applied to the **steps leading to a throne**, and by extension to the **throne** and its encumbent, i.e. the **emperor** and hence **majesty**. Note in passing that the seemingly inappropriate use of below/ bottom 下 7 in the term HEIKA/ majesty stems from the fact that most persons granted an audience with the emperor did not in fact speak directly with the emperor but with his advisers, who were positioned at the foot of the steps to the throne. Thus heika literally means those at the foot of the steps, but eventually came to represent the emperor himself.

Mnemonic: **HIS MAJESTY'S THRONE COMPARES TO EARTHEN HILL**

968 閉
HEI, to*jiru*, shi*maru/meru*
CLOSE, SHUT
11 strokes

閉店 HEITEN   closing store
閉口 HEIKŌ   dumbfounded
閉め出す SHIMEDASU   shut out

門 is **door/ gate** 211. 才 is **talent** 126 q.v.; here used in its literal sense of **dam** and by extension **barrier**. Thus **barred gate**, leading to **shut** and **close**. Suggest taking 才 as a **cross** 十 with **prop** ⟋.

Mnemonic: **CLOSE GATE WITH PROPPED CROSS**

---

969 片
HEN, kata
ONE SIDE, PIECE
4 strokes

断片 DANPEN   fragment
片手 KATATE   one hand
片付ける KATAZUKERU   tidy up

A pictograph of a **tree** 屮 / 木 69 **cut in half**, giving **one side** and also **(cut) piece**. See also 1389.

Mnemonic: **ONE SIDE OF A TREE IS SOME PIECE!**

---

970 補
HO, ogina*u*
MAKE GOOD, STOPGAP
12 strokes

補助 HOJO   support
補充 HOJŪ   supplementation
補強 HOKYŌ   reinforcement

衤 is **clothing** 420. 甫 is an NGU character meaning **begin**. It was originally written , showing **use** 甪 / 用 215 and a **hand holding a tool** 又 (actually known to be an ax, though in practice to all intents and purposes a variant of hand holding stick 又101/ 197), and meant **start to use an ax** and later **start work** and just **start/ begin**. In compounds it often lends connotations of **hasty work** and by extension **temporary work**. Here it lends such connotations as well as lending its sound to express **patch**. 970 originally referred to the hasty repairing of clothing by **patching**, and then came to mean **stopgap** and **make good** in a broader sense (particularly supplement and compensate). Suggest taking 十 as **needle** 十 33 and **point** 丶.

Mnemonic: **USE NEEDLE POINT TO MAKE GOOD TORN CLOTHES**

---

971 宝
HŌ, takara
TREASURE
8 strokes

宝石 HŌSEKI   jewel
財宝 ZAIHŌ   riches
子宝 KODAKARA   children

Formerly 寶. 宀 is **roof/ house/ building** 28. 王/玉 is **jewel** 102. 貝 is **shell/ money/ precious item** 90. 缶 is **can** 1095 q.v., here lending its literal idea of **(securely) contain**. Thus **building securely containing jewels and other precious items**. Eventually building faded, leaving just **treasure**.

Mnemonic: **TREASURE HOUSE CONTAINS JEWELS**

972

HŌ, otozu*reru*, tazu*neru*
VISIT, INQUIRE
11 strokes

訪問 HŌMON　　　　visit
来訪者 RAIHŌSHA　　visitor
探訪 TANBŌ　　　　inquiry

言 is words/ speak 274. 方 is side/ direction 204, here acting phonetically to express **ask widely** and possibly also lending an idea of **line**. 972 originally referred to **asking widely in order to follow a line of inquiry**. This involved **visiting** many people. Visit has come to prevail as the major meaning, while tazuneru in the sense of **inquire** is now usually (but not always) expressed by 1451.

Mnemonic: **VISIT SOMEONE TO HAVE WORDS ON THE SIDE**

973 亡

BŌ, MŌ, nai/kunaru
DIE, ESCAPE, LOSE
3 strokes

死亡 SHIBŌ　　　　death
亡者 MŌJA　　　　deceased
亡命 BŌMEI　　　　exile

Once written 𠃜 and 亡, showing **person** 人 / 亻 / 𠆢 39 and a **corner** ∟ 349, here indicating **concealment**. It originally meant a **person no longer able to be seen**, and referred to **escaping**. It later also came to mean **lose** and **die**, from the idea of no longer being visible/ actively present.

Mnemonic: **DEAD PERSON LOST IN CORNER**

974 忘

BŌ, wasu*reru*
FORGET, LEAVE BEHIND
7 strokes

忘却 BŌKYAKU forgetfulness
忘恩 BŌON　　　ingratitude
忘れ勝ち WASUREGACHI
　　　　　　　forgetful

心 is **heart** 147. 亡 is **die** 973 q.v., here used in a sense of **no longer actively present**. Thus **that which is no longer actively present in the heart**, i.e. something **forgotten**.

Mnemonic: **"DEAD IN ONE'S HEART" MEANS FORGOTTEN**

975

BŌ
POLE, BAR, CLUB
12 strokes

心棒 SHINBŌ　　　axle, shaft
棒グラフ BŌGURAFU　bar graph
棒紅 BŌBENI　　　lipstick

木 is **tree/ wood** 69. 奉 is **offer up** 1793 q.v., here acting phonetically to express **staff** as well as lending its literal meaning of **hold something in both hands**. Thus **wooden staff held in both hands**, i.e. a **large pole or club**. Suggest taking 夫 as **big** 大 53 plus **two** 二 61, and 龶 as a **club with nails through it**.

Mnemonic: **TWO BIG WOODEN CLUBS WITH NAILS THROUGH**

308

976		MAI SHEET COUNTER 8 strokes	一 枚 ICHIMAI	one sheet
			二 枚 舌 NIMAIJITA	duplicity
			二 枚 貝 NIMAIGAI	bivalve

攵 is **hand holding stick** 101, with attention drawn to the stick itself by the addition of **wood** 木 69. The original meaning was **wooden stick**, and it was also used for **counting wooden sticks** (still very occasionally found in this meaning). It is not fully clear how it later came to be used as a **counter for thin flat objects**, but some scholars feel that it may stem from the fact that 976 was particularly used to refer to a special thin flat stick used for goading horses.

Mnemonic: **HAND HOLDS THIN FLAT WOODEN STICK FOR COUNTING**

977		MAKU, BAKU CURTAIN, TENT, ACT 13 strokes	天 幕 TENMAKU	curtain, tent
			開 幕 KAIMAKU	opening scene
			幕 府 BAKUFU	Shogunate

巾 is **threads/ cloth** 778. 莫 is **sun sinking among plants** 788 q.v., here lending its meaning of **conceal**. Some scholars feel that 莫 also acts phonetically to express **conceal**. Thus **cloth which conceals**, a reference to a **curtain**. **Tent** is an associated meaning. **Act** is also an associated meaning, from the curtain long associated with the theater. Note that since 'tent government' was a reference to the **Shogunate**, 977 itself is sometimes used to refer to the Shogunate. Suggest taking 莫 as **grass** 艹 9, **sun** 日 62, and **big** 大 (variant 大 53).

Mnemonic: **BIG CURTAIN OF THREADED GRASS SHADES OUT SUN**

978		MITSU, hiso*ka* DENSE, SECRET 11 strokes	密 度 MITSUDO	density
			密 輸 MITSUYU	smuggling
			綿 密 MENMITSU na	detailed

山 is **mountain** 24. 宓 is a CO character meaning both **quiet** and **stop**. It comprises **building** 宀 28, here meaning **temple**, and **necessarily** 必 568 q.v., here acting phonetically to express **comb** and also lending an idea of being **tightly packed** from its literal meaning of packed and bound halberd. Thus 宓 originally referred to **temples tightly 'packed' together in a cluster like teeth in a comb**. This presented an effective barrier to the outside world (hence **stop**), and was a place associated with **other-worldliness** and **quietness**. When combined with mountain 山 the meaning became one of **mountains clustered tightly/ densely together**, forming a mysterious and impenetrable (i.e. **secretive**) domain. Hence the present meanings of **dense** and **secret**. It also has connotations of **hushed**.

Mnemonic: **BUILDING IN DENSE MOUNTAINS NECESSARILY SECRET**

979 | MEI | 連盟 RENMEI | federation
| ALLIANCE, PLEDGE | 同盟 DŌMEI | alliance
| 13 strokes | 加盟 KAMEI | affiliation

Once written 盃 and 盟, showing that **blood** 血/血 270 and **dish/ bowl** 皿/皿 1307 have long been interchanged. The present form uses bowl though in fact blood is the more appropriate. The old forms show that 日 derives from 日, an element felt to show a **mouth and teeth** and indicating **taking in through the mouth** (possibly a variant of mortar 臼 648). 979 originally meant to **sup blood from a bowl**, which was a symbol of **making a pledge** and by association **forming an alliance**. It seems likely that the later addition 夕 was originally intended to show **meat** 夕/月 365, to emphasise the idea of blood, but it appears to have become confused with **moon** 夕/月 16, almost certainly under the influence of **bright** 明 208. (The latter properly has an old form ☉, being an ideograph combining sun ☉/日 62 with moon 夕/月 , though some scholars feel that a character 明 existed as a virtual variant, with 日 acting phonetically to express shine brightly to give brightly shining moon.) Suggest taking 明 as **bright**.

Mnemonic: **BRIGHT ALLIANCE PLEDGED OVER BOWL OF BLOOD**

---

980 | MO, BO | 模型 MOKEI | model, mold
| COPY, MODEL, MOLD | 模写 MOSHA | copy, copying
| 14 strokes | 規模 KIBO | scale

木 is **tree/ wood** 69. 莫 is sun sinking among plants (variant 莫 788 q.v.), here acting phonetically to express **standard** and possibly also lending an idea of envelop / **enclose**. 980 originally referred to a **wooden mold/ frame that ensured standardisation** (of those items that it **enclosed**?). **Model** and **copy** are associated meanings. Suggest taking 莫 as **plant** 艹 9, **sun** 日 62, and **big** 大 53.

Mnemonic: **PLANT COPIES MODEL TREE AND GROWS BIG IN SUN**

---

981 矢 | ya, SHI | 矢先 YASAKI arrowhead, point
| ARROW | 矢印 YAJIRUSHI arrow mark
| 5 strokes | 一矢 ISSHI return shot, riposte

From a pictograph of an **arrow**. There was a range of such pictographs, such as 矢, 矢, 矢, 矢, and the highly stylised and somewhat confusing 矢. Some appear to show exaggerated tailfeathers, some material bound to the shaft, and others material bound to the tip. The modern form probably derives from the stylised 矢. Suggest remembering by association with **big** 大 53, taking 丿 as a **broken tip** (A).

Mnemonic: **BIG ARROW WITH BROKEN TIP**

982

YAKU, wake
TRANSLATION, MEANING
11 strokes

翻訳 HONYAKU　　translation
通訳 TSŪYAKU　　interpreting
言い訳 IIWAKE　　excuse

Formerly 譯. 言 is **words** 274. 睪 is eye watching prisoners 233 q.v., here acting phonetically to express **change** and probably also lending an idea of **link/ succession**. Thus to **change words (in a linked succession?)**, i.e. to **translate**. **Meaning** is an associated idea. Suggest taking the modern form 尺 as **person** 人 39 with a **pack/ load** on their back ⊐.

Mnemonic: **PERSON TRANSLATING CARRIES A LOAD OF WORDS**

983

YŪ
MAIL, RELAY STATION
11 strokes

郵便 YŪBIN　　mail
郵送 YŪSŌ　　mailing
郵亭 YŪTEI　　relay station

阝 is **village** 355. 垂 is **dangle/ hang down** 907, acting phonetically to express **billowing flag** and possibly also lending connotations of **hanging**. 983 originally referred to a **relay station** on a messenger route, such a place being indicated by a flag (that was hung there and billowed). Messages were often written on the flag. It then came to mean **communication** in a general sense, and **mail** in modern times.

Mnemonic: **MAIL IN VILLAGE LEFT DANGLING**

984

YŪ, yasashii, sugureru
SUPERIOR, GENTLE,
ACTOR
17 strokes

優秀 YŪSHŪ　　excellence
優先 YŪSEN　　priority
女優 JOYŪ　　actress

亻 is **person** 39. 憂 is **grief** 1871 q.v., here acting phonetically to express **dance with gestures** and also lending its own connotations of **moving slowly**. 984 originally referred to a **dancer performing a slow ritual dance**, then came to mean **actor**. Some scholars take **superior** and **gentle** to be borrowed meanings, but it seems more likely that they derive from the idea of a masterful performance of a slow and dignified ritual dance.

Mnemonic: **GENTLE ACTOR'S SUPERIOR DISPLAY OF PERSON'S GRIEF**

311

985

YŌ, osana*i*
INFANCY
5 strokes

幼児 YŌJI — infant
幼時 YŌJI — infancy
幼子 OSANAGO — infant

幺 is **short thread** 111, here meaning **tiny/ little/ limited**. 力 is **strength** 74. Of **little strength** was a reference to a **young child/ infant**.

Mnemonic: **INFANT SHORT ON STRENGTH, LIKE TINY THREAD**

986

YŌ, hitsuji
SHEEP
6 strokes

羊皮 YŌHI — sheepskin
羊水 YŌSUI — amniotic fluid
羊飼い HITSUJIKAI — shepherd

Stylised derivative of a pictograph of a **sheep's head and horns** 𦍌 (later 羊). In compounds usually found as ⺶. Often lends connotations of **fine/ praiseworthy**, since a sheep was a prized animal. Suggest remembering in particular the **three cross-strokes** 三, taking them as **stripes**.

Mnemonic: **SHEEP WITH FINE HORNS MARKED WITH THREE STRIPES**

987 欲

YOKU, ho*shii*
GREED, DESIRE
11 strokes

欲望 YOKUBŌ — desire
食欲 SHOKUYOKU — appetite
物欲しげ MONOHOSHIGE — wistful

欠 is **lack** 471 q.v., here in its literal sense of **person with gaping mouth**. 谷 is **valley** 122 q.v., acting phonetically to express **continuous** and almost certainly also lending connotations of **big receptacle** and thereby reinforcing 欠. Thus **person with continuously gaping mouth**, symbolising a **person constantly desiring food** and hence **greedy**, with **desire** being an associated meaning. Some scholars feel that 谷 actually serves a double phonetic role in that it also expresses **cereal**, symbolising **food** and thus clarifying the meaning of gaping mouth.

Mnemonic: **GREEDY PERSON LACKS VALLEY SO DESIRES ONE**

988

YOKU
NEXT (OF TIME)
11 strokes

翌日 YOKUJITSU — next day
翌朝 YOKUCHŌ — next morning
翌翌年 YOKUYOKUNEN — two years later

羽 is **wings** 812. 立 is **stand/ rise/ leave** 73, here acting phonetically to express **fly** and also lending an idea of **rise and leave**. 988 originally referred to a **bird flying off**. Its present meaning is borrowed, though it may be helpful to think of it as a figurative reference to the **wings of time** (not unlike the Japanese 'version' of day 曜 216, q.v.).

Mnemonic: **WINGS OF TIME LEAVE, TILL THE NEXT TIME**

989

RAN, mida*reru/su*
DISORDER, RIOT
7 strokes

乱暴 RANBŌ   violence
反乱 HANRAN   rebellion
乱れ足 MIDAREASHI out of step

Formerly 亂. 𤔔 is **hands untying tangled threads** 500, symbolising **putting in order/ bringing under control**. ∟ is **person kneeling** 413, symbolising a **person being made to submit**. 989 originally referred to **bringing rebellious persons to submission** and thus **bringing a disturbance under control**. For some reason, however, the idea of **disturbance** and **disorder** prevailed, and in Japanese has now entirely replaced the idea of bringing under control. Somewhat confusingly, both meanings co-exist in Chinese, with 989 able to mean both bring about order and bring about disorder, but the latter is overwhelmingly the major meaning. Suggest taking 舌 as **tongue** 732.

Mnemonic: **KNEELING FIGURE PUTS TONGUE OUT -- LEADS TO RIOT**

990

RAN, tamago
EGG, ROE
7 strokes

卵黄 RANŌ   yolk
産卵 SANRAN   spawning
生卵 NAMATAMAGO raw egg

Somewhat obscure. For many centuries an early form 卯 has been interpreted as a stylised depiction of either **fish eggs** or **frogspawn**. However, some scholars now believe this to be a variant of **treadle** 卯 444, along with another early form 卯. **Egg/ roe** is then taken to be a purely borrowed meaning.

Mnemonic: **ANGULAR BACK-TO-BACK FISH EGGS?!**

991

RAN
SEE, LOOK
17 strokes

御覧 GORAN   look, try
回覧 KAIRAN   circulation
観覧 KANRAN   inspection

Formerly 覽. 臨 is **watch over** 1111, here meaning just **look/ watch**, and 見 is **look/ see** 18. Thus **look and see**. It is not clear why such an apparently unnecessary character should have evolved, especially in view of the complexity of its strokes. Suggest taking 臣 as **staring eye** 512, and 𠂉 as **person** 丿 39 and **one** 一 1.

Mnemonic: **PERSON WITH ONE STARING EYE SEES ALL**

992 RI, ura
REVERSE SIDE, REAR,
INSIDE, LINING
13 strokes

裏面　RIMEN　　　　inside, back
裏毛　URAKE　　　　fleece lining
裏付ける　URAZUKERU　back up

Formerly also 裡 . ネ/ 衣/衣 is **clothing** 420. 里 is **village** 219, used purely phonetically to express **inside/ reverse side**. 992 originally referred to the **inside/ reverse side of clothing**, i.e. **lining**, but is now also used in a general sense.

Mnemonic: **CLOTHING MADE AT REAR OF VILLAGE HAS GOOD LINING**

---

993 RITSU, RICHI
LAW, CONTROL
9 strokes

法律　HŌRITSU　　　　law
規律　KIRITSU　　　discipline
律義　RICHIGI　　　integrity

彳 is **road/ move** 118, here acting in the figurative sense of **path**. 聿 is a variant of **brush in hand** 聿 142, and here indicates **writing** and by extension **prescribing**, as well as lending its sound to express **one**. Thus **the one (and only) prescribed path** (to follow), i.e. **the law**. **Control** is an associated meaning.

Mnemonic: **MOVING HAND WRITES DOWN THE LAW**

---

994 RIN, nozom*u*
FACE, VERGE ON,
ATTEND, COMMAND
18 strokes

臨時　RINJI　　　　temporary
臨海　RINKAI　　　　seaside
臨席　RINSEKI　　attendance

臥 is a variant of 臥 , an NGU character meaning **bend down/ be prostrate** (literally **staring eye** 臣 512 and **person** ト /人 39, indicating a person bending down to stare). 品 is **goods/ group of people** 382, acting phonetically to express **cliff** and possibly also lending a meaning of **group of people**. 994 originally meant (**a group of people?) crouched on a cliff top looking down**. This has given rise to a range of associated and extended meanings, such as **verge, face, command** (a view), **be in a certain place** and hence **attend**, and **be in a high position** (including figuratively of rank).

Mnemonic: **PERSON FACES GOODS AND STARES**

995

RŌ, hoga*raka*
CLEAR, FINE, CHEERFUL
10 strokes

明朗 MEIRŌ na   bright, clean
朗報 RŌHŌ   good news
朗読法 RŌDOKUHŌ   elocution

月 is **moon** 16. 良 is **good** (variant 良 598). A **good moon** is a **clear** one (in fact, some scholars feel 良 also acts phonetically to express **clear**), with **bright** and **cheerful** being associated meanings.

Mnemonic: **GOOD MOON IS CLEAR AND BRIGHT**

996

RON
ARGUMENT, OPINION
15 strokes

論文 RONBUN   thesis
理論 RIRON   theory
論理 RONRI   logic

言 is **words/ speak** 274. 侖 is **arrange neatly** 601 q.v., which according to some scholars also acts phonetically to express **sequence/ order**. Thus to **speak while arranging one's words neatly in order**, a reference to the presentation of an **argument**. Suggest taking 侖 literally as **capped** 亼 121 and **aligned/** stacked (bamboo tablets) 冊 874.

Mnemonic: **ARGUMENT OF NEATLY CAPPED AND ALIGNED WORDS**

END OF SIXTH GRADE

THE 949 GENERAL USE CHARACTERS

997
A
NEXT, SUB-, ASIA
7 strokes

亜熱帯 ANETTAI subtropics
欧亜 ŌA Eurasia
亜流 ARYŪ follower

Formerly 亞. Popularly thought to derive from some assumed pictograph of (hatted) **hunchbacks** facing each other, such as 㒼. 997 did indeed mean hunchback at one stage, leading to associated ideas such as **ugly** and **inferior** and hence **secondary/ next** and **sub-**. However, very old forms such as and depict a particular type of underground dwelling with a central chamber and various passages and/or smaller chambers on each side. This came to acquire associated meanings such as **angular/ not straight/ crooked,** and was eventually applied to **hunchbacks,** leading to the evolution of meaning outlined above. Somewhat surprisingly, despite its negative associations it is also borrowed phonetically to express the first syllable of **Asia.** Suggest remembering by association with **two** 二 61 and **center** 中 55. See also 222.

Mnemonic: **TWO ASIAN SUB-CENTERS NEXT TO EACH OTHER**

998
AI, aware/remu
SORROW, PITY
9 strokes

悲哀 HIAI sadness
哀歌 AIKA dirge, elegy
物の哀れ MONONOAWARE pathos

Mouth/ say 口 20 and **clothing** 衣 420. The latter is used primarily for its sound, which is now **I** but was once somewhere between **I** and **AI,** to express the sound of **wailing** and **lamenting.** It may also be felt to lend an extended figurative idea of **covering** (cf. English cloaked/clothed in sorrow). Thus to **say the sorrowful sound I/ AI,** symbolising **sorrow** and **pity.**

Mnemonic: **MOUTH WAILS, CLOTHED IN SORROW**

999
AKU, nigiru
GRASP, GRIP
12 strokes

握手 AKUSHU handshake
握り屋 NIGIRIYA miser
握り飯 NIGIRIMESHI rice-ball

扌 is **hand** 32. 屋 is **store(keeper)** 236 q.v., here acting phonetically to express **seize** and possibly also lending some suggestion of **reaching** through its element 至 (reach 875). Thus to **(reach out and?) seize by the hand.** Though now also sometimes used in a broader sense, 999 still generally retains connotations of seizing with the hand.

Mnemonic: **GRASP STOREKEEPER BY THE HAND**

| 1000 | | atsuka*u*, ko*ku*
TREAT, HANDLE,
THRESH
6 strokes | 取り扱い TORIATSUKAI handling
扱き使う KOKITSUKAU keep busy
客扱い KYAKUATSUKAI
hospitality |

扌 is **hand** 32. 及 is **reach** 1148, here acting phonetically to express **control** and almost certainly also lending an idea of reach/ **attain**. Thus **attain something by controlling with the hand**, i.e. **handle**. As with the English term, this is also used figuratively in the sense of **treat/ deal with**. **Thresh** is a minor associated meaning.

Mnemonic: **REACH WITH HAND, THEN HANDLE CAREFULLY**

| 1001 | 依 | I, E, yor*u*
DEPEND, AS IS
8 strokes | 依頼 IRAI request
依然 IZEN as before
依こ地 EKOJI spite |

Person イ 39 and **clothing** 衣 420. The latter acts phonetically to express **deformity**, though any semantic role is unclear. Thus a **deformed person**. Such a person was **dependent** on others, leading to **depend** in general. (Some scholars feel rather that the deformed person **leaned** on a physical support/ crutch, with **depend** being a figurative extension of lean.) It is not clear how the lesser meaning of **as is** was acquired, though it is possibly an associated meaning from the idea of lack of movement.

Mnemonic: **PERSON DEPENDS ON CLOTHING**

| 1002 | | I, odos*u*
AUTHORITY, THREATEN
9 strokes | 威力 IRYOKU authority
威厳 IGEN dignity
威し文句 ODOSHIMONKU threat |

Once written 𢦏, showing **woman** ㄠ / 女 35 and broad bladed **halberd** 㦰/ 戊 515/ 246. The latter acts phonetically to express **fearsome**, as well as lending similar connotations of its own. Thus **fearsome woman** (cf. English slang battle ax), originally used as a term of address by a new bride towards her mother-in-law (and still very occasionally found in this sense in Chinese). **Authority** and **threaten** are associated meanings.

Mnemonic: **AUTHORITATIVE WOMAN THREATENS WITH HALBERD**

317

1003 為

I, su*ru*, na*su*, tame
DO, PURPOSE
9 strokes

行為	KŌI	action, act
為筋	TAMESUJI	patron
為過ぎる	SHISUGIRU	overdo

Formerly 爲 and earlier . 爫 is hand reaching down 303, here meaning just **hand** (and depicted as such in the older form, as ), while  is the prototype of **elephant** 象 533 q.v. That is, 為 is a variant of 象. Some scholars have interpreted the character as referring to a controlling hand **training an elephant**, which involves **doing** the same **action** over and over again and thus by association gives the present meanings. However, other scholars take 為/象 to be used in its sense of **form/ image/ resemble**, to express the idea of a hand making a shape which resembles something. This came to mean **imitate someone's gestures**, which involved **doing** the gestures **over and over again/ practice**, with **purpose/ benefit** being an associated idea. The fact that the addition of person 亻 39 gives imitate (literally imitating person) 偽 1135 suggests that the latter theory is correct. Suggest remembering 為 by association with **bird** 鳥 174.

Mnemonic: **DO PRACTICE FOR PURPOSE OF IMITATING FUNNY BIRD**

1004 尉

I
MILITARY RANK
11 strokes

大尉	TAII	captain
小尉	SHŌI	ensign
尉官	IKAN	company officer

Once written 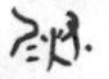. ⺕ is a hand, later replaced with measure/ **hand** 寸 909 q.v. to emphasise careful use of the hand. 火 is fire 8, here meaning **heat**.  is a variant of benevolent 仁 906 q.v., here acting phonetically to express **press down** and probably also lending its own idea of pressing down through its assumed early meaning of a person bent down under a double load. 1004 originally meant **press down with something hot**, a reference to **ironing**. This meaning is now conveyed by the NGU character 熨, which adds an extra fire 火. Just as with the English term iron out, by figurative extension 1004 came to mean **smooth out creases/ put into shape**, and was eventually applied to a **lower ranking officer** given the task of 'knocking' new recruits into shape. Suggest taking  as **corpse** 尸 236 and **show** 示 695.

Mnemonic: **HAND SHOWS CORPSE TO BE SOLDIER OF RANK**

1005	偉	I, erai GREAT, GRAND 12 strokes	偉大 IDAI	grandeur
			偉人 IJIN	hero, prodigy
			偉物 ERABUTSU	great person

イ is **person** 39. 韋 is opposed feet 422 q.v., here acting phonetically to express **differ** and also lending similar connotations of **going against the norm**. Thus a **person different from normal persons**, a reference to an **outstanding/ great person**. Suggest remembering 韋 by association with **differ** 違 1006 q.v.

Mnemonic: **GREAT PERSON DIFFERS FROM OTHERS**

1006	違	I, chigau DIFFER 13 strokes	相違 SŌI	difference
			違反 IHAN	infringement
			言い違い IICHIGAI	misstatement

辶 is **movement** 129. 韋 is opposed feet 422 q.v., here acting phonetically to express **part from** and also lending its own connotations of **moving away**. Thus to **move away from something**, leading by extension to **differ**. Suggest taking 口 as **opening** 20, with a play on the word opening, 屮 as **'almost' five** 五 19, and 中 as **'almost' year** 年 64.

Mnemonic: **AFTER ALMOST FIVE YEARS, OPENING MOVE DIFFERS**

1007	維	I FASTEN, ROPE, SUPPORT 14 strokes	維持 IJI	upkeep
			維新 ISHIN	restoration
			繊維 SENI	fiber

糸 is **thread** 27, here meaning **cord**. 隹 is **bird** 216, here acting phonetically to express **pull** and also lending connotations of **forward movement**. 1007 originally referred to a **rope fastened to something in order to pull it forward**. Thus **rope** and **fasten**, while **support** is an associated meaning, from the idea of helping along.

Mnemonic: **ROPE THREADED THROUGH BIRD HELPS SUPPORT IT**

1008 **I, nagusa**mi/mu/meru
COMFORT, CONSOLE,
AMUSEMENT
15 strokes

慰問 IMON   condolence
慰安 IAN   solace, amusement
慰み物 NAGUSAMIMONO
           plaything

Heart/ **feelings** 心 147 and soldier of rank 尉 1004 q.v. Some scholars take the latter to have been used from the outset in its sense of **smooth out**, to give **smooth out someone's feelings**, i.e. **comfort/ console** them. Others take it to have originally been used phonetically to express **resentment**, as well as lending its literal connotations of **burning pressure**, to give **feelings of smoldering resentment**. It is then felt to have acquired its present meanings as a result of the popular reinterpretation of its elements as discussed above (i.e. smooth out someone's feelings). As with 1004, suggest taking 尉 as **corpse** 尸 236, **show** 示 695, and **hand**/ measure 寸 909.

Mnemonic: **SHOWN CORPSE'S HAND TO CONSOLE FEELINGS?!**

1009 **I**
HORIZONTAL, WEFT
16 strokes

緯度 IDO   latitude
経緯儀 KEIIGI   theodolite
緯糸 NUKIITO *   weft

糸 is **thread** 27. 韋 is opposed feet 422 q.v., here acting in a dual phonetic role to express both **cover** and **differ** and in a dual semantic role to lend supporting connotations both of **surrounding** (and hence **covering**) and **going in a different direction**. Thus **thread that covers by going in a different direction**, a reference to the **weft** relative to the warp. Suggest remembering 韋 by association with **differ** 違 1006.

Mnemonic: **HORIZONTAL WEFT THREADS DIFFER FROM WARP**

1010 **ITSU, so**reru/rasu
ESCAPE, GO ASTRAY,
FAST, EXCEL
11 strokes

逸品 IPPIN   fine article
逸れ矢 SOREYA   stray arrow
逸出 ISSHUTSU
        escape, excellence

Formerly 逸, showing that 兎 is not **escape** 1849 q.v. but a simplification of the NGU character **hare** 兔, which derives from a pictograph 兔 (though the simplification was almost certainly influenced by confusion with escape 免). This was combined with **movement** 辶 129 to express the idea of a **hare's movement**, which is **fast** and associated with **escaping**. **Go astray** is derived from escape, while **excel** is derived from fast. Suggest remembering by association with **escape** 兎.

Mnemonic: **MOVE FAST AND ESCAPE**

1011 芋	imo POTATO 6 strokes	里芋 SATOIMO	taro
		芋貝 IMOGAI	cone shell
		焼き芋 YAKIIMO	baked potato

艹 is **plant** 9. 于 is **emerge** 811, here also acting phonetically to express **big**. Thus **big (leaved) plant which emerges (from the ground)**, a somewhat vague reference to the **potato**. As with 811, suggest taking 于 as a **'stiff'** (i.e. dead) version of **child** 子 25.

Mnemonic: **CHILD IN RIGOR MORTIS AFTER EATING POTATO PLANT**

1012 姻	IN MARRIAGE 9 strokes	婚姻 KONIN	marriage
		姻せき INSEKI	in-laws
		姻族閥 INZOKUBATSU	
			nepotism

女 is **woman** 35. 因 is **depend on** 614 q.v., here probably lending its assumed specific meaning of **become dependent on a person in whose house one stays**. Thus **woman becoming dependent** (on her new family), a reference to **marriage**. Suggest taking 因 as **big man** 大 53 in **confinement** 囗 (see 123).

Mnemonic: **BIG MAN CONFINED BY WOMAN AFTER MARRIAGE**

1013 陰	IN, kage SHADOW, SECRET, NEGATIVE 11 strokes	陰気 INKI	gloom, sadness
		陰部 INBU	private parts
		陰口 KAGEGUCHI	backbiting

阝 is **hill** 229. 侌 is a now defunct character meaning **obscure/ secret/ shadow**. It comprises now 今 125 q.v., used in its literal sense of **cover**, and say 云 78 q.v., used in its literal sense of **vapors**. Thus something **covered in vapors/ mist**. When combined with hill 阝 the meaning became **misty/ shaded side of a hill**, as opposed to the sunny side of the hill seen in 陽 406 q.v. It also retained its connotations of **secret**. Whereas 406 connotes the positive (yang), 1013 connotes the **negative (yin)**. Note that kage/ shade is also expressed by the NGU character 蔭, that adds plant 艹 9 and technically means shaded plants. Suggest remembering 侌 as a combination of **now** 今 and **meet** 会 87.

Mnemonic: **NOW MEET IN SECRET IN SHADOW OF HILL**

1014

IN, kaku*reru*/*su*
HIDE
14 strokes

隠居 INKYO   retirement
隠者 INJA   hermit
隠れ家 KAKUREGA   refuge

Formerly 隱 . 阝 is **hill** 229. 慁 is a CO character meaning **compassion/ care**. Its exact etymology is unclear but it comprises **heart/ feelings** 心 147, **reaching hand** 𠬤 303, a further **hand** 彐 , and what appears to be tile/ weight/ **press down** 工 944. Thus presumably hands pressing down on heart, indicating compassion. In the case of 1014 慁 acts phonetically to express **cover**, and possibly lends similar connotations from the idea of hands covering the heart. Thus **covered by a hill**, i.e. obscured from view and hence **hidden/ hide**.

Mnemonic: **HILL CAN'T HIDE FEELINGS -- NEED HANDS OVER HEART**

1015

IN
RHYME, TONE
19 strokes

韻文 INBUN   poetry
韻律 INRITSU   rhythm
音韻 ONIN   phoneme

音 is **sound** 6. 員 is **member** 228 q.v., here acting phonetically to express **round** and also lending its literal meaning of **round object** but in a figurative sense. Thus **rounded sound**, i.e. **rhyme/ rhythm**.

Mnemonic: **MEMBER'S RHYME DISPLAYS ROUNDED SOUNDS**

1016

EI, yom*u*
POEM, RECITE,
COMPOSE
12 strokes

詠歌 EIKA   composition
詠草 EISŌ   draft of poem
詠史 EISHI   epic

Formerly also 咏 . **Words/ speak** 言 274 (or **mouth/ say** 口 20) and **long** 永 615, to convey the idea of **drawing out a verbal statement** (in the dramatic sense). Thus **recitation**, with **poem** and **compose** being associated meanings.

Mnemonic: **RECITED POEM CONTAINS LONG WORDS**

322

1017

EI, kage
SHADOW, LIGHT,
IMAGE
15 strokes

影響 EIKYŌ　　　　influence
影像 EIZŌ　　　shadow, image
影武者 KAGEMUSHA
　　　　　　　general's double

景 is scene/ **bright** 469 q.v., here in its early sense of **open to the sunlight**. 彡 is **delicate hairs** 93 q.v., here in an extended sense of **delicate pattern**. (Some scholars see 彡 as **rays of sunlight**, as in 144/618, and it is indeed highly likely that there was some confusion between hairs and sunrays, or even a deliberate merging of the two.) Thus the **delicate pattern formed by sunlight**, i.e. **dappling** or **shading**.　This led to both **shadow** and **light**, though the former is by far the commoner meaning, while the idea of the pattern/ shape of the shadowing led to **form** and **image**.　Suggest taking 景 literally as **sun(light)** 日 62 and **capital** 京 99, with 彡 as **streaming sunlight**.

Mnemonic: **SUN STREAMS DOWN ON CAPITAL, FORMING SHADOWS**

1018

EI, surudoi
SHARP, KEEN
15 strokes

鋭利 EIRI na　　　sharp, keen
鋭角 EIKAKU　　　acute angle
精鋭 SEIEI　　　elite, 'crack'

金 is **metal** 14. 兌 is **exchange** 524 q.v., which acts phonetically to express **small**. According to some scholars 兌 also lends an extended idea of reduction and hence **taper** from its connotations of dispersing.　This does not seem particularly convincing, however, and it may be felt more likely that it lends a loose idea of **penetrativeness** from its literal meaning of a person dispersing words by way of explaining, instructing, or preaching. Thus **small (tapered?/ penetrating?) piece of metal**, namely a **tip**, symbolising something **sharp**. This is also used figuratively, i.e. **keen**. Suggest taking 兌 as **elder brother** 兄 267 and **out** ⌄ 66.

Mnemonic: **ELDER BROTHER IS SHARP WHEN MONEY GIVEN OUT**

1019

EKI, YAKU
EPIDEMIC
9 strokes

防疫 BŌEKI　　　disinfection
悪疫 AKUEKI　　　plague
疫病 EKIBYŌ/ YAKUBYŌ
　　　　　　　　epidemic

Illness 疒 381 and **strike** 殳 153, to give **illness that strikes**. Some scholars feel that 殳 also acts phonetically to express **succession**, giving **illness that strikes people in succession**.

Mnemonic: **EPIDEMIC IS ILLNESS THAT STRIKES**

1020

ETSU
JOY
10 strokes

喜悦 KIETSU joy
悦楽 ETSURAKU enjoyment
満悦 MANETSU delight

忄 is **heart/ feelings** 147. 兑 is **exchange** 524 q.v., here acting phonetically to express **burst forth** and also lending an idea of **proclaim** from its literal meaning of person dispersing words. Thus **feelings which burst forth and are proclaimed**, namely **joy**. Suggest taking 兑 as **elder brother** 兄 267 and **out** 丷 66.

Mnemonic: **ELDER BROTHER GIVES OUT FEELINGS OF JOY**

1021

ETSU, koeru/su
CROSS, EXCEED, EXCEL
12 strokes

優越 YŪETSU superiority
越境 EKKYŌ border violation
追い越す OIKOSU overtake

走 is **run** 161. 戉 is **halberd/** battle ax 515, which acts phonetically to express **fleet/ swift** and probably also lends an idea of **aggression**. Thus **to run swiftly** (like warriors attacking?). The idea of running swiftly led to the idea of **exceeding** (not unlike 629 q.v.) and thus **crossing**, as well as **excelling**. Scholars who emphasise the ideographic role of the elements feel that the present meanings stem from warriors **crossing** into other territory, with **excel** stemming from the idea of triumph. This theory is a useful mnemonic.

Mnemonic: **RUN WITH HALBERD AND CROSS BORDER**

1022

ETSU
AUDIENCE (WITH RULER)
15 strokes

拝謁 HAIETSU audience
謁見 EKKEN audience
謁見室 EKKENSHITSU
audience chamber

Formerly 謁 . 言 is **words/ speak** 274. 曷 is a CO character now used to indicate a range of **interrogatives**, and in compounds it often lends an idea of **ask** and/or **threaten**. It comprises **say** 曰 /日 688, **encircle/ surround** 勹 655, and **person** 人 39 **in a corner** ㇄ 349 (see also 973). Its etymology is unclear, but it appears to indicate a person (possibly an escapee) trapped in a corner surrounded by interrogators, which would account for its connotations both of threaten and of the interrogative. However, it is also possible that person in a corner 匕 is used in its sense of dead person (973), particularly in view of the fact that the modern form uses fallen person 匕 238, to give talking persons surrounding a dead person. In such case it is not clear how it came to acquire its various connotations. (Note that 匂 exists as a 'made in Japan' NGU character meaning smell, but this is also of unclear etymology.) In the case of 1022 曷 acts phonetically to express **state clearly**, and is also believed to lend connotations of **demand**, combining with words 言 to give **make a clear verbal demand**. This led by association to **audience**. Suggest taking 曰 as **sun** 62, with 勹 as **cover** and 匕 as **sitting person/ man**.

Mnemonic: **MAN SITS COVERED IN SUNSHINE AFTER WORDY AUDIENCE**

1023 **ETSU**   閲兵 EPPEI   troop review
INSPECTION   検閲 KENETSU   censorship
15 strokes   閲覧室 ETSURANSHITSU

                                                 reading room

門 is **gate** 211, here in an extended sense of **emerge in succession** (i.e. from a gate). 兌 is exchange 524 q.v., here acting phonetically to express **count** and possibly also lending its idea of speaking person. Thus to **count things emerging in succession** (i.e. troops who answer when called?), leading to **inspection**. Suggest taking 兌 as **elder brother** 兄 267 and **out** ⳿ ✓ 66.

Mnemonic: **INSPECT ELDER BROTHER WHEN HE COMES OUT OF GATE**

1024 **EN, honō**   火炎 KAEN   flame, blaze
FLAME   脳炎 NŌEN   encephalitis
8 strokes   炎天 ENTEN scorching weather

Fire/ flame 火 8 doubled for emphasis. It often has connotations of **excessive fire/ heat**.

Mnemonic: **TWO FIRES CAN MEAN TOO MUCH FLAME**

1025 **EN, utage**   宴会 ENKAI   banquet
BANQUET   宴楽 ENRAKU   revelry
10 strokes   酒宴 SHUEN   drinking bout

宀 is **house**/ building 28. 晏 is a now defunct character meaning **attractive woman**. The latter comprises **woman** 女 35 and **sun/ bright** 日 62, and literally means **dazzling woman**. This was often used as a euphemistic reference to **prostitutes** and what might be termed professional party-goers. (Note that woman 女 combined with bright 昌 508 [double sun 日] gives the NGU character prostitute 娼 .) Thus, depending on one's level of interpretation, **house of prostitutes/ brothel** or **house of beauties**. By association this led to **revelry** and **banquet**.

Mnemonic: **BANQUET HOSTED BY WOMAN IN SUNNY HOUSE**

| 1026 | | EN
HELP
12 strokes | 援助 ENJO
応援 ŌEN
声援 SEIEN | assistance
backing, aid
vocal support |

爰 is draw to oneself 932 q.v., here in its literal sense of one person **helping** another by means of a rope. **Hand** 扌 32 draws emphasis to the 'helping hand', giving **help**. As with 932, suggest taking 爰 as **three hands** (hand 爫 303, hand 又 , and 'hand' 𠂇 [taken as variant hand 手 32]), thus giving **four hands** in total.

Mnemonic: **FOUR HANDS PROVIDE HELP**

| 1027 | | EN, kemuri, kemui/tai
SMOKE, FEEL AWKWARD
13 strokes | 煙突 ENTOTSU
禁煙 KINEN
煙草 TABAKO* | chimney
'no smoking'
tobacco |

火 is **burn/ fire** 8. 垔 is a CO character meaning embankment/ **block**. It comprises **ground/ earth** 土 60 and **west** 西 152, the latter being used phonetically to express **block** to give **earth that blocks**. Thus 1027 means literally **fire that blocks. Smoke** is felt to be an associated meaning, from the idea of blocking vision and breathing. 1027 is now also sometimes used to refer to **mist** or **haze** in a broad sense. It is not fully clear how in Japanese it also came to mean **feel awkward/ shy**, but it seems likely that this is an associated figurative meaning, from the idea of not being able to see properly and hence not knowing which way to turn or how to proceed. Note that there is an occasionally encountered variant form 烟, which uses depend on/ cause 因 614. The latter acts phonetically to express block and also lends its meaning of cause. Thus that which is caused by fire and blocks.

Mnemonic: **SMOKE FROM BURNING GROUND IN WEST**

| 1028 | | EN, saru
MONKEY, APE
13 strokes | 類人猿 RUIJINEN
野猿 YAEN
猿真似屋 SARUMANEYA | anthropoid
wild monkey
copycat |

Formerly 猨 , which is the correct form. 犭 is dog 17, here meaning **animal**. 爰 is **pull up by hand** 932. Thus **animal which pulls itself up by hand**, a reference to the **monkey** and its tree-climbing agility. The later use of long robe 袁 79 is almost certainly the result of miscopying, but since it has the same pronunciation as 爰 it may be considered a phonetic substitution for the latter. Suggest remembering 袁 by association with **distant** 遠 79.

Mnemonic: **ANIMAL IN DISTANCE IS MONKEY**

326

1029

EN, namari
LEAD
13 strokes

亜鉛 AEN zinc
黒鉛 KOKUEN graphite
鉛筆入れ ENPITSUIRE pencil case

金 is **metal** 14. 分 is hollowed out 158, here acting phonetically to express **white** and possibly also lending an idea of **extraction** from its literal elements **source/ opening** 口 20 and **out of** ハ 66. Thus **(extracted?) white metal**, a reference to **lead**. White metal is also the description of silver 銀 263 q.v., but it should be noted that the latter is specifically white metal that is <u>scrutinised</u> (to distinguish it from similar metals, such as lead). Some scholars feel that white is in fact a reference not to the color per se but to **cosmetics** (white and cosmetics conceptually overlapping and in Japanese sharing the same word shiro), since it is known that in ancient times many cosmetics were lead based. Thus the interpretation of 1029 then becomes **metal associated with cosmetics**. A combination of both theories is not impossible, i.e. **white metal associated with cosmetics**. Suggest taking 口 as **hole**.

Mnemonic: **METAL POURING OUT OF HOLES IS LEAD**

1030

EN, fuchi
RELATION(S), TIES,
FATE, EDGE
15 strokes

縁側 ENGAWA veranda
縁縫い FUCHINUI hemming
縁談 ENDAN offer of marriage

Formerly 緣. 糸 is **thread** 27. 彖 is a CO character meaning running pig/ hedgehog, and is to all intents and purposes a variant of **pig** 豕 1670. Here it acts phonetically to express **edge**, to give **threads used for edging/ hemming**. Why such a character should have been chosen as a phonetic is not clear, but it may possibly have been confused with and/or likened to streamers 勿 387, i.e. to suggest tassels. Edging came to mean **edge** in general. **Relation(s)**, **ties**, and **fate** are taken by some scholars to be the result of borrowing, but it seems more likely that the combination of threads and edge suggested **bringing things into contact**, and that they are therefore extended/ associated meanings. Fate is certainly a meaning figuratively associated with ties. Suggest taking 彖 as **pig with tusks**.

Mnemonic: **TUSKED PIG TIED WITH THREAD SUFFERS SAD FATE**

1031

O, kega*reru/su/rawashii*,
yogo*reru/su*, **kitanai**
DIRT, DISHONOR
6 strokes

汚染	OSEN	pollution
汚職	OSHOKU	bribery
汚れ物	YOGOREMONO	laundry

Also written 汙. ; is **water** 40. 于/亐 is **emerge** 811 q.v., acting phonetically to express **dip/ hollow** and possibly also lending its own idea of **emerge** (though it may be felt that the **waterweed** element 亐 [see also 281] is the dominant connotation). 1031 originally referred to **water which collected in a hollow**, possibly having seeped (i.e. emerged) from the ground and/or becoming covered with waterweed. Unlike the pure connotations of spring 泉 915, it acquired connotations of **stagnancy** (still found as a meaning in Chinese) and hence **impurity** and eventually **dirt** and the figurative **dishonor**. As with 811, suggest taking 于 as a 'stiff' (i.e. **dead**) version of **child** 子 25, with 亐 as '**almost' stiff/ dead child**.

Mnemonic: **CHILD ALMOST DEAD AFTER DRINKING DIRTY WATER**

1032

凹

Ō, **kubo, boko, heko***mu*
HOLLOW, CONCAVE,
DENT
5 strokes

凹面	ŌMEN	concave
凹地	KUBOCHI	hollow, pit
凹み	HEKOMI	dent

A symbolic representation of **concavity**. Suggest remembering by association with a **box** 口.

Mnemonic: **HOLLOW BOX DENTED, NOW RATHER CONCAVE**

1033

Ō, os*u*
PUSH
8 strokes

押収	ŌSHŪ	confiscation
押し入れ	OSHIIRE	closet
手押し車	TEOSHIGURUMA	barrow

扌 is **hand** 32. 甲 is **shell/ casing** 1243, here acting phonetically to express **press/ push** and probably also lending its own connotations of **thrust** and **force** from its literal meaning of a seed bursting forth from its casing. Thus **press/ push with hand**.

Mnemonic: **HAND PUSHES SHELL**

1034 **Ō**

EUROPE, EU-

8 strokes

欧州 ŌSHŪ   Europe

欧米 ŌBEI   the West

欧氏管 ŌSHIKAN

Eustachian tube

Formerly 歐 . 欠 is **lack** 471 q.v., here in its literal sense of **gaping mouth**. 區/区 is ward/ **section** 465 q.v. Though the 品 of 區 probably referred initially to various enclosures/ sub-sections, because of the similarities with **mouth** 口 20 區 was often chosen as a phonetic in words relating to the mouth. Here it is used to express the sound Ō. (Though as an independent character 區 is now invariably read KU it is also listed as having a minor reading Ō, both readings appearing to stem from an original reading of YOKU/ EOKU/ EUKU or similar.) Thus to **make the sound Ō (EO/EU) with a gaping mouth**, a reference to **groaning while vomiting**. It can still be used to mean vomit in Chinese, while in Japanese this is expressed by the NGU character 嘔 , which uses an ordinary mouth 口 instead of gaping mouth 欠 . The character was also chosen as the phonetic for the **EU** of **Europe**, as well as Eustachian, Euclid, etc. Why a character with such emetic connotations should be chosen to represent Europe is a matter of some conjecture. While it is true that there are very few characters with a reading of this particular type of Ō (EU/EO, as opposed to OO, OU, etc.), it should be noted that there is a perfectly good NGU character 謳 (言 is words 274), which is read Ō/EU/EO and has a meaning of praise/ extol.

Mnemonic: **SECTION OF EUROPE LACKING**

1035 **Ō**, nagu*ru*

HIT, BEAT, ASSAULT

8 strokes

殴打 ŌDA   blow, assault

殴り込み NAGURIKOMI gang raid

殴り合う NAGURIAU trade blows

Formerly 毆 . 殳 is **hand holding weapon/ strike** 153. 區/区 is **ward/** section 465, here acting phonetically to express **beat** and possibly also suggesting through its sound Ō the groans and wails of someone being beaten (see 1034). Thus **strike (with weapon) and beat**.

Mnemonic: **ASSAULT IN WARD INVOLVING WEAPON**

1036 Ō, sakura   桜桃 ŌTŌ   cherry fruit
CHERRY (BLOSSOM)   桜色 SAKURAIRO   pink
10 strokes   桜肉 SAKURANIKU

                                                    horsemeat

Formerly 櫻 . 木 is **tree** 69. 嬰 is an NGU character meaning **baby (girl)**, comprising **woman** 女 35 and the CO character **string of shells/ pearls** 賏 (a doubling of **shell** 貝 90). In Chinese 嬰 also has connotations of **roundness**. That is, plump baby girls were likened to a string of pearls. In combination with tree 木 the meaning became **tree that produces a string/ cluster of baby round things**. The peach (see 1646) was one of the commonest fruits, and the **cherry** was considered 'baby' relative to this. In Chinese 1036 is hardly used, but it is a popular character in Japanese. It should be noted that, despite the fact that 1036 was first applied to the cherry <u>fruit</u>, fruiting cherries appear to have become rare (certainly in Japan), and in Japanese it is now used almost exclusively of the <u>flowering</u> cherry. The cherry fruit is now often referred to as the 'Western fruit-cherry' (Seiyōmizakura 西洋実桜). Suggest taking the ソ of the modern form as a **'half'** variant of **claw** ⺤ 303.

Mnemonic: **WOMAN HALF CLAWS WAY UP TREE TO GET CHERRY BLOSSOM**

1037 翁 Ō, okina   老翁 RŌŌ   old man
OLD MAN, VENERABLE   村翁 SONŌ   village elder
10 strokes   げん翁 GENOKINA

                                               Old Man Gen

羽 is wings/ **feathers** 812. 公 is **public** 277 q.v., acting phonetically to express **head**. 1037 originally referred to the (soft) **plumage on either side of a hawk's head**. In view of this rather specific meaning it is possible that 公 was chosen as the phonetic for its suggestion of a **nose** 厶 134 (though technically 277 derives from 㕣 , 口 was from an early stage often abbreviated to 厶), with ハ then becoming symbols of **either side**. Some scholars feel that the present meaning of **old man** is purely the result of borrowing, while others feel that an early form 翁 of 1037 became graphically confused with an early form 耂 of old man 老 609. However, it seems equally possible that 1037 was applied by association to whiskered old men and/or those who had gone bald on top of the head and had hair left only on the sides.

Mnemonic: **OLD MAN RUFFLES FEATHERS IN PUBLIC**

1038

Ō, oku
DEEP INSIDE
12 strokes

奥底 OKUSOKO inner depths
奥様 OKUSAMA wife
奥義 ŌGI/ OKUGI mysteries

Formerly 奥 and earlier 奧. 禾 and 屮 show the same apparent confusion between **rice** 米 201and **rice plant** 禾 81 as seen in 196, though the modern form has opted for **rice** 米. 冂 is clearly a variant of roof/ **building** 冖 28. 大 is not **big** 大 53, though it may be useful to take it as such, but clearly a simplification of a pair of hands 𠫓, which here indicate **pushing**. 1038 originally referred to **rice stored** (literally pushed) **deep inside a building**, with the idea of **deep inside** eventually prevailing as the meaning. Note that the reading OKU is believed by many scholars to be an ON (i.e. Chinese) reading, of which Ō is taken to be an abbreviated form , but it is officially classified as a KUN (i.e. Japanese) reading, and probably has etymological connections with the verb oku meaning to put in place (see 545). Further evidence for the KUN classification includes the fact that when used in compounds 1038 never lends a reading OKU. It does, however, very occasionally have an ON reading IKU.

Mnemonic: **BIG AMOUNT OF RICE DEEP INSIDE BUILDING**

1039

OKU
THINK, REMEMBER
16 strokes

記憶 KIOKU memory
追憶 TSUIOKU reminiscence
憶測 OKUSOKU speculation

Thought/ think 意 226 and **heart**/ feelings 忄 147, conveying the idea of **a thought kept in the heart**, such as a lingering **memory**. Nowadays often interchanged in practice with the NGU character 臆, which uses flesh/ of the body 月 365 instead of heart 忄, but technically 臆 has connotations of timidity and hesitation.

Mnemonic: **A THOUGHT IN THE HEART IS A THOUGHT REMEMBERED**

1040

osore, GU
FEAR, ANXIETY
13 strokes

憂虞 YŪGU distress
不虞 FUGU unexpected
虞美人草 GUBIJINSŌ poppy

虍 is **tiger** 281. 吳 is **give** 1237 q.v., acting phonetically to express **contrast** (of color) and probably also lending connotations of **not proven fact** from its literal meaning of a person not telling the truth. 1040 originally referred to a **mythical tiger-like creature** with black spots against a white background. Its present meanings result from confusion with **concern** 慮 1904.

Mnemonic: **TIGER GIVES ONE FEAR AND ANXIETY**

1041

乙

OTSU, ITSU
ODD, B, 2ND, STYLISH
1 stroke

乙種 OSSHU　　　　B Class
乙女 OTOME*　　　　maiden
乙に OTSUNI　　　　strangely

From a pictograph of a **double bladed sword** (held in the middle). This was an **unusual** weapon, leading to **odd**. **Stylish** is felt to be a loosely associated meaning, from the idea that something unusual is something outstanding, with stylish being an associated meaning with outstanding. **Second/ B** is a borrowed meaning (First/ A being 甲 1243 and Third/ C being 丙 1773).

Mnemonic: **ODD DOUBLE BLADED SWORD IS B-GRADE STYLE**

1042

卸

oro*su*, oroshi
WHOLESALE, GRATE
9 strokes

卸売 OROSHIURI　　wholesale
卸商 ORISHISHŌ　　wholesaler
卸し大根 OROSHIDAIKON
　　　　　　　grated radish

Of unusual etymology in that it is formed from a larger character, without reference to which 1042 cannot be understood. The character in question is **honorable** 御 1158 q.v., used in its meaning of **drive a cart**. This has had **road/ movement** 彳 118 removed from its **moving foot/ movement** element 辵 129 q.v., to leave just **foot** 止 129, which changed to its meaning of **stop**. In combination with the **'drive a cart'** element 卸 (which confusingly only became drive a cart in combination with movement, since there is no cart element proper) this produced a meaning of **stop (driving) a cart**. This came to mean **unload**, which is its main meaning in Chinese. In Japanese there is a semantic overlap between unloading a vehicle and **selling wholesale** (i.e. selling there and then at the roadside rather than through a retail outlet), with the verb orosu meaning both lower/ unload and sell wholesale depending on the character (generally 下 7 is used for lower/ unload). 1042 is also sometimes used to express a separate homophonic word orosu meaning to **grate** (vegetables), though this is normally expressed by 下 7. Suggest remembering by association with **honorable** 御 1158, minus its **movement** radical 彳.

Mnemonic:**WHOLESALE MARKET HONORABLE BUT LACKS MOVEMENT**

1043
ON, odayaka
PEACE, MODERATION
16 strokes

穏和 ONWA — moderation
穏当 ONTŌ na — reasonable
平穏 HEION — calm

Formerly 穩. 禾 is **rice plant** 81, while 急 / 急 is **care/ compassion** 1014 q.v. The latter acts phonetically to express **soften** and probably also lends connotations of **pressing** from its assumed original meaning of hands pressed to heart. 1043 originally referred to **softening rice by pressing it**. Some scholars take its present meanings to result from borrowing, while others see them as extended meanings, feeling that **soften rice** came to mean **soften** in a broad sense, leading to **make amenable** and thus **advocate peace** and **moderation**. Suggest taking 急 literally as **hands** (hand 〵 303 and hand ヨ) clasped to **heart** 心 147.

Mnemonic: **HANDS HOLD RICE PLANT TO HEART AS TOKEN OF PEACE**

1044
KA
BEAUTIFUL, GOOD
8 strokes

佳人 KAJIN — a beauty, belle
絶佳 ZEKKA — superb
佳作 KASAKU — a fine work

亻 is **person** 39, here meaning **woman**. 圭 is **edge/ jewel** 819, here acting phonetically to express **beautiful** and possibly also lending its meaning of **jewel**. Thus a **beautiful (jewelled?/ jewel-like?) woman**. This later became **beautiful/ fine/ good** in a broad sense. Suggest taking 圭 literally as a **doubling** of **ground** 土 60.

Mnemonic: **GOOD PERSON COVERS TWICE AS MUCH GROUND**

1045
KA, kakaru/keru
BUILD, SPAN, FRAME
9 strokes

架道橋 KADŌKYŌ — overbridge
書架 SHOKA — bookshelf
架空 KAKŪ — aerial, fanciful

木 is **tree/ wood** 69, here meaning **timber**. 加 is **add** 431, here also acting phonetically to express **build up**. Thus to **build up by adding timber**, a reference to **constructing a frame/ support**, usually with connotations of height and **spanning** (as a bridge).

Mnemonic: **ADD WOOD TO BUILD UP SPAN OF FRAME**

1046

KA, GE, hana
FLOWER, SHOWY,
CHINA
10 strokes

華美 KABI   splendor, color
中華 CHŪKA-   Chinese-
華華しい HANABANASHII
       brilliant

Originally 蒅, showing a **richly leafed plant coming into bud** 蒅 with a reinforcing **plant** radical ΨΨ/艹 9. A later form 華 shows the plant radical on top and a simplified leafy plant 本, with the idea of coming into bud conveyed by **emerge** 亏 811. It is from this later form that the modern character derives. 1046 is now generally used in the figurative sense of **flowery/ showy**, with the physical flower being conveyed by 花 9. It is also used as a reference to **China**. Suggest taking 華 as an **eight-leaved plant** 華 with the number being confirmed by **eight** 丶丿 66.

Mnemonic: **SHOWY CHINESE FLOWER IS PLANT WITH EIGHT LEAVES**

1047

KA
FRUIT, CAKE
11 strokes

菓子 KASHI   candy, cake
製菓 SEIKA   confectionery
水菓子 MIZUGASHI   fruit

Fruit 果 627 with **plant** 艹 9 added after the the meaning of 627 became vague. **Cake** is an associated meaning, from the idea of sweet refreshment. Suggest taking 果 as **tree** 木 69 and **field** 田 59.

Mnemonic: **TREE PLANTED IN FIELD PRODUCES FRUIT FOR CAKE**

1048

KA, uzu
WHIRLPOOL, EDDY
12 strokes

渦巻き UZUMAKI   eddy, vortex
渦線 UZUSEN   spiral line
渦中 KACHŪ   maelstrom

Formerly 渦, comprising **water/ river** 氵 40 and **pass/ flexible movement** 過 629. 1048 is used as a proper noun to refer to a certain river in China, and some scholars feel that **whirlpool** results either from borrowing or from the particular nature of the river in question. Others feel that whirlpool is the older meaning, from the idea of **flexibly moving water**, and that the river in question was so named because of this. **Movement** 辶 129 has disappeared in the present form, which may be a useful mnemonic.

Mnemonic: **WATER IN WHIRLPOOL PASSES WITH DISAPPEARING MOVEMENT**

1049	**KA, yome, totsug***u* **MARRY, BRIDE** 13 strokes	花嫁 HANAYOME 嫁資 KASHI 転嫁 TENKA	bride dowry buck passing

Woman 女 35 and **house** 家 83, indicating a **woman going to a (new) house**, i.e. as a **bride**. Some scholars feel that 家 also acts phonetically to express **make-up**, to refer specifically to a bride making herself up before going to her new home.

Mnemonic: **MARRIED WOMAN GOES TO NEW HOME**

1050	**KA, hima** **LEISURE, FREE TIME** 13 strokes	休暇 KYŪKA 余暇 YOKA 暇取る HIMADORU	holiday leisure be tardy

日 is **day** 62. 叚 is false 625, known to act here phonetically to express **space** but of unknown semantic role. Thus **day of space**, meaning a day of **leisure**. Suggest taking 𠂤 as **doorsteps** (door 尸 [variant 戸 108] and steps ニ), and 又 as a variant of **hand holding tool/ weapon** 殳 153 (i.e. **repair**).

Mnemonic: **USE HANDY TOOL TO REPAIR DOORSTEPS ON FREE DAY**

1051	**KA, wazawai** **CALAMITY** 13 strokes	禍福 KAFUKU 災禍 SAIKA 禍根 KAKON	ups and downs calamity root of evil

Formerly 禍. 示/ネ is altar/ **of the gods** 695. 咼 is the somewhat unclear 'backbone' element 629 q.v., which is known to act here phonetically to express **rebuke** but is of unknown semantic role. Thus **rebuke from the gods**, a reference to a **calamity**. Suggest remembering 咼 by association with **pass** 過 629, taking it to be **'almost' pass**.

Mnemonic:**ALMOST PASS ALTAR -- COULD HAVE BROUGHT CALAMITY**

1052	**KA, kutsu** **SHOE** 13 strokes	製靴 SEIKA 靴下 KUTSUSHITA 長靴 NAGAGUTSU	shoemaking sock boot

Leather 革 821 and **change/convert** 化 238. **Shoes** are **'converted'** from **leather**. Leather footwear was in fact quite rare in ancient China, and was used primarily for riding. Thus 1052 originally meant riding boots before coming to mean **shoe** in general.

Mnemonic: **SHOES ARE CONVERTED LEATHER**

335

1053

KA
FEW, MINIMUM, WIDOW
14 strokes

寡黙 KAMOKU   silence
寡婦 KAFU/ YAMOME widow
寡言 KAGEN   reticence

An old form 寡 shows a **house** 冂/宀 28, a **face** 頁/直/頁 93 (here meaning **person**), and **divide** 刀/分/分 199 (here meaning **separate**), indicating a **person separated from others and alone in a house**. This was a reference to a **widow**, but also conveyed the idea of **minimum** since one person is a minimal 'family'. **Few** is an associated meaning.

Mnemonic: **FEW SMILES ON FACE OF WIDOW IN DIVIDED HOUSE**

1054

KA, KO
ITEM (COUNTER)
14 strokes

箇条書 KAJŌGAKI itemisation
箇所 KASHO   place, point
一箇 IKKO   one item

竹 is **bamboo** 170. 固 is **hard** 476, here acting phonetically to express **straight** and almost certainly also lending an idea of solid physical presence (i.e. actual existence). 1054 was originally used as a **counter for straight bamboo slats**, but later came to be used of other items. It has long been confused with 個 669 q.v.

Mnemonic: **COUNT ITEMS OF HARD BAMBOO**

1055

KA, kase*gu*
WORK, EARN MONEY
15 strokes

稼業 KAGYŌ   one's trade
稼ぎ手 KASEGITE breadwinner
共稼ぎ TOMOKASEGI
            dual income

禾 is **rice plant** 81, while 家 is **house/ home** 83. Popularly interpreted as **bringing home the rice**, which is seen as an assumed equivalent to the English term **breadwinner**. A useful mnemonic, but incorrect. 家 is used primarily phonetically, to express **very big**, and also lends an idea of a **safe building** and by extension **storehouse**. 1055 originally meant a **crop of rice big enough to fill a (store)house**. It then also came to mean by association **work hard enough to produce such a crop**. In Chinese it still means harvested crop or work on the land, but in Japanese the idea of **working in order to achieve wealth** has come to prevail.

Mnemonic: **WORK TO EARN MONEY AND 'BRING HOME THE RICE'**

1056

ka, BUN
MOSQUITO
10 strokes

蚊針 KABARI   flyhook
大蚊 GAGANBO*   crane fly
蚊遣り火 KAYARIBI   smudge fire

虫 is **insect** 56. 文 is **text** 68, here used purely for its sound **BUN**. Thus **insect that makes a BUN sound**, a reference to the whine/ hum of a **mosquito**.

Mnemonic: **TEXT DESCRIBES MOSQUITO AS INSECT THAT GOES 'BUN'**

1057

GA
ELEGANCE, 'TASTE'
13 strokes

優雅 YŪGA   elegance
雅号 GAGŌ   pen name
雅趣 GASHU   artistry

隹 is **bird** 216. 牙 is **fang** 434, used for its sound **GA**, and according to some scholars also lending connotations of **ugly** and/or **unpleasant**. Thus **(unpleasant?) bird that makes a GA sound**, a reference to the cawing of a **crow**. 216 can still mean crow in Chinese, though generally this is expressed by a character 鴉 which uses bird 烏 174 instead of bird 隹 and which is also found in Japanese as an NGU character. Somewhat surprisingly, 1057 was later borrowed phonetically to express **elegant/ tasteful**, though it is unclear why a character with such connotations should have been chosen.

Mnemonic: **FANGED BIRD IS AN ELEGANT CROW**

1058

GA, ueru
STARVE
15 strokes

飢餓 KIGA   starvation
餓鬼 GAKI   hungry imp, brat
餓死 GASHI   starving to death

Somewhat obscure. 食 is **food/ eat** 146. 我 is **I/ self** 817, felt by some scholars to act purely phonetically to express **empty/ lacking**, to give **lacking food**. However, it seems more likely that 我 was originally used in error instead of entrust 委 423. 餧 is a CO character meaning both **feed** and **be hungry/ starve**, in which 委 acts phonetically to express empty/ lacking and may at the same time lend connotations either of **food** through its rice plant element 禾 (see 81) or **give** through its later meaning of entrust. There seems to have been a conceptual association between starving and feeding, through the basic concept of being hungry (i.e. depending on whether one intransitively suffers the hunger or transitively reacts to it). However, 1058 is used only in the sense of **starve**.

Mnemonic: **I'M STARVING AND NEED FOOD**

1059 **KAI** 介入 KAINYŪ intervention
MEDIATE, SHELL 介殻 KAIKAKU sea shell
4 strokes 自己紹介 JIKOSHŌKAI
self-introduction

Originally 𠆢丨, showing a **person** 𠆢 39 **encased**)丨, indicating a **person wearing armor** (front and back). This led on the one hand to the idea of **casing**, including eventually even **sea shell**, and on the other to the idea of **being between things**, giving by extension **mediate**. Suggest taking 介 as an **arrow**.

Mnemonic: **SHELL PROTECTS MEDIATOR FROM ARROW**

1060 **KAI, imashi***meru* 警戒 KEIKAI caution
COMMAND, ADMONISH 戒律 KAIRITSU commandment
7 strokes 戒行 KAIGYŌ penance

Originally 戒, showing **two hands** 廾 holding a **halberd/ weapon** 𢦏 493. This indicated a **threat**, leading to the ideas of **commanding** someone to do something and of **rebuking/ punishing** them. Suggest taking 廾 as two **tens** 十 33.

Mnemonic: **TWENTY HALBERDS ENFORCE COMMAND**

1061 **KAI, KE, aya***shii/shimu* 怪談 KAIDAN ghost story
WEIRD, SUSPICIOUS 怪物 KAIBUTSU monster
8 strokes 怪しげ AYASHIGE questionable

忄 is **feelings** 147. 圣 is not the usual simplification of warp threads 坙/巠 269. It was formerly written 圣, showing a **hand** ユ over **earth/ ground** 土 60, and exists as a CO character meaning **work on the land**. However, it has long been used in Chinese as a simplification of **sacred** 聖 911, and consequently in the case of 1061 almost certainly lends 'borrowed' connotations of **otherworldliness** and **mysteriousness**. It also lends its sound to express **unusual**. 1061 originally meant **one's feelings when encountering something strange**, but, like the English term **suspicious**, it also came to be applied to the object itself.

Mnemonic: **WEIRD HAND ON GROUND GIVES SUSPICIOUS FEELING**

338

1062

KAI
DECEIVE, KIDNAP, BEND
8 strokes

拐帯者 KAITAISHA   absconder
誘拐 YŪKAI   abduction
拐じょう KAIJŌ   crooked staff

Formerly also written 拐 or, correctly, 拐. 扌 is **hand** 32, here meaning **arm**. 另 is the same variant of bone 咼 867 seen in split 別 579. Here it acts phonetically to express **bend**, and may also lend loose connotations of **flexibility** through its associations with the backbone (see also 629). 1062 originally meant to **bend one's arm around something and thus acquire it**. This usually meant to acquire in a furtive and/or illegal manner, leading to **deceive** and **kidnap**, while the minor meaning of **bend** derives from bent arm. Some scholars feel that bent arm in itself may also have symbolically suggested furtive or deviant behavior (cf. English crooked). Suggest taking 另 as **mouth** 口 20 and **cut** 刀 181.

Mnemonic: **RECEIVE CUTS TO HAND AND MOUTH IN KIDNAP**

1063

KAI, ku*yamu*, ku*yashii*, ku*iru*
REGRET, REPENT,
VEXED
9 strokes

後悔 KŌKAI   regret
悔しさ KUYASHISA   vexation
悔やみ状 KUYAMIJŌ   letter of condolence

忄 is **feelings** 147. 毎 is **every** 206, here acting phonetically to express **resent** but of unknown semantic role. Thus **feelings of resentment**. For some reason this came in particular to mean **resentment against oneself**, leading to **remorse** and hence **repent/regret**. Like the English term regret, it is now also used in a broad sense of **feel sorry**.

Mnemonic: **EVERY PERSON HAS FEELINGS OF REGRET**

1064

皆

KAI, min[n]a
ALL, EVERYONE, FULL
9 strokes

皆済 KAISAI   full payment
皆無 KAIMU   none at all
皆様 MINASAMA   everyone

Once written 皆 and earlier 𣬈, showing **compare/ people lined up** 比 771 and **speak/ say** 白/曰 (old form and variant respectively of 曰 688: see also 307). 1064 originally meant **people in a row talking**, but gradually the idea of **all the people** came to prevail, leading to the present meanings. Note that 1064 is also used of **all** in the general sense of **full or complete**, and is not necessarily restricted to people. The use of **white** 白 65 in the present form appears to result from miscopying.

Mnemonic: **EVERYONE LINED UP, ALL IN WHITE**

339

1065

KAI, katamari
LUMP, CLOD, MASS
13 strokes

金塊 KINKAI   gold bullion
塊鋼 KAIKŌ   steel ingot
山塊 SANKAI   massif

Somewhat obscure. Once written simply as 凷, namely **mass of earth in a container** 948, leading to **mass/ lump** in a broad sense. For reasons that are not clear the simple container 凵 (which technically existed as an independent character with a reading KI) was replaced by **devil** 鬼 1128 (also read KI), used apparently as a purely phonetic replacement. **Earth** 土 60 was then placed alongside the new element.

Mnemonic: **DEVILISH LUMP OF EARTH**

1066

KAI, kowa*reru/su*
BREAK, DESTROY, RUIN
16 strokes

破壊 HAKAI   destruction
壊滅 KAIMETSU   destruction
壊血病 KAIKETSUBYŌ   scurvy

Formerly 壞 and earlier 壌. 土 is **earth**, here meaning **earthen rampart**. 褱/裏 is a CO character meaning wrap/ conceal/ carry in the sleeve. Its etymology is unclear, but it comprises **clothing** 衣/衣 420 and an element 罒 that includes eye 罒/目 72 and is possibly a variant of multitude 眾/衆 705 q.v. (thus giving many things enveloped by one's clothing?). In the case of 1066 褱 acts phonetically to express **destroy**, but any semantic role is unclear. Thus to **destroy/ break down an earthen rampart**, now **destroy/ break** in a broad sense. Suggest taking 亞 as **ten** 十 33 and **four** 罒 (variant 四 26), i.e. **fourteen**.

Mnemonic: **RUIN CLOTHES DESTROYING FOURTEEN EARTHEN WALLS**

1067

KAI, futokoro, natsu*kashii*
BOSOM, YEARN, FOND
16 strokes

懐中 KAICHŪ-   pocket-
懐手 FUTOKORODE   idleness
述懐 JUKKAI   reminiscence

Formerly 懷. 忄 is **heart/ feeling** 147. 褱/裏 is the somewhat unclear character **carry in the sleeve** 1066 q.v. It should be noted that both in Chinese and Japanese there is a conceptual overlap between sleeve (or in the case of western clothes pocket) and **bosom**, both loosely meaning that part of the person which carries things. Thus 1067 came to mean the **feeling carried in one's bosom**, a reference to **yearning**. **Fond** is an associated meaning. 1067 is also used to refer to **bosom/ pocket**. There is an alternative but less likely theory that 褱 means simply carry, to give that carried in the heart. Suggest taking 褱 as **clothes** 衣 420, **ten** 十 33, and **four** 罒 (variant 四 26).

Mnemonic: **YEARNING FEELING FOR FOURTEEN SETS OF CLOTHES**

1068 **GAI**
INVESTIGATE (WRONG)
8 strokes

弾劾者 DANGAISHA denunciator
弾劾 DANGAI impeachment
劾奏 GAISŌ
reporting offense to ruler

力 is strength/ **effort** 74. 亥 is pig 865, here used phonetically to express **examine thoroughly**. Thus **examine thoroughly and with great effort**. This came to acquire particular connotations of **investigating wrongdoing**. Suggest taking 亥 as a 'broken' variant of (short) thread 幺 111.

Mnemonic: **MAKE EFFORT TO INVESTIGATE BREAKING OF THREAD**

1069 涯 **GAI**
SHORE, EDGE
11 strokes

生涯 SHŌGAI life
際涯 SAIGAI limits
天涯 TENGAI horizon

氵 is **water** 40. 厓 is an NGU character meaning (tall) **cliff**, comprising **cliff** 厂 45 and **raised earth** 圭 819 (literally a doubling of **earth** 土 60). Thus **waterside cliff**, a reference to the **shoreline** and by association **edge** of the land/ water. Now also used of **edge** in a general sense. Note that cliff is now usually conveyed by an NGU character 崖, which adds hill/ mountain 山 24.

Mnemonic: **CLIFF OF RAISED EARTH STANDS AT WATER'S EDGE**

1070 **GAI**
LAMENT, DEPLORE
13 strokes

慨嘆 GAITAN lamentation
感慨 KANGAI deep emotion
慨然 GAIZEN to indignantly

Formerly 慨. 忄 is **heart/ feelings** 147. 既/既 is **already** 1126 q.v., acting phonetically to express **anger / detestation** and possibly also lending connotations of **something ceasing to be**. Thus **feelings of anger (at something ceasing to be?)**, a reference to **lamenting/ deploring**.

Mnemonic: **ALREADY HAVE FEELINGS OF LAMENT**

341

1071 **GAI**
RELEVANCE, THE SAID-
13 strokes

該当 GAITŌ   relevance
当該 TŌGAI-   the relevant-
該博 GAIHAKU   profundity

言 is **words** 274. 亥 is **pig** 865, here acting phonetically to express **binding**. 1071 originally referred to a **binding agreement**, then as a result of a reinterpretation of its elements (some scholars see it as a pure borrowing) came to mean **words that are bound to something**, i.e. that are **relevant**. Suggest taking 亥 as a **'broken'** variant of (short) **thread** 幺 111.

Mnemonic: **THREAD BINDING SAID WORDS HAS BEEN BROKEN**

1072 **GAI,** ōmu*ne*
ROUGHLY, IN GENERAL
14 strokes

概念 GAINEN   general idea
概略 GAIRYAKU   outline
大概 TAIGAI   in general

Formerly 槩. 木 is **tree/ wood** 69. 旡/既 is **already** 1126 q.v., acting phonetically to express **rub across** and possibly also lending a loose idea of finished/ **complete**. 1072 originally referred to a **strickle**, which is a piece of wood passed across the top of a filled open container (usually of grain) in order to ensure an approximately full (i.e. complete) measure. It still retains this meaning in Chinese. **Rough measure** came to mean **rough/ roughly** and by association **in general**.

Mnemonic: **ALREADY ROUGHLY MEASURED WITH PIECE OF WOOD**

1073 **kaki**
FENCE, HEDGE
9 strokes

垣根 KAKINE   fence, hedge
生け垣 IKEGAKI   hedge
垣間見る KAIMAMIRU*   peep

Ground/ earth 土 60 and **go around** 亘 913, to give **earth that goes around** (a building), namely a **wall** and later, by association, a **hedge**. Suggest taking 亘 as **sun** 日 62 and **two** 二 61.

Mnemonic: **SUNNY GROUND BETWEEN TWO FENCES**

| 1074 | 核 | **KAKU**
CORE, NUCLEUS,
NUCLEAR
10 strokes | 核心 KAKUSHIN core, kernel
結核 KEKKAKU tuberculosis
核兵器 KAKUHEIKI
nuclear weapon |

木 is **tree/ wood** 69. 亥 is pig 865, here acting phonetically to express **(hard) casing**. 1074 originally referred to an item with a **hard wooden casing**, i.e. a **box**, then as a result of a reinterpretation of its elements (some scholars see it as a pure borrowing) it came to mean **that with a hard casing found on a tree**, a reference to the stone/ **kernel** of some fruits. This also came to mean **nucleus** and in modern times **nuclear**. Suggest taking 亥 as a **'snapped'** variant of **(short) thread** 幺 111.

Mnemonic: **TREES SNAPPED LIKE THREADS IN NUCLEAR BLAST**

| 1075 | 殻 | **KAKU, kara**
SHELL, HUSK, CRUST
11 strokes | 貝殻 KAIGARA sea shell
甲殻 KŌKAKU shell
地殻 CHIKAKU earth's crust |

Formerly 殻 and in ancient times 𣪊, showing a **hand** ㄐ holding a **gong/striker** ℓ and striking a **large hanging bell** 肖. ㄐ later became graphically confused with **striking hand holding weapon/ tool** 殳 / 攴 153, while the bell and its supporting ropes became stylised to 肖, 壴, then finally 壳. Bell gave rise to the idea of **hard cover**, leading to the present meanings. Suggest taking 士 as **samurai** 494, 冖 as **cover**, and 几 as **desk** 832, with 殳 as **strike a blow**.

Mnemonic: **SAMURAI COVERS DESK AGAINST BLOWS, SAVES SHELL**

| 1076 | 郭 | **KAKU**
QUARTER, ENCLOSURE
11 strokes | 輪郭 RINKAKU outlines
城郭 JŌKAKU citadel
遊郭 YŪKAKU gay quarter |

阝 is **village** 355, here meaning **settlement**. 享 is receive 1162 q.v., here in its original meaning of **well guarded castle**. 1076 originally referred to a **settlement within a castle** (or under its protection), such as a **citadel**. It later came to mean **enclosed area** or **quarter** in a broader sense, though it is still occasionally used in the sense of fortification and can mean castle walls in Chinese. Suggest taking 享 as lid/ **cover** 亠, **child** 子 25, and **entrance** 口 20.

Mnemonic: **CHILD COVERS ENTRANCE TO VILLAGE ENCLOSURE**

1077 較 **KAKU, KŌ**
COMPARISON
13 strokes

比較	HIKAKU	comparison
較量	KŌRYŌ	comparison
大較	TAIKŌ	approximation

Once written 較, showing that 交 is not crossed legs/ exchange 交 115 but a derivative of (or confusion with) **crossed sticks** 爻 10 q.v., which in itself contains the idea of **matching** and thus by association **comparing.** 車 is **carriage/ vehicle** 31. 1077 originally referred to small **cross-spars built out from the shaft of a dignitary's carriage,** used for boarding and alighting. Symmetrical spars were a sign of good workmanship, and were thus the object of scrutiny and **comparison**. Some scholars see comparison as resulting from confusion with check 校 21 q.v., but it seems more likely to be an extended meaning from matching cross-spars. Note that in Chinese 1077 still retains a minor meaning of state carriage. Suggest taking 交 as **exchange** 115.

Mnemonic: **EXCHANGE VEHICLES FOR COMPARISON**

1078 隔 **KAKU, heda*taru*/*teru***
SEPARATE, INTERPOSE
13 strokes

隔離	KAKURI	quarantine
間隔	KANKAKU	spacing
隔週	KAKUSHŪ	fortnightly

Formerly 隔, and earlier 隔 and 隔. 阝/阝 is **hill** 229. 鬲 is a CO character meaning **large pot/ cauldron**, comprising the large **pot** itself 画/口 and a **stand** 冂 (stand 丁, as in altar 示 695 q.v., and frame 冂 with cross- supports 八). Here 鬲 acts phonetically to express **block,** and probably also lends connotations of **obstacle** (being a bulky item that would occupy considerable space in a house). Thus **hills that block,** leading to **screen/ separate/ interpose**. Suggest remembering by association with **one/ single** 一 1 and **round** 口 (see also 228).

Mnemonic: **SEPARATED BY SINGLE HILL LIKE ROUND POT ON STAND**

1079 獲 **KAKU, e*ru***
OBTAIN, GAIN, SEIZE
16 strokes

獲得	KAKUTOKU	acquisition
漁獲	GYOKAKU	fishing
獲物	EMONO	prey

犭 is **dog** 17, while 蒦 is **seize** (crested) **bird** (in hand) 670. Thus a **dog seizing a bird**, leading to **seize/ obtain** in a broad sense but still also occasionally found with specific hunting connotations. Suggest taking 蒦 as **grass** 艹 9, **bird** 隹 216, and **paws** (literally hand) 又.

Mnemonic: **DOG SEIZES BIRD IN GRASS WITH PAWS**

1080

嚇

KAKU, odo*su*/*kasu*
THREATEN, MENACE
17 strokes

威嚇　IKAKU　　　　threat
嚇怒　KAKUDO　　　　fury
威嚇的　IKAKUTEKI　threatening

口 is mouth/ say 20. 赫 is an NGU character meaning **bright/ intense/ sudden** and comprises a doubling of **red** 赤 46, used in its literal sense of big fire (cf. English flare up). Here 赫 acts phonetically to express **round on/ retort**, and also lends connotations of **sudden** and **intense**. Thus to **round suddenly and intensely on someone verbally**, and by extension **speak angrily** (again cf. English flare up). It came to acquire particular associations with **threatening**.

Mnemonic: **THREATENING WORDS MAKE ONE SEE RED TWICE OVER**

1081

KAKU
HARVEST
18 strokes

収穫　SHŪKAKU　　　harvest
多穫　TAKAKU　　　good crop
収穫高　SHŪKAKUDAKA　yield

禾 is **rice plant** 81. 蒦 is **seize a crested bird in hand** 670, here meaning simply **take/ obtain**. Thus **obtained rice plants**, namely the **harvest**. Suggest taking 蒦 as **plants** 艹 9, **bird** 隹 216, and **hand** 又 .

Mnemonic: **HARVEST OF RICE PLANTS BETTER THAN BIRD IN HAND**

1082

GAKU, take
PEAK, IMPOSING
8 strokes

山岳　SANGAKU　　mountains
岳父　GAKUFU　father-in-law
雲ぜん岳　UNZENDAKE
　　　　　　　Mount Unzen

Formerly also written 嶽 , though technically they are separate characters. 岳 comprises **mountain** 山 24 and **hill** 丘 1149, the latter probably being used in its early sense of **hills in the plural**. Thus **many hills and mountains**, a reference to an **imposing mountain range** and hence the present meanings of **peak** and **imposing**. 嶽 comprises **mountain** 山 and **prison** 獄 1274 q.v., here acting phonetically to express **tower up** and almost certainly also lending connotations of **fearsome** and/or **daunting** from its early meanings of fight and litigation. Thus **(fearsome/ daunting?) towering mountain(s)**.

Mnemonic: **IMPOSING PEAK OF HILL TOWERS OVER MOUNTAIN!**

1083

kakari, ka*karu*/keru 掛かり人 KAKARIBITO hanger-on
BE CONNECTED,APPLY, 見掛け MIKAKE appearance
HANG,DEPEND,COST 腰掛ける KOSHIKAKERU sit
11 strokes

扌 is **hand** 32. 卦 is an NGU character meaning **divination point**, comprising **divination** 卜 91 q.v. and **angle**/ edge 圭 819. 1083 originally referred to divination by hanging various bamboo strips from the hand and interpreting the groupings formed as they hung. Thus **hang (together)**, leading by figurative extension to a range of associated and extended meanings as listed above. Suggest taking 卜 literally as **crack** and 圭 literally as a **doubling** of **earth**/ **soil** 土 60.

Mnemonic: **CRACK IN HAND CONNECTED WITH DOUBLE LOAD OF SOIL**

1084

kata, SEKI 干潟 HIGATA tidal flat
BEACH, LAGOON 潟湖 SEKIKO lagoon
15 strokes 新潟市 NIIGATASHI Niigata City

氵 is **water** 40. 烏 is the somewhat obscure **bird** element seen in 寫 297 q.v. It acts here phonetically to express **salt**, and may also lend an idea of **take**. 1084 originally referred to **salty water** as in a **saltmarsh**, i.e. water which has taken in salt. Its meaning has now broadened to include **lagoon** and **beach**, and it is also sometimes used of **creek** and **flats**. Suggest taking 烏 as **bird** 勹 (simplified variant 鳥 174) and **talons** 臼 .

Mnemonic: **LAGOON TRAPS WATER LIKE BIRD TRAPS WITH TALONS**

1085

括

KATSU, kuku*ru* 一括 IKKATSU (en) bloc
BIND, WRAP, FASTEN 括弧 KAKKO parentheses
9 strokes 包括的 HŌKATSUTEKI blanket-

扌 is **hand** 32. 舌 is not tongue 舌 732 but, as an old form 括 shows, the same corruption of hollowed out space 呉 seen in 活 244 q.v. Here 舌 acts phonetically to express **bind**, but any semantic role is unclear. Thus to **bind the hands** (some scholars feel rather bind <u>with</u> the hand, i.e. with hand 扌 playing a purely clarifying role), later **bind**/ **fasten**/ **wrap** in a broader sense. Suggest taking 舌 as **tongue**.

Mnemonic: **HAND BINDS AND WRAPS TONGUE**

1086

喝 KATSU
SHOUT, SCOLD
11 strokes

喝さい KASSAI — applause
恐喝 KYŌKATSU — threat
一喝 IKKATSU — yell, roar

Somewhat obscure. Formerly 喝. 口 is **mouth/ say**. 曷/曷 is the somewhat obscure interrogative element seen in 謁 1022 q.v. Some scholars feel that 曷 is used purely phonetically to express **dry up** (as in 1087), to give **dried up voice/ hoarse**, and take **shout/ scold** to be a borrowing. However, if it is indeed the case that 1086 originally meant hoarse, it might be felt that shout/ scold is an associated meaning, as in shouting oneself hoarse. Others scholars take 曷 to act semantically in its assumed early meaning of **interrogate/ threaten**, with **shout/ scold** thus being an extended meaning. The latter theory seems the more likely. Suggest taking 曷 as **person/ man sitting** ヒ 238 **covered** 勹 in **sunshine** 日 62.

Mnemonic: **MAN SITS COVERED IN SUNSHINE, SHOUTS OPEN MOUTHED**

1087

渴 KATSU, kawa*ku*
THIRST, PARCHED
11 strokes

渴水 KASSUI — water shortage
渴望 KATSUBŌ — craving
渴き KAWAKI — thirst

Formerly 渴. 氵 is **water** 40. 曷/曷 is the somewhat obscure interrogative element seen in 謁 1022 q.v., here acting phonetically to express **dry up** and possibly also lending its assumed connotations of **threaten/** menace. Thus a **(threatening?) drought**, now used of **dry up** and **parched** in a broader sense, including **thirst**. Suggest taking 曷 as **person/ man sitting** ヒ 238 **covered** 勹 in **sunshine** 日 62.

Mnemonic: **MAN SITS COVERED IN SUNSHINE, THIRSTING FOR WATER**

1088

滑 KATSU, sube*ru*, name*raka*
SLIP, SLIDE, SMOOTH
13 strokes

円滑 ENKATSU — smoothness
滑走路 KASSŌRO — runway
滑り易い SUBERIYASUI — slippery

氵 is **water** 40. 骨 is **bone** 867 q.v., here acting phonetically to express **emerge** and possibly also lending some idea of flexibility and hence **smoothness** from its association with the backbone (see also 1048). Thus **water emerging (smoothly?)**, i.e. **flowing**. The flowing of water suggested by association a smooth **sliding/ gliding** movement and by further association the idea of **slip** and **slippery**.

Mnemonic: **WATER ON BONES MAKES THEM SMOOTH AND SLIPPERY**

1089 **KATSU** 褐色 KASSHOKU brown
BROWN, COARSE CLOTH 褐炭 KATTAN lignite
13 strokes 褐夫 KAPPU ragged beggar

Formerly 褐. 衤 is **clothing/ cloth** 420. 曷／曷 is the somewhat obscure interrogative element seen in 謁 1022 q.v., here used as a simple form of 葛. The latter is an NGU character meaning arrowroot/ strong vine/ **strong fiber**. It comprises plant 艹 9 and 曷, which is here used phonetically to express bind but is of unknown semantic role. Thus binding plant. In the case of 1089 曷 itself thus means **strong fiber**, giving **cloth of strong (coarse) fiber**. This was a reference to a popular type of **brown cloth**, and hence the acquisition of the meaning **brown**. Suggest taking 曷 as **person/ man sitting** ヒ 238 **covered** ㄇ in **sunshine** 日 62.

Mnemonic: **MAN IN COARSE BROWN CLOTHING SITS COVERED IN SUNSHINE**

1090 **KATSU** 所轄 SHOKATSU jurisdiction
CONTROL, LINCHPIN 管轄 KANKATSU jurisdiction
17 strokes 統轄 TŌKATSU control

車 is **vehicle** 31. 害 is **harm** 437 q.v., here acting phonetically to express **lock** and almost certainly also lending connotations of **cover/ cap** (firmly). 1090 originally referred to a wedge-shaped **linchpin** inserted in the end of an axle to lock the wheel in place. Just like the English term linchpin, it came to mean **vital element** and hence by extension controlling element and eventually **control**.

Mnemonic: **VEHICLE HARMED -- CONTROLLING LINCHPIN REMOVED**

1091 **ka*tsu*, SHO, SO** 且つ又 KATSUMATA moreover
FURTHERMORE, BESIDES 且つ KATSU besides
5 strokes こう且 KŌSHO for a while

From a pictograph of a **cairn** 昌, the piled up stones of which came to mean **one thing on top of others** and hence **in addition/ furthermore**. Suggest remembering as **three layers and a base**.

Mnemonic: **FURTHERMORE, CAIRN HAS THREE LAYERS AND A BASE**

1092		karu **REAP, CUT, SHEAR** 4 strokes	刈り入れ KARIIRE harvesting 刈り込む KARIKOMU crop, trim 草刈り機 KUSAKARIKI mower

Originally 㓞 and later 㹡. 㹡 (now 乂) depicts a pair of **shears**, with **cut** 刀/刂 181 added later for clarity. Thus **cut with shears**.

Mnemonic: **CUT WITH CROSSED SHEARS**

1093	甘	KAN, amai/eru/yakasu **SWEET, PRESUME UPON** 5 strokes	甘酒 AMAZAKE sweet sake 甘言 KANGEN sweet words 甘え AMAE presumption

Originally 甘, showing a **mouth** 𠙵/口 20 with **something held in it** 一. (Note that the same combination of elements can confusingly indicate a tongue in a mouth and mean speak or vocalise, as in 6/688 etc.) Something held in the mouth suggests something **savored**, i.e. something **sweet**. Suggest taking 甘 as an **'exaggerated'** mouth 口.

Mnemonic: **MOUTH EXAGGERATEDLY SAVORS SWEET THING**

1094		KAN, ase, asebamu **SWEAT** 6 strokes	発汗 HAKKAN sweating 汗顔 KANGAN shame 汗水 ASEMIZU heavy sweat

氵 is **water** 40, here meaning **watery liquid**. 干 is **dry** 825 q.v., here acting phonetically to express **scatter**. 1094 thus means literally **scattered watery liquid**, a somewhat vague reference to **sweat** (which is scattered by/over the body).

Mnemonic: **WATERY SWEAT DRIES**

1095		KAN, kama **CAN, BOILER** 6 strokes	缶詰 KANZUME canned goods 缶切り KANKIRI can opener 汽缶 KIKAN steam boiler

Formerly also written 罐, though technically they are separate characters. 缶 derives from 𦈢, a pictograph of a **vessel** 凵 with a **double lid** 仐, the double lid indicating security (see also 258). 雚 is heron 445, acting phonetically to express **pour** and possibly also lending loose connotations of accommodate/ take in (from a heron's ability to consume large quantities of fish). Thus 罐 means a **secure vessel for pouring liquid into**. It is not clear how it later developed particular associations with **metal** containers, but it is possible that 缶 became confused with **metal** 金 14. Suggest taking 缶 as a combination of **noon** 午 110 and mountain 山 24.

Mnemonic: **OPEN CAN FOR NOON PICNIC ON MOUNTAINTOP**

1096 KAN, kimo   肝臓 KANZŌ   liver
LIVER, COURAGE   肝心 KANJIN   vital
7 strokes   肝っ玉 KIMOTTAMA guts, pluck

月 is **meat/of the body** 365. 千 is **dry** 825, acting phonetically to express **vital**. Thus **that which is vital to the body**, a somewhat vague reference to the **liver**. Also used figuratively to refer to **courage** (cf. English slang **guts**).

Mnemonic: **DRIED MEAT PROVES TO BE LIVER**

1097 KAN, kanmuri   王冠 ŌKAN   royal crown
CROWN   栄冠 EIKAN   laurels
9 strokes   冠毛 KANMŌ   crest, plume

冖 is **cover**, here meaning **on top of**. 寸 is **hand/ measure** 909 q.v., here meaning **careful use of the hand**. 元 is **origin** 106 q.v., here in its literal sense of **head**. Thus **something placed carefully on a head**, a reference to a **crown**.

Mnemonic: **MEASURE ORIGINAL CROWN TO ENSURE COVERS HEAD**

1098 KAN, ochiiru   陥没 KANBOTSU   cave-in
COLLAPSE   欠陥 KEKKAN   defect
10 strokes   陥落 KANRAKU   surrender

Formerly 陷 . 阝 is **hill** 229, here meaning **high place**. 臽 is a CO character meaning **hole**, comprising **stumbling person** 勹 / 人 39 and mortar 臼 648, the latter indicating a **hollow/ hole**. 臽 acts here phonetically to express **fall**, and also lends an idea of **low place**. Thus **to fall from a high place to a low place**, i.e. **collapse**. Suggest taking 𦥑 as **old** 648.

Mnemonic: **OLD PERSON STUMBLES AND COLLAPSES ON HILL**

1099 乾 KAN, kawaku   乾電地 KANDENCHI dry battery
DRY   乾燥器 KANSŌKI   drier
11 strokes   乾いた KAWAITA   dry, dried

乙 is **odd** 1041 q.v., here in its sense of **twisted**. 倝 is **rising sun** 637 q.v., here acting phonetically to express **straighten** and probably also lending similar connotations of **straight/ undeviating** by association with the course of the rising sun. Thus 1099 originally meant **to straighten something twisted**. **Dry** is generally seen as a borrowing, but may stem from the idea of becoming hot and drying out associated with the rising sun, with 乙 (at one stage written 乀) possibly being taken to be **vapors/ steam** (see 11). Suggest taking 𠦝 as **sun** 日 62 rising through **plants** ⧺ 9, with 𠂉 as **person** 39.

Mnemonic: **ODD PERSON DRIED BY SUN RISING THROUGH PLANTS**

1100

KAN
ENDURE, CONSIDER,
INVESTIGATE, SENSE
11 strokes

勘弁 KANBEN　　pardon
勘定 KANJŌ　　bill, account
勘違い KANCHIGAI
　　　　　misjudgment

力 is strength/ effort 74. 甚 is **great/ exceedingly** 1449 q.v., acting phonetically to express **endure/ tolerate** and probably also lending connotations of great emotion. Thus **make an effort to endure something** (very emotional?), leading to the idea of **great tolerance** and **perseverance** and in turn to such ideas as **strive to understand**.

Mnemonic: **MAKE EXCEEDINGLY GREAT EFFORT TO INVESTIGATE**

1101

KAN, wazura*u*
DISEASE, BE ILL
11 strokes

患者 KANJA　　patient, victim
患部 KANBU　　diseased part
長患い NAGAWAZURAI
　　　　　long illness

心 is **heart/ feelings** 147. 串 is an NGU character meaning **skewer/ pierce** (often taken to comprise two items 吕 pierced | , which is a useful mnemonic, but an old form 串 suggests rather that it derives from hands 串 thrusting a stake |). Thus **pierced heart**, meaning to **grieve** (still a meaning in Chinese). This came to mean **be afflicted** in a broad sense (also a meaning in Chinese) before coming to acquire particular associations with **being afflicted by an illness/ disease** (despite the absence of the sickness radical 疒 381).

Mnemonic: **FALL ILL AFTER SKEWER PIERCES HEART**

1102

KAN, tsuranu*ku*
PIERCE
11 strokes

貫通 KANTSŪ　　penetration
縦貫 JŪKAN　　traversing
貫流 KANRYŪ
　　　　　flowing through

Originally 毌 , showing **two shells/ units of money** 貝/ 貝 90 **threaded/pierced** | . 1102 originally referred to **money threaded on a string or stick,** but then came to mean **thread/ pierce** in general. Suggest taking 毌 as a variant of **mother** 母 203.

Mnemonic: **MOTHER PIERCED BY SHARP SHELL**

351

1103

KAN, wame*ku*
SHOUT, YELL
12 strokes

喚問 KANMON　　　summons
叫喚 KYŌKAN　　cry, scream
喚き声 WAMEKIGOE shout, yell

口 is **mouth/ say** 20. 奐 is a CO character meaning lively and excellent, originally written 竒. 冎/冏 is a **woman's genitals** (bending person 𠆢 39 and spread thighs 冂 317 [see also 1849 and 1105]), while ⺌ is a **pair of hands**. The original meaning appears to have been **spread a woman's thighs with the hands**, with connotations both of **intercourse** and **childbirth**. In the case of 1103 奐 acts phonetically to express **cry out**, reinforced by mouth/ say 口 , but it is not clear whether it connotes a woman crying out during childbirth or during intercourse. It now means **shout** or **cry out** in a broad sense. Suggest taking 奐 as **big** 大 53, **hole** 冗 (variant 穴 849), and **stumbling person/man** 勹 (see also 1098), with 口 in its sense of **opening/open**.

Mnemonic: **MAN SHOUTS AS HE STUMBLES INTO BIG OPEN HOLE**

1104

KAN, TAN, ta*eru*
ENDURE, WITHSTAND
12 strokes

堪忍 KANNIN　　　patience
堪能 TANNŌ　　　　skill
堪え難い TAEGATAI unendurable

土 is **earth** 60. 甚 is **great/ exceedingly** 1449, here acting phonetically to express **thrust (up)** and probably also lending an idea of **great**. Thus a **great upthrusting of earth**, a reference to **raised ground**. Its present meaning of **endure/ withstand** stems from confusion with **endure** 勘 1100 q.v.

Mnemonic: **EXCEEDINGLY LARGE EARTHEN MOUND WILL ENDURE**

1105

KAN, ka*eru*
EXCHANGE
12 strokes

換気 KANKI　　　ventilation
換え着 KAEGI　　spare clothes
交換学生 KŌKANGAKUSEI
　　　　　　　exchange student

扌 is **hand** 32. 奐 is **woman with spread legs** 1103 q.v. The latter acts phonetically to express **exchange**, and is also felt by some scholars to lend an idea of **careful handling** from an assumed meaning of assisting in the delivery of a child. Thus to **exchange something (carefully?) by hand**, later **exchange** in a broad sense. Suggest taking 奐 as **big** 大 53, **hole** 冗 (variant 穴 849), and **falling person/man** 勹 (see 1103).

Mnemonic:**MAN FALLS INTO BIG HOLE DURING EXCHANGE OF HANDS**

1106

敢

KAN, ae*te*, ae*nai*
DARING, TRAGIC
12 strokes

勇敢 YŪKAN   bravery, valor
敢然 KANZEN   bravely
敢なく AENAKU   tragically

Of very distorted graphic evolution. Originally 𝄡, showing **two hands** pulling (symbolised by ⌒) **something** - out of a **container** ∪. The original meaning was to **pull out with both hands**. This came to mean **make a great effort**, leading to the idea of a **make-or-break effort** and hence **do something daring**. **Tragic** is a negatively associated meaning. The present form results from a stylised intermediate form 敄, amongst other things showing confusion with **strike** 攴 153 (now **strike** 攵 101). Suggest remembering 耳 by association with **ear** 耳 29, taking it as **top of the ear**.

Mnemonic: **DARING STRIKE TO TOP OF EAR -- TRAGIC RESULTS**

1107

棺

KAN, hitsugi
COFFIN
12 strokes

棺おけ KANOKE   coffin, casket
石棺 SEKKAN   sarcophagus
棺台 HITSUGIDAI   bier

木 is tree/ **wood** 69. 官 is **official** 441 q.v., here acting phonetically to express **coffin** and possibly also lending a loose suggestion of **that which covers a corpse** through its elements roof/ building 宀 28 (which can mean cover) and buttocks 㠯 350 (which can mean corpse [see 236]). Thus **wooden coffin**, now **coffin** in a general sense.

Mnemonic: **OFFICIAL RESTS IN WOODEN COFFIN**

1108

款

KAN
FRIENDSHIP, CLAUSE,
ENGRAVE
12 strokes

借款 SHAKKAN   loan, credit
落款 RAKKAN   signature
款待 KANTAI   hospitality

Somewhat obscure. Formerly also written 欵. 示 is **altar/ of the gods** 695. 欠 is **lack** 471 q.v., here used to mean **open** from its literal meaning of **gaping mouth**. Old forms such as 祟 and 祟 show that 木 / 士 derives from a **thickly growing plant** 屮 or 𡳞. 𣎳 is believed to have been a variant of **rice plant** 𥝌 / 禾 81, but has the same form as tree 朩 / 木 69. 𡳞 is an old form of **growing plant** 生 42, but has long been confused with emerge 出 34 q.v. Note that it has this 'emerge' form in the NGU character 祟 , which has evolved from 祟 and now means **curse**. It literally depicts **plants placed on an altar** and originally meant **make an offering to the gods by way of supplication** to them, possibly acquiring its modern meaning in similar fashion to the English term oath, which can either mean sincere statement or curse depending on the circumstances. In the case of 1108 it appears in the form 素 and lends a meaning of **sincere wish**, as well as acting phonetically to express **open** and thus reinforcing 欠. 1108 originally meant an **open and sincere statement of a wish**, with open having the same connotations of **sincerity** and **earnestness** as in English, and it can still mean earnest wish in Chinese. Some scholars see its present meaning of **friendship** as an association/ extension of earnest/ open statement, i.e. a situation in which there is no duplicity and only goodwill, while others see it as a borrowing. **Engrave** is likewise seen as a borrowing by some scholars, and by others as an alternative line of semantic evolution from the emphasised idea of open, leading to open up a hole and thus by association engrave (i.e. make a groove). While the latter theory seems somewhat unlikely it should be noted that in Chinese 1108 can also mean empty/ hollow. **Clause** is felt to be an associated meaning with engrave, from the idea of a piece of writing that is endowed with permanence. Suggest taking 士 as **samurai** 494, with 示 in its other meaning of **show**. It should also be noted that 1108 is occasionally encountered written as 欵 , resulting from graphic confusion between 素 and the 'lost person' element of doubt 矣 835.

Mnemonic: **SAMURAI SHOWS LACK OF FRIENDSHIP**

1109		**KAN** **LEISURE, QUIET** 12 strokes	閑静 **KANSEI**	tranquility
			閑散 **KANSAN**	leisure, quiet
			閑人 **KANJIN**	idle person

木 is tree/ **wood** 69, while 門 is gate 211. 1109 originally referred to a **piece of wood used to bar a gate**, and meant **block/ obstruct/ defend** (meanings still found in Chinese). **Leisure** results from confusion with **space** 閒 / 間 92, which once had an associated meaning of **free time**, while **quietude/ quiet** is in turn an associated meaning with leisure.

Mnemonic: **BUILD WOODEN GATE IN A QUIET MOMENT OF LEISURE**

1110	寛	**KAN, kutsurog*u*** **MAGNANIMOUS, RELAX** 13 strokes	寛大 **KANDAI**	liberality
			寛容 **KANYŌ**	tolerance
			寛衣 **KANI**	loose clothes

Somewhat obscure. Formerly 寬 . 宀 is **house/ roof** 28. 莧 is found as a CO character with the unhelpful meaning of vegetables, but it is not certain that this is the same character as the 莧 / 莧 element of 1110. (If it is, then its present meaning is presumably borrowed.) The latter was once written 寬, showing that 卄 is not grass/ plant 艸 9 but apparently a derivative of a **crest** of some sort 艿. 見 is the old form 見 of (**bend down to**) **look** 見 18, with ヽ / ・ possibly some form of **support**. Its meaning is unclear, though in the case of 1110 it is known to have acted phonetically to express **big**, thus giving a meaning of **big house**. By association this came to mean a place where one could **relax**, i.e. where one was not cramped, and it also developed associated figurative connotations of **'easy going'/ largesse/ magnanimity**. Suggest taking 見 as **see** and 卄 as **grass**, with 宀 as **cover**.

Mnemonic: **SEE GRASS COVERED SPOT AND RELAX THERE**

1111

KAN
SUPERVISE, WATCH
15 strokes

監視 KANSHI　　　observation
総監 SŌKAN　　　superintendent
監禁 KANKIN　　　imprisonment

Once written 監, showing a **person** ル/ト 39 bending over to **stare** 臣/臣 512 q.v. at the **surface of water** 一 in a **bowl** 皿/皿 1307. The person was **staring at his reflection**, which was the original meaning of 1111, but this then came to mean **look carefully** and hence **supervise/ watch**. Suggest taking 臣 literally as **staring eye**, and 一 as **one** 1. See also 991.

Mnemonic: **PERSON WITH ONE STARING EYE WATCHES BOWL**

1112

KAN, yurui/mu/meru/yaka
LOOSE, EASY, SLACK
15 strokes

緩和 KANWA　　　mitigation
緩流 KANRYŪ　　gentle current
緩緩 YURUYURU　　leisurely

糸 is **thread** 27, here meaning **cord**. 爰 is draw to oneself 932 q.v., here acting phonetically to express **loose(ly)** and also lending an idea of **pulling on a rope/ cord** and hence **bind**. Thus to **bind something loosely with cord**. **Slack** is now also used figuratively, in the sense of **easy**. Suggest taking 爰 as **three hands** (i.e. reaching hand ⺧ 303, hand 又, and hand 于 [variant 手 32]).

Mnemonic: **THREE HANDS RESULT IN LOOSELY TIED THREAD**

1113

KAN, uramu
REGRET
16 strokes

遺憾 IKAN na　　　regrettable
憾恨 KANKON　　　grudge
憾み URAMI　　　regret

Heart/ feeling 忄 147 and (intense) feeling 感 246, to give **doubly intense feeling**. An intense feeling is one that lingers in the heart, a somewhat vague reference to **regret**. (Some scholars feel that 感 also acts phonetically to express **regret**, thus clarifying the meaning.) See also 1277, and note the overlap between resent and regret.

Mnemonic: **REGRET IS DOUBLY STRONG FEELING**

355

1114		KAN RETURN 16 strokes	還元 KANGEN	restoration
			生還者 SEIKANSHA	survivor
			返還 HENKAN	restitution

辶 is **movement** 129, here meaning **go**. 睘 is a CO character meaning **gaze in terror**. Its etymology is not fully clear but it appears to comprise **eye** 罒/目 72, here presumably meaning **look**, and a variant 袁 of **sorrow** 哀 998, and presumably originally meant **look of sorrow**. Here it acts phonetically to express **turn back**, and may possibly also have originally lent connotations of **alarm** and/or **despair**. Thus to **go back/ return (in alarm/ despair?)**, now **return** in a broad sense.

Mnemonic: **RETURN, MOVING WITH SORROWFUL LOOK**

1115	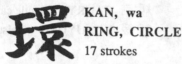	KAN, wa RING, CIRCLE 17 strokes	指環 YUBIWA	finger ring
			環状線 KANJŌSEN	loop line
			環境 KANKYŌ	environment

Jewel 王 102 and **gaze in terror** 睘 1114 q.v. The latter acts phonetically to express **fit**, and may possibly also lend an idea of **looking in awe** (i.e. at something **wondrous**). 1115 originally referred to a **jeweled ring or bracelet (of wondrous quality?) that fitted perfectly**, and later came to mean **ring** or **circle** in a broad sense. Suggest taking 睘 in its assumed literal meaning of **sorrowful** 袁 (variant sorrow 哀 998) **look** 罒 (variant eye 目 72).

Mnemonic: **JEWELED RING EVOKES SORROWFUL LOOK**

1116		KAN WARSHIP 21 strokes	軍艦 GUNKAN	warship
			艦隊 KANTAI	fleet
			艦種 KANSHU	warship class

舟 is **boat/ ship** 1354. 監 is **watch (over)** 1111, here acting phonetically to express **protected** (by cladding) and possibly also lending its own idea of **watch over**. Thus a **ship which is protected (and which watches over other ships?)**, i.e. a **warship**.

Mnemonic: **SHIP THAT WATCHES OVER OTHERS IS A WARSHIP**

1117 KAN, kanga*miru* 年鑑 NENKAN yearbook
TAKE NOTE, HEED 鑑賞 KANSHŌ appreciation
23 strokes 鑑みて KANGAMITE in view of

金 is **metal** 14. 監 is **watch** 1111 q.v., here with its literal meaning of **stare at one's reflection**. Thus to **stare at one's reflection in a metal mirror** (metal mirror still being listed as a meaning in Chinese). This came to mean **scrutinise** and hence **take note of/ heed**. Note that the verb kangamiru derives from kagami (mirror) and miru (look).

Mnemonic: **WATCH SELF IN METAL MIRROR, HEEDING REFLECTION**

1118 GAN, fuku*mu*/*meru* 包含 HŌGAN inclusion
INCLUDE, CONTAIN 含有量 GANYŪRYŌ content
7 strokes 含めて FUKUMETE including

口 is **mouth** 20. 今 is **now** 125 q.v., here in its literal sense of **cover**. Thus **covered by the mouth**, i.e. **contained in the mouth**, leading to **contain** and by association **include**. See also 1182.

Mnemonic: **NOW CONTAINED IN THE MOUTH**

1119 GAN 頑固 GANKO stubbornness
STUBBORN 頑健 GANKEN robust health
13 strokes 頑張る GANBARU persevere

頁 is **head** 93. 元 is **origin** 106 q.v., here rather unusually acting in three roles. First, it lends its literal meaning of **head**, and by extension **brain** and **thought**. 106 also often has connotations of **roundness**, partly because of the round shape of the head and partly because its sound (GAN) is the same as the sound for round (GAN 丸 830), and its second role in the case of 1119 is to lend such connotations (and/or it may be taken to act phonetically to express round). Third, it lends its later meaning of **origin**. 1119 could literally mean a **person with a round head**, but it was also used to refer to a person whose **thinking went round in circles** (i.e. back to the origin), i.e. a **stubborn** person.

Mnemonic: **STUBBORN HEAD GOES ROUND AND BACK TO ORIGIN**

1120	KI, kuwada*teru* **PLAN, UNDERTAKE** 6 strokes	企業 KIGYŌ	enterprise
		企画 KIKAKU	plan
		企て KUWADATE	plot, scheme

人 is a variant of **person** 人 39. 止 is **foot** 129, here also acting phonetically to express **precarious**. 1120 originally meant **person of precarious footing**, a reference to a person **standing on tiptoe** (still a meaning in Chinese). Stand on tiptoe led to a wide range of associated/ extended meanings, such as stand erect, look out, and be alarmed (all still found in Chinese), while in Japanese the idea of **standing up in some alarm** led to **take action**, which in turn led to **undertake** and by association **plan**. Suggest taking 止 in its commoner meaning of **stop**.

Mnemonic: **PERSON STOPS AND PLANS UNDERTAKING**

1121	KI **FORK** 7 strokes	岐路 KIRO	forked road
		分岐 BUNKI	divergence
		多岐 TAKI	many directions

山 is **mountain** 24. 支 is **branch** 691, here acting phonetically to express **fork** and probably also lending an idea of **branching/ bifurcation**. 1121 originally referred to a specific mountain in ancient China noted for its **twin peaks**, then came to mean **forked mountain** in general and eventually just **fork**.

Mnemonic: **BRANCHED MOUNTAIN IS FORKED**

1122 忌	KI, i*mu*/*mawashii* **MOURN, ABHOR,** **ODIOUS** 7 strokes	忌中 KICHŪ	mourning
		禁忌 KINKI	taboo
		忌み嫌う IMIKIRAU	detest

心 is **heart**/feeling 147. 己 is **self** 855 q.v., here acting phonetically to express **abhor** and possibly also lending an idea of **thoroughly** from its literal meaning of thread from end to end. Thus **feeling of (total?) abhorrence**. **Odious** is an associated meaning. **Mourn** is also seen as an associated meaning, since something abhorred was usually something shunned, which came to mean something taboo. Taboos were frequently associated with conventions observed during mourning. Note that there is an occasionally encountered form 忌, which appears to have mistaken 己 for bending body/ serpent 己 (see 250) and used a variant form 巳 of this (also 250).

Mnemonic: **ABHOR ONESELF IN ONE'S HEART**

| 1123 | KI
STRANGE, ODD
8 strokes | 奇数 KISŪ
新奇 SHINKI
奇形 KIKEI | odd number
novelty
deformity |

Somewhat obscure, though its elements are clearly **big** 大 53 q.v. and **can** 可 816 q.v. Some scholars take the latter to act phonetically to express **one-legged** and take 大 to mean literally **standing person**, thus giving **person standing on one leg**, which is something **strange**. Note that there is a CO character 踦 which means one-legged, combining 1123 with the foot/ leg radical 足 51. It is possible that in the latter case 奇 itself acts phonetically to express one-legged (as well as lending a meaning of strange), or else that leg 足 was simply added to 奇 (assuming for argument's sake that this does mean one-legged) for clarity. However, it seems unlikely that a spoken word meaning one-legged existed, and more likely that 可 lent its connotations of **twisted** (and possibly also acted in some unclear phonetic role), giving either a **person standing in a twisted fashion** or else something **greatly twisted**. In view of the association between twisted and odd (see 1041), the 'greatly twisted' theory seems the most likely. (踦 would then mean greatly twisted leg, leading to cripple and presumably later also amputee.)

Mnemonic: **SOMETHING BIG CAN BE SOMETHING STRANGE**

| 1124 | KI, ino*ru*
PRAY, HOPE
8 strokes | 祈念 KINEN
祈とう KITŌ
祈り合う INORIAU | prayer
prayer
pray together |

Formerly 祈. 示/ネ is **altar/ of the gods** 695. 斤 is **ax** 1176, acting phonetically to express **desire/ wish**. Thus **desire something of the gods**, i.e. **pray** or **hope**.

Mnemonic: **AX AT ALTAR ENFORCES PRAYER**

| 1125 | KI
TRACK, RUT, WAY
9 strokes | 軌道 KIDŌ
無軌道 MUKIDŌ no
常軌 JŌKI | track, orbit
wayward
normal way |

車 is **vehicle** 31. 九 is **nine** 12, acting phonetically to express **parallel**. Thus **that which is parallel and associated with a vehicle**, a somewhat vague reference to its **tracks/ ruts**. Later **track/ path** in a broad sense.

Mnemonic: **TRACK RUTTED AFTER NINE VEHICLES PASS**

1126		KI, sude	既 製 KISEI	ready-made
		ALREADY, FINISHED	既 婚 KIKON	married
		10 strokes	既 定 KITEI	established

Formerly 旣. 皀/皀 are variants of food/ eat 食 146. 旡 is without 688 q.v. Thus **without food**, indicating that one has **already finished** it. Suggest taking 旡 literally as **long haired kneeling man**.

Mnemonic: **HAIRY KNEELING MAN HAS ALREADY FINISHED EATING**

1127		KI, u*eru*	飢 寒 KIKAN	hunger and cold
		STARVE, HUNGER	飢 え 死 に UEJINI	death from hunger
		10 strokes	飢 餓 行 進 KIGAKŌSHIN	
				hunger march

食 is **food/ eat** 146. 几 is **table** 832, acting phonetically to express **few/ little** and probably also lending its meaning of **table**. Thus **little food (on the table?)**, indicating **hunger** and **starvation**.

Mnemonic: **FOOD ON THE TABLE, BUT STILL STARVING**

1128		KI, oni	鬼 界 KIKAI	nether world
		DEVIL, DEMON, GHOST	鬼 籍 KISEKI	the dead
		10 strokes	鬼 ごっこ ONIGOKKO	tag (game)

From a pictograph 鬼, showing a **person crouching** ﾉﾚ/ﾉﾚ 39 wearing a **mask** ⊕/ 甶 807. This was actually a **death-mask**, worn in a religious ritual in which contact was made with **spirits of the dead**. Thus the masked figure came to represent **spirits/ ghosts**, which for some reason came to acquire frequently malicious connotations. The later addition ム is seen by some scholars as a graphic derivative of the kneeling figure's lower leg, but by others as nose/self 134 used phonetically to express **dead/ death** and thus clarify the nature of the mask. Suggest remembering by association with think/ **thought** 思 131 q.v., taking ﾉ凵 as a **'distorted' heart** 心 (147).

Mnemonic: **DISTORTED HEART PRODUCES DEVILISH THOUGHT**

| 1129 | | KI, iku-
HOW MANY, HOW MUCH
12 strokes | 幾何学 KIKAGAKU geometry
幾つ IKUTSU how many?
幾ら IKURA how much? |

幺幺 is a doubling of (short) thread 111, the doubling indicating many. 戈 is a variant of **broad bladed halberd** 515/ 246 q.v., here used in its sense of **trim/ put into shape** and also lending its sound to express **control**. Thus **that which controls threads and puts them into shape**, i.e. a **loom**. This is now conveyed by 機 453, which adds wood 木 69, while 1129 itself has undergone a convoluted change of meaning. Controlling threads on a loom came to represent **predictable movement**, which by association came to mean **predictable quantity** and hence **how many/ how much**.

Mnemonic: **HOW MANY SHORT THREADS CAN A HALBERD TRIM?**

| 1130 | 棋 | KI
(ORIENTAL) CHESS
12 strokes | 棋士 KISHI go/shogi player
将棋 SHŌGI Japanese chess
棋敵 KITEKI chess opponent |

Formerly also 棊 . 木 is **wood** 69. 其 is **winnowing device** 251, here acting phonetically to express **little** and possibly also lending loose connotations of **selecting**. Thus **little wooden pieces (which are selected?)**, a reference to **chess pieces** and hence **chess** itself. See also 1240.

Mnemonic: **PLAY WITH WOODEN CHESS PIECES WHILE WINNOWING**

| 1131 | | KI, su*teru*
ABANDON, RENOUNCE
13 strokes | 放棄 HŌKI abandonment
棄権 KIKEN abstention
棄児 KIJI abandoned child |

Once written 棄 , showing **newborn child** 古 / 云 227 (literally inverted child 子 / 子 25) and **hands** 廾. The hands are actually **throwing away** the child, though since this is not especially clear later forms such as 棄 (the prototype of the modern form) added a **broom** 箒, which symbolised **clearing away/ disposing**. To **abandon a child** came to mean **abandon** in general. Suggest remembering by association with **leaf** 葉 405, from which distinguish.

Mnemonic: **ABANDON CHILD, TOSSING AWAY LIKE A LEAF**

1132		KI, kagaya*ku*/*kashii*	光輝 KŌKI	luster, splendor
		SPARKLE, SHINE	輝石 KISEKI	pyroxene
		15 strokes	輝き KAGAYAKI	light

Correctly written 煇 , though in practice **fire** 火 8 was some time ago replaced by **light** 光 116. 軍 is **army** 466, acting phonetically to express **light** but of unknown semantic role. Thus **firelight**, now **shine/ sparkle** in a broad sense.

Mnemonic: **ARMY PROVIDES SHINING LIGHT**

1133		KI	騎士 KISHI	rider, knight
		RIDER	騎兵 KIHEI	cavalry
		18 strokes	一騎打ち IKKIUCHI	single combat

馬 is **horse** 191. 奇 is **strange** 1123, acting phonetically to express **straddle** but of unknown semantic role. Thus to **straddle a horse**, i.e. **ride**, though now usually found in the sense of **rider**.

Mnemonic: **RIDER ON STRANGE HORSE**

1134		GI, yoro*shii*	適宜 TEKIGI	suitability
		GOOD, RIGHT	便宜 BENGI	convenience
		8 strokes	宜しく YOROSHIKU	
				well, best regards

Though long written as **roof/ building** 宀 28 and **furthermore/ cairn/ pile up** 且 1091, very old forms such as 〔〕 show (a bird's eye view of) **meat** 冉 / 月 / 肉 365 (doubled to indicate considerable quantity) on the **sacrificial slab** 臼 of an altar (= presumably being **grooves** to let blood drain). 1134 is to all intents and purposes a variant of the NGU character 俎 , which also means sacrificial altar (and in modern times chopping board) and shows a similar miscopying resulting in pile up 且, with 仌 being additional meat (technically the grains 仌 of meat seen in 肉). **Good/ right** is an associated meaning, i.e. offering meat in a sacrifice being **proper** behavior.

Mnemonic: **FURTHERMORE, GOOD BUILDING IS RIGHT FOR SACRIFICE**

1135 偽	GI, nise, itsuwaru FALSE, LIE 11 strokes	偽物 NISEMONO	forgery
		偽善 GIZEN	sacrifice
		偽り者 ITSUWARIMONO	liar

Formerly 僞 . イ is **person** 39. 爲/爲 is **do/ purpose** 1003 q.v., here acting phonetically to express **change** and almost certainly also lending connotations of **imitate**. 1135 originally referred to a **person changing his appearance in order to imitate** someone, and thus came to mean **deception** and **falsehood**.

Mnemonic: **PERSON LIES TO SUIT OWN PURPOSES**

1136 欺	GI, azamuku CHEAT, DECEIVE 12 strokes	詐欺 SAGI	fraud
		欺まん GIMAN	deception
		欺き取る AZAMUKITORU	defraud

欠 is **lack** 471 q.v., here in its literal sense of **gaping mouth/ yawn**. 其 is **winnowing device** 251, here acting phonetically to express **exhaustion** but of unclear semantic role. Thus to **yawn with exhaustion**. **Cheat/ deceive** is a borowed meaning.

Mnemonic: **LACK WINNOWING DEVICE SO RESORT TO CHEATING**

1137 儀	GI CEREMONY, RULE, CASE 15 strokes	儀式 GISHIKI	ceremony
		儀典 GITEN	rite, ritual
		礼儀 REIGI	etiquette

Person イ 39 and **righteousness** 義 645, to give a **righteous person**. The meaning gradually changed to refer to the **way in which a person becomes righteous**, i.e. **rules, norms,** and **conventions**. **Ceremony** is an associated meaning.

Mnemonic: **RIGHTEOUS PERSON OBEYS RULES IN CEREMONY**

1138 戯	GI, tawamureru PLAY, FROLIC, JOKE 15 strokes	遊戯的 YŪGITEKI	playful
		戯画 GIGA	caricature
		戯言 TAWAGOTO*	gibberish

Formerly also written 戲 . 戈 is **halberd** 493. 虛 is **empty/ hollow** 1156 q.v., here acting phonetically to express **play** and almost certainly also lending figurative connotations of **not in earnest** (虐 fulfils the same phonetic role and probably the same semantic role, with vessel 豆 1640 replacing hollow crowned tall hill 业 1149). Thus **halberd used in play/ sport** (and not in earnest), leading to **play/ frolic** in general.

Mnemonic: **EMPTY THREATS WITH HALBERD -- JUST A JOKE**

1139 GI 模擬 MOGI imitation
IMITATE, MODEL 擬勢 GISEI bluff
17 strokes 擬声 GISEI onomatopoeia

扌 is **hand** 32. 疑 is **doubt** 835 q.v., here acting phonetically to express **confusion** and also lending similar connotations of its own. Thus to **cause confusion with the hands**, meaning to **make something resembling something else**, i.e. **imitate/ model**.

Mnemonic: **MAKE DOUBTFUL IMITATION BY HAND**

1140 GI 犠牲 GISEI sacrifice
SACRIFICE 犠打 GIDA baseball sacrifice hit
17 strokes 犠牲制度 GISEISEIDO
sacrificial system

Formerly also 犠. 牛 is **cow/ bull** 97. 義 is a CO character now meaning breath. Its etymology is somewhat obscure, but its elements are sheep/ excellent ⺷ 986 q.v., halberd/ cut 戈 493, rice plant 禾 81, and seek exit 丂 281 (possibly here meaning grow), and it may originally have meant cut excellently grown rice, i.e. a **fine crop**. Breath may be a borrowed meaning, or else an associated meaning from the idea of life-giving. Here it acts phonetically to express **good**, and probably also lends similar connotations. The later form uses **righteousness** 義 645, which likewise acts phonetically to express **good** and also lends similar connotations. Thus **good bull**, a reference to a bull of outstanding quality which was chosen as a **sacrifice** (see also 760).

Mnemonic: **RIGHTEOUS BULL IS JUST RIGHT FOR SACRIFICE**

1141 KIKU 野菊 NOGIKU aster
CHRYSANTHEMUM 菊花 KIKKA chrysanthemum
11 strokes 菊判 KIKUBAN small octavo

Plant 艹 9, **encircle** 勹 655 (here meaning **circle**), and **rice grains/ head of rice** 米 201 (here meaning **head of plant**). Thus **plant with a circular head**, a reference to the **chrysanthemum**.

Mnemonic: **CHRYSANTHEMUM PLANT ENCIRCLED BY RICE**

1142 吉 KICHI, KITSU   吉日 KICHINICHI   lucky day
GOOD LUCK, JOY   吉報 KIPPŌ   good news
6 strokes   不吉 FUKITSU   ill omen

Of confused etymology. Once written 吉, showing a **double-lidded** 士 **container**
口. Such a container potentially symbolised **plenty** and hence **good fortune** and **contentment**. In the case of go/ leave 去 258 q.v. it confusingly suggests the opposite, but
in the case of 1142 the auspicious connotations appear to have been reinforced by confusion with an ancient character 台, in which 口 is **mouth** 20 and 夅 is a variant of the
early form ϙ of **dam** 土 126 q.v., here meaning **block** and thus giving **blocked
mouth**. This is potentially confusing in itself but is known to have been a reference to **full
mouth**, and hence also symbolised contentment and good fortune. Another ancient character 台 seems to have confused block 夅 with a lid or stopper 今, and it is not clear
whether it means full mouth or lidded container. However, it clearly shows the overlap between **full mouth**, **lidded container**, and **good fortune/ contentment**. **Joy** is an
extension of contentment. Suggest taking 口 as **open mouth** and 士 as **samurai** 494.
See also 1159.

Mnemonic: **SAMURAI OPEN MOUTHED WITH JOY AFTER GOOD LUCK**

1143 喫 KITSU   喫煙 KITSUEN   smoking
INGEST, RECEIVE   喫茶店 KISSATEN   cafe
12 strokes   喫水線 KISSUISEN   waterline

口 is **mouth** 20. 契 is **pledge** 1195 q.v., here acting phonetically to express **chew** and
probably also lending reinforcing connotations of **bringing jagged edges together**.
Thus to **chew in the mouth**, later just **take in/ ingest through the mouth** and also
by extension **take in/ receive** in a broader sense.

Mnemonic: **MOUTH PLEDGED TO INGEST**

1144 詰 KITSU, tsu*mu*/*maru*/*meru*   詰問 KITSUMON   grilling
PACK, PACKED, FULL   詰まり TSUMARI   in short
13 strokes   詰め込む TSUMEKOMU   cram

言 is **words** 274. 吉 is **good luck/ joy** 1142 q.v., here in its meaning of **full mouth/
container** and also acting phonetically to express **extremely**. Thus a **mouth extremely
full of words**, which was originally a reference to grilling/ 'bombarding' with questions
but later came to mean just **full to bursting** in general.

Mnemonic: **WORDS PACKED WITH JOY**

1145

KYAKU, ka*ette*
(ON THE) CONTRARY
7 strokes

却下 KYAKKA　　　rejection
退却 TAIKYAKU　　retreat
却説 SATE*　　　 well now

去 is go/ leave 258. ﾖ is **bending person** 425, here meaning **person on their knees**. Thus to **leave on one's knees**, meaning to leave the presence of a superior. Some scholars take **contrary** to be a borrowing, others an associated meaning from the idea of **withdrawing** and thus **going away from**. The latter seems more likely.

Mnemonic: **LEAVE ON BENDED KNEES, JUST TO BE CONTRARY**

1146

KYAKU, KYA, ashi
LEG, FOOT
11 strokes

脚下 KYAKKA　　at one's feet
脚立 KYATATSU　stepladder
脚荷 ASHINI　　　ballast

却 is **on the contrary** 1145 q.v., here in its literal sense of **leave on one's knees**. 月 is **flesh/ of the body** 365, serving to draw attention to the part of the body involved. Thus the **knee** and by association **leg**, especially the **lower leg** and thus sometimes **foot**.

Mnemonic: **LEG CAN BE CONTRARY TO BODY**

1147

GYAKU, shiita*geru*
CRUELTY, OPPRESS
9 strokes

虐殺 GYAKUSATSU massacre
虐待 GYAKUTAI maltreatment
残虐 ZANGYAKU　　cruelty

Once written 𧇍, showing a **tiger** 白 / 虍 281 **clawing** ﾋ / ∈ **a person** 人 39. This came to represent **cruelty**, with **oppress** being an associated meaning. Person has disappeared in the modern form.

Mnemonic: **TIGER'S CLAWS SYMBOLISE CRUELTY**

1148

及

KYŪ, oyo*bu/bosu/bi*
REACH, EXTEND, AND
3 strokes

及第点 KYŪDAITEN　pass mark
追及 TSUIKYŪ　　　catch up
及び腰 OYOBIGOSHI bent back

Originally 乁𡗗, showing a **person** 乁 39 and a **hand** 又 **reaching** out to seize them. Later forms such as 乁又 show a stylised <u>bent</u> person, the bending being felt to emphasise the idea of the person's attempt to escape. Reach out for an escaping person came to mean **reach** in general, with **extend** being an associated meaning. **And** is also an associated meaning, from the idea of a range of items extending to include an additional one. Note that very occasionally 1148 still appears to retain connotations of bending. Suggest remembering partly by association with **movement** 辶 129.

Mnemonic: **HAND REACHES OUT FOR BENT PERSON MOVING OFF**

366

1149

KYŪ, oka
HILL
5 strokes

砂丘 SAKYŪ   sand dune
丘しん KYŪSHIN   pimple
丘辺 OKABE   near a hill

Originally ᗰ , depicting two **hills**. Later greatly stylised to ᭵ and eventually miscopied as two **persons back to back** 北 / 北 (丿 being person 39), from which the present shape derives. Suggest taking 斤 as **ax** 1176 and — as **ground level**.

Mnemonic: **REDUCE HILL TO GROUND LEVEL WITH AX!**

1150

KYŪ, kuchiru
DECAY, ROT
6 strokes

老朽 RŌKYŪ   decrepitude
不朽 FUKYŪ   imperishability
朽ち葉 KUCHIBA   dead leaves

木 is **tree**/ **wood** 69. 丂 is seek an exit / **twisting waterweed** 281 q.v., acting phonetically to express **rot** and possibly also lending an idea of **twisting**. Thus **rotting (twisted?) wood**, now **rot** in general.

Mnemonic: **TWISTING WEED ON ROTTING TREE**

1151

KYŪ
ENTWINE, EXAMINE
9 strokes

紛糾 FUNKYŪ   complication
糾弾 KYŪDAN   impeachment
糾明 KYŪMEI   examination

糸 is **thread** 27. 丩 is **intertwined threads** 703. Thus **many intertwined threads**, indicating a **tangle** or **complication**. **Examine** is felt by some scholars to be a borrowing, and by others to be an associated meaning. Suggest taking 丩 as a **pitchfork**.

Mnemonic: **EXAMINE ENTWINED THREADS WITH PITCHFORK**

1152

窮

KYŪ, kiwamaru/meru
EXTREME, SUFFER
15 strokes

窮極 KYŪKYOKU   ultimate
窮境 KYŪKYŌ   predicament
窮屈 KYŪKUTSU   constraint

Formerly 竆 . 躬/躳 is an NGU character meaning body. 躬 comprises **body** (of a pregnant woman) 身 323 and backbone 呂 256, and originally referred to a pregnant woman's body **pulling** against the backbone. 弓 is bow 836, here used to convey the same idea of **pulling/distorting**. In the case of 1152 躬 / 躳 acts phonetically to express **extreme** and also lends similar connotations (i.e. from extremely pregnant), as well as lending connotations of **discomfort**. It combines with **hole** 穴 849 q.v., here in its literal sense of **primitive dwelling**, to refer to **uncomfortable** quarters in the **extreme** innermost part of such a dwelling. It later came to mean **be in an extreme situation**, including the idea of **suffering/ constraint**, and can also mean **extreme** in general.

Mnemonic: **BODY BOWED IN HOLE -- EXTREME SUFFERING**

1153		**KYO**	巨人	KYOJIN	giant
		HUGE, GIANT	巨大	KYODAI na	massive
		5 strokes	巨費	KYOHI	great cost

Once written 𠃜 . Some authoritative Japanese scholars take this to be a hole in the base of an ax head into which the handle was inserted, and take **huge** to be a borrowed meaning. Others take it to be a tool similar to a **carpenter's square** 工 113, characterised by its **large** size. Since 1153 has a minor meaning of carpenter's square in Chinese, and since it often lends relevant connotations in compounds (e.g. measuring square 矩 342), the latter theory seems the more likely. The present form appears to have used only half of the character (as 969 etc.), but the reason for this is not clear. Suggest remembering by association with **staring eye** 臣 512, from which distinguish.

Mnemonic: **GIANT CHARACTERISED BY HUGE STARING EYE**

1154		**KYO, koba***mu*	拒絶	KYOZETSU	refusal
		REFUSE, RESIST	拒否	KYOHI	denial
		8 strokes	拒止	KYOSHI	refusal

扌 is **hand** 32. 巨 is **huge** 1153 q.v., here acting phonetically to express **block/ prevent** and possibly also lending loose connotations of **impediment** from its assumed depiction of a huge and presumably cumbersome tool (see also 1078). 1154 originally meant to **hold in check with the hand,** but then came to mean **refrain/ restrain** and hence **refuse** and **resist.**

Mnemonic: **REFUSAL ENFORCED BY HUGE HAND**

1155		**KYO, KO, yo***ru*	根拠	KONKYO	base, basis
		BASE, BASIS	証拠	SHŌKO	proof
		8 strokes	拠り所	YORIDOKORO	grounds

Formerly 攄 and 據 . 扌 is **hand** 32. 處 /処 is **place/ deal with** 896 q.v., here acting phonetically to express **take hold of/ use as a support** and almost certainly also lending its literal meaning of **resting/ leaning upon.** 豦 is tiger attacking pig 848, which acts in a similar phonetic role and also lends connotations of taking hold of. Thus **that which one takes hold of with the hand by way of support,** i.e. a **prop,** with **base/ basis** being an extended meaning.

Mnemonic: **HANDS IN PLACE, GIVING FIRM BASE**

368

| 1156 虚 | KYO, KO, uro
EMPTY, HOLLOW, DIP
11 strokes | 虚偽 KYOGI　　　falsehood
虚空 KOKŪ　　empty space
虚無主義 KYOMUSHUGI nihilism |

Formerly 虛 and earlier 虘. 北/业 are early forms of **hill** 丘 1149 q.v. 臼/虍 is **tiger** 281, here acting phonetically to express **big** and possibly also lending connotations of **awesome**. 1156 originally meant **large and imposing hill**. The shape of 北 suggested a hill with a **hollow crown**, such as an extinct volcano, and this came to mean **empty/ hollow** in a broad sense. Note that 1156 can mean specifically a **hollow/ dip in the ground**. Note also that this is read uro, and distinguish both this reading and the character itself from the similar NGU character uso 嘘 , which combines empty with mouth/ say 口 20 and means a lie. Suggest remembering 业 by association with row/ **line up** 並 1775.

Mnemonic: **EMPTY TIGERS LINED UP IN HOLLOW**

| 1157 距 | KYO
DISTANCE, COCKSPUR
12 strokes | 距離 KYORI　　　distance
距骨 KYOKOTSU anklebone
測距儀 SOKKYOGI range finder |

足 is leg/ **foot** 51. 巨 is **huge** 1153, here acting phonetically to express **spear**/ lance and also lending a meaning of **big**. Thus **big spear on the foot**, a reference to a **cockspur**. It still retains this as a lesser meaning in Chinese, and it is also found very occasionally in related meanings in Japanese (e.g. see anklebone above). Cockspur came to mean by association **repel**, which in turn came to mean **keep at a distance** and hence **distance** in a broader sense.

Mnemonic: **HUGE FOOT COVERS GREAT DISTANCE**

| 1158 | GYO, GO, o[n]-, mi-
HANDLE, DRIVE,
HONORABLE, YOUR
12 or 11 strokes | 御者 GYOSHA　　　driver
御用 GOYŌ　　your business
御中 ONCHŪ　　　Messrs |

A combination of **movement (along a road)** 彳 118/129 q.v. and 卸 . The latter is a now defunct character meaning **pound/ soften**, comprising **bending person** 卩 425 and **pestle** 午 110. Pound/ soften came by figurative extension to mean **make tractable/ manageable**, and thus **handle/ control**. In combination with movement along a road 彳 it came to mean **drive a team of horses/ vehicle**, either being confused with or deliberately merged with 馭, the prototype of a character 馭 . This shows **horse** 馬

369

/馬 191 and **striking hand** 攵 (technically 攴 101, but now simply hand 又). In Chinese 馭 is interchangeable with 1158, but in Japanese it exists as a separate NGU character meaning **drive horses**. 1158 itself can still mean specifically **drive a cart/ carriage**, especially with connotations of tradesman's cart, and also retains connotations of **handling** and **controlling** in a more general sense. It later came to acquire a meaning of **imperial** as a result of its being used instead of the more complex 禦 , an NGU character meaning prevent/ bar. This comprises **drive a cart** 御 and 示 , which is not show 示 695 but a simplification of **prohibit** 禁 654, and its original meaning was equivalent to the modern expression **"tradesmen's vehicles prohibited"**. This was originally a reference to the **grounds of the imperial palace**, but the character later became used as a reference to **imperial** in a broad sense. In Chinese it still has a strong meaning of imperial, but in Japanese has come by extension to be used as a general **honorific prefix**. See also 1042.

Mnemonic: **BENDING PERSON HANDLES HONORABLE PESTLE WITH UNUSUAL MOVEMENT**

1159		KYŌ	凶 悪	KYŌAKU na	atrocious
		BAD LUCK, DISASTER	凶 作	KYŌSAKU	bad harvest
		4 strokes	吉 凶	KIKKYŌ	one's fortune

凵 is a **container** (some scholars see it as a variant of **mouth** 口 20), while 乂 is a symbol **drawing attention**, in this case to the inside of the container/ mouth. This was a potentially confusing reference to the fact that the container/ mouth was **empty** (some scholars feel that 乂 also acted phonetically to express empty, thereby clarifying the meaning). By contrast with full container/ mouth 吉 1142, which indicated good fortune, the **empty container/ mouth** of 1159 indicated **ill fortune**.

Mnemonic: **X INDICATES BOX IS EMPTY -- WHAT BAD LUCK**

1160		KYŌ, sakebu	絶 叫	ZEKKYŌ	scream
叫		**SHOUT, YELL**	叫 び 声	SAKEBIGOE	shout, yell
		6 strokes	叫 び 出 す	SAKEBIDASU	cry out

口 is **mouth/ say** 20. 丩 is entwined threads 703, here acting phonetically to express **sudden** and possibly also lending connotations of complication/ **difficulty**. Thus to **make a sudden sound with the mouth**, i.e. **cry out (in difficulty?)**. Suggest taking 丩 as a **pitchfork**.

Mnemonic: **PITCHFORK IN MOUTH EVOKES YELL**

1161 狂 **KYŌ, kuru*u*** 狂人 KYŌJIN lunatic
LUNATIC, MAD 狂言 KYŌGEN farce
7 strokes 狂った KURUTTA crazy

Once written 犭㞷. 犭/犬 is **dog** 17. 㞷 is a variant of the prototype 㞷 of emperor 皇 861 q.v., which literally shows a crown 白 on a **king** 王 5, and in the modern form only king 王 has been retained. 㞷 / 王 acts here phonetically to express **convulsion**, but any semantic role is unclear. 1161 originally referred to a **convulsing dog**, i.e. a **mad dog**, and later came to mean **mad** in general.

Mnemonic: **THE KING IS A MAD DOG**

1162 享 **KYŌ** 享受者 KYŌJUSHA recipient
RECEIVE, HAVE 享有 KYŌYŪ possession
8 strokes 享楽 KYŌRAKU enjoyment

From an ideograph 亯 (later 亯 and hence the modern form), showing a **castle watchtower** 高 extending in two directions to indicate **on both sides/ on all sides.** This was a representation of a **well guarded castle**, which was the original meaning. The present meaning is a borrowing. Suggest taking 亠 as a **lid**, 口 as **mouth** 20, and 子 as **child** 25.

Mnemonic: **CHILD RECEIVES LID OVER MOUTH**

1163 況 **KYŌ, ma*shite*** 状況 JŌKYŌ situation
MORE SO, SITUATION 実況 JIKKYŌ real situation
8 strokes 況んや IWANYA* still more

Formerly also written 况, i.e. with ice 冫 378 instead of **water** 氵 40. 兄 is **elder brother** 267, here acting phonetically to express **very cold** and possibly also lending connotations of big. 1163 originally referred to (a big expanse of?) **icy cold water**. Its present meanings are borrowed, though in the case of **more so** it technically appears to have been used as a simplification of two talking persons 兄兄 475 q.v., which could be used to represent the idea of plurality and addition and hence moreover/ more so.

Mnemonic: **WET SITUATION -- FOR ELDER BROTHER EVEN MORE SO**

1164

KYŌ
RAVINE, GORGE
9 strokes

峡谷 KYŌKOKU ravine, gorge
地峡 CHIKYŌ isthmus
海峡 KAIKYŌ strait(s)

Formerly 峽 . 山 is **mountain** 24. 夾 is an NGU character meaning **insert**, deriving from a (big) **person** 大 53 **squeezed between** two other **persons** 人 39. Thus **that which is squeezed between mountains**, i.e. a **ravine/ gorge**. Suggest taking 夾 as **man** 夫 573 and **out of** ㇏ 66.

Mnemonic: MAN TRIES TO GET OUT OF MOUNTAIN GORGE

1165

KYŌ, hasa*maru/mu*
INSERT, PINCH,
SQUEEZE BETWEEN
9 strokes

挟撃 KYŌGEKI pincer attack
板挟み ITABASAMI dilemma
挟み虫 HASAMIMUSHI earwig

Formerly 挾 . 扌is **hand** 32. 夾 is **insert/ squeeze** between 1164 q.v. Thus to **squeeze by hand**, now **squeeze in/ squeeze between** in general. Note that the addition of metal 金 14 to 夾 gives the NGU character hasami/ scissors 鋏 . Suggest taking 夾 as **man** 夫 573 and **away** ㇏ 66.

Mnemonic: MAN SQUEEZED BY HAND CAN'T GET AWAY

1166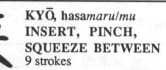

KYŌ, sema*i*
NARROW, SMALL
9 strokes

狭義 KYŌGI narrow sense
広狭 KŌKYŌ extent, area
狭苦しい SEMAKURUSHII
cramped

Formerly 狹 and earlier 陜 , showing that **dog** 犭 17 is a miscopying of **hill** 阝/阝 229. 夾 is **insert/ squeeze** 1164 q.v. Thus the original meaning of 1166 was **that squeezed between hills**. Although 'that squeezed between mountains' referred to a gorge (see 1164), this was a reference to a **narrow strip of (arable) land**. It now means **narrow** in a general sense. Suggest taking 夾 as **man** 夫 573 and **away** ㇏ 66.

Mnemonic: MAN TRIES TO GET AWAY FROM DOG IN NARROW LANE

1167

KYŌ, oso*reru/roshii*
FEAR, AWE
10 strokes

恐怖 KYŌFU fear
恐英病 KYŌEIBYŌ Anglophobia
恐れ入る OSOREIRU be awed, sorry

心 is **heart/ feelings** 147. 卭 is **hand striking instrument** 751, here acting phonetically to express **fear** and possibly also lending a meaning of **strike**. Thus **(struck by?) feelings of fear**. **Awe** is an associated meaning. Suggest taking 卭 as **work/ worker** 工 113 and **mediocre** 凡 1827.

Mnemonic: STRIKE FEAR INTO HEART OF MEDIOCRE WORKER

1168		**KYŌ, uyauya***shii* **RESPECTFUL** 10 strokes	恭順 KYŌJUN 恭敬 KYŌKEI 恭謙 KYŌKEN	obedience respect deference

小 is a variant of **heart/ feelings** 心 147. 共 is **together** 460 q.v., here in its literal sense of **hands offering up a precious object**. The **feelings of the giver** symbolise **respectfulness**.

Mnemonic: **RESPECTFUL FEELINGS GO TOGETHER WITH GIVING**

1169		**KYŌ, odo***[ka]su,* **obiya***kasu* **THREATEN, COERCE** 10 strokes	脅迫 KYŌHAKU 脅威 KYŌI 脅かして ODOKASHITE	threat threat, menace by threats

劦 is **strong arm/ strength** 力 74 trebled for emphasis, indicating **great force/ pressure**. 月 is **flesh/ of the body**. Thus **(put) great pressure upon the body**, now used figuratively as **threaten/ coerce**.

Mnemonic: **THREE STRONG ARMS THREATEN ONE'S BODY**

1170		**KYŌ, ta***meru* **STRAIGHTEN, FALSIFY** 17 strokes	矯正的 KYŌSEITEKI 奇矯 KIKYŌ 矯め直す TAMENAOSU	corrective eccentricity correct

矢 is **arrow** 981. 喬 is tall structure bent at the tip 259, here meaning simply **bent at the tip**. 1170 originally referred to a **bent arrow**, which symbolised something **not straight** and thus by figurative extension **false** and by association **falsify**. Confusingly, it also came to mean an **arrow in need of straightening** and thus eventually by association to **straighten/ correct**. Rather like disturbance 乱 989, which in Chinese can mean both disorder and (bring) order (to chaos), both meanings are still prominent in Chinese despite the fact that they are opposites. In Japanese **straighten/ correct** is by far the major meaning. Suggest remembering 喬 by association with **(arched) bridge** 橋 259.

Mnemonic: **STRAIGHTEN ARROW BENT LIKE ARCHED BRIDGE**

1171

KYŌ, hibik*u*
RESOUND, ECHO,
EFFECT
20 strokes

響き渡る HIBIKIWATARU resound
悪影響 AKUEIKYŌ bad influence
交響曲 KŌKYŌKYOKU
　　　　　　　　symphony

Formerly 響 . 音 is **sound** 6. 郷/鄉 is **village** 841 q.v., here in its sense of **village feast**. Thus the **sound of a village feast**, i.e. the noise and hubbub of a crowd of people. This was a **far-reaching noise**, giving **resound** and **echo**, with **effect/ repercussion** being a figurative extension of this.

Mnemonic: **SOUND OF VILLAGE FEAST ECHOES AFAR**

1172

KYŌ, odoro*ku/kasu*
SURPRISE
22 strokes

驚異 KYŌI 　　miracle, wonder
驚がく KYŌGAKU 　　　　shock
驚くべき ODOROKUBEKI startling

馬 is **horse** 191. 敬 is **respect/ respectful** 846 q.v., here acting phonetically to express **startle** and possibly also lending connotations of **timidity/ nervousness** or of **forcing obedience**. Thus a **startled horse** (which is **nervous?**/ which one **attempts to control?**), leading to **startle/ surprise** in general.

Mnemonic: **SURPRISINGLY RESPECTFUL HORSE**

1173

GYŌ, KŌ, ao*gu*, *ōse*
LOOK UP, STATE,
RESPECT
6 strokes

仰天 GYŌTEN 　　amazement
信仰 SHINKŌ 　　faith, creed
仰せ出す ŌSEDASU 　　proclaim

卬 is a CO character meaning **raise**. It was once written 卬 , showing **bending person** Ʒ 145 (now bending person 卩 425) **looking up respectfully** at another **person** ┌ 39. A further person 亻 39 was added later, though its role tends to confuse and look 見 18 or eye 目 72 would have seemed a more logical choice (giving 䁈 or 䀐). **State** is an associated meaning, from the idea of being granted an audience with one's lord.

Mnemonic: **BENDING PERSON LOOKS UP RESPECTFULLY AT OTHERS**

1174	**GYŌ**, akatsuki	暁天 GYŌTEN	dawn
	DAWN, LIGHT, EVENT	通暁 TSŪGYŌ	conversancy
	12 strokes	暁星 GYŌSEI	Venus, rarity

Formerly 曉 . 日 is **sun/ day** 62. 堯 is **high** 509, here acting phonetically to express **clear** and almost certainly also lending a meaning of **rise**. Thus **when the sun rises and the day becomes clear**, i.e. **dawn**. Also used figuratively in the sense of **enlightenment**. **Event** is a minor associated meaning. Suggest remembering 堯 by association with **burn** 焼 509.

Mnemonic: **BURNING SUN RISES AT DAWN**

1175	**GYŌ**, ko*ru/rasu*	凝視 GYŌSHI	stare
	STIFF, ENGROSSED,	凝り性 KORISHŌ	fastidiousness
	ELABORATE	凝った KOTTA	elaborate
	16 strokes		

冫 is **ice** 378. 疑 is **doubt** 835 q.v., here acting phonetically to express **stiff/ immobile** and also lending connotations of **not moving** (from its literal meaning of not knowing how to proceed). Thus **firmly frozen ice**. Ice has now faded as a semantic element, leaving just **stiff** and **immobile**. Like the English term stick/ stickler, it also has connotations of **fastidiousness** (i.e. not budging), and by further figurative extension **elaborate** (i.e. from attention to detail). **Engrossed** is an associated meaning, from the idea of not moving from something.

Mnemonic: **DOUBT IF ICE IS STIFF ENOUGH**

1176	**KIN**	斤量 KINRYŌ	weight
	AX, WEIGHT	斤目 KINME	weight
	4 strokes	ふ斤 FUKIN	ax

From a pictograph of an **ax with a shaped handle** 𠂆 . Ax is nowadays usually conveyed by an NGU character 斧, which adds **striking hand** 父 197. 1176 was borrowed to express the **kin weight** (600 grams). Suggest taking it as resembling a **hacksaw** 𠂆 .

Mnemonic: **HACKSAW-LIKE AX**

1177		KIN FUNGUS, BACTERIA 11 strokes	細菌 SAIKIN	bacteria
			菌類 KINRUI	fungi
			保菌者 HOKINSHA	germ carrier

サ is **plant** 9. 囷 is a CO character meaning granary, comprising **rice plant** 禾 81 q.v. and **enclosure** 囗 123. It acts here phonetically to express **shade** and also lends connotations of a **plant with prominent head** (the literal meaning of 禾) growing in a **delineated** (i.e. **given/ certain**) **area**. Thus a **plant with prominent head growing in a certain shaded area**, a reference to the **mushroom** and other **fungi**. **Bacterium/ bacillus** is an associated meaning.

Mnemonic: **RICE PLANT IN ENCLOSURE DEVELOPS FUNGUS**

1178		KIN, koto KOTO (HARP) 12 strokes	手風琴 TEFŪKIN	accordion
			琴線 KINSEN	heartstrings
			琴づめ KOTOZUME	plectrum

Somewhat obscure. Once written 瑟, taken by some scholars to be a pictograph of an instrument with **strings with bridges** 王王 and a **shaped base** 𝒬, though the positioning of these elements is a little baffling. There is also a theory that the present form 琴 shows the **strings** 王王 and KIN/ **now** 今 125, the latter acting phonetically to express **closed over** and possibly also lending similar connotations from its original meaning of **covered**, thus giving (**instrument with**) **strings and closed over** (**wooden box**), the latter being a reference to the base. Another old form 琴 shows a different arrangement of strings 𝍅 and an early form 金 of KIN/ **gold** 金 14, used in a similar phonetic role but of unclear semantic role. The existence of this second form suggests that the 'strings plus phonetic' theory is correct, but in such case the meaning of 𝒬 is unclear.

Mnemonic: **KOTO HARP NOW HAS STRINGS**

1179		KIN TIGHT, COMPACT 15 strokes	緊張 KINCHŌ	tension
			緊急 KINKYŪ	crisis
			緊密 KINMITSU	compactness

糸 is **thread** 27. 臤 is an NGU character meaning both **hard** and **wise**, though how it acquired these meanings is not clear. It comprises staring eye 臣 512 and hand 又, and may possibly have originally meant a hand pressed hard against an eye, while **wise** might result from its being used as a simplification of **wise** 賢 1221. In any event, it acts here phonetically to express **entwine** and almost certainly also lends a meaning of **hard/ compact**. 1179 thus referred to **threads tangled in a tight knot**, leading to **tight/ compact** in a broad sense. It is also used figuratively in similar fashion to the English term knotted up, i.e. to refer to a highly strung state of nerves or similar.

Mnemonic: **EYE STARES AT HAND BINDING THREAD TIGHT**

1180		KIN, tsutsushi*mu* CIRCUMSPECT 17 strokes	謹厳 KINGEN	seriousness

謹厳 KINGEN — seriousness
謹啓 KINKEI — Dear Sirs
謹んで TSUTSUSHINDE — respectfully

言 is **words** 274. 堇 is the obscure element violet/ **few**/ season 842 q.v., here acting phonetically to express **few** and almost certainly lending similar connotations of its own. Thus **few words**, a reference to **circumspect** behavior. Suggest remembering 堇 by association with **work** 勤 842.

Mnemonic: **BE CIRCUMSPECT AT WORK, USING FEW WORDS**

1181		KIN, eri COLLAR, NECK, HEART 18 strokes

胸襟 KYŌKIN — bosom
襟度 KINDO — magnanimity
襟首 ERIKUBI — nape of neck

衤 is **clothing** 420. 禁 is **forbid**/ **ban** 654, here acting phonetically to express **closed** and almost certainly also lending similar connotations of **not open**. Thus **that part of the clothing which is closed**, a somewhat vague reference to the **collar**. Later **neck area** in a more general sense, including a figurative meaning of **bosom**/ **heart**.

Mnemonic: **COLLARS ARE BANNED ITEMS OF CLOTHING**

1182	吟	GIN RECITE 7 strokes

吟詠 GINEI — recital
吟味 GINMI — scrutiny
吟遊詩人 GINYŪSHIJIN — minstrel

口 is **mouth**/ **say** 20. 今 is **now** 125 q.v., here acting phonetically to express **howl** and possibly also lending loose connotations of **suppress**/ **stifle** from its literal meaning of **cover**. 1182 originally referred to a **howl of pain** (**which one has tried to suppress?**), and later came to mean **drawn out vocal emission** in a broader sense but with particular associations with **recitation**. Note that the same elements of mouth 口 and now 今 are found in include 含 1118 q.v.

Mnemonic: **MOUTH NOW USED FOR RECITING**

1183

KU, ka*keru*, ka*ru*
GALLOP, SPUR ON
14 strokes

先駆者 SENKUSHA   pioneer
駆り出す KARIDASU   flush out
駆け落ち KAKEOCHI   elopement

Formerly 驅 . 馬 is **horse** 191. 區 /区 is **ward**/ section 465/1034 q.v. here acting phonetically to express **strike/ beat** and almost certainly also lending its sound (once **EO/ Ō**) to refer to the cries of exhortation of a rider urging on his horse (now OI/ Ō in Chinese, though confusingly the similar sounding English whoa is intended to have the opposite effect). Thus **beating a horse (and crying Ō)**, i.e. **spurring it on** at the **gallop**.

Mnemonic: **SPURRED ON HORSE GALLOPS THROUGH THE WARD**

1184

GU, oroka
FOOLISH
13 strokes

愚人 GUJIN   fool
愚図る GUZURU   grumble
愚行 GUKŌ   foolish act

心 is **heart/ feelings** 147. 禺 is a CO character now meaning **begin**, though in compounds it often seems to lend a meaning of **not clear** or **not open**. Its etymology is somewhat obscure, but an old form 禺 shows what appears to be a 'clawless' version of **scorpion with twisting tail** 禺 392 (the prototype of **ten thousand** 萬 392), and it is possible that the idea of **twisting** came to symbolise something **convoluted** and hence **obscure/ not clear**. In the case of 1184 it acts phonetically to express **unclear** and almost certainly lends similar connotations of its own. Thus **unclear feelings**. This came to mean **incomprehensible feelings**, and hence by association **irrational** and then **foolish feelings**. Now **foolish** in general. Suggest taking 禺 as a combination of **insect** 虫 56 and **field** 田 59, with 冂 as **long legs**.

Mnemonic: **LONG-LEGGED INSECT IN FIELD GIVES FOOLISH FEELING**

1185

GŪ
BY CHANCE, SPOUSE,
DOLL
11 strokes

偶然 GŪZEN   by chance
偶像 GŪZŌ   idol, image
配偶者 HAIGŪSHA   spouse

亻 is **person** 39. 禺 is the somewhat obscure **begin** 1184 q.v., here acting phonetically to express **meet (by chance)** and possibly also lending connotations of **not predictable** (i.e. not planned). Thus **persons meeting by chance**. On the one hand this led to **by chance** in a general sense, and on the other to **companion**. Companion in turn led to **spouse**. **Doll/ effigy** is believed to stem from the ancient practice of burying effigies with dead persons of rank as companions for them in the after-life. That is, it is taken to be an associated meaning with companion. Suggest taking 禺 as a combination of **insect** 虫 56 and **field** 田 59, with 冂 as **long legs**.

Mnemonic: **BY CHANCE, PERSON FINDS LONG-LEGGED FIELD INSECT**

1186 **GŪ**   奇遇 KIGŪ   chance meeting
     MEET, RECEIVE, TREAT   待遇 TAIGŪ   reception
     12 strokes   不遇 FUGŪ   misfortune

As 偶 1185 q.v., but with person 亻 39 replaced by **movement (along a road)** 辶 129. Thus to **meet (by chance) while moving along a road**. Whereas 1185 developed associations with chance and companionship, 1186 developed associations rather with the **act of meeting**. Eventually the by chance connotation largely disappeared, and ironically 1186 even came instead to have not infrequent connotations of a planned meeting/ reception, leading to **receive/ treat**. As with 1185 and 1184, suggest taking 禺 as a combination of **insect** 虫 56 and **field** 田 59, with 冂 as **long legs**.

Mnemonic: **MEET LONG-LEGGED INSECT MOVING ALONG IN FIELD**

1187 **GŪ, sumi**   一隅 ICHIGŪ   corner, nook
     CORNER, NOOK   隅石 SUMIISHI   cornerstone
     12 strokes   片隅 KATASUMI corner, nook

阝 is **terraced hill** 229. 禺 is the somewhat obscure begin 1184 q.v, here acting phonetically to express **fold/ recess** and almost certainly also lending connotations both of **twisting/ undulating** and **not clear/ not visible**. 1187 originally referred to a **hidden recess/ hollow in a terraced/ undulating hillside**, then came to mean **nook** and by association **corner**. As with 1184/5/6, suggest taking 禺 as a combination of **insect** 虫 56 and **field** 田 59, with 冂 as **long legs**.

Mnemonic: **LONG-LEGGED INSECT IN CORNER OF HILLSIDE FIELD**

1188 **KUTSU**   屈服 KUPPUKU   surrender
     SUBMIT, CROUCH   不屈 FUKUTSU   unyielding
     8 strokes   屈折 KUSSETSU   refraction

Usually explained simply as **buttocks** 尸 236 and **put out** 出 34, to give **thrust out the buttocks** and thereby **crouch**, with crouch leading by association to **adopt a position of humility/ submit**. A useful mnemonic, but incorrect. Old forms such as 屈 show that , while 出 is indeed put out 出 (屮 being its old form), 尸 is in fact a simplification of **tail** 尾 1734 q.v. This was not infrequently used as a reference to the genitals, especially the **testicles**, and here it has such a meaning. 出 acts phonetically to express **remove**, as well as lending its meaning of **put out** (but in the sense of put out an eye), to give **put out/ remove the testicles**, i.e. **castrate**. This was a form of **punishment**, and thus **submit** is seen as an associated meaning (i.e. submit to punishment). **Crouch** is in turn taken to be an associated meaning, since crouching was a gesture of submission.

Mnemonic: **PUT OUT BUTTOCKS IN SUBMISSIVE CROUCH**

1189	**KUTSU,** hor*u* **DIG** 11 strokes	発掘 HAKKUTSU 掘り出す HORIDASU 採掘 SAIKUTSU	excavation unearth mining

才 is **hand** 32. 屈 is **crouch** 1188 q.v., here acting phonetically to express **dig** and also lending its connotations of **remove** (and possibly also of **crouch**). Thus to **(crouch down to?) dig by hand and remove soil**, i.e. **dig a hole**.

Mnemonic: **CROUCH AND DIG BY HAND**

1190	**kur*u*** **REEL, TURN** 19 strokes	繰り糸 KURIITO 繰り越す KURIKOSU 繰り返す KURIKAESU	silk reeling transfer repeat

Of disputed etymology. Formerly also written 繰, though according to some scholars this is a separate character. 糸 is **thread** 27. 巢/巢 is **nest** 1521, here symbolising **gathering of birds** and by extension **gathering** in general. 喿 is **birds in a tree** 922, felt by some scholars similarly to symbolise **gathering** (conceptually as 309) but by others to act phonetically to express **dark blue**. 繰 is thus an ideograph meaning to **gather threads**, and by association **reel/ turn**. Some scholars feel that from the outset 繰 was a variant ideograph of similar meaning. Others feel that 繰 originally meant **dark blue threads** before becoming confused with 繰. The variant ideograph theory seems the more convincing. Suggest taking 木 as **wood** 69 and 品 as **three boxes**.

Mnemonic: **PUT REELED THREADS INTO THREE WOODEN BOXES**

1191	**KUN** **MERIT** 15 strokes	勲章 KUNSHŌ 殊勲 SHUKUN 勲位 KUNI	medal great merit order of merit

Formerly 勳, and in ancient times 勳. 力/力 is **strength/ effort** 74. 熏 is an NGU character meaning **smoke**, comprising **black** 黑/黑/黑 124 q.v., here with its original connotations of **burning**, and 屮, a variant of **growing plant** 生 42 but here with a meaning of **emerge** (as a plant emerges from the ground). That which emerges during burning is smoke. (Note also the more common NGU character for **smoke**, 燻, which adds a further **fire** 火 8.) 熏 often has connotations of **pleasant-smelling smoke** (see 1192), being a controlled fire usually associated with cooking. In the case of 1191 熏 acts phonetically to express **many**, and possibly also lends loose associated connotations of **desirable/ good**. Thus **many (good?) efforts**, i.e. **meritorious service**. The graphic evolution of the present form has almost certainly been influenced by **heavy/ pile up** 重 311, suggesting **piled up/ accumulated efforts**. Suggest using this as a mnemonic, with ⺣ literally as fire/ burn 8.

Mnemonic: **BURN SELF OUT WITH HEAVY EFFORT -- GREAT MERIT**

1192

薰

KUN, kao*ri*
AROMA, FRAGRANCE,
AURA
16 strokes

薰香 KUNKŌ　　　　incense
薰育 KUNIKU　　　　education
薰風 KUNPŪ　　　　balmy breeze

Formerly 薰 . 艹 is **plants** 9. 熏/薰 is **(pleasant-smelling) smoke** 1191 q.v., here acting phonetically to express **fragrant** and also lending similar connotations. Thus the **fragrant smell of plants** (possibly originally the **fragrant smell of burning plants**), later **fragrance/ aroma** in a broader sense. **Aura** is a minor associated meaning. Suggest taking 重 as **heavy** 311, with 、、、、 as fire/ **burn** 8.

Mnemonic: **BURNING PLANTS PRODUCE HEAVY FRAGRANCE**

1193 刑

KEI
PUNISH
6 strokes

処刑 SHOKEI　　　　punishment
死刑 SHIKEI　　　　death penalty
刑事 KEIJI penal case, detective

刂 is **sword/ cut** 181. 开 derives from 井 , which is not **well** 井 1470 but **grille/ lattice window** 104. Here 井/开 acts phonetically to express **injure**, and may also suggest **shackles** or similar instruments of punishment. Thus to **injure someone with a sword**, which came to refer to cutting with a sword by way of **punishment** and eventually **punish** in a general sense. Suggest taking 开 as a **well-frame**.

Mnemonic: **CUT UP WHILE IN WELL-FRAME -- WHAT A PUNISHMENT!**

1194

茎

KEI, kuki
STALK, STEM
8 strokes

球茎 KYŪKEI　　　　bulb
地下茎 CHIKAKEI　　root stock
歯茎 HAGUKI　　　　the gums

Formerly 莖 . 艹 is **plant** 9. 巠/圣 is **warp threads** 269 q.v., here acting phonetically to express **straight** and also lending its own connotations of **straight** and possibly also of **bare**. Thus the **straight (and bare?) part of a plant**, i.e. its **stalk/ stem**. Suggest taking 圣 as **hand** ㄡ and **earth** 土 60.

Mnemonic: **HAND PLUCKS PLANT STEM FROM THE EARTH**

1195

KEI, chigi*ru*
PLEDGE, JOIN
9 strokes

契約 KEIYAKU   contract
契機 KEIKI   opportunity
契印 KEIIN   joint seal

㓞 is **serrated tally** 659 q.v. Joining the tallies indicated the conclusion of an **arrangement** or **pledge**. **Big** 大 53 suggests an **important** arrangement/ pledge. 1195 also has connotations of **joining**. Suggest taking 㓞 literally as **serrated/ notched wood** 丯 and **cut** 刀 181.

Mnemonic: **JOINING CUT NOTCHED WOOD HONORS BIG PLEDGE**

1196

KEI, E, megu*mu*
BLESSING, KINDNESS
10 strokes

恵与 KEIYO   bestowal
知恵 CHIE   wisdom
恵み深い MEGUMIBUKAI merciful

Formerly 惠 , with a variant 恵 . 心 is **heart/ feeling** 147. 叀 is the same spinning weight seen in 専 /專 914 q.v., here acting phonetically to express **give** and possibly also lending an idea of **all around**. Thus **heart which gives (all around?)**, i.e. a **generous** and **kind** heart. **Blessing** is an associated meaning. Suggest taking 由 as **ten** 十 33 and **field** 田 59.

Mnemonic: **KIND HEARTED PERSON BLESSED WITH TEN FIELDS**

1197

KEI
ENLIGHTEN, STATE
11 strokes

啓発 KEIHATSU enlightenment
啓示 KEIJI   revelation
拝啓 HAIKEI Dear.. (in letters)

Formerly 啓 . 启 is to all intents a variant of **door** 戸 531 q.v. (comprising **door** 月 / 尸 /戸 108 and **open/ opening** 口 20), here acting phonetically to express **open** and also lending connotations of **open a door**. 攵 is **force/ coerce** 101, here acting as a causative element. Thus **to force someone to open a door**, later just **open up** in a broad sense and eventually in particular in the figurative sense of **enlighten**. **State** is felt to be an associated meaning, from the idea of explain/ inform.

Mnemonic: **FORCE OPEN DOOR AND SHED LIGHT**

1198	KEI, kaka*geru* DISPLAY, HOIST, PRINT 11 strokes	掲示板 KEIJIBAN notice board 前掲 ZENKEI aforementioned 掲揚 KEIYŌ hoisting

Formerly 揭 . 扌 is **hand** 32. 昜/曷 is the somewhat obscure interrogative seen in 1022 q.v, here acting phonetically to express **hoist/ hold aloft** and possibly also lending connotations of aggression and hence defiance. Thus to (defiantly?) **hold something aloft in the hand,** now **hoist** in general. **Display** and **print** are associated meanings. Suggest taking 曷 as **sun** 日 62, **cover** 勹 , and **sitting person/man** 匕 238.

Mnemonic: **MAN SITS COVERED IN SUNSHINE, DISPLAYING HAND**

1199	KEI VALLEY, GORGE 11 strokes	渓谷 KEIKOKU valley, gorge 雪渓 SEKKEI snowy valley 渓流 KEIRYŪ mountain stream

Formerly 溪 , and correctly 谿 . 谷 is **valley** 122. 奚 is a CO character now used as an interrogative expressing doubt. Its etymology is not clear, but it comprises **hand reaching down** 爫 303, and either **short thread** 幺 111 plus **big** 大 53 or a variant 糸 of **thread** 糸 27, and may originally have had a meaning of **twisting threads** (short threads together to make bigger thread?). Certainly it often appears to lend a meaning of **twisting** in compounds. Here it acts phonetically to express **blocked**, and may also lend connotations of **twisting**. Thus (**twisting?**) **valley that is blocked**, i.e. a **blind ravine** and later **gorge/ valley** in a general sense. (Note that the use of mountain 山 24 gives a CO character 嵠, which also means mountain gorge [literally that which twists through the mountains?].) The character 溪 , which adds **water/ river** 氵 40 and appears to mean literally a **twisting stream/ river**, exists in Chinese as a separate character with that very meaning, but in Japanese it has been used as a simpler substitute for 谿 . Suggest taking 奚 as **hand/ claw** 爫 303 and **man** 夫 573.

Mnemonic: **MAN CLAWS WAY ALONG WATERY GORGE**

1200	KEI, hotaru FIREFLY 11 strokes	螢光 KEIKŌ fluorescence 螢雪 KEISETSU studying 螢狩り HOTARUGARI catching fireflies

Formerly 螢 . 炒 is **covered in fire/ light** 427 (fire 火 8 and cover 冖), while 虫 is **insect** 56. Thus **insect covered in fire/ light**, i.e. a **firefly**. Suggest taking 𭕄 as an **ornate cover**.

Mnemonic: **FIREFLY IS INSECT ORNATELY COVERED IN FIRE**

1201　傾　KEI, katamuku/keru　傾向 KEIKŌ　tendency
INCLINE, DEDICATE　傾倒 KEITŌ　devotion
13 strokes　傾斜度 KEISHADO　gradient

頃 is an NGU character now used to mean **about** (of time), but is in fact the prototype of 1201. It comprises **head** 頁 93 and **fallen/slumped person** 匕 238, to indicate **slumped head** and by extension a **person slumped** or **fallen to one side. Person** 亻 39 was added for emphasis at this stage. However, despite this addition the person element presently faded from the meaning, leaving just **fall to one side** and hence **incline. Dedicate** is an associated meaning, from the idea of bias/ concentration. Suggest remembering by partial association with **change** 化 238.

Mnemonic: **FALLEN PERSON CHANGES INCLINATION OF HEAD**

1202　携　KEI, tazusawaru/eru　携帯 KEITAI-　portable
CARRY, PARTICIPATE　提携 TEIKEI　cooperation
13 strokes　必携 HIKKEI

　　　　indispensable, handbook

Formerly 攜 and 擕. 扌 is **hand** 32. 雟/雟 is obscure, though 雟 (and a variant form 雟, of which 凹 is almost certainly a variant of 冏 [old forms such as 雟 show 冏 to be the earlier]) exists as a CO character meaning **fatty/ fleshy/ fine**. 崔 appears to be a **crested bird** (not unlike crested bird 雀/雚 634), i.e. a variant of **bird** 隹 216, rather than bird 隹 plus **mountain** 山 24 (but see 1293). It would seem likely that 冏 is **vagina** 317 q.v., here used for its **fleshy thighs** element 冂 (i.e. with hole/ opening 口 20 redundant), to give **plump thighed bird** and thereby **fatty/ fleshy/ fine**. The later 乃 may thus be a variant of **(plump) buttocks** 尻 350 q.v. In any event, in the case of 1202 雟 is used phonetically to express **carry**, to give **carry in the hand**, though originally it almost certainly would have also lent its assumed meaning of plump bird to give carry a plump bird in the hand. **Participate** is a minor associated figurative meaning, from the idea of involvement (i.e. having something [business] in one's hands). Suggest remembering 乃 as **plump buttocks**.

Mnemonic: **CARRY PLUMP-BUTTOCKED BIRD IN HAND**

1203

KEI, tsu*gu*, mama-
INHERIT, FOLLOW,
JOIN, STEP-, PATCH
13 strokes

継続 KEIZOKU   continuation
継子 MAMAKO   stepchild
継ぎ足し TSUGITASHI   extension

Formerly 繼 . 糸 is **thread** 27. 𢆶/𠛱 is **cut threads** 750. Though the combination of these elements is somewhat vague, 1203 is an ideograph referring to the **splicing** of small cut threads into a larger whole thread. Its core meaning is thus to **join threads**, leading on the one hand to the idea of physically mending and **patching** and on the other to figurative associated meanings such as **inheriting** and **following**. Suggest taking 迷 as **rice** 米 201 in a **corner** ∟ 349.

Mnemonic: **FOLLOW THREAD TO INHERIT RICE PILED IN CORNER**

1204

KEI
JOY
15 strokes

慶祝 KEISHUKU   celebration
慶事 KEIJI   happy event
慶賀 KEIGA   congratulation

Of convoluted and disputed etymology. 严 is a simplification of 鹿, an NGU character meaning **deer** which derives with much stylisation from a pictograph 𢉖. 严 was combined with 与, to all intents and purposes a simplification of **horse** 馬 191, to give 麀, a CO character referring to a fabulous beast which was a cross between a horse and a deer and which represented **goodness** (see also 1499). Some scholars feel that 麀 was simplified back to 严, i.e. the same form as the simplification for deer but this time indicating the beast of goodness and by extension goodness itself, and that it was combined with a simplification of **love** 愛 417, namely 爱, to give the present character 慶. The core meaning of this is thus taken to be **love and goodness**, with **joy** being an associated meaning. However, other scholars feel that old forms such as 𢠘 suggest strongly that 爱 is not a variant of love 愛, but that 庹 is a variant of 麀, and that this combines with **heart/ feeling** 忄/心 147 to give **goodness in the heart**. Such a core meaning might logically suggest virtue but appears to have evolved rather into **joy**, with some scholars attributing this to the fact that 麀 had the same pronunciation as the word for **feasting** (again see 1499) and thus suggested by association **happiness** and **contentment**. Suggest taking 严 as a combination of **building** 广 114 and 'funny' **west** 西 152, with 爱 as a variant of **love** 愛 .

Mnemonic: **LOVE AND JOY IN FUNNY WESTERN BUILDING**

1205 憩 **KEI, ikou**
REST
16 strokes

休憩 KYŪKEI rest, recess
少憩 SHŌKEI brief rest
憩い IKOI rest, spell

A combination of **breath/ rest** 息 332 q.v. and **hollowed space** 舌 244. The latter acts phonetically to express **stop and rest**, and may also lend an associated idea of not being busy/ having free time (see 1109). Thus **stop and rest/ stop and 'take a breather'**. Suggest taking 舌 as **tongue** 732, and 息 literally as **heart** 心 147 and **nose** 自 134.

Mnemonic: **TONGUE, NOSE, AND HEART ALL TAKE A REST**

1206 鶏 **KEI, niwatori**
CHICKEN, HEN, COCK
19 strokes

鶏卵 KEIRAN hen's egg
鶏舎 KEISHA henhouse
鶏鳴 KEIMEI cockcrow

Formerly 鷄. 鳥 is **bird** 174. 奚/奚 is the obscure element seen in valley 渓 1199 q.v., here used as a phonetic substitute for a more complex character meaning **cockscomb**. It is not clear why a still simpler character was not chosen as the phonetic, and it may be the case that 奚 also lent reinforcing connotations of twisting and by association undulating, or else, from an earlier form 奚, graphically suggested a cock and comb. In any event, **bird with cockscomb** refers to a **cock/ hen/ chicken**. There is also an occasionally encountered variant form 雞, which uses bird 隹 216. Suggest taking 爪 as **talons** (see 303), and 大 as **man** 573.

Mnemonic: **BIRD SEIZING MAN IN TALONS IS A CHICKEN!?**

1207 **GEI, mukaeru**
GREET, WELCOME,
MEET
7 strokes

歓迎会 KANGEIKAI reception
迎合 GEIGŌ ingratiation
迎え酒 MUKAEZAKE 'hair of dog'

辶 is **movement** 129. 卬 is **raise** 1173 q.v., here acting phonetically to express **greet** and also lending similar connotations from its literal meaning of one person being respectful in an encounter with another. 1207 originally meant to **move (out of one's house) to greet someone**, and now means **meet/ greet** in a broad sense. Suggest taking 卬 literally as **person** ⌐ 39 (originally 𠂉) and **bending person** 卩 425.

Mnemonic: **BENDING PERSON MOVES TO GREET ANOTHER**

| 1208 | GEI, kujira
WHALE
19 strokes | 鯨油 GEIYU
捕鯨 HOGEI
座頭鯨 ZATŌKUJIRA | whale oil
whaling

humpback whale |

魚 is **fish** (or more exactly fishlike creature) 98. 京 is **capital** 99, here acting phonetically to express **big** and also lending an idea of **chief/ principal**. Thus **principal big 'fish'**, i.e. **whale**.

Mnemonic: **THE WHALE IS A CAPITAL 'FISH'**

| 1209 | GEKI, utsu
STRIKE, ATTACK, FIRE
15 strokes | 狙撃 SOGEKI
攻撃 KŌGEKI
早撃ち HAYAUCHI | sniping
attack
rapid firing |

Formerly 擊 , and earlier 撃 . 殳 is **strike** 153. 軎 depicts a **vehicle** 車 31 with attention drawn to its **axle/ hub** ○ . 轂 referred to a **vehicle striking its own axle**, i.e. (constantly) rubbing or chafing. **Hand** 手 32 was added to give the idea of **(persistently) striking with the hand**, leading by association to **attack**. For some reason it has also developed particular associations with **discharging a firearm**.

Mnemonic: **ATTACK VEHICLE BY STRIKING WITH HAND**

| 1210 | GEKI, hageshii
AGITATED, INTENSE
16 strokes | 感激 KANGEKI
激化 GEKKA
激しさ HAGESHISA | deep emotion
intensification
intensity |

氵 is **water** 40. 敫 is a CO character meaning **strike/ beat**. It comprises **release** 放 391q.v., here with its literal connotations of **strike** (a person), and **white** 白 65, which acts phonetically to express **beat** (as in 1695). 1210 originally referred to **water striking** against something (and according to some scholars, who interpret 敫 as also acting phonetically to express **leap**, sending spray leaping into the air). This indicated **agitated water**, i.e. **'fierce' water**, and hence 1210 came to mean **agitated** as well as **fierce/ intense**.

Mnemonic: **FIERCELY AGITATED WATER RELEASES WHITE SPRAY**

387

1211

傑

KETSU
OUTSTANDING
13 strokes

傑士 KESSHI   hero
傑出 KESSHUTSU excelling
傑作 KESSAKU

          masterpiece, blunder

亻 is **person** 39. 傑 is a CO character meaning **bird's roost, cruel**, and **heroic**. It was once written 桀, showing the same combination of **opposed feet** 北/タキ 422 (タ being a variant of 止) and **tree** 米/木 69 as seen in climb 桀/乗 320 q.v., and similarly meant **person in treetop**. Bird's roost derives from the idea of treetop, while heroic comes from the associated idea of **outstanding** (i.e. a person higher than others). Cruel is a misleading meaning derived from association with a particular tyrant in ancient China, noted both for his outstanding prowess as a warrior and for his cruelty. In the case of 1211 桀 lends only its meaning of **outstanding**, combining with **person** 亻 to give **outstanding person** and eventually **outstanding/ excellent** in a broad sense. Suggest taking タ as **evening** 44 and 舛 as a variant of **well(-frame)** 井 1470, with 木 in its sense of **wooden**.

Mnemonic: **OUTSTANDING PERSON BUILDS WOODEN WELL NIGHTLY**

1212

KEN, kata
SHOULDER
8 strokes

肩章 KENSHŌ   epaulette
比肩 HIKEN   comparison
肩書き KATAGAKI title of rank

Flesh/ of the body 月 365 and **door** 戸 108. Though the oldest forms of 1212 found to date do show door, it is believed to be a miscopying of some earlier pictograph of a **shoulder**, such as 𠃍 . Thus the **shoulder part of the body**.

Mnemonic: **USE FLESHY SHOULDER AGAINST DOOR**

1213

KEN
THRIFTY, FRUGAL
10 strokes

倹約 KENYAKU   frugality
節倹 SEKKEN   frugality
勤倹 KINKEN   thrift

Formerly 儉. 亻 is **person** 39. 僉/㑒 is **combine/ judge** 475 q.v., here acting phonetically to express **few** and possibly also lending associated connotations of avoidance of duplication (i.e. from the idea of combining things). 1213 referred to a **person of few possessions**, which came to symbolise **thrift** and **frugality**. Suggest taking 㑒 as a combined variant of **elder brother** 兄 267 and cover/ **cap** 亼 87/121.

Mnemonic: **ELDER BROTHER WEARS ONLY A CAP -- THRIFTY PERSON**

1214		KEN, tsurugi SWORD, BAYONET 10 strokes	剣道 KENDŌ	kendo
			剣舞 KENBU	sword dance
			短剣 TANKEN	dagger, dirk

Formerly 劍. 刂 is **sword** 181, while 僉/僉 is **combine/** judge 475 q.v. The latter acts phonetically to express **taper(ed)**. Any semantic role is not clear, but it is possible that it lends an idea of combining the function both of a sword and a dagger. Thus **tapered sword**, i.e. a **short stabbing sword,** though it is occasionally used in a wider sense. Suggest taking 僉 as a combined variant of **elder brother** 兄 267 and **cover** 亼 87.

Mnemonic: **ELDER BROTHER PUTS COVER ON SWORD**

1215		KEN, noki EAVES, HOUSE COUNTER 10 strokes	一軒 IKKEN	one house
			軒灯 KENTŌ	eaves lantern
			軒先 NOKISAKI	frontage

Carriage/ vehicle 車 31 and **dry/ forked weapon** 干 825 q.v. The latter acts phonetically to express **high/ raised** and probably also lends its idea of forking to refer to the forked support of a **canopy over a carriage**. 1215 originally referred to such a **raised canopy**, and can still be used in this sense in Chinese, where it can also mean raised/ high in a broader sense. In Japanese it was applied by association to the **canopy of a house**, i.e. the **roof,** and eventually came by further association to mean **eaves**. It is also used for counting houses.

Mnemonic: **VEHICLE KEPT DRY UNDER EAVES**

1216		KEN RANGE, SPHERE, ZONE 12 strokes	成層圏 SEISŌKEN	stratosphere
			圏外 KENGAI	outside bounds
			共産圏 KYŌSANKEN	
				Communist Bloc

Formerly 圈. 囗 is **enclosure** 123. 卷/巻 is **roll (up)** 826 q.v., here acting phonetically to express **block** and also lending its own idea of **containment**. Thus **that contained by a blocking enclosure**, i.e. **zone, range,** etc.

Mnemonic: **ENCLOSURE IS ROLLED AROUND ZONE**

389

1217

KEN, kata*i*
FIRM, SOLID, HARD
12 strokes

堅実 KENJITSU   reliable
堅固 KENGO   firm, steady
中堅 CHŪKEN   mainstay

Earth/ ground 土 60 and **hard** 臤 1179. Originally **firm ground**, later **firm/ hard/ solid** in a broad sense, including reliable. Suggest taking 臤 literally as **staring eye** 臣 512 and **hand** 又 .

Mnemonic: **HAND THROWS HARD EARTH AT STARING EYE**

1218

KEN, GEN, kira*u/i***, iya**
DISLIKE(D)
13 strokes

嫌悪 KENO   loathing
機嫌 KIGEN   mood
嫌嫌 IYAIYA   reluctantly

女 is **woman** 35. 兼 is **combine/ do two things at once** 850, here acting phonetically to express **dissatisfaction** and almost certainly also lending its own idea of **two at once**. 1218 originally referred to a **woman's feelings of dissatisfaction**, and, to judge from the fact that in Chinese it can also mean suspicion and jealousy, almost certainly referred specifically to her feelings at sharing her husband's affections with another woman. Now **dislike/ disliked** in a general sense.

Mnemonic: **WOMAN DISLIKES BEING COMBINED WITH ANOTHER**

1219

KEN, KON
DEDICATE, PRESENT
13 strokes

献上 KENJŌ   presentation
献立 KONDATE   menu, plan
献身 KENSHIN   dedication

Formerly 獻 . 鬳 is a now defunct character referring to a particular type of **dog used in sacrifices**, a dog presumably considered to have **tiger-like** attributes (虍 is **tiger** 281) and **eaten** after the sacrifice (鬲 is **cooking pot on stand** 1078). **Dog** 犬 17 was added later for clarity. Sacrificial dog came to symbolise **sacrifice** and the idea of **dedicating/ presenting** in general. The modern form uses **south** 南 190 as a simplification of 鬳 .

Mnemonic: **SOUTHERN DOG IS VERY DEDICATED**

1220

KEN, tsuka*u*, ya*ru*
SEND, USE, DO
13 strokes

派遣 HAKEN   dispatch
小遣い KOZUKAI pocket money
遣り直す YARINAOSU   redo

追 is a variant of **pursue** 追 350 q.v., here used in the sense of **follow**. 虫 is **gather** 834. 1220 originally referred to a **gathering of followers**, i.e. a retinue, then came to be used of **retainer/ servant**. Probably because of the presence of the movement radical 辶 129, it became particularly associated with a **messenger**, i.e. someone sent on errands, and thus came to mean **send**. In Japanese it also developed connotations of **use**, which later broadened to **act/ do** in general, whereas in Chinese send came to mean send off/ banish and thus acquired the connotations which 追 350 itself later acquired in Japanese. Suggest taking 虫 as **middle/ midst** 中 55 and **one** 一 1. See also 331.

Mnemonic: **USE ONE FROM AMIDST FOLLOWERS TO SEND IN PURSUIT**

1221

KEN, kashiko*i*
WISE
16 strokes

賢者 KENJA   sage
賢明 KENMEI   wisdom
賢立て KASHIKODATE
          pretence of wisdom

貝 is shell/ **money** 90, here meaning **assets/ wealth**. 臤 is **hard/ wise** 1179 q.v., here acting phonetically to express **bountiful** but of unclear semantic role due to its somewhat obscure nature. 1221 originally referred to **great wealth** in terms of tangible assets, but was later applied figuratively to a person endowed with a **wealth of wisdom**. Suggest taking 臤 literally as **staring eye** 臣 512 and **hand** 又 .

Mnemonic: **WISE PERSON STARES HARD AT MONEY IN HAND**

1222

KEN, herikuda*ru*
HUMBLE, MODEST
17 strokes

謙そん KENSON   humility
謙虚 KENKYO   modesty
謙譲 KENJŌ   humility

言 is words/ **speak** 274. 兼 is combine/ **be unable** 850, here acting phonetically to express **awe** as well as lending its meaning of **be unable**. Thus to **be awed and unable to speak**, as in the presence of a great superior. This later came to mean **be respectfully reserved**, leading to **humble** and **modest**.

Mnemonic: **MODEST PERSON UNABLE TO SPEAK**

1223

KEN, mayu
COCOON
18 strokes

繭ちゅう KENCHŪ　　pongee
大繭　OMAYU　double cocoon
空繭　KARAMAYU

waste cocoon

Formerly 蘭. 糸 is **thread** 27, while 虫 is **insect** 56. 芇 derives from an ideograph
茮, which combines a **cocoon** ∩ with 丷, a simplification of a ram's horns (see 986)
used to symbolise **symmetry/ equal on both sides.** 1223 thus literally means **symmetrical cocoon of thread-making insect.** Suggest taking 芇 as **grass** 艹 9 and a
double chambered cocoon 冂.

Mnemonic: **INSECT THREADS DOUBLE COCOON UNDER GRASS**

1224

顕

KEN, arawa*reru*
MANIFEST, VISIBLE
18 strokes

顕著　KENCHO　　noticeable
顕要　KENYŌ　　prominence
顕微鏡 KENBIKYŌ microscope

Formerly 顯. 頁 is **head** 93, though old forms of 1224 such as 㬎兄 reveal that this is
a miscopying of **look/ see** 見 18. 㬎 is a CO character meaning **motes** (small particles
of dust) and by association **minute.** It comprises **sun(-light)** 日 62 and 絲, which is a
simplified doubling of **thread** 糸 27 and here means **small things.** Thus **small things
(showing up) in sunlight,** i.e. motes. In the case of 1224 㬎 acts phonetically to express **clear/ visible** and almost certainly also lends a similar meaning of being visible (if
small). Thus something **(small but) visible upon looking,** leading to **visible** in general and hence also **manifest.** Suggest taking 业 as a variant of **line up** 並 1775.

Mnemonic: **ODD LINE UP OF HEADS VISIBLE IN SUN**

1225

懸

KEN, KE, ka*karu*/*keru*
ATTACH, HANG, APPLY
20 strokes

懸命　KENMEI　　eagerness
懸念　KENEN　　anxiety
命懸け INOCHIGAKE perilous

縣 is the old form of **prefecture** 県 273 q.v., here in its early sense of **attach/ hang.**
心 is **heart** 147. Thus **that which hangs on the heart,** i.e. a **worry/ anxiety.** It can
still have this meaning in Chinese, but in Japanese it has mostly lost its heart connotations
to leave just **hang** in a broad sense, being virtually interchangeable with 掛 1083.

Mnemonic: **HEART STILL ATTACHED TO OLD PREFECTURE**

1226

GEN, maboroshi
ILLUSION, MAGIC
4 strokes

幻想 GENSŌ — illusion
幻像 GENZŌ — phantom
幻術 GENJUTSU — magic

Originally written 𢆯, being an inversion of **weaving shuttle** 甩 403 q.v. and having a similar meaning. Its highly stylised present form clearly shows confusion with **short thread** 幺 111. Its present meanings result from borrowing, to an extent involving confusion with occult 玄 1227 q.v. Suggest taking ㇉ as a **hook**.

Mnemonic: **SHORT THREAD BECOMES HOOK!? -- A MAGICAL ILLUSION**

1227

GEN
OCCULT, BLACK
5 strokes

玄妙 GENMYŌ — mystery
玄関 GENKAN — porch
玄人 KURŌTO* — expert

Of very extended semantic evolution. 幺 is **short thread** 111. 亠 is the same **twisting device** seen in 率 803 q.v. (for twisting bits of thread into rope). Thus 1227 originally meant **short thread suitable for twisting**. It then came to mean something **very small** and by association something **hard to see**, leading to **obscure** both in the physical sense of **dark/ black** and in the figurative sense of **mysterious**, including **occult**.

Mnemonic: **TWISTED BLACK THREAD SYMBOLISES OCCULT**

1228

GEN, tsuru
(BOW)STRING
8 strokes

正弦 SEIGEN — sine (of angle)
弓弦 YUMIZURU — bowstring
弦楽器 GENGAKKI
— stringed instrument

弓 is **bow** 836. 玄 is occult/ black 1227 q.v., here in its sense of **twisted thread** and by association **cord twisted taut**, and also acting phonetically to express **attach**. Thus **cord attached to bow and twisted taut**, i.e. **bowstring**. Now also **string** in a broader sense.

Mnemonic: **BOW HAS STRING OF TWISTED BLACK THREAD**

1229

KO
ORPHAN, LONELY
9 strokes

孤児院 KOJIIN — orphanage
孤独 KODOKU — loneliness
孤立 KORITSU — isolation

子 is **child** 25. 瓜 is an NGU character meaning **melon** (once written 𤓰, thought to be a pictograph of a melon hanging from a frame). The latter acts phonetically to express **alone**, and may possibly also lend similar connotations from its depiction of a single melon. Thus **child alone**, i.e. an **orphan**. Also **alone/ lonely** in a wider sense.

Mnemonic: **LONELY ORPHAN CHILD GIVEN MELON**

1230	KO ARC, ARCH, BOW 9 strokes	弧形 KOKEI 弧状 KOJŌ 弧灯 KOTŌ	arc arcuate arc light

弓 is **bow** 836. 瓜 is **melon** 1229, here acting phonetically to express **rounded** and also lending similar connotations of its own from the shape of the melon. 1230 originally referred to a particularly **curved type of bow**, but later, like the English term **bow**, came to mean **arc/ arch** in a general sense.

Mnemonic: **BOW ARCHED AS ROUND AS A MELON**

1231	KO, ka*reru*/*rasu* WITHER, DECAY 9 strokes	枯死 KOSHI 冬枯れ FUYUGARE 枯れ葉 KAREHA	withering away winter decay dead leaf

木 is **tree** 69. 古 is **old** 109 q.v., acting phonetically to express **bone** (and by extension **skeleton**) and almost certainly also lending similar connotations from its assumed literal meaning of ancient skull. Thus a **tree reduced to a skeleton**, symbolising **decaying** and **withering**.

Mnemonic: **WITHERED OLD TREE**

1232	KO, yato*u* EMPLOY, HiRE 12 strokes	雇用 KOYŌ 雇い人 YATOININ 解雇 KAIKO	employment employee dismissal

Bird 隹 216 and **door** 戸 108. 1232 originally referred to a bird whose wings flapped like the leaves of a door, i.e. in a somewhat stiff and ungainly fashion, specifically a type of **quail** (still retained in Chinese). **Employ/ hire** is generally assumed to be a purely borrowed meaning, but it is possible that it was used by association of an apprentice ungainly in his work.

Mnemonic: **PUT BIRD UNDER DOOR TO GAIN EMPLOYMENT**

1233	KO, hoko*ru* PROUD, BOAST 13 strokes	誇大 KODAI 誇示 KOJI 誇り顔 HOKORIGAO	exaggeration ostentation proud look

夸 is a CO character meaning **brag/ boast** (**big** 大 53 and **emerge** 亏 811), here reinforced by **words/ speak** 言 274. Thus **boastful words**, with **proud** being an associated meaning.

Mnemonic: **BIG WORDS EMERGE IN PROUD BOAST**

1234 鼓	KO, tsuzumi DRUM 13 strokes	鼓動 KODŌ	beating
		大鼓 TAIKO	big drum
		小鼓 KOTSUZUMI	hand drum

支 is **branch** 691q.v., here meaning literally **hand holding bamboo stick**. 壴 is edible plants in a food vessel 450 q.v. The latter was used for its sound (generally believed to have been **CHŪ** at the time in question [or **SHOKU** by some scholars], though **KO** might seem more appropriate), and almost certainly also for its elements, with **food vessel on a stand** 豆 1640 q.v. being likened to a drum on a stand, and plant 土 / 屮 (variant 生 42) probably being reinterpreted as **emerge** (an occasional connotation of plant 生, which emerges from the ground). Thus 1234 literally means **instrument resembling a food vessel on a stand from which the sound CHŪ (SHOKU? KO?) emerges when struck with a bamboo stick**, i.e. a **drum**. Suggest taking 士 as **samurai** 494.

Mnemonic: **SAMURAI WIELDS BRANCH, USING FOOD POT AS DRUM**

1235 顧	KO, kaerimiru LOOK BACK 21 strokes	顧慮 KORYO	concern
		回顧 KAIKO	retrospection
		顧問 KOMON	adviser

頁 is **head** 93. 雇 is **employ**/ quail 1232 q.v., here acting phonetically to express **turn around** and possibly also lending connotations of ungainly movement (as in a panic or similar). Thus to **turn the head around** (in a panic?), now **look back** in a broad sense including the figurative.

Mnemonic: **EMPLOY HEAD TO LOOK BACK**

1236 互	GO, tagai MUTUAL 4 strokes	相互 SŌGO-	mutual
		互助 GOJO	mutual aid
		互い違い TAGAICHIGAI	alternately

From a pictograph 玄, showing a **special spool used for evenly crosswinding** thread. It thus came to symbolise **balance** and **symmetry**, and hence by association **equality, mutuality, reciprocity**, etc. Note the similarity of shape to reel/ **five** 五 19, which may be useful as a mnemonic.

Mnemonic: **MUTUALITY AWKWARD FROM FIVE**

1237

GO, ku*reru*
GIVE, WU CHINA
7 strokes

呉服 GOFUKU — drapery
呉呉も KUREGUREMO earnestly
呉れ手 KURETE — donor

Formerly 吳 and in ancient times ꝏ. ㇓/口 is **mouth/ say** 20, deliberately tilted in the original form to reinforce 夭, which shows a **man** 大 53 with his **head tilted at an angle** ⌒. This expressed the idea of **deviating from the truth**, as in **bragging**, and was also used to express putting the head back and bawling (still found in Chinese). For reasons that are not clear it was later used to refer to a **district in China**, and in Japanese was also borrowed to express **give** (to an inferior). Suggest taking 矢 as a combination of **corner** ∟ 349 and **six** 六 76, with 口 as a **box**.

Mnemonic: **GIVEN A CHINESE BOX WITH SIX CORNERS**

1238

GO
PLEASURE, AMUSEMENT
10 strokes

娯楽 GORAKU — pleasure
歓娯 KANGO — pleasure
娯楽品 GORAKUHIN — plaything

女 is **woman** 35. 呉 is **give** 1237 q.v., here acting phonetically to express **talk** and possibly also lending its literal meaning of **brag**. Thus to **talk with (brag to?) a woman**, which came to symbolise **pleasure** and **amusement**.

Mnemonic: **WOMAN GIVES PLEASURE AND AMUSEMENT**

1239

GO, sato*ru*
PERCEIVE, DISCERN
10 strokes

悟性 GOSEI — wisdom
覚悟 KAKUGO — mental resolve
悟り SATORI — enlightenment

忄 is **heart/ feelings** 147. 吾 is **I/me** 112 q.v., here acting phonetically to express **enlightenment** and possibly also lending connotations of balance and by extension proper proportion. Thus **enlightenment in the heart** (seeing things in proper proportion?), leading to **perceive** and **discern**. Suggest taking 吾 as **five** 五 19 and **mouth** 口 20.

Mnemonic: **I LISTEN TO FIVE MOUTHS AND PERCEIVE FEELINGS**

1240

GO
(THE GAME OF) GO
13 strokes

碁石 GOISHI — go stone
碁盤 GOBAN — checkerboard
碁打ち GOUCHI — go player

As **chess** 棋 1130 q.v., but with **wood** 木 69 replaced by **stone** 石 45.

Mnemonic: **'GO' IS A TYPE OF CHESS PLAYED WITH STONES**

396

1241

KŌ, ana
HOLE, CONFUCIUS
4 strokes

鼻孔 BIKŌ — nostril
気孔 KIKŌ — pore
孔子 KŌSHI — Confucius

Once written 孚孔, showing **child** 孚/孑 25 and a semi-abstract depiction of a **cavity** 𠃌, later confusingly stylised to し and retaining the convex rather than concave element. 1241 originally meant the **cavity/ hole through which children emerge**, i.e. the **vagina**, but then came to mean **hole** in general. It was also borrowed phonetically to express the first syllable of **Confucius**. Suggest taking し as a **hook**, for an irreverent mnemonic.

Mnemonic: CONFUCIUS SAY CHILD WHO PLAY WITH HOOK GET HOLE

1242

巧

KŌ, takumi
SKILL
5 strokes

技巧 GIKŌ — skill
巧言 KŌGEN — flattery
精巧 SEIKŌ — elaborateness

工 is **work/ carpenter's square** 113, here meaning **accurate carpentry**. 丂 is **twisting waterweed** 281, here with its meaning of **flat/ level** (see 388). 1242 originally referred to a carpenter **planing a piece of wood till it was exactly flat/ level**, and this eventually came to symbolise **skilled work** and **skill** in general.

Mnemonic: WORK WITH WATERWEED CALLS FOR SKILL

1243

甲

KŌ, KAN, kōra
SHELL, ARMOR,
HIGH, 1ST, A
5 strokes

甲虫 KŌCHŪ — beetle
甲種 KŌSHU — Grade A
甲高い KANDAKAI — shrill

Once written 田 or simply +, indicating a **hard-shelled seed** ○ with a **split** + (see 162) in its case. |, which represents a sprout, was added later to clarify the meaning, giving 甲. Though the original emphasis was on sprouting, in time 1243 came to refer rather to the **case** of the seed, giving **shell** and **armor**. **1st/ A** and **high** are borrowed meanings. Suggest taking 甲 as a combination of **field** 田 59 and the **figure 1**.

Mnemonic: AN 'A 1' FIELD

1244

KŌ, e
INLET, RIVER
6 strokes

入り江 IRIE — creek, inlet
江湖 KŌKO — world, public
江戸 EDO — Edo, old Tokyo

氵 is **water** 40, here meaning **river**. 工 is **carpenter's square** 113, here acting phonetically to express **huge** and possibly also indirectly lending similar connotations of its own (see 1153). Thus **huge river**, which was also applied to an **arm of the sea/ inlet**.

Mnemonic: FIND CARPENTER'S SQUARE IN WATERS OF INLET

397

1245 坑 KŌ
MINE, PIT, HOLE
7 strokes

炭坑 TANKŌ coal mine
坑夫 KŌFU miner
坑道 KŌDŌ mine shaft

Of confusing semantic evolution. Originally written 阬, showing **hill** ß / β 229 and **high/ straight** 亼/兀 479. The latter also acted phonetically to express **high**, thus giving **steep high hill**. This came to mean **sheer** and **precipitous**, which by a confusing process of assocation came in turn to mean a **precipitous drop,** and hence eventually **deep hole** and the present meanings. **Ground/ earth** 圡 60 was later used as an alternative to hill ß , eventually prevailing in Japanese though in Chinese 阬 and 坑 are interchangeable. Suggest taking 亠 as a **top** and 几 as **desk** 832, with 土 as **soil/ dirt.**

Mnemonic: **HOLE IN DESKTOP FULL OF DIRT**

1246 抗 KŌ
RESIST, OPPOSE
7 strokes

対抗 TAIKŌ opposition
抗議 KŌGI protest
抗争 KŌSO dispute

扌 is **hand** 32. 亢 is **high/ straight** 479, here acting phonetically to express **block** and also lending loose connotations of obstacle/ **obstruct** from its idea of rising sheer. Thus to **block with the hand,** leading to **resist** and by association **protest**. Suggest taking 亠 as a **top** and 几 as **desk** 832.

Mnemonic: **HAND THUMPED ON DESKTOP SHOWS OPPOSITION**

1247 攻 KŌ, semeru
ATTACK
7 strokes

攻撃者 KŌGEKISHA aggressor
専攻 SENKŌ specialty
攻め入る SEMEIRU invade

攵 is **strike** 101. 工 is **carpenter's square** 113, here acting phonetically to express **strike/ beat** and possibly also lending connotations of an implement resembling a weapon. Thus to **strike and beat,** leading to **attack**.

Mnemonic: **ATTACK, STRIKING WITH CARPENTER'S SQUARE**

1248 KŌ, sara, fu*keru*/*kasu*
ANEW, CHANGE,
AGAIN, GROW LATE
7 strokes

更新 KŌSHIN　　　　renewal
今更 IMASARA now, belatedly
夜更け YOFUKE　　late at night

Formerly 甦 . 攴 is **striking hand/ coerce** 101, here meaning **(en)force**. 丙 is third rate 1773 q.v., here acting phonetically to express **change** and also, from its literal meaning of sturdy altar, lending an idea of being **firmly planted**, which was a reference to a **guard**. 1248 originally referred to an **enforced change of guard**, then came to refer to **unavoidable duty rosters**. The **night watch** (still a meaning in Chinese) was one such duty, leading to **stay up late** and **grow late**. On the other hand, change of guard led to **change** in general, including **renew/ anew** and by association **(yet) again**. Suggest taking 日 as **day** 62 and 乂 as a variant of **force** 攵 101.

Mnemonic: **DAY GROWS LATE, FORCING CHANGE**

1249 KŌ, kakawa*ru*
SEIZE, ADHERE TO
8 strokes

拘束 KŌSOKU　　　restriction
拘引 KŌIN　　arrest, custody
拘らず KAKAWARAZU
　　　　　　　　　regardless

扌 is **hand** 32, here meaning **arm**. 句 is **phrase** 655 q.v., here acting phonetically to express **stop** and also lending connotations of **encircle** through its element 勹. Thus to **stop with the arms by encircling**, i.e. **seize/ cling**, now also in a figurative sense.

Mnemonic: **SEIZE ONTO A HANDY PHRASE**

1250 KŌ
CONSENT, AGREE, VITAL
8 strokes

首肯 SHUKŌ consent, assent
肯定 KŌTEI　　　affirmation
肯けい KŌKEI　　　the point

Once written 冎. 夕/月 is **meat/ of the body** 365. 冂 is an abbreviation of **bone** 咼 867 q.v. Thus to all intents and purposes 1250 is a variant of **bone** 骨 867. Its present major meaning of **consent/ agree** is a borrowing, felt to stem from confusion with 可/ 可 816 q.v. Its early meaning of **bone** is still seen indirectly in some compounds, as in the CO character **gnaw** 啃, which adds **mouth** 口 20, and in the minor meaning of **vital part/ substance**. The reason for the later use of **stop** 止 129 is not clear. Some scholars feel it refers to meat stopping on the bone, but it is more likely to have been used in some now unclear phonetic role.

Mnemonic: **CONSENT TO MEAT STOPPAGE**

1251 恒 **KŌ, tsune**   恆常 **KŌJŌ**   constancy
      ALWAYS, CONSTANT   恆久 **KŌKYŪ**   perpetuity
      9 strokes   恆例 **KŌREI**   common usage

Formerly 恆. 忄 is **heart/ feelings** 147. 亙 is a CO character meaning **limit**, showing a **moon** 月/月 16 between **two boundaries** 二 (see 913). The boundaries symbolised limits and fixed course, and 亙 originally referred to the **fixed trajectory of the
moon**. In combination with heart 忄 it expressed the idea of **fidelity/ constancy**, now
constant in a general sense. The later use of around 亘 913 q.v. almost certainly results
from a misinterpretation of 日 as **sun** 62 (though it is actually a derivative of vortex ℮),
to give an alternative idea of fixed trajectory of the sun (sun and moon often being interchanged, as in 間/閒 92 etc.). Suggest taking 日 as **day** 62, with 二 as **two** 61.

Mnemonic: **FEELINGS CONSTANT OVER TWO DAYS**

1252 **KŌ**   洪水 **KŌZUI/ ŌMIZU***   flood
      FLOOD, VAST   洪積層 **KŌSEKISŌ**   diluvium
      9 strokes   洪大 **KŌDAI na**   vast

氵 is **water** 40. 共 is **together** 460 q.v., here acting phonetically to express **big** and
probably also lending an idea of coming together. Thus a **big body/ volume of water**
(coming together from various sources?), leading to **flood** and occasionally **vast** in a general sense.

Mnemonic: **WATERS COME TOGETHER IN VAST FLOOD**

1253 **KŌ, arai, areru/rasu**   荒天 **KŌTEN**   stormy weather
      ROUGH, WILD, WASTE 荒れ地 **ARECHI**   wasteland
      9 strokes   荒波 **ARANAMI**   rough sea

艹 is **grass** 9. 㐬 is a CO character meaning **(vast) watery waste**, comprising **river**
川L/川 48 and **death** 亡 973, which acts phonetically to express **vast** as well as lending
connotations of death and by association **destruction**. In combination with grass 艹 it
meant **grassy waste**, i.e. a place once inhabited but now **ruined** and **overgrown with
grass**. Thus **uncared for, rough, wild**, etc.

Mnemonic: **RIVER AND DEAD GRASS IN WILD WASTELAND**

1254 **KŌ**
SUBURBS
9 strokes

郊外 KŌGAI　　suburbs
近郊 KINKŌ　　suburbs
郊野 KŌYA　　suburban field

阝 is **village/ settlement** 355, while 交 is **mix/ cross/** exchange 115. Thus **settlement at crossing** (i.e. crossroads). Whereas the similar 街 819 q.v. came to mean town, 1254 came rather to mean community <u>outside</u> a town, giving **suburbs**.

Mnemonic: **VILLAGE MIXED WITH SUBURBS**

1255 **KŌ, ka, kao***ru/ri*
FRAGRANCE, INCENSE
9 strokes

香水 KŌSUI　　perfume
香気 KŌKI　fragrance, aroma
色香 IROKA　woman's charms

日 is a simplification of **sweet** 甘 1093, while 禾 is rice plant/ **grain plant** 81. 1255 originally referred to a certain type of **aromatic millet**, and then came to mean delicate flavor and eventually **fragrance** and **incense**. Suggest taking 日 as **sun** 62.

Mnemonic: **SUN BRINGS OUT FRAGRANCE OF GRAIN PLANT**

1256 **KŌ**
MARQUIS, LORD
9 strokes

侯爵 KŌSHAKU　　marquis
太田侯 ŌTAKŌ　Marquis Ota
王侯 ŌKŌ　　royalty

Somewhat obscure, having become etymologically confused with **sign/ ask** 候 478 q.v. It appears to be a variant of **meet/ greet** (humbly) 矦 (also 478), with ノ becoming **person** 亻 39, but from an early stage meant **archery** or **target range** (still in fact a lesser meaning in Chinese), apparently having become confused with target range 矦 (also 478). It was borrowed phonetically to express **marquis**. Unfortunately there is no easy mnemonic for the character, but suggest remembering by partial association with **arrow** 矢 981, taking 矦 as a **'fancy' arrow**.

Mnemonic: **PERSON WITH FANCY ARROW IS MARQUIS**

1257 **KŌ, KU, mitsu***gu*
TRIBUTE
10 strokes

貢献 KŌKEN　　contribution
年貢 NENGU　　tax, dues
貢ぎ物 MITSUGIMONO　tribute

貝 is shell/ **money** 90, here meaning **assets**. 工 is **work** 113, here also acting phonetically to express **offer up**. Thus **offer up assets and work** (i.e. corvee), namely the **tribute** paid to one's lord.

Mnemonic: **BOTH WORK AND MONEY OFFERED AS TRIBUTE**

1258

KŌ, hika*eru*
REFRAIN, WRITE DOWN,
HAVE NEAR, WAIT
11 strokes

控え所 HIKAEJO waiting room
控訴 KŌSO legal appeal
控え書き HIKAEGAKI memo, note

Of broad and somewhat unclear semantic evolution. 扌 is **hand** 32. 空 is **sky** 15, here acting phonetically to express **pull back** and possibly also lending an idea of space (i.e. distance). Thus to **pull back with the hand** (over a distance?). This originally meant to pull back a bow or to pull on reins (both meanings still found in Chinese). However, just like the English pull back, it also came to mean **refrain**, **wait**, and **be patient**. **Have near** is taken to be an associated meaning, from the idea of pulling something towards oneself. **Write down** is felt to derive from the idea of keeping something (i.e. as a record), which in turn derives from association with holding back.

Mnemonic: **REFRAIN, HANDS REACHING FOR THE SKY**

1259

KŌ, awa*teru*/*tadashii*
BE FLUSTERED
12 strokes

恐慌 KYŌKŌ panic, scare
大慌て ŌAWATE big fluster
慌て者 AWATEMONO blunderer

忄 is **heart**/ **feelings** 147. 荒 is **wild** 1253, here acting phonetically to express **unclear**/ **incomprehensible** and almost certainly also lending an idea of wild. Thus **wild incomprehensible feelings**, a reference to a state of being **panicked** or **flustered**.

Mnemonic: **WILD FEELINGS SHOW ONE IS FLUSTERED**

1260

KŌ, kata*i*
HARD
12 strokes

硬化 KŌKA hardening
硬貨 KŌKA coin
硬水 KŌSUI hard water

石 is **rock**/ **stone** 45. 更 is **change** 1248 q.v., here acting phonetically to express **solid** and possibly also lending an idea of change to suggest petrification. Thus (become?) **solid as a rock**, i.e. **hard**.

Mnemonic: **CHANGE TO STONE AND BECOME HARD**

1261 絞 KŌ, shi*boru*, shi*meru*
STRANGLE, WRING
12 strokes

絞首台 KŌSHUDAI　　gallows
絞め殺す SHIMEKOROSU strangle
絞り出す SHIBORIDASU
　　　　　　　　squeeze out

糸 is thread 27, here essentially meaning **cloth**. 交 is **mix/ cross/ exchange** 115 q.v., here acting phonetically to express **twist** and also lending an idea of **criss cross**. Thus to **put cloth over something in a criss cross fashion and twist** (in order to squeeze out the contents), giving **wring** and later **strangle**.

Mnemonic: **STRANGLED WITH MIXED THREADS**

1262 頂 KŌ, unaji
CLAUSE, ITEM, NAPE
12 strokes

項目 KŌMOKU　　clause, item
事項 JIKŌ　　　　matters
条項 JŌKŌ　　　　articles

頁 is **head** 93. 工 is **work** 113, here acting phonetically to express **rear/ back**. Thus the **back of the head**, and by extension **back of the neck** (i.e. **nape**). Rather like the English term **heading**, it also came to be used figuratively of an **item** or **clause**.

Mnemonic: **WORK HEADINGS INCLUDE SUNDRY ITEMS**

1263 溝 KŌ, mizo, dobu
DITCH, CHANNEL
13 strokes

下水溝 GESUIKŌ　　　drain
溝切り MIZOKIRI　　grooving
溝ねずみ DOBUNEZUMI sewer rat

氵 is **water** 40. 冓 is **build up/ accumulation** 675 q.v., here acting phonetically to express **criss cross** and probably also lending an idea of **accumulation/ plurality**. 1263 originally referred to (a number of?) **crisscrossing irrigation channels**, giving the present meanings. Suggest taking 冓 literally as **pile of baskets**.

Mnemonic: **BUILD WATER CHANNEL WITH PILE OF BASKETS?!**

1264 綱 KŌ, tsuna
CABLE, LINE, PRINCIPLE
14 strokes

要綱 YŌKŌ　　　　　gist
大綱 TAIKŌ　　main principles
綱引き TSUNABIKI　tug-of-war

糸 is **thread** 27, here meaning **cord**. 岡 is **(towering) hill** 864 q.v., here acting phonetically to express **strong** and probably also lending an idea of **formidable**. Thus **strong (and formidable?) cord**, i.e. a **rope** or **cable**. **Line** is an associated meaning, with **principle** being a figurative associated meaning with line/ thread (cf. English thread of argument etc.).

Mnemonic: **CABLE THREADS WAY UP HILLSIDE**

1265	酵	KŌ	酵母 KŌBO	yeast
		FERMENT, YEAST	酵素 KŌSO	enzyme
		14 strokes	発酵 HAKKŌ	fermentation

酉 is **wine jar** 302, here meaning **alcohol**. 孝 is **filial piety** 860 q.v., here acting phonetically to express **yeast** and probably also suggesting the process of **aging** through its elements of young (i.e. child 子 25) and old (i.e. old man 耂 117). (Aging) yeast is involved in the process of **fermentation** in the production of alcohol.

Mnemonic: **FILIAL PIETY IS A JAR OF FERMENTED ALCOHOL**

1266	稿	KŌ	原稿 GENKŌ	manuscript
		MANUSCRIPT, STRAW	投稿 TŌKŌ	contribution
		15 strokes	草稿 SŌKŌ	rough draft

Formerly also 稾 . 禾 is **rice plant / grain plant** 81, while 高 is **tall** 119. The tall part of a grain plant is its **stem**, which was the original meaning of 1266, with **straw** being an associated meaning. Nowadays straw is usually conveyed by the NGU character 藁, which adds plant 艹 9. **Manuscript** is a borrowed meaning.

Mnemonic: **MANUSCRIPT ABOUT TALL RICE PLANTS**

1267	衡	KŌ, kubiki	均衡 KINKŌ	balance
		SCALES, YOKE	平衡 HEIKŌ	equilibrium
		16 strokes	衡器 KŌKI	scales

大 is **big man** 53, here meaning simply **man**. 甶 is a simplification of **horn** 角 243. 行 is **go** 118 q.v., here acting phonetically to express **crosswise** and also lending similar connotations from its literal meaning of crossroads. 1267 originally referred to a **piece of wood fixed across a cow's horns** to prevent them from goring the herdsman. It was later also used to refer to a **yoke**, though technically this is a different device. **Balance/scales** is felt by some scholars to be a borrowed meaning, and by others to derive from the fact that the piece of wood was fixed horizontally and thus suggested a set of scales. Suggest remembering 甶 as a **'stumpy' horn**, with 大 in its commoner sense of **big**.

Mnemonic: **BIG STUMPY HORN GOES ON TO THE SCALES**

1268 購	KŌ BUY 17 strokes	購入 KŌNYŪ	purchase
		購買 KŌBAI	buying
		購読 KŌDOKU	subscription

貝 is **shell/ money** 90. 冓 is build up/ **piled up baskets** 675 q.v., here acting phonetically to express **desire** and almost certainly also lending connotations of **pile/ large amount**. 1268 originally referred to **desiring something to the extent of paying out (a large amount of?) money for it**, and eventually came to mean **buy** in a broad sense.

Mnemonic: **USE SHELL-MONEY TO BUY PILE OF BASKETS**

1269 拷	GŌ TORTURE, HIT 9 strokes	拷問 GŌMON	torture
		拷責 GŌSEKI	torture
		拷問台 GŌMONDAI	the rack

扌 is **hand** 32. 考 is **consider** 117 q.v., here acting phonetically to express **beat/ hit** and possibly also lending its connotations of bent figure. Thus to **beat someone with the hand** (causing them to double up?), which also came to mean **hurt** and later, by association, **torture**.

Mnemonic: **CONSIDER HOW TO USE HAND TO TORTURE**

1270 剛	GŌ STRENGTH 10 strokes	剛健 GŌKEN	fortitude
		剛毛 GŌMŌ	bristle
		剛直 GŌCHOKU	integrity

刂 is **sword/ cut** 181. 岡 is **(towering) hill** 864 q.v., here acting phonetically to express **strong** and almost certainly also lending connotations of **formidable**. Thus a **strong (and formidable?) sword**, which later came to symbolise **strength** and **power** in general.

Mnemonic: **CUTTING DOWN A HILL TAKES STRENGTH**

1271	GŌ STRENGTH, SPLENDOR, AUSTRALIA, BRUSH 14 strokes	豪雨 GŌU 豪壮 GŌSŌ 豪州 GŌSHŪ	heavy rain splendor Australia

Of confusing semantic evolution. A modified combination of **pig/ pig-like creature** 豕 1670 and **tall** 高 119. The latter acts phonetically to express **fearsome sword-like weapon** (in effect being a phonetic substitute for strong sword 岡刂 1270) and almost certainly also originally lent its meaning of tall. Thus **pig-like creature with (tall?) fearsome sword-like weapons**. This was technically a reference to the **porcupine** (a meaning still found in Chinese and very occasionally in Japanese), but was apparently also used to refer to the **wild boar**, thus leading to **strength** (and in Chinese prowess) and the occasionally encountered associated meanings of **mane** and **bristle** (including **writing brush**) and by further confusing association **down** and **plumage**. **Splendor** is felt to be an associated meaning with plumage. Of late 1271 has also been used instead of the NGU character moat 濠 (i.e. water 氵 40 plus 豪 in its sense of formidable) to refer to **Australia**. Suggest taking 豪 as a combination of **tall** 高 and **house** 家 83.

Mnemonic: **AUSTRALIA BOASTS SPLENDID STRONG TALL HOUSES**

1272	KOKU CONQUER, OVERCOME 7 strokes	克服 KOKUFUKU subjugation 克己 KOKKI self-denial 克明 KOKUMEI diligence

Somewhat obscure. 儿 is **bending person** 39. 古 is **old** 109 q.v., here in its assumed literal meaning of **skull-like mask**. 1272 originally appeared to refer to a person bending under the weight of a heavy ceremonial mask, then came by association to mean **withstand** (i.e. the weight of the mask) and eventually **overcome/ conquer**.

Mnemonic: **OVERCOME BENT OLD PERSON**

1273	KOKU SEVERE, INTENSE, CRUEL, HARSH 14 strokes	酷使 KOKUSHI exploitation 残酷 ZANKOKU cruelty 酷暑 KOKUSHO intense heat

酉 is **wine jar/ alcohol** 302. 告 is **proclaim** 481 q.v., here acting phonetically to express **strong** and possibly also lending connotations of reeking from its idea of emerging from the mouth. Thus **strong alcohol**, leading to **strong/ intense/ astringent** in a general sense, with **cruel/ harsh** being an associated meaning.

Mnemonic: **CRUEL PROCLAMATION ABOUT ALCOHOL**

1274 **GOKU** 　　獄門 GOKUMON　prison gate
PRISON, LITIGATION 　地獄 JIGOKU　hell
14 strokes 　　　　　疑獄 GIGOKU　criminal case

Two **dogs** 犭/犬 opposed to each other, indicating a **fight**, with **words/ speak** 言 274. 1274 originally referred to a **dispute**, then came to mean **litigation** (still a strong meaning in Chinese). This gradually broadened to mean **going through the legal process**, leading to **imprisonment** and **prison**.

Mnemonic: **WORDS IN DOG FIGHT LEAD TO LITIGATION AND PRISON**

1275 *komu/meru* 　　見込み MIKOMI　prospect
PUT IN, BE CROWDED 人込み HITOGOMI　crowd
5 strokes 　　　　　込め物 KOMEMONO　stuffing

Movement 辶 129 and **enter/ put in** 入 63, giving **move into/ put into** and by association **be crowded**. A 'made in Japan' character.

Mnemonic: **IT BECOMES CROWDED AS PEOPLE MOVE TO ENTER**

1276 **KON** 　　　昆虫 KONCHŪ　insect
MULTITUDE, INSECT, 昆布 KONBU　kelp
DESCENDANTS 　後昆 KŌKON　descendants
8 strokes

A long-misinterpreted character. Usually taken to comprise **sun/ day** 日 62, in the sense of **time**, and compare 比 771 q.v., in its literal sense of **line of people**, to give **line of people over time**, i.e. **descendants**, with **multitude** being an associated meaning and **insect** taken to be an associated meaning in turn from the idea of swarm. However, very old forms such as 𩠐 show that 1276 is in fact a pictograph of an **insect** with **legs** 𣎳/ 比 and **carapace** ⊡/日. Thus insect is the original meaning. However, since early times it was miscopied as day 日 and people 比, thus giving descendants and multitude as per the interpretation cited above, but somewhat incongruously the original meaning of insect was retained.

Mnemonic: **DESCENDANTS LINE UP OVER MANY DAYS, LIKE INSECTS**

1277

KON, ura*mu*
RESENT, REGRET
9 strokes

悔恨 KAIKON   remorse
遺恨 IKON   grudge
恨み言 URAMIGOTO   grievance

忄 is heart/ **feelings** 147. 艮 is **stop and stare/ turn round and stare** 263, here acting phonetically to express **contrary** and also lending similar connotations of **turning against**. 1277 originally meant to have **contrary feelings/ be opposed**. Possibly because of the idea of staring contained in 艮 (as opposed to voicing), it came to acquire particular (but not exclusive) connotations of opposition kept in the heart rather than openly expressed, giving **resentment** and by association **regret**.

Mnemonic: **STOP AND STARE WITH RESENTFUL FEELINGS**

1278

KON
MARRIAGE
11 strokes

婚約 KONYAKU   engagement
結婚式 KEKKONSHIKI wedding
新婚夫婦 SHINKONFŪFU
               newly weds

Somewhat obscure. 女 is **woman** 35. 昏 is an NGU character meaning dim/ **sunset**. It comprises **sun** 日 62 and **scoop** 氏 495 q.v., though the role of the latter element is unclear (some scholars take it to be an abbreviation of bottom 氐 548, giving sun at the bottom [of its trajectory] and hence sunset). Woman 女 and sunset 昏 are popularly interpreted as being used ideographically to refer to some supposed practice of **wedding ceremonies being held at sunset**, but there is no historical foundation for this. Some authoritative Japanese scholars take 昏 to be used purely phonetically to express **root** (KON 根 282), which was a euphemism for **male organ**, and thus take 婚 to refer to the **penetration of a woman**. As in Western societies, this was a symbol of the **consummation of marriage**. Suggest taking 氏 in its meaning of **Mr.** (It is remotely possible, but chronologically unlikely, that 昏 was deliberately chosen as a phonetic with 氏 in its later sense of Mr, to give a balance between man and woman.)

Mnemonic: **WOMAN MARRIES MISTER, WITH SUN SINKING BELOW**

1279 紺

KON
DARK BLUE, DYE
11 strokes

紺色 KONIRO   dark blue
紺屋 KONYA   dyer
濃紺 NŌKON   dark blue

糸 is **thread** 27. 甘 is **sweet** 1093, here acting phonetically to express **dark blue**. Thus **threads (dyed) dark blue**, later **dark blue** in general, with **dye** a minor meaning.

Mnemonic: **THREADS DYED A SWEET DARK BLUE**

1280

KON, tama, tamashii
SOUL, SPIRIT
14 strokes

霊魂 REIKON　　　　soul
商魂 SHŌKON　salesmanship
魂消る TAMAGERU* be shocked

鬼 is **ghost**/ demon 1128 q.v., here meaning **spirit of a dead person**. 云 is **say**/ speak 78 q.v., here acting phonetically to express move/ **swirl** and also lending its literal meaning of **vapors**. Thus **swirling vapors which are the spirit of a dead person**, later **spirit** and **soul** in a broader sense. Suggest taking 云 as **two** 二 61 **noses** ム 134.

Mnemonic: **GHOST WITH TWO NOSES IS A FUNNY SPIRIT**

1281

KON
CULTIVATE, RECLAIM
16 strokes

開墾 KAIKON　　reclamation
墾田 KONDEN　　new fields
未開墾地 MIKAIKONCHI

　　　　　　　virgin land

Somewhat obscure. Formerly 墾, and in earlier times 𥃅. 艮 is **stop and stare** 263. 堇 is the obscure element seen in 漢 442 q.v., and is taken by some scholars to have originally meant **beast**. In this case it does indeed appear to have been interchangeable with beast 豸 (see below). In combination with stop and stare 艮 it gives the NGU character **difficult** 艱, though it is not clear how these elements are used. 堇 was later replaced by **pig** 豕 1670, presumably meaning simply beast, and later still by 豸. This is a CO character used of a range of mythical beasts. It shows **claws** 爫 303 and **dog**/ **beast** 犭 17, and is generally known as the **clawed beast** (affectionately Claude Beast) or **clawed dog** radical. In the case of 1281 艱/ 豤/ 貇 acts phonetically to express **difficult** and also lends a similar meaning, combining with **earth**/ **ground** 土 60 to give **earth that is difficult (to till/ cultivate)**. This was a reference to **virgin land**, leading by association to **reclaim** and **cultivate**.

Mnemonic: **STOP AND STARE AT CLAWED BEAST ON RECLAIMED GROUND**

1282
KON, nengoro
COURTESY, CORDIALITY,
EARNEST WISH
17 strokes

懇談 KONDAN — chat
懇願 KONGAN — entreaty
懇意 KONI kindness, friendship

心 is **heart/ feelings** 147. 狠 is the somewhat obscure element seen in 銀 1281 q.v., here acting phonetically to express **wish/ request** and possibly also lending connotations of difficulty. Thus a **wish/ request from the heart** (which is difficult to make?). In Chinese earnest wish/ beseech is a major meaning, but in Japanese the idea of **earnestness/ sincerity** gave rise to the associated meanings of **cordiality** and hence **courtesy**, which are now the major meanings. Suggest taking 狠 literally as **clawed beast** (claws 爫 303 and beast 豸 17) and **stop and stare** 艮 263.

Mnemonic: **STOP AND STARE AT CLAWED BEAST, CORDIALITY IN HEART**

1283
S A
ASSIST, ASSISTANT
7 strokes

補佐 HOSA — assistance
佐官 SAKAN — field officer
大佐 TAISA — colonel

Left 左 22 q.v., here with its original meaning of **assist**, with **person** 亻 39. Originally **assistant**, but now also **assist/ assistance**.

Mnemonic: **ASSISTED BY PERSON ON ONE'S LEFT**

1284
SA, sosonokasu, sosoru
ENTICE, INCITE
10 strokes

示唆 SHISA — suggestion
教唆 KYŌSA — incitement
教唆者 KYŌSASHA — abettor

口 is **mouth/ say** 20. 夋 is **linger** 689, here acting phonetically to express **coerce/ exhort** but of unclear semantic role. Thus to **urge someone to do something**, often with connotations of wrongdoing. Suggest taking 口 in its extended sense of **words**.

Mnemonic: **LINGERING WORDS OF ENTICEMENT**

1285
S A
LIE, DECEIVE
12 strokes

詐欺師 SAGISHI — swindler
詐取 SASHU — fraud
詐称 SASHŌ misrepresentation

Words/ speak 言 274 and **make/ make up** 乍 127 q.v., which also lends its later connotations of **deceit**. Thus **made up deceitful words**, i.e. a **lie** or similar.

Mnemonic: **MAKE UP WORDS IN DECEITFUL LIE**

1286 SA, kusari
CHAIN, LINK
18 strokes

鎖国 SAKOKU closed country
連鎖 RENSA chain, series
鎖止め KUSARIDOME sprocket

金 is **metal** 14. 𧶠 is an element meaning **chain/ link**, comprising **shell** 貝 90 and **small** ⺌/小 36 (small shells being strung together in a chain). Some scholars feel that 𧶠 also acts phonetically to express **connect**. Thus **metal chain** (of small connected links). 1286 was also formerly written 鏁, though this is technically a separate character of similar meaning using nest 巢 1521, the latter acting in a similar phonetic role to 𧶠 and possibly also lending connotations of round and hollow. Suggest taking 金 in its meaning of **gold**.

Mnemonic: **CHAIN OF SMALL GOLD SHELLS**

1287 SAI, kuda*ku/keru*
BREAK, SMASH
9 strokes

砕氷船 SAIHYŌSEN icebreaker
砕片 SAIHEN fragment
砕けた KUDAKETA informal

Formerly 碎. 石 is **stone/ rock** 45. 卒 is **soldier** 537, here acting phonetically to express **smash/ break up** but of unknown semantic role. Thus **smash rock**, later **smash/ break up** in a broader sense. Suggest taking 卆 as **nine** 九 12 and **ten** 十 33.

Mnemonic: **SMASH ROCK INTO NINETEEN FRAGMENTS**

1288 SAI
ADMINISTER
10 strokes

主宰者 SHUSAISHA leader
宰領 SAIRYŌ management
宰相 SAISHŌ prime minister

宀 is **house/ building** 28. 辛 is **needle** 1432 q.v., but is known to have symbolised **prisoner** and thus derives from the variant 辛/辛 that appears to have been an instrument of torture. Thus **prisoners in a building**. This was actually a reference to prisoners being <u>made to work</u> in a building (at one stage strike 殳 153 was added to act as a causative particle, giving 𢨺, which is still found in Chinese as a variant of 1288). In Chinese 1288 can also mean to slaughter animals, which appears to be a reference to one of the tasks usually assigned to prisoners. In general , however, the idea of prisoners at work led by association to the idea of **supervising** such work, giving supervisor/ ruler in Chinese and **administer** in Japanese. Suggest taking 辛 in its sense of **sharp**.

Mnemonic: **BUILDING HOUSES SHARP ADMINISTRATION**

411

1289		SAI PLANTING 10 strokes	栽培 SAIBAI 盆栽 BONSAI 前栽 SENZAI*	cultivation bonsai garden

木 is **tree** 69. 𢦏 is **cut/ fancy halberd** 872, here acting phonetically to express **plant** and possibly also loosely lending similar connotations from the occasional practice of thrusting a halberd/ lance into the ground as a crude marker (see 698). Thus to **plant trees**, later **plant/ planting** in a broader sense.

Mnemonic: **PLANT TREES USING FANCY HALBERD!?**

1290		SAI, irodoru COLOR 11 strokes	色彩 SHIKISAI 淡彩 TANSAI 彩雲 SAIUN	color(ing) light coloring glowing clouds

彡 is **delicate hairs** 93, here meaning **attractive adornment**. 采 is **hand plucking from tree** 483 (literally hand 爫 303 and tree 木 69), here acting phonetically to express **variety** and possibly also lending similar connotations (采 does in fact have a lesser meaning of variety of color, but it is not clear whether this is a meaning acquired in its own right, such as by extension from a bouquet of picked blossoms or similar, or whether it results from its use as a simplification of color 彩 1290). Thus **attractive and varied adornment**, which later came to mean in particular an **attractive variety of color** and finally just **coloration/ color**. Suggest taking 彡 as the **hairs of a brush**.

Mnemonic: **BRUSH PAINTS COLORS OF BLOSSOMS TAKEN FROM TREE**

1291	斎	SAI PURIFICATION, ABSTAIN, WORSHIP, A STUDY 11 strokes	斎戒 SAIKAI 書斎 SHOSAI 潔斎 KESSAI	purification a study abstinence, purification

Formerly 齋 . 礻 is a variant of **altar/ of the gods** 示 695. 斉 is a variant of similar 齊 1473 q.v., here acting phonetically to express **pure/ purified** and also lending similar connotations from its literal meaning of **food arranged for offering**. Thus **purified food for offering to the gods**, leading to **purification** and **worship**. By association it also came to mean **abstain**, from the fact that priests ate only purified foods and abstained from others. **Study** derives from 1291's use as a simplification of a now defunct character 齋 , which added building 广 114 to give place of worship. This came to mean (room in a) temple, which was a place of contemplation/ study. Suggest taking the modern form 斎 as **altar** 示 , **text** 文 68, and a **frame** ||.

Mnemonic: **TEXT ON PURIFICATION USING FRAMED ALTAR**

1292	債	SAI	債務 SAIMU	liabilities
		DEBT, LOAN	債券 SAIKEN	debenture
		13 strokes	債権者 SAIKENSHA	creditor

Liability 責 728 q.v., here in its literal meaning of **money which can be demanded**, and **person** 亻 39, here referring to the person doing the demanding. Thus **money demanded by a person**, namely a **debt/ loan**.

Mnemonic: **DEBT IS A PERSON'S LIABILITY**

1293	催	SAI, moyō*su*	主催 SHUSAI	sponsorship
		ORGANISE, MUSTER	催促 SAISOKU	urging
		13 strokes	催眠 SAIMIN	hypnosis

Obscure. 亻 is **person** 39. 崔 is a CO character meaning **high mountain**, thus suggesting that the character comprises two distinct elements of **mountain** 山 24 and **bird** 隹 216 and is not one of the graphically similar crested bird characters (see 1202). The etymology of 崔 is not clear, but 隹 presumably suggests height (either from a bird soaring or a high place where birds gather) and probably also plays some unclear phonetic role. In the case of 1293 the role of 崔 is also unclear. Some scholars feel that it originally acted phonetically to express **forge** (metal), giving **person who forges metal**, i.e. **swordsmith**, and that it was later borrowed to express **organise/ muster**. However, the evidence for this is not entirely convincing. An alternative hypothesis might be that 崔 acts phonetically to express **administer/ supervise** (see 1288), in a sense of **control**, and also lends connotations of **gathering** (birds occasionally symbolising this), thus giving a **controlled gathering of persons** and hence both **organise** and **muster**.

Mnemonic: **PERSON MUSTERS AND ORGANISES BIRDS ON MOUNTAIN**

1294	歳	SAI, SEI	二歳 NISAI	two years old
		YEAR	歳費 SAIHI	annual expenses
		13 strokes	歳暮 SEIBO	year-end gift

Old forms such as 歲 show 止, the old form of **walk** 步 202 q.v., and **halberd/ trimming tool** 戌 246 (now halberd/ trimming tool 戊 515). The latter acts phonetically to express **circuit** and may also lend supporting figurative connotations of cut/ cut off (cutting often being associated with halberds -- see 493), as in the English term cut-off point. 1294 originally referred to **walking one lap/ circuit**, but was then applied to the **completion of a cycle of time**, specifically a **year**. Suggest taking 止 as **foot** 129, 示 as a variant of **altar** 示 695, and 戊 as **halberd**.

Mnemonic: **EVERY YEAR HALBERDS PLACED AT FOOT OF ALTAR**

413

1295		SAI, noru/seru LOAD, CARRY 13 strokes	積載 SEKISAI	loading
			掲載 KEISAI	publication
			記載 KISAI	mention

車 is **vehicle** 31. 戈 is **fancy halberd/ cut** 872 q.v., here acting phonetically to express **load** and almost certainly also lending connotations of **trim/ adjust**. Thus **that which is loaded onto a vehicle (and adjusted?)**, i.e. **load/ cargo**, now **load/ carry**.

Mnemonic: **VEHICLE CARRIES LOAD OF FANCY HALBERDS**

1296		ZAI MEDICINE, DRUG 10 strokes	薬剤師 YAKUZAISHI pharmacist
			薬剤 YAKUZAI	drug
			緩下剤 KANGEZAI	laxative

Formerly 劑. 刂 is **sword/ cut** 181, here meaning **trim**. 齊/斉 is **similar** 1473 q.v., here acting phonetically to express **put in order** and also lending its own connotations of **arrange and make similar**. 1296 originally referred to **fine trimming something until all aspects were similar**, and thus came to mean **adjust/ regulate/ make just right**. This was later applied to **medicines/ drugs**, which regulate the body (some scholars feel rather that the adjustment was carried out on the drugs themselves, to ensure the optimal mix). Suggest remembering **similar** 斉 by partial association with **text** 文 68.

Mnemonic: **TEXT SAYS DRUGS CAN BE SIMILAR IN EFFECT TO SWORD**

1297		saki, KI CAPE, STEEP 11 strokes	長崎 NAGASAKI	Nagasaki
			島崎 SHIMAZAKI	a surname
			崎く KIKU	steep road

Mountain 山 24 and **strange** 奇 1123. The latter acts phonetically to express **dangerous** and almost certainly also lends connotations of **unusual/ exceptional**. Thus **(exceptionally?) dangerous mountain**, i.e. one that is very **steep**. In Japanese it has come to mean **promontory/ cape**, being a reference to a steep mountain rising from the sea.

Mnemonic: **CAPE FORMED BY STRANGE STEEP MOUNTAIN**

| 1298 削 | SAKU, kezuru
PARE, REDUCE
9 strokes | 削除 SAKUJO deletion
削減 SAKUGEN reduction
削り取る KEZURITORU shave off |

Of disputed etymology. 刂 is **sword/ cut** 181, while 肖 is **be like** 1391 q.v. Some scholars feel that the latter acts phonetically to express **put in**, giving **that into which one puts a sword**, i.e. a **scabbard**, and take **pare/ reduce** to be a borrowing. (In such case 肖 might also be felt to lend an idea of similarity [of shape], i.e. the scabbard matching the sword.) There is some evidence to support this theory in that the use of leather 革 821 instead of sword 刂 gives the CO character scabbard/ sheath 鞘 . However, other scholars take 肖 to lend connotations of **reduce** from its original meaning of miniature version, as well as possibly acting phonetically to express **few/ little** (see 消 316), to give **reduce by cutting**. It is possible that both theories are correct, in that 1298 may originally have meant scabbard, but that pare/ reduce results from a reinterpretation of its elements (in similar fashion to the reinterpretation of 1276) rather than a simple borrowing. Suggest taking 肖 literally as **small** ⺌ /小 36 and **flesh** 月 365.

Mnemonic: **TO CUT AWAY SMALL BITS OF FLESH IS TO PARE**

| 1299 索 | SAKU
ROPE, SEARCH
10 strokes | 索引 SAKUIN index
思索 SHISAKU speculation
鉄索 TESSAKU cable |

Old forms such as show **hands** 屮屮 and **thread** 幺 /糸 27. The hands are in fact **plaiting** the thread into **rope**. **Search** is a borrowed meaning. Suggest taking 十 as a roof with a cross, i.e. a **church roof**.

Mnemonic: **SEARCH FOR ROPE: FIND THREAD UNDER CHURCH ROOF**

| 1300 酢 | SAKU, su, suppai
VINEGAR, SOUR
12 strokes | 酢酸 SAKUSAN acetic acid
酢の物 SUNOMONO pickles
酢づけ SUZUKE pickling |

酉 is **wine jar/ alcohol** 302, here meaning **wine**. 乍 is **make** 127, here also acting phonetically to express **passage of time**. Thus **that which is made from wine with the passage of time**, i.e. **vinegar**.

Mnemonic: **VINEGAR IS MADE FROM WINE**

1301

SAKU, shibo*ru*
WRING, PRESS
13 strokes

搾取 SAKUSHU　exploitation
圧搾 ASSAKU　　pressure
搾り取る SHIBORITORU　extract

A 'made in Japan' character comprising **hand** 扌 32 and 窄, an NGU character meaning **squeeze**/ make narrow (from **hole** 穴 849 and **make** 乍 127) which also acts here phonetically to express **press**. Thus **press and squeeze with the hand**, now **press/ wring** in a broader sense.

Mnemonic: **MAKE HOLE BY PRESSING WITH HAND**

1302

SAKU
MIX UP, CONFUSE
16 strokes

錯誤 SAKUGO　　mistake
錯覚 SAKKAKU　　illusion
倒錯 TŌSAKU　　perversion

金 is **metal** 14. 昔 is **olden times** 1481 q.v., here acting phonetically to express **cover** and almost certainly also lending its connotations of duplicate. Thus to **cover with metal** (thereby making a second surface?), i.e. to **plate** and by association **inlay** (still a minor meaning in Chinese). Some scholars take **mix up/ confuse** to be a borrowed meaning, while others take it to be an associated meaning from the idea of mixing elements involved in inlaying/ plating.

Mnemonic: **IN OLDEN TIMES METALS WERE OFTEN MIXED UP**

1303

saku
BLOOM, BLOSSOM
9 strokes

四季咲き SHIKIZAKI　perennial
遅咲き OSOZAKI　late blooming
咲き残る SAKINOKORU

stay in bloom

Formerly 唉. 口 is **mouth/ say** 20. 关/关 is not raise repeatedly 关 1603 but a variant or miscopying of (drooping?) **thistle** 実 900 q.v., as is clear from an old form 口关. 关/关/关 acts phonetically to express **crease** and almost certainly also lends connotations of **thin** (from the stem of the thistle), to give (thin) **creases around the mouth**. This was a reference to **smiling** and **laughing**, the original meanings of 1303 (and still its only meanings in Chinese). In Japanese the idea of laughing led by association to the idea of a **plant opening its mouth**, giving **blossom/ bloom**, while smile/ laugh has disappeared. Suggest taking 关 as **heaven** 天 58 and out of/ **forth** ⺍ 66, with 口 in its literal sense of **open mouth**.

Mnemonic: **HEAVENLY FLOWERS OPEN MOUTHS TO BLOSSOM FORTH**

1304	**SATSU, fuda**	札入れ SATSUIRE billfold
	TAG, BILL, NOTE	名札 NAFUDA nameplate, tag
	5 strokes	千円札 SENENSATSU
		1000 yen note

木 is **tree/ wood** 69. し is not **praying figure** し 413, though it may be helpful to remember it as such, but a variant of **odd** 乙 1041, here used purely phonetically to express **slice/ shave thinly**. Thus **thinly shaved piece of wood**, i.e. **a tag**, which was later also applied to **money bills/ notes**.

Mnemonic: **PERSON PRAYS AT TREE FOR MONEY BILLS**

1305	**SATSU, toru, tsumamu**	撮影 SATSUEI photography
	PLUCK, TAKE	撮り直す TORINAOSU retake
	15 strokes	撮み食い TSUMAMIGUI 'graft'

扌 is **hand** 32. 最 is **most** 484 q.v., here in its literal sense of **take by force**. Thus **take by force with the hand**, i.e. **snatch/ pluck**, often with connotations of theft or improper possession. It is also used of **taking photographs**, probably from the idea of quick action.

Mnemonic: **TAKE MOSTLY BY HAND**

1306	**SATSU, suru/reru, kosuru**	擦過傷 SAKKASHŌ abrasion
	RUB, CHAFE, BRUSH	擦れ違う SURECHIGAU brush past
	17 strokes	擦り込む SURIKOMU rub in

扌 is **hand** 32. 察 is **realise** 489 q.v., here acting phonetically to express **rub** and possibly also lending an idea of scouring from its assumed early connotations of purify. Thus to **rub with the hand**, now **rub** in a broader sense.

Mnemonic: **REALISE HAND IS CHAFED**

1307	**sara**	灰皿 HAIZARA ashtray
	DISH, BOWL, PLATE	大皿 ŌZARA large dish
	5 strokes	皿洗い SARAARAI dishwashing

Stylised derivative of a stemmed **bowl** with exaggerated lip ᴗ. Suggest taking ‖ as **fluting**, with ㅛ as a **dish on a plate**.

Mnemonic: **FLUTED DISH ON PLATE**

417

1308		SAN	桟橋 SANBASHI	jetty
		SPAR, BEAM, FRAME	桟敷 SAJIKI*	stand, box
		10 strokes	桟道 SANDŌ	
			walkway made of planks	

Formerly 棧. 木 is tree/ wood 69. 戔 is lances/ halberds 493, here acting phonetically to express interweave and probably also lending an idea of pole. Thus interwoven pieces of wood, a reference to a frame and the spars/ beams forming it. Suggest taking 戔 as two 二 61 lances 戈 493.

Mnemonic: FRAME MADE USING TWO WOODEN LANCES AS SPARS

1309		SAN, ZAN, mugo*i*, miji*me*	惨劇 SANGEKI	tragedy
		CRUEL, MISERABLE	惨殺 ZANSATSU	massacre
		11 strokes	悲惨 HISAN	misery

忄 is heart/ feelings 147. 参 is attend/ go 490 q.v., here acting phonetically to express needle/ pierce and probably also lending reinforcing connotations of needle/ pin from its original meaning of woman with ostentatious hairpins. Thus to pierce the heart (figuratively with a needle), i.e. torment, symbolising cruelty from one point of view and misery from another.

Mnemonic: CRUELTY ATTENDED BY FEELINGS OF MISERY

1310		SAN, kasa	傘下 SANKA-	affiliated
		UMBRELLA, PARASOL	雨傘 AMAGASA	umbrella
		12 strokes	日傘 HIGASA	parasol

A pictograph of an umbrella/ parasol showing its frame 十, hood 人, and supports 仌仌. Suggest taking 人 as a cover (see 87), 仌仌 as four persons 人 39, and 十 as ten 33.

Mnemonic: UMBRELLA COVERS FOURTEEN PERSONS!

1311

暫

ZAN, shibaraku
A WHILE, BRIEFLY
15 strokes

暫定的 ZANTEITEKI　　tentative
暫時 ZANJI　　short time
暫くして SHIBARAKUSHITE
after a while

日 is **sun/ day** 62, here meaning **time**. 斬 is an NGU character meaning **behead/ kill**. Its exact etymology is unclear, but it comprises **vehicle** 車 31 and **ax/ cut** 斤 1176, and may possibly have originally referred to cutting someone down in their carriage/ palanquin. Here it acts phonetically to express **brief/ quick**, and presumably also lends similar connotations from the swiftness associated with beheading. Thus **brief time**. Confusingly, but in exactly the same way as the English term **a while**, in practice it can also mean a **considerable time**.

Mnemonic: **AX TAKES A WHILE -- A DAY -- TO CHOP UP VEHICLE**

1312

旨

SHI, mune, umai
TASTY, GOOD, GIST
6 strokes

要旨 YŌSHI　　gist
趣旨 SHUSHI　　spirit
旨旨 UMAUMA　　nicely

日 is a simplification of **sweet** 甘 1093 q.v., here also with its connotations of **lingering in the mouth**. ヒ is **spoon** 910. Thus **something sweet which is spooned into the mouth and (whose taste) lingers**. This came to mean **tasty**, and **good** in a broad sense. **Gist** is a borrowed meaning, resulting from 1312's being used instead of 恉, a CO character meaning gist which combines 旨 with **heart/ feelings** 忄 147 and presumably means literally that which (is good and?) lingers in the heart. Suggest taking 日 as **sun** 62 and ヒ as **sitting person** 238.

Mnemonic: **GIST IS THAT PERSON THINKS IT'S GOOD TO SIT IN SUN**

1313

伺

SHI, ukagau
VISIT, SEEK, ASK,
HEAR
7 strokes

伺い事 UKAGAIGOTO　　inquiry
伺候 SHIKŌ　　courtesy call
伺い探る UKAGAISAGURU
spy out

亻 is **person** 39. 司 is **administer/ official** 497 q.v., here acting phonetically to express **observe**. Since 1313 is a character of relatively recent origin it is probable that 司 also lends its later meaning of **official** (as opposed to its original meaning of anus). Thus **(an official?) person who observes**, actually a reference to an **investigator**. The present meanings are all derived from the idea of investigating.

Mnemonic: **OFFICIAL PERSON VISITS AND ASKS**

1314

SHI, sa*su*/sa*ru*, toge
PIERCE, STAB, THORN
8 strokes

名刺 MEISHI   name card
刺身 SASHIMI   sashimi
刺抜き TOGENUKI   tweezers

刂 is **sword/ cut** 181. 朿 is **thorn** 873 q.v., here also used in a general sense to indicate something **sharp** and **piercing**. 1314 originally meant **stab with a sword** before coming to mean **pierce/ stab** in general, and it is also occasionally found as **cut** in a broader sense (e.g. sashimi [sliced fish]). As with 873, suggest taking 朿 as a **tree** 木 69 with **droopy branches** ⌐.

Mnemonic: **CUT PIERCING THORNS FROM DROOPY BRANCHED TREE**

1315

SHI, eda
BRANCH
8 strokes

枝隊 SHITAI troop detachment
枝角 EDAZUNO   antlers
枯れ枝 KAREEDA   dead branch

Branch 支 691 q.v. with **tree** 木 69. Whereas 691 is now used largely in a figurative sense 1315 is largely (but not exclusively) used literally.

Mnemonic: **TREE BRANCH**

1316

SHI
WELL-BEING,
HAPPINESS
8 strokes

祉福 SHIFUKU   well-being
福祉 FUKUSHI   welfare
福祉国家 FUKUSHIKOKKA
              welfare state

Formerly 祉. 示/ネ is **altar/ of the gods** 695, while 止 is **foot/ stop** 129. The latter acts phonetically to express **bestow** but any semantic role is unclear. Thus **that bestowed by the gods**, a reference to **happiness/ well-being**.

Mnemonic: **FIND HAPPINESS AT FOOT OF ALTAR**

1317 肢

SHI
LIMB, PART
8 strokes

肢体 SHITAI   the limbs
下肢 KASHI   lower limbs
選択肢 SENTAKUSHI   option

Flesh/ of the body 月 365 and **branch** 支 691. The **branches of the body** are the **limbs**.

Mnemonic: **LIMBS ARE BRANCHES OF THE BODY**

1318

SHI, SE, hodoko*su*
PERFORM, CHARITY
9 strokes

施設　SHISETSU　facilities
実施　JISSHI　implementation
施薬　SEYAKU　free medicine

方゛ is **fluttering flag** 333.　也 is **twisting creature** 167, here acting phonetically to express **wave/ billow** and almost certainly also lending its own similar connotations of undulating. Thus **billowing flag**. **Perform** and **charity** (which both derive from the same core concept of doing an action for someone) result from borrowing. Suggest taking 方゛ as **side** 方 204 and **person** ト 39.

Mnemonic: **PERSON SHOWS CHARITY TO TWISTING CREATURE AT SIDE**

1319

SHI, abura, yani
FAT, GREASE, RESIN
10 strokes

脂肪　SHIBŌ　fat
脂気　ABURAKE　greasiness
脂目　YANIME　gummy eyes

Meat/ of the body 月 365 and **tasty** 旨 1312. **Fat** was often considered tastier than lean meat.

Mnemonic: **FAT IS TASTY MEAT**

1320

SHI, murasaki
PURPLE, VIOLET
12 strokes

紫煙　SHIEN　tobacco smoke
紫色　MURASAKIIRO　purple
紫外線　SHIGAISEN
　　　　ultraviolet rays

糸 is **thread** 27. 此 is an NGU character meaning **this/ here**, and comprises **foot/ stop** 止 129 and **sitting person** ヒ 238 (both presumably indicating not moving from a given point). 此 acts here phonetically to express **purple**, but any semantic role is unclear. Thus **purple threads**, now simply **purple**.

Mnemonic: **PERSON SITS AND TIES PURPLE THREAD ON FOOT**

1321

SHI, tsug*u*
HEIR, SUCCEED TO
13 strokes

嗣子 SHISHI — heir
後嗣 KŌSHI — heir
皇嗣 KŌSHI — crown prince

Of somewhat confused and obscure evolution. Originally written 𤔲, showing **bound bamboo writing-tablets** 卅/冊/冊 874 and the component parts of **administer/ official/ anus** 司 497 q.v., namely (reversed) **buttocks** 𠃌 and hole/ **opening** 口 20. The reason for the dislocation of these elements is not clear. When an opening 口 was later put under buttocks 𠃌, giving the proper form 司, the original opening 口 was also left over the bound tablets element 冊, giving the present form 嗣. It is not clear whether this was simply an error or whether it was left there deliberately to serve some special and presumably different purpose, such as perhaps suggesting encircling (with binding). 司 is known to have acted phonetically to express **control**, and probably (at least at the stage at which 𠃌 became written as 司) also lent similar connotations of its own (though since administer is a later meaning, it is possible that at the time of the earliest form 𠃌 it still meant anus, in which case any semantic role is unclear). Thus to **control bound tablets**, a reference to **binding them together particularly securely**. This came to mean **bind/ join** in general, with **inherit** and **succeed (to)** being associated meanings (as tsugu 継 1203). These associated meanings have now prevailed over bind/ join. Suggest taking 司 in its sense of **official**, and 口 as **circular/ round** (see 228).

Mnemonic: **OFFICIAL HEIR TO BOUND CIRCULAR TABLETS**

1322

SHI, ka*u*
REAR ANIMALS
13 strokes

飼育 SHIIKU — breeding
飼い主 KAINUSHI — owner
飼い犬 KAIINU — pet dog

食 is **food/ eat** 146. 司 is **administer/ official** 497, here acting phonetically to express **give** and almost certainly also lending its meaning of administer/ supervise. Thus to **give food to people** (under one's supervision?). In Chinese it still has this meaning, and is interchangeable with a CO character 飤 (food/ eat 食 and person 人 39), but in Japanese it came to refer rather to **feeding animals**, and thus by extension to **rearing** them.

Mnemonic: **REAR ANIMALS BY ADMINISTERING FOOD TO THEM**

1323

SHI, mesu, me
FEMALE
14 strokes

雌雄 SHIYŪ — gender, outcome
雌牛 MEUSHI — cow, heifer
雌犬 MEINU — bitch

隹 is **bird** 216. 此 is **this/ here** 1320, here acting phonetically to express **small** but of unclear semantic role. The smaller bird of a pair is generally the **female**. Suggest taking 此 literally as **stop** 止 129 and **sitting person** 匕 238.

Mnemonic: **FEMALE PERSON STOPS AND SITS ON BIRD**

1324 賜	SHI, tamawa*ru* BESTOW 15 strokes	賜暇 SHIKA furlough 恩賜 ONSHI imperial gift 賜物 TAMAMONO* gift, boon

貝 is shell/ **money** 90, here meaning **valuable item**. 易 is **easy**/ divination 618 q.v, here acting phonetically to express **great volume** and possibly also lending an idea of dazzling from its literal meaning of iridescent. 1324 originally referred to a **voluminous and valuable** (and dazzling?) **reward bestowed by a ruler**, leading to **bestowal**. It still retains occasional connotations of an imperial bestowal.

Mnemonic: **BESTOWAL IS EASY MONEY**

1325	SHI, haka*ru* CONSULT, INQUIRE 16 strokes	諮じゅん SHIJUN consultation 諮問 SHIMON inquiry 諮問機関 SHIMONKIKAN advisory body

咨 is an NGU character meaning **investigate/ inquire**. It comprises **mouth/ say** 口 20 and **next** 次 292 q.v., here acting phonetically to express **consult/ inquire** and almost certainly also lending connotations of sequence. Thus to **inquire verbally** (and in sequence, i.e. systematically?). 1325 adds **words/ speak** 言 274 for emphasis. Nevertheless, the verbal aspect has now faded, leaving just **inquire/ consult**.

Mnemonic: **IN INQUIRY, ONE MOUTH SPEAKS, THEN THE NEXT**

1326	JI, samurai, habe*ru* ATTEND (UPON) 8 strokes	侍従 JIJŪ chamberlain 侍女 JIJO lady-in-waiting 侍僧 JISŌ acolyte

亻 is **person** 39. 寺 is **temple** 133, here acting phonetically to express **serve** and also lending its connotations of **clerical work**. Thus **person serving in a clerical capacity**, later **servant/ attendant** in general, including **samurai**.

Mnemonic: **PERSON IN ATTENDANCE AT TEMPLE IS SAMURAI**

| 1327 | | JI
LUXURIANT, RICH,
STRENGTHEN, ENLIVEN
12 strokes | 滋養 JIYŌ
滋味 JIMI
滋雨 JIU | nourishment
savoriness
welcome rain |

Somewhat obscure. Formerly 滋. 氵 is **water/ river** 40, while 玆/兹 is the somewhat obscure double twisted thread element seen in 磁 881 q.v. Its role is unclear. Some scholars feel that it originally acted phonetically to express the name of a certain river, and take the present meanings to have derived from the life-giving nature of the river in question. However, it may be felt to have acted phonetically to express **rear/ grow** (as in 1328), as well as possibly lending connotations of mysteriousness and/or draw (see 881), to give **water/ river that brings growth** (and draws forth the mysterious power of life?), with any use as a proper noun stemming from this. Suggest remembering 玆 by association with **double** (short) **thread** 幺 111.

Mnemonic: **DOUBLE THREAD OF RIVER BRINGS LUXURIANT GROWTH**

| 1328 | | JI, itsuku*shimu*
LOVE, PITY, AFFECTION
13 strokes | 慈悲 JIHI
慈善 JIZEN
慈愛 JIAI | mercy
charity
benevolence |

Formerly 慈. 心 is **heart/ feelings** 147. 玆/兹 is the somewhat obscure double twisted thread element seen in 磁 881 q.v., here acting phonetically to express **rear/ raise** and probably also lending connotations of **small** and hence **child** (from the early meaning of very small of 玄 [see 1227]). 1328 originally referred to the **tender feelings** involved in **caring for a small child** (and in Chinese still retains connotations of motherhood), and then came to mean **(show) affection** in a general sense, including **love** and **pity**. Suggest remembering 玆 by association with **double** (short) **thread** 幺 111.

Mnemonic: **DOUBLE THREADS OF LOVE AND PITY IN HEART**

| 1329 | | JI
IMPERIAL SEAL
19 strokes | 御璽 GYOJI
国璽 KOKUJI
印璽 INJI | imperial seal
seal of state
imperial seal |

Once written 壐. 爾 is an NGU character now borrowed to express **you** and **so**, but it originally pictographically depicted a **device used in spinning** 㸚. Here it acts phonetically to express **press**, combining with **earth** 土 60 (here in the sense of **clay**) to express **that pressed into clay**, a reference to a **seal**. It is not clear why such a complex character was chosen as a phonetic, but it is possible that its complexity suggested the intricacy of a seal of a person of high rank. Earth 土 was later replaced by **jewel/ jade** 玉 102, symbolising **nobility** (particularly the **imperial house**). Unfortunately there is no easy mnemonic for 爾, but suggest remembering it by partial association with **four crosses** 㸚.

Mnemonic: **JEWELED IMPERIAL SEAL INCLUDES FOUR CROSSES**

1330		**JIKU**	車軸 SHAJIKU	axle
		AXLE, SHAFT, SCROLL	地軸 CHIJIKU	earth's axis
		12 strokes	軸物 JIKUMONO scroll picture	

車 is **vehicle** 31. 由 is **reason** 399, here acting phonetically to express **support** but of unclear semantic role. Thus **that which supports a vehicle**, a reference to its **axle(s)**. This later gave **spindle/ shaft** in a broad sense and, by association (of shape), **scroll**.

Mnemonic: **AXLE IS REASON VEHICLE MOVES**

1331		**SHITSU**	疾患 SHIKKAN	disease
		ILLNESS, SWIFTLY	疾走 SHISSŌ	scamper
		10 strokes	疾つく TOKKU ni*	long since

Once written 疾, showing a **person** 大 (see 53) hit by an **arrow** 一 981 and indicating a **sudden strike/ affliction**. The present form uses **arrow** 矢 981 and the **sickness** radical 疒 381. It can also be used of **swiftness** unrelated to illness.

Mnemonic: **ILLNESS STRIKES SWIFTLY AS AN ARROW**

1332		**SHITSU, SHŪ, tor*u***	執筆 SHIPPITSU	writing
		TAKE, GRASP	執念 SHŪNEN	tenacity
		11 strokes	執り成す TORINASU	mediate

Very old forms such as 𡙇 clearly show **shackles** 㚔/幸 233 and **kneeling person with outstretched arms** 彐/丸 470. Thus to **shackle a prisoner**, leading to **seize/ grasp** and **take**. Note that the addition of **thread/ cord** 糸 27 gives the CO character **fetter** 縶. Suggest taking 幸 as **happiness** 279 and 丸 as **round** 830.

Mnemonic: **HAPPINESS ROUNDED OFF BY TAKING A PRISONER**

1333		**SHITSU, shime*ru/su***	湿度 SHITSUDO	humidity
		DAMP, MOIST, HUMID	湿地 SHITCHI	marshland
		12 strokes	湿っぽい SHIMEPPOI damp, dismal	

Formerly 濕. 氵 is **water/ river** 40. 㬎/㬎 is **motes/ small particles** 1224 q.v., here acting phonetically to express **wet** and also lending its connotations of **small bits of thread**. 1333 originally referred to a **river broken up into pools** (i.e. not flowing in a continuous thread), giving **wetland/ marshland** and later **damp** in a broad sense. Note that very old forms such as 㬎 show that 㬎 is either a miscopying of or deliberate substitution for **cut threads** 幽 750 (㬎 being an old form of this), but both elements clearly play a similar role. Suggest taking 日 as **sun** 62 and 业 as a variant of **row** 並 1775.

Mnemonic: **SUN ON ROW OF WATERY DROPS MAKES IT HUMID**

1334 　SHITSU, urushi　　漆器 SHIKKI　　lacquerware
　　　　　LACQUER, VARNISH　漆黒 SHIKKOKU　jet black
　　　　　14 strokes　　　　漆塗り URUSHINURI lacquering

Formerly 桼 and earlier 桼, showing a **tree** 木/木 69 with **droplets of moisture** ⁚⁚ to indicate **resin/ sap**. This was a reference to **lacquer** (the sap of the lacquer-tree), with **varnish** being an associated meaning. **Water** 氵 40 was added to emphasise the liquid. Suggest taking 氺 as a variant of **water** 水 40, with 人 as **extra branches**.

Mnemonic: **EXTRA WATERY LACQUER FROM EXTRA BRANCHED TREE**

1335 　shiba　　　　芝生 SHIBAFU*　　　lawn
　　　　　TURF, LAWN　　芝居 SHIBAI　　drama, show
　　　　　6 or 5 strokes　芝刈り機 SHIBAKARIKI
　　　　　　　　　　　　　　　　　　　　　lawnmower

艹 is **plant/ grass** 9. 之 is an NGU character now borrowed to mean **this**, but it is in fact a highly stylised derivative of the variant 止/屮 of **plant** 生 42 q.v., and at one stage meant **emerge** (as a plant emerges from the ground) and by association **from**. In the case of 1335 it is used literally to mean (emerging) **plant**, with plant/ grass 艹 acting as a reinforcing element. In Japanese it has come to mean specifically **grass** (especially in the sense of **turf/ lawn**), but note that in Chinese it means lily. Suggest taking 之 as a **zig-zag path**.

Mnemonic: **ZIGZAG PATH CROSSES GRASSY LAWN**

1336 赦　SHA　　　　容赦 YŌSHA　　forgiveness
　　　　　FORGIVENESS　赦免 SHAMEN　　clemency
　　　　　11 strokes　　恩赦 ONSHA　　amnesty

攵 is **strike with stick/ beat** 101. 赤 is **red** 46 q.v., which acts phonetically to express **abandon/ stop** and may possibly also lend connotations of **raging** (from its literal meaning of large fire). Thus to **beat someone (in a rage?) and then stop**, with the act of stopping coming to symbolise **forgiveness**.

Mnemonic: **BEAT TILL RED, THEN SHOW FORGIVENESS**

426

1337

SHA, nana*me*

SLANTING, DIAGONAL

11 strokes

斜面 SHAMEN slope
斜方形 SHAHŌKEI rhombus
斜め継ぎ NANAMETSUGI

miter joint

斗 is **measure/ ladle** 1633. 余 is **ample/** excess 800, here acting phonetically to express **scoop out** and also lending its meaning of **ample**. Thus to **scoop out an ample measure. Slanting/ diagonal** is essentially a borrowed meaning, with 1337 being used instead of a more complex character with that meaning, but it may be that the borrowing process was influenced by the slope of the cross stroke in 斗 and the idea of ample contained in 余 (a diagonal giving the amplest measure across a square).

Mnemonic: **DIAGONAL GIVES AMPLEST MEASURE**

1338

SHA, ni*ru/eru/yasu*

BOIL, COOK

12 strokes

煮沸 SHAFUTSU boiling
生煮え NAMANIE undercooked
煮立てる NITATERU bring to boil

Formerly 煮. ⋯ is **fire** 8. 者/者 is **person** 298 q.v., here acting phonetically to express **boil** and also lending its early meaning of **various things**. Thus **boil various things over a fire.**

Mnemonic: **PERSON BOILS THINGS OVER FIRE**

1339

SHA, saegir*u*

OBSTRUCT,

INTERRUPT

14 strokes

遮二無二 SHANIMUNI recklessly
遮光幕 SHAKŌMAKU a shade
遮断器 SHADANKI circuit-
breaker, crossing-gate

辶 is **movement** 129. 庶 is **various** 1381 q.v., here acting phonetically to express **put** and also lending similar connotations from its early meaning of put things on a fire. Thus to **put something in the way of movement**, i.e. **obstruct**, with **interrupt** being an associated meaning.

Mnemonic: **VARIOUS THINGS CAN OBSTRUCT MOVEMENT**

1340	JA	邪悪 JAAKU	wickedness
	WICKEDNESS	無邪気 MUJAKI	innocence
	8 strokes	風邪 FŪJA/KAZE	a cold

Somewhat obscure. 阝 is **village** 355, while 牙 is **fang** 434. The role of the latter is not clear, since 1340 was originally used as a proper noun referring to a specific village in ancient China. It is also not clear whether the present meaning of **wickedness** derives from association with the village in question (cf. etymology of terms such as sodomy), or whether it is a borrowed meaning.

Mnemonic: **FANGS ARE BARED IN VILLAGE OF WICKEDNESS**

1341	JA, DA, hebi	蛇管 JAKAN	hose
	SNAKE, SERPENT	蛇行 DAKŌ	meandering
	11 strokes	蛇皮 HEBIKAWA	snakeskin

虫 is **insect** 56 q.v., here in its original meaning of **large headed (or hooded) snake**. 它 is a CO character now borrowed for a confusing range of meanings such as hang down and impute, but it derives from a pictograph of a **large headed snake** 它 and is to all intents and purposes a variant of 虫 56. Suggest taking 它 as **house/ roof** 宀 28 and **sitting person/ man** 匕 238.

Mnemonic: **MAN IN HOUSE SITS ON 'INSECT' -- REALLY A SNAKE!**

1342	SHAKU	一勺 ISSHAKU	one shaku
	LADLE, MEASURE	三勺 SANSHAKU	three shaku
	3 strokes	十勺 JISSHAKU	ten shaku

Also written 勺. From a pictograph of a **ladle/ scoop** 勺 (also 勹), with 丶/一 indicating the **contents**. It is now used almost exclusively to mean **scoopful** (specifically a **measure** of 0.02 liters), while ladle/ scoop is conveyed by the NGU character 杓 , which adds wood 木 69.

Mnemonic: **TILTED LADLE STILL KEEPS MEASURE OF CONTENTS**

1343 SHAKU, ku*mu*
SERVE WINE, LADLE,
SCOOP, DRINK
10 strokes

酌婦 SHAKUFU　　　waitress
晩酌 BANSHAKU　　'nightcap'
酌量 SHAKURYŌ
　　　　　　consideration

Ladle/ measure 勺 1342 and **wine (jar)** 酉 302. **A ladleful of wine** represented both **serving** and **drinking**. 1343 is also occasionally used to mean **scoop up**, including in the figurative sense of taking all circumstances into account, but this is generally conveyed by the NGU character 汲 (water/ liquid 氵 40 and reach 及 1148).

Mnemonic: **DRINK WINE SERVED BY LADLEFUL**

1344 SHAKU
PEERAGE
17 strokes

爵位 SHAKUI　　　　peerage
授爵 JUSHAKU　ennoblement
男爵 DANSHAKU　　　baron

Somewhat obscure, and of confused graphic evolution. Originally written 爵, showing an ornate **vessel used for pouring wine** (apparently with three legs, two handles, and a spout, and, according to some scholars, shaped like a bird with spread wings). Note that in Chinese 1344 still retains a minor meaning of wine vessel. Its evolution became confused with the addition and deletion of sundry sometimes obscure elements. The present form is best taken as an ideograph comprising **hand** 爫 303 (though in fact this is a miscopying of wood 木 69), dish/ **bowl** 皿 (variant 皿 1307), here meaning **vessel**, **food/ eat** 艮 146, here meaning **ingest**, and measure/ **hand** 寸 909 q.v. (apparently a miscopying of an ordinary hand 手, though it is possible that it is a deliberate substitution to suggest careful use of the hand). Thus a **vessel whose contents are ingested and which is lifted with two hands**. It is not clear how 1344 came to mean **peerage**. It does not appear to be a borrowing, and it is possible that the particular wine vessel was a symbol of high rank and hence nobility.

Mnemonic: **PEER'S HANDS CLUTCH FOOD BOWL**

1345 JAKU, SEKI, sabi, sabi*shii*
QUIET, LONELY
11 strokes

静寂 SEIJAKU　　　silence
寂ばく SEKIBAKU no　desolate
寂しさ SABISHISA　loneliness

宀 is roof/ **building** 28. 叔 is **uncle** 1367, here acting phonetically to express **quiet** but of unclear semantic role. Thus **quiet building**, now **quiet/ lonely** in a broader but usually melancholy sense.

Mnemonic: **UNCLE LONELY IN QUIET BUILDING**

1346	SHU	朱色 SHUIRO	vermilion
	VERMILION, RED	朱肉 SHUNIKU	red ink pad
	6 strokes	朱筆 SHUHITSU	
			red pen, correction

Once written 米 and later 朱, showing tree 朱/朱/木 69 and a symbol ○/一 indicating **center** (here in the sense of **inside**). The **inside of a tree(trunk)** is often **red**, and hence 1346 came to acquire this meaning. Somewhat surprisingly it came to acquire particular connotations of bright orange-red/ **vermilion**, though a pinkish red might have seemed more appropriate. Distinguish from immature/ treetop 未 794. Suggest in fact taking 1346 as a **treetop** (tree 木 69 with extra branches 一), with ノ as a **ribbon**.

Mnemonic: **BRIGHT RED RIBBON IN TREETOP**

1347	SHU, karu/ri	狩猟 SHURYŌ	hunting
	HUNT	狩犬 KARIINU	hunting dog
	9 strokes	狩り込み KARIKOMI	round-up

犭 is **dog** 17. 守 is **protect** 300 q.v., here acting phonetically to express **on all sides** and also lending a meaning of **be attentive and protective**. Thus a **dog which protects (its master) and is attentive on all sides**, i.e. a **hunting dog** (still a meaning in Chinese). Hunting dog came to symbolise **hunt** in general.

Mnemonic: **DOG PROTECTS MASTER WHEN OUT HUNTING**

1348	SHU, koto	特殊 TOKUSHU	special
	ESPECIALLY	殊勝 SHUSHŌ na	laudable
	10 strokes	殊更 KOTOSARA	especially

歹 is **bare bones/ death** 286. 朱 is **red** 1346 q.v., here acting phonetically to express **cut down/ attack** and almost certainly also lending its own connotations of inside the body/ trunk. 1348 originally meant to **cut someone to the very bone** (i.e. inside the body) and **kill them** (still a meaning in Chinese). This symbolised an **extreme attack**, giving **extremely** and hence **especially**.

Mnemonic: **RED BARE BONES ARE ESPECIALLY RARE**

1349

SHU
JEWEL, PEARL
10 strokes

珠玉 SHUGYOKU jewel, gem
真珠 SHINJU   pearl
数珠 JUZU*   rosary

王 is **jewel** 102. 朱 is **red** 1346 q.v., here acting phonetically to express **round** and almost certainly also lending its connotations of **inside**. Thus **round jewel/ pearl** (a pearl being a jewel inside a shell).

Mnemonic: **PEARL IS A RED JEWEL!?**

1350

SHU, omomuki
GIST, TENDENCY
15 strokes

趣味 SHUMI   hobby
趣意 SHUI   gist, view
趣向 SHUKŌ   scheme, plan

Run 走 161 and **take/ grasp** 取 301, to give a meaning of **run after something to take hold of it**. This came to mean **hurry after something** (still a meaning in Chinese), and then by association **go in a certain direction**. In the physical sense this is now usually conveyed by omomuku 赴 1751, whereas 1350 has come to be used rather in the abstract sense of **incline towards** and hence **tend/ tendency**. In Japanese it has also come to mean by association the **'drift'** or **gist** of an argument.

Mnemonic: **TENDENCY TO HAVE TO RUN FAST TO GRASP GIST**

1351

JU, kotobuki
LONG LIFE,
CONGRATULATION
7 strokes

寿命 JUMYŌ   life span
長寿 CHŌJU   longevity
米寿 BEIJU   88th birthday

Somewhat obscure. Formerly written 壽. 士 is a simplification of **old man** 老 117 (now usually 耂). 吾 is a simplification of 畺. This is an unclear element that was once written 畳, indicating perhaps **continuity/ flow** (possibly a symbol of flowing 乙 and **mouths/ openings** 口 20, though to judge from another form 畳, showing **speak** 曰 688, the bottom one of the mouths was originally a separate element meaning **speak**). 吾 is known to have acted phonetically to express **long time**, though any semantic role is unclear, with **hand/ measure** 寸 909 (a relatively late addition) playing a similar phonetic role for reinforcement. Thus an **old man who has lived a long time**. A **long life** is cause for **congratulation**. Note that eighty-eight is considered a particularly felicitous age, owing to the fact that the character for rice (a symbol of bounty and the life-force), 米 201, can be graphically interpreted as **ten** 十 33, times **eight** ハ 66, with a further **eight** ハ 66. Suggest taking 𦰩 as a variant of **hand** 手 32, and 寸 also in its sense of **hand**.

Mnemonic: **PUT HANDS TOGETHER TO CONGRATULATE LONG LIFE**

1352	JU	儒教 JUKYŌ	Confucianism
	CONFUCIANISM	儒者 JU SHA	Confucianist
	16 strokes	儒学 JUGAKU	Confucianism

イ is **person** 39. 需 is **demand** 887 q.v., here acting phonetically to express **gentle** and possibly also lending similar connotations of soft through its original meaning of **wet beard**. Thus **gentle person**, later applied to **followers of Confucius** and hence **Confucianism** itself.

Mnemonic: **CONFUCIANIST IS PERSON IN DEMAND**

1353	SHŪ	囚人 SHŪJIN	prisoner
	PRISONER	囚役 SHŪEKI	prison labor
	5 strokes	死刑囚 SHIKEISHŪ	
			condemned prisoner

A **person** 人 39 inside an **enclosure** 囗 123, indicating an **imprisoned person**.

Mnemonic: **PERSON CONTAINED WITHIN ENCLOSURE IS PRISONER**

1354	SHŪ, fune, funa-	舟航 SHŪKŌ	navigation
	BOAT, SHIP	舟遊び FUNAASOBI	boating
	6 strokes	小舟 KOBUNE	little boat

Once written 𠂤, pictographically depicting a **boat with raised stern and raised pointed prow**. Often found in early compounds as 𠂤 or 𠂤, and occasionally lends a meaning of **convey(ance)**. Popularly likened to a **sternless rowing boat** ∏ viewed from above, with **two people** ∶ sitting in it, an **oar** ─ laid across it, and a **mooring rope** ∕.

Mnemonic: **MOORED STERNLESS BOAT WITH TWO ROWERS AND OAR**

1355	SHŪ, hii*deru*	秀才 SHŪSAI	able student
	EXCEL, EXCELLENT	秀逸 SHŪITSU	excellence
	7 strokes	秀美 SHŪBI	great beauty

禾 is **rice plant** 81 (literally plant with head of grain). 乃 derives from a **bending person** 儿 (normally simplified to 儿 39, but in this case deliberately exaggerated to emphasise **bending**, and possibly showing some graphic influence from reach 及 1148). Thus **rice plant bent (under exceptionally heavy head)**, indicating an **excellent plant/ crop** and thus **excel/ excellent** in general.

Mnemonic: **GREATLY BENT RICE PLANT MEANS EXCELLENT CROP**

1356

SHŪ, kusa*i*
SMELL, SMACK
9 strokes

臭気 SHŪKI   bad odor
俗臭 ZOKUSHŪ   vulgarity
臭味 KUSAMI   smell, smack

Formerly 臭 , showing **dog** 犬 17 and **nose** 自 134. 1356 originally referred to a dog using its nose to follow a scent when hunting, but now means **smell** in a broader but frequently unpleasant sense. Also used figuratively as **smack (of)**. Suggest taking 大 as **big** 53.

Mnemonic: **BIG NOSE GOOD FOR SMELLS**

1357

SHŪ, urei/*eru*
GRIEF, SADNESS
13 strokes

愁傷 SHŪSHŌ   grief
哀愁 AISHŪ   sorrow
愁い顔 UREIGAO   sad face

心 is **heart/ feelings** 147. 秋 is **autumn** 140, here acting phonetically to express **grief** and possibly also lending its own connotations of melancholy. Thus **feelings of grief/ sadness**.

Mnemonic: **AUTUMNAL FEELINGS OF SADNESS**

1358

SHŪ
REWARD, TOAST, REPLY
13 strokes

報酬 HŌSHŪ   reward
応酬 ŌSHŪ   response
献酬 KENSHŪ

     exchange of sake cups

酉 is **wine jar/ alcohol** 302. 州 is **province/** sandbank 304, here acting phonetically to express **toast/ exchange drinking cups** and possibly also lending loose connotations of **flowing** from its **river** element 川 (see 48). 1358 originally referred to a **toast** (involving an exchange of cups), then came by extension to mean **recognise something worthy of toasting**, leading eventually to **reward**. **Reply/ response** is an associated meaning.

Mnemonic: **GAIN REWARD OF PROVINCIAL ALCOHOL**

1359		SHŪ, miniku*i* UGLY, SHAMEFUL 17 strokes	醜悪 SHŪAKU 醜聞 SHŪBUN 醜さ MINIKUSA	foulness scandal ugliness

Somewhat obscure. 酉 is **wine jar/ alcohol** 302. 鬼 is **devil** 1128 q.v. Some scholars take the latter to act literally to mean **crouching person wearing a death-mask**, and by extension simply **crouching/ bending person**, and take 酉 to act phonetically to express **bent**. Thus **doubly bent person**, a reference to a **hunchback** and by extension **ugly** (see 997). However, although both the earliest and the latest forms of 1359 do show a wine jar it seems possible that these present meanings result rather from confusion at some point with **hunchback/ ugly** 亞 997 q.v., which at one stage had a stylised form 𠇷 that closely resembled a (wine) jar. The original meaning may have been **person wearing a death mask offering wine (to the ancestor-gods)**, i.e. in some religious ceremony (see also 386). **Shameful** is an associated meaning with ugly.

Mnemonic: **UGLY DEVIL WITH ALCOHOL**

1360		SHŪ, oso*u* ATTACK, INHERIT 22 strokes	襲来 SHŪRAI 空襲 KŪSHŪ 世襲 SESHŪ	invasion air raid heredity

衣 is **clothing** 420. 龍 is **dragon** 1899, here used phonetically to express **fold**. 1360 originally referred to a type of **burial garment with the collar folded over (in a special way)**, the folding having a certain religious significance. It still retains this meaning in Chinese, and in Japanese is very occasionally used in the associated sense of wearing double layers of clothing. It is not clear why such a complex character was chosen as a phonetic. The idea of **religious ritual** led to ritual and **convention** in a broad sense, and eventually to the associated idea of **inheriting** (something from the past). **Attack** stems from confusion with a now defunct character 褻, which combines clothing 衣 with grasp 執 1332 and originally meant grapple/ scuffle.

Mnemonic: **DRAGON ATTACKS INHERITED CLOTHES**

1361		JŪ, shiru JUICE, SOUP, LIQUID 5 strokes	果汁 KAJŪ 墨汁 BOKUJŪ 味そ汁 MISOSHIRU	fruit juice India ink miso soup

氵 is **water** 40, here meaning **liquid**. 十 is **ten** 33, here acting phonetically to express **liquid** and thus reinforcing 氵. Now used for a range of liquids (but not water).

Mnemonic: **JUICE MIXED WITH TEN PARTS OF WATER**

1362 JŪ, *ateru*, mi*tasu*   充分 JŪBUN   enough
FULL, FILL, PROVIDE   充実 JŪJITSU   fullness
6 strokes   充てがう ATEGAU   allot, apply

Once written 㐬. 古/ㄊ is **new born child** 227 (literally inverted child 㐂/子 25). ノL
is **crouching person/ bent legs** 39, here acting phonetically to express **grow** and possibly
also lending its own connotations of **big** (see 267). Thus a **new born babe growing
(big?)**, which later came to refer by association to something **becoming full**. **Allot/
provide** is an associated meaning with fill.

Mnemonic: **NEWBORN BABE HAS FULL SET OF LEGS, IF BENT**

1363 JŪ, NYŪ, yawa*rakai*   柔道 JŪDŌ   judo
SOFT, GENTLE, WEAK   柔弱 NYŪJAKU   weakness
9 strokes   柔らか物 YAWARAKAMONO

    silks

矛 is **halberd/ lance** 1843, while 木 is **tree/ wood** 69. Usually explained to the effect
that a **wooden lance** is **weak** (relative to a metal one), and that weak led by association to
soft and **gentle**. A useful mnemonic, but almost certainly incorrect. It seems more likely
that 木 acts in its sense of **tree**, and that 矛 acts phonetically to express **newborn** as
well as lending connotations of **thrust**. Thus **newborn growth that thrusts forth
from a tree**, a reference to **new shoots**. Such shoots symbolised **softness** and **weakness**, with **gentle** being an associated meaning.

Mnemonic: **WOODEN LANCE IS WEAK, INDEED SOFT**

1364 JŪ, shibui/*ru*   渋滞 JŪTAI   delay
HESITATE, ASTRINGENT   渋味 SHIBUMI   astringency
11 strokes   渋渋 SHIBUSHIBU grudgingly

Formerly 澁, showing **water/ liquid** 氵 40 and an emphatic trebling of **stop** 止 129.
The original meaning was **not flow smoothly**, which came to mean by association **be
tardy** and hence **delay/ hesitate**. **Astringent** is felt by some scholars to be a **borrowing**, and by others to stem from the idea of preventing the juices flowing. Suggest taking 氵
as (four) **drops**.

Mnemonic:**ASTRINGENCY MAKES WATER DROPS HESITATE AND STOP**

1365		JŪ	小銃	SHŌJŪ	rifle
		GUN	銃剣	JŪKEN	bayonet
		14 strokes	銃火	JŪKA	gunfire

金 is **metal** 14. 充 is **fill** 1362, here acting phonetically to express **hole** and also lending its meaning of **fill**. 1365 originally referred to the **hole in a metal ax head** (which is filled by the handle). It was later applied to **firearms**, by association with the hole in the barrel (which is filled by the ammunition).

Mnemonic: **GUN IS FILLED WITH METAL**

1366	獣	JŪ, ke[da]mono	獣医	JŪI	veterinarian
		BEAST	獣的	JŪTEKI	bestial
		16 strokes	鳥獣	CHŌJŪ	wildlife

Somewhat obscure. Formerly 獸, and earlier 獸 and 獸. 犬/犬 is **dog** 17. As shown by the early forms, 単 is an abbreviation of **simple** 單/単 542 q.v., here used phonetically to express **guard/ protect** and probably also lending similar connotations from its original meaning of forked weapon. Thus **dog that protects** (see also 1347), i.e. **guard dog**. The role of the later addition **mouth/ say** 口 20 is not clear. Some scholars take 嘼 to be a now defunct character meaning **beast**, though the evolution of such a meaning is not clear. Moreover, if 嘼 did exist as an independent character with a meaning of beast, then it may well be a derivative of beast 獸 1366 (see below). It should be noted that a different arrangement of the same elements gives the CO character **snort** 嘽 (with 單 presumably acting in some unclear phonetic role), and thus it is possible that 嘼 replaced 嘽 to give a meaning of **snorting/ snarling dog**, thereby emphasising its fearsomeness and efficacy as a guard dog. It is not clear how (snarling?) guard dog came to mean **beast**. Dog and beast have long overlapped conceptually (see 17), and it may just be an extension of this, particularly if the dog were indeed seen as snarling and fierce. Suggest taking 単 as 'seeming like' **simple** 単, with 口 as **say** (i.e. **bark**).

Mnemonic: **DOG'S BARK MAKES IT SEEM A SIMPLE BEAST**

1367

SHUKU	叔父 OJI*	uncle
UNCLE, YOUNG BROTHER	叔母 OBA*	aunt
8 strokes	伯叔 HAKUSHUKU	uncles

Once written 尗, showing a **hand** ㄨ pulling up a **potato** 朱 (plant ㇄ [variant 业/
屮/生 42] with tuber ┃ and side roots ⼋). Note that in Chinese it can still mean gather
vegetables. Some scholars see the present meanings as borrowings, but others feel that the
task of pulling up potatoes came to symbolise following a row, leading by association to
(line of) **younger brothers** (see 177), with **uncle(s)** being one's parents' younger
brothers. Younger brother is now rare. Suggest taking 朱 as 'almost' **walk** 步 202.

Mnemonic: **WITH HELPING HAND, UNCLE CAN ALMOST WALK**

1368

淑

SHUKU	貞淑 TEISHUKU	chastity
PURE, GRACEFUL	淑女 SHUKUJO	lady
11 strokes	私淑 SHISHUKU	admiration

氵 is **water** 40. 叔 is **uncle** 1367, here acting phonetically to express **pure** but of unclear
semantic role. Thus **pure water**, later **pure** in the figurative sense of **virtuous**
(especially of women). **Graceful** is an associated meaning.

Mnemonic: **UNCLE DRINKS PURE WATER**

1369

SHUKU	粛然 SHUKUZEN	to solemnly
SOLEMN, QUIET	自粛 JISHUKU	self-control
11 strokes	厳粛 GENSHUKU	solemnity

Formerly 肅. 聿 is a variant of **hand holding brush** 聿 142. It acts here phonetically
to express **dark**, but is of unclear semantic role. 淵 represents a **deep pool** (now usually
conveyed by an NGU character 淵, which adds water 氵 40), of unclear etymology but
apparently comprising inner chamber 龹 (variant 呂 997) and confines ｜ ｜, with old
forms such as 淵 also showing water 丶. 1369 originally referred to a **dark deep pool**,
which came to symbolise something **hushed** and rather **foreboding**, with **solemn** being
an associated meaning. Suggest taking 米 as **rice** 201, ｜ ｜ as an **open container**, and
聿 as a **hand holding a stick** (to **pound**).

Mnemonic: **HAND SOLEMNLY POUNDS RICE IN OPEN CONTAINER**

437

1370   JUKU   塾生 JUKUSEI   juku student
JUKU, PRIVATE SCHOOL   塾則 JUKUSOKU   juku rules
14 strokes   私塾 SHIJUKU

                                                 home-based juku

Though 孰 has now acquired the same form and sound as boil 孰 894 q.v., old forms such as 𦥑 show that it is in fact **castle** 拿 / 畲 / 享 1162 q.v. plus **person bending with outstretched arms** 卩 / 月 / 丸 470 q.v. The person is in fact **building the castle walls**, with **earth** 土 60 being the material used. Thus **castle walls built of earth**. 1370 originally referred to a **walled settlement**, then later came to mean **walled compound** and eventually, by association, **school**. In Japanese it has come in particular to refer to a **private after-hours 'cramming' school** (known as a **juku**). Suggest taking 享 as **child** 子 25, **top hat** 亠, and **mouth** 口 20, with 丸 as **round** 830.

Mnemonic: **EARTHY PRIVATE SCHOOL FOR ROUND-MOUTHED TOP-HATTED CHILDREN**

1371   SHUN   俊才 SHUNSAI   genius
EXCELLENCE, GENIUS   俊傑 SHUNKETSU   hero
9 strokes   俊童 SHUNDŌ   prodigy

亻 is **person** 39. 夋 is **linger** 689. The latter acts phonetically to express **stand apart from**, thus giving **person who stands apart from others**, but its meaning would confusingly appear to connote someone who stood apart from others in the sense of being behind rather than leading. There is a similarly confusing NGU character 駿, which uses **horse** 馬 191 instead of person 亻, and means fast horse rather than tardy/ slow horse. Thus it would appear that in both these cases linger 夋 has connotations of **giving others a start but still being able to outstrip them**. Note that in most other cases 夋 means linger in a less confusing sense, such as the NGU character fall back 逡 (which uses **movement** 辶 129), the CO character fall back/ stop/ hop 踆 (which uses **foot** 足 51), and the CO character remains of a meal 餕 (which uses **food/eat** 食 146).

Mnemonic: **GENIUS IS PERSON WHO EXCELS DESPITE LINGERING**

| 1372 | SHUN, matata*ku*
FLASH, TWINKLE,
BLINK
18 strokes | 一瞬 ISSHUN an instant
瞬間 SHUNKAN instant
瞬く間 MATATAKUMA ni
in the twinkling of an eye |

Once written 眹 (still found as a variant in Chinese), showing **eye** 目 72 and **arrow** 矢 981. The latter indicates **rapidity**, to give an ideograph referring to the rapid movement of the eye, i.e. **blinking**, with **twinkle** and **flash** being associated meanings. Arrow 矢 was later replaced by straighten an arrow 寅 621, which was used phonetically to express blink and also retained connotations of arrow, and this was in turn replaced by 舜. The latter is a CO character meaning wise and is also used of a legendary ruler. Its etymology is unclear, though its elements appear to be **hand reaching down to convey** 爫 303 and **opposed feet** 舛 1211. It appears to have been used phonetically to express **blink**, but any semantic role is unclear. It is also unclear why the seemingly straightforward ideograph 眹 was modified with increasing complexity. Suggest taking 爫 as **hand reaching down**, 冖 as **cover**, and 舛 as **splayed feet**.

Mnemonic: **IN BLINK OF AN EYE HAND REACHES DOWN TO COVER SPLAYED FEET**

| 1373 | JUN
TEN DAY PERIOD
6 strokes | 上旬 JŌJUN first part of month
中旬 CHŪJUN middle of month
下旬 GEJUN last part of month |

日 is **sun/ day** 62. 勹 is **encircle** 655, here acting phonetically to express cycle and almost certainly also lending similar reinforcing connotations of **circle**. Thus **cycle of days**, a rather vague reference to a **ten day cycle** which was a standard unit of time in ancient China.

Mnemonic: **TEN DAY CYCLE OF CIRCLING SUN**

| 1374 | JUN, megur*u*
GO AROUND
6 strokes | 巡回 JUNKAI tour, patrol
巡査 JUNSA policeman
一巡り HITOMEGURI one round |

辶 is **movement** 129. 巛 is **river** (variant 川 48: see also 680), here acting phonetically to express **see** and also lending its own connotations of movement. Thus to **move and see**, a reference to an **inspection**, leading to **go around**. Suggest remembering 巛 as a **river with sharp bends**.

Mnemonic: **MOVING RIVER GOES AROUND SHARP BENDS**

1375

JUN, tate
SHIELD, PRETEXT
9 strokes

矛盾 MUJUN　contradiction
後盾 USHIRODATE　backing
盾突く TATETSUKU　oppose

目 is **eye** 72, here meaning **look**. ｢ is a **shield**. Thus 自 means **shield from be-hind which one looks out**. The meaning of ┿ is unclear. Since no very early forms of this character have been discovered it is possible that it derives from some earlier depiction of a **hand** holding the shield ⻌, but it is also possible that it lends the same idea of **piercing** as in 直 349 q.v. (i.e. look piercingly/ intently out from behind a shield). Suggest taking it as **ten** 十 33. Note that the physical shield is now usually conveyed by an NGU character 楯, which adds **wood** 木 69, whereas 1375 is usually used in a figurative sense.

Mnemonic: **TEN EYES LOOK OUT FROM BEHIND SHIELD**

1376

JUN
QUASI-, CONFORM,
PERMIT
10 strokes

准尉 JUNI　warrant officer
批准 HIJUN　ratification
准許 JUNKYO　approval

Technically the same character as quasi/ conform 準/準 709 q.v., of which it is a simplified form. However, for reasons that are not clear, 1376 also came to acquire connotations of **permission**, presumably from some association with conforming. Its elements are **ice/ freeze** ⼎ 378 and **bird** 隹 216.

Mnemonic: **FREEZE BIRD IN CONFORMITY WITH STANDARDS**

1377

JUN
DUTIFUL DEATH
10 strokes

殉死 JUNSHI　dutiful death
殉教者 JUNKYŌSHA　martyr
殉職 JUNSHOKU
　　　　death at one's post

歹 is **bare bones/ death** 286. 旬 is **ten day period** 1373, here acting phonetically to express **conform/ follow** and probably also lending loose connotations of **being fixed/ inexorable**. Thus to **follow (inexorably?) in death**, a reference to the suicide of a retainer upon the death of his lord.

Mnemonic: **DUTIFUL DEATH, BUT BARE BONES AFTER TEN DAYS**

1378  JUN 　　　因循 INJUN　　　indecision
FOLLOW 　　循環 JUNKAN　　cycle, circle
12 strokes 　　悪循環 AKUJUNKAN

vicious circle

彳 is **movement** 118. 盾 is **shield** 1375, here acting phonetically to express **follow** and probably also lending similar connotations (from the idea of moving forward behind a shield).

Mnemonic: **FOLLOW, MOVING BEHIND SHIELD**

1379 JUN, uruou/su 　　潤滑 JUNKATSU　lubrication
MOISTEN, ENRICH 　利潤 RIJUN　　　　profit
15 strokes 　　　潤沢 JUNTAKU　　moisture,

profit, plenty, gloss

氵 is **water** 40. 閏 is an NGU character meaning **intercalation/ insert(ed) between**. It comprises **gate/ doorway** 門 211 and **king** 王 5 (though some old forms show **standing person** 壬 1610). Thus **king/person between doorposts**, a reference to **someone/ something coming between things**. (Note that 閏 can have the specific meaning of illegitimate reign, i.e. an unlawful 'king' coming between two lawful reigns.) In the case of 1379 閏 acts phonetically to express **wet** and probably also lends connotations of **coming between** (as water seeping through cracks etc.). Thus **make wet (with water)**, i.e. **moisten**, with **enrich** being an associated meaning.

Mnemonic: **KING AT GATE MOISTENED WITH ENRICHING WATER**

1380 JUN 　　　遵守 JUNSHU　　observance
FOLLOW, OBEY 　遵奉 JUNPŌ　　observance
15 strokes 　　　遵法 JUNPŌ　　law abiding

辶 is **movement (along a road/path)** 129. 尊 is **respect/ esteem** 927, here acting phonetically to express **follow** and possibly also lending an idea of **respected**. Thus **follow a path** (possibly follow after someone respected or follow a respected path), with **obey** being an associated meaning.

Mnemonic: **WHEN MOVING, OBEDIENTLY FOLLOW RESPECTED PATH**

1381	SHO MULTITUDE, VARIOUS ILLEGITIMATE 11 strokes	庶民 SHOMIN the masses 庶務 SHOMU general affairs 庶子 SHOSHI illegitimate child

Of somewhat unclear etymology. Once written 度. 火 /··· is **fire** 8, but it is not clear whether 庐 /庐 is a stylised variant of **stone** 石 45, used phonetically to express **put (on)**, or whether it is a combination of **building** (in the sense of **house**) 广 114 and an **object** 廿/口. The former theory seems more likely. In any event, the early meaning is known to have been **put things on a fire** (in a house?). It then appears to have become confused with **boil various things over a fire** 煮 1338 q.v., and to have come to mean **various things. Various** came to mean sundry and hence common, leading to commoners/ the masses/ **multitude**. 1381 was also borrowed to express concubine (still a minor meaning in Chinese), leading by association to **illegitimate**. Suggest taking 广 as **building/ house**, and 廿 as an **object**.

Mnemonic: **VARIOUS OBJECTS BURN IN HOUSE FIRE**

1382	SHO, CHO, o BEGINNING, CORD, CLUE, CONNECTION 14 strokes	一緒 ISSHO together 端緒 TANSHO beginning 鼻緒 HANAO clog thong

Formerly 緒. 糸 is **thread** 27. 者/者 is **person** 298 q.v., here acting phonetically to express **end/ beginning** (conceptually the same in the case of a thread) and almost certainly also lending its early connotations of **various** (things). Thus the **start/ end of a thread** (sticking out from amongst various threads?). This gave rise to a range of meanings, such as **thread/ cord** and **beginning**, and also to the idea of starting to unravel a tangle, giving **clue** and **connection**.

Mnemonic: **PERSON FOLLOWS THREAD FROM BEGINNING**

1383 如	JO, NYO, gotoku SIMILAR, EQUAL 6 strokes	如上 JOJŌ no aforesaid 如実 NYOJITSU realism 如何 IKAGA* how?

口 is **mouth/ say** 20, here meaning **tell** (someone to do something). 女 is **woman** 35, here acting phonetically to express **comply** and also lending connotations of compliance and submissiveness. Thus to **comply with what one is told**. The idea of doing (the same) as one is requested to do led to the associated ideas of **similar** and **equal** (cf. English slang do <u>like</u> one is told).

Mnemonic: **WOMEN'S MOUTHS ARE SIMILAR**

1384

JO
DESCRIBE, CONFER
9 strokes

叙術 JOJUTSU   description
叙情的 JOJŌTEKI   lyrical
叙勲 JOKUN

conferment of decoration

Formerly also written 敘 and 敍, i.e. with **striking hand** 攵/攴 101 (here indicating **coercion**) instead of a simple **hand** 又. 余 is **ample/** excess 800, here acting phonetically to express **sequence/ order** but of unclear semantic role. Thus to **make someone put things in order**, i.e. **arrange** (still a meaning in Chinese). This was applied by association to the idea of relating a series of events in their proper order, giving **describe**. It is not fully clear how the meaning of **confer** evolved, but it may relate to conferring things in a set order.

Mnemonic: **AMPLE DESCRIPTION OF HAND**

1385

JO, omomu*ro*
SLOWLY, GRADUALLY
10 strokes

徐行 JOKŌ   going slowly
徐徐 JOJO ni   slowly
徐歩 JOHO   walking slowly

彳 is **movement** 118. 余 is **ample/ excess** 800, here acting phonetically to express **slowly** and probably also lending a meaning of **excessive/ very**. Thus **move (excessively?) slowly**, with **gradually** being an associated meaning.

Mnemonic: **MOVE EXCESSIVELY SLOWLY**

1386

SHŌ, masu
LIQUID MEASURE
4 strokes

升目 MASUME   measure
二升 NISHŌ   two shō
一升びん ISSHŌBIN one shō bottle

Once written 𦫳, showing a **scoop/ ladle** 𠦝 with **contents** ‾. Now a standardised **liquid measure** of 1.8 liters, particularly associated with sake. Suggest taking 丿 as **person** 39 and 十 as a variant of **ten** 十 33.

Mnemonic: **LIQUID MEASURE ENOUGH FOR TEN PEOPLE**

| 1387 | SHO, mes*u*
 SUMMON, PARTAKE,
 WEAR
 5 strokes | 召集 SHŌSHŪ summons, call
 召喚 SHŌKAN summons
 召し使い MESHITSUKAI servant |

Of disputed etymology. An old form 召 is interpreted by some scholars as an ideograph combining **mouth/ say** ㅂ /口 20 and **bending person** 人 39, to give a **person/ servant bending** (a symbol of humility) **as they answer their master's summons.** **Sword/ cut** 刀 181 is thus taken to be a miscopying. Other scholars feel that 刀 is simply a variant of the old form 勹 of 刀, and take this to be used purely phonetically to express **summon.** Thus **summon verbally** (i.e. with the mouth). The former theory seems more likely. In either case, **partake** and **wear** are associated meanings, relating to actions for which a master might summon a servant.

Mnemonic: **CUT MOUTH AND SUMMON HELP**

| 1388 | SHŌ
 CRAFTSMAN, PLAN
 6 strokes | 師匠 SHISHŌ master
 巨匠 KYOSHŌ great master
 意匠 ISHŌ idea, design |

匚 is a **container** (see 225), here meaning **box.** 斤 is **ax** 1176, here indicating **tool.** Thus **tool box,** a symbol of an **artisan** and by extension **craftsman.** **Plan** is felt to be an associated meaning, from the way in which a craftsman sets about his work.

Mnemonic: **CRAFTSMAN KEEPS AX IN BOX**

| 1389 | SHŌ, toko, yuka
 BED, FLOOR, ALCOVE
 7 strokes | 病床 BYŌSHŌ sickbed
 床張り YUKABARI flooring
 床の間 TOKONOMA <br> ornamental alcove |

Formerly 牀 and 牀. 爿/ 뉘 is a **plank of wood,** being a mirror image of **piece of wood** 片 969 q.v. (literally one side of a tree 朩/ 木 69), and came by association to mean **bed** (originally sickbed [see 381] but later bed in general). In Japanese it also refers to **flooring/ floor** and an **alcove,** the latter now used for ornamental purposes but originally a place where a bed was placed. The reason for the later use of **building/** house 广 114 is unclear. It is taken by some scholars to be a miscopying of (or simplification of) 爿, by others to be a miscopying of the sickness radical 疒 381, and by still others to be a deliberate attempt to indicate being indoors.

Mnemonic: **BUILDING HAS WOODEN FLOOR AND BED IN ALCOVE**

1390	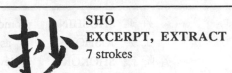 SHŌ EXCERPT, EXTRACT 7 strokes	抄本 SHOHON — extract 詩抄 SHISHŌ — selected poems 抄訳 SHŌYAKU — abridged translation

A later variant of the similar meaning NGU character 鈔. 金 is **metal** 14. 少 is **few/ little** 143, here acting phonetically to express **take** and also lending its meaning of **little**. 1390 originally referred to **extracting a little of something by removing it with a metal tool** (felt by some scholars to be specifically a pair of scissors). Metal 金 was later replaced by **hand** 扌 32, giving **take away a little by hand**. Now **extract/ excerpt** in a broad sense.

Mnemonic: **EXTRACT A LITTLE BY HAND**

1391	SHŌ, ayaka*ru* BE LIKE, BE LUCKY 7 strokes	肖像 SHŌZŌ — portrait 不肖 FUSHŌ — unlike, I/me 肖り者 AYAKARIMONO — lucky person

月 is **flesh/ of the body** 365. ⺌ is a variant of **little/ small** 小 36, which also lends its sound to express **resemble**. 1391 originally referred to **offspring resembling their parents** (i.e. being little versions of their body), but later came to mean **be like** in a broader sense. For some reason it also acquired connotations of **being** (as) **lucky** (as anyone else).

Mnemonic: **LITTLE ONE IS LIKE PARENTS IN BODY AND IN LUCK**

1392	SHŌ, nao, tatto*bu* FURTHERMORE, ESTEEM 8 strokes	尚早 SHŌSŌ — prematurity 高尚 KŌSHŌ — loftiness 尚尚 NAONAO — still more

Of broad semantic evolution. Formerly 尚 and earlier 尙, showing a combination of **out of/ away** ハ/ ソ 66 and **face (towards)** 向/向 (here 向) 278 q.v., the latter being used in its literal sense of **house with window**. 1392 originally referred to **smoke rising out of the window of a house**, and thus came to symbolise **height** and **rising/ raising to a height**. **Esteem** is an extension of the latter. **Furthermore** is seen as an associated meaning, from the idea of rising ever higher (i.e. giving one thing on top of all others: see also 1091).

Mnemonic: **FURTHERMORE, FACING AWAY IS A SIGN OF ESTEEM!**

445

1393

SHŌ, nobo*ru*
RISE, ASCENT
8 strokes

昇進 SHŌSHIN   promotion
上昇 JŌSHŌ   ascent
昇降機 SHŌKŌKI   elevator

日 is **sun** 62. 升 is (liquid) **measure** 1386, here acting phonetically to express **rise** and possibly also lending a loose idea of **measurably**, i.e. **noticeably**. Thus **sun rising (noticeably?) high**, later **rise/ ascend** in a broad sense. Sugest taking 升 as **person** 亻 39 and **ten** 十 (variant 十 33).

Mnemonic: **SUN RISES, MEASURED BY TEN PERSONS**

1394

SHŌ, matsu
PINE
8 strokes

松葉 MATSUBA   pine needle
松原 MATSUBARA pine grove
松竹梅 SHŌCHIKUBAI
           pine-bamboo-plum

木 is **tree** 69. 公 is **public** 277, here acting phonetically to express **needle** and probably also lending connotations of **common**. Thus **(common?) tree bearing needles**, a reference to the **pine**.

Mnemonic: **PINE IS A PUBLIC TREE**

1395

SHŌ, numa
SWAMP, MARSH
8 strokes

沼気 SHŌKI   methane
沼沢 SHŌTAKU swamp, marsh
沼地 NUMACHI   marshland

氵 is **water** 40, here meaning **body of water**. 召 is **summon** 1387 q.v., here acting phonetically to express **little**. Thus **little body of water** (i.e. a small volume of water relative to a lake or river), a reference to a **swamp/ marsh**. Since there is no obvious reason why the simpler SHŌ **little** 小 36 or SHŌ **little** 少 143 were not used, 召 presumably also lent some meaning, but this is not clear. It may perhaps suggest **gathering**, i.e. a **place where water gathers/** collects (though still smaller in volume than a river).

Mnemonic: **SUMMON WATERS OF SWAMP**

1396

宵

SHŌ, yoi
EVENING
10 strokes

徹宵 TESSHŌ　　　　all night
宵月 YOIZUKI　　evening moon
宵越し YOIGOSHI　　　overnight

Somewhat obscure. Formerly 宵 . 宀 is **roof/ house** 28, here meaning **indoors**. 肖/ 肖 has for many centuries been interpreted as **be like** 1391 q.v., which is assumed to act phonetically to express **vanish** to give **vanishing (light) indoors**, i.e. **evening**. Indeed, there is a very old form 宵, clearly showing **meat** 夕 / 月 365 and **little** 小 36, the component elements of 1391. However, since there is no element specifically meaning **light** this has never been a fully convincing explanation. In fact, the very oldest form of all, 宵, shows clearly that **meat** 夕 / 月 is a longstanding miscopying of **moon** 夕/ 月 16, which presumably indicated **light** (though **sun** 日 62 may have been more appropriate). Thus it seems most likely that 1396 was originally an ideograph meaning **little light indoors**, rather than vanishing light, though both result in **evening**.

Mnemonic: **SMALL MOON SEEN UNDER ROOF AS EVENING ARRIVES**

1397

症

SHŌ
SYMPTOM, ILLNESS
10 strokes

症状 SHŌJŌ　　　　symptoms
炎症 ENSHŌ　　inflammation
恐怖症 KYŌFUSHŌ　　phobia

疒 is **sickness/ illness** 381. 正 is **correct/ proper** 41, here acting phonetically to express **sign** and probably also lending its meaning of **proper** and by extension **authentic**. Thus the (**authentic?**) **signs of an illness**, i.e. the **symptoms**, as well as the **illness** itself.

Mnemonic: **PROPER SYMPTOMS OF ILLNESS**

1398

祥

SHŌ
GOOD FORTUNE, OMEN
10 strokes

発祥地 HASSHŌCHI　birthplace
吉祥 KISSHŌ　　　good omen
不祥事 FUSHŌJI
　　　　　bad omen, scandal

Formerly 祥 . 示/ネ is **altar/ of the gods** 695. 羊 is **sheep** 986 q.v., here acting phonetically to express **auspicious (sign)** and possibly also lending its own connotations either of **fine** or of **sacrifice**. **Auspicious sign from the gods** was a good **omen**, symbolising **good fortune**.

Mnemonic: **SHEEP SACRIFICED ON ALTAR TO BRING GOOD FORTUNE**

1399

SHŌ

CROSS OVER, LIAISE

11 strokes

交渉 KŌSHŌ negotiations
干渉 KANSHŌ interference
渉外 SHŌGAI public relations

Formerly also written 渉. 氵 is **water** 40, here meaning **river**, while 歩/歩 is **walk** 202. To **walk across a river**, i.e. ford it, came to mean **cross carefully from one side to another** in a broader sense, including that of **liaise**.

Mnemonic: **LIAISON CAN INVOLVE WALKING ON WATER**

1400

SHŌ

INTRODUCE, INHERIT

11 strokes

紹介 SHŌKAI introduction
紹介者 SHŌKAISHA introducer
紹介状 SHŌKAIJŌ
letter of introduction

糸 is **thread** 27. 召 is **summon** 1387, here acting phonetically to express **join** and possibly also lending supporting connotations of **gather/ muster** and thus **bring together**. 1400 originally meant to **join threads**, and was later used by association to mean **put people together**, i.e. to **introduce** them. **Inherit** is an associated meaning, from the idea of joining threads in a figurative sense.

Mnemonic: **THREAD ONE'S WAY TO INTRODUCTION AFTER SUMMONS**

1401

SHŌ

ACCUSE, SUE

11 strokes

訴訟 SOSHŌ litigation
訴訟人 SOSHŌNIN plaintiff
訴訟費用 SOSHŌHIYŌ court costs

言 is **words/ speak** 274. 公 is **public** 277, here acting phonetically to express **dispute** and probably also lending its meaning of **public**. Thus **words spoken in a (public?) dispute**, with **accuse** being an associated meaning and **sue** being a further association.

Mnemonic: **PUBLIC WORDS OF ACCUSATION LEAD ONE TO SUE**

1402

SHŌ, tanagokoro

CONTROL, PALM (HAND)

12 strokes

掌中 SHŌCHŪ in one's hand
車掌 SHASHŌ conductor
職掌 SHOKUSHŌ duties

手 is **hand** 32. 尚 is **furthermore** 1392, here acting phonetically to express **hold** but of unclear semantic role. Thus **that part of the hand which holds**, a somewhat vague reference to the **palm** rather than the fingers. **Control** is an associated meaning, from the idea of handling/ manipulating.

Mnemonic: **FURTHERMORE, PALM OF HAND CONTROLS**

1403

SHŌ
CRYSTAL, CLEAR,
BRIGHT
12 strokes

水晶　SUISHŌ　　crystal, quartz
晶化　SHŌKA　　crystallisation
結晶　KESSHŌ　　crystallisation

A trebling of **sun/ light** 日 62, to mean **many points of light** (and at one stage applied to stars: see 154). This came to mean **bright** and then by association **clear**, and was eventually used to refer to **crystals**.

Mnemonic: **THREE SUNS MAKE IT BRIGHT AND CRYSTAL CLEAR**

1404

SHŌ, ko*geru/gasu*, a*seru*, *jireru*
SCORCH, FRET
12 strokes

焦土　SHŌDO　　scorched earth
焦心　SHŌSHIN　　impatience
黒焦げ　KUROKOGE　　charring

An ideograph showing a **bird** 隹 216 **roasting** over a **fire** 灬 8. This came to acquire associated connotations of **scorching** and **charring**, and was also applied figuratively to the idea of **fretting**. There is an alternative theory that 隹 acts purely phonetically to express blacken, to give blacken with fire, but this is not convincing.

Mnemonic: **BIRD FRETS WHEN SCORCHED OVER FIRE**

1405

硝

SHŌ
NITER, GUNPOWDER
12 strokes

硝酸　SHŌSAN　　nitric acid
硝薬　SHŌYAKU　　gunpowder
硝子　GARASU*　　glass

石 is **rock** 45. 肖 is **be like** 1391 q.v., here acting phonetically to express **digest** and possibly also lending connotations of **growing from** as an extension of its literal meaning of small version of a (bigger) body. Thus **that associated with rock and digestion** (which grows out from rock?), a reference to **niter**. Niter is found as an incrustation on rock (cf. English term saltpeter, meaning literally salt of rock), and is also used medicinally to aid digestion as well as in the making of gunpowder.

Mnemonic: **NITER IS LIKE A ROCK**

1406	SHŌ ADORN, MAKE UP 12 strokes	化粧 KESHŌ make-up 化粧品 KESHŌHIN cosmetics 化粧室 KESHŌSHITSU powder room

A character of relatively recent origin, with a history of only six hundred years or so. Nevertheless, its etymology is somewhat confused. 米 is **rice** 201, here symbolising **white** and by association **face powder** (see 1029). 庄 is an NGU character meaning manor/ cottage, popularly believed to comprise **building** 广 114 and **ground/ earth** 土 60 but in fact a variant/ miscopying of manor/ villa 荘 1515 q.v. (though its graphic evolution may well have been influenced by 广 and 土). Here it acts phonetically to express **adorn**, giving **adorn oneself with face powder**. Note that in Chinese 荘 1515 can also be interchanged with 1406 to mean adorn/ make up. Note also that 荘 is often interchanged with its principal component manly 壮 1514 q.v., which has an assumed literal meaning of erect male organ in bed (male organ 士 494 and bed 丬 1389) and thus strong sexual connotations. 壮 is itself the 'male equivalent' of 牀, a CO character literally meaning woman in bed (woman 女 35 and bed 丬/爿 1389) which is also interchangeable in Chinese with 1406. Thus originally 1406 clearly had strong connotations of making oneself up with a specific view to increasing sexual allure, though nowadays it is usually used in a general esthetic sense. Suggest taking 庄 as **building** 广 and **earth** 土.

Mnemonic: **ADORN EARTHEN FLOOR OF BUILDING WITH RICE**

1407	SHŌ, mikotonori IMPERIAL EDICT 12 strokes	詔書 SHŌSHO imperial edict 詔令 SHŌREI imperial edict 大詔 TAISHŌ imperial edict

言 is **word/ speak** 274. 召 is **summon** 1387 q.v., here especially with its connotations of a high ranking person summoning a lower ranking person. 1407 became particularly associated with an **emperor's summons/ edict**.

Mnemonic: **SUMMONED TO HEAR WORDS OF IMPERIAL EDICT**

1408

SHŌ
URGE, ENCOURAGE
13 strokes

奨励 SHŌREI encouragement
推奨 SUISHŌ recommendation
奨学金 SHŌGAKUKIN
scholarship

Of somewhat confused evolution. Formerly 奬, showing **command** 將/将 899 q.v. and **big** 大 53. However, older forms such as 獎 and 獎 show clearly that the modern forms stem from a miscopying of the elements **bed** 爿/爿/丬 1389, **meat** 夕/夕/月 365, and **dog** 犬/犬 17. There is a theory that 將 was from an early stage a simplification of command 將, giving **command a dog** and hence **order** and by association **urge/ encourage**, but it seems equally if not more likely that 爿 acts phonetically to express **offer** (as in 899 itself), and that 1408 thus originally meant **offer meat to a dog**, thereby leading to **encourage** and by association **urge**. Suggest taking 奨 as **command(er)** 将 and big/ **great** 大.

Mnemonic: **URGED ON BY GREAT COMMANDER**

1409

SHŌ, kuwashii
DETAILED
13 strokes

詳細 SHŌSAI details
未詳 MISHŌ unclear
詳しく KUWASHIKU in detail

言 is **word** 274, here meaning **talk/ discuss**. 羊 is **sheep** 986, here acting phonetically to express **examine thoroughly** and possibly also loosely lending similar connotations (a sheep being a prized object that would necessarily be examined carefully prior to purchase). Thus to **discuss with a view to examining thoroughly**, with thorough examination/ discussion leading by association to **detailed**.

Mnemonic: **DETAILED TALK ABOUT SHEEP**

1410

SHŌ
MANIFEST,
OPENLY ACKNOWLEDGE
14 strokes

表彰 HYŌSHŌ commendation
顕彰 KENSHŌ manifestation
彰徳 SHŌTOKU public praise

彡 is **delicate hairs** 93 q.v., here in its sense of **attractive decoration**. 章 is **badge** 318 q.v., here in its sense of **attractive pattern**. 1410 originally referred to an **attractive decorative pattern**, and in Chinese still retains lesser meanings of beautiful and ornamental. By association it also came to mean **display something attractive**, with the idea of display leading by further association to **manifest** and **make something clear to the world at large**, i.e. **openly acknowledge** (often in the sense of praise).

Mnemonic: **OPENLY ACKNOWLEDGE BADGE HAS THREE HAIRS ON IT**

1411	SHŌ	衝突 SHŌTOTSU	collision
	COLLIDE, CLASH, ROAD	衝動 SHŌDŌ	impulse
	15 strokes	折衝 SESSHŌ	negotiations

Somewhat obscure. Once written 衝. 行 is **move/ go** 118 q.v, here with its literal meaning of **road(s)**. 童 is **child/ slave** 363 q.v., here acting phonetically to express **pass**. Thus **road that (people) pass along**. It is not clear whether 童 also plays any semantic role, though its complexity would suggest that it does. It may possibly lend its literal connotations of slaves bearing loads, i.e. porters, and thereby suggest a file of people moving along, or it may simply suggest people from the outset. It is also possible that it lends figurative associations of heavy usage (cf. English term heavy traffic), though this is unlikely. The modern form uses the simpler **heavy** 重 311 q.v., which at one stage had the same pronunciation as 童 (then SHŌ) and thus plays a similar phonetic role, as well as having the same (possibly relevant) literal connotations of persons bearing loads. **Road** is now a minor meaning. **Collide/ clash** is taken by some scholars to be a purely borrowed meaning, but it may stem from a reinterpretation of the elements 童/重 and 行 as **heavy** and **move** respectively, suggesting **heavy objects coming together**.

Mnemonic: **COLLISION OF HEAVY OBJECTS MOVING ON ROAD**

1412	SHŌ, tsugunau	償金 SHŌKIN	reparation
	RECOMPENSE, REDEEM	償却 SHŌKYAKU	redemption
	17 strokes	弁償 BENSHŌ	compensation

亻 is **person** 39. 賞 is **prize** 511 q.v., here acting phonetically to express **return/ back** and also lending its connotations of **bestowing money**. 1412 originally referred to **buying back a person**, i.e. **redeeming** a slave by **recompensing** the owner. It now means **redeem** and **recompense** in a broader sense.

Mnemonic: **PERSON RECOMPENSED WITH PRIZE**

1413	SHŌ	岩礁 GANSHŌ	reef
	(HIDDEN) REEF	暗礁 ANSHŌ	hidden reef, snag
	17 strokes	さんご礁 SANGOSHŌ	coral reef

Of relatively recent origin. 石 is **rock** 45. 焦 is **scorch/ fret** 1404, here acting phonetically to express **tapered** and almost certainly also lending a meaning of **fret/ worry**. Thus **tapered rock (that causes worry?)**, a somewhat vague reference to a **submerged rock/ reef** of which only the tip is visible above the water. It is not clear why water 氵/ 水 40 was not added for clarity, to give 瀳 or similar.

Mnemonic: **FRET OVER ROCKY REEF**

452

1414 SHŌ, kane 警鐘 KEISHŌ alarm bell
BELL 釣鐘堂 TSURIGANEDŌ belfry
20 strokes 鐘乳石 SHŌNYŪSEKI stalactite

Of disputed etymology, though its elements are clearly **metal** 金 14 and **child/ slave** 童 363 q.v. Some scholars take the latter to lend its connotations of **heavy**, to give **heavy metal object**, a rather vague reference to a **large hanging bell**. Others take 童 (once pronounced SHŌ) to be used essentially phonetically to express **handle** (with any semantic role unclear), to give **metal object with a handle**, a similarly vague reference to a **hand bell**. Though confusingly 1414 does nowadays usually refer to a large and unwieldy type of bell, the latter theory seems the more likely. Evidence for this includes the fact that 1414 is interchangeable with an NGU character 鉦, which uses SHŌ correct 正 41 in an apparently similar phonetic role, and the fact that there exists a CO character 鍾, which uses heavy 重 311 (also once pronounced SHŌ and sometimes interchanged with 童 [see 1411]) in a similar role, though it actually means large goblet rather than bell (i.e. handle becoming interpreted as stem). Suggest taking 童 as **stand** 立 73 and **village** 里 219.

Mnemonic: **METAL BELLS STANDS IN VILLAGE**

1415 JŌ, take 丈夫 JŌBU sturdy, robust
LENGTH, STATURE, 背丈 SETAKE height
MEASURE 方丈 HŌJŌ abbot's chamber,
3 strokes abbot, ten feet square

Once written 㐱, showing **hand** 又 and **ten** 十 33. A hand represented the **span of one hand**, namely **one shaku** (30.3 cms) 尺 884 q.v. Thus **ten shaku/ one jō**, namely a **measure** of approximately **ten feet**. It is now also used of **length** and **height** in a more general sense, including a person's **stature** (clearly initially with some degree of exaggeration). Suggest taking 丈 as a **hand** 乂 holding a **stick** ‾.

Mnemonic: **HAND HOLDS STICK TEN FEET IN LENGTH**

1416 JŌ 冗談 JŌDAN joke
SUPERFLUOUS 冗長 JŌCHŌ verbosity
4 strokes 冗語 JŌGO redundant word

Formerly also written 冗, and earlier 冘. ∩/⌒ is **house** (variant 宀 28), while 𠆢/ ノL/几 is **crouching person** 39 (probably a **hunchback**). **Person (/hunchback?) at home** was a reference to a **person with no work**, presumably as a result of incapacity, which came to mean **superfluous person** and eventually **superfluous** in a broad sense. Note that in Chinese it can by extension mean tramp/ vagrant, and also mean potter about and do various things, leading by association to a somewhat confusing and paradoxical meaning of various duties/ business. Suggest taking 几 as **table** 832 and ⌒ as **cover**.

Mnemonic: **COVER UP SUPERFLUOUS TABLE**

1417	JŌ	浄化 JŌKA	purification
浄	PURE, CLEAN	不浄 FUJŌ	filth
	9 strokes	浄水 JŌSUI	clean water

Formerly 淨 . 氵 is **water** 40. 爭/争 is **vie/** conflict 529, here acting phonetically to express **pure** and possibly also lending connotations of something that is vied for and hence desirable. Thus (desirable?) **pure water**.

Mnemonic: **VIE FOR PURE, CLEAN WATER**

1418	JŌ, amatsusae	剰余 JŌYO	surplus
剰	SURPLUS, BESIDES	余剰 YOJŌ	surplus
	11 strokes	過剰 KAJŌ	surplus, excess

Formerly 剩 . Obscure, though its elements are clearly **sword/ cut** 刂 181 and **ride/ mount** 乘/乗 320. Some authoritative Japanese scholars believe it to be a later simplification/ miscopying of the CO character **surplus** 賸 , with which it is indeed interchangeable in Chinese. This comprises shell/ money/ valuable item 貝 90 and royal we 朕/朕 1603 q.v., here acting phonetically to express **give** and also lending its own supporting connotations of **raise/ offer (up)**. Thus to **give valuables**. Some scholars take surplus to be a borrowed meaning, while others see it as an extended meaning, either from the idea of giving away surplus items or the idea of giving items away with excessive generosity. In any event, the theory that 剰 is a simplification/ miscopying of 賸 is by no means convincing. The forms are too distinct for a miscopying or deliberate variation to be likely, and 剰 is too complex to be used as a simplification. It seems more likely that 剰 did exist as a primitive character in its own right, but that no primitive forms have yet been discovered. A possible explanation of its etymology might be that 刂 meant **cut (away)**, with 乘 acting phonetically to express **surplus/ superfluous** (see 1416) and possibly also lending supporting connotations of **extremity** (from its original connotations of treetop). Thus a **superfluous part (such as an extremity?) which is cut away**, leading eventually to **surplus**.

Mnemonic: **RIDE WITH SURPLUS SWORD**

1419

JŌ, tatami, tata*mu*
TATAMI MAT, SIZE,
FOLD, PILE, REPEAT
12 strokes

畳句 JŌKU   repeated phrase
二畳 NIJŌ   two-mat (size)
畳み込む TATAMIKOMU   fold up

Formerly 疊 and 疉. 宜 is a variant of good/ **meat piled on altar** 宜 1134 q.v., here meaning **pile up** in a broad sense. 畾 is a CO character meaning divided fields, being a trebling of **field** 田 59, while 晶 is bright 1403, being a trebling of sun 日 62. Both 畾 and 晶 are used for their trebled composition simply to indicate **quantity** and **repetition**, thus reinforcing 宜. 1419 originally meant to **pile something up layer upon layer**, giving by association **fold** and **repeat**. In Japanese it also came to be applied to **matting** (which can be folded and stored), especially the **tatami mat,** and is also used as a **unit of size** based upon the tatami (approximately six feet by three feet). Suggest taking 宜 as **cover** ⌐ and **besides/ cairn/ pile** 且 1091.

Mnemonic: **BESIDES, PILE OF FOLDED MATS IN FIELD IS COVERED**

1420

JŌ, nawa
ROPE, CORD
15 strokes

沖縄 OKINAWA   Okinawa
縄張り NAWABARI cordon, area
自縄自縛 JIJŌJIBAKU
         falling in one's own trap

Formerly 繩. 糸 is **thread** 27. 黽 derives from a pictograph 黽 of a type of **fly** with bulging eyes, double wings, and tail/ sting. (Note that fly in a general sense is now conveyed by the NGU character 蠅 /蝿, which adds insect 虫 56.) 黽 acts here phonetically to express **twist (together)**. It is not clear why it was chosen as a phonetic, but it may possibly also lend loosely associated connotations of **many** (from the swarming associated with flies). Thus **(many?) threads twisted together,** giving **rope/ cord.** Suggest taking 黽 as **two days** 日 62 and a **(long) rope** し.

Mnemonic: **THREADING ROPE TAKES LONGER THAN TWO DAYS**

1421 **壌** **JŌ** **EARTH, SOIL** 16 strokes

土壌	DOJŌ	earth, soil
壌土	JŌDO	earth, soil
天壌	TENJŌ	heaven and earth

Somewhat obscure. Formerly 壤. 土 is **earth/ ground/ soil** 60. 襄 is a CO character with a confusing range of meanings, such as disrobe, assist, high, yoke, and change position. Its exact etymology is unclear, but its earliest form was 㗊. This is known to have comprised a trebling of **mouth/ say** ㅂ/口 20 and a symbol of **reciprocity/ mutuality** 乂, and to have meant **people accusing one another** (see also 1424). 㗊 later became 𠾂, with plural mouths ㅂㅂ, symbols of reciprocity 爻, and 卂. 卂 is known to be a simplification of 𦥑, the obscure element seen in 1351 q.v. which appears to mean (here) **flowing from one mouth to another**. Thus 𠾂 also appears to have meant **mutual accusations**. At some later point **clothing** 衣/衣 420 was added and 𠾂 became abbreviated to 丵, thus giving the semi-modern form 襄. Unfortunately the role of clothing 衣 is not clear, though it obviously relates to the meaning disrobe and also appears to have lent connotations of softness and pliancy, since these sometimes seem associated with 襄 in compounds. In the case of 1421 襄/𮅕 acts phonetically to express **soft**, and may also lend similar connotations of its own. Thus **soft earth**, i.e. **rich earth**, though now it is used of **earth/ soil** in a broader sense. Suggest taking 六 as **six** 76, 井 as a variant of **well** 井 1470, and 𧘇 as a variant of **clothing/ clothe** 衣.

Mnemonic: **GROUND AROUND SIX WELLS CLOTHED IN RICH SOIL**

1422 **嬢** **JŌ** **YOUNG LADY, DAUGHTER** 16 strokes

令嬢	REIJŌ	young lady
愛嬢	AIJŌ	beloved daughter
お嬢さん	OJŌSAN	young lady, daughter

Formerly 孃. 女 is **woman** 35. 襄/𮅕 is the somewhat obscure element seen in 1421 q.v., here acting phonetically to express **control** according to some scholars and **upper** according to others (though both have the same result). It may possibly also lend its own connotations of **high** and thus reinforce upper. 1422 originally referred to the **upper woman in a house**, i.e. the **lady in control/ principal lady** of the house. Initially this was used as a polite reference to a **mother**, but later, not unlike the English term Mistress, it was applied to women in general, and came to acquire particular associations with **young ladies** (**daughter** being an associated meaning). As with 1421, suggest taking 𮅕 as **six** 六 76, **well** 井 (variant 井 1470), and **clothes** 𧘇 (variant 衣 420).

Mnemonic: **YOUNG LADY HAS ENOUGH CLOTHES TO FILL SIX WELLS**

| 1423 | 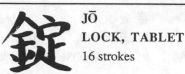 JŌ
LOCK, TABLET
16 strokes | 錠前 JŌMAE
手錠 TEJŌ
錠剤 JŌZAI | lock
handcuffs
pill, tablet |

Somewhat obscure. 金 is **metal** 14. 定 is **fix/ establish** 351 q.v. Often explained as **metal that fixes in place**, i.e. a **lock**. This is a useful mnemonic but possibly an over-simplification, since it does not have a meaning of lock in Chinese (though it can mean an-chor, which can be interpreted as a metal object that fixes in place [but see below]). It seems more likely that it originally referred to a **slab of metal forming the foundation/ base** of something, thus using the similar connotations of framework/ starting-point of 定, and in Chinese it does indeed have a principal meaning of slab or ingot (with anchor presumably an associated meaning from the idea of heavy metal). Some scholars feel that the 正 element of 定, namely correct/ lower leg 41, lent particular connotations of base, and also feel that 1423 was initially used specifically to refer to a metal goblet/ dish with a broad base. Its Japanese meanings of **lock** and **tablet** are taken by some scholars to be borrowings, but it seems more likely that lock results either from a reinterpretation of the elements as outlined above (i.e. metal that fixes in place) or from the associated idea of a heavy metal base/ slab keeping something firmly in place. Tablet may similarly result from an association (of shape) with ingot.

Mnemonic: **LOCK IS METAL OBJECT THAT FIXES IN PLACE**

| 1424 | 讓 JŌ, yuzuru
HAND OVER, YIELD
20 strokes | 譲歩 JŌHO
譲渡 JŌTO
親譲り OYAYUZURI | concession
transfer
patrimony |

Formerly 讓, and originally simply 㘟. The latter is the prototype of the somewhat ob-scure element 襄/襄 (see 1421), and is here used in its original meaning of **people ac-cusing each other**. After the meaning of 襄 became vague **words/ speak** 言 274 was added to stress the idea of **dispute/ argument**. **Yield** is felt by some scholars to be a borrowing, and by others to be an associated meaning, from the idea of yielding in an ar-gument. **Hand over** is an associated meaning in turn with yield. Suggest taking 襄 as **six** 六 76, **well** 井 (variant 丼 1470), and **clothes** 衣 (variant 衣 420).

Mnemonic: **YIELD TO WORDS -- HAND OVER CLOTHES AND SIX WELLS**

1425

JŌ, kamo*su*
BREW, CAUSE
20 strokes

醸造 JŌZŌ   brewing
醸成 JŌSEI   brew, cause
醸し出す KAMOSHIDASU   cause

Formerly 釀. 酉 is **alcohol** 302. 襄/襄 is the somewhat obscure element seen in 1421 q.v., here acting phonetically to express **brew** and possibly also lending loose connotations of **change** or of **soften/ break down**. Thus **brew alcohol**, with **cause** being an associated meaning (cf. English brew up trouble etc.). Suggest taking 襄 as **six** 六 76, **well** 井 (variant 井 1470), and **clothes** 衣 ('ruined' variant 衣 420).

Mnemonic: **BREW ALCOHOL IN SIX WELLS AND RUIN CLOTHES**

1426

殖

SHOKU, fu*eru/yasu*
INCREASE, ENRICH
12 strokes

生殖 SEISHOKU   procreation
利殖 RISHOKU money making
殖え高 FUEDAKA   increment

歹 is **bare bones/ death** 286. 直 is **direct** 349, here acting phonetically to express **soft/ pulpy** but of unclear semantic role. 1426 originally referred to a **corpse putrefying**, and in Chinese still retains occasional connotations of bones. **Enrich** is a borrowed meaning, with **increase** being an associated meaning with enrich.

Mnemonic: **INCREASED BARE BONES DIRECTLY ENRICH GROUND**

1427

SHOKU, kaza*ru*
DECORATE
13 strokes

装飾 SŌSHOKU   decoration
首飾り KUBIKAZARI   necklace
飾り物 KAZARIMONO

                decoration

巾 is **cloth** 778. 飣 is a variant of **feed** 食人 1322, here acting phonetically to express **rub** but of unclear semantic role. Thus to **rub with a cloth**, meaning to **polish/ make clean** and by extension to **beautify/ decorate**. Suggest taking 飣 literally as food/ **eat** 食 146 and **person** ト 39.

Mnemonic: **PERSON USES DECORATIVE CLOTH WHEN EATING**

1428	**SHOKU, fu**_reru_, **sawa**_ru_	触手 SHOKUSHU	feeler
	TOUCH, FEEL, CONTACT	接触 SESSHOKU	contact
	13 strokes	触れ合う FUREAU	contact

Formerly 觸 . 角 is **horn** 243. 蜀 is **caterpillar** 744 q.v., here acting phonetically to express **make contact** and also lending its own similar connotations. 1428 originally referred to **horns making contact** with something/ someone, i.e. **goring**. It still has this meaning in Chinese, including derived figurative meanings such as insult, arouse, etc. In Japanese also it can occasionally have connotations of conflict (in similar fashion to brush in the English term brush with the law etc.), but in general it has come to mean **make contact** in a much broader sense, including **feel** and **touch**. The modern form uses **insect** 虫 56 instead of caterpillar 蜀 .

Mnemonic: **TOUCHED HORNED INSECT -- UNFORGETTABLE FEEL!**

1429	**SHOKU**	委嘱 ISHOKU	commission
	REQUEST, ENTRUST	嘱望 SHOKUBŌ	expectation
	15 strokes	嘱託 SHOKUTAKU	
			commission

Formerly 囑 . 口 is **mouth/ say** 20. 屬/属 is **belong** 744 q.v., here acting phonetically to express **bring into contact/ join** and probably also lending its own connotations of **join**. Thus **verbally enjoin**, leading to **request, charge, entrust**, etc.

Mnemonic: **ENTRUSTED TO SAY WHAT BELONGS**

1430	**JOKU, hazuka**_shimeru_	侮辱 BUJOKU	insult
	INSULT, HUMILIATE	屈辱 KUTSUJOKU	humiliation
	10 strokes	雪辱 SETSUJOKU	vindication

Clam(shell) 辰 366 q.v., here in its sense of **cutting tool**, and **hand/ measure** 寸 909 q.v., here meaning **careful use of the hand**. Thus **careful use of a cutting tool**, a reference to **using a scythe/ sickle**. Some scholars take **insult/ humiliate** to be a borrowing, but it seems equally if not more likely to be a figurative extension (cf. English cutting remark etc.).

Mnemonic: **HAND OUT INSULTS AS CUTTING AS CLAMSHELL**

| 1431 | 伸 | SHIN, nobiru/basu
STRETCH, EXTEND
7 strokes | 伸縮 SHINSHUKU elasticity
追伸 TSUISHIN postscript
背伸び SENOBI stretch on tiptoe |

イ is **person** 39. 申 is **say** 322 q.v., here used phonetically to express **stretch**. 申 may also lend its own suggestion of stretching/ straightening through its early form , which is actually a stylisation of a jagged bolt of lightning but looks very similar to hands straightening a stick ((see hands straightening an arrow 寅 621, and see also 1439). Thus a **person stretching**, now **stretch/ extend** in a broad sense.

Mnemonic: **PERSON STRETCHES OUT WHAT HE HAS TO SAY**

| 1432 | 辛 | SHIN, karai, tsurai
SHARP, BITTER
7 strokes | 辛苦 SHINKU hardship
辛味 KARAMI sharp taste
辛うじて KAROJITE barely |

Also written 辛, and earlier 辛 or 辛, and depicting a **tattooist's needle**. ∨ is an exaggeration of a barb, generally felt to be used symbolically to emphasise the idea of **piercing** but it should be noted that there appears to have been a type of needle used as an instrument of torture. This is usually found as a variant form 辛 or 辛 (e.g. see 1288). Both this variant form and the conventional tattooist's needle could symbolise **prisoners** and **slaves**, who were variously tortured and tattooed (e.g. see 318/ 340). 1432 also symbolised **sharpness** and by figurative association **bitterness**, both in the sense of taste and of hardship. Suggest taking 辛 as **stand** 立 73 and **ten/ needle** 十 33.

Mnemonic: **STAND ON TEN SHARP NEEDLES -- BITTER EXPERIENCE**

| 1433 | 侵 | SHIN, okasu
INVADE, VIOLATE
9 strokes | 侵入 SHINNYŪ invasion
侵害 SHINGAI violation
侵略 SHINRYAKU aggression |

Once written , showing that 彐 is a simplification of **hand holding broom** 帚 96. 入/イ is **person** 39. ㇒ is a further **hand**, presumably indicating sweeping with both hands though in reality redundant. Thus a **person sweeping**. **Invade/ violate** is taken by some scholars to be a borrowing, but it seems equally likely that the idea of sweeping led to that of moving gradually forward, which in turn led to **encroach** (still a strong meaning in Chinese) and hence **invade/ violate**. Suggest taking 彐 as **hand**, ㇒ as another **hand**, and ⌐ as **cover**.

Mnemonic: **INVADED BY PERSON WITH COVERED HANDS**

460

1434		SHIN, tsu HARBOR, CROSSING 9 strokes	津津 SHINSHIN	brimful
			津波 TSUNAMI	tidal wave
			津津浦浦 TSUTSUURAURA	
				throughout the land

氵 is **water** 40, here meaning **river** or **body of water**. 聿 is **brush in hand** 993/ 142, here acting phonetically to express **advance** and possibly also lending its own similar connotations (from the movement of a hand when writing). Thus to **advance across water**, leading to **cross** and **crossing (place)**. In Japanese crossing also led by association to **harbor/ port**, from the idea of a safe stretch of water.

Mnemonic: **CROSS WATERS OF HARBOR, BRUSH IN HAND**

1435	唇	SHIN, kuchibiru LIP(S) 10 strokes	唇音 SHINON	labial sound
			口唇 KŌSHIN	lips
			紅唇 KŌSHIN	red lips

Somewhat obscure, though its elements are clearly **mouth/ say** 口 20 and **clam** 辰 366. Some scholars feel that the latter acts phonetically to express **tremble** and also lends its own connotations of **closing**, thus giving **that part of the mouth which trembles and closes**, i.e. the **lips**. Other scholars feel that 1435 originally referred ideographically to the mouth of a clam, i.e. the edges of its shells and thus by association lips. The former theory is supported by the existence of the NGU character lip 脣 (to all intents and purposes interchangeable with 1435), which uses **meat/ of the body** 月 365. It is unlikely that this could mean mouth of a clam (though meat of a clam is a possibility), and it would seem to be the case that 辰 again acts phonetically to express tremble and also lends its own connotations of closing, to give that part of the body which trembles and closes.

Mnemonic: **LIPS SHUT MOUTH LIKE A CLAM**

1436	娠	SHIN PREGNANCY 10 strokes	妊娠 NINSHIN	pregnancy
			妊娠可能 NINSHINKANŌ	fertile
			妊娠検査 NINSHINKENSA	
				pregnancy test

女 is **woman** 35. 辰 is **clam(shell)** 366, here acting phonetically to express **duplicate** and probably also lending its own connotations of a living thing contained within a casing. Thus **woman duplicating**, a reference to **pregnancy**.

Mnemonic: **PREGNANT WOMAN IS LIKE CLAM**

461

1437
SHIN, fu*ri*/*ru*/*ruu*
WAVE, SWING,
AIR, MANNER, AFTER
10 strokes

振動 SHINDŌ   swing
振り切る FURIKIRU   shake off
二年振り NINENBURI
                                    after two years

Of broad semantic evolution. 扌 is **hand** 32. 辰 is **clam/ cutting tool** 366 q.v., here acting phonetically to express **shake/ wave** and possibly also lending its own connotations of **swing** from the action of using a scythe. Thus to **shake/ swing/ wave the hands,** with the hand element later fading. **Air/ manner** (often in the sense of **pretense**) is felt to be an extended figurative meaning, from the idea of brandish (i.e. show off/ put on airs and graces). It is not clear how 1437 came to acquire the meaning of **after** (in the sense of something happening after a period of not happening), but this may possibly be an associated figurative meaning from the idea of rousing/ bringing about action after inertia.

Mnemonic: **WAVE CLAM IN HAND IN STRANGE MANNER**

1438
SHIN, hita*su*/*ru*
SOAK, IMMERSE
10 strokes

浸食 SHINSHOKU   erosion
浸水 SHINSUI   inundation
水浸し MIZUBITASHI flooding

氵 is **water** 40. 㑒 is the simplified **hands holding broom** seen in 1433 q.v., here acting phonetically to express **advance** and probably also lending similar connotations of its own. Thus **water advancing,** a reference to **flooding** and hence the associated meanings of **soak** and **immerse.** Suggest taking ヨ as **hand,** 又 as another **hand,** and 冖 as **cover.**

Mnemonic: **SOAK HANDS, COVERING THEM WITH WATER**

1439
SHIN
GENTLEMAN, BELT
11 strokes

紳士 SHINSHI   gentleman
紳商 SHINSHŌ rich merchant
紳士録 SHINSHIROKU
                                    Who's Who

糸 is **thread** 27, here meaning **cloth.** 申 is **say** 322, here acting phonetically to express **pull/stretch** and possibly also lending a similar suggestion through its early form 㬥 (see 1431). Thus **cloth which is pulled/ stretched,** a reference to a **waistband/ belt.** It later came to acquire associations with a **gentleman.**

Mnemonic: **FINE THREADS ON BELT SAY HE'S A GENTLEMAN**

1440

SHIN, mi*ru*
DIAGNOSE, EXAMINE
12 strokes

診断 SHINDAN diagnosis
診察 SHINSATSU examination
往診 ŌSHIN house call

言 is **words/ speak/ state** 274. 㐱 is a CO character meaning **hair**, being to all intents and purposes **hair** 彡 93 plus **person** 人 39. Here 㐱 acts phonetically to express **examine**, and may also lend loose suggestions of delicate and hence in (fine) detail (see 93). It is not clear whether 1440 originally meant to **examine someone's words** or, more likely, to **examine and then make a pronouncement** (i.e. diagnosis), but from a very early stage it became associated with a **medical examination**.

Mnemonic: **PERSON EXAMINED: DIAGNOSIS STATES TOO HAIRY**

1441

SHIN, ne*ru*/*kasu*
SLEEP, LIE DOWN
13 strokes

寝室 SHINSHITSU bedroom
寝入る NEIRU fall asleep
寝かし物 NEKASHIMONO
unsold stock

宀 is **roof/ building** 28. 丬 is **(sick)bed** 1389, here indicating someone being 'laid up' with sickness (see also 381). 㑴 is the simplified **hands holding broom** seen in 1433 q.v., here acting phonetically to express **cleanse** and also lending similar connotations of sweep away/ remove impurities. 1441 originally referred to a type of temple outbuilding where sick persons were laid to be cleansed of the evil spirit believed to be causing their sickness. It later came to mean **rest** or **lie down** in a broad sense, and is now also often used of **sleep**. Suggest taking 㑴 as **hand** ヨ, another **hand** ㄨ, and **cover** 冖.

Mnemonic: **SLEEP IN BUILDING, HANDS OUT OF BED-COVER**

1442

SHIN, tsutsushi*mu*
BE DISCREET, REFRAIN
13 strokes

慎重 SHINCHŌ prudence
勤慎 KINSHIN good conduct
慎み深い TSUTSUSHIMIBUKAI
discreet

Formerly 愼. 忄 is **heart/ feelings** 147. 眞/真 is **true** 514 q.v., here acting phonetically to express **constrain/ restrain** and possibly also lending connotations of **proper** (or, less likely, **true**). Thus to (**act properly and?**) **restrain one's (true?) feelings**, i.e. **refrain**, with **be discreet** being an associated meaning.

Mnemonic: **DISCREETLY REFRAIN, MASKING TRUE FEELINGS**

1443 SHIN
JUDGE, INVESTIGATE
15 strokes

審議 SHINGI deliberation
不議 FUSHIN doubt
審判 SHINPAN
judging, refereeing

宀 is roof/ **building** 28. 番 is **number** 196 q.v., here acting phonetically to express **know (thoroughly)** and possibly also lending connotations of **systematic/ in order**. Unlikely as it may seem, 1443 originally referred to having a **thorough (and systematic?) knowledge of a building**, later coming to mean **have a thorough knowledge** in general. **Judge** and **investigate** are associated meanings.

Mnemonic: **INVESTIGATE HOUSE NUMBERS PRIOR TO JUDGING**

1444 SHIN, furu*u/eru*
SHAKE, TREMBLE
15 strokes

地震 JISHIN earthquake
身震い MIBURUI trembling
震え声 FURUEGOE
trembling voice

雨 is **rain** 3, here meaning **storm**. 辰 is **clam/ cutting tool** 366 q.v., here acting phonetically to express **shake/ wave/ tremble** and possibly also lending its own connotations of (swinging) movement from the action of using a scythe. 1444 originally referred to a **violent storm causing things to shake and sway**, then later came to mean **shake/ tremble/ sway** in a general sense.

Mnemonic: **RAIN MAKES CLAM SHAKE AND TREMBLE?!**

1445 SHIN, takigi, maki
FIREWOOD, KINDLING
16 strokes

薪炭 SHINTAN fuel
薪小屋 TAKIGIGOYA woodshed
薪割り MAKIWARI
woodchopping

新 is **new** 148 q.v., here in its original meaning of **chop down a tree/ chop wood**, with **plant** 艹 9 added to draw attention to the wood itself. It came to acquire connotations of small pieces of wood, i.e. **firewood/ kindling**, rather than timber/ lumber.

Mnemonic: **USE NEWLY CHOPPED PLANTS AS KINDLING**

1446		JIN, ha, yaiba BLADE, SWORD 3 strokes	白刃 HAKUJIN drawn sword 刃物 HAMONO bladed object 両刃 RYŌBA double blade

Sword 刀 181 with a **mark** 丶 to indicate the **blade**. Note that the blade is on the <u>inside</u> edge of the sword, unlike the now famed katana which is also expressed by 181.

Mnemonic: **SWORD WITH MARKED BLADE**

1447		JIN, tsukiru/kusu USE UP, EXHAUST 6 strokes	尽力 JINRYOKU effort(s) 尽未来 JINMIRAI forever 心尽くし KOKOROZUKUSHI care

Formerly 盡 and originally 蓋. 皿/皿 is **dish** 1307. 戈/聿 is **hand holding brush** (old form/ variant 聿 142), here acting phonetically to express **empty** and almost certainly also lending connotations of **soaking up**. **Fire** 灬 8 was added later, presumably to lend a supporting idea of **dry**. 1447 originally meant **dry and empty bowl**, with **use up/ exhaust** being an associated meaning. Suggest taking 尺 of the modern form as **person** 人 39 with **back-pack** ユ, and 〻 as a variant of **two** 二 61, with a play on the word **exhaust**.

Mnemonic: **PERSON EXHAUSTED BY CARRYING TWO BACK-PACKS**

1448		JIN, hayai FAST, INTENSE 6 strokes	迅速 JINSOKU rapidity 迅雷 JINRAI thunderclap 奮迅 FUNJIN great rage

辶 is **movement** 129. 卂 is an obscure element, once written 卂 and apparently comprising **bending person** 丨 39 and needle/ **ten** 十 33 but of unclear meaning. It is however known to act here phonetically to express **fast**, giving **fast movement**. **Intense** is an associated meaning. Suggest taking 乚 as a **sprinter kneeling (at the blocks)**.

Mnemonic: **TEN KNEELING SPRINTERS, READY TO MOVE FAST**

1449		JIN, hanahada[shii] GREAT(LY), EXTREME 9 strokes	甚大 JINDAI na immense 甚六 JINROKU dunce 幸甚 KŌJIN very glad

A combination of **sweet** 甘 1093 (here 甘) and **match/ matched pair** 匹 1736. Unlikely as it may seem, **sweet matched pair** was a reference to a **pair of lovers**, and symbolised **great happiness**. Eventually **great** came to prevail over happiness.

Mnemonic: **SWEET MATCHED PAIR GREATLY IN LOVE**

1450 **JIN**

POSITION, CAMP

10 strokes

陣頭 JINTŌ — van of army

陣地 JINCHI — position

陣痛 JINTSŪ — labor pains

Hill 阝 229 and **vehicle** 車 31. **Vehicles drawn up around a hill** indicated an **army encampment** (see 466 and 540). Now also **position** in a broader sense.

Mnemonic: **VEHICLES POSITIONED AROUND HILL SHOW ARMY CAMP**

1451 **JIN, tazu*neru*, hiro**

INQUIRE, NEXT,

USUAL, A FATHOM

12 strokes

尋問 JINMON — questioning

尋常 JINJŌ — normal

尋ね出す TAZUNEDASU — seek out

Once written 𩙿. 彐 is **right hand** 2. 彡 is a derivative of 𠂇, an old form of **left hand** 左 22. 屮/寸 is **hand/ measure** 909, here also acting phonetically to express **stretch**. 1451 originally referred to the **span between two outstretched arms/ hands**, to give a measure of **one fathom** (six feet or 1.82 m. in Japan [as England] but an exaggerated eight feet in China: note the similar etymology of the English term fathom, which in Old English literally means the span of the arms). Outstretched arms also came to symbolise **making an appeal**, leading to **inquire/ ask**. **Usual** is felt to stem from the usual/ standard span of the arms (though ironically the Japanese and Chinese interpretations have been seen to differ). It is not clear how **next** evolved. Suggest taking 彐 as **hand**, 寸 as another **hand**, 口 as **opening** 20, and 工 as **work** 113.

Mnemonic: **INQUIRE ABOUT OPENING FOR WORKING HANDS**

1452 **SUI, fuk*u***

BLOW, BREATHE OUT

7 strokes

鼓吹 KOSUI — advocacy

吹雪 FUBUKI* — snowstorm

吹き倒す FUKITAOSU — blow down

口 is **mouth** 20 while 欠 is **lack** 471 q.v., here in its literal meaning of **gaping mouth**. 1452 is a somewhat vague ideograph indicating a **person letting out a big breath**, with **blow** being an associated meaning.

Mnemonic: **LACK MOUTH, BUT BREATHE AND BLOW NONETHELESS?**

466

| 1453 | 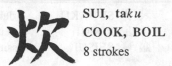 | SUI, ta*ku*
 COOK, BOIL
 8 strokes | 炊事 SUIJI — cooking
 飯炊き MESHITAKI cook, maid
 自炊 JISUI cooking for self |

火 is **fire** 8. 欠 is **lack/ gaping mouth** 471 q.v., here acting phonetically to express **blow** (i.e. to all intents and purposes a simplification of blow 吹 1452 q.v.). 1453 referred to **blowing on a fire to make it flare up prior to cooking,** and thus by extension symbolised **cooking/ boiling.**

Mnemonic: **LACK FIRE, BUT COOK NONETHELESS?**

| 1454 |  | SUI
 COMMANDER
 9 strokes | 統帥 TŌSUI supreme command
 元帥 GENSUI field marshal
 将帥 SHŌSUI commander |

𠂤 has long been confused with **hill** 𠂤 (see 師 693, from which distinguish), but in fact old forms of 1454 such as ｜⃫飞 show it to be a **pair of hands** 彐 and a **stick** ｜. 巾 is **cloth** 778. 1454 originally referred to a **person waving a stick with a piece of cloth attached,** i.e. a **banner-waver** and by association **leader.** Suggest taking 𠂤 as **hill.**

Mnemonic: **COMMANDER CARRIES CLOTH BANNER UP HILL**

| 1455 | | SUI, iki
 PURE, ESSENCE, 'STYLE'
 10 strokes | 粋美 SUIBI true beauty
 粋事 IKIGOTO romance
 粋人 SUIJIN man of taste, <br> man about town |

Formerly 粹. 米 is **rice** 201. 卒 is **soldier** 537, here acting phonetically to express **pure** but of unclear semantic role. Thus **pure rice,** later **pure/ quintessential** in a broader sense. From association with **essence** it also came to acquire connotations of knowing just the right thing to do, in particular in the sense of being worldlywise, and thus also came to mean **style** (as in the English to have style). Suggest taking 卆 as **nine** 九 12 and **ten** 十 33.

Mnemonic: **NINETEEN GRAINS OF PURE RICE**

467

1456 SUI, otoro*eru*
WEAKEN, WANE
10 strokes

衰弱 SUIJAKU　debility
老衰 RŌSUI　senility
盛衰 SEISUI　vicissitudes

Once written 衺 , showing **clothing** 会/衣/衣 420 and 㐅. The latter shows two **plants** 屮 (inverted variant 屮 9 or 生 42), here indicating **straw**, joined together ∩. Rather like thatching a roof, (inverted) straw was fashioned into a topcoat for keeping out rain and cold, and 1456 originally meant **straw raincoat**. This meaning is now conveyed by the NGU character 蓑 , which adds plant 艹 9. Its present meaning of **weaken/ wane** results from borrowing. Suggest taking 甴 as a **pierced** 一 **hole**/ opening 口 20.

Mnemonic: **CLOTHING WEAKENED AFTER HOLE PIERCED**

1457 SUI, *you*
DRUNK, DIZZY
11 strokes

麻酔 MASUI　anesthesia
酔払い YOPPARAI　drunkard
船酔い FUNAYOI　seasickness

Formerly 醉 , showing **wine jar**/ alcohol 酉 302 and **soldier**/ **end** 卒 537. The latter acts phonetically to express **finish** and probably lends its own similar connotations. Thus to **finish off a wine jar**, meaning to **become drunk**. In Japanese also **become dizzy** in a broader sense. Suggest taking 卆 as **nine** 九 12 and **ten** 十 33.

Mnemonic: **DRUNK AND DIZZY AFTER NINETEEN WINE JARS**

1458 SUI, tog*eru*, tsui
ATTAIN, FINALLY
12 strokes

遂行 SUIKŌ　attainment
未遂 MISUI no　attempted
仕遂げる SHITOGERU　accomplish

豕 is an element meaning **(group of) pigs moving**. It comprises **pig** 豕 1670 and **away**/ **out of** ハ 66, to refer to the action of pigs when moving out of an enclosure, and often has connotations of pushing and jostling. Here the idea of movement is reinforced by **movement** 辶 129. Pigs moving in a group came to refer to **group movement** in general, especially in the sense of **attaining a goal through the brute force of the group** (not unlike the English term bulldoze one's way). Now **attain** in a general sense, with **finally** being an associated meaning. Suggest taking ハ in its meaning of **eight**.

Mnemonic: **EIGHT MOVING PIGS FINALLY ATTAIN GOAL**

1459 SUI, nemu*ru*
SLEEP
13 strokes

睡眠 SUIMIN　sleep
熟睡 JUKUSUI　sound sleep
午睡 GOSUI　nap, siesta

Eye 目 72 and **droop** 垂 907. **Droopy eyes** indicate **sleepiness** and hence **sleep**.

Mnemonic: **DROOPY EYES LEAD TO SLEEP**

1460	SUI, ho EAR/ SPEAR (OF GRAIN) 15 strokes	穂状 SUIJŌ 稲穂 INAHO 穂先 HOSAKI	spear shape ear of rice spear

Formerly 穗 . 禾 is **rice plant/ grain plant** 81. 心 is **heart** 147, here meaning **main part**. 叀 /甶 is spinning weight 914 q.v., here acting phonetically to express **hang** and also lending its own connotations of **hanging weight**. Thus **that which hangs heavily down from a grain plant and is its main part**, namely the **head/ ear/ spear**. Suggest taking 甶 as **ten** 十 33 and **field** 田 59.

Mnemonic: **HEARTENED BY EARS ON GRAIN PLANTS IN TEN FIELDS**

1461	SUI, tsumu, omori SPINDLE, SINKER 16 strokes	紡錘 BŌSUI 錘状 SUIJŌ 丸錘 MARUOMORI	spindle spindle shape ball sinker

Metal 金 14 and **hang down** 垂 907, giving **metal object that hangs down**, i.e. **plumb-bob, spindle, sinker**, etc.

Mnemonic: **SINKER IS METAL OBJECT THAT HANGS DOWN**

1462	ZUI FOLLOW, RANDOM 12 strokes	随筆 ZUIHITSU random notes 随行員 ZUIKŌIN attendant 随分 ZUIBUN considerably

Formerly 隨 . 辶 is **movement** 129. 隋 is a CO character now meaning both **fall** and **scraps of meat**. It comprises **hill** 阝 229 and an element meaning **falling scraps of meat** 肯 (**meat** 月 365 and [left] **hand** 𠂇 22, to indicate scraps of meat falling from the hand). The combination of hill 阝 and falling scraps of meat 肯 indicates a hillside falling/ crumbling, i.e. a **landslide**, but clearly this meaning was eventually replaced by the meanings properly belonging to 肯 itself (i.e. with hill 阝 becoming redundant). Note that the addition of earth 土 60 gives **fall/ landslide** 墮 /堕 1539. In the case of 1462 隋 acts phonetically to express **follow**, and almost certainly also lends connotations of **unstoppable movement** from its literal meaning of landslide. Thus **move and follow (in unstoppable fashion)**. On the one hand this has led to connotations of great momentum and inexorability, and on the other to doing what one wishes regardless, somewhat paradoxically often with its own connotations of acting in a capricious or desultory manner (thus giving **random**). Suggest taking 有 as **exist** 401.

Mnemonic: **MOVEMENT EXISTS TO FOLLOW HILLS AT RANDOM**

1463 ZUI
MARROW
19 strokes

骨 髄 KOTSUZUI bone marrow
脳 髄 NŌZUI brain
真 髄 SHINZUI essence

Of confused and somewhat obscure etymology. Formerly 髓遀 , and in ancient times 骼髐 with an occasionally encountered variant 骨脔. 骨/骨 is **bone** 867. 阝/阝 is **hill** 229. 垚 is a doubling of **left hand** 22. As an element 垚 is obscure, but it seems most likely that 隓 is a variant or miscopying of **landslide/ fall/ scraps of meat** 隋 1462 q.v. In the case of 1463 隋/隓 acts phonetically to express **fat**, here meaning **fatty meat**, and almost certainly also lends connotations of **bits of meat**. Thus **fatty meat within the bones**, i.e. **marrow**. The modern form replaces hill 阝 with **movement** 辶 129, probably a miscopying under the influence of 随 1462. Suggest taking 有 as **exist** 401.

Mnemonic: **MARROW EXISTS IN MOVING BONES**

1464 SŪ, toboso
PIVOT, DOOR
8 strokes

枢 軸 SŪJIKU axis
枢 要 SŪYŌ importance
中 枢 CHŪSŪ center, pivot

Formerly 樞. 木 is **tree/ wood** 69. 區/区 is **ward/ section** 465 q.v., here acting phonetically to express **important** and almost certainly also lending connotations of **hole** and **container** (since the elements of 區 can be reinterpreted as opening/ hole 口 20 and container 匸 225). 1464 originally referred to a **hole containing/seating an important shaft,** namely the **pivot** on which a certain type of **door** swung. It thus came to be used of the **pivot** itself, and occasionally also of **door**. As in the English term pivot, it has connotations of importance.

Mnemonic: **PIVOT IS IMPORTANT SECTION OF WOODEN DOOR**

1465 SŪ, aga*meru*
LOFTY, NOBLE, REVERE
11 strokes

崇 拝 SŪHAI worship
崇 高 SŪKŌ na sublime
崇 敬 SŪKEI reverence

山 is **mountain** 24. 宗 is **religion** 889, here acting phonetically to express **duplicate/ layer** and also lending its connotations of **respect/ awe**. 1465 originally referred to a **tall mountain towering over others** (i.e. forming another layer of mountain). It is still occasionally found in this sense of **lofty peak**, but is usually found in a figurative sense of **something lofty and noble which inspires respect and awe**.

Mnemonic: **RELIGIOUSLY REVERE LOFTY MOUNTAIN**

1466 据	su*eru*/*waru* **SET, PLACE, SIT** 11 strokes	据え置く SUEOKU	leave as is
		据え物 SUEMONO	ornament
		据え付け SUETSUKE	installation

扌 is **hand** 32. 居 is **be**/ reside 649 q.v., here with its literal meaning of **be fixed in a place**. Thus to **fix something in a place by hand**, i.e. **set**/ **place**, with **sit** being an associated meaning that overlooks the presence of hand 扌 (note that in English also set and sit are etymologically related).

Mnemonic: **SET SOMETHING DOWN WHERE HAND IS**

1467	sugi **CRYPTOMERIA, CEDAR** 7 strokes	杉あや SUGIAYA	herringbone
		杉垣 SUGIGAKI	cedar hedge
		杉並木 SUGINAMIKI	
			avenue of cedars

木 is **tree**/ wood 69. 彡 is (delicate) **hairs** 93, here acting phonetically to express **enduring** and also lending its shape to suggest **hair-like leaves**. Thus **enduring tree with hair-like leaves**, a reference to the **cedar**/ **cryptomeria**.

Mnemonic: **CEDAR IS TREE WITH HAIR-LIKE LEAVES**

1468 畝	se, une **RIDGE,** **SQUARE MEASURE** 10 strokes	畝立て UNEDATE	furrowing
		二畝 NISE	two se
		畝織り UNEORI	ribbed fabric

Formerly 畂, showing **field** 田 59, **lasting** 久 647, and what appears to be ten 十 33. 久 acts phonetically to express **ridge**, and may also lend connotations of permanence. The role of 十 is not clear, but it may possibly lend its shape to suggest intersecting paths. 1468 originally referred to the **ridges running through/ separating fields**. It later also came to be used of a **square measure** (presumably the area between ridges), specifically a standard 99.3 sq.m. in Japanese but of variable size in Chinese. Suggest taking 亠 as a symbol of **top**.

Mnemonic: **MEASURED FIELDS TOPPED BY LASTING RIDGES**

1469 se
SHALLOWS, RAPIDS
19 strokes

浅 瀬 ASASE　　shoal, shallows
瀬 戸 SETO　　strait, channel
瀬 戸 物 SETOMONO　　porcelain

Formerly 瀨 . ⺡ is **water/ river** 40. 賴/頼 is **rely/ request** 1889 q.v., here acting phonetically to express **fast** and probably also lending its connotations of **dividing**. Thus **where a river (divides and?) flows fast**, a reference to **shallows/ rapids**.

Mnemonic: **RELY ON WATER HAVING SHALLOWS**

1470 SEI, SHŌ, i
WELL
4 strokes

油 井 YUSEI　　oil well
天 井 TENJŌ　　ceiling
井 戸 IDO　　well

From a pictograph of a **well crib/ well frame** 井 . Once also written 丼, with ・ indicating water within the well, but 丼 is now a separate character meaning receptacle/ bowl (see 43).

Mnemonic: **WELL WITH FRAME**

1471 SEI, SHŌ
SURNAME
8 strokes

姓 名 SEIMEI　　surname
改 姓 KAISEI　　name change
百 姓 HYAKUSHŌ　　farmer

Woman 女 35 and **birth** 生 42. Often interpreted as children being given (at birth) the family name of their mother rather than father, this practice being connected with an attempt to preserve the mother's lineage in a polygamous situation. There may have been some truth to this at some stage, but it seems more likely that 女 indicates **female children** rather than mother, since in ancient China it was generally only women who used a family name. Thus **that given a female child at birth**, i.e. a **family name**.

Mnemonic: **WOMAN GIVEN SURNAME AT BIRTH**

1472 SEI
SUBJUGATE, TRAVEL
8 strokes

征 服 SEIFUKU　　subjugation
遠 征 ENSEI　　expedition
征 衣 SEII　　traveling clothes, military clothes

彳 is **movement (along a road)** 118. 正 is **proper** 41 q.v., here in its literal meaning of lower leg/ **foot**. Thus **to set foot on a road/ move off**. This can mean **travel** in a general sense, but has particular connotations of **setting forth on a military campaign**, with **subjugate** being an associated meaning.

Mnemonic: **MOVE OFF PROPERLY TO SUBJUGATE**

1473
SEI, hito*shii*
EQUAL, SIMILAR
8 strokes

一斉 ISSEI　　all together
斉一 SEIITSU　　equality
斉唱 SEISHŌ singing in unison

Formerly 齊 . The earliest form 𝖘𝖙𝖙 shows **similar heads of grain** (arranged for religious offering). The idea of similarity and belonging to the same category was reinforced by the addition of a symbol ＝ , giving 𝖕𝖕 , which was later stylised to 𝖌 and eventually became 齊 . **Similarity/ equality** came to prevail over the original meaning of religious offering of grain. Suggest taking 文 as **text** 68 and 爿 as a 'partially eclipsed' **moon** 月 16.

Mnemonic: **TEXTS ABOUT LUNAR ECLIPSE ALL VERY SIMILAR**

1474
SEI
SACRIFICE
9 strokes

犠牲者 GISEISHA　　victim
犠牲 IKENIE*　　live sacrifice
犠牲的 GISEITEKI self-sacrificing

牛 is **cow/ bull** 97. 生 is **live** 42, here also acting phonetically to express **purify**. A **purified cow** was offered as a **live sacrifice**. Now **sacrifice** in a general sense. See also 1140.

Mnemonic: **SACRIFICE OF LIVE COW**

1475
SEI, yu*ku*
DIE, PASS ON, DEATH
10 strokes

逝去 SEIKYO　　death
急逝 KYŪSEI　　sudden death
長逝 CHŌSEI　　death

辶 is **movement** 129. 折 is **bend/ break** 522 q.v., here acting phonetically to express **sever** and also lending similar connotations of its own from its literal meaning of **chop down**. Thus a **movement that severs**, a reference to **passing on/ death**.

Mnemonic: **MOVEMENT BREAKS DOWN THROUGH DEATH**

1476
SEI, JŌ, mo*ru*, sakaru/n
PROSPER, HEAP, SERVE
11 strokes

全盛期 ZENSEIKI　　golden age
大盛り ŌMORI　　large helping
燃え盛る MOESAKARU　　flare up

皿 is **dish** 1307. 成 is **become** 515 q.v., here acting phonetically to express **pile up** and probably also lending connotations of completion and by extension fullness. Thus a **piled up dish**, leading to **heap** and **serve** and by figurative association **grow/ prosper**.

Mnemonic: **SERVE HEAPED DISHES WHEN ONE BECOMES PROSPEROUS**

1477

SEI, muko
SON-IN-LAW
12 strokes

女婿 JOSEI　　　　son-in-law
花婿 HANAMUKO bridegroom
婿入り MUKOIRI

marrying heiress

Formerly also written 壻, i.e. with **male** 士/土 494 instead of **woman** 女 35. 胥 is a CO character with a range of confusing meanings, such as together, assist, wait, examine, distant, clerk, store, and minced crabs. Its etymology is unclear, though its elements are **meat**/ of the body 月 365 and **proper**/ lower leg 足/正 41 (though technically the variant 疋 has become a separate NGU character now used as a cloth measure and animal counter). Here 胥 acts phonetically to express **partner**, but any semantic role is unclear. Thus 壻 means a **male who is a partner (for a woman)**, while 婿 means a **partner for a woman**, both being references to a **husband**. In particular it has come to mean husband viewed from the standpoint of the woman's parents, i.e. an adopted husband/ **son-in-law**.

Mnemonic: **MEATY SON-IN-LAW IS PROPER PARTNER FOR WOMAN**

1478

SEI, chika*u*
PLEDGE, VOW, OATH
14 strokes

誓約 SEIYAKU　　　　pledge
宣誓 SENSEI　　　　oath
誓い言 CHIKAIGOTO　pledge

言 is **word** 274. 折 is bend/ **break** 522 q.v., here acting phonetically to express **cut/ sever** and also lending similar connotations of its own from its literal meaning of chop down. A **broken/ severed word** rather confusingly suggests the very opposite of a **pledge**, but in fact the character refers to the practice of **cutting a piece of wood in two as tallies** to be joined again upon completion of a (verbal) arrangement or similar (see 1195), and thus symbolises a **pledge**.

Mnemonic: **BROKEN WORD IS ACTUALLY A PLEDGE!**

1479

SEI, SHIN, k*ou*, u*keru*
REQUEST, UNDERTAKE
15 strokes

請求 SEIKYŪ　　　　request
普請 FUSHIN　　construction
請負人 UKEOININ　contractor

言 is **word/ speak** 274. 青 is green/ **blue** 43, here acting phonetically to express **audience** but of unclear semantic role. 1479 originally referred to a **person requesting an audience**, and later came to mean **request** in a broader sense. **Undertake** is an associated meaning (cf. connotations of English tender [a bid etc.]).

Mnemonic: **EXPRESS REQUEST IN BLUE WORDS**

1480	SEKI, shirizo*keru* **REPEL, REJECT** 5 strokes	排斥 HAISEKI — boycott 斥候 SEKKŌ — scout, patrol 斥力 SEKIRYOKU — repulsive force

Once written 庐. 广 is **building** 114. 屰 is **reverse** 646 q.v., here acting phonetically to express **empty** and probably also lending its connotations of opposite to normal. 1480 originally referred to an **empty building** (i.e. one normally occupied), and **repel/ reject** is a borrowed meaning. Suggest taking the modern form 斥 as **ax** 斤 1176 plus a down stroke ＼ indicating **coming down** (see 下 7).

Mnemonic: **REPELLED BY AX COMING DOWN**

1481	SEKI, SHAKU, mukashi **OLDEN TIMES, PAST** 8 strokes	昔日 SEKIJITSU — old days 昔風 MUKASHIFŪ — oldstyle 今昔 KONJAKU — past and present

Once written 㫺. ⊙/日 is **sun/ day** 62, while ≈ is an abstract symbol felt to express the idea of piling up/ **accumulating** (possibly originally some variant of mountains 山 24). Thus **accumulation of days**, i.e. **history/ the past**. Suggest taking 昔 as a combination of **two tens** 廾 33 and **one** — 1.

Mnemonic: **TWENTY-ONE DAYS AGO IS WELL IN THE PAST**

1482	SEKI **DIVIDE, ANALYSE** 8 strokes	分析 BUNSEKI — analysis 解析 KAISEKI — analysis 析出 SEKISHUTSU — eduction

Tree/ wood 木 69 and **ax** 斤 1176, here with its connotations of **chop**. Thus to **chop up a tree/ wood**, leading to the idea of **reduce to small bits** and hence **divide** and by association **analyse**.

Mnemonic: **ANALYSE TREE BY CHOPPING AND DIVIDING WITH AX**

1483

SEKI
ONE OF A PAIR,
SHIP COUNTER
10 strokes

隻手 SEKISHU   one arm
一隻 ISSEKI   one ship/ boat
一隻眼 ISSEKIGAN discernment

Bird 隹 216 and **hand** 又. **A bird in the hand** indicated **one bird** (especially of a pair/ brace), as opposed to two birds in the hand/ pair 雙/双 1513 q.v., and 1483 has thus come to mean **one of a pair** in a broad sense. Also originally a counter for birds, though for some reason it has now become a **counter for ships/ boats** (possibly through a figurative reference to sails, which are frequently likened in poetry to wings).

Mnemonic: **ONLY ONE BIRD IN THE HAND**

1484

SEKI, oshii/shimu
REGRET, BE LOATH TO
11 strokes

痛惜 TSŪSEKI   deep regret
惜し気 OSHIGE   regret
骨惜しみ HONEOSHIMI
            sparing oneself

忄 is **heart/ feelings** 147. 昔 is **past** 1481, here acting phonetically to express **pierce** and possibly also lending connotations of the past. Thus **pierced heart** (over a matter in the past?), a somewhat vague reference to **feelings of regret**, with **reluctance/ being loath to** an associated meaning. Note that in the case of 1101 q.v. pierced heart means grieve/ be afflicted.

Mnemonic: **FEELINGS FOR THE PAST ARE FULL OF REGRET**

1485

SEKI, ato
TRACE, REMAINS
13 strokes

追跡 TSUISEKI   pursuit
足跡 ASHIATO   footprint
遺跡 ISEKI   ruins

足 is **foot** 51, here meaning **footprint**. 亦 is again 212 q.v., here acting phonetically to express **accumulate** and probably also lending its own connotations of duplication. Thus **accumulation of footprints**, namely a trail, being the **traces/ remains** of someone's passing. Note that there is an NGU character 迹, i.e. using movement 辶 129 instead of foot 足, which is identical in pronunciation and meaning to 1485. Suggest taking 亦 as 'partly' **red** 赤 46.

Mnemonic: **THE ONLY REMAINS ARE A PARTLY RED FOOT**

1486 籍 SEKI
REGISTER
20 strokes

書籍 SHOSEKI publications
戸籍 KOSEKI family register
国籍 KOKUSEKI nationality

⺮ is **bamboo** 170. 耤 is a CO character meaning **rely on/ avail**. Its exact etymology is unclear, but it appears to comprise **past** 昔 1481 and serrated piece of wood/ tally/ **pledge** 耒 (tally 丰 659 and wood 木 69), and may mean literally a **pledge given in the past upon which one can rely**. (耒 may however be the variant of plow seen in 673, in which case its etymology is even less clear.) In the case of 1486 耤 acts phonetically to express **write**, and if taken to be pledge would almost certainly also lend connotations of a piece of wood on which something is written. Thus **bamboo for writing on**, a reference to **bamboo tablets used for keeping records**, with **register** being an extended meaning. Suggest taking 耒 as a **'heavily branched' tree** 木 69.

Mnemonic: **REGISTER OF BAMBOO AND BRANCHED TREES FROM PAST**

1487 拙 SETSU, tsutanai, mazui
CLUMSY, POOR
8 strokes

拙者 SESSHA I, me
拙劣 SETSURETSU na clumsy
拙速 SESSOKU
rough-and-ready

扌 is **hand** 32. 出 is **put out** 34, here acting phonetically to express **clumsy** but of unclear semantic role. Thus **clumsy hand**, later **clumsy/ poor** in a broad sense.

Mnemonic: **PUT OUT A CLUMSY HAND**

1488 窃 SETSU, nusumu, hisoka
STEAL, STEALTHY
9 strokes

窃盗 SETTŌ theft
票窃 HYŌSETSU plagiarism
窃取 SESSHU theft

Formerly 竊 and in ancient times . 宀/穴 is **hole** 849, with 口 being an additional **hole/ opening** 20 to emphasise **depth** and by extension **secrecy**. 米/釆 is **rice** 201/196. Thus 窩 indicates **rice (stored away) in a deep hole/ hidden place**. 禼/离 is a variant of **scorpion** 虿/萬 392, here acting phonetically to express **take** and almost certainly also lending connotations of **grasp/ clutch**. 1488 originally referred to **taking someone's stored rice**, then came to mean **steal** in general. **Stealthy** is an associated meaning (as in English). The modern form uses **cut** 切 156 as a simpler phonetic to express **take**, retaining **hole** 穴 .

Mnemonic: **STEALTHILY CUT HOLE TO STEAL CONTENTS**

1489 **SETSU**   摂取 SESSHU   intake

TAKE, ACT AS PROXY   摂政 SESSHŌ   regency, regent

13 strokes   摂生 SESSEI   health care

Formerly 攝. 扌 is **hand** 32. 聶 is a trebling of **ear** 耳 29, and forms an NGU character meaning whisper (i.e. something whispered to a succession of ears). Here 聶 acts phonetically to express **pull** but is of unclear semantic role. 1489 orginally referred to **pulling something out by hand**, later coming to mean **take out** and eventually just **take**. **Act as proxy** is an associated figurative meaning, from the idea of taking on a role/ duties. Though the use of the same elements of hand and ear as in **take** 取 301 is coincidental, this may be helpful in remembering 1489. Suggest taking 丶丶 as **four marks**.

Mnemonic: **TAKE EAR IN HAND TO EARN FOUR MARKS**

1490 **SEN**   仙人 SENNIN   hermit, wizard

HERMIT, WIZARD   酒仙 SHUSEN   hard drinker

5 strokes   水仙 SUISEN   narcissus

A **person** 亻 39 who lives in the **mountains** 山 24, i.e. a **recluse/ hermit**, with **wizard** being an associated meaning.

Mnemonic: **HERMIT IS PERSON LIVING IN MOUNTAINS**

1491 占 **SEN, urana*u*, shi*meru***   独占 DOKUSEN   monopoly

DIVINE, OCCUPY   占い者 URANAISHA   diviner

5 strokes   占めた SHIMETA   Good!

卜 is a variant of **divination (cracks)** 卜 91 q.v., while 口 is mouth/ **say** 20. Thus **that which is said by a diviner**, namely a prediction, symbolising **divining**. **Occupy** is a borrowed meaning.

Mnemonic: **TO DIVINE IS TO SAY WHAT CRACKS MEAN**

1492 **SEN, ōgi, ao*gu***   扇子 SENSU   (folding) fan

FAN   扇風機 SENPŪKI   electric fan

10 strokes   扇形 ŌGIGATA/ SENKEI

                                         fan shape

Door 戸 108 and **wings** 羽 812. Thus the **wings of a door**, i.e. very similar etymologically to door/ gate 門 211 or (wings of a) door 扉 1730, but in this case used by association to refer to **flapping action** and **fan**.

Mnemonic: **WINGS OF DOOR ACT AS FAN**

| 1493 | | SEN
STOPPER, PLUG, TAP
10 strokes | 栓抜き SENNUKI corkscrew
給水栓 KYŪSUISEN water tap
消火栓 SHŌKASEN fire hydrant |

木 is **wood** 69. 全 is **complete** 330, here also acting phonetically to express **insert**. Thus **wooden item inserted (into a hole), completely (filling it)**, i.e. a **bung/ stopper**. Now used of a range of stopping devices.

Mnemonic: **WOODEN STOPPER DOES JOB COMPLETELY**

| 1494 | | SEN
ROTATE, TURN
11 strokes | 旋回 SENKAI rotation
旋盤 SENBAN lathe
周旋 SHŪSEN mediation |

疋 is the variant of **proper** 正 41 seen in 1477, here meaning **set foot (on a road)/ travel** from its literal meaning of lower leg (see also 1472). 㫃 is fluttering flag 333, here (unusually) acting phonetically to express **return** and possibly also lending a loose idea of **following**, from its associations with rallying under a banner. 1494 originally referred to **returning along a road** (still a meaning in Chinese), with **return** later coming to mean **turn** in a broad sense, including **rotate**. Suggest taking 㫃 as **person** 亻 39 and **side** 方 204.

Mnemonic: **PERSON TURNS PROPERLY ON SIDE**

| 1495 | | SEN, fum*u*
STEP, ACT
13 strokes | 実践 JISSEN practice
実践的 JISSENTEKI practical
実践主義 JISSENSHUGI activism |

Formerly 踐 . 足 is **foot/ leg** 51. 㦮 is a doubling of **halberd** 戈 493, here acting phonetically to express **tread** and possibly also lending an idea of **decisiveness** from its connotations of cutting (see also 750). Thus to **tread/ step (with the foot) (decisively?)**, later also to **take action** in a broader sense. Suggest taking 㦮 as **halberd** 戈 and **two** 二 61.

Mnemonic: **FOOT STEPS ON TWO HALBERDS, LEADING TO ACTION**

1496 銑 **SEN, zuku** / **PIG IRON** / 14 strokes

銑鉄 SENTETSU pig iron
銑鋼 SENKŌ pig iron
溶銑 YŌSEN molten iron

金 is **metal** 14. 先 is precede/ **tip** 49, here acting phonetically to express **dull gleam** and almost certainly also lending connotations of **prior** (i.e. prior to refining). Thus **metal with dull gleam (prior to refining?)**, a reference to **pig iron**.

Mnemonic: **METAL TIP OF PIG IRON**

1497 潜 **SEN, hiso*mu*, mogu*ru*** / **DIVE, LURK, HIDE** / 15 strokes

潜在 SENZAI latency
潜水 SENSUI diving
潜り込む MOGURIKOMU 'hole up'

Formerly 濳. 氵 is **water** 40. 朁 is if/ supposing 688, here acting phonetically to express **sink** and probably also lending connotations of uncertainty. Thus to **sink in water** (and thus become of uncertain whereabouts?). The meaning has now broadened to include the idea of **lurking/hiding**. Suggest taking 朁 as **sun(light)** 日 62 and two **men** 夫 573.

Mnemonic: **TWO MEN DIVE INTO SUNLIT WATERS**

1498 遷 **SEN, utsu*ru*** / **SHIFT, MOVE, CHANGE** / 15 strokes

遷延 SENEN procrastination
変遷 HENSEN changes
遷化 SENGE death of dignitary

Once written 䙴. 䙴 (also 䙴) is a CO character meaning **soar on high/ go to heaven/ die**. 囟/西 is the somewhat obscure element seen in 票 570 q.v., and as in 570 seems to lend a meaning of upper part and by extension **raised/ high**. 𦥑/六 is hands offering up, an element often used to indicate **raising** and by extension **height**. 卪/己 is **bending person** (see 45), with a variant form 䙴 using curling person 㔾 768. It is not clear whether 己/㔾 depicts a **person offering** (from a position of humility) or, more likely, a **slumped person** (symbolising a **dead person**). Thus 䙴/䙴 means to **raise/ rise to a height**, a reference to **dying and moving to heaven** (of dignitaries). 1498 emphasises the idea of **moving** by adding **movement** 辵/辶 129. Moving to heaven later came to mean **move to a high place/ climb** and eventually **move/ shift/ change** in a broader sense, though 1498 occasionally still reveals connotations of dying. Suggest taking 西 as **west** 152, 六 as a variant of **big** 大 53, and 己 as **self** 855.

Mnemonic: **MOVE ONESELF IN BIG SHIFT TO WEST**

1499

SEN, susu*meru*, komo
RECOMMEND, MAT
16 strokes

推 薦 SUISEN recommendation
薦 骨 SENKOTSU sacrum
自 薦 JISEN

self-recommendation

⼨ is **grass** 9. 鷹 is **fabulous beast between horse and deer** 1204, here acting as a rather elegant reference simply to **grazing beasts** and also lending its sound to express both **fresh** and **feast/ eat**. 1499 originally meant **fresh grass such as eaten (first) by grazing beasts**, and in Chinese still retains choice grazing grass as a minor meaning. Good/ selected grass led on the one hand to **grass mat** (now a minor meaning) and on the other to the idea of **selecting the best** in a broad sense, leading in turn to **recommend**. Suggest taking 庀 as a modified combination of **building** 广 114 and **west** 西 152, with .⺝ as a 'short' variant of **horse** 馬 191.

Mnemonic: **SHORT HORSE RECOMMENDS GRASS MATS IN WESTERN BUILDING**

1500

SEN
FINE, SLENDER
17 strokes

繊 維 SENI fiber
繊 細 SENSAI fine, delicate
繊 毛 SENMŌ cilia, fine hair

Formerly 纖 . 糸 is **thread** 27. 韱 is a CO character meaning wild onion/ leek. 韭 is to all intents and purposes a variant of 韮 (also found simply as 非), an NGU character similarly meaning **leek** (韭 deriving from a pictograph of a leafy leek and ⼨ being **grass/ plant** 9). 戈 is **halberd/ lance** 493, here almost certainly lending connotations of **thrusting** and presumably also acting in some unclear phonetic role. Thus **leek that thrusts up** (from the ground). In the case of 1500 韱 acts phonetically to express **fine/ slender** and almost certainly lends similar connotations from the shape of the leek. Thus **fine, slender thread**, now **fine/ slender** in a general sense. Suggest taking the modern form as a combination of **red** 赤 (variant 赤 46), **one** 一 1, and **halberd** 戈 493.

Mnemonic: **CUT ONE SLENDER RED THREAD WITH HALBERD**

1501

SEN, aza*yaka*
FRESH, VIVID, CLEAR
17 strokes

鮮 魚 SENGYO fresh fish
鮮 明 SENMEI na clear, vivid
朝 鮮 CHŌSEN Korea

魚 is **fish** 98. 羊 is **sheep** 986, here lending its connotations of **fine**. Thus **fine fish**, a reference to **fresh fish** and hence **fresh** in general. **Clear/ vivid** is a borrowing.

Mnemonic: **SHEEP LIKES FISH TO BE FRESH**

1502 **ZEN** 　　座禅 ZAZEN　　meditation
ZEN, MEDITATION 禅宗 ZENSHŪ　　zen sect
13 strokes 　　禅寺 ZENDERA　　zen temple

Formerly 禪. 示/ネ is **altar/ of the gods** 695. 單/単 is **simple** 542 q.v., here acting phonetically to express **clear land** and possibly also lending a meaning of **simple**. 1502 originally referred to **clearing land in order to build a (simple?) altar**, and still retains this as a minor meaning in Chinese. The present meanings are felt by some scholars to be borrowed, but may in fact result from a reinterpretation of the character as an ideograph meaning **simple religion**, i.e. **zen** based on **meditation**.

Mnemonic: **ZEN ENTAILS SIMPLE MEDITATION AT ALTAR**

1503 **ZEN** 　　漸次 ZENJI　　gradually
GRADUAL ADVANCE 漸進的 ZENSHINTEKI　gradual
14 strokes 　　東漸 TŌZEN eastwards advance

氵 is **water** 40, here meaning **river**. 斬 is behead 1311 q.v., which acts phonetically to express **advance** and presumably originally lent connotations of **rapidity** and/or **force**. 1503 was originally used as a proper noun to refer to a river in ancient China, probably one associated with flowing swiftly and powerfully. In time the assumed connotations of **rapid advance** became **gradual advance**, though the reasons for such a change are not clear. Suggest taking 斬 literally as **vehicle** 車 31 and **ax/ chop/ cleave** 斤 1176.

Mnemonic: **VEHICLE GRADUALLY ADVANCES, CLEAVING THROUGH WATER**

1504 **ZEN, tsukuro**u 　　修繕 SHŪZEN　　repair(s)
REPAIR, MEND 修繕工 SHŪZENKŌ　repairman
18 strokes 　　繕い飾る TSUKUROIKAZARU
cover up, conceal error

糸 is **thread** 27, here meaning **clothes**. 善 is **good** 735, here also acting phonetically to express **repair**. Thus to **repair clothes and make them good (again)**, now **mend/ repair** in general.

Mnemonic: **MEND WITH GOOD THREAD**

482

1505

阻

SO, haba*mu*
OBSTRUCT, HINDER
8 strokes

阻止 SOSHI   hindrance
阻外 SOGAI   obstruction
険阻 KENSO na   steep

阝 is **hill** 229. 且 is **furthermore** 1091 q.v., here with its literal meaning of **pile (up)**. Thus **piled up hills**, indicating a **hindrance/ obstruction** to travelers.

Mnemonic: **FURTHERMORE, HILL CAN BE A HINDRANCE**

1506

租

SO
LEVY, TITHE
10 strokes

租税 SOZEI   taxes, rates
租借 SOSHAKU   lease
租借権 SOSHAKKEN   leasehold

禾 is **rice plant** 81, here indicating **harvested rice**. 且 is **furthermore** 1091 q.v., here acting phonetically to express **pay** and almost certainly also lending its connotations of accumulate and hence burden. 1506 originally referred to **rice paid as a tithe**, and now means **levy/ tithe** in general.

Mnemonic: **FURTHERMORE, THERE IS A LEVY ON RICE**

1507

措

SO
PLACE, DISPOSE
11 strokes

措置 SOCHI   step, action
措辞 SOJI   phraseology
挙措 KYOSO   behavior

扌 is **hand** 32. 昔 is **past** 1481, here acting phonetically to express **dispose** but of unclear semantic role. Thus to **dispose of something with the hand**, meaning both physically **place** and figuratively **handle/ manage** (cf. English dispose).

Mnemonic: **HAND FROM PAST PLACED AT ONE'S DISPOSAL**

1508

粗

SO, ara*i*
COARSE, ROUGH
11 strokes

粗末 SOMATSU   coarseness
粗糖 SOTŌ   raw sugar
粗筋 ARASUJI   rough outline

米 is **rice** 201. 且 is **furthermore** 1091 q.v. here acting phonetically to express **neglect** and almost certainly also lending its connotations of accumulate. 1508 originally referred to (spilled) **rice left neglected** (in a corner of a storehouse), and later came to mean **poor quality/ coarse/ rough** in a broad sense.

Mnemonic: **FURTHERMORE, RICE IS COARSE**

1509

疎

SO, utoi/*mu*
DISTANT, SHUN,
COARSE
12 strokes

疎隔 SOKAKU   alienation
疎開者 SOKAISHA   evacuee
疎疎しい UTOUTOSHII unfriendly

Correctly written 疏, as seen from an earlier form 疎, though 疏 is now technically a separate NGU character with identical readings and meanings. 足/正 is **foot** 51/ 41/ 1477, here (unusually) acting phonetically to express **emerge** and possibly also lending its connotations of movement. 㐬/流 is **child being born** 409. 1509 originally referred to a **child emerging from its mother**, indicating the moment of **parturition**. This later came to mean **(become) separate** in a broader sense, and for unclear reasons also came to acquire negative connotations such as **shunning**. **Coarse** is a borrowed meaning. The modern form uses **bundle** 束 1535.

Mnemonic: **SHUN COARSE BUNDLE AT ONE'S FEET**

1510

訴

SO, utta*eru*
SUE, APPEAL
12 strokes

訴訟事件 SOSHŌJIKEN   lawsuit
告訴 KOKUSO   legal action
哀訴 AISO   appeal

言 is **word/ speak** 274. 斥 is **reject** 1480, here acting phonetically to express **appeal** (to a higher authority) and possibly also lending an idea of rejection. Thus to **appeal verbally** (following a rejection? / only to be rejected?), leading by association to **take legal action** in a general sense.

Mnemonic: **WORDS OF REJECTION LEAD ONE TO APPEAL AND SUE**

1511

塑

SO
MODEL, FIGURINE
13 strokes

塑像 SOZŌ   figure, figurine
彫塑 CHŌSO   plastic arts
可塑性 KASOSEI   plasticity

土 is **earth** 60, here meaning **clay**. 朔 is an NGU character meaning **new moon/ north**, comprising **moon** 月 16 and **inversion/ reversal** 屰 646 q.v.(here indicating change of form) to give **change of moon**. Here 朔 acts phonetically to express **model/ copy** and probably also lends connotations of change of form/ shape. Thus **clay model**, now **model** in a wider sense. Suggest remembering 屰 as a sign of **inversion**.

Mnemonic: **EARTHEN MODEL OF INVERTED MOON**

1512 SO, ishizue　　　　礎石 SOSEKI foundation stone
FOUNDATION STONE　　基礎 KISO　　　　　　basis
18 strokes　　　　　基礎的 KISOTEKI　elementary

石 is **stone** 45. 楚 is an NGU character now meaning **cane/ rod**. It comprises **foot** 疋 51/ 41/ 1477 and a doubling of **tree** 木 69, and originally referred to the **foot of a tree** (i.e. the lower part without branches, hence **cane/ rod**). Here it acts phonetically to express **place/ lay**, and also lends a meaning of **foot of a wooden pillar**. Thus **stone laid at the foot of a wooden pillar**, now **foundation stone** in general.

Mnemonic: **FOUNDATION STONE LAID AT FOOT OF TWO TREES**

1513 SŌ, futa-　　　　双方 SŌHŌ　　　　both sides
PAIR, BOTH　　　　無双 MUSŌno　　matchless
4 strokes　　　　　双子 FUTAGO　　　　twins

Formerly 雙, showing **two birds** 隹 216 in a **hand** 又 (as opposed to one bird in a hand 隻 1483). This came to represent **pair/ both** in a broad sense. The modern form uses **two hands** 又.

Mnemonic: **PAIR OF HANDS MEANS BOTH HANDS**

1514 SŌ　　　　　　　　壮大 SŌDAI　　　　grandeur
MANLY, STRONG,　　強壮 KYŌSŌ　　robustness
GRAND, FERTILE　　壮者 SŌSHA　man in prime
6 strokes

Formerly 壯. 爿/爿 is **bed** 1389, while 士 is **samurai/ male/ erect male organ** 494. Some scholars take 爿 to act phonetically to express **big**, and take 士 in its sense of **male**, thus giving **big male** and hence **manly/ strong** etc. This is not convincing, especially in view of the existence of the CO character woman in bed 牀 (see 1406). While 爿 may express **big**, it almost certainly also lends its meaning of **bed**, and 士 almost certainly acts in its literal meaning of **erect male organ**. Thus **(big?) erect male organ in bed**, a reference to copulation and by extension **virility/ fertility/ manliness** etc. That is, it is a 'male equivalent' to woman in bed 牀.

Mnemonic: **MANLY SAMURAI IN BED**

485

1515 荘

SŌ, SHŌ
VILLA, MANOR,
SOLEMN, MAJESTIC
9 strokes

荘厳 SŌGON   majesty
荘園 SHŌEN   manor
別荘 BESSŌ   country villa

Formerly 莊. 艹 is **grass** 9. 壯/壮 is **manly/ fertile** 1514, here acting phonetically to express **keep in order** and also lending its connotations of **fertile**. Thus **place where grass is fertile but kept in order**, a reference to a **country estate/ manor**. It is not clear how 1515 also acquired the meanings of **majestic** and **solemn**, but it is possible that majestic was applied to a grand estate, with solemn then being a later associated meaning with majestic. Note that 1515 is occasionally interchanged with **manly/ fertile** 壮 1514, and in Chinese is also interchanged with **make up/ adorn** 粧 1406. Suggest taking 壮 literally as **samurai** 士 494 and **bed** 丬 1389.

Mnemonic: **SAMURAI BEDS DOWN IN MAJESTIC GRASSY MANOR**

1516 捜

SŌ, sagas*u*
SEARCH
10 strokes

捜査 SŌSA   investigation
捜索 SŌSAKU   search
捜し出す SAGASHIDASU seek out

Formerly 搜. 叟 is an NGU character now borrowed to express **old man**, but it originally meant **search**. It derives from 𝇌, showing a **hand** 又 holding up a **torch/ fire** 火 8 inside a **building** ∩, and meant literally to **search for something by torchlight in a building**. **Hand** 扌 32 was added to emphasise holding the torch. Suggest taking 申 as **field** 田 59 and **stick** | .

Mnemonic: **SEARCHING HANDS PROBE FIELD WITH STICK**

1517 挿

SŌ, sas*u*
INSERT
10 strokes

挿入 SŌNYŪ   insertion
挿話 SŌWA   episode
挿し絵 SASHIE   illustration

Formerly 插. 臿 is a CO character meaning **grind**, comprising **mortar** 臼 648 and **pestle** 千 (variant 午 110). **Hand** 扌 32 was added to emphasise the idea of **thrusting** the pestle into the mortar, leading to **insert** in a general sense. Suggest taking 臿 as a combination of **thousand** 千 47 and **sun/ day** 日 62.

Mnemonic: **HAND INSERTS A THOUSAND ITEMS PER DAY**

1518

SŌ, kuwa
MULBERRY
10 strokes

桑園 SŌEN   mulberry farm
桑色 KUWAIRO   light yellow
桑畑 KUWABATA

               mulberry field

A stylised derivative of 桒 , a pictograph of a **mulberry bush**. Suggest taking 木 as **tree** 69 and 叒 as **three hands** 又 .

Mnemonic: **THREE HANDS TEND MULBERRY TREE**

1519

SŌ, ha*ku*
SWEEP
11 strokes

掃除機 SŌJIKI   vacuum cleaner
一掃 ISSŌ   sweeping away
掃き出す HAKIDASU   sweep out

Hand holding broom 帚 96, with **hand** 扌 32 added to emphasise the action of **sweeping**.

Mnemonic: **HOLD BROOM IN TWO HANDS TO SWEEP**

1520

SŌ, ZŌ
OFFICIAL, COMPANION
11 strokes

法曹 HŌSŌ   lawyer
軍曹 GUNSŌ   sergeant
曹司 ZŌSHI   cadet

Once written 曹. 日 is **say** 688. 棘 is a doubling of **east/ sack** 184 q.v., here acting phonetically to express **equal/ match** and also graphically lending an idea of **two**. 1520 originally referred to **two well matched people/ parties on opposed sides in a debate**, and thus became used of **lawyers/ legal officials** and later **official** in a broader sense. **Companion** is felt to be an associated meaning, from the idea of one's legal representative/ ally, but it probably also reflects the influence of the two sacks <u>side by side</u> 棘. Suggest taking 曹 as **two suns** 日 62 and a **'long'** version 廿 of **grass** 艹 9.

Mnemonic: **OFFICIAL SAYS DOUBLE SUN MAKES GRASS GROW LONG**

1521

SŌ, su
NEST
11 strokes

帰巣 KISŌ   homing
巣箱 SUBAKO   nesting box
巣立つ SUDATSU   leave nest

Formerly 巢. 木 is **tree** 69. 甾 derives from 甶, namely the old form of **basket** 由 399. Some scholars feel that 甾 also acts phonetically to express **gather**. Thus **basket in a tree (where [birds] gather?)**, namely a **nest**. Suggest taking 果 as **fruit (tree)** 627 and ⺍ as **three sticks**.

Mnemonic: **THREE STICKS ATOP FRUIT TREE FORM NEST**

1522

SŌ, mo
MOURN, LOSS, DEATH
12 strokes

喪失 SŌSHITSU   loss
喪服 MOFUKU mourning dress
喪中 MOCHŪ   in mourning

Somewhat obscure. Old forms such as 器 clearly show **die** 匕 / 亡 973 and **vessel** 器/器 452 q.v. The latter is itself somewhat obscure, but is believed to show a **dog wheeling around open mouthed (i.e. barking) to face all quarters**. Thus 1522 appears to be an ideograph indicating a **dog acting frantically upon the death of its master**, later coming to mean **mourn** on the one hand and **loss/ death** on the other. Suggest taking 喪 as **ten** 十 33 and **two mouths** 口 20 (i.e. **twelve mouths**), and 𧘇 as a **'missing' variant of clothes** 衣 420.

Mnemonic: **TWELVE MOUTHS MOURN MISSING CLOTHES**

1523

葬

SŌ, hōmu*ru*
BURY
12 strokes

葬式 SŌSHIKI   funeral
葬儀屋 SŌGIYA   undertaker
葬歌 SŌKA   dirge

死 is **death** 286 q.v., here meaning **dead person**. 艹 is **grass** 9, while 廾 (formerly 𡴞) is also **grass**. Thus **surround/ cover a dead person with grass**, i.e. **bury** (originally a reference to covering the corpse with grass rather than interment in the ground, but now bury in a broad sense).

Mnemonic: **DEATH FOLLOWED BY BURIAL SURROUNDED BY GRASS**

1524

SŌ, SHŌ, yoso*u*
WEAR, CLOTHING, GEAR
12 strokes

装置 SŌCHI   device
衣装 ISHŌ   clothing
変装 HENSŌ   disguise

Formerly 裝 . 衣 is **clothing** 420. 壯/壮 is **manly/ grand** 1514, here acting phonetically to express **wrap** and almost certainly also lending its meaning of **grand**. Thus **wrap (oneself) in (grand?) clothing**, i.e. **wear**. (Wear) clothing came by extension to mean **gear/ equipment** in a broad sense, including even mechanical devices. Suggest taking 壯 literally as **samurai** 士 494 and **bed** 爿 1389.

Mnemonic: **SAMURAI WEARS CLOTHES IN BED**

488

1525 SŌ

PRIEST

13 strokes

僧院 SŌIN   monastery, temple
高僧 KŌSŌ   high priest
僧職 SŌSHOKU   priesthood

Formerly 僧. 亻 is **person** 39. 曾/曽 is **formerly**/ build up 741, here acting phonetically to express the first syllable of sangha, a Sanskrit word for **priest**. Since 1525 is of relatively recent origin 曽 may possibly also lend its later meaning of **formerly**. Thus **person who is a priest** (possibly priest-person who was formerly a lay person). Suggest taking 曾 as **away** ∨ 66, **field** 田 59, and **day** 日 62.

Mnemonic: **PERSON TAKEN AWAY DAILY FROM FIELD IS PRIEST**

1526 SŌ, a*u*

ENCOUNTER, MEET

14 strokes

遭遇 SŌGŪ   encounter
遭難 SŌNAN   accident
遭難信号 SŌNANSHINGŌ   SOS

辶 is **movement** 129. 曹 is official/ **companion** 1520, here acting phonetically to express **meet**/ **encounter** and possibly also lending connotations of **falling in with**. Thus to **encounter while moving**, later **encounter**/ **meet** in a broader sense. Suggest remembering companion 曹 by association with **grass** 廾 (variant ⁺⁺ 9) and (double) **sun** 日 62.

Mnemonic: **ENCOUNTER COMPANION MOVING ON SUNNY GRASS**

1527 SŌ

TANK, TUB, VAT

15 strokes

水槽 SUISŌ   water tank
浴槽 YOKUSŌ   bathtub
歯槽 SHISŌ   tooth socket

木 is **wood** 69, here meaning **wooden item**. 曹 is official/ **companion** 1520 q.v., here acting phonetically to express **damaged grain** and possibly also lending loose connotations of **dumping** and/or **containing** from the double sack element 棘 in its early form 轡. 1527 originally referred to a **wooden tub used for holding damaged grain**, but later came to mean **tub/ vat/ receptacle** in a broader sense. Suggest remembering companion 曹 by association with **grass** 廾 (variant ⁺⁺ 9) and two **days** 日 62.

Mnemonic: **COMPANION SPENDS TWO DAYS IN WOODEN TUB ON GRASS**

| 1528 | SŌ
 DRY, PARCH
 17 strokes | 乾燥 KANSŌ — dryness
 焦燥 SHŌSŌ — impatience
 高燥地 KŌSŌKI <br> high and dry ground |

火 is **fire** 8. 喿 is birds chirping in tree 922 q.v., here acting phonetically to express **dry** and possibly also lending loose connotations of intensity. Thus to **dry by fire**, later giving **dry/ parch** in a broad sense. Suggest taking 木 as **wood** 69 and 品 as **three boxes**.

Mnemonic: **DRY THREE WOODEN BOXES BY FIRE**

| 1529 | SŌ, shimo
 FROST
 17 strokes | 霜害 SŌGAI — frost damage
 霜夜 SHIMOYO — frosty night
 霜降り肉 SHIMOFURINIKU <br> marbled beef |

雨 is **rain** 3, here meaning loosely **moisture associated with weather**. 相 is **mutual** 530 q.v., here acting phonetically to express **freeze/ frozen** and possibly also lending a loose idea of appearance. Thus (the appearance of?) **frozen moisture**, i.e. **frost**.

Mnemonic: **MUTUAL RELATIONSHIP BETWEEN RAIN AND FROST?**

| 1530 | SŌ, sawagu/gashii
 NOISE, DISTURBANCE
 18 strokes | 騒音 SŌON — cacophony
 騒動 SŌDŌ — disturbance
 大騒ぎ ŌSAWAGI uproar, chaos |

Formerly 騷. 馬 is **horse** 191. 蚤 is an NGU character meaning **flea**, comprising **insect** 虫 56 and **hand** 叉 (from 𠬶, and variant 又), and presumably meaning insect found on hand or insect squashed with hand/ fingers. In the case of 1530 蚤 acts phonetically to express **confusion** and also lends its connotations of **troublesome insect**. Thus **confusion caused by insect troubling horse**, now **noise/ disturbance** in general.

Mnemonic: **HAND SLAPS INSECT ON HORSE: DISTURBANCE FOLLOWS**

1531

SŌ, mo
WATERWEED, SEAWEED
19 strokes

藻抜け MONUKE　cast off skin
海藻 KAISŌ　seaweed
詞藻 SHISŌ rhetorical flourish

艹 is grass/ plant 9. 氵 is water 40. 喿 is birds chirping in tree 922, here acting phonetically to express **gather** and also lending similar connotations of its own. Thus **waterplant that gathers (in clusters)**, originally a reference to a particular type of **waterweed** but now also **waterweed/ seaweed** in a broader sense. Suggest taking 木 as **wood** 69 and 品 as **three boxes**.

Mnemonic: **THREE WOODEN BOXES OF PLANTS ARE ALL WATERWEED**

1532

ZŌ, niku*mu/i/shimi*
HATE(FUL)
14 strokes

憎悪 ZŌO　malice, hatred
憎らしい NIKURASHII　hateful
憎み合う NIKUMIAU mutually hate

Formerly 憎. 忄 is heart/ **feelings** 147. 曾/曽 is formerly/ **build up** 741 q.v., here acting phonetically to express **hatred** and almost certainly also lending its connotations of **accumulation**. Thus **(accumulated?) feelings of hatred**. Suggest taking 曽 as **away** ソ 66, **field** 田 59, and **day** 日 62.

Mnemonic: **FEEL HATE ON DAY FIELD TAKEN AWAY**

1533

ZŌ, SŌ, oku*ru*
PRESENT, GIVE
18 strokes

贈与 ZŌYO　presentation
寄贈 KIZŌ/ KISŌ　donation
贈り物 OKURIMONO　present

Formerly 贈. 貝 is shell/ **money/ valuable item** 90. 曾/曽 is formerly/ **build up** 741 q.v., here acting phonetically to express **send/ give** and almost certainly also lending its connotations of accumulation and hence **large volume**. Thus **send/ give (large volume of?) vaulable items**, later just **present/ give**. Suggest taking 曽 as **away** ソ 66, **field** 田 59, and **day** 日 62.

Mnemonic: **ONE DAY GIVE AWAY FIELD AND MONEY**

1534	SOKU, sunawa*chi* **IMMEDIATE, NAMELY,** **ACCESSION** 7 strokes	即位 SOKUI enthronement 即刻 SOKKOKU immediately 即席 SOKUSEKI impromptu

Formerly 卽 and in ancient times 皀, showing **food** 豆 / 皀 / 艮 /食 146 and **kneeling/ bending person** 入 / 卩 39/ 425. 1534 originally referred to **taking one's place at the table**, later coming to mean take one's (rightful) place and thus **accede**. **Immediate** is felt to be an associated meaning from the idea of being prompt, while **namely** is felt to be an associated meaning from the idea of things being proper/ as they should be.

Mnemonic: **UPON ACCESSION PERSON IMMEDIATELY KNEELS BY FOOD**

1535	SOKU, taba[*neru*], tsuka[*neru*] **BUNDLE, MANAGE** 7 strokes	結束 KESSOKU bond, union 花束 HANATABA bouquet 束の間 TSUKANOMA moment

An old form 朿 has led to the popular interpretation that 1535 originally depicted **trees** 米 /木 69 being **bound together** ○. However, in view of the fact that only one tree is shown this is rather unconvincing. In fact, other old forms such as 栐 suggest strongly that it is merely a variant of east/ **sack** 東 /東 184 q.v. Putting things into a bundle led by figurative association to the idea of **handling/ managing**. Suggest taking 木 as **tree** and 口 as **box**.

Mnemonic: **MANAGE TO PUT BOX-LIKE BUNDLE IN TREE**

1536	SOKU, unaga*su* **URGE, PRESS** 9 strokes	促進 SOKUSHIN promotion 催促 SAISOKU demand 促成 SOKUSEI growth, promotion

Of disputed etymology, though its elements are clearly **person** 亻 39 and **foot/ leg** 足 51. Some scholars feel that 足 acts phonetically to express **shorten/ compress** and also lends its meaning of **leg**, to give **person with short(ened) legs**. This later came to mean **be short/ make short** in general, with **press down** being an associated meaning that later led to **press** in a general sense. Opinion is then divided as to whether **urge** is a borrowed meaning or an associated figurative meaning with press. An alternative theory is that 足 is used in its associated sense of **set foot/ set off** (see 1494), giving **person setting off**, with **urge** and **press** being either associated or borrowed meanings.

Mnemonic: **PERSON URGED TO PRESS WITH FOOT**

492

1537 ZOKU
REBEL, PLUNDER,
INJURE
13 strokes

海賊 KAIZOKU   pirate
盗賊 TŌZOKU   thief
賊軍 ZOKUGUN   rebel army

Once written 賊, showing that 貝十 is a miscopying of rule 則 742 q.v., here acting phonetically to express **injure** and also lending its early connotations of **cutting**. 戈 is **halberd** 493, here meaning **cutting weapon**. Thus to **cut and injure with a weapon**, later also used to refer to a person associated with perpetrating such injuries, namely a **bandit** and by further association **rebel**. **Plunder** is another associated meaning. Suggest taking 貝 as shell/ **money** 90 and 十 as **ten** 33.

Mnemonic: **TEN REBELS WITH HALBERDS PLUNDER MONEY**

1538 DA
PEACE, SETTLED
7 strokes

妥当 DATŌ na   appropriate
妥協 DAKYŌ   compromise
妥結 DAKETSU   agreement

Of disputed etymology, though its elements are clearly **hand** (reaching down) 爫 303 and **woman** 女 35. Some scholars take 爫 to be a miscopying of **rice plant** 禾 81. That is, 1538 is taken to be a variant of entrust 委 423 q.v., whose literal meaning of **be soft and pliant** is felt to have led to the idea of **being peaceful and settled**. Other scholars take 爫 to act purely phonetically to express **soft and delicate**, giving **soft and delicate woman** and hence soft/ pliant and peaceful/ settled as above.

Mnemonic: **WOMAN'S HAND SYMBOLISES PEACE**

1539 DA
FALL(EN), DEGENERATE
12 strokes

堕落 DARAKU   depravity
堕胎 DATAI   abortion
堕落坊主 DARAKUBŌZU
               apostate priest

Formerly 隓. 隋 is **fall/ landslide** 1462. **Earth** 土 60 was added after the original meaning of 隋 (i.e. landslide) became vague. However, landslide has now disappeared and 1539 has come to mean **fall/ slip** in a broad sense, but particularly in moral terms. Suggest taking 隋 as **hill** 阝 229 and **exist** 有 401.

Mnemonic: **EARTH FALLS BUT HILL STILL EXISTS**

1540 **DA**
LAZY, INERT
12 strokes

惰力 DARYOKU　　inertia
怠惰 TAIDA　　　laziness
惰気 DAKI　　　indolence

忄 is heart/ **feelings** 147. 𡐔 is **fall** 1462, here acting phonetically to express **listless** and probably also lending connotations of slumping and heaviness. Thus **listless feelings**, a reference to **laziness**, with **inertia** being an associated meaning. See also listless feelings/ laziness/ neglect 怠 1543. Suggest taking 𡐔 as **left hand** 左 22 and **meat** 月 365.

Mnemonic: **FEEL LAZY AND EAT MEAT WITH LEFT HAND**

1541 **DA**
PACK-HORSE,
POOR QUALITY
14 strokes

駄物 DAMONO　cheap goods
駄馬 DABA　　　pack-horse
無駄 MUDA　　　waste

Formerly also written 馱, which is technically the correct form. 馬 is **horse** 191, while 大 is **big** 53. The modern form uses **fat/ big** 太 164. **Big horse** was a reference to a **pack-horse**. Since this was not considered an especially valuable beast, 1541 also came to symbolise **poor quality/ cheap**.

Mnemonic: **FAT PACK-HORSE OF POOR QUALITY**

1542 **TAI, ta**eru
ENDURE, BEAR
9 strokes

耐久 TAIKYŪ　　endurance
耐火 TAIKA　　　fireproof
耐え難い TAEGATAI　unbearable

而 is **beard** 887. 寸 is **measure/ hand** 909 q.v., here meaning **careful use of the hand**. 1542 is a somewhat vague ideograph referring to **shaving off a beard**. This was a minor official punishment (the next grade being to shave the hair), and thus symbolised something **not too bad** and **bearable**. Suggest taking 而 as a **rake**.

Mnemonic: **CAN ONE BEAR TO PUT HAND ON RAKE?**

1543 **TAI, okota**ru, **nama**keru
BE LAZY, NEGLECT
9 strokes

怠業 TAIGYŌ　　　go-slow
怠け者 NAMAKEMONO　idler
怠り勝ち OKOTARIGACHI
　　　　　　　　neglectful

心 is heart/ **feelings** 147. 台 is **stand** 166, here acting phonetically to express **listless** but of unclear semantic role. Thus **listless feelings**, giving **laziness** and by association **neglect** (as opposed to listless feelings/ laziness/ inertia in the case of 惰 1540 q.v.).

Mnemonic: **FEEL TOO LAZY TO MOUNT THE STAND**

494

| 1544 | 胎 | TAI WOMB 9 strokes | 胎児 TAIJI 受胎 JUTAI 胎盤 TAIBAN | fetus conception placenta |

月 is **flesh/ of the body** 365. 台 is stand/ **platform** 166, here acting phonetically to express **pregnancy** but of unclear semantic role. Thus **that part of the body associated with pregnancy**, i.e. the **womb**.

Mnemonic: **WOMB IS A SORT OF FLESHY PLATFORM**

| 1545 | | TAI CALM, SERENE, BIG, THAI 10 strokes | 泰然 TAIZEN 安泰 ANTAI 泰西 TAISEI | composure peace Occident |

Obscure. Once written 㣊, showing **big** 大/大 53, **hands** 𦥑, and **water** 氺/水 (old form/ variant 水 40). Some scholars believe that 大 acts phonetically to express **slip/ lose**, and that 1545 originally referred to **losing something while washing it** (i.e. have it slip from the hands). **Calm/ serene** and **big** are assumed to be borrowed meanings (though the presence of big 大 53 raises the possibility of some now unclear association), and the character has also been borrowed to refer to **Thailand**. In Chinese it can also mean extravagant/ liberal, which is similarly assumed to be a borrowing. Suggest taking 夫 as a combination of **two** 二 61 and **big man** 大 53.

Mnemonic: **TWO BIG THAI MEN SIT CALMLY BY WATER**

| 1546 | | TAI, fukuro BAG, POUCH 11 strokes | 郵袋 YŪTAI 有袋類 YŪTAIRUI 手袋 TEBUKURO | mailbag marsupial gloves |

衣 is **clothing** 420, here meaning **cloth**. 代 is **replace** 338, here acting phonetically to express **container** but of unclear semantic role. Thus **cloth container**, i.e. **bag/ pouch**.

Mnemonic: **REPLACE ONE'S CLOTHES WITH A BAG!?**

1547 TAI 逮捕 TAIHO — arrest
CHASE, SEIZE 逮捕者 TAIHOSHA — captor
11 strokes 逮夜 TAIYA — (eve of) anniversary of death

辶 is **movement** 129. 隶 is a CO character now meaning fox cub. It was once written 隸, showing a **hand** ⺕ **seizing/ holding a tail** 人 (hair ⺓/毛 210, but here representing tail 尾 1734), and thus 隶 originally meant **seize an animal by the tail**. The addition of movement 辶 gives 1547 a meaning of **chase** and **seize**.

Mnemonic: **MOVE IN CHASE AND SEIZE TAIL BY HAND**

1548 替 TAI, *kaeru/waru* 代替 DAITAI — substitution
EXCHANGE, SWAP 両替え RYŌGAE money changing
12 strokes 取り替え TORIKAE — swapping

Somewhat obscure. Originally written 暜, showing **two standing men** 竝 (see stand 立 73) and **say** 臼/日/曰 688. The modern form uses two **men** 夫 573. It is not clear how these elements are used. Some scholars feel that 曰 acts phonetically to express **lean/ fall**, to give **falling persons** and by extension **fall/ collapse** in a general sense, with **exchange** being a borrowed meaning. Other scholars feel that 1548 ideographically referred to **one person speaking for another**, i.e. **in place of another**, with **exchange** deriving from **in place of**. The latter theory seems the more helpful. Suggest taking 曰 as **day** 62.

Mnemonic: **ONE DAY, ONE MAN EXCHANGED FOR ANOTHER**

1549 滞 TAI, *todokōru* 滞在 TAIZAI — sojourn, stay
STOP, STAGNATE 停滞 TEITAI — stagnation
13 strokes 滞納 TAINŌ — non-payment

Formerly 滯. 氵 is **water** 40. 帶/帯 is **belt** 539, here acting phonetically to express **stop** and almost certainly also lending its own connotations of contain/ restrict. 1549 originally referred to **a flow of water stopping**, and now means **stop/ stagnate** in a general sense.

Mnemonic: **USE BELT TO STOP WATER**

496

1550 taki
CASCADE, WATERFALL
13 strokes

清滝 KIYOTAKI clear cascade
滝川 TAKIGAWA rapids
華厳滝 KEGONDAKI
Kegon Falls

Formerly also written 瀧. 氵 is **water/ river** 40. 龍 / 竜 is **dragon** 1899, here acting phonetically to express **fall** and probably also lending connotations of **fearsome** and/or **flying**. Thus **(fearsome?) falling water/ river (that flies through the air?)**, i.e. **waterfall/ cascade**.

Mnemonic: **WATER-DRAGON LIVES IN WATERFALL**

1551 **TAKU**, era*bu*, yo*ru*
CHOOSE, SELECT
7 strokes

採択 SAITAKU adoption
選択 SENTAKU choice
選択科目 SENTAKUKAMOKU
elective subject

Formerly 擇. 扌 is **hand** 32, here meaning by extension **take in the hand**. 睪 is **watch over (file of) prisoners** 233 q.v., here acting phonetically to express **arrange** and probably also lending supporting connotations of putting in sequence. 1551 originally referred to **taking things in the hand and putting them in order**, then later came by association to mean **pick out by hand** and then **select** in a broad sense. Suggest taking 尺 as **person** 人 39 with **back-pack** コ .

Mnemonic: **PERSON CARRIES HANDY BACK-PACK**

1552 **TAKU**, sawa
MARSH,MOISTEN,MUCH,
MANY,BENEFIT,GLISTEN
7 strokes

光沢 KŌTAKU luster
沢山 TAKUSAN much, many
沢地 SAWACHI marshland

Formerly 澤. 氵 is **water** 40. 睪 is **watch over (file of) prisoners** 233 q.v., here acting phonetically to express **confusion** and probably also lending an idea of stretching out in a line. 1552 originally referred to an **area where land and water became confused** (though the fact that it contains no element to indicate land is itself a source of confusion), i.e. **marshland** (where pools of water stretch out ahead? -- see 1333). Some scholars take **much/ many** to be a borrowed meaning, but in fact 1552 has long had connotations of much water/ many pools (especially in Japanese, where since classical times the word sawa has had a secondary meaning of many/ much). **Moisten** is an associated meaning, with **glisten** and **enrich/ benefit** being further associations (see also 1379). Suggest taking 尺 as **person** 人 39 with **back-pack** コ .

Mnemonic: **PERSON CARRIES PACK THROUGH WATER OF MARSH**

497

1553

TAKU
TABLE, EXCEL, HIGH
8 strokes

卓球 TAKKYŪ　　table tennis
卓越 TAKUETSU　　excellent
食卓 SHOKUTAKU

dining table

Obscure. The earliest form is 𣎳, but the meaning of this is unclear. Some scholars take 早 to be **early** 早 50 q.v., and indeed it has been copied as such for many centuries, but the upward tilt of the lower cross-stroke(s) indicates that this is incorrect. It is more likely to be **sun** ⊙ / 日 62 and possibly **plant** Y (variant 屮 9), and may suggest the **sun rising high** (i.e. above the plants). Certainly 1553 has long had a core meaning of **high**, with **prominent/ excellent** being an associated meaning. The meaning of ⼘ / ⼘ is unknown. At one stage it was written ⼘, suggesting a variant of slumped figure ⼖ 238, and this has led to a theory that it indicated a lame person (reinforced by the fact that the pronunciation of 早 was the same as that of a word for cripple). Lame person is said to have symbolised leaning and unevenness, with the latter eventually leading by association to height. This does not seem at all convincing, though it is a theory favored by authoritative Japanese scholars. In any event, **table** is categorically a borrowed meaning. Specifically, 1553 was borrowed as a simpler version of the NGU character 棹. This combines high 卓 with wood 木 69 (here meaning wooden item) to give high wooden item, a reference to a table. Confusingly, while 棹 still means table in Chinese, in Japanese it now means oar/ pole. Suggest taking 早 as **early** and ⼘ as a variant of **cracks** ⼘ 91.

Mnemonic: **EXCELLENT TABLE CRACKED AT EARLY STAGE**

1554

TAKU
RECLAIM, CLEAR, RUB
8 strokes

拓殖 TAKUSHOKU colonising
開拓 KAITAKU　　reclamation
魚拓 GYOTAKU　　fish print

扌 is **hand** 32. 石 is **stone** 45, here also acting phonetically to express **remove**. Thus to **remove stones by hand**, i.e. **clear/ reclaim land**. From an early stage its elements were also interpreted as **remove by hand from stone**, a reference to **taking a rubbing from a stone inscription**, leading to **rub/ make a print** in a broader sense.

Mnemonic: **HAND PICKS UP STONES TO CLEAR LAND**

1555

TAKU
ENTRUST, COMMIT
10 strokes

託宣 TAKUSEN　　　oracle
託送 TAKUSŌ　consignment
委託 ITAKU　　commission

言 is **words/ speak** 274. ⺄ is **plant taking root** 928, here acting phonetically to express **commit/ entrust** and possibly also lending connotations of firmness. Thus (firmly?) **entrust verbally**, later **entrust/ commit** in a broad sense. Suggest taking ⺄ as **seven** 七 30 and **top** ⼃.

Mnemonic: **COMMIT SEVEN TOP WORDS TO MEMORY**

1556		**TAKU**	洗濯 SENTAKU	washing
		WASH, RINSE	洗濯機 SENTAKUKI	washer
		17 strokes	洗濯物 SENTAKUMONO	laundry

氵 is **water** 40. 翟 is **bird's wings/ plumage** 216 (bird 隹 216 and wings 羽 812), here acting phonetically to express **beat** and probably also lending its own connotations of **beat/ flap.** Thus to **beat in water**, a reference to **washing** (clothes).

Mnemonic: **WASH BIRD'S WINGS IN WATER**

1557		**DAKU**	受諾 JUDAKU	acceptance
		CONSENT, AGREE	承諾 SHŌDAKU	consent
		15 strokes	快諾 KAIDAKU	ready consent

若 is **young** 886 q.v., here in its original meaning of **compliant words/ agree.** **Words/ speak** 言 274 was added after 若 lost its original meaning.

Mnemonic: **AGREE WITH YOUNGSTER'S WORDS**

1558		**DAKU, nigoru/su**	濁流 DAKURYŪ	turbid stream
		IMPURE,TURBID,VOICED	濁音 DAKUON	voiced sound
		16 strokes	濁り江 NIGORIE	muddy creek

氵 is **water** 40. 蜀 is **caterpillar** 744, here acting phonetically to express **impure** and probably also lending connotations of **unpleasant.** Thus **(unpleasant?) impure water.** Also used of a **voiced** sound (cf. English thick). In Chinese it has much stronger connotations of unpleasantness, and its meanings include foul and corrupt.

Mnemonic: **TURBID WATER, FULL OF CATERPILLARS**

1559		tada*shi*, **TAN**	但し書き TADASHIGAKI	proviso
		BUT, HOWEVER	但し付き TADASHIZUKI	condition
		7 strokes	但島 TAJIMA*	a place-name

Of convoluted etymology. 亻 is **person** 39. 旦 is **dawn** 929, here acting phonetically to express **naked** and probably also lending its own connotations of **expose.** Thus **naked man**, a reference to a person stripped of outward signs of rank and thus **merely a man.** **Merely** came to prevail as a meaning, leading eventually to merely in the sense of "the only thing is....", i.e. **but/ however** (cf. range of nuances of tada). Suggest taking 日 as **sun** 62 and 一 as **one** 1.

Mnemonic: **SUN SHINES ON ONE PERSON, BUT.... (HE'S NAKED!)**

499

1560

DATSU, nu*gu*
TAKE OFF, SHED, ESCAPE
11 strokes

脱衣 DATSUI   undressing
脱皮 DAPPI   emergence
脱出 DASSHUTSU   escape

Formerly 脫. 月 is **flesh/ of the body** 365. 兌/兑 is exchange 524 q.v., here acting phonetically to express **lose** and probably also lending its own connotations of **disperse**. Thus to **lose flesh**. This was originally a reference to losing weight, but was also later applied by association to a range of **things leaving the body**, such as a child during parturition and clothes. **Escape** is also an associated meaning, from the extended idea of losing something in one's possession (i.e. expressed intransitively). Suggest taking 兑 as **elder brother** 兄 267 and **away/ off** 丷 66.

Mnemonic: ELDER BROTHER TAKES CLOTHES OFF BODY AND ESCAPES

1561

DATSU, uba*u*
SNATCH, CAPTIVATE
14 strokes

奪取 DASSHU   seizure
奪回 DAKKAI   recovery
奪い去る UBAISARU   carry off

隹 is **bird** 216. 寸 is **hand/ measure** 909, here meaning **hand** (it is not clear why the simpler hand 又 was not used). 大 is **big** 53, here also acting phonetically to express **lose**. Thus to **lose a big (i.e. prized) bird from the hand**. This came to mean lose from the hand in general, and by association have something **snatched** from the hand. Now **snatch** in a broad sense, with **captivate** being an associated figurative meaning. Distinguish from 奮 966, and note the different etymology of 雀.

Mnemonic: BIG BIRD IS SNATCHED FROM HAND

1562

棚

tana
SHELF, TRELLIS
12 strokes

戸棚 TODANA   cupboard
本棚 HONDANA   bookshelf
ぶどう棚 BUDŌDANA

     grapevine trellis

Somewhat obscure. Formerly 棚 and earlier 棚. 米/木 is **wood/ tree** 69. 拜 is felt to show **strings of matching jewels** 丰 (see 102), the strings themselves also being attached to each other 乙, and to symbolise **matching**. (Note that 朋/朋 exists as an NGU character meaning match and by association companion.) In the case of 1562 拜/朋/朋 acts phonetically to express **join** and also lends its connotations of **matching**. Thus **matched and joined pieces of wood**, a reference to **trellis**. In Japanese it is also applied by association to **shelves**, whereas in Chinese it can mean a crude shed. The modern form uses two **moons** 月 16, almost certainly a miscopying but one that retains an idea of matching. Suggest taking 月 in its meaning of **month**.

Mnemonic: TAKE TWO MONTHS TO PUT UP WOODEN SHELVES

1563

丹

TAN, ni
RED, SINCERE
4 strokes

丹念 TANNEN — diligence
丹精 TANSEI — assiduity
丹塗り NINURI — painted red

Somewhat obscure. Originally 丹, with a meaning of **red earth/ clay**, and believed to be a variant of **contents of well** 井 1470/ 43 q.v. but with the contents extended to clay rather than water. **Sincere** is a borrowed meaning. Suggest remembering 丹 by association with **boat** 舟 1354, taking it as 'half' a boat.

Mnemonic: **ONLY HALF THE BOAT IS RED**

1564

TAN, kimo
LIVER, GALL, COURAGE
9 strokes

大胆 DAITAN — bravery
胆石 TANSEKI — gallstone
落胆 RAKUTAN — discouragement

Formerly 膽 . 月 is **flesh/ of the body** 365. 詹 is the obscure element seen in 擔/担 929 q.v., here acting phonetically to express **jar** but of unclear semantic role. Thus the **jar of the body**, a reference to the (jar shaped) **liver**. **Gall** is an associated meaning, while **courage** is a figurative association. As with 929, the modern form uses **dawn** 旦 (see 929) as a simple phonetic. Suggest taking this as **one** 一 1 **day** 日 62.

Mnemonic: **BODY NEEDS LIVER TO SURVIVE EVEN ONE DAY**

1565

TAN, awai
PALE, LIGHT, FAINT
11 strokes

淡水 TANSUI — freshwater
淡色 TANSHOKU — light color
淡雪 AWAYUKI — light snow

氵 is **water** 40. 炎 is **flame(s)** 1024 (literally a doubling of **flame/ fire** 火 8), here acting phonetically to express **plain** but of unclear semantic role. Thus **plain water**, i.e. water with nothing mixed in. While this may seem logically to suggest pure water, in fact it came rather to mean insipid and uninteresting (still meanings in Chinese), with **light/ faint/ pale** being associated meanings.

Mnemonic: **WATER ON FLAMES MAKES THEM FAINT AND PALE**

1566

TAN, nage*ku*/*kawashii*
LAMENT, ADMIRE
13 strokes

嘆息 TANSOKU   sigh
驚嘆 KYŌTAN   admiration
嘆き叫ぶ NAGEKISAKEBU   wail

Formerly 嘆. 口 is **mouth/ say** 20, here meaning **cry out**. 莫/糞 is the obscure element seen in 442 q.v., here acting phonetically to express **stifle** but of unclear semantic role. Thus **stifled cry**. This usually indicates a gasp of **despair** or **alarm**, but occasionally of **admiration**. Suggest taking 莫 as **man** 夫 573, **grass** ⺿ 9, and **hole** 口 20.

Mnemonic: **CRY OF LAMENT OVER MAN IN GRASSY HOLE**

1567

TAN, hashi, hata, ha
EXTREMITY, EDGE,
BIT, UPRIGHT
14 strokes

極端 KYOKUTAN   extreme
端正 TANSEI   upright
道端 MICHIBATA   roadside

立 is **stand** 73. 耑 is a CO character now borrowed to express **only**. Its etymology is unclear, but some scholars interpret an old form 耑 as a **bushy plant** growing vigorously, while others note the similarity of the lower half to beard 而/而 887, take 𠂉 to be flowing hair (see 173), and take 耑 to mean **divided beard**. The bushy plant theory seems the more likely. In any event, in the case of 1567 耑 acts phonetically to express **upright** and may possibly also lend similar connotations of upright/ vertical (either from a plant growing upright or a beard hanging vertically). Thus **stand upright**, later **upright** in a broad sense including the moral one. The other meanings are borrowed. Suggest taking 山 as **mountain** 24 and 而 as a **rake**.

Mnemonic: **RAKE STANDS UPRIGHT ON EDGE OF MOUNTAIN**

1568

TAN
BIRTH, DECEIVE
15 strokes

誕生日 TANJŌBI   birthday
荒誕 KŌTAN   lie, nonsense
降誕 KŌTAN   holy/royal birth

言 is **words** 274. 延 is **stretch/ extend** 814, here also acting phonetically to express **big**. Thus **big stretched words**, a reference to **bragging/ exaggeration** and hence **deception**. Its main modern meaning of **birth** is a borrowing, specifically being felt to derive from the term kōtan (see above). This originally meant to 'make a fuss'/ talk big about a holy/royal birth and thus established an association between 1568 and birth.

Mnemonic: **USE STRETCHED WORDS TO DECEIVE ABOUT BIRTH**

1569 TAN, kita*eru* 鍛工所 TANKŌJO smithy
FORGE, TRAIN 鍛練 TANREN forge, train
17 strokes 鍛金 TANKIN beating gold

金 is **metal** 14. 段 is **step** 931 q.v., here acting phonetically to express **beat** and possibly also lending its own similar connotations. Thus to **beat metal**, i.e. **forge/ temper**, with **train** being an associated figurative meaning.

Mnemonic: **FORGING METAL IS A STEP IN ONE'S TRAINING**

1570 DAN, hi*ku*, hazu*mu*, tama 弾薬 DANYAKU ammunition
BULLET, SPRING, PLAY 弾力 DANRYOKU elasticity
12 strokes 弾き手 HIKITE player

Formerly 彈 and in ancient times ᘚ. ß / 弓 is **bow** 836, here meaning by association **catapult**, while • shows a **small round object** used as a projectile. Later forms use **simple/ weapon** 單 / 単 542 q.v., here acting phonetically to express **small round object** and probably also lending its connotations of weapon. The action of **using a catapult** led to **spring** and by further association **pluck/ play** a stringed instrument, while **bullet** derives from projectile.

Mnemonic: **BULLET SPRINGS FORTH FROM SIMPLE BOW?!**

1571 DAN, TAN 花壇 KADAN flower bed
STAGE, PLATFORM 壇場 DANJŌ stage
16 strokes 土壇場 DOTANBA
execution scaffold

土 is **earth/ ground** 60. 亶 is a CO character now meaning indeed/ truly, but its etymology is unclear. Its original meaning appears to have been **raised/ built up/ high**, and it is possibly a variant of **high/ watchtower** 髙 / 高 119. Here it acts phonetically to express **high/ raised**, and possibly lends similar connotations of its own. Thus **raised earth/ ground**, leading to **stage** and **platform**. Suggest taking 亠 as **top**, 回 as **rotate/ revolve** 86, 日 as **day** 62, and 一 as **one** 1.

Mnemonic: **EARTHY SHOW ONE DAY ATOP REVOLVING STAGE**

1572

CHI, haji, ha*jiru*/*zukashii*
SHAME, ASHAMED
10 strokes

恥辱 CHIJOKU   disgrace
無恥 MUCHI   shamelessness
恥じ入る HAJIIRU   be ashamed

心 is **heart**/ **feelings** 147. 耳 is **ear** 29, here acting phonetically to express **shrink** but of unclear semantic role. Thus **shrinking heart**, a reference to **feeling ashamed** (cf. English feel small).

Mnemonic: **FEEL ASHAMED TO HAVE HEART NO BIGGER THAN EAR**

1573 致

CHI, ita*su*
DO, SEND, CAUSE
10 strokes

一致 ITCHI   unity, accord
致命的 CHIMEITEKI   fatal
致し方 ITASHIKATA   means

Once written 䂓, i.e. with **upturned foot** 夂 438 q.v. (here in its sense of **visit and stop**) rather than **striking hand**/ **coerce** 攵 101. 夂 is correct, as seen from an old form 𣪠 that shows person 儿 39 and upturned foot 夂. 𡈼/至 is **arrive**/ **reach** 875. 1573 originally referred to a **person reaching their destination and stopping**. However, the miscopying of 夂 as 攵 brought about causative connotations, giving **make someone visit** and hence **send**. As with send/ do 遣 1220 q.v., send broadened to **act**/ **do** in general. 1573 is also occasionally used to mean **cause**.

Mnemonic: **COERCIVELY SEND SOMEONE, WHO DOES ARRIVE**

1574

CHI, oku*reru*, oso*i*
TARDY, SLOW, LATE
12 strokes

遅刻 CHIKOKU   lateness
遅遅 CHICHI   slowly
遅咲き OSOZAKI   late blooming

Formerly 遟. 辶 is **movement** 129. 犀 is an NGU character now used to mean rhinoceros. It comprises **tail** 尾 1734 and **cow** 牛 97, and originally referred to **bovine beasts** in general. Here it acts phonetically to express **slow**, and also lends similar connotations of its own (cf. English bovine). Thus **slow movement**. The modern form uses **sheep** 羊 986, primarily as a graphic simplification. Suggest taking 尸 as **corpse** 236.

Mnemonic: **MOVE LIKE A SHEEP'S CORPSE -- SLOWLY!**

504

1575

CHI
FOOLISH
13 strokes

白痴 HAKUCHI   idiot
愚痴 GUCHI   idle complaint
痴情 CHIJŌ   infatuation

Formerly 癡. 疒 is **illness** 381, here meaning affliction/ **impairment**. 疑 is **doubt** 835 q.v., here acting phonetically to express **slow(-witted)** and probably also lending its connotations of being in doubt/ dithering. Thus **impairment associated with slow-wittedness** (and dithering?), a reference to **stupidity/ foolishness**. The modern form uses **know** 知 169, giving **impaired knowledge**.

Mnemonic: **ILLNESS IMPAIRS KNOWLEDGE, LEAVES ONE FOOLISH**

1576

CHI
YOUNG, IMMATURE
13 strokes

稚魚 CHIGYO   fish fry
稚拙 CHISETSU   naivety
幼稚園 YŌCHIEN   kindergarten

禾 is **rice plant** 81. 隹 is **bird** 216, here acting phonetically to express **slow** but of unclear semantic role. 1576 originally referred to **rice that was slow to mature,** and later came to mean **immature** in general.

Mnemonic: **BIRD FINDS IMMATURE RICE**

1577

CHIKU
LIVESTOCK
10 strokes

家畜 KACHIKU   livestock
畜生 CHIKUSHŌ beast, Damn!
畜産 CHIKUSAN

              stockbreeding

田 is **field** 59. 玄 is occult 1227 q.v., here acting phonetically to express **store/ accumulate** and possibly also lending connotations of mysterious (power). 1577 originally referred to **leaving a field fallow** in order for its fertility to be (mysteriously?) regenerated. Fallow fields were often used for **grazing,** and hence 1577 came to represent **livestock**. It still also retains connotations of accumulate/ regenerate, and is sometimes interchanged with accumulate 蓄 1579 q.v. Suggest remembering 玄 by association with **short thread** 幺 111.

Mnemonic: **LIVESTOCK TETHERED IN FIELD BY SHORT THREAD**

1578   CHIKU, *ou*   駆逐 KUCHIKU   driving off
CHASE, PURSUE   逐一 CHIKUICHI   one by one
10 strokes   逐語的 CHIKUGOTEKI   literal

Move 辶 129 and **pig** 豕 1670, meaning to **pursue a pig** and later **pursue/ chase** in a broad sense. Distinguish 遂 1458, q.v.

Mnemonic: **MOVE IN PURSUIT OF PIG**

1579   CHIKU, *takuwaeru*   貯蓄 CHOCHIKU   savings
ACCUMULATE, STORE   蓄電 CHIKUDEN   charging
13 strokes   蓄積 CHIKUSEKI
                    stockpiling, accumulation

畜 is **livestock** 1577 q.v., here with its original connotations of **leaving a field fallow** in order to **regenerate**, with **grass/ plants** 艹 9 added to emphasise growth. The idea of regeneration gradually broadened, and 1579 came by association to mean **accumulate/ store** in general.

Mnemonic: **LIVESTOCK CONSUMES STORED GRASS**

1580   CHITSU   秩序 CHITSUJO order, system
ORDER, STIPEND   官秩 KANCHITSU official rank
10 strokes   秩ろく CHITSUROKU   stipend

禾 is **rice plant** 81, here meaning harvested rice. 失 is **lose** 501, which acts here phonetically to express **arrange/ put in order** and probably originally also lent its meaning of lose. 1580 originally referred to **putting in order rice paid as a tithe** (i.e. rice 'lost' from the farmer's point of view), and eventually the idea of **putting in order** came to prevail. **Order/ rank** is now 1580's sole meaning in Chinese, but in Japanese it is also occasionally used in the sense of **stipend**, i.e. in effect reversing the assumed original viewpoint of donor to that of recipient.

Mnemonic: **LOSE RICE IN ORDERLY FASHION!?**

1581   CHITSU   窒死 CHISSHI   asphyxia
BLOCK UP, PLUG   窒息 CHISSOKU   suffocation
11 strokes   窒素 CHISSO   nitrogen

穴 is **hole** 849. 至 is **reach** 875 q.v., here acting phonetically to express **block** and probably also lending connotations of cover a given area. Thus **block a hole**.

Mnemonic: **REACH INTO HOLE AND PLUG IT**

506

1582		CHAKU	嫡子	CHAKUSHI	legal heir
		LEGITIMATE HEIR	廃嫡	HAICHAKU	disinherit
		14 strokes	嫡妻	CHAKUSAI	legal wife

女 is **woman** 35. 商 is base/ starting point 755 q.v., here acting phonetically to express **dutiful** and probably also lending connotations of **appropriate**. An **(appropriately?) dutiful woman** refers to a **legitimate wife**, as opposed to a concubine. In Japanese 1582 has by extension now come mainly to mean **legitimate offspring**, and hence **heir**. Suggest taking 商 as a combination of **emperor** 帝 1616 and **old** 古 109.

Mnemonic: **OLD EMPEROR'S WIFE PRODUCES LEGITIMATE HEIR**

1583	沖	CHŪ, oki	沖天	CHŪTEN	ascendancy
		OPEN SEA, SOAR	沖合い	OKIAI	offshore
		7 strokes	沖づり	OKIZURI	offshore fishing

氵 is **water** 40. 中 is **middle** 55, here acting phonetically to express **move/ be unsettled** and originally also lending a meaning of **middle**. 1583 originally referred to **unsettled waters in the middle** (of a channel). In Japanese it has now come to mean rather waters far from land, i.e. the **open sea**, whereas in Chinese the idea of moving/ distant waters has led to a range of extended and associated meanings such as seethe, be restless, wander, dash against, and **fly in the air/ soar** (from dash against). **Soar** is also occasionally found in Japanese.

Mnemonic: **WATER IN THE MIDDLE OF THE SEA IS OPEN WATER**

1584	抽	CHŪ	抽出	CHŪSHUTSU	extraction
		PULL, DRAW OUT	抽象	CHŪSHŌ	abstraction
		8 strokes	抽せん	CHŪSEN	lottery

扌 is **hand** 32. 由 is **reason** 399 q.v., here acting phonetically to express **pull** and almost certainly also lending its early connotations of **from**. Thus **pull something by hand** (out from somewhere?), now **pull/ extract** in a broad sense.

Mnemonic: **THERE'S A REASON FOR PULLING BY HAND**

507

1585

衷

CHŪ
INNER FEELINGS
9 strokes

折衷 SETCHŪ　compromise
衷心 CHŪSHIN　true feelings
苦衷 KUCHŪ　anguish

Once written 褱, showing **clothing** 仌/衤/衣 420 and **middle/ inside** 中/中 55 (here 屮). 1585 originally referred to **inner clothing**, i.e. **underwear**, and still retains this meaning in Chinese. However, it became confused with **loyalty/ inner feelings** 忠 936 q.v. (literally middle/ inner 中 and heart/ feelings 心 147), and came to acquire the meaning of **inner feelings** (but not necessarily loyalty).

Mnemonic: **INNER FEELINGS KEPT INSIDE ONE'S CLOTHES**

1586

鋳

CHŪ, iru
CAST, FOUND, MINT
15 strokes

鋳造 CHŪZŌ　casting
鋳鉄 CHŪTETSU　cast iron
鋳型 IGATA　mold

Formerly 鑄. 金 is **metal** 14. 壽/寿 is **long life** 1351, though in fact 壽 is a longstanding miscopying of 𤔲, which shows **hands** 𦥑 **inverting a vessel** 宀 and **pouring** 乚 (/ causing to flow: see also 1421) into another **vessel** 皿 1307. Thus to **pour out metal into a vessel**, i.e. **cast**.

Mnemonic: **CAST METAL HAS LONG LIFE**

1587

駐

CHŪ
STOP, STAY
15 strokes

駐車 CHŪSHA　parking
駐在 CHŪZAI　residence
駐日 CHŪNICHI
resident in Japan

馬 is **horse** 191. 主 is **master** 299 q.v., here acting phonetically to express **stop/ stay** and possibly also loosely lending similar connotations from its original depiction of a lamp which was generally fixed in one (central) place in a house. 1587 was originally a reference to a **horse stopping**, and later came to mean **stop/ stay** in a broader sense.

Mnemonic: **MASTER'S HORSE STOPS**

1588

CHŌ, tomura*u*
MOURN
4 strokes

敬弔 KEICHŌ   condolence
弔問 CHŌMON   sympathy call
弔い合戦 TOMURAIGASSEN
               battle of revenge

Obscure. The numerous early forms sometimes show a **snake coiled round a person**, as 𣎴 or 𣎳 (person 𠂉 / 亻 39), and sometimes a **snake coiled round a stick**, as 𣎴 or 𣎳. It is not clear which is the very earliest form, and thus not clear if stick is a mis-copying of person or vice-versa. Some scholars have taken 1588 to be a variant of younger brother/ binding on a stake 𣎳 / 弟 177 q.v., but the 'binding' in the case of 1588 is cate-gorically a snake and thus any overlap between 1588 and 177 seems unlikely. Other schol-ars have assumed snake round person to be the older version, and take this to be an ideo-graph depicting a **person killed by a snake**, thus leading by association to **mourning**. Still others have similarly assumed snake round person to be the older form, but have taken the snake to indicate twisting, giving twisted person/ hunchback. Mourn is then assumed to be a borrowed meaning. The 'person/ man killed by snake' theory seems the most helpful.

Mnemonic: **MOURN MAN CRUSHED LIKE STICK BY TWISTING SNAKE**

1589

CHŌ, idom*u*
CHALLENGE, DEFY
9 strokes

挑発 CHŌHATSU provocation
挑戦 CHŌSEN   challenge
挑戦的 CHŌSENTEKI aggressive

扌 is **hand** 32. 兆 is sign/ **trillion** 939, here acting phonetically to express **stir** but of un-clear semantic role. Thus **stir by hand**. Later stir in a figurative sense, i.e. **rouse**, with **challenge/ defy** being an associated meaning.

Mnemonic: **TRILLION HANDS RAISED IN DEFIANCE**

1590

CHŌ, hor*u*
CARVE, SCULPTURE
11 strokes

彫刻 CHŌKOKU   carving
彫像 CHŌZŌ   sculpture
手彫り TEBORI   hand carving

彡 is **hairs** 93, q.v., here in its sense of delicate/ attractive and by extension **decorative/ patterned**. 周 is **around**/ circumference 504 q.v., here acting phonetically to express **cut/ carve** and possibly also lending connotations of all around. Thus **decorative/ pat-terned carving** (all around, i.e. three-dimensional?). Suggest taking 彡 as **three lines**.

Mnemonic: **THREE LINES CARVED AROUND SCULPTURE**

| 1591 | CHŌ, naga*meru*
GAZE, LOOK
11 strokes | 眺望 CHŌBŌ view, outlook
眺め NAGAME view
眺望絶景 CHŌBŌZEKKEI
fine view |

目 is **eye** 72, here meaning **look**. 兆 is **sign/ trillion** 939, here acting phonetically to express **distance** but of unclear semantic role. Thus to **look into the distance**, i.e. **gaze**.

Mnemonic: **TRILLION EYES GAZING**

| 1592 | CHŌ, tsu*ru/ri*
FISH, LURE, CHANGE
11 strokes | 釣り場 TSURIBA fishing spot
釣魚 CHŌGYO fishing
釣り銭 TSURISEN change, coin |

金 is **metal** 14. 勺 is **ladle/ measure** 1342, here acting phonetically to express **catch/ snare** and almost certainly also lending its shape to suggest a **hook**. Thus to **catch with metal (hook)**, i.e. **fish**. Now also used to mean **lure/ trap** in a broad sense. It is not clear how it also came in later times to mean **change/ coin**.

Mnemonic: **FISH WITH LADLE-LIKE METAL HOOK**

| 1593 | CHŌ, fuku*ramu/reru*
SWELL, BULGE
12 strokes | 膨脹 BŌCHŌ expansion
脹れ面 FUKUREZURA pout
脹らし粉 FUKURASHIKO*
baking powder |

月 is **flesh/ of the body** 365. 長 is **long** 173, here acting phonetically to express **swell** and probably also lending connotations of **stretch**. Thus **swollen (and stretched?) body**. This was originally a reference to a certain type of illness (and at one stage was written 痕, i.e. with the sickness radical 疒 381, which in Chinese is still interchangeable with 脹), but it later came to mean **swollen** in a broader sense.

Mnemonic: **BODY SWELLS A LONG WAY**

| 1594 超 | CHŌ, ko*eru/su*
EXCEED, CROSS, SUPER-
12 strokes | 超人 CHŌJIN superman
超過 CHŌKA excess, surplus
入超 NYŪCHŌ imports excess |

走 is **run** 161. 召 is **summon** 1387, here acting phonetically to express **leap high (in a dance)** and possibly also lending connotations of being requested (to dance). To **run and leap high** came by association to mean **go beyond a normal level** in a broad sense, including in the sense of **exceed** and of the prefix **super-**.

Mnemonic: **SUPERFAST RUNNER SUMMONED FOR EXCEEDING LIMIT**

1595

CHŌ, ha*neru*, to*bu*
SPRING, JUMP, LEAP
13 strokes

跳躍 CHŌYAKU spring, jump
跳び板 TOBIITA springboard
跳ね返る HANEKAERU rebound

足 is foot/ leg 51. 兆 is sign/ **trillion** 939, here acting phonetically to express **leap high** but of unclear semantic role. Thus to **leap using the legs**, now **leap/ spring** in a broad sense.

Mnemonic: **TRILLION LEGS LEAPING**

1596

CHŌ, shirushi
SIGN, SUMMON, LEVY
14 strokes

象徴 SHŌCHŌ symbol
徴収 CHŌSHŪ levy
特徴 TOKUCHŌ characteristic

Somewhat obscure. Formerly 徴 and earlier 徵 徵 is the early form of small/ **secretive** 㣲/ 微 1735 q.v., while 土 is a simplification of the early form 呈 of **person standing** (attentively) 壬 1610. The latter is believed to have also been used phonetically to express **reveal**, thus giving 1596 a meaning of **reveal something to a person in a secretive manner**, as by a **sign**. **Summon** is felt to derive from the associated idea of searching for a sign, which came to mean search/ seek in general and eventually by extension summon. **Levy** is then taken to be an associated meaning with summon. Suggest taking 彳 as **go** 118, 山 as **mountain** 24, 王 as **king** 5, and 攵 as coerce/ **force** 101.

Mnemonic: **SIGN FORCES KING TO GO TO MOUNTAIN**

1597

CHŌ, su*mu*/*masu*
CLEAR, SETTLE
15 strokes

清澄 SEICHŌ na clear
澄み切る SUMIKIRU be clear
澄まし顔 SUMASHIGAO
smug look

氵 is **water/ river** 40. 登 is **climb** 360, here acting phonetically to express transparent/ **clear** and possibly also loosely lending a suggestion of upstream/ headwaters. Thus **clear water** (at head of river?), later **clear** in a broad sense. **Settled** is an associated meaning with clear.

Mnemonic: **WATER CLEARS AS ONE CLIMBS UP RIVER**

| 1598 | CHŌ, ki*ku*
 LISTEN (CAREFULLY)
 17 strokes | 聴講 CHŌKŌ attending lecture
 盗聴 TŌCHŌ wiretapping
 聴心器 CHŌSHINKI stethoscope |

Formerly 聽 . 耳 is **ear** 29, here meaning **listen**. 壬 is **person standing still** (variant 壬 1610). Thus 耳 means **person standing still listening** (see also 911). 恵 /恵 is **virtue** 762. Thus **stand listening virtuously**, i.e. attentively, now **listen carefully** in a broader sense. Suggest taking 十 as **ten** 33, 罒 as **eye** 72, and 心 as **heart** 147.

Mnemonic: **EAR IS WORTH TEN EYES WHEN LISTENING TO HEART**

| 1599 | CHŌ, ko*riru*/*rasu*
 CHASTISE, LEARN
 18 strokes | 懲罰 CHŌBATSU punishment
 懲戒 CHŌKAI reprimand
 懲り懲り KORIKORI to one's cost |

心 is **heart**/ feelings 147. 徴 is **sign** 1596, here acting phonetically to express **reform** and possibly also lending an idea of sign/ visible evidence. Thus to **reform in one's heart**, i.e. mend one's ways (publicly?). This suggested by association reforming after learning the error of one's old ways, and hence 1599 came to mean **learn** by some unfortunate experience. Probably because of the presence of the causative element 攵 (see 101), 1599 also came to mean cause to reform, i.e. **chastise**.

Mnemonic: **SIGN THAT CHASTISED HEART HAS LEARNED LESSON**

| 1600 | CHOKU
 IMPERIAL EDICT
 9 strokes | 勅語 CHOKUGO imperial edict
 勅旨 CHOKUSHI imperial will
 勅任 CHOKUNIN
    imperial appointment |

Formerly 敕 , i.e. with strike/ force/ cause 攵 101 instead of strength/ **power** 力 74. 束 is **bundle**/ **manage** 1535, here acting phonetically to express **correct** as well as lending its meaning of **manage**. Thus to **manage a situation by making someone act correctly**. All **imperial pronouncements** were considered to be of this nature, i.e. of setting people on the right course.

Mnemonic: **IMPERIAL EDICTS COME IN POWERFUL BUNDLE**

| 1601 | | CHIN, shizumu/meru
SINK
7 strokes | 沈没 CHINBOTSU sinking
沈滞 CHINTAI stagnation
沈下 CHINKA subsidence |

氵 is **water** 40. 宀 is a CO character now meaning **move in**, but its original meaning was **hang down** (etymology unclear, but originally written 冘, suggesting a bending person 人 39 and what is possibly a symbol of drooping/ hanging 卅). Thus to **hang down in the water**, i.e. to **sink**. Suggest taking 宀 as **big man** 大 53 with **broken arms** 冖 and **broken leg** 乚.

Mnemonic: **BIG MAN WITH BROKEN ARMS AND LEG SINKS IN WATER**

| 1602 | | CHIN, mezurashii
RARE, CURIOUS
9 strokes | 珍奇 CHINKI na novel, rare
珍品 CHINPIN rarity, curio
珍本 CHINPON rare book |

王 is **jewel** 102. 㐱 is **person and hair** 1440 (person 人 39 and delicate hairs 彡 93 q.v.), here acting phonetically to express pure/ **unblemished** and probably also lending connotations of **attractive** from its delicate hairs element 彡. Thus an (**attractive?**) un-blemished jewel, which was a relatively **rare** item. Now **rare/ curious** in general.

Mnemonic: **PERSON HAS RARE JEWEL WITH CURIOUS HAIR-LIKE PATTERN**

| 1603 | 朕 | CHIN
(ROYAL) WE
10 strokes | 朕 CHIN We
朕の CHIN no Our
朕徳 CHINTOKU Our virtue |

Formerly 朕. The oldest form 月卅 shows that 月 is derived from **boat** 月/舟 1354 and that 关 is derived from **two hands** 卅 **holding up an item** ‡. The latter is be-lieved by some scholars to be a spigot or tool, and by others to be a pestle, but in any event 卅 is known to have had a core meaning of **work with the hands** and strong connotations both of **raising** and **repetitiveness**/ continuity. The original meaning of 1603 was to **repair a boat**, but it was later borrowed as a **first person pronoun**, and in practice is now almost exclusively used as a **royal 'we'**. Suggest taking 月 as flesh/ (of the) **body** 365 and 关 as **from**/ out of 丷 66 **heaven** 天 58.

Mnemonic: **OUR ROYAL BODY DESCENDS FROM HEAVEN**

1604

CHIN
STATE, SHOW, OLD
11 strokes

陳情 CHINJŌ　　petition
陳列 CHINRETSU　exhibition
新陳代謝 SHINCHINTAISHA
　　　renewal, metabolism

阝 is **hill** 229, here meaning **mound of earth**. 東 is **east** 184, here acting phonetically to express **encircling embankment** but of unclear semantic role. 1604 originally referred to the **raised earthen path around a field** (and still has a minor meaning of path in Chinese). **Raised** gradually led by association to **show/ expose**, with **express/ state** being a further association (though some scholars feel these meanings are borrowed). It is not clear how the meaning of **old/** of long standing was acquired, but it may relate to an idea of permanence possibly attributed to such ridges (see 1468).

Mnemonic: **STATEMENT SHOWS EASTERN HILLS ARE OLD**

1605

CHIN, shizu*maru*/*meru*
CALM, SUPPRESS,
WEIGHT
18 strokes

鎮痛剤 CHINTSŪZAI　painkiller
鎮静 CHINSEI　　calm, quiet
文鎮 BUNCHIN　　paperweight

Formerly 鎭. 金 is **metal** 14. 眞/真 is **true** 514 q.v., here acting phonetically to express **heavy** and almost certainly also lending its early meaning of **upside-down**. 1605 originally meant **(inverted?) heavy metal weight**, leading by association to **press down** and hence the figurative meanings of **suppress** and **quieten/ calm**.

Mnemonic: **SUPPRESS WITH TRULY HEAVY METAL WEIGHT**

1606

TSUI
FALL
15 strokes

墜落 TSUIRAKU　　　　fall
撃墜 GEKITSUI shooting down
墜死 TSUISHI　falling to death

隊 is **corps/ unit** 540 q.v., here with its original meaning of **fall down a hill** reinforced by earth/ **ground** 土 60. Now **fall** in a broader sense.

Mnemonic: **CORPS FALLS TO GROUND**

1607

tsuka, CHŌ
MOUND, TUMULUS
12 strokes

貝塚 KAIZUKA　shell mound
塚穴 TSUKAANA　　　grave
宝塚 TAKARAZUKA
　　　　place-name

Formerly also 塚. 土 is **earth** 60. 冖 is **roof/ cover** (variant 宀 28), here meaning **cover**. 豖/豕 is **pig** 1670, here acting phonetically to express **pile** but of unclear semantic role. Thus **pile of earth that covers**, i.e. a **tumulus**.

Mnemonic: **EARTHEN MOUND COVERS PIG**

1608 tsu*karu*/*keru*, SHI 漬け物 TSUKEMONO pickles
PICKLE, SOAK 茶漬け CHAZUKE tea on rice
14 strokes 塩漬け SHIOZUKE salting

氵 is **water/ liquid** 40. 責 is **blame** 728 q.v., here acting phonetically to express **build up** and possibly also lending similar connotations of **accumulate**. Thus to **build up in water/ liquid**, a reference to leaving layers of items to **soak/ pickle**.

Mnemonic: **TAKE BLAME FOR WATERY PICKLES**

1609 tsubo, HEI 建坪 TATETSUBO floor space
TSUBO, 五坪 GOTSUBO five tsubo
SQUARE MEASURE 坪数 TSUBOSŪ area
8 strokes

Ground 土 60 and **flat/ level** 平 388, giving **level ground**. In Chinese this is 1609's only meaning, but in Japanese it has come to be used principally to refer to a **tsubo**, a **square measure** of 3.31 sq.m.

Mnemonic: **TSUBO IS MEASURED ON FLAT GROUND**

1610 廷 **TEI** 宮廷 KYŪTEI court
COURT, 法廷 HŌTEI law court
GOVERNMENT OFFICE 廷臣 TEISHIN courtier
7 strokes

廴 is **movement** 129. 壬 is a CO character now borrowed for a range of meanings such as artful and great, but it derives from 𡈼, showing a **person** 人 39 **standing** (still) on the **ground** 土 60. Thus **move to (take up) a standing position on the ground**, a rather vague reference to people at **court** moving to take up their designated position as the emperor appeared. Suggest taking 壬 as a **hatted** ノ **samurai** 士 494.

Mnemonic: **HATTED SAMURAI MOVES TO COURT**

1611 呈 **TEI** 呈上 TEIJŌ presentation
PRESENT, OFFER 贈呈 ZŌTEI donation
7 strokes 進呈 SHINTEI presentation

Formerly 呈. 口 is **mouth/ say** 20. 壬 is **person standing** (at court) 1610, here acting phonetically to express **reveal** and also lending connotations of a person in the presence of a dignitary. 1611 originally referred to a **person giving a revealing (i.e. detailed) verbal statement** to a dignitary, i.e. **presenting a report**, but now means **present/ offer** in a broad sense. Suggest taking 王 as **king** 5.

Mnemonic: **PRESENT ITEM FOR KING'S MOUTH**

1612	TEI RESIST, MATCH 8 strokes	抵抗 TEIKŌ	resistance
		抵当 TEITŌ	mortgage
		大抵 TAITEI	generally

扌 is hand 32. 氐 is bottom of hill 548, here acting phonetically to express **push back** (with equal force) but of unclear semantic role. Thus to **push back with the hand**, leading to **resist** and **match/ prove equal**. Suggest taking 氐 as **clan** 氏 495 and **one** 一 1.

Mnemonic: **RESIST CLAN WITH ONE HAND**

1613	TEI MANSION, RESIDENCE 8 strokes	邸宅 TEITAKU	mansion
		邸内 TEINAI	premises
		官邸 KANTEI official residence

Of confusing etymology. 阝 is **village** 355, felt by some scholars to be used here in an extended sense of metropolis/capital (i.e. as an abbreviation of capital 都 355) and by others to indicate person from a village. 氐 is **bottom of hill** 548, here acting phonetically to express **reside** and also lending an idea of **house at the bottom of a hill** (see 548). Normally a house at the bottom of a hill was associated with a commoner, while a house on a hilltop was associated with a noble (see 99 and 548). Confusingly, however, some low ranking provincial nobles (i.e. those from villages) were unable to secure hilltop residences in the capital, and were thus obliged to live in houses at the bottom of hills. 1613 originally referred to such a residence, i.e.**'townhouse'** (at the foot of a hill) where a low ranking provincial noble resided when in the capital. In Chinese it can still mean **noble's townhouse in the capital**, while in Japanese it has come to mean **residence** in a broader sense, usually of a reasonably impressive nature such as a **mansion**. Suggest taking 氐 as **clan** 氏 495 and **one** 一 1.

Mnemonic: **CLAN LIVES IN ONE MANSION IN VILLAGE**

1614	亭 TEI PAVILION, INN 9 strokes	亭主 TEISHU	host, husband
		旅亭 RYOTEI	inn
		料亭 RYŌTEI	restaurant

高 is a simplification of **tall** 高 119 q.v., here with its connotations of **tall edifice/ building**. 丁 is exact/ **nail** 346, here acting phonetically to express **stay/ stop**. Thus **tall (/large) building where people stay**, a reference to an **inn**. **Pavilion** is an associated meaning.

Mnemonic: **NAIL SUPPORTS TALL PAVILION**

1615 **TEI** 貞操 TEISŌ chastity
CHASTITY, VIRTUE 貞節 TEISETSU chastity
9 strokes 貞実 TEIJITSU fidelity

Once written 鼑. ⺊ is a variant of **divination (crack)** ⼘ 91. 鼑/貝 is a simplified **round kettle** 鼎 228, here acting phonetically to express **request/ seek** but of unclear semantic role. 1615 originally referred to **seeking to learn the will of the gods by means of divination**, and can still have this meaning in Chinese. Some scholars feel that **chastity/ virtue** is a borrowed meaning, while others see it as an extended meaning, i.e. seeking to act in a manner approved by the gods (cf. English godly). It has now acquired particular connotations of **female virtue**. Suggest taking 貝 as **shell** 90, and ⺊ in its literal meaning of **crack**.

Mnemonic: **CRACKED SHELL A SYMBOL OF CHASTITY?**

1616 **TEI** 帝国 TEIKOKU empire
EMPEROR 帝王 TEIŌ emperor
9 strokes 帝王切開 TEIŌSEKKAI caesarian

Formerly 帝 and earlier 帝, showing a large **two-tier table** 帀 supported by **cross-struts** ✕ with an **item** ─ placed on top. The (firm) table was used in religious services and is to all intents and purposes an elaborate variant of **altar** ⊤ / 示 695 q.v., with similar connotations of **relating to the gods**. **Ruler/ emperor** is taken by some scholars to be a borrowed meaning, but seems more likely to be an associated meaning with god. Suggest taking 帝 as a combination of **stand** 立 73 and **broom** 帚 96.

Mnemonic: **EMPEROR STANDS OVER BROOM**

1617 **TEI** 訂正 TEISEI correction
CORRECT, REVISE 改訂 KAITEI revision
9 strokes 改訂版 KAITEIBAN
revised edition

言 is **words/ speak** 274. 丁 is exact 346, here acting phonetically to express **fair/ just**. 1617 originally meant to **make a fair statement (and thereby settle an issue)**. In Chinese it still means settle, but in Japanese it has come rather to mean **amend/ revise/ correct**.

Mnemonic: **USE EXACT WORDS IN CORRECTION**

517

1618 **TEI**
RELAY, IN SEQUENCE
10 strokes

逓送 TEISŌ forwarding
逓信 TEISHIN communications
逓次 TEIJI in succession

Formerly 遞. 辶 is **movement (along a road)** 129. 虒 is a CO character referring to a **mythical beast** resembling a **tiger** 虎 281 with a large curved **horn** ⌒ (now ⺄), and was also used of a certain district in ancient China. Here it acts phonetically to express **change**, but its semantic role is unclear. Thus **change in those moving along a road**, a reference to a change of messengers and hence the present meanings of **relay** and **in sequence**. Suggest taking 㡭 as a combination of **ten** 十 33 and **city** 巿 130, with ⌒ as **building/ house** (variant 厂 114).

Mnemonic: **MOVE TO RELAY IN SEQUENCE TO HOMES IN TEN CITIES**

1619 **TEI**
SPY, INVESTIGATE
11 strokes

探偵 TANTEI detection
内偵 NAITEI secret inquiry
偵察 TEISATSU reconnaissance

亻 is **person** 39. 貞 is **chastity** 1615 q.v., here in its literal sense of **seeking to know the will of the gods by divination**. Thus person who seeks to know by divination, i.e. a **diviner**. This later came to mean **investigator/ investigate** in a broader sense, but still retains connotations of acting in an esoteric and hence secretive manner (i.e. **spy**).

Mnemonic: **SPY ON PERSON'S CHASTITY**

1620 **TEI, tsutsumi**
EMBANKMENT
12 strokes

防波堤 BŌHATEI breakwater
堤防 TEIBŌ levee, dike
堤防伝い TEIBŌZUTAI along bank

土 is **earth** 60. 是 is **proper** 910, here acting phonetically to express **firm** but of unclear semantic role. **Firm earth** was a reference to an **embankment**.

Mnemonic: **USE PROPER EARTH FOR EMBANKMENT**

1621 **TEI**
BOAT
13 strokes

艦艇 KANTEI naval vessel
艇庫 TEIKO boathouse
救命艇 KYŪMEITEI lifeboat

舟 is **boat** 1354. 廷 is **court** 1610, here acting phonetically to express **small** but of unclear semantic role. Thus **small boat**, now **boat** in a broader sense.

Mnemonic: **COURT HAS ITS OWN BOAT**

1622		**TEI, shi***maru***/***meru*	締め切り	SHIMEKIRI	deadline
		BIND, TIGHTEN, CLOSE	締約	TEIYAKU	treaty
		15 strokes	締め出し	SHIMEDASHI	shutout

糸 is **thread** 27, here meaning **cord**. 帝 is **emperor** 1616 q.v., here acting phonetically to express **bind** and possibly also lending loose connotations of **firmly** from its original meaning of firmly braced table. Thus to **bind (firmly?) with cord**, later also **tighten/ shut** and figuratively as **tie up/ conclude**.

Mnemonic: **BIND EMPEROR WITH THREAD**

1623		**DEI, doro, nazu***mu*	泥土	DEIDO	mud, mire
		MUD, ADHERE TO	拘泥	KŌDEI	adherence
		8 strokes	泥足	DOROASHI	muddy feet

Somewhat obscure. 氵 is **water** 40, here meaning **river**. 尼 is **nun** 1674 q.v. Some scholars feel the latter is used purely phonetically to express the name of a certain river in ancient China, with **mud** being either an associated meaning or a borrowing. However, it seems equally if not more likely that 尼 acts phonetically to express **stop** (originally being pronounced SHI, as in stop SHI 止 129) and also lends its own early connotations of **stop**. Thus a **river which stops flowing**, i.e. leaving an expanse of **mud**. In either case, **adhere to** is an associated meaning with mud, from the idea of sticking.

Mnemonic: **NUN IN MUDDY WATER**

1624		**TEKI, fue**	汽笛	KITEKI	steam whistle
		FLUTE, WHISTLE	笛手	TEKISHU	flutist, flautist
		11 strokes	口笛	KUCHIBUE	whistle

竹 is **bamboo** 170. 由 is **reason** 399 q.v., here acting phonetically to express **pure/ clear (sound)** and almost certainly also lending its connotations of **from**. Thus **bamboo from which pure/clear sound (emerges)**, i.e. a **flute**. Now also **whistle** in a broad sense.

Mnemonic: **THERE'S A REASON FOR MAKING FLUTE FROM BAMBOO**

1625 摘 **TEKI, tsu***mu***, tsuma***mu*
PLUCK, PICK, EXTRACT
14 strokes

摘要 TEKIYŌ summary
摘発 TEKIHATSU exposure
摘み取る TSUMITORU pluck, pick

扌 is **hand** 32. 啇 is starting point 755 q.v., here acting phonetically to express **pick** and possibly also lending connotations of **appropriate**. Thus to **pick (something appropriate?) by hand**. It was originally used in a physical sense, as in picking/ plucking flowers or fruit, but is now often used in a figurative sense, such as **extracting** or **revealing**. Suggest taking 啇 as a combination of **emperor** 帝 1616 and **old** 古 109.

Mnemonic: **PICKED BY OLD EMPEROR'S HAND**

1626 滴 **TEKI, shizuku, shitata***ru*
DROP, DRIP
14 strokes

水滴 SUITEKI water drop
一滴 ITTEKI one drop
滴下 TEKIKA dripping

氵 is **water** 40. 啇 is **starting point** 755, here acting phonetically to express **tap/ strike** and possibly also lending its connotations of starting point. Thus **water which taps against something**, namely a **drip** (the starting point of a larger flow?). Suggest taking 啇 as a combination of **emperor** 帝 1616 and **old** 古 109.

Mnemonic: **WATER DRIPS ONTO OLD EMPEROR**

1627 迭 **TETSU**
ALTERNATE, ROTATE
8 strokes

更迭 KŌTETSU reshuffle
迭立 TETSURITSU alternating
迭起 TEKKI alternate occurrence

辶 is **movement (along a road)** 129. 矢 is **lose** 501, here acting phonetically to express **change** but of unclear semantic role. Like 遞 1618, 1627 originally referred to **changing those moving along a road**, i.e. messengers, and later came to mean **alternate/ rotate** in a broader sense.

Mnemonic: **ALTERNATING CAN INVOLVE LOSS OF MOVEMENT**

1628 哲 **TETSU**
WISDOM
10 strokes

哲学 TETSUGAKU philosophy
哲人 TETSUJIN sage
先哲 SENTETSU sage of old

口 is **mouth/ say** 20, here meaning **words**. 折 is **break** 522 q.v., here acting phonetically to express **correct** and probably also lending connotations of **understanding** from its original meaning of chop and hence divide/ analyse (see also 199). Thus **correct words** (full of understanding?), a symbol of **wisdom**.

Mnemonic: **SPEECH BROKEN BUT STILL SHOWS WISDOM**

1629

徹

TETSU
GO THROUGH, CLEAR,
REMOVE
15 strokes

徹夜 TETSUYA　　　　all night
徹底的 TETTEITEKI　　thorough
貫徹 KANTETSU　　fulfillment

Of confused evolution. Originally written 㝵又, showing **hand** 又 and **pot on a stand** 㝵 (a very early form of 鬲 1078). It originally meant to **remove a pot from a stand**, and still retains connotations of **remove** (though remove is nowadays usually conveyed by 撤 1630, with which 1629 is sometimes interchanged). Remove came to mean **clear away**, and then by association **have a clear passage** (note that pot on a stand was almost certainly also a symbol of an impediment -- see 1078). Like 通 176, this then came to mean **pass clear through**, with **road/ go** 彳 118 being added for clarity. Thus **road that passes clear through/ go clear through**. Pot on stand 㝵/鬲 was later miscopied as child being born/ **educate** 育 227, and hand 又 miscopied as striking hand/ **force** 攵 101.

Mnemonic: **FORCED TO GO CLEAR THROUGH ONE'S EDUCATION**

1630

撤

TETSU
REMOVE, WITHDRAW
15 strokes

撤収 TESSHŪ　　　　removal
撤去 TEKKYO　　　　removal
撤回 TEKKAI　　withdrawal

Remove a pot 㪠 1629 q.v. (correctly 敊) with **hand** 扌 32 added after the meaning had become vague. Now **remove/ withdraw** in a broader sense. Suggest taking 育 as **educate (a child)** 227 and 攵 as **force** 101.

Mnemonic: **FORCE EDUCATED CHILD TO REMOVE HAND**

1631

添

TEN, so*u/eru*
ACCOMPANY, ADD
11 strokes

添加 TENKA　　　　addition
添付 TENPU　　　appending
添え木 SOEGI　　splint, brace

氵 is **water** 40. 忝 is an NGU character meaning grateful/ embarrassed, though in Chinese it has stronger meanings of ashamed/ disgraced (literally the **feelings** 小ヽ [variant 心 147] of a **person/ man with head bowed** 夭 279). Here 忝 acts phonetically to express **fill**, but any semantic role is unclear. Thus to **fill with water**. Add water later came to mean **add** in a broad sense, with the intransitive version coming to mean **join/ accompany** (not unlike 431). Since no early forms of 添 have been found some scholars conclude that it is in fact a later variant of 沾, an NGU character meaning moisten/ add water which uses divine/ occupy 占 1491 in a similar phonetic role to 忝, but this is not especially convincing.

Mnemonic: **MAN WITH BOWED HEAD FEELS NEED FOR ADDED WATER**

1632		DEN, TEN	宮 殿 KYŪDEN	palace
		PALACE, LORD, MR	御 殿 GOTEN	palace
		13 strokes	殿 様 TONOSAMA	lord

Somewhat obscure. Once written 㲉. 殳 is **strike** 153, 尸 is **buttocks**/ slumped figure 236, while 仄 is obscure. However, 肙 appears to have meant **buttocks**, and also to have lent its sound (known to have once been **TON**). Thus to **strike someone on the buttocks with a TON sound**. Note that in Chinese 1632 can still mean **rear**. **Palace** is a borrowed meaning, specifically resulting from 1632's being used in place of a now defunct character 壂 . This combines **earth/ ground** 土 60 with 殿 , which is known to have acted phonetically to express **raised** (any semantic role being unclear), thus giving **raised earth/ ground**. This originally referred to **earthen ramparts**, which came to symbolise **castle**, with **palace** being an associated meaning. In Japanese 1632 is also used by further association to refer to the person living in a palace/ castle, namely a **lord**, and is also used as a general term of respect. Suggest taking 共 as **together** 460.

Mnemonic: **STRIKE BUTTOCKS TOGETHER AT LORD'S PALACE**

1633		TO	北 斗 星 HOKUTOSEI Big Dipper
		DIPPER, MEASURE	斗 酒 TOSHU gallons of sake
		4 strokes	泰 斗 TAITO an authority

To all intents and purposes a variant of **ladle** 升 1386 q.v., being a derivative of a highly stylised variant 㪺 of 1386's early form 斗 (a pictograph of a ladle) but technically without the contents ˙ . Confusingly, however, while 1386 has become a standard measure of 1.8 liters, 1633 is a **measure** ten times that amount, namely 18 liters.

Mnemonic: **BIG DIPPER HAS SLOPING CROSS AND TWO DOTS?!**

1634		TO, haku	吐 剤 TOZAI	emetic
		DISGORGE, VOMIT	吐 き 気 HAKIKE	nausea
		6 strokes	吐 息 TOIKI	gasp, sigh

口 is **mouth** 20. 土 is **soil/ ground** 60, here acting phonetically to express **pour forth** and possibly also lending extended connotations of **filth**. Thus to **pour forth (filth?) from the mouth**, i.e. **vomit/ disgorge**.

Mnemonic: **DISGORGE VOMIT FROM MOUTH TO GROUND**

1635		TO ROAD, WAY 10 strokes	途中 TOCHŪ	on the way
			途端 TOTAN	verge, point
			前途 ZENTO	future

辶 is **movement (along a road)** 129. 余 is **ample** 800, here also acting phonetically to express **road/ way**. Thus **ample road (permitting) (easy) movement**, now **road/ way** in a general sense including the figurative.

Mnemonic: **ROAD PERMITTING AMPLE MOVEMENT**

1636		TO, wata*ru/su* CROSS, HAND OVER 12 strokes	渡航 TOKŌ	passage, crossing
			渡世 TOSEI	livelihood
			言い渡す IIWATASU	sentence

シ is **water** 40, here meaning **river**. 度 is **degree** 356 q.v., here acting phonetically to express **span** and possibly also loosely lending similar connotations from its literal meaning of measure with the hand. Thus to **span a river**, later **cross (over)** in a general sense. **Hand over** is the transitive version.

Mnemonic: **CROSS WATER BY DEGREES**

1637		TO, nu*ru* PLASTER, COAT, PAINT 13 strokes	塗り物 NURIMONO	lacquerware
			塗装 TOSŌ	painting
			塗り薬 NURIGUSURI	ointment

Once written simply as 涂, which still exists in Chinese as a variant of 塗. シ is **water** 40, here meaning **river**. 余 is **ample/ excess** 800. Thus **ample/ excessive river**, a reference to a **large river prone to flood**. This came by association to mean **leave a coating of mud**, with **earth** 土 60 being added for clarity. Now to **coat** in a general sense, but note that in Chinese 1637 can still mean mud.

Mnemonic: **EXCESS RIVER-WATER LEAVES COATING OF EARTHY MUD**

1638	奴	DO, yatsu, yakko, -me SLAVE, SERVANT, GUY 5 strokes	奴隷 DOREI	slave
			奴等 YATSURA	those guys
			奴様 YAKKOSAN *	that guy

Somewhat obscure, though its elements are clearly **hand** 又 and **woman** 女 35. Some scholars feel that woman 女 symbolises **compliance** and hand 又 symbolises **work**, to give a meaning of **work compliantly** and by association **be a slave/ servant**. Other scholars take woman 女 to be used literally and hand 又 to indicate **control**, to give **woman under one's control**, a reference to a **slave-girl**. The former theory seems the more likely. 1638 is also used as a pejorative suffix and slang reference to a **person**.

Mnemonic: **HAND-MAIDEN IS A SLAVE**

1639 怒 **DO, ika*ru*, oko*ru***
ANGER, RAGE
9 strokes

怒気	DOKI	anger
怒鳴る	DONARU	shout, bawl
怒り狂う	IKARIKURUU	rage madly

心 is heart/ **feelings** 147. 奴 is **slave** 1638, here acting phonetically to express **anger** and possibly also suggesting feelings associated with being a slave or (more likely) directed towards a slave. Thus **feelings of anger** (directed towards a slave?). Now **anger/ rage** in a broad sense.

Mnemonic: **SLAVE'S FEELINGS ARE OF ANGER**

1640 豆 **TŌ, ZU, mame**
BEANS, MINIATURE
7 strokes

豆腐	TŌFU	beancurd
大豆	DAIZU	soybean
豆本	MAMEHON	miniature book

Once written 豆, showing a **monopedal table-cum-food vessel** (known as takatsuki in Japanese) 豆 with **contents** 一. Some scholars take **bean** to be a borrowing, while others see it as an associated meaning with food in general, which was in turn associated with food vessel 豆 (see also 146). In compounds 1640 is often used to indicate both food and vessel/ container in a broader sense. Confusingly, depending on one's point of view the takatsuki could be considered quite tall (i.e. relative to a normal dish), and occasionally it seems to lend such connotations (as in 360), but in general it was considered short (i.e. relative to a table) and usually lends these connotations (see 342). **Miniature** is an associated meaning with short. It also occasionally appears to lend connotations of fixed height/ dimensions (again see 342). Suggest taking 一 as **one** 1, 口 as a **box**, and 䒑 as a variant of **stand** 立 73.

Mnemonic: **ONE MINIATURE BOX ON STAND, FULL OF BEANS**

1641 到 **TŌ, ita*ru***
GO, REACH, ARRIVE
8 strokes

到来	TŌRAI	arrival, advent
到達	TŌTATSU	arrival
到底	TŌTEI	absolutely

Once written 到, showing that **sword**/ cut 刂 181 is actually a miscopying of **person** 人 / 亻 39. 至/至 is **arrive/ reach** 875 q.v., here in its literal sense of arrow falling upside-down and thus indicating being **upside-down**. 1641 originally referred to a **person being upside-down**, i.e. **falling**. This meaning is now conveyed by 倒 1643 q.v., which adds a further person 亻. The meaning of 1641 itself evolved in similar fashion to that of 至 875, i.e. to give **reach/ arrive**.

Mnemonic: **REACH SWORD**

1642		TŌ, ni*geru*/*gasu*, noga*reru*/*su* **ESCAPE, EVADE, MISS** 9 strokes	逃亡者 TŌBŌSHA	fugitive
			見逃す MINOGASU	overlook
			逃げ道 NIGEMICHI	escape route

辶 is **movement** 129. 兆 is sign/ **trillion** 939 q.v., here acting phonetically to express **escape** and possibly also lending supporting connotations of separation. Thus to **move and escape**.

Mnemonic: **ESCAPE THROUGH A TRILLION MOVES**

1643		TŌ, tao*reru*/*su* **FALL, TOPPLE, INVERT** 10 strokes	倒産 TŌSAN	bankruptcy
			面倒 MENDŌ	trouble
			倒置 TŌCHI	inversion

Reach 到 1641 q.v., here in its literal sense of **person fallen over/ upside-down**, with **person** イ 39 added for clarity. Suggest remembering reach 到 by association with **reach** 至 875 and **sword** 刂 181.

Mnemonic: **REACH FALLEN PERSON WITH SWORD**

1644		TŌ, kŏ*ru*, kogo*eru* **FREEZE** 10 strokes	冷凍剤 REITŌZAI	refrigerant
			凍結 TŌKETSU	freezing
			凍り付く KŌRITSUKU	freeze to

冫 is **ice** 378. 東 is **east** 184 q.v., here acting phonetically to express **hard** and possibly also lending loose connotations of mass from its early meaning of heavy sack. **Hard ice** symbolises **freezing**.

Mnemonic: **ICE FREEZES OVER EAST**

1645		TŌ, kara **(T'ANG) CHINA** 10 strokes	唐本 TŌHON	Chinese book
			毛唐人 KETŌJIN	foreigner
			唐手 KARATE	karate

Formerly 唐 and earlier 啻 , showing **mouth/ say** 口 20 and hands holding a pestle 庚 480. The latter acts phonetically to express **brag/ boast** but is of unclear semantic role. Thus to **speak boastfully** (still a meaning in Chinese). It was later borrowed to refer to **T'ang** and by extension **China** in general (and from a Japanese perspective can also mean **foreign**), but the reason for the borrowing is not clear. Suggest taking 广 as **building** 114 and 肀 as a **hand** ヨ holding a **stick** l , with 口 in its sense of opening/ **entrance**.

Mnemonic: **HAND HOLDS STICK AT ENTRANCE TO CHINESE BUILDING**

1646

桃

TŌ, momo
PEACH
10 strokes

白桃　HAKUTŌ　　white peach
桃色　MOMOIRO　　　　pink
桃原境　TŌGENKYŌ　Shangri-La

木 is **tree** 69. 兆 is **sign/ trillion** 939 q.v., here in its meaning of **sign**. In the ancient Orient the peach was a **symbol of fertility/ pregnancy**, partly for the similarity of its appearance to female genitalia (cf. the Japanese legend of Momotarō, the Peach Boy) and partly for the fact that, along with the plum (see 1689), it was a favorite fruit of pregnant women. Thus the **peach tree** was literally a **'pregnancy-sign tree'**. Note that in Chinese 1646 can also mean marriage, clearly showing its procreative associations.

Mnemonic: **TREE BEARING A TRILLION PEACHES**

1647

透

TŌ, su*ku/kasu/keru*
CLEAR, TRANSPARENT
10 strokes

透明　TŌMEI　　transparency
透写　TŌSHA　　　　tracing
透き通る　SUKITŌRU　　be clear

辶 is **movement** 129. 秀 is **excel** 1355, here acting phonetically to express **lead** and also lending similar associated connotations of its own. 1647 originally referred to a **person leading another** in a physical sense. Some scholars feel its present meanings are borrowed, while others feel that **lead the way** came by association to mean **clear the way** and eventually **clear** in a broad sense (not unlike 1629). **Transparent** is an associated meaning. Note that 1647 can still be used in the sense of **clear/ unobstructed**, though it is usually used in the sense of **clear/ transparent**.

Mnemonic: **EXCELLENT MOVEMENT CLEARS WAY**

1648

悼

TŌ, itam*u*
GRIEVE, MOURN
11 strokes

哀悼　AITŌ　　　　mourning
追悼　TSUITŌ　　　mourning
悼むべき　ITAMUBEKI　lamentable

忄 is **heart/ feelings** 147. 卓 is **excel/ table** 1553, here acting phonetically to express **sway/ move** but of unclear semantic role. Thus to **have one's heart swayed**, a somewhat vague reference to **mourning/ grieving**.

Mnemonic: **GRIEVE WITH HEART ON THE TABLE**

1649		TŌ, nusum*u*	盗用	TŌYŌ	appropriation
		STEAL	強盗	GŌTŌ	robbery
		11strokes	盗人	NUSUBITO *	thief

Formerly 盜 , showing that 次 is not **next** 次 292 -- though it may be useful to remember it as such -- but a miscopying/ simplification of 次. The latter is a CO character meaning **saliva** (literally **water** 氵 40 and **gaping mouth** 欠 471). A **watering mouth** is a universal symbol of **desire for food**, here reinforced by **dish** 皿 1307. 1649 originally meant to **have a strong desire to eat**. The idea of having a strong desire for something came to prevail, leading to **desiring to acquire at any cost** and eventually to **appropriating/ stealing**.

Mnemonic: **STEAL DISH NEXT**

1650		TŌ	陶器	TŌKI	ceramic ware
		CERAMIC, HAPPY,	薫陶	KUNTŌ	education
		EDUCATE	陶然	TŌZEN	enraptured
		11 strokes			

Of confused etymology. Correctly written simply as 匋, which still exists in Chinese and is interchangeable with 陶. 匋 comprises **surround/ womb** 勹 655 and **can/ vessel** 缶 1095, and originally ideographically indicated an **outer covering protecting an inner vessel**. 缶 originally referred to a pottery vessel, and thus 匋 meant **protected pottery vessel**, eventually coming to mean **pottery/ ceramic** in a broad sense. The idea of protection also led by association to **care for/ rear/ educate**. In the case of 阝匋, **hill** 阝 229 combines with **pottery** 匋, which also acts phonetically to express **successive**, to refer to a type of **kiln** build in successive stages up a hillside (a type still found in China and Japan). It can still mean kiln in Chinese, and also came to refer to a hill with terracing. Eventually, however, 陶 and 匋 became confused. It is not clear how the lesser meaning of **happy** was acquired.

Mnemonic: **HILL SURROUNDED BY CANS AND CERAMIC VESSELS**

1651		TŌ	石塔	SEKITŌ	tombstone
		TOWER, MONUMENT	卒塔婆	SOTŌBA *	stupa
		12 strokes	五重の塔	GOJŪNOTŌ	
					five storied pagoda

土 is **earth** 60. 荅 is a CO character now used in a range of confusing meanings such as undertake and iron spike. Its etymology is obscure, though it appears to comprise **grass/ plants** 艹 9 and **join together/ fit** 合 121. Here it acts phonetically to express **build up**, to give **build up (a mound of) earth**. 1651 was then borrowed phonetically to express the **'tu'** sound of stupa (see above), a Sanskrit term for **shrine** (presumably also being felt to be semantically appropriate). **Monument** and **tower** are associated meanings.

Mnemonic: **JOIN PLANTS AND EARTH TOGETHER TO MAKE MONUMENT**

1652 搭	TŌ LOAD, BOARD 12 strokes	搭載 TŌSAI	loading
		搭乗 TŌJŌ	boarding
		搭乗券 TŌJŌKEN	boarding pass

扌 is **hand** 32. 荅 is the obscure element seen in 塔 1651 q.v., here similarly acting phonetically to express **build up**. Thus **build up with the hands**, a reference to placing one thing on top of another and hence **load**. **Board** is the intransitive version of load. Suggest taking 荅 as **plants** 艹 9 and **join together** 合 121.

Mnemonic: **HANDS JOIN PLANTS TOGETHER FOR LOADING**

1653	TŌ, mune, muna- RIDGEPOLE, BUILDING 12 strokes	病棟 BYŌTŌ	ward
		棟木 MUNAGI	ridgepole
		別棟 BETSUMUNE	outbuilding

木 is **tree/ wood** 69. 東 is **east** 184 q.v., here acting phonetically to express **center** and also lending its original connotations of **supporting pole**. Thus **central wooden supporting pole**, a reference to a **ridgepole**. Also used later to refer to a **building**.

Mnemonic: **WOOD FROM EAST BEST FOR BUILDING'S RIDGEPOLE**

1654 痘	TŌ SMALLPOX 12 strokes	天然痘 TENNENTŌ	smallpox
		水痘 SUITŌ	chicken pox
		種痘 SHUTŌ	vaccination

A character of relatively recent origin (approximately the fourth century A.D.). 疒 is **sickness** 381. 豆 is food vessel/ **beans** 1640, here unusually used in its later sense of **beans** to refer to **bean-like pustules**. Thus **sickness producing bean-like pustules**, a reference to **smallpox**.

Mnemonic: **SMALLPOX IS ILLNESS WITH BEAN-LIKE PUSTULES**

1655	TŌ, tsutsu TUBE, CYLINDER 12 strokes	円筒 ENTŌ	cylinder
		筒抜け TSUTSUNUKE	directly
		筒形 TSUTSUGATA	cylindrical

竹 is **bamboo** 170. 同 is **same** 187 q.v., here acting phonetically to express **pass (clear) through** and according to some scholars also lending connotations of having the same diameter at all points, i.e. being round. Thus (round?) **bamboo with a clear passage through it**, a reference to a **bamboo tube**. Later **tube/ cylinder** in general .

Mnemonic: **CYLINDER IS SAME SHAPE AS BAMBOO**

| 1656 稲 | TŌ, ine, ina
RICE (PLANT)
14 strokes | 水稲 SUITŌ
稲作 INASAKU
早稲田 WASEDA* | paddy rice
rice crop
place-name |

Formerly 稻. 禾 is **rice plant** 81. 舀/臽 is a CO character now meaning to bale. It comprises **hand** 爪/爫 303 and **mortar** 臼/旧 648 and appears to have originally meant hand holding mortar/ bowl. Here it acts phonetically to express **soft** and may also lend similar connotations (from the idea of material being ground in a mortar). Thus **soft rice (plant)**. Since rice plant 禾 in itself has connotations of soft, 舀 is in effect redundant. Suggest taking 旧 as **old** 648.

Mnemonic: **HAND PICKS OLD RICE PLANT**

| 1657 踏 | TŌ, fumu/maeru
TREAD, STEP ON
15 strokes | 踏破 TŌHA
踏み込む FUMIKOMU
足踏み ASHIBUMI | tramping
step into
step, standstill |

足 is **foot** 51. 沓 is a CO character meaning **connect** (etymology unclear, but apparently comprising **water** 氺 40 and **sun** 日 62 and possibly referring ideographically to the connection between these elements in the scheme of the universe). Here 沓 acts phonetically to express **come into contact with,** and almost certainly also lends similar connotations of its own. Thus **foot coming into contact with (the ground)**, a reference to **treading/ stepping on**.

Mnemonic: **FOOT STEPS ON SUNLIT WATER**

| 1658 謄 | TŌ
COPY
17 strokes | 謄本 TŌHON
謄写 TŌSHA
謄写機 TŌSHAKI | manuscript
copy
copier |

言 is **words** 274. 朕 is **royal we** (variant 朕 1603 q.v.), here acting phonetically to express **write** and probably also lending its connotations of **repetition**. Thus to **write words (repetitively?)**, i.e. **copy**. Suggest taking 月 as **moon(light)** 16, and 关 as **two** 二 61 and **fire** 火 8.

Mnemonic: **COPY TWO FIERY WORDS BY MOONLIGHT**

529

1659 TŌ, tataka*u*   闘志 TŌSHI   fighting spirit
FIGHT   闘士 TŌSHI   fighter
18 strokes   戦闘機 SENTŌKI   fighter plane

Somewhat obscure. Formerly 鬭 and earlier 鬥, showing that 鬥 is not **door/ gate** 門 211 but a derivative of 鬥. This shows **two people facing each other** 〳 〵 (variants **person** ⺅/亻 39) and **hands** 丰 (variant 屮 / 手 32), and in turn derives from a pictograph 鬥, the prototype of 1659 which clearly shows **two people hitting each other**. The later addition 斲 is a CO character meaning **carve/cut**, comprising **ax** 斤 1176 and an unclear element 豖. Here 斲 acts phonetically to express **hit** and almost certainly also lends connotations of **strike with a weapon**. 斲 was later replaced with 斗 . It is not clear if this is intended as a combination, in which case it is possibly a variant of plant upright 壴 888 (lending an idea of standing erect/ **squaring up**), or whether the elements (**food vessel** 豆 1640 q.v. and measure/ **hand** 寸 909) are used individually, in which case both could act phonetically to express **fight**, 豆 could also lend connotations of standing erect/ **squaring up**, and 寸 could lend connotations of **hand to hand** (combat). In any event, 1659 clearly has its origins in the depiction of two persons fighting each other, but now means **fight** in a broad sense. Suggest taking 鬥 as **doorway**.

Mnemonic: **FIGHT IN DOORWAY OVER HANDY FOOD VESSEL**

1660 TŌ   騰貴 TŌKI   (price-) rise
RISE, LEAP   騰落 TŌRAKU   fluctuations
20 strokes   暴騰 BŌTŌ   sharp rise

馬 is **horse** 191. 朕 is **royal we** (variant 朕 1603 q.v), here acting phonetically to express **leap** and almost certainly also lending its own connotations of raise/ rise. 1660 originally referred to a **horse leaping**. It is now used of **rise/ leap** in a broader sense, but especially of price rises. Suggest taking 月 as **moon** 16 and 关 as **two** 二 61 **fires** 火 8.

Mnemonic: **HORSE LEAPS TWO FIRES AS MOON RISES**

1661 DŌ, hora   洞察 DŌSATSU   insight
CAVE, PENETRATE   空洞 KŪDŌ   cavern, cavity
9 strokes   洞くつ DŌKUTSU   cave

氵 is **water** 40, here meaning **river/ stream**. 同 is **same** 187 q.v., here acting phonetically to express **pass clear through** and according to some scholars also lending loose connotations of round. Thus **that** (round thing?) **which a stream passes clear through**, a somewhat vague reference to a **cave**, with **penetrate** being an associated meaning. It is not clear why cliff 厂 45 or hole 穴 849 was not added for clarity, giving 峒 or 窬 or similar.

Mnemonic: **SAME WATER PENETRATES CAVE**

| 1662 | DŌ **BODY, TRUNK, TORSO** 10 strokes | 胴体 DŌTAI body, trunk
双胴船 SŌDŌSEN catamaran
胴回り DŌMAWARI girth |

月 is **flesh/ of the body** 365. 同 is **same** 187 q.v., here acting phonetically to express **big** and according to some scholars also lending loose connotations of round. The **big** (round?) **part of the body** is the **trunk/ torso**.

Mnemonic: **TORSO IS OF SAME FLESH AS BODY**

| 1663 | tōge **PASS, CREST, CRISIS** 9 strokes | 峠道 TŌGEMICHI pass
う水峠 USUITŌGE Usui Pass
四十の峠 YONJŪNOTŌGE
mid-life crisis |

A 'made in Japan' character combining **mountain** 山 24 with **up** 上 37 and **down** 下 7, to refer to **that which goes up and down a mountain**, i.e. a **pass**. **Crest** and **crisis** are associated meanings.

Mnemonic: **PASS GOES UP AND DOWN MOUNTAIN**

| 1664 | TOKU **CONCEAL** 10 strokes | 匿名 TOKUMEI pseudonym
隠匿 INTOKU concealment
秘匿 HITOKU concealment |

匚 is **box/ container** 225. 若 is **young** 886 q.v., here acting phonetically to express **put** and possibly also lending connotations of bend from its early meaning of pliant. Thus to **put something in a container** (by bending it?), which came to indicate **concealing**.

Mnemonic: **YOUNG PERSON CONCEALED IN BOX**

| 1665 | TOKU **SUPERVISE, URGE** 13 strokes | 監督 KANTOKU supervision
督励 TOKUREI encouragement
督促 TOKUSOKU urging |

目 is **eye** 72. 叔 is **uncle** 1367 q.v., here acting phonetically to express **fix (on)** and probably also lending an idea of uncle or similar senior person. Thus (uncle?) **fixing an eye** (on someone), meaning to **supervise**. **Encourage/ urge** is an associated meaning.

Mnemonic: **UNCLE'S EYE SUPERVISES**

1666		**TOKU**	篤志 TOKUSHI	benevolence
		SINCERE, SERIOUS	危篤 KITOKU	seriously ill
		16 strokes	篤と TOKUTO	seriously

馬 is **horse** 191. 竹 is **bamboo** 170, here unusually acting as a phonetic to express **step** and possibly also lending connotations of strong but supple. 1666 originally referred to a **horse stepping surefootedly** (with suppleness and strength?). **Sincere** and **serious** are borrowed meanings.

Mnemonic: **SINCERE HORSE SERIOUS ABOUT BAMBOO**

1667		**TOTSU, deko**	凸面 TOTSUMEN	convexity
		CONVEX, PROTRUSION	凸凹 DEKOBOKO	unevenness
		5 strokes	凹凸 ŌTOTSU	unevenness

A symbolic representation of **convexity**, being the opposite of concavity 凹 1032.

Mnemonic: **BOX HAS BIT PROTRUDING, MAKING IT CONVEX**

1668		**TOTSU, tsuku**	突然 TOTSUZEN	suddenly
		THRUST, LUNGE,	突入 TOTSUNYŪ	plunge
		PROTRUDE	突っ込む TSUKKOMU	thrust in
		8 strokes		

Of disputed etymology. Formerly 突 , showing **dog** 犬 17 and **hole** 穴 849. For many centuries taken to be an ideograph indicating a **dog bolting from a hole**, with the present meanings thus being seen as extended and/or associated meanings. However, some authoritative Japanese scholars take dog 犬 to be used purely phonetically to express **protrude**, to give a paradoxical **hole that protrudes**. This is seen as a reference to an ancient style of **chimney**, which instead of emerging from the roof **protruded** from the side of a dwelling. Thus **thrust out/ protrude** are seen as ancient meanings, with **lunge** being an associated meaning. The ideographic theory seems the more helpful . However, in the case of the modern form suggest taking 大 as **big** 53.

Mnemonic: **THRUST INTO BIG HOLE**

532

1669

TON	屯営 TONEI	barracks
BARRACKS, CAMP, POST	駐屯 CHŪTON	posting
4 strokes	駐屯地 CHŪTONCHI	post

Of somewhat obscure evolution, though it clearly derives from a pictograph 屯, showing a **sprouting plant** ⺗ 928 with a **bud** •. In Chinese it can still mean sprout/ shoot. Confusingly, though in compounds it sometimes lends an idea of **fresh** from its depiction of a budding plant (e.g. 895), it also seems at times to refer to a **bud that fails to open** (e.g. 1671). Some scholars believe that the latter is in fact its principal meaning, and that this led to the idea of **failing to progress** and hence **being stationary**, giving by association such meanings as **camp/ barracks/ post**. Others see the present meanings as borrowings, which seems more likely. Suggest remembering by association with **hair** 毛 210.

Mnemonic: **HAIR-LIKE SPROUTING PLANT FOUND IN CAMP**

1670

TON, buta	豚毛 TONMŌ	pig bristle
PIG, PORK	豚肉 BUTANIKU	pork
11 strokes	豚カツ TONKATSU	pork cutlet

豕 is an NGU character meaning **pig**, deriving from a rather confusingly stylised pictograph 豕. The addition of **meat**/ of the body 月 365 suggests that 1670 originally meant **pig meat/ pork**, but it is now also used of **pig** in general instead of the simpler 豕.

Mnemonic: **PIG MEAT IS PORK**

1671

鈍

DON, nibui/ru	鈍感 DONKAN	insensitivity
BLUNT, DULL	鈍才 DONSAI	stupidity
12 strokes	鈍色 NIBUIRO	dull gray

金 is **metal** 14, here meaning **metal implement**. 屯 is camp/ sprout 1669 q.v., here acting phonetically to express **blunt** and almost certainly also lending connotations of **failing to do what is expected** (from a bud that fails to blossom). Thus **blunt (and ineffective?) metal implement**, i.e. a **dull blade**. Also used of **dull** in an extended sense, as of wits and colors. Suggest remembering 屯 by association with **hair** 毛 210.

Mnemonic: **METAL BLADE TOO BLUNT TO CUT HAIR-LIKE SPROUT**

| 1672 曇 16 strokes | DON, kumoru TO CLOUD, DIM, MAR | 曇天 DONTEN cloudy sky
曇り勝ち KUMORIGACHI cloudy
花曇り HANAGUMORI
hazy spring sky |

Sun 日 62 and cloud 雲 78, to give **sun obscured by cloud**. As in English, to **cloud** is also used in extended senses such as **dim** and **mar**.

Mnemonic: **SUN IS DIMMED BY CLOUD**

| 1673 軟 11 strokes | NAN, yawarakai SOFT | 軟化 NANKA softening
軟水 NANSUI soft water
軟弱 NANJAKU weakness |

Formerly 輭. 車 is **vehicle** 31, while 耎 is a CO character meaning **soft** (comprising big 大 53 and beard 而 887, a beard being a symbol of softness). 1673 originally referred to the practice of **wrapping reeds around the wheels of a vehicle to soften the ride**, and now means **soft** in a general sense. The modern form uses **lack** 欠 471, apparently as a graphic simplification.

Mnemonic: **VEHICLE LACKS SOFTNESS**

| 1674 尼 5 strokes | NI, ama NUN, PRIESTESS | 尼僧 NISŌ priestess, nun
尼寺 AMADERA convent
比丘尼 BIKUNI *
Buddhist priestess |

尸 is **corpse/ slumped figure** 236, here meaning **injured/ maimed person**. 匕 is similarly a **slumped figure** 238, here also acting phonetically to express **stop**. 1674 originally referred to a **person too badly injured/ maimed to move**, and later came to mean **not move/ stop** in a broad sense (still a minor meaning in Chinese). It was borrowed phonetically to express the **'ni'** of **bikuni**, a Sanskrit term for **priestess** (see above), and may possibly also have been considered to lend suitable extended connotations of unswerving/ dedicated.

Mnemonic: **SLUMPED CORPSE OF NUN**

| 1675 尿 7 strokes | NYŌ URINE | 糖尿病 TŌNYŌBYŌ diabetes
尿素 NYŌSO urea
尿意 NYŌI nature's call |

Once written 屎. 屎 is **tail** 尾 1734 q.v., here in its extended sense of **genitals**. 水 is **water** 40. Thus **water from genitals**, i.e. **urine**. The modern form uses **buttocks** 尸 236 as a simplification.

Mnemonic: **'BUTTOCK WATER' REFERS TO URINE**

1676

NIN, hara*mu*
PREGNANT, SWOLLEN
7 strokes

妊婦 NINPU   pregnant woman
不妊症 FUNINSHŌ   infertility
妊娠調節 NINSHINCHŌSETSU
birth control

女 is **woman** 35. 壬 is spindle 764 q.v., here acting phonetically to express **swell** and possibly also lending its connotations of **bearing/ carrying**. Thus **swollen (carrying?) woman**, i.e. a **pregnant woman**. Suggest taking 壬 as a **hatted** ノ **samurai** 士 494.

Mnemonic: **WOMAN MADE PREGNANT BY HATTED SAMURAI**

1677

NIN, shino*bu*
ENDURE, STEALTH
7 strokes

忍耐 NINTAI   patience
忍者 NINJA   ninja (spy)
忍び込む SHINOBIKOMU
sneak into

心 is **heart/ feelings** 147. 刃 is **blade** 1446, here acting phonetically to express **bear** and also lending connotations of something **sharp and painful**. Thus to **bear something painful in the heart**, i.e. **endure**. Concealing one's pain led to the idea of being secretive and hence by association **being stealthy**.

Mnemonic: **ENDURE PAIN OF BLADE IN THE HEART**

1678

NEI, mushi*ro*
PEACE, PREFERABLY
14 strokes

安寧 ANNEI   public peace
丁寧 TEINEI   civility, care
寧日 NEIJITSU   quiet day

Once written 寍 . 宀 is **roof/ house** 28. 寍 is a now defunct character meaning **peace**. Its etymology is unclear, but it comprises **heart/ feelings** 心 147, **dish** 皿 /皿 1307, and **twisting waterweed/ seek an exit** 丂 281, and may have originally referred to **feelings of contentment when one has food** (with 丂 in some unclear phonetic role). Thus 1678 means **peace at home**. **Preferably/ rather** is an associated meaning, i.e. peace being a preferred situation. Suggest taking 丁 as **nail** 346 and 皿 as **eye** 72.

Mnemonic: **FEEL PEACEFUL HOME PREFERABLE TO NAIL IN EYE**

535

1679

粘

NEN, nebaru
STICKY, GLUTINOUS
11 strokes

粘土 NENDO   clay
粘着 NENCHAKU   adhesion
粘り強い NEBARIZUYOI tenacious

Formerly 黏 . 黍 is an NGU character meaning **(glutinous) millet**, once written 黍 and comprising **grain plant** 朿 / 朿 (variant 禾 81) and **water/ liquid** 氺 / 氺 (old form/ variant 水 40). (Distinguish 黍 from lacquer 桼 / 桼 1334, and note the different etymology.) 占 is occupy/ **divine** 1491, here acting phonetically to express **adhere/ stick** but of unclear semantic role. Thus **glutinous millet that sticks**, now **sticky/ glutinous** in general. The modern form uses **rice** 米 201.

Mnemonic: **DIVINE USING STICKY RICE?**

1680

悩

NŌ, nayamu/masu/mashii
WORRY, DISTRESS,
TEASE
10 strokes

苦悩 KUNŌ   distress
悩殺 NŌSATSU   captivation
おう悩 ŌNŌ   torment

Formerly 悩 and earlier 嫐 . 女 is **woman** 35. 甾 / 凶 is head 954 q.v., here meaning **brain/ mind** and also acting phonetically to express **torment**. According to some scholars 嫐 originally referred to the torment on a woman's mind, but in view of the connotations of nayamashii, nōsatsu (see above) bonnō (see 1717) etc., which refer to a **woman teasing/ tormenting a man**, it is far more likely that it referred from the outset to a **man being tormented by having a woman on his mind**. Though it still retains strong connotations of sexual torment it can also mean **torment/ distress** in a broader sense. The modern form uses **heart/ feelings** 忄 147. Suggest remembering 凶 as **brain** (i.e. a simplification of brain 脳 954).

Mnemonic: **WORRY AFFECTS BOTH HEART AND BRAIN**

1681

濃

NŌ, koi
THICK, DEEP, RICH
16 strokes

濃化 NŌKA   thickening
濃厚 NŌKŌ no   rich, intense
脂濃い ABURAKOI   fatty

氵 is **water** 40. 農 is **farming** 366, here also acting phonetically to express **abundant**. Thus **abundant water for farming**, which came to indicate **fertile land** and then **rich** in general. **Thick** and **deep** are associated meanings.

Mnemonic: **RICH WATER AIDS FARMING**

1682 把 HA, *toru*, -*wa*
TAKE, GRASP, BUNDLE
7 strokes

把握 HAAKU grasp
把住 HAJŪ retention
把手 TOTTE handle

扌 is **hand** 32. 巴 is **crouching figure** 145, here acting phonetically to express **grasp** and possibly also lending connotations of bending down . Thus (bend down and?) **grasp in the hand**, later **grasp** in a broad sense including the figurative. It is also used to count **armfuls/ bundles**.

Mnemonic: **CROUCHING FIGURE GRASPS BUNDLE IN HAND**

1683 HA
DOMINATION, RULE
19 strokes

覇権 HAKEN domination
覇気 HAKI ambition
制覇 SEIHA supremacy

Formerly 覇 , comprising **moon** 月 16 and 霸 . The latter is a now defunct character meaning bleach and by extension **white**. It shows **leather/ hide** 革 821 being exposed to the weather -- symbolised by **rain** 雨 3 -- and refers to a carcass being reduced to bleached white bones. Thus 覇 originally meant **white moonlight**. It acquired the meaning of **domination/ rule** as a result of its being borrowed as an elegant substitute for count/ principal person 伯 1694 q.v. (literally person 亻 39 and white 白 65, though technically white 白 is used to mean principal). Principal person came to mean ruler/ dominant person, and thus symbolised rule/ domination. The modern form uses **west** 西 152 as a simplification of rain/ weather 雨 . Suggest taking 月 as meat/ (of the) **body** 365.

Mnemonic: **BODIES IN WESTERNS DOMINATED BY LEATHER**

1684 BA, baba
OLD WOMAN
11 strokes

老婆 RŌBA old woman
産婆 SANBA midwife
鬼婆 ONIBABA witch, hag

女 is **woman** 35. 波 is **wave** 367, here acting phonetically to express **white** and also lending connotations of **white and billowing**. 1684 originally referred to an **old woman with billowing white hair**. Now **old woman** in general.

Mnemonic: **WOMAN SINKING UNDER WAVES IS OLD WOMAN**

1685

HAI, sakazuki
WINECUP, CUP(FUL)
8 strokes

玉杯 GYOKUHAI   jade cup
一杯 IPPAI   cup, full, all
杯事 SAKAZUKIGOTO
    exchange of cups

木 is **wood** 69, here meaning **wooden item**. 不 is calyx/ **not** 572 q.v., here acting phonetically to express **hold**. Thus **wooden item for holding**, i.e. a **wooden vessel**. From the outset this was associated with a **wooden winecup/ goblet**, suggesting that 不 may also have been chosen for its shape, since its early form 又 may be felt to be similar to a goblet or to the early form 🝯 of dish/ vessel 皿 1307. Note that both 盃 and 桮 are found as variants of 杯. 1685 is now also used to refer to **cup(ful)** in a broad sense.

Mnemonic: **WINECUP NOT NECESSARILY OF WOOD**

1686

排

HAI
REJECT, EXPEL,
PUSH, ANTI-
11 strokes

排除 HAIJO   removal
排水 HAISUI   drainage
排気ガス HAIKIGASU exhaust gas

扌 is **hand** 32. 非 is **not/ spreading wings** 773 q.v., here acting phonetically to express **open** and also lending its own connotations of **spread apart/ open up**. Thus to **push apart with the hands and open up**, as of doors etc. (see 1730). Later used in a range of extended/ associated meanings, such as **push aside, reject, expel**, and **anti-**.

Mnemonic: **REJECTED, BUT NOT NECESSARILY WITH THE HANDS**

1687

HAI, sutaru/reru
ABANDON(ED),
OBSOLETE
12 strokes

廃止 HAISHI   abolition
廃寺 HAIJI   ruined temple
廃り物 SUTARIMONO
    obsolete thing

Formerly 廢. 广 is **building** 114. 發/発 is discharge/ **leave** 370 q.v., here acting phonetically to express **abandon(ed)** and also lending similar connotations of **leave**. Thus an **abandoned building**, now **abandoned/ obsolete** in general.

Mnemonic: **LEAVE BUILDING TO BE ABANDONED**

| 1688 | | **HAI** **FELLOW, COMPANION,** **LINE** 15 strokes | 我輩 WAGAHAI I, me
先輩 SENPAI one's senior
輩出 HAISHUTSU
successive appearance |

車 is **vehicle** 31. 非 is **not/ spreading wings** 773 q.v., here acting phonetically to express **line up** and also lending its own connotations of **spread out**. 1688 originally referred to a **procession of vehicles**, and came to mean **line/ file** on the one hand and **co-traveler/ companion** on the other. It is also used to refer to **person(s)** in general.

Mnemonic: **COMPANIONS IN A LINE, IF NOT IN VEHICLES**

| 1689 | | **BAI, ume** **PLUM** 10 strokes | 梅花 BAIKA plum blossom
梅酒 UMESHU plum wine
梅雨 BAIU/ TSUYU*
summer rain |

Formerly 梅. 木 is **tree** 69. 每/每 is **every/** each 206 q.v., here in its early sense of **fertile growth**. Like the **peach** 桃 1646 q.v., the plum was a favorite fruit of pregnant women and was thus associated with pregnancy and hence procreation/ fertility. 1689 means literally **tree of fertility**, i.e. **plum tree**. There is a theory that 每 is used purely phonetically to express big, giving big tree, and that plum is a pure borrowing, but this is far from convincing.

Mnemonic: **EVERY TREE SHOULD BE A PLUM TREE**

| 1690 | | **BAI, tsuchikau** **CULTIVATE, GROW** 11 strokes | 培養 BAIYŌ cultivation
栽培者 SAIBAISHA grower
培地 BAICHI culture (medium) |

土 is **soil/ ground** 60. 咅 is the obscure element spit 384, here acting phonetically to express **build up** but of unclear semantic role. 1690 originally referred to **building up soil (to ensure fertility)**, and later came to mean **cultivate/ grow** in a broad sense. Suggest taking 立 as **stand** 73 and 口 as opening/ **hole** 20.

Mnemonic: **STAND IN HOLE TO CULTIVATE GROUND**

539

| 1691 | | **BAI** **ATTEND, ACCOMPANY** 11 strokes | 陪席者 BAISEKISHA attendant 陪審 BAISHIN jury 陪音 BAION harmonics |

阝 is **hill** 229. 咅 is the obscure element spit 384, here acting phonetically to express **build up** but of unclear semantic role. 1691 originally referred to **one hill 'built on' another**, i.e. a **range of hills**. By association it was later applied to **groups of things** in general, especially people, and thus came to mean **one person added to others in a group**, i.e. an **attendant/ accompanying person**. Suggest taking 立 as **stand** 73 and 口 as **opening/ hole** 20.

Mnemonic:**ACCOMPANYING ATTENDANT STANDS IN HOLE IN HILLSIDE**

| 1692 | | **BAI** **INTERMEDIARY** 12 strokes | 媒介 BAIKAI mediation 触媒 SHOKUBAI catalyst 媒体 BAITAI medium |

女 is **woman** 35. 某 is **a certain** 1811 q.v., here acting phonetically to express **seek/ inquire** and also lending its connotations of **liaison** and **matchmaking**. 1692 originally referred to making an **inquiry about a (pregnant?) woman's suitability as a prospective marriage partner** (some scholars feel rather inquiry about a woman's feelings towards marriage). From this it came to mean (be an) **intermediary** in a broad sense. See also 1818.

Mnemonic: **ACT AS INTERMEDIARY REGARDING A CERTAIN WOMAN**

| 1693 | 賠 | **BAI** **COMPENSATE** 15 strokes | 賠償 BAISHŌ compensation 賠償金 BAISHŌKIN damages 損害賠償 SONGAIBAISHŌ indemnity |

貝 is **shell/ money** 90. 咅 is the obscure element spit 384, here acting phonetically to express **compensate** but of unclear semantic role. Thus to **compensate with money**. Suggest taking 立 as **stand** 73 and 口 as **opening/ hole** 20.

Mnemonic: **COMPENSATED WITH MONEY FOR STANDING IN HOLE**

1694 伯	HAKU	伯爵 HAKUSHAKU count, earl
	COUNT, SENIOR FIGURE	伯父 OJI* uncle
	7 strokes	画伯 GAHAKU master artist

亻 is **person** 39. 白 is **white** 65 q.v., here in its literal sense of **thumb(nail)**. Since a thumb was the principal finger it often symbolised **principal/ leading**, as here. Thus **principal person**, a reference to a leader. It is now applied to a range of 'leading persons'/ **senior figures** such as elder brother, uncle, chief official etc., but is used in particular of **count/ earl**.

Mnemonic: **COUNT IS A WHITE PERSON**

1695 拍	HAKU, HYŌ	拍手 HAKUSHU hand clapping
	BEAT, TAP, CLAP	拍子 HYŌSHI beat, rhythm
	8 strokes	拍車 HAKUSHA spur

扌 is **hand** 32. 白 is **white** 65 q.v., here acting phonetically to express **beat/ tap**. It is not clear whether 白 also plays any semantic role, but it may possibly suggest either **leading** or **fingernail** (from its original meaning of thumbnail: see also 1694). Thus to **tap with the hand** (fingernail?), a reference to tapping out a beat/ tune (thereby leading a rhythm?). Now **beat/ tap** in a broader sense, as well as **clap**.

Mnemonic: **CLAP TILL HANDS GO WHITE**

1696 泊	HAKU, tomaru/meru	宿泊 SHUKUHAKU lodging
	STAY, LODGE	泊まり番 TOMARIBAN night duty
	8 strokes	一泊 IPPAKU overnight, one night's stay

氵 is **water** 40. 白 is **white** 65, here acting phonetically to express **shallow**. It is possible that originally 白 also lent its meaning of white, since white water is generally associated with shallows. However, from an early stage 1696 became associated with shallow water suitable for an **anchorage**, then came to mean **stopping place** and eventually **stop/ stay** in general.

Mnemonic: **STAY IN WHITE WATER?!**

541

1697

HAKU, sema*ru*
PRESS, DRAW NEAR
8 strokes

迫害 HAKUGAI   oppression
迫力 HAKURYOKU   force
切迫 SEPPAKU   pressure

辶 is **movement** 129. 白 is **white** 65, here acting phonetically to express **draw near** but of unclear semantic role. Thus **move and draw near**, later also used figuratively in the sense of **press/ be imminent/ be compelling.**

Mnemonic: **PRESSING MOVEMENT TURNS ONE WHITE**

1698

HAKU
SHIP, SHIPPING
11strokes

船舶 SENPAKU   shipping
舶来 HAKURAI   importation
舶用 HAKUYŌ   marine-

舟 is **boat** 1354. 白 is **white** 65, here acting phonetically to express **large** and possibly also lending a suggestion of principal/ chief (see 1694). Thus **large boat** (principal of fleet?), i.e. a **ship**, with **shipping** being an associated meaning.

Mnemonic: **WHITE BOAT USED FOR SHIPPING**

1699

HAKU, usu*i/maru/meru*
THIN, WEAK,
SHALLOW, LIGHT
16 strokes

薄着 USUGI   light clothes
軽薄 KEIHAKU   frivolity
薄皮 USUKAWA   thin skin

Formerly 薄. 艹 is **plants** 9. 溥/溥 is a CO character meaning **extensive/** pervasive, comprising **water** 氵 40 and **spread** 尃/専 564 and presumably originally meaning extensive body of water. 1699 originally meant **extensive vegetation**, i.e. **luxuriant/ dense growth**, and still retains this as a minor meaning in Chinese. Its present core meaning of **sparse/ insubstantial**, which confusingly is the opposite of its real meaning, results from borrowing. It is unclear why such a seemingly inappropriate character was borrowed.

Mnemonic: **THIN PLANT COVERING SPREAD OVER SHALLOW WATER**

542

1700	BAKU VAGUE, VAST, DESERT 13 strokes	漠然 BAKUZEN	vague
		漠漠 BAKUBAKU	vast, vague
		砂漠 SABAKU	desert

シ is **water** 40. 莫 is sun sinking in grass 788 q.v., here acting phonetically to express **smothered/ covered** and also lending its own similar connotations of **hidden**. A place where the **water is hidden/** covered (i.e. inaccessible) is a **desert**. **Vast** is an associated meaning, with **vague/ undelineated** being a further association. Suggest taking 艹 as **plant** 9, 日 as **sun** 62, and 大 as **big** 53.

Mnemonic: **IN VAST DESERT, BIG PLANTS NEED SUN AND WATER**

1701	BAKU, shibar*u* BIND 16 strokes	束縛 SOKUBAKU	restraint
		捕縛 HOBAKU	capture
		縛り首 SHIBARIKUBI	hanging

Formerly also 縛. 糸 is **thread** 27, here meaning **cord**. 尃/専 is **spread** 564 q.v., here acting phonetically to express **bind** and probably also lending connotations of **extensive**. Thus to **bind (extensively?) with cord**, now **bind** in a broad sense.

Mnemonic: **BIND WITH SPREAD THREADS**

1702	BAKU BURST, EXPLODE 19 strokes	爆発 BAKUHATSU	explosion
		爆弾 BAKUDAN	bomb
		原爆 GENBAKU	atom bomb

火 is **fire** 8. 暴 is **violence/** expose 793 q.v., here acting phonetically to express **burn** and possibly also lending connotations of **heat** and/or **violent action**. 暴 also lends its sound **BAKU** in an onomatopoeic sense. 1702 originally referred to something **burning in a fire and bursting/ exploding (violently?) with a BAKU sound**. Now **burst/ explode** in general.

Mnemonic: **VIOLENT FIRE CAUSES EXPLOSION**

1703	hako, SŌ BOX 15 strokes	小箱 KOBAKO	little box
		箱舟 HAKOBUNE	ark
		箱入り HAKOIRI	boxed

ケケ is **bamboo** 170. 相 is **mutual** 530, here acting phonetically to express **both sides** and also lending similar connotations. 1703 originally referred to bamboo frames put on either side of a cart, then came to mean **container/ box** in a broad sense.

Mnemonic: **BAMBOO SIDES MUTUALLY OPPOSED IN BOX**

1704	hada, KI **SKIN, TEXTURE, GRAIN** 6 strokes	肌色 HADAIRO flesh color 素肌 SUHADA bare skin 肌理 KIME * texture, grain

月 is **meat/ of the body** 365. 几 is **table/ desk** 832, here acting phonetically to express **cover** and possibly also lending a similar suggestion through its shape (cover often being represented by ⌒). **That which covers the meat/ body** is the **skin**. **Texture** and **grain** are associated meanings.

Mnemonic: **BODY AT DESK COVERED IN SKIN**

1705	**HACHI, HATSU** **BOWL, POT, SKULL** 13 strokes	植木鉢 UEKIBACHI plant pot 鉢巻き HACHIMAKI headband 衣鉢 IHATSU master's mantle

A relatively recent character, but of obscure and disputed etymology due to a dearth of earlier forms. 金 is **metal** 14. 本 is taken by some scholars to be **root/ source** 70, here in a sense of **base**. Thus **item with metal base**, a rather vague reference to a **bowl**. Other scholars believe that 本 derives from 米, an element felt to show a **thickly growing plant**, and that it acts here phonetically to express **big** as well as possibly lending connotations of **edible plant**. Thus **big metal item (for vegetables?)**, a similarly vague reference to a **bowl**. Neither of these theories seems especially convincing. It is equally likely that 本 is root 70 (usually pronounced HON) acting phonetically to express **basket**, specifically the NGU character HON basket 畚 (etymology unclear, but 由 is basket 399). Thus **metal basket**, i.e. **metal bowl**. The pronunciation may have changed to HATSU/ HACHI under the influence of a now defunct character with those readings 盋, which also meant (big) bowl (vessel 皿 1307 and the obscure element 犮 [see 1706], the latter acting phonetically to express big). 1705 clearly originally referred to a metal vessel, but is now used of a range of vessels, including the **skull**.

Mnemonic: **ROOTED IN METAL BOWL**

1706	**HATSU, kami** **HAIR** 14 strokes	頭髪 TŌHATSU the hair 散髪 SANPATSU haircut 髪型 KAMIGATA hairstyle

Formerly 髪. 髟 is a CO character meaning **hair**, comprising **hairs** 彡 93 and **long** 長 (variant 镸 173). 犮 is an obscure element, though an early form 犮 appears very similar to an early form 犬 of dog 犬 17. Here 犮 acts phonetically to express **grow**, while any semantic role is unclear. Thus **growing hair**, now simply **hair**. Suggest taking 友 as **friend** 214, and 彡 as **three strands**.

Mnemonic: **FRIEND'S HAIR INCLUDES THREE LONG STRANDS**

1707

BATSU, HATSU
ATTACK, CUT DOWN
6 strokes

伐採 BASSAI　　　　felling
征伐 SEIBATSU　　punishment
殺伐 SATSUBATSU na　brutal

Person 亻 39 and **halberd** 戈 493, meaning to **cut down a person with a halberd** and hence **attack**. Now also **cut down** in a broad sense. The Japanese reading BATSU/ HATSU (originally FUA, and in Chinese now FA) is onomatopoeic, expressing the sound of a sword/ halberd cutting a person down. It is also related to the adverb bassari, used of cutting people down.

Mnemonic: **PERSON ATTACKED AND CUT DOWN WITH HALBERD**

1708

BATSU, nu*ku/karu/keru/kasu*
PLUCK, EXTRACT,
MISS
7 strokes

抜群 BATSUGUN preeminence
抜け穴 NUKEANA　　loophole
手抜かり TENUKARI　omission

Formerly 拔. 扌 is **hand** 32. 友 is the obscure element seen in 1706, here acting phonetically to express **extract** but of unclear semantic role. Thus to **extract with the hand**, now **extract/ pluck** in a broad sense. **Miss (out)** is an associated meaning. Suggest taking 友 as **friend** 214.

Mnemonic: **PLUCK FRIEND AWAY BY THE HAND**

1709

BATSU, BACHI
PUNISHMENT
14 strokes

罰金 BAKKIN　　　　fine
処罰 SHOBATSU　punishment
罰当り BACHIATARI no damned

刂 is **sword/ cut** 181. 詈 is an NGU character meaning ridicule/ **criticise**, comprising **net** 罒 193 (here meaning **trap/ ensnare**) and **words** 言 274. Here 詈 acts phonetically to express **threaten** and also lends its meaning of **criticise**. Thus to **threaten someone with sword and critical words**, meaning to **rebuke**. This later came to mean **punish**.

Mnemonic: **NETTED, THEN PUNISHED WITH WORDS AND SWORD**

1710		BATSU FACTION, CLAN, LINEAGE 14 strokes	門閥 MONBATSU	lineage
			閥族 BATSUZOKU	clan
			財閥 ZAIBATSU	zaibatsu

門 is door/ **gate** 211, here symbolising **house** in a broad sense. 伐 is **cut down** 1707 q.v., here acting phonetically to express **emerge** but of unclear semantic role. The **house from which one emerges** indicates one's **clan** and by extension **lineage**, with **faction** being an associated meaning. It is not clear why a character with such sinister overtones as 伐 should be chosen as a phonetic. Though its reading BATSU is perfectly valid, it seems possible that it was confused with the graphically and phonetically similar BATSU 友` 1706, which unfortunately is an element of unclear meaning.

Mnemonic: **CLAN MEMBER CUT DOWN AT GATE**

1711		HAN, ho SAIL 6 strokes	帆船 HANSEN	sailboat
			帆柱 HOBASHIRA	mast
			帆掛ける HOKAKERU	set sail

巾 is **cloth** 778. 凡 is common/ **mediocre** 1827, here acting as a simplification of **wind** 風 198 q.v. and almost certainly also used for its shape (which may be felt to suggest a sail). Thus **'wind cloth'**, i.e. **sail**.

Mnemonic: **MEDIOCRE CLOTH USED FOR SAIL**

1712	伴	HAN, BAN, tomonau ACCOMPANY 7 strokes	同伴者 DŌHANSHA	companion
			伴奏者 BANSŌSHA	accompanist
			相伴う AITOMONAU	accompany

Of disputed etymology, though its elements are clearly **person** イ 39 and **half** 半 195 q.v. Some scholars believe that 半 originally acted phonetically to express **fat** (as well as lending similar connotations from its literal meaning of half a cow?), and that 1712 original-ly meant **fat person** before being borrowed to express **accompany**. Other scholars feel that 半 acts phonetically to express **accompany** and also lends a suggestion of **less than whole**, i.e. to the effect that **one person alone is less than whole** and thus needs **company**. The latter theory seems the more helpful.

Mnemonic: **PERSON ONLY HALF COMPLETE UNLESS ACCOMPANIED**

1713

HAN, aze
RIDGE, EDGE
10 strokes

池畔 CHIHAN edge of pond
湖畔 KOHAN lakeside
湖畔詩人 KOHANSHIJIN

Lake Poet

田 is **(paddy) field** 59. 半 is **half** 195 q.v., here in its literal meaning of **divide**. Thus **that which divides a (paddy) field**, i.e. **ridge/ raised path**. **Edge** is an associated meaning.

Mnemonic: **RIDGE DIVIDES FIELD IN HALF, FROM EDGE TO EDGE**

1714

HAN
GENERAL, TIME, CARRY
10 strokes

一般 IPPAN general
全般 ZENPAN the whole
過般 KAHAN recently

舟 is **boat** 1354 q.v. 殳 is **striking hand** 153, here acting as a causative element. 1714 originally meant to **cause a boat (to move)**, i.e. **to sail.** Since boats were also associated with **conveying** it also came to mean **convey/ carry** (a meaning now largely assumed by 搬 1716, which adds hand 扌 32). The present main meaning of **general** and the lesser meaning of **time** are both borrowed. Suggest remembering by a play on the words **hand** (as in worker) and **strike** (as in go on strike).

Mnemonic: **HAND ON BOAT GOES ON GENERAL STRIKE**

1715 販

HAN
SELL, TRADE
11 strokes

販売 HANBAI selling
市販 SHIHAN marketing
販路 HANRO market

貝 is **shell/ money** 90. 反 is **oppose** 371 q.v., here acting phonetically to express **accumulate** and also lending connotations of **exchange** from its literal meaning of turning over the hand (cf. English term turn-over). Thus to **accumulate money by exchanging** (goods for money), i.e. **sell/ trade.**

Mnemonic: **OPPOSED TO USE OF MONEY IN SELLING?!**

1716

HAN
CARRY, TRANSPORT
13 strokes

運搬 UNPAN transportation
搬送 HANSŌ conveyance
搬送帯 HANSŌTAI conveyor belt

General/ carry 般 1714 q.v., here in its original meaning of **carry**, with the addition of **hand** 扌 32. Thus to **carry by hand**, now **carry** in a broad sense.

Mnemonic: **GENERAL TRANSPORT CAN INCLUDE CARRYING BY HAND**

1717

HAN, BON, wazurau/**washii**   煩雑 HANZATSU complication

TROUBLE, PAIN,   煩悩 BONNŌ   carnal desire

TORMENT   煩労 HANRŌ   trouble, worry

13 strokes

Fire 火 8 in the **head** 頁 93, indicating **fever** and by association **torment** and **pain**. **Trouble** is a further associated meaning.

Mnemonic: **FIRE IN HEAD CAUSES TORMENT AND PAIN**

1718

HAN   頒布 HANPU   distribution

DISTRIBUTE, DIVIDE   頒行 HANKŌ   distribution

13 strokes   頒白 HANPAKU   graying hair

頁 is **head** 93, here meaning **mind**. 分 is **divide** 199. Thus a **divided mind**, later **divide** in general. **Distribute** is an associated meaning. Some scholars believe that 分 acts phonetically to express big and that 1718 originally meant big head (in a physical sense), with divide and distribute being borrowed meanings. This is not convincing.

Mnemonic: **DIVIDED HEAD DISTRIBUTES THOUGHTS**

1719

HAN   模範 MOHAN   model

MODEL, NORM, LIMITS   規範 KIHAN   standard, norm

15 strokes   範囲内 HANINAI   within limits

Obscure. 竹 is **bamboo** 170, 車 is **vehicle** 31, and 巳 is **slumped person** 768. The original meaning is believed to have been **purify a vehicle** (as part of a religious ceremony), thus indicating that 車 acts semantically. It is not clear whether the phonetic element (expressing **purify**) is 笵 or 巳 alone. There does not appear to have been any character 笵, though it is possible that it is a variant of the CO character 竾, which means bamboo fence (巴 being bending figure 145, thus giving bending bamboo, and possibly also playing some unclear phonetic role). In any event, **model** is a borrowed meaning, with **norm** being an associated meaning with model. **Limit(s)** is felt to be a further association in turn with norm (i.e. from the idea of guidelines).

Mnemonic: **PERSON SLUMPED BESIDE BAMBOO MODEL OF VEHICLE**

1720

HAN, shige*ru*
PROFUSE, RICH,
COMPLEX
16 strokes

繁盛 HANJŌ　　　　prosperity
繁雑 HANZATSU　complexity
繁殖 HANSHOKU propagation

Somewhat obscure. Formerly 每糸 . 糸 is **thread** 27. 每 is **every** 206 q.v., here acting phonetically to express **intertwine** and also lending connotations of **profusion** from its original meaning of fertile growth. 1720 originally referred to **strong cord made by intertwining numerous threads**. The reason for the later addition of **striking hand/ cause** 攵 101 is unclear, but it is believed to draw attention to the <u>making up</u> of such cord. Some scholars see the present meanings as borrowings, but it seems equally likely that the **profusion of threads** associated with 每 gave rise to the idea of **profusion** in general, with **rich** and **complex** being further associated meanings.

Mnemonic: **HAND STRIKES EVERY THREAD IN PROFUSELY COMPLEX TANGLE**

1721

HAN
FIEF, CLAN, FENCE
18 strokes

藩主 HANSHU　　　feudal lord
藩べい HANBEI　　　　　fence
加賀藩 KAGAHAN
　　　　　　　　　Kaga Clan/Fief

艹 is **grass/ plants** 9, here meaning **brushwood** (as 904). 潘 is a CO character used to refer to a tributary of the Han River. It comprises **water/ river** 氵 40 and **turn/ number** 番 196 q.v., the latter being used as the phonetic HAN but almost certainly also being used for its literal elements of **rice** 釆 (variant 米 201) and **field** 田 59, thus combining with water/ river 氵 to give a strong and appropriate suggestion of **fertile area**. In the case of 1721 潘 acts phonetically to express **fence** and almost certainly also lends a suggestion of fertile area. Thus **brushwood fence** (around fertile area?). It is still occasionally used in this meaning, but is generally used in the associated meaning of **fief** (i.e. the [fertile?] area enclosed by a fence) or the further associated meaning of **clan**.

Mnemonic: **CLAN TAKES TURNS TO USE GRASS AND WATER OF FIEF**

1722	蛮 BAN BARBARIAN 12 strokes	蛮人 BANJIN	barbarian
		蛮行 BANKŌ	barbarism
		野蛮 YABAN	barbarism

Formerly 蠻 . 虫 is **snake/ insect** 56 q.v., while 絲 is **tied together/ complicated** 581. 絲 was also used to refer to a **certain region in southern China** (largely for phonetic reasons, but it presumably also lent connotations of troublesome), a region considered **barbarous/** uncivilised, and thus it is technically the correct prototype of 1722. **Snake** 虫 was added to refer to a snake associated with the region in question (still retained as a minor meaning of 1722 in Chinese), but in time 蠻 came like 絲 to refer to the region itself and hence to symbolise **barbarity/ barbarism**. Suggest remembering 亦 by association with **red** 赤 46, taking it as **reddish**.

Mnemonic: **'REDDISH INSECT' REFERS TO BARBARIAN**

1723	BAN TRAY, BOARD, BOWL, PLATE 15 strokes	円盤 ENBAN	disc, discus
		基盤 KIBAN	base
		水盤 SUIBAN	bowl

General/ carry 般 1714 q.v., here in its original meaning of **carry**, with **dish/ bowl/ plate** 皿 1307 added. Thus **dish/ bowl/ plate for carrying things**. Later also **board/ plate** in a broader sense.

Mnemonic: **DISH IS GENERALLY CARRIED ON TRAY**

1724	HI QUEEN, PRINCESS 6 strokes	王妃 ŌHI	queen, empress
		妃殿下 HIDENKA	Her Highness
		皇太子妃 KŌTAISHIHI	crown princess

女 is **woman/ women** 35. 己 is **self/ thread** 855, here acting phonetically to express **line** and also lending similar connotations of thread/ sequence. Thus **women in a line**, a reference to **imperial consorts** and by association **queen/ princess**.

Mnemonic: **WOMAN THINKS HERSELF A PRINCESS**

| 1725 | | HI, kare, kano, are, ano
HE, THAT,
DISTANT GOAL
8 strokes | 彼氏 KARESHI he, boyfriend
彼女 KANOJO she, girlfriend
彼岸 HIGAN equinox,
other shore, goal |

亻 is **movement** (along a road) 118. 皮 is **skin** 374 q.v., here acting phonetically to express **distance** and probably also lending connotations of part (from its literal meaning of parting the skin from the flesh). Thus to **move into the distance** (thus parting?), a reference to **heading for a distant destination/ goal**. It also came to mean **yonder**, and hence **that** (over there). Its use as a **third person pronoun** results from the associated idea of **that person**.

Mnemonic: **HE HAS MOVING SKIN, DOES THAT PERSON!**

| 1726 | | HI
OPEN, DISCLOSE
8 strokes | 披見 HIKEN perusal
披歴 HIREKI disclosure
披露 HIRŌ announcement |

扌 is **hand** 32. 皮 is **skin** 374 q.v., here acting phonetically to express **open** and almost certainly also lending connotations of **pull off cover** (from its literal meaning of pulling the skin off an animal). Thus (**pull?**) **open by hand**, now **open/ disclose** in a broad sense.

Mnemonic: **SKIN ON HAND OPENED UP**

| 1727 | | HI, iyashii/shimu
LOWLY, MEAN, DESPISE
9 strokes | 卑下 HIGE humility
卑屈 HIKUTSU baseness
卑近 HIKIN na common |

Once written 畀, showing a **hand** 又 holding a **wine-pressing basket** 甶 (variant 甴 / 由 399) upside-down, in order to extract the last drops. This was considered **mean** and **petty**, leading to **mean/ lowly** in a general sense. **Despise** is an associated meaning. Suggest taking 田 as **field** 59, 十 as a variant of **ten** 十 33, and 丿 as **bits**.

Mnemonic: **MEAN AND LOWLY PERSON PICKS BITS FROM TEN FIELDS**

1728

HI, tsuka*reru*
TIRE, EXHAUSTION
10 strokes

疲労 HIRŌ   fatigue
疲れ目 TSUKAREME eyestrain
疲れ切る TSUKAREKIRU
                    be worn out

广 is **sickness** 381, here indicating **being unwell/ lacking vitality**. 皮 is **skin** 374 q.v., here indicating break down/ **collapse** and probably also lending supporting connotations of a body breaking into pieces (from its literal meaning of skin being separated from the meat). Thus to **collapse and lack vitality**, a rather vague reference to **exhaustion**.

Mnemonic: **SKIN SICKNESS CAN BE TIRESOME**

1729

HI, kō*muru*, ō*u*
SUSTAIN, COVER, WEAR
10 strokes

被害者 HIGAISHA   victim
被服 HIFUKU   clothing
被告人 HIKOKUNIN defendant

衤 is **clothing** 420. 皮 is **skin** 374, here acting phonetically to express **cover** and almost certainly lending similar connotations of its own. Thus **cover (oneself) with clothes**, i.e. **wear**. Now also used in a range of associated and extended meanings, such as **don, take on, sustain, suffer** etc.

Mnemonic: **SUSTAINED BY CLOTHES COVERING SKIN**

1730

HI, tobira
DOOR, FRONT PAGE
12 strokes

開扉 KAIHI   opening of door
門扉 MONPI   doors of gate
扉絵 TOBIRAE frontispiece

戸 is **door** 108. 非 is **not/ spreading wings** 773, here meaning literally **spreading wings/ flaps**. 1730 technically refers to the **flaps/ wings of a door**, but is generally used to refer to the **door** in its entirety, and is also used by association of **pages** (especially the **front page**).

Mnemonic: **A DOOR IS NOT A DOOR!? MUST MAKE THE FRONT PAGE!**

1731

HI
TOMBSTONE, MONUMENT
14 strokes

碑銘 HIMEI   epitaph
石碑 SEKIHI   tombstone
記念碑 KINENHI   monument

石 is **stone/ rock** 45. 卑 is **lowly** 1727, here acting phonetically to express **upright** but of unclear semantic role. 1731 originally referred to a **rock/ stone placed upright in the ground as a primitive sundial**, and then came to mean **upright stone** in a broader sense, eventually coming to mean in particular **tombstone** and **monument**.

Mnemonic: **TOMBSTONE IS A LOWLY STONE**

1732	HI, maka*ru*	罷業 HIGYŌ	strike
	CEASE, LEAVE, GO	罷免 HIMEN	dismissal
	15 strokes	罷り通る MAKARITŌRU	pass

罒 is **net** 193. 能 is **ability/ bear** 766 q.v., here acting phonetically to express **set/ leave** and possibly also lending its early meaning of **bear**. Thus to **set/ leave a net** (**for a bear?**), a very similar meaning to that of put 置 545. However, in the case of 1732 the idea of leaving something broadened to give a range of extended and associated meanings, such as **leave a place** and thus **go**, and also **abandon** and thus **cease** (doing something). Suggest taking 能 in its sense of **bear**.

Mnemonic: **CEASE WORK, LEAVING BEAR IN NET**

1733	HI, sa*keru*	回避 KAIHI	avoidance
	AVOID	不可避 FUKAHI	unavoidable
	16 strokes	避妊 HININ	contraception

辟 is an NGU character with a wide range of meanings, such as false, punish, crime, law, and ruler, while in Chinese (even after discounting the obvious borrowings) it can also mean punish, castrate, execute, wail, perverse, specious, flattery, decadent, remove, twist, open, develop, summon, and appoint. It comprises **buttocks** 尸 236, **opening/ hole** 口 20, and **needle/ sharp** 辛 1432 q.v. Buttocks 尸 and hole 口 clearly combine to give **anus**, as in 后 858 q.v. Needle 辛 is used in its sense of **pierce/ penetrate**, to give **anal penetration** (see also vaginal penetration 商 317). This core meaning gave rise on the one hand to a range of meanings associated with **torture/ punishment**, which also symbolised **law** and **authority**, and on the other to meanings associated with **sodomy**, which when used in relation to a male partner was also a symbol of **flattery**. (Note that when combined with woman 女 35 it gives an NGU character 嬖, which in Chinese means sexual partner/ lecherous/ depraved [though in Japanese it is listed with the euphemistic meaning of agreeable person]. When 嬖 is itself combined with child 童 363 it gives in Chinese a compound term meaning catamite.) In the case of 1733 辟 acts phonetically to express **evade**, though its semantic role is a matter of conjecture, and combines with **movement** 辶 129 to give **evasive movement**.

Mnemonic: **MOVE TO AVOID NEEDLE IN ANUS**

| 1734 | | **BI, o**
 TAIL
 7 strokes | 尾骨 BIKOTSU
 交尾 KŌBI
 しっ尾 SHIPPO* | coccyx <br> copulation <br> tail |

Buttocks 尸 236 and **hair** 毛 210, a reference to a **tail**. Also sometimes used to refer to **genitals** (especially male). In compounds often found as 屁 (or, early on, simply 木).

Mnemonic: **TAIL IS HAIR BELOW BUTTOCKS**

| 1735 | | **BI**
 TINY, OBSCURE,
 FAINT, SECRETIVE
 13 strokes | 微細 BISAI
 微光 BIKŌ
 微行 BIKŌ | minuteness <br> faint light <br> traveling incognito |

Once written 溦, showing **movement (along a road)** 彳 118, **hand holding stick/ force** 攴/攵 101, and **bent old man** 長 (variant 耂 117/ 173, and here meaning simply **crouched**). Thus to **make someone move (along a road) in a crouched fashion**, i.e. so as to avoid detection and hence **secretively**. The causative aspect presently faded, leaving just **move secretively**. Though this meaning is still occasionally encountered (see bikō above), 1735 is usually used in the associated meanings of **obscure, faint**, and **tiny** (i.e. from the idea of being hard to see -- see also 1227). Suggest taking 山 as **mountain** 24 and 几 as a variant of **table** 几 832.

Mnemonic: **FORCED TO MOVE TINY TABLE UP MOUNTAIN IN SECRET**

| 1736 | | **HITSU, hiki**
 MATCH,COMMON,CLOTH
 ANIMAL COUNTER
 4 strokes | 匹敵 HITTEKI
 匹夫 HIPPU
 一匹 IPPIKI | match <br> common man <br> one animal |

Once written 𠥓, showing that 匚 is not container 匚 225 but a stylised miscopying of 厂. This is itself a simplification of oppose/ **(roll of) cloth** 反 371 q.v., here in its sense of **roll of cloth**. 𠫔 shows **two rolls of cloth of equal length**. It is in effect a doubling of 厂, and in fact can refer to a specific quantity of cloth twice the length of 反 (i.e. approximately 20 m.), but is generally used in the extended sense of **equal/ match**. **Common** is an associated meaning with equal, i.e. one item much the same as any other. It is not clear how 1736 also came to be used as a **counter for animals**. Note that hiki is a Japanese (i.e. kun) reading, and not a Chinese (i.e. on) reading as popularly believed. Suggest remembering 匹 by association with **four** 四 26.

Mnemonic: **COUNT MATCHING ANIMALS -- NOT QUITE FOUR?!**

1737

HITSU, HI
FLOW, SECRETE
8 strokes

分泌 BUNPITSU   secretion
泌尿 HINYŌ   urination
泌尿器科 HINYŌKIKA   urology

氵 is **water** 40. 必 is **necessarily** 568, here acting phonetically to express **unceasingly** and possibly also lending supporting connotations of **inexorably**. Thus **unceasingly (flowing) water**. In Chinese **steady flow** is 1737's only meaning, but in Japanese it has also come by association to mean **secrete/ ooze**.

Mnemonic: **WATER NECESSARILY SECRETED**

1738

hime, KI
PRINCESS, LADY,
LITTLE, PRETTY
10 strokes

姫宮 HIMEMIYA   princess
姫垣 HIMEGAKI   low fence
洋子姫 YŌKOHIME
             Princess Yōko

Somewhat obscure. Formerly 姫匝 and earlier 𦥯, showing **woman** 夂/女 35 and also showing that **staring eye/ retainer/ guard** 臣/臣 512 q.v. is a miscopying of 𠂤/匝. Unfortunately the latter element is of obscure origin, but is known to have acted phonetically to express the name of a certain river (the **River Chi**), near which the legendary emperor **Huangti** (third millenium B.C.) is believed to have been born. 𠂤/匝 thus came to symbolise **Huangti**. 1738 originally meant **woman of the Huangti imperial family/ line**, and later came by extension to mean **princess/ noble lady** in general. **Pretty** and **little** are associated meanings. The miscopying of 匝 (intermediate form 匝) as 臣 may well have been influenced by an assumption that 1738 was intended to indicate ideographically a woman who is guarded/ protected or a woman with retainers.

Mnemonic: **EYE STARES AT PRETTY LITTLE WOMAN -- A PRINCESS**

1739

HYŌ, tadayou
FLOAT, DRIFT, BOB
14 strokes

漂白 HYŌHAKU   bleaching
漂着 HYŌCHAKU drift ashore
漂流者 HYŌRYŪSHA   castaway

氵 is **water** 40. 票 is **sign/ vote** 570 q.v., here acting phonetically to express **float/ bob** and possibly also lending loose connotations of **bobbing/ dancing** from its original meaning of **leaping flames**. Thus **float/ bob on water**.

Mnemonic: **FLOATING VOTE DRIFTING ON WATER?!**

1740 苗 BYŌ, MYŌ, nae, nawa   種苗 SHUBYŌ   seedlings
SEEDLING, OFFSPRING   苗字 MYŌJI   family name
8 strokes   苗木 NAEGI   sapling

Plants 艹 9 still in the **field** 田 59, i.e. not yet ready for cropping. **Young plants/ seedlings** also came by association to refer to human **offspring**.

Mnemonic: **PLANTS IN FIELD ARE SEEDLINGS**

1741 BYŌ, egaku   描写 BYŌSHA   depiction
DEPICT, DRAW, WRITE   点描 TENBYŌ   sketch
11 strokes   描き出す EGAKIDASU   delineate

扌 is **hand** 32. 苗 is **seedling** 1740, here acting phonetically to express **copy** and possibly also originally lending a suggestion of incomplete. Thus **copy by (free-)hand** (roughly?), now **draw/ depict** in a broader sense including the figurative.

Mnemonic: **DRAW SEEDLINGS FREEHAND**

1742 BYŌ, MYŌ, neko   愛貓 AIBYŌ   pet cat
CAT   貓背 NEKOZE   a stoop
11 strokes   シャム貓 SHAMUNEKO
     Siamese cat

Formerly 貓, i.e. with **clawed beast** 豸 1281 rather than dog/ **beast** 犭 17. 苗 is **seedling** 1740, here acting phonetically (MYŌ in Japanese, MIAO in Chinese) to express **the sound of a cat's call/ miaow** and possibly also lending connotations of little. Thus **(little?) clawed beast that cries MIAO**, i.e. **cat**.

Mnemonic: **BEAST AMONGST SEEDLINGS IS CAT**

1743 浜 HIN, hama   海浜 KAIHIN   seashore
BEACH, SHORE   浜辺 HAMABE   beach, shore
10 strokes   浜跳び虫 HAMATOBIMUSHI
     sand-hopper

Formerly 濱. 氵 is **water** 40. 賓 is **guest** 1744 q.v., here acting phonetically to express **edge** and almost certainly also lending its early meaning of **display of shells**. Thus **edge of water (where shells are to be seen?)**, i.e. **beach/ shore**. The modern form uses **soldier** 兵 578.

Mnemonic: **SOLDIERS COME BY WATER AND MAKE BEACH LANDING**

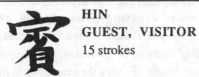

1744

HIN
GUEST, VISITOR
15 strokes

主賓 SHUHIN　　guest of honor
来賓 RAIHIN　　　guest, visitor
賓客 HINKYAKU

　　　　　　　　guest of honor

Somewhat obscure, and of confused etymology. Formerly 賓 . 貝 is **shell/ money/ valuable item** 90. (One early form 賓 shows kettle 鼑 / 鼎 / 貝 228, but this appears to be a one-off miscopying: still earlier and later forms all show shell.) 宷/宷 is a now defunct character meaning **guest**. 宀 is **roof/ house** 28, but otherwise the etymology of 宷/宷 is rather obscure. It appears to use different elements at different stages. The earliest forms such as 宷 show 丂 , which is believed to be a variant of **twisting weed** 丁 / 丂 281 q.v. and may have acted symbolically to indicate **reaching and stopping** (from its characteristic of reaching the surface and then stopping -- see the parallel with inverted foot below). Later forms such as 宷 show what appears to be a stylised version of **foot** 止 /正 129 q.v./ 41, possibly in its meaning of **stopping** and thus being similar to stopping/ inverted foot 夂 438 q.v. and giving a similar character to guest/ visitor 客 252 q.v. Note however that there is a CO character 宀 meaning curtain/ hidden/ **protected** (of unclear etymology, but possibly itself a version of foot 止 /正 -- see also 1805), and it is possible that 少 /少 derives from this, to give a literal meaning to 宷/宷 such as **person protected under a roof**. In any event, in the case of 1744 宷/宷 is known to have acted phonetically to express **display**, and probably also originally lent connotations of visitor. 1744 originally referred to **displaying shells/ valuable items** (believed to have been literally shells at first, as these were primitive symbols of wealth and ostentation, but later valuable items in general), probably on the occasion of a visit to one's home. It later came to mean **display** in a broader sense, but at a still later stage became confused with **guest/ visitor** 宷 /宷 and eventually replaced this (despite being the more complex of the two). Suggest taking 少 as a combination of **one** 一 1 and **few** 少 143.

Mnemonic: **JUST ONE OR A FEW SHELLS TO SHOW VISITOR TO HOME**

1745

HIN, shiki*ri*
FREQUENTLY, FROWN
17 strokes

頻繁 HINPAN ni　　frequently
頻発 HINPATSU　　frequency
頻度 HINDO　　　　frequency

Of confused evolution. At one early stage the same character as the NGU character 瀕, which now means **verge/ shore**. The key elements are **head** 頁 93 and **cross water** 涉 1399 q.v. (**water** 氵 40 and **walk** 歩 202). 涉 originally acted phonetically to ex-

557

press **wave/ ripple** and also lent connotations of **crossing**. Thus **ripples which cross the head**, a reference to **wrinkles** (and by association **frown**). However, the strong presence of 渉 led to 瀕 also being used to mean **cross water**, and thus at one stage 瀕 meant both wrinkles and cross water. Water 氵 was then removed to distinguish between the meanings, with the 'waterless' 頻 being used to represent wrinkles while 瀕 developed its acquired meaning of cross water, eventually coming by association to mean shore/ verge. It is not fully clear how 頻 then came to mean **frequently**. Some scholars feel it is a borrowed meaning, but it seems equally likely to be an associated meaning with wrinkle through a linking concept of many/ numerous. Confusingly, 頻 is still very occasionally interchanged with 瀕 to mean shore. It is now used only rarely to mean wrinkles/ frown, this meaning having been largely assumed by an NGU character 顰 which adds lowly 卑 1727 (the role of the latter unclear).

Mnemonic: **FREQUENTLY WALK ON ONE'S HEAD**

1746

敏

BIN
AGILE, ALERT, QUICK
10 strokes

敏速 BINSOKU   alacrity
鋭敏 EIBIN   sharpness
機敏 KIBIN   smartness

攵 is **hand holding stick/ striking hand** 101, here used to indicate a **moving hand**. 毎 is **every** 206 q.v., here acting phonetically to express **quick** and possibly also loosely lending an associated idea of rapidity from its connotations of rapid/ fertile growth. 1746 originally referred to **deftness in performing manual tasks**, then came to mean **deft/ quick/ agile** in a broader sense, including the mental.

Mnemonic: **EVERY HAND THAT STRIKES SHOULD BE AGILE**

1747

BIN, kame
BOTTLE, JUG, JAR
10 strokes

瓶詰め BINZUME   bottling
花瓶 KABIN   flower vase
釣瓶 TSURUBE*   well-bucket

Formerly 瓶. 幷/并 is **put together/ pair** 1774. 瓦 is an NGU character meaning **tile** in Japanese but also **earthenware/ vessel** in Chinese (deriving from 瓦, felt by some scholars to show interlocking tiles but by others to show two outer items 瓦 interlocking to contain an inner item 丶). 1747 originally referred to **well-buckets**, which were often earthenware and used in tandem, but now refers to a range of vessels (particularly **jar** and **bottle**). Suggest taking 丶 as **out of** 66 and 幵 as a variant of **well** 井 1470.

Mnemonic: **TILES, BOTTLES AND JARS TAKEN OUT OF WELL**

1748 扶 **FU**
HELP, SUPPORT
7 strokes

扶助 FUJO　　　　　aid
扶養 FUYŌ　　　　support
扶育 FUIKU　raising children

扌 is **hand** 32. 夫 is **man/ adult male** 573, here acting phonetically to express **help** and probably also lending its meaning. Thus **helping hand (of an adult male?)**, now generally **help/ support** in a less physical sense.

Mnemonic: **MAN GIVES HELPING HAND**

1749 怖 **FU, kowa**_i_
FEAR, AFRAID
8 strokes

恐怖症 KYŌFUSHŌ　　phobia
い怖 IFU　　　　dread, awe
恐怖小説 KYŌFUSHŌSETSU
　　　　　　　　horror story

忄 is **heart/ feelings** 147. 布 is **cloth** 778, here acting phonetically to express **fear** and possibly also lending an associated suggestion of wrapping/ **enveloping**. Thus **feelings of fear** (which envelop the heart?).

Mnemonic: **FEAR WRAPS HEART LIKE CLOTH**

1750 附 **FU**
ATTACH
8 strokes

附属 FUZOKU-　　affiliated
寄附 KIFU　　contribution
附近 FUKIN　　　vicinity

阝 is **hill** 229. 付 is **attach** 574, here acting phonetically to express **swelling** and also lending its meaning of **attach**. 1750 originally referred to a **swelling/ hillock on the side of a larger hill** (i.e. attached to it), but has now become confused with 付 itself. That is, hill 阝 has become redundant.

Mnemonic: **ATTACHED TO HILL**

1751 **FU, omomu**_ku_
PROCEED, GO
9 strokes

赴援 FUEN　　going to rescue
赴任 FUNIN　taking up post
赴任地 FUNINCHI　post, posting

走 is **run** 161, here meaning **rush**. 卜 is **divination** 91, here acting phonetically to express **announce** and also lending similar extended connotations of its own. Thus to **rush to announce** something (still a minor meaning in Chinese), later **rush to do** something in a broad sense and hence **proceed (quickly)/ go**. It has become particularly associated with proceeding to a new posting.

Mnemonic: **DIVINATION PROMPTS ONE TO PROCEED AT RUN**

1752		FU, u*ku*/*kabu*/*kaberu*/*kareru*	浮力 FURYOKU	buoyancy
		FLOAT, FLEETING, GAY	浮気 UWAKI*	inconstancy
		10 strokes	浮き世 UKIYO	fleeting world

氵 is **water/ liquid** 40. 孚 is a CO character now meaning **hatch/ brood** (over eggs). It comprises **reaching hand** 丷 303 and **child** 子 25, and is clearly related to hand reaching for child to remove it from the vagina 乳 951 q.v. It presumably has a core meaning of **assist at birth** (with hatch/ brood an associated meaning). Here 孚 acts phonetically to express **float**, and almost certainly also originally lent a meaning of **reach for a child at birth**. That is, it is almost certain that water 氵 represented **amniotic fluid** (see 409 and 227), and that 1752 originally meant **reach for a child at birth to help it 'float' forth**, before later coming to mean **float** in a general sense. **Fleeting** is an associated meaning with floating (note that in English fleet and float are etymologically the same word), with **gay** felt to be a further association with fleeting (from fleeting pleasures).

Mnemonic: **HAND PLUCKS FLOATING CHILD FROM WATER**

1753		FU	切符 KIPPU	ticket
		TALLY, SIGN	符号 FUGŌ	symbol, code
		11 strokes	符合 FUGŌ	agreement

竹 is **bamboo** 170, here indicating a **bamboo tally** cut in two and then joined upon fulfillment of an agreement (see 1195). 付 is **attach** 574, here meaning **join**. Thus 1753 originally meant **join tallies**, but later came to refer rather to the **tally** itself. **Sign** is an associated meaning.

Mnemonic: **ATTACH BAMBOO TALLIES TOGETHER**

1754	普	FU, amane*ku*	普通 FUTSŪ	ordinary
		WIDELY, GENERALLY	普遍 FUHEN	universality
		12 strokes	普及 FUKYŪ	diffusion

日 is **sun(light)** 62. 並 is **line/ row** 1775, here acting phonetically to express **weak** and almost certainly also lending connotations of **spread out**. Thus **(spread out?) weak sunlight**. Some scholars see **widely/ generally** as a borrowed meaning, others as an extended meaning from the idea of **diffuse**. Suggest taking 日 in its meaning of **day**.

Mnemonic: **GENERALLY, ONE DAY FOLLOWS ANOTHER IN A ROW**

560

1755 FU, kusaru/reru 腐心 FUSHIN pains, trouble
ROT, DECAY, BAD 腐敗 FUHAI decay, rot
14 strokes 腐れ KUSARE- worthless

肉 is **meat** 365. 府 is **government center** 575 q.v., here acting phonetically to express **rot** and possibly also lending its original meaning of storehouse. Thus **meat rotting** (in a storehouse?), now **rot/ decay** in a broad sense. Like the English term rotten, it is also used figuratively to mean **worthless**.

Mnemonic: **MEAT IN GOVERNMENT CENTER IS ROTTEN**

1756 敷 FU, shiku 敷設 FUSETSU laying
SPREAD, LAY 敷き物 SHIKIMONO rug
15 strokes 屋敷 YASHIKI residence

Formerly 尃攵 . 攵 is **striking hand/ force** 101, here meaning **apply the hand**. 尃 is **spread** 564, here also acting phonetically to express **cloth**. 1756 originally meant to **spread a cloth and apply the hand to smooth it**, later **spread/ lay** in a broader sense. Suggest taking 尃 as **beside** 方 204, **field** 田 59, **ten** 十 33, and a **bit** 丶 .

Mnemonic: **FORCED TO SPREAD OUT BESIDE TEN AND A BIT FIELDS**

1757 FU, hada 皮膚炎 HIFUEN dermatitis
SKIN 完膚 KANPU utterly
15 strokes 膚着 HADAGI underwear

Popularly believed to comprise **belly/ stomach** 胃 424 q.v. and **tiger** 卢 281, the latter being assumed to be a miscopying of **skin** 皮 374, thus giving **skin over belly** and later **skin** in general. A useful mnemonic, but incorrect (apart from the link with the belly). Old forms such as 膚 show that 田 derives from **basket** 甴 399 (now usually 由) and not belly ⊕ 424. 膚 is in fact a simplified variant of a CO character 臚 , which shows **(of the) body** 月 365 and **container** 盧 1934 q.v. (the latter comprising **basket** 田 , **vessel** 皿 1307, and **tiger** 卢/虍 , the role of which is unclear) and means both **belly** (literally **body's container**) and **skin**. That is, 1757 is 臚 minus vessel 皿 and with (of the) body 月 in a different position. The relationship between belly and skin is not fully clear. Some scholars believe it is a natural association (the belly showing an expanse of skin), while others feel that because 膚 had the same pronunciation as a word for **cover**, 膚 could also be interpreted as that **which covers the body**.

Mnemonic: **SKIN FROM A TIGER'S BELLY**

1758		FU **LEVY, TRIBUTE, ODE** 15 strokes	賦課 FUKA	levy, tax
			賦詩 FUSHI	writing poetry
			月賦 GEPPU	monthly payment

貝 is **shell/ money** 90, here meaning **valuable item(s)**. 武 is **warrior** 781, here acting phonetically to express **divide** and probably also originally lending its connotations of soldier. Thus to **divide valuable assets**, probably originally a reference to soldiers sharing the spoils of a campaign. Giving out valuable items led by association to **paying tribute**, both in the form of a **levy** and in the eulogistic form of an **ode**.

Mnemonic: **WARRIOR PAYS TRIBUTE IN SHELL-MONEY**

1759		FU **NOTATION, GENEALOGY** 19 strokes	楽譜 GAKUFU	musical score
			系譜 KEIFU	genealogy
			年譜 NENPU	
				chronological record

言 is **words/ speak** 274, here meaning **express/ state**. 普 is **widely** 1754 q.v., here acting phonetically to express **in sequence** and possibly also lending its own similar connotations of **in a line** from its row/ line element 並 (1775). Thus to **state/ express in sequence**, leading to **chronology/ genealogy** on the one hand and **(musical) notation** on the other.

Mnemonic: **GENEALOGY WIDELY SPOKEN OF**

1760		BU, anado*ru* **SCORN, DESPISE** 8 strokes	侮辱的 BUJOKUTEKI	insulting
			軽侮 KEIBU	contempt
			侮慢 BUMAN	offense, insult

イ is **person** 39. 每 is **every** 206 q.v., here acting phonetically to express **ridicule/ insult** and possibly also lending connotations of profusely. Thus to **insult a person** (profusely?), with **scorn/ despise** being an associated meaning.

Mnemonic: **DESPISE EVERY PERSON**

1761		BU, ma*u* **DANCE, FLIT** 15 strokes	舞台 BUTAI	stage
			舞子 MAIKO	dancing girl
			振舞い FURUMAI	behavior

Dancing person 無 796 and **opposed feet** 舛 1211, the latter indicating **footwork** and thus reinforcing 無. Suggest taking 無 as a **wheatsheaf**, 夕 as **night** 44, and 中 as a variant of **well** 井 1470.

Mnemonic: **DANCE NIGHTLY AMONGST WHEATSHEAFS BESIDE WELL**

1762 封 **FŪ, HŌ**　　　封筒 FŪTŌ　　　envelope
CLOSE OFF, FIEF　封鎖 FŪSA　　　blockade
9 strokes　　　　封建 HŌKEN　　　feudalism

Once written 半殳 and originally 半, showing that 圭 is not doubled/piled **earth** 土 60 (see also 819) -- though this would be semantically appropriate -- but a derivative of a **bushy branched** (and originally thick trunked) **tree** 半 / 半 (tree normally written 木 / 木 69). The tree was used to **block a road**, thus giving **close off** and by extension **closed off area**, with **fief** being an associated meaning. **Hand**/ measure 寸 909 q.v. was added later to show **deliberate action** (with the hand). Suggest taking 圭 as **double earth**.

Mnemonic: **HAND DOUBLES UP EARTH TO CLOSE OFF FIEF**

1763 伏 **FUKU, fusu/seru**　　起伏 KIFUKU　　undulations
CROUCH, HIDE, AMBUSH　潜伏 SENPUKU hiding, lurking
6 strokes　　　　　伏して FUSHITE　　humbly

Obscure, though its elements are (and have been since its ancient origin) **person** 亻 39 and **dog** 犬 17. Its oldest known meaning is **crouch**, and some authoritative Japanese scholars believe it is an ideograph intended to indicate a **dog crouching low when barking at a person**. However, as an ideograph it clearly has a vast range of potential meanings, and one such specific interpretation seems a little forced. It seems equally likely that 犬 once acted phonetically to express **crouch**, thus giving **crouching person** (possibly one crouching like a dog). In any event, **hide** is an associated meaning with crouch, and **ambush** is a further association.

Mnemonic: **DOG CROUCHES TO AMBUSH PERSON**

1764 **FUKU, haba**　　　振幅 SHINPUKU　　amplitude
WIDTH, SCROLL　画幅 GAFUKU　picture scroll
12 strokes　　　横幅 YOKOHABA　　breadth

巾 is **cloth** 778. 畐 is **full** 386, here also acting phonetically to express **width**. Thus the **full width of (a roll of) cloth**, later **width** in general. **Scroll** is an associated meaning with roll of cloth. Suggest taking 畐 as **field** 田 59, opening/ **entrance** 口 20, and **one** 一 1.

Mnemonic: **ONE CLOTH SPANS WIDTH OF ENTRANCE TO FIELD**

1765   FUKU, ōu, kutsugaeru/su 覆面 FUKUMEN   mask
OVERTURN, COVER   転覆 TENPUKU   overturn
18 strokes   覆水 FUKUSUI   spilt water

Correctly written 覆 , showing 西 rather than **west** 西 152. 西 derives from a pictograph of an **upturned dish** 丙. 復 is **again/ return** 782 q.v., here acting phonetically to express **invert/ overturn** and also lending its own connotations of reverse. Thus to **turn a dish over**, giving both **overturn** and **cover**. Overturn is now also used in a figurative sense.

Mnemonic: **WEST OVERTURNED AGAIN**

1766 払 FUTSU, harau   払い戻す HARAIMODOSU   refund
PAY, SWEEP AWAY, RID   払底 FUTTEI   shortage
5 strokes   払い出す HARAIDASU   drive out

Formerly 拂 . 扌 is **hand** 32. 弗 is **unwind/ disperse** 567, here acting phonetically to express **sweep** and also lending similar connotations of **remove**. 1766 originally referred to **sweeping something away with the hand,** and was later also used to mean **rid** in a broad sense. It is particularly used of ridding oneself of a debt, i.e. by means of **paying**. Suggest taking ム as **nose** 134.

Mnemonic: **HAND GIVES SWEEPING BLOW TO NOSE TO GET PAYMENT**

1767 沸 FUTSU, waku/kasu   沸点 FUTTEN   boiling point
BOIL, GUSH   沸き立つ WAKITATSU   seethe
8 strokes   沸き出る WAKIDERU   gush forth

氵 is **water** 40. 弗 is **unwind/disperse** 567, here acting phonetically to express **emerge** and also lending its own connotations of **away/ out**. 1767 originally referred to **water gushing out (of the ground)**, but is now more commonly found in the associated meaning of **boil** (from the idea of bubbling up).

Mnemonic: **WATER 'UNWINDS' WHEN IT BOILS**

1768		FUN, magi*reru/rasu/rawashii*	紛失 FUNSHITSU	loss
		CONFUSION, STRAY	紛争 FUNSŌ	dispute
		10 strokes	紛紛 FUNPUN	in confusion

糸 is **thread** 27. 分 is **divide** 199 q.v., here acting phonetically to express **sort/ arrange** and probably also lending similar connotations of **bringing about order by separation**. Thus to **(separate and?) sort threads**. The present meaning of **stray/ be confused** is a borrowing.

Mnemonic: **DIVIDED THREADS GO ASTRAY, CAUSING CONFUSION**

1769		FUN	雰囲気 FUNIKI	atmosphere
		ATMOSPHERE, AIR	霧雰 MUFUN	misty air
		12 strokes	霜雰 SŌFUN	frosty air

雨 is **rain** 3, here indicating **weather conditions** in a broad sense and by extension **atmosphere**. 分 is **divide** 199, here acting phonetically to express **powder** (namely 粉 577, of which it can in effect be considered a simplification). 1769 refers to **conditions in which the atmosphere becomes 'powdery'**, such as when it snows, sleets, drizzles, is misty, etc. It is also used of **unclear air**, and of **atmosphere** in a figurative sense. Note that in Chinese 1769 has now been largely replaced by 氛 , a CO character (of long standing) which uses vapors 气 11 instead of rain/ weather/ atmosphere 雨 .

Mnemonic: **RAIN DIVIDES THE ATMOSPHERE**

1770		FUN, fu*ku*	噴火 FUNKA	eruption
		EMIT, SPOUT, GUSH	噴水 FUNSUI	fountain
		15 strokes	噴き出す FUKIDASU	spurt out

Somewhat obscure due to the obscure nature of 賁 This is an NGU character with a meaning of decorate/ ornament, but in Chinese it can also mean large, strenuous, bright, honor, and defeated. Its early form 賁 shows **shell/ money** 貝 90 and what appears to be **three plants** 艸 (plant 屮 9: note that 艸/卉 is an NGU character meaning **grass/ plants**). Its core meaning is not clear, but in compounds it often seems to be associated with **swelling/ rising/ building up**, suggesting that either the plants symbolised growth and by extension growing big/ swelling or else they became reinterpreted as hands 丫 raising/ offering something up. In any event, in the case of 1770 賁 is known to have lent its sound (originally **PON**) onomatopoeically, combining with **mouth/ say** 口 20 to give **make a PON sound with the mouth**, i.e. **snort** or **puff** (i.e. a sound building up within the mouth and then bursting forth?). Snort and puff are still retained as minor meanings in Chinese. By extension this came to mean **vent/ emit** in a broad sense, including **spout/ gush**. Suggest taking 卉 as a **trebling of ten** 十 33 and 口 in its sense of **opening**.

Mnemonic: **THIRTY SHELLS GUSH FROM OPENING**

565

1771	FUN	古墳 KOFUN	tumulus
	(BURIAL-) MOUND	墳墓 FUNBO	tomb
	15 strokes	墳墓の地 FUNBONOCHI	
			birthplace

土 is **earth/ ground** 60. 賁 is the obscure element seen in 1770 q.v., here acting phonetically to express **swelling** but of unclear semantic role (though it may possibly lend its own connotations of swelling). Thus a **swelling of earth**, i.e. **mound**. It is now used especially of **burial mounds**. Suggest taking 卉 as a trebling of **ten** 十 33 and 貝 as **shell** 90.

Mnemonic: **THIRTY SHELLS FOUND IN EARTH OF BURIAL MOUND**

1772	FUN, ikidō*ru*	憤慨 FUNGAI	indignation
	INDIGNANT, ANGRY	憤怒 FUNDO	rage
	15 strokes	義憤 GIFUN	
			righteous indignation

忄 is **heart/ feelings** 147. 賁 is the obscure element seen in 1770 q.v., here acting phonetically to express **overflow/ burst forth** but of unclear semantic role (though it may possibly lend its own connotations of building up). Thus **feelings bursting forth**, indicating **indignation**. Suggest taking 卉 as a trebling of **ten** 十 33 and 貝 as **shell** 90.

Mnemonic: **THIRTY SHELLS CAUSE INDIGNANT FEELINGS**

1773	HEI	丙種 HEISHU	C class
	C, 3RD	甲乙丙 KŌOTSUHEI	ABC/ 123
	5 strokes	丙 HINOE*third calendar sign

In ancient times written as 冈 or 内, showing a **(large) altar with sturdy legs**. Later forms such as 丙 show an **item** 一 placed on the altar (as altar 丁 / 示 695 q.v.). 1773 was later borrowed to express **third** in a sequence. Suggest taking it as **inside** 内 364 and **one** 一 1, with a play on 'one'.

Mnemonic: **THIRD ONE INSIDE IS RATED C**

1774

HEI, awa*seru*
UNITE, JOIN
8 strokes

合併 GAPPEI   merger
併用 HEIYŌ   joint use
併発 HEIHATSU complication

Formerly 倂 or 併. イ is **person** 39. 幵/幷 is an NGU character meaning **put together**. Some scholars take its earliest form 幵 to show **two** stylised **persons** 𠆢 (variant 𠆢 39) **linked** by the symbol **two** ニ 61, here doubled for emphasis. However, since 千 could mean two thousand (see 47) it is unlikely that it would be used in a totally different sense here, and it seems more likely that 幵 shows **two persons** 𠆢 and **matching stakes** 幵/开 272 (especially in view of the existence of fence 屏 1777 q.v.), thus giving the idea of **matching persons** and hence **going together**. In any event, the original meaning was clearly **two persons together**, with the later person イ presumably merely for emphasis. This came to symbolise **uniting** in a broad sense. Suggest taking ヽ/ as **out of** 66 and 开 as a variant of **well** 井 1470.

Mnemonic: **UNITE TO GET PERSON OUT OF WELL**

1775

HEI, nami, nara*bu/beru/bi*
ROW, LINE, RANK WITH,
ORDINARY
8 strokes

並行 HEIKŌ   parallelism
並木 NAMIKI   line of trees
月並 TSUKINAMI
    commonplace

Formerly 竝, showing a doubling of **standing person** 立 73. 1775 originally meant **line of standing people**, and now means **row/ line** in a broad sense. It also came to mean **rank alongside** and by association **be ordinary** (cf. English term rank and file). Suggest taking 业 as a Roman **two** and ヽ/ and ヽ/ as **eight** 66 (i.e. two eights).

Mnemonic: **LINE UP IN TWO ROWS OF EIGHT**

1776

HEI, gara, e
HANDLE, PATTERN,
POWER, NATURE
9 strokes

黄柄 ŌHEI   arrogance
家柄 IEGARA   pedigree
大柄 ŌGARA big frame/ pattern

木 is **wood** 69. 丙 is **third** 1773 q.v., here acting phonetically to express **grasp** and probably also lending connotations of **sturdy** from its literal meaning of sturdy altar. Thus **(sturdy?) wooden part that is grasped**, a reference to a **handle**. It is not clear how it acquired its other meanings, but they are assumed to be borrowings (though **power** may result from the idea of a lever).

Mnemonic: **WOOD OF THIRD RATE NATURE USED FOR HANDLE**

1777		**HEI**	板塀 ITABEI	board fence
		FENCE, WALL	土塀 DOBEI	earthen wall
		12 strokes	塀越し HEIGOSHI	over fence

Formerly 土屛. A 'made in Japan' character formed by adding **earth** 土 60 to the NGU character **fence/ wall/ screen** 屛/屏 . The latter comprises **corpse** 尸 236, here acting as a simplification of **building** 屋 236, and put together 幷/并 1774 q.v., here acting phonetically to express **block/ screen** and probably also lending connotations of **matching stakes** from its 幵/开 element (see also 272). Thus 屛 literally means **that (matching stakes?) screening a building**, i.e. a **fence**, later **wall/ screen** in a broader sense. Despite the addition of earth 土 in the case of 塀 1777, presumably originally intended to give wall but not fence, 1777 can now also be used of fence. Suggest taking ⺍ as **out of** 66 and 开 as a variant of **well** 井 1470.

Mnemonic: **CORPSE TAKEN OUT OF WELL BEHIND EARTHEN WALL**

1778		**HEI**	紙幣 SHIHEI	paper money
		OFFERING, MONEY	貨幣 KAHEI	coin, money
		15 strokes	御幣 GOHEI	paper strips
				in Shinto shrine

Of confused evolution. Formerly also written 㡀攵. 攵 is striking hand 101, here meaning simply **use of the hand** (though it is not clear why hand/ careful use of the hand 寸 909 q.v. was not used). Opinion is divided as to whether 㡀 is **cloth** 巾 778 plus four (small) **bits** ⺍ or a slightly modified combination of cloth 巾, two bits 八, and **small** 小/⺌ 36 (the latter seeming the more likely). 敝 referred to the practise of **cutting up (i.e. by hand) small bits of cloth (later paper) as symbolic offerings to the gods**, now associated with Shintoism but also once found in ancient China. It also came to mean **my/ humble**, by association with the idea of making a humble offering (note that 敝 does in fact exist independently in Chinese with a main meaning of my/ humble, whereas in Japanese this is now conveyed by 弊 1779 q.v.). A further cloth 巾 was added at some stage, presumably to draw attention to the offering itself. Cloth/ paper offering was later applied by association to **paper money**, and eventually was used of **money** in a broad sense including coin. The idea of making an offering to the gods also came to symbolise repentance over a wrongdoing, and later confusingly to symbolise **wrongdoing** itself, but this meaning is now conveyed by 弊 1779 q.v. Suggest taking 攵 in its sense of **force**.

Mnemonic: **FORCED TO MAKE OFFERING OF MONEY AND BITS OF CLOTH**

1779		**HEI** **MY (HUMBLE), EVIL, EXHAUSTION** 15 strokes	弊社 HEISHA	our company
			疲弊 HIHEI	exhaustion
			弊害 HEIGAI	evil, abuse

Formerly 獘, with **dog** 犬 17 (at one stage miscopied as big 大 53) and **hand cutting cloth/ paper strips** 敝 1778 q.v. The latter acts phonetically to express **collapse** and may also lend connotations of breaking into pieces (see 1728). 1779 originally referred to **collapsing like a dog**, i.e. with **exhaustion** (cf. English dog tired). It is still occasionally used in this sense, but became confused with 幣 1778 q.v. and adopted the latter's one-time meanings of **my/ humble** and **wrongdoing/ evil,** which are now its main meanings. Suggest taking 廾 as a stylised combination of two **tens** 十 33 (i.e. **twenty**), and 敝 as **cloth** 巾 778, **bits** 丷, and **force** 攵 101.

Mnemonic: EVILLY FORCED TO CUT MY CLOTH INTO TWENTY STRIPS

1780		**HEKI, kabe** **WALL** 16 strokes	壁画 HEKIGA	mural
			岩壁 GANPEKI	rock face
			壁紙 KABEGAMI	wallpaper

土 is **earth** 60, here meaning **earthen embankment**. 辟 is anal penetration 1733 q.v., here acting phonetically to express **surround** but of unclear semantic role (though it may possibly lend its later connotations of turn). Thus **earthen embankment that surrounds (a building)**, a reference to a **wall** (now in a broad sense). Suggest taking 辟 literally as **anus** 启 (buttocks 尸 236 and opening/ hole 口 20) and **needle** 辛 1432.

Mnemonic: SITTING ON EARTHEN WALL CAN BE LIKE NEEDLE IN ANUS

1781		**HEKI, kuse** **HABIT, KINK** 18 strokes	盗癖 TŌHEKI	kleptomania
			習癖 SHŪHEKI	habit
			癖毛 KUSEGE	kinky hair

An indelicate character. 疒 is **sickness** 381. 辟 is **anal penetration/ sodomy** 1733 q.v., here acting phonetically to express **build up** and also lending an idea of **blocked anus.** 1781 originally referred to **constipation**, and can still mean this in Chinese. It later acquired a meaning of (pathologically?) **deviant habits** as a result of the strong presence of **sodomy** 辟 and of confusion with female sexual partner 嬖 1733 (literally sodomy 辟 with a woman 女 35) and its male equivalent 僻, an NGU character now meaning prejudice/ bias but in Chinese still having connotations of dissolute behavior (combining person 亻 39 [here meaning man] and sodomy 辟). **Deviant habits** then led on the one hand to **habits** in general and on the other to **kink,** i.e. something not straight/ normal (which like the English term is used both physically and figuratively). Suggest taking 辟 literally as **anus** 启 (buttocks 尸 236 and opening/ hole 口 20) and **needle** 辛 1432.

Mnemonic: SICK AND KINKY HABIT OF NEEDLE IN ANUS

1782 **HEN, kata***yoru*
INCLINE, BIAS
11 strokes

偏向 HENKŌ inclination
偏見 HENKEN prejudice
偏屈 HENKUTSU bigotry

亻 is **person** 39. 扁 is **doorplate** 785 q.v. (literally **door** 戸 108 and **writing tablets** 冊 874), here acting phonetically to express **incline/ lean** and possibly also lending its own connotations of **to one side**. 1782 originally referred to a **person who leans to one side/ limps**, i.e. a **cripple**, but later came to mean **lean/ incline** in a broader sense, including **bias**. Cripple/ limp is now conveyed by the NGU character 蹁, which uses foot/ leg 足 51.

Mnemonic: **PERSON INCLINED TO LEAVE WRITING TABLETS AT DOOR**

1783 **HEN, amane***ku*
WIDELY, EVERYWHERE
12 strokes

普遍性 FUHENSEI universality
遍在 HENZAI ubiquity
一遍 IPPEN (all at) once

辶 is **movement** 129. 扁 is **doorplate** 785 q.v. (literally **door** 戸 108 and **writing tablets** 冊 874), here acting phonetically to express **roundabout/ indirect** and possibly also lending its own connotations of **to one side** (and thus not straight). Thus **move in a roundabout fashion**, leading by association to **widely** and **everywhere**. Note that 1783 can be interchanged with an NGU character 徧, which uses movement 彳 118 instead of movement 辶.

Mnemonic: **MOVE WIDELY, LEAVING WRITING TABLETS AT DOORS**

1784 **HO, to***ru*/**ra***eru*,
tsuka*maru*/*maeru*
SEIZE, CAPTURE
10 strokes

捕獲 HOKAKU seizure
捕らえ所 TORAEDOKORO point
捕まえ所 TSUKAMAEDOKORO
hold

扌 is **hand** 32. 甫 is **begin** 970 q.v., here acting phonetically to express **envelop** but of unclear semantic role. Thus to **envelop with the hand**, i.e. **seize/ capture**. Suggest taking 甫 as **use** 用 215, **needle** 十 33, and **point** ヽ.

Mnemonic: **HAND SEIZES NEEDLE TO USE POINT**

1785 浦 **HO, ura** / **COAST, INLET, BAY** / 10 strokes

浦波 URANAMI breaker
浦風 URAKAZE bay breeze
浦里 URAZATO coastal village

氵 is **water** 40. 甫 is **begin** 970 q.v., here acting phonetically to express **edge** but of unclear semantic role (though it may possibly lend loose connotations of **beginning/ edge**). Thus the **water's edge**. In Chinese usually associated with the bank of a river, but in Japanese with the shore of the sea. Suggest taking 甫 as **use** 用 215, **needle** 十 33, and **point** 丶.

Mnemonic: **USE COMPASS NEEDLE POINT TO FIND INLET AND WATER**

1786 舖 **HO** / **SHOP, LAY, PAVE** / 15 strokes

店舖 TENPO shop, store
舖装 HOSŌ paving
舖装道路 HOSŌDŌRO sealed road

Of confused and somewhat obscure evolution. Once written 鋪, showing **metal** 金 14 and **begin** 甫 970 q.v. The latter is felt by some scholars to have been used phonetically to express **turn** (with any semantic role unclear), to give **metal item that turns**, a reference to a type of **lock**. This is then assumed to have been borrowed to express **lay/ spread**. However, there is little evidence to support this, and it seems equally likely that 甫 is used as a simplification of **spread** 尃 564 q.v., and that 1786 originally meant **spread metal** (i.e. gild, plate, or similar) before coming to mean **spread/ lay** in a broader sense. In any event, in Japanese **spread/ lay** came in particular to have associations with **paving**. **Shop** is a later borrowing, and as a result of this new meaning metal 金 14 was replaced by the semantically more appropriate **quarters/ building** 舎 700. Note that in Chinese 鋪 still exists and is used to mean **spread/ lay**, while 舖 is used to mean **shop**. Suggest taking 甫 as **use** 用 215, **needle** 十 33, and **point** 丶.

Mnemonic: **USE NEEDLE POINT TO PAVE SHOP QUARTERS?!**

1787 募 **BO, tsunoru** / **GATHER, RAISE, ENLIST** / **GROW INTENSE** / 12 strokes

募集 BOSHŪ recruitment
募金 BOKIN fund raising
応募 ŌBO response to call

力 is **strength/ effort** 74. 莫 is **sun sinking among plants** 788 q.v., here acting phonetically to express **seize/ take** and probably also lending its connotations of **cover/ enfold**. 1787 originally meant to **make efforts to bring someone into one's fold**, and thus came to mean **raise/ enlist/ gather**. Like the English term **gather** in expressions such as a gathering storm, it also came to mean **grow intense/ strong**. Suggest taking 莫 as **grass** 艹 9, **sun** 日 62, and **big** 大 (variant 大 53).

Mnemonic: **BIG EFFORT TO GATHER GRASS WHILE SUN SHINES**

1788 BO, shita*u* 慕情 BOJŌ　　　longing
　　　YEARN, ADORE, DEAR　敬慕 KEIBO　　admiration
　　　14 strokes　　　　　　慕心 BOSHIN　　yearning

小 is **heart/ feelings** (variant 心 147).　莫 is sun sinking among plants 788 q.v., here acting phonetically to express **seek** and possibly also lending its connotations of envelop. Thus to **seek something with the heart** (something which envelops the heart?), a reference to **yearning/ longing**. **Dear** and **adore** are associated meanings. Suggest taking 莫 as **grass** サ 9, **sun** 日 62, and **big** 大 (variant 大 53).

Mnemonic: **BIG YEARNING IN HEART TO LIE ON SUNNY GRASS**

1789 BO, ku*reru/rasu* 暮春 BOSHUN　　late spring
　　　LIVE, SUNSET, END　夕暮れ YŪGURE　　evening
　　　14 strokes　　　暮らし方 KURASHIKATA lifestyle

Sun setting among plants 莫 788 q.v. with an extra **sun** 日 62 added after the original meaning became vague. Thus **sunset**, with **end** being an associated meaning. **Live** is also felt to be an associated meaning, from the idea of surviving/ seeing out another day (it still generally has connotations of making a living/ getting by). Suggest taking 莫 as **plants** サ 9, **sun** 日, and **big** 大 (variant 大 53), with the extra 日 in its sense of **day**.

Mnemonic: **LIVE TO SEE SUN SET AMONG BIG PLANTS AT END OF DAY**

1790 BO, HAKU　　　　　名簿 MEIBO　　(name) register
　　　REGISTER, RECORD(S)　簿記 BOKI　　　bookkeeping
　　　19 strokes　　　　　　帳簿 CHŌBO　　register, lease

Formerly 簿 . 竹 is **bamboo** 170, here indicating **bamboo tablets used for keeping records**. 溥 / 溥 is **extensive** 1699, here acting phonetically to express **bind** and probably also lending its meaning of **extensive**. 1790 originally referred to an (extensive?) **collection of bamboo tablets bound together**, i.e. a **register/ set of records**. Suggest taking 溥 literally as **water** 氵 40 and **spread** 專 564.

Mnemonic: **WATER SPREADS OVER BAMBOO REGISTER**

1791 芳 HŌ, kanbashii　　　　芳香 HŌKŌ　　　fragrance
FRAGRANT, GOOD, YOUR 芳志 HŌSHI　your kindness
7 strokes　　　　　　　芳紀 HŌKI　　　girl's age

艹 is **plant** 9. 方 is **side/ direction** 204, here acting phonetically to express **fragrant** and possibly also lending its meaning of direction. Thus **fragrant plant** (fragrance from direction of plant?), now **fragrant** in a broad sense. Also used of **good** in a broad sense, and as a polite reference to the **second person/ you.**

Mnemonic: **FRAGRANT SMELL FROM DIRECTION OF PLANT**

1792 邦 HŌ　　　　　　　邦画 HŌGA　Japanese picture
COUNTRY, JAPAN　連邦 RENPŌ　　　federation
7 strokes　　　　　本邦 HONPŌ　　our country

 is a variant of **bushy tree used as barrier** ‡ / ‡ / ‡ 1762 q.v., while β is **village** 355. Thus **village of barred access**, indicating a **guarded area**. This later broadened to mean **region** or **country**. In Japanese only it has also acquired associations with **one's own country**, i.e. **Japan**. Suggest taking ‡ as a **(bent) telegraph pole.**

Mnemonic: **JAPAN A COUNTRY WHERE VILLAGES HAVE BENT TELE-GRAPH POLES**

1793 奉 HŌ, BU, tatematsuru　　奉仕 HŌSHI　　　service
OFFER, RESPECTFUL　奉納 HŌNŌ　　　offering
8 strokes　　　　　信奉 SHINPŌ　faith, belief

Once written 𡴭, showing **two hands** 𠂇𠂇 **offering** up a **thickly growing plant** 𡳾 (variant 㞢 42), either as tribute to a lord or in a religious ritual. Later forms such as 𡴭 show an additional **hand** 𠂇 32 (now 手). This came to mean **offer** in general and by association **show respect**. Note that there is an NGU character 捧, which adds yet another hand 扌 32 and is to all intents and purposes interchangeable with 1793. Suggest taking 夫 as **two** 二 61 and **big** 大 53, and 丰 as **a club with nails through it.**

Mnemonic: **RESPECTFULLY OFFER CLUB WITH TWO BIG NAILS**

1794 抱 HŌ, [i]daku, kakaeru　抱き付く DAKITSUKU　　hug
EMBRACE, HUG, HOLD　抱懐 HŌKAI　cherishing
8 strokes　　　　　抱え込む KAKAEKOMU　hold

扌 is **hand** 32, here meaning **arm(s)**. 包 is **wrap/ envelop** 583. Thus to **wrap/ envelop with the arms**, i.e. **hug/ embrace**. Also used figuratively.

Mnemonic: **TO EMBRACE IS TO ENVELOP WITH THE ARMS**

| 1795 | | HŌ, awa
FROTH, BUBBLE, FOAM
8 strokes | 気泡 KIHŌ
発泡 HAPPŌ
泡立つ AWADATSU | air bubble
foaming
bubble, froth |

冫 is **water** 40. 包 is **wrap/ envelop** 583. In Chinese 1795 can mean either to **envelop with water**, i.e. **immerse**, or **that which envelops water**, i.e. **froth/ foam**, but in Japanese almost always has the latter meaning.

Mnemonic: **WATER WRAPPED IN FROTHY BUBBLES**

| 1796 |  | HŌ
PLACENTA, WOMB
9 strokes | 胞子 HŌSHI
胞衣 HŌI/ ENA*
細胞 SAIBŌ | spore
placenta
cell |

Flesh/ of the body 月 365 and **wrap/ envelop** 包 583. **That part of the body which envelops** is the **womb**, with **placenta** being an associated meaning.

Mnemonic: **WOMB IS PART OF THE BODY THAT ENVELOPS**

| 1797 | | HŌ
SALARY, PAY
10 strokes | 俸給 HŌKYŪ
年俸 NENPŌ
俸ろく米 HŌROKUMAI | salary, pay
annual salary

rice allowance |

Offer 奉 1793 with **person** 亻 39 added to indicate the **person offering**. The meaning has now changed rather to **that which is offered a person**, a reference to **salary/ pay**. Suggest taking 夫 as **two** 二 61 and **big** 大 53, and 丰 as a **club with nails**.

Mnemonic: **PERSON USES CLUB WITH TWO BIG NAILS TO GET PAY**

| 1798 | 倣 | HŌ, narau
IMITATE, FOLLOW
10 strokes | 模倣 MOHŌ
模倣者 MOHŌSHA
倣い削り NARAIKEZURI | imitation
imitator
profiling |

Not **person** 亻 39 and **release** 放 391, though this may be useful as a mnemonic, but **strike/ force** 攵 101 plus the NGU character 仿 . The latter comprises **person** 亻 and **side** 方 204, which is used phonetically to express **resemble** (semantic role unclear), and originally meant **resemble a person**. The causative element 攵 thus gave 倣 a meaning of **make to resemble a person**, i.e. **imitate/ follow**. 仿 itself then became confused with 倣 and also came to mean imitate/ follow, and in Chinese is now interchangeable with 1798. 仿 is listed in some Japanese dictionaries (but without illustration) as having meanings of wander and stand still, but the reason for this listing is not clear.

Mnemonic: **RELEASED PERSON MUST IMITATE OTHERS**

1799	HŌ, mine	主峰 SHUHŌ	main peak
	PEAK, TOP	連峰 RENPŌ	mountain range
	10 strokes	峰打ち MINEUCHI	striking with
			back of sword

Formerly 峯. 山 is **mountain** 24. 夆 is a CO character meaning **butt/ gore**. It was once written 鉤, showing a stylised upturned foot 夂 (early form 夂 438 q.v.) -- here meaning **go back** -- and cow's horns 半 (variant 半/牛 97), and thus literally means **person sent back by cow's horns**. In compounds 夆 can lend connotations both of **go back** and/or of **tapered/ sharp**. In the case of 1799 it means **sharp**, thus giving **sharp part of mountain**, i.e. **peak**. It can also mean **top** in a wider sense, somewhat confusingly including the back of a sword (which is the opposite of the sharp part). Suggest taking 夂 as **sitting crosslegged** and 丰 as a **telegraph pole**.

Mnemonic: **SIT CROSSLEGGED ON TELEGRAPH POLE ON MOUNTAIN PEAK**

1800	HŌ	砲丸 HŌGAN	cannonball
	GUN, CANNON	鉄砲 TEPPŌ	firearms
	10 strokes	大砲 TAIHŌ	gun, cannon

石 is **rock/ stone** 45. 包 is **wrap/ envelop** 583, here acting phonetically to express **release/ discharge** and probably also lending a meaning of **encircling/ encasing**. 1800 originally referred to a **primitive type of cannon which fired small rocks through a tube,** said to be in use from as early as the fifth century B.C.

Mnemonic: **ENVELOPED IN ROCKS DISCHARGED FROM CANNON**

1801	HŌ, kuzu*reru/su*	崩壊 HŌKAI	collapse
	CRUMBLE, COLLAPSE	雪崩 NADARE*	avalanche
	11 strokes	山崩れ YAMAKUZURE	landslide

Formerly 崩 and in ancient times 阝崩, showing that 朋 derives from the somewhat obscure **matching jewels** 棚/朋 1562. Here it acts phonetically to express **collapse**, combining with **mountain** 山 24 (or in the ancient form **hill** 阝/阝 229) to give **collapsing mountainside** (/hillside). Now **collapse/ crumble** in a broader sense. Suggest taking 月 as **month** 16.

Mnemonic: **MOUNTAIN CRUMBLES AWAY IN JUST TWO MONTHS**

1802		HŌ, aku/kiru/kasu	飽和 HŌWA	saturation
		TIRE, SATIATE	飽食 HŌSHOKU	satiation
		13 strokes	飽き性 AKISHŌ	fickleness

食 is **food/ eat** 146. 包 is **wrap/ envelop** 583, here acting phonetically to express **full** and possibly also lending supporting connotations of **smothered**. Thus **satiated with food**, now **satiated/ tired** in a broader sense.

Mnemonic: **TIRED OF WRAPPED FOOD**

1803		HŌ, homeru	褒章 HŌSHŌ	medal
		PRAISE, REWARD	褒美 HŌBI	praise, reward
		15 strokes	褒め言葉 HOMEKOTOBA	praise

衣 is **clothing** (variant 衣 420). 保 is **preserve** 787, here acting phonetically to express **long** but of unclear semantic role. 1803 originally referred to a special **long robe** presented by the emperor to deserving officials, and hence symbolises **praise** and **reward**. 襃 is an occasionally encountered variant form.

Mnemonic: **PRAISED AND REWARDED FOR PRESERVING CLOTHES**

1804		HŌ, nuu	縫合 HŌGO	stitching
		SEW, STITCH	縫い物 NUIMONO	needlework
		16 strokes	縫い目 NUIME	seam, stitch

糸 is **thread** 27. 逢 is an NGU character now meaning **meet**, but in Chinese it also means **penetrate**. It comprises **movement** 辶 129 and **gore** 夆 1799 q.v., the latter lending its connotations of **sharpness**, and literally means **penetrative movement** (in order to attain something). Here 逢 acts phonetically to express **join** and also lends its connotations of **penetration**. Thus to **join by penetrating with thread**, i.e. **sew/ stitch**. Suggest taking 夂 as **sit crosslegged** and 丰 as **a telegraph pole**.

Mnemonic: **SIT CROSSLEGGED ON MOVING TELEGRAPH POLE, SEWING WITH THREAD**

1805 乏 BŌ, toboshii   欠乏 KETSUBŌ   dearth
SCARCE, DESTITUTE   貧乏 BINBŌ   poverty
4 strokes   耐乏 TAIBŌ   austerity

Obscure. Felt by some scholars to derive from an ancient character 乏 , though it is not fully clear that this is in fact the prototype of 1805. 乏 is said to be a mirror image of **hidden/ curtain/ protected** 乍 1744, which is itself obscure and may or may not be a variant of **foot** 止 / 止 /正 129/ 41 (the mirror image possibly being intended to emphasise reversal of movement , a view supported by the fact that the curtain in question is believed to have been used to ward off [i.e. send back] arrows in an archery range -- see also 478). **Scarce/ destitute** is then taken to be a borrowing, specifically resulting from 1805's being used in place of the NGU character 貶. This now means look down upon/ belittle, but originally referred to **lacking money/ destitute** (shell/ **money** 貝 90 and 乏, the latter acting phonetically to express **lack** and possibly also lending similar connotations of **not existing** from its assumed meaning of **hidden**: see also the similar link between hidden and not existing in the case of 莫 788). Other scholars believe that 1805 is a variant of **this/ emerging plant** 之 1335, though agree that the present meanings are borrowings involving 貶. Suggest taking 之 as a **zigzag path** and / as a variant of **one** 一 1.

Mnemonic: **LIFE OF A DESTITUTE LIKENED TO ONE ZIGZAG PATH**

1806 忙 BŌ, isogashii   多忙 TABŌ na   very busy
BUSY   繁忙 HANBŌ pressure of work
6 strokes   忙殺 BŌSATSU
     being worked to death

忄 is **heart/ feelings** 147. 亡 is **die** 973, here acting phonetically to express **be busy** and possibly also lending a figurative meaning of die. 1806 originally referred to **one's heart being busy** (to the point where it 'dies'/ can take no more?), a reference to being **flustered/ pressured**. Now **busy** in a broader sense, with particular connotations of **work** (as opposed to traffic etc.).

Mnemonic: **HEART DEATH THROUGH BEING TOO BUSY**

1807 坊 BŌ   坊主 BŌZU*   priest
PRIEST, BOY, TOWN   坊や BŌYA   boy
7 strokes   坊間 BŌKAN   around town

Earth/ ground 土 60 and **side** 方 204. 1807 originally referred to the (**raised**) **earth at the side of a river**, i.e. an **embankment**, and by association later came to mean **town** (towns often being built on riverbanks). It was later borrowed to refer to an **acolyte**, thus giving both **boy** and **priest** (and very occasionally [by association] **temple**).

Mnemonic: **BOY-PRIEST FOUND AT SIDE OF EARTHEN BANK IN TOWN**

1808		BŌ, samata*geru*	妨害 BŌGAI	obstruction
		HAMPER, OBSTRUCT	防止 BŌSHI	prevention
		7 strokes	妨げなし SAMATAGENASHI	
				without hindrance

女 is **woman** 35. 方 is **side** 204, here acting phonetically to express **vilify** and possibly also originally meaning beside. 1808 originally referred to a **woman** (possibly initially a woman at a lord's side) **vilifying** someone and thereby **hampering** the progress/ request of that person. Now **hamper/ obstruct** in general.

Mnemonic: **WOMAN AT SIDE CAUSES OBSTRUCTION**

1809		BŌ, fusa	房室 BŌSHITSU	chamber
		ROOM, WIFE, TUFT	房房 FUSAFUSA	fleecy
		8 strokes	世話女房 SEWANYŌBŌ	
				devoted wife

戸 is **door** 108, here meaning **partition**, and 方 is **side** 204. 1809 originally referred to a **little room partitioned off at the side of a larger room**. On the one hand this led to **room** in general, and on the other to a range of extended and associated meanings based on ideas such as **being appended** (giving concubines and **wives**) and **sticking out** (giving **tuft**).

Mnemonic: **DOOR TO ONE SIDE LEADS TO WIFE'S ROOM**

1810		BŌ	脂肪 SHIBŌSŌ	fat layer
		FAT	脂肪過多 SHIBŌKATA	obesity
		8 strokes	脂肪組織 SHIBŌSOSHIKI	
				fatty tissue

月 is **meat** 365, here meaning **lean meat**, while 方 is **side** 204. **That found at the side of lean meat is fat.**

Mnemonic: **FAT IS FOUND AT SIDE OF MEAT**

1811 某	**BŌ, BAI, nanigashi**	某氏 BŌSHI	a certain man
	A CERTAIN-, SOME-	某所 BŌSHO	a certain place
	9 strokes	太田某 ŌTANANIGASHI*	a certain Mr Ōta

木 is **tree** 69. 甘 is **sweet** 1093, here meaning literally **something tasty** (and therefore **favorite**) kept in the mouth. 1811 originally referred to the **favored produce of certain trees**, specifically the plums and peaches favored by **pregnant women** (see 1646 and 1689). It thus became a symbol of **pregnancy**. This led to its becoming associated with **rumor** (and matchmaking -- see 1692), and thus it came to acquire its present meaning of **a certain somebody**. Also used as a general prefix meaning **a certain-**.

Mnemonic: **SOMEBODY IS SWEET ON FRUIT OF A CERTAIN TREE**

1812 冒	**BŌ, oka*su***	冒険 BŌKEN	adventure
	DEFY, RISK, ATTACK	感冒 KANBŌ	a cold
	9 strokes	冒して OKASHITE	at the risk of

Formerly 冐 and earlier 冃, with the original form being [glyph]. [glyph]/冃/冂/日 is a **protective helmet**, while [glyph]/目 is **eye** 72. Thus **protective helmet worn over the eyes**, a symbol of a **fighting man**. By association this came to mean **attack**, with **risk** and **defy** being further associations. Suggest taking 日 as **sun** 62.

Mnemonic: **RISK SUN ATTACKING EYES**

1813 剖	**BŌ**	解剖 KAIBŌ	dissection
	DIVIDE, CUT UP	解剖学 KAIBŌGAKU	anatomy
	10 strokes	生体解剖 SEITAIKAIBŌ	vivisection

刂 is **sword/ cut** 181. 咅 is the obscure element spit 384, here acting phonetically to express **open up** but of unclear semantic role. Thus **cut open**, with **cut up** and **divide** associated meanings. Suggest taking 立 as **stand** 73 and 口 as opening/ **entrance** 20.

Mnemonic: **STAND AT ENTRANCE AND GET CUT UP BY SWORD**

1814 紡	**BŌ, tsumu*gu***	紡機 BŌKI	spinning machine
	SPIN (YARN)	紡毛 BŌMŌ	carded wool
	10 strokes	紡績業 BŌSEKIGYŌ	spinning industry

糸 is **thread** 27. 方 is **side/ direction** 204, here acting phonetically to express **twist together** and possibly also lending loose connotations of **in a given way**. Thus to **twist threads together** (in a given way?), a reference to **spinning**.

Mnemonic: **SPIN THREADS ON THE SIDE**

1815 傍 **BŌ, katawara**
SIDE, BESIDE(S)
12 strokes

傍聴 BŌCHŌ attendance
傍観 BŌKAN looking on
傍注 BŌCHŪ margin notes

Somewhat obscure, and of confused evolution. Once written 𠆢旁, showing **person** 亻/亻 39 and 旁/旁. The latter is an NGU character meaning **side**, felt to show two **boats** 方/方 (taken to be a simplification of boat 舟 1354: see also 204) tethered **side by side** but confusingly depicted as one overlaid by the other in highly stylised mirror image fashion. (The reason for this stylisation is not clear.) Thus 旁 had a core meaning of **boats side by side**. As an independent character it eventually came to mean simply **side**, but in the case of 1815 lent a meaning rather of **at the side of boats**, to give **person at the side of boats/ boatman**. In time, however, 傍 became confused with 旁, and eventually took on the latter's later meaning of **side/ beside**. As is the case in English, **beside** also came to be used in the sense of **in addition to**, i.e. **besides**. Suggest taking 旁 as **side** 方 204 and **stand** 立 (variant 立 73).

Mnemonic: **PERSON STANDING AT SIDE**

1816 帽 **BŌ**
CAP, HEADGEAR
12 strokes

帽子 BŌSHI hat
帽章 BŌSHŌ cap badge
学帽 GAKUBŌ school cap

冒 is **attack** 1812 q.v., here in its literal sense of **helmet/ cap** (but without its connotations of battle helmet). **Cloth** 巾 778 -- here in the sense of **apparel** -- was added after 冒 underwent a change of meaning. Suggest taking 日 as **sun** 62 and 目 as **eye** 72.

Mnemonic: **WEAR CLOTH CAP TO SHADE EYES FROM SUN**

1817 膨 **BŌ, fuku*ramu/reru***
SWELL, EXPAND
16 strokes

膨大 BŌDAI swelling
膨満 BŌMAN inflation
膨脹弁 BŌCHŌBEN expansion valve

月 is flesh/ **of the body** 365. 彭 is an NGU character meaning **swell/ drumbeat/ strong**. It is believed to comprise **emerge from a drum/ vessel** 壴 1234 and **delicate (hairs)** 彡 93, the latter meaning **delicate** and also serving graphically to indicate **regular repetition**. 彭 thus indicates a **drumbeat starting delicately and rising steadily to a crescendo, i.e. swelling in intensity**. In the case of 1817 it lends its meaning of **swell**, to give **swelling body**, used initially of pregnancy but now **swell/ expand** in a broad sense. Suggest taking 壴 as **samurai** 士 494 and **beans** 豆 (variant 豆 1640).

Mnemonic: **SAMURAI'S BODY SWELLS AFTER EATING HAIRY BEANS**

1818

謀

BŌ, MU, hakaru, hakarigoto
PLOT, STRATAGEM
16 strokes

陰謀 INBŌ   plot, intrigue
謀反 MUHON*   insurrection
謀略 BŌRYAKU   stratagem

言 is **word/ speak** 274. 某 is **a certain** 1811 q.v., here acting phonetically to express **seek** and also lending connotations of a **secret relationship**. 1818 originally meant to **seek a confidential discussion with someone,** and came by association to mean **plot/ conspire. Stratagem** is also an associated meaning.

Mnemonic: **PLOT HINGES ON A CERTAIN WORD**

1819

朴

BOKU, hŏ
SIMPLE, MAGNOLIA
6 strokes

純朴 JUNBOKU   simplicity
素朴 SOBOKU   artlessness
朴の木 HŌNOKI   magnolia

木 is **tree/ wood** 69. 卜 is **divination crack** 91, here acting phonetically to express **tear** and probably also lending connotations of split. 1819 originally referred to **treebark,** i.e. **that which is torn from a tree.** It became particularly associated with a type of **magnolia** (hypoleuca), presumably because its bark was used for some now unclear purpose. **Simple** is a borrowing.

Mnemonic: **MAGNOLIA WOOD SIMPLY CRACKS**

1820

僕

BOKU, shimobe
(MAN)SERVANT, I
14 strokes

公僕 KŌBOKU   public servant
奴僕 DOBOKU   manservant
僕ら BOKURA   we/ us

Once written , clearly showing a **slave** 㒒 (person 𠆤, with tail/ **testicles** 㞢 1734 q.v. to indicate a **male** and **tattooist's needle** 辛 1432 q.v. to indicate **slave status**) carrying a **container** ⊌ with **bits** ⋅⋅⋅ in it . ⊌ is taken by some authoritative Japanese scholars to be specifically a **chamber-pot and turds,** but in any event the pictograph clearly depicts a slave performing a (menial) task. **Slave/ manservant** then came to mean **servant** in general (though is still used largely of males), and was also used as a **humble reference to oneself** (though now considered rather colloquial). **Person** 亻 39 was added at a later stage for clarity. The modern form 業 derives from a simplified 㒒, showing **hands** 䒑, **needle/ slave** 丵 , and **basket/ container** 凵 (see 399). In compounds 業 often lends an idea of **rough/ crude,** but note that it is listed as a CO character with the rather confusing meaning of **thicket.** This is presumably either a borrowing or an associated meaning with **rough** (i.e. rough area). Suggest remembering 業 by association with **profession** 業 260, taking it as an **'odd'** variant of this.

Mnemonic: **I'M A PERSON WITH ODD PROFESSION -- MANSERVANT**

581

1821		**BOKU, sumi**	筆墨 HITSUBOKU stationery
		INK, INKSTICK	白墨 HAKUBOKU chalk
		14 strokes	墨絵 SUMIE ink drawing

Formerly 墨 . 土 is **earth** 60. 黑/黒 is **black** 124 q.v., here with its literal meaning of **soot**. 1821 originally referred to a type of **ink** formed by mixing **soot** with a certain kind of **earth** (plus water -- it is not clear why water 氵 40 was not added to the character). Now **ink/ writing wherewithal** in a broader sense.

Mnemonic: **BLACK EARTH MAKES INK**

1822		**BOKU**	打撲 DABOKU strike, blow
		STRIKE, BEAT	相撲 SUMŌ* sumo
		15 strokes	撲殺 BOKUSATSU
			beating to death

扌 is **hand** 32. 業 is **servant** 1820, here acting phonetically to express **beat** and almost certainly also originally lending its meaning of **servant**. Thus to **beat (a servant?) with the hand**, now simply **beat/ strike**. Suggest taking 業 as a 'sort of' variant of **profession** 業 260.

Mnemonic: **BEATING WITH HAND IS A SORT OF PROFESSION**

1823		**BOTSU**	没収 BOSSHŪ forfeiture
		SINK, DISAPPEAR,	日没 NICHIBOTSU sunset
		DIE, LACK, NOT	没後 BOTSUGO after death
		7 strokes	

Formerly 沒 and earlier 沕殳. 氺/氵 is **water/ river** 40, 又 is a **hand**, and 回 is a **vortex/ whirlpool** 86. 1823 originally referred to a **whirlpool where the hand can find no hold**, and thus came to mean **disappear and die by sinking into a whirlpool**. Disappear/ die led by association to **not (be present)/ be lacking**. Suggest taking 殳 as **strike** 153.

Mnemonic: **STRIKE WATER AND SINK, DISAPPEAR, AND DIE**

1824 hori, KUTSU 　　　　外堀 SOTOBORI 　outer moat
MOAT, DITCH, CANAL 　つり堀 TSURIBORI fishing pond
11 strokes 　　　　　堀川 HORIKAWA 　　　canal

土 is **earth** 60. 屈 is **crouch/ submit** 1188 q.v., here acting phonetically to express **dig** and probably also lending its meaning of crouch (and possibly also connotations of remove). Thus (crouch down and?) **dig earth** (thereby removing it?), i.e. **dig a hole/ ditch**. At one stage 1824 was interchangeable with dig 掘 1189, but eventually it came to indicate the noun (i.e. **that which is dug**) rather than the verb (dig). Now **moat/ ditch** rather than just any shape of hole.

Mnemonic: **CROUCH IN EARTHEN MOAT**

1825 HON 　　　　　奔走 HONSŌ 　　　　bustle
RUN, BUSTLE 　　奔放 HONPŌ na 　uninhibited
8 strokes 　　　　出奔 SHUPPON 　absconding

Once written 㚟, showing a **man running** 大 161 and **three footprints** 止 129, thus indicating a **man running and leaving a trail of footprints** (suggesting distance). However, as a result of the confusing similarity of growing plant 㞮 42 q.v., from an early stage the three footprints 㞢 became confused with **three plants** 㞢/卉/卉 1770 q.v., giving **man running over plants/ grass** (see also plants/ grass 屮 9). However, the core meaning of **run** remained unchanged. **Bustle** is an associated meaning. Suggest taking 大 as **big man** 53 and 卉 as a combined **trebling** of ten 十 33.

Mnemonic: **THIRTY BIG MEN RUNNING AND BUSTLING**

1826 HON, hirugae*ru/su* 　　翻訳家 HONYAKUKA translator
FLAP, CHANGE 　　　翻意 HONI 　　changing mind
18 strokes 　　　　　翻って HIRUGAETTE
　　　　　　　　　　　　　　　on second thought

Formerly 飜, i.e. with **fly/ spread wings** 飛 566 q.v. instead of **wings** 羽 812. 番 is **number/ turn** 196 q.v., here acting phonetically to express **reverse/ change** and also lending connotations of **in turn/ sequence**. Thus to **change the wings in turn** (in flight), i.e. **flap**. Now **flap/ flutter/ change** in a broad sense.

Mnemonic: **WINGS FLAP, CHANGING IN TURN**

1827 **BON, HAN,** oyo*so* 平凡 HEIBON mediocrity
MEDIOCRE, COMMON, 凡戦 BONSEN dull game
ROUGHLY, IN GENERAL 凡例 HANREI
3 strokes explanatory notes

Formerly also 凡 and originally 𠘨 . 𠘨 indicates a **shallow tray**. 〳/ 丶 is taken by some scholars to indicate contents, but it is far more likely to be the displaced bottom stroke of 𠘨 . The present core meaning of **commonplace** (with **mediocre** and **[in] general** being associated meanings, and **roughly** being a further association in turn of in general) is felt by some scholars to be a borrowing, while others feel that the simple tray in itself symbolised something commonplace. Suggest taking 几 as **table** 832 and 丶 as a **mark**.

Mnemonic: **IT'S COMMON FOR MEDIOCRE TABLES TO BE MARKED**

1828 **BON** 盆地 BONCHI land basin
TRAY, BON FESTIVAL 盆踊り BONODORI Bon Dance
9 strokes 盆景 BONKEI tray landscape

Formerly also 盆. 皿 is **dish** 1307. 分/分 is **divide/ understand** 199 q.v., here acting phonetically to express big/ **wide** and probably also lending its own connotations of opened up/ out. Thus **wide dish** (opened out?), i.e. **tray**. In Japan it was also borrowed to refer to the **Bon Festival**, a lantern festival held in summer to welcome the spirits of the dead (from the Sanskrit Ura<u>bon</u>).

Mnemonic: **UNDERSTAND DISH TO BE TRAY USED IN BON FESTIVAL**

1829 **MA,** asa 麻布 MAFU/ ASANUNO linen
HEMP, FLAX, NUMB 麻薬 MAYAKU narcotic
11 strokes 麻綱 ASAZUNA hemp rope

Formerly also 麻, and in ancient times 麻. 广 is a simplification of oppose 反 371 q.v., here in its meaning of **cloth**, while 林 indicates **plants/** bushes (variant tree/ bush 朮/木 69). **'Cloth plant'** was a reference to **hemp** or **flax**. The later use of **building** 广 114 instead of cloth 广 is felt by some scholars to be an error and by others to be an attempt to indicate the storing of hemp cloth indoors. As a result of the narcotic potential of hemp 1829 is also used to refer to **narcotics** and **numbness**. Suggest taking 林 as **forest** 75.

Mnemonic: **FOREST OF HEMP AND FLAX GROWN IN BUILDING**

1830

MA, su*ru*　　　　　摩天楼 MATENRŌ　skyscraper
RUB, GRAZE, SCRAPE　摩擦 MASATSU　friction
15 strokes　　　　　摩擦音 MASATSUON　fricative

Hand 手 32 and **hemp/ flax** 麻 1829. 1830 originally referred to **rubbing hemp/ flax by hand** in order to separate the fibers, and now means **rub** in a broad sense. Often interchanged with rub 磨 1831.

Mnemonic: **HAND RUBS HEMP**

1831

MA, miga*ku*　　　研磨 KENMA　grinding
POLISH, SCOUR, RUB　磨滅 MAMETSU　wear and tear
16 strokes　　　　靴磨き KUTSUMIGAKI
　　　　　　　　　　　　　　　　shoeshine

A simplification of 礦. 石 is **stone** 45. 靡 is an NGU character now used in a wide range of confusing meanings such as wave and yield, but in Chinese it can mean **separate** and clearly relates to the act of **separating** 非 773 q.v. the fibers of **hemp/ flax** 麻 1829. It thus originally had a meaning very similar to that of **separate fibers/ rub** 摩 1830 q.v., with the addition of stone 石 giving 1831 a meaning of **rub hemp/ flax with a stone** (as opposed to by hand in the case of 1830, though the two are often interchanged). Now **grind/ scour/ rub** in a broad sense, with **polish** being an associated meaning.

Mnemonic: **RUB HEMP WITH A STONE, TO POLISH IT!?**

1832

MA　　　　　悪魔 AKUMA　　　devil
DEMON, DEVIL　魔法 MAHŌ　magic, sorcery
21 strokes　　　魔羅 MARA　demon, penis

鬼 is **devil/ demon** 1128. 麻 is **hemp/ flax** 1829, here used phonetically to express **mara**, a Sanskrit term for a particularly evil **demon** (see above). In Japanese mara is also used to refer to the penis (but note that it is an extremely vulgar term which should be avoided).

Mnemonic: **HEMP CAN BE A DEVIL**

585

1833 MAI, u[zu]*maru/meru/moreru* 埋葬 MAISŌ burial
BURY 埋め立て UMETATE reclamation
10 strokes 埋れ木 UMOREGI fossil wood

土 is **earth** 60. 里 is **village** 219 q.v., here acting phonetically to express **cover** and possibly also lending loose connotations of **mound of earth** from its own original connotations of raised earthen path. Thus to **cover with earth**, i.e. **bury**. Now used in a broad sense.

Mnemonic: **VILLAGE BURIED IN EARTH**

1834 MAKU 鼓膜 KOMAKU eardrum
MEMBRANE 網膜 MŌMAKU retina
14 strokes 膜質 MAKUSHITSU
membranous

月 is **flesh/ meat** 365. 莫 is **sun sinking among plants** 788 q.v., here acting phonetically to express **wrap** and also lending its own connotations of **envelop**. Thus **that which wraps/ envelops flesh**, a reference to **membrane**. Suggest taking ⧾ as **grass** 9, 日 as **sun** 62, and 大 as **big** 53.

Mnemonic: **BIG FLESHY MEMBRANE STRETCHED OVER SUNNY GRASS**

1835 mata 又は MATAWA or
AGAIN 又と無い MATATONAI unique
2 strokes 又貸し MATAGASHI sublease

Formerly 又, deriving from a pictograph of a (right) **hand** 又. **Again** is a borrowed meaning.

Mnemonic: **HAND APPEARS AGAIN**

1836 抹 MATSU 抹殺 MASSATSU erasure
ERASE, RUB, PAINT 抹茶 MATCHA powdered tea
8 strokes 一抹 ICHIMATSU tinge

扌 is **hand** 32, here meaning **action with the hand**. 末 is **tip/ end** 587 q.v., here acting phonetically to express **paint over/ coat** but of unclear semantic role. Thus **paint over (using the hand)**, with **erase** and **rub out** being associated meanings. Rub out later broadened to mean **rub** in a general sense. Suggest taking 末 literally as **treetop** (tree 木 69 and top 一).

Mnemonic: **HAND TRIES TO ERASE TREETOP BY PAINTING OVER**

586

1837 MAN
LAZY, RUDE, BOASTFUL
14 strokes

怠慢 TAIMAN   neglect
自慢 JIMAN   vanity
慢性 MANSEI   chronic

忄 is heart/ feelings 147. 曼 is an NGU character now meaning full/ **expansive**. Its etymology is unclear, but old forms such as 曼 appear to show a variant 冒 of attack/ helmet (over eye) 冒 / 冒 1812 plus **hand** 又 , and it may have originally meant either cover with the hand or (less likely) attack with the hand. In the case of 1837 曼 acts phonetically to express **loose** and may also lend similar connotations of spread (i.e. as opposed to constrained). **Loose feelings** indicated being **easy-going** and **unconcerned**, giving **lazy** and by association **rude** (cf. English term **sloppy**). It is not fully clear how it also acquired the meaning of **boastful**, but this may be an associated meaning with rude. Suggest taking 日 as **sun** 62, with 皿 literally as **eye** 72.

Mnemonic: **FEEL LAZY AS HAND SHADES EYE FROM SUN**

1838 MAN, sozo*ro*
RANDOM, DIFFUSE,
INVOLUNTARY
14 strokes

漫画 MANGA   cartoon, comic
散漫 SANMAN na   diffuse
漫ろ言 SOZOROGOTO rambling

氵 is **water** 40. 曼 is **expansive** 1837, here acting phonetically to express **spread** and probably also lending an idea of widely. 1838 originally referred to **water spreading** (widely?), i.e. **flooding** (still a major meaning in Chinese). Since flooding water generally spreads **indiscriminately** and **inexorably** 1838 also came to acquire these connotations, the former leading to **diffuse/ random** and the latter to **involuntar(il)y**. Suggest taking 日 as **sun** 62, 皿 as **eye** 72, and 又 as **hand**.

Mnemonic: **HAND INVOLUNTARILY SHADES EYE WATERING IN DIFFUSE SUNLIGHT**

1839 MI
BEWITCH, CHARM
15 strokes

魅力 MIRYOKU charm, appeal
魅惑 MIWAKU   fascination
魅了 MIRYŌ   charm

鬼 is **devil/ demon** 1128. 未 is **immature** 794, here acting phonetically to express **beast**. Thus **beast-like demon**, a reference to a particular demon with human face but four legs (a meaning still listed for 1839 in some Chinese dictionaries). **Bewitch/ charm** is an associated meaning (demons being believed to possess the power of bewitching).

Mnemonic: **BEWITCHED BY CHARMING IMMATURE DEVIL**

587

1840	misaki, saki, KŌ	岬角 KŌKAKU	point, spit
	PROMONTORY, CAPE	岬湾 KŌWAN	indentations
	8 strokes	コッド岬 KODDOMISAKI	
			Cape Cod

Of disputed etymology, though its elements are clearly **mountain** 山 24 and **grade A/ high** 甲 1243. Some scholars believe that 甲 originally acted phonetically to express **insert/ be between** (as well as possibly lending connotations of **high**), and that 1840 originally referred to a **valley between (high?) mountains** before coming to mean simply **mountainous** and then by association **promontory**. Other scholars feel that 甲 lent its meaning of **high** and played no phonetic role (though its pronunciation necessarily became 1840's [on/ Chinese] reading), thus giving a meaning from the outset of **high mountain** and then by association **promontory**. The latter theory seems the more helpful.

Mnemonic: **PROMONTORY CONTAINS GRADE 'A' HIGH MOUNTAINS**

1841	MYŌ	妙案 MYŌAN	great idea
	EXQUISITE, ODD	微妙 BIMYŌ	subtlety
	7 strokes	奇妙 KIMYŌna	odd

女 is **woman** 35. 少 is **few/ little** 143, here acting phonetically to express **delicate** and probably also lending similar connotations of not bulky. 1841 originally referred to an **exceptionally willowy and graceful woman**. On the one hand such beauty led to **exquisite**, and on the other hand its exceptional nature led to **unusual** and **odd**.

Mnemonic: **FEW WOMEN ARE AS EXQUISITE, OR AS ODD**

1842	MIN, nemuru/i	不眠症 FUMINSHŌ	insomnia
	SLEEP, SLEEPY	眠気 NEMUKE	sleepiness
	10 strokes	居眠り INEMURI	doze, nap

目 is **eye** 72. 民 is the somewhat obscure **people/ populace** 590 q.v., here acting phonetically to express **close**. Thus **close the eyes**, a reference to **sleeping**. It is not clear whether 民 also plays any semantic role. It may lend connotations of **not using the eyes** through a possible early meaning of blind, but since 1842 is a character of relatively late origin it is more likely that any connotations lent by 民 would relate to its later meaning of populace, such as perhaps **common to all**.

Mnemonic: **POPULACE CLOSES ITS EYES IN SLEEP**

1843

MU, BŌ, hoko

HALBERD, LANCE,

SPEAR

5 strokes

矛げき BŌGEKI   spear, halberd

矛先 HOKOSAKI   spearpoint

矛盾した MUJUNSHITA

contradictory

From a pictograph of a **barbed lance** 𢍐 (earlier simply a **spear** ↑). It is not clear whether the lower extra stroke ⁄ is an additional **barb** or, more likely, a **hand-guard**. **Lance** and **halberd** conceptually overlap (see also 493).

Mnemonic: **LANCE WITH TWO POINTS AND HAND-GUARD**

1844

MU, yume

DREAM

13 strokes

夢中 MUCHŪ   absorbed

悪夢 AKUMU   nightmare

夢見る YUMEMIRU fancy,dream

Somewhat obscure. Once written 𦱀, showing **evening** ⼣ / 夕 44, **encircle/ cover** ⼌ / ⼍ (see 655), **eye** ⼞ / ⽥ / ⽬ 72, and an obscure element 𣎳. Its earliest meaning is known to have been **dark night when one cannot see**, so presumably 𦴦 originally referred to the **eye when covered by the night** (or similar). **Dream** is taken by some scholars to be a borrowing, and by others to be an associated meaning (either from the idea of that 'seen' by the eye when it cannot really see or from the idea of covered eye, giving sleep and then dream). Suggest taking ⺧ as **grass** 9.

Mnemonic: **COVER EYES AT NIGHT AND DREAM OF GRASS**

1845

MU, kiri

MIST, FOG

19 strokes

霧笛 MUTEKI   foghorn

濃霧 NŌMU   thick fog

朝霧 ASAGIRI   morning mist

Once written 𩃦 . 雨 is **rain** 3, here meaning **rain-like conditions**. 敄/務 is **perform/ duty** 795, here acting phonetically to express **cover** but of unclear semantic role. Thus **rain-like conditions that cover**, a reference to **fog/ mist**.

Mnemonic: **PERFORM DUTIES IN RAIN, MIST, AND FOG**

| 1846 | musume, JŌ
GIRL, DAUGHTER
10 strokes | 小娘 KOMUSUME young girl
娘子軍 JŌSHIGUN amazons
娘盛り MUSUMEZAKARI
prime of womanhood |

Of recent origin, combining **woman** 女 35 and **good** 良 598 to give **good woman**, meaning a **(young) woman in her prime. Daughter is an associated meaning with girl/ young woman.**

Mnemonic: **ONE'S DAUGHTER IS A GOOD WOMAN**

| 1847 | MEI
INSCRIBE, SIGN
14 strokes | 銘柄 MEIGARA brand
銘記 MEIKI remembering
銘銘 MEIMEI severally |

Metal 金 14 and **name** 名 71. 1847 originally meant to **inscribe a name in metal** (at first a dead person's, later one's own), giving both **inscribe** and **sign**. It can also symbolise an **individual/ person.**

Mnemonic: **INSCRIBE ONE'S NAME IN METAL**

| 1848 | METSU, horobiru/bosu
DESTROY
13 strokes | 絶滅 ZETSUMETSU extinction
滅亡 METSUBŌ collapse
破滅 HAMETSU destruction |

威 is a CO character which is interchangeable (in Chinese) with 滅. It comprises **broad bladed halberd** 戌 246, here meaning **weapon/ attack**, and **fire** 火 8. It is not clear whether it originally meant attack with halberd and fire or attack with (the weapon of?) fire, but in any event it meant **attack and destroy**. In combination with **water** 氵 40 it technically meant **destroy water (-supply)**, but has come to mean **destroy** in a general sense.

Mnemonic: **DESTROYED BY HALBERD, FIRE, AND WATER**

1849	兔	MEN, manuka*reru*	免除 MENJO	exemption
		ESCAPE, AVOID	免税 MENZEI	tax-exempt
		8 strokes	放免 HŌMEN	acquittal

Formerly also written 兔. 囚 and 囧 derive from 夃, namely **woman's genitals/ spread legs** 1103, while ルレ is **bending/ crouching person** 39. 1849 originally referred to a **woman squatting with legs apart striving to give birth** (birth still being retained as a meaning in Chinese, but now usually conveyed by 娩 [which adds woman 女 35] or 挽 [which adds child 子 25] -- see 390). **Escape** is believed to be an associated meaning with parturition, i.e. the 'escaping' of the child from the woman, with **avoid** being a further association with escape. However, some scholars believe that it stems from confusion with the similar character **hare** 兔 1010 q.v., which symbolised fleetness and hence escaping. Suggest taking ク as **crouching person** 39/ 145, ル as **another crouching person** 39, and ロ as **boxes**.

Mnemonic: TWO PERSONS ESCAPE BY CROUCHING BEHIND BOXES

1850	茂	MO, shige*ru*	繁茂 HANMO	thick growth
		GROW THICKLY	茂林 MORIN	dense forest
		8 strokes	茂み SHIGEMI	thicket

艹 is **grass/ plants** 9. 戊 is **broad bladed halberd** 515, here acting phonetically to express **flourishing** and possibly also lending an idea of thrusting. Thus **flourishing plants** (thrusting forth?), indicating **thick growth**.

Mnemonic: PLANTS GROW THICKLY, THRUSTING LIKE HALBERDS

1851	妄	MŌ, BŌ, midari	妄言 BŌGEN	harsh words
		IRRATIONAL, RASH	妄想 MŌSŌ	delusion
		6 strokes	迷妄 MEIMŌ	fallacy

女 is **woman** 35. 亡 is **die** 973 q.v., here acting phonetically to express **blind** and almost certainly also lending its own connotations of **unable to see**. 1851 originally referred to a **man 'blinded' by his infatuation with a woman**, and hence came to symbolise **loss of reason** and **irrational/ rash** behavior.

Mnemonic: ACT IRRATIONALLY AFTER DEATH OF WOMAN

1852

MŌ, mekura
BLIND
8 strokes

盲目 **MŌMOKU** blindness
文盲 **MONMŌ** illiteracy
盲判 **MEKURABAN**
'rubber stamp'

Eye 目 72 and **die/ cease to exist** 亡 973. Thus **no eyes/ blind**.

Mnemonic: **DEAD EYES ARE BLIND**

1853

MŌ, KŌ
WASTE, DECREASE
10 strokes

消耗 **SHŌMŌ** consumption
損耗 **SONMŌ** wastage, loss
心神耗弱 **SHINSHINKŌJAKU**
feeble minded

Correctly written 耗. 禾 is **rice plant/ grain plant** 81. 毛 is **hair** 210, here acting phonetically to express **not/ cease to be** and possibly also suggesting a wispy and insubstantial plant. 1853 originally referred to a **failed crop**, with **waste** and **decrease** being associated meanings. The modern form uses **plow** 耒 673 q.v. (which may itself once have depicted a plant), felt by some scholars to be a simple miscopying. Suggest taking 耒 as a **heavily branched** variant of **tree** 木 69.

Mnemonic: **HEAVILY BRANCHED TREE WASTES AWAY TO HAIRS**

1854

MŌ
FIERCE, RAGING, BRAVE
11 strokes

猛烈 **MŌRETSU na** fierce
猛獣 **MŌJŪ** fierce animal
猛者 **MOSA*** a stalwart

犭 is **dog** 17. 孟 is an NGU character meaning **chief/ first**. Its etymology is unclear, but it combines **child** 子 25 and **dish** 皿 1307, and the fact that in Chinese it can also mean eldest, rude, and rush forward suggests that it may originally have been an ideograph depicting the eldest child rushing rudely to eat. Here it acts phonetically to express **spirited** and possibly also lends loose connotations of aggression, thus giving **spirited dog**. This came to mean **spirited** in a broader sense, eventually leading by association to **fierce**, **raging**, and **brave**.

Mnemonic: **FIERCE DOG BEATS BRAVE CHILD TO DISH**

592

1855

網

MŌ, ami
NET, NETWORK
14 strokes

漁網 GYOMŌ　　fishing net
網戸 AMIDO　　screen door
通信網 TSŪSHINMŌ
　　　　　　　news network

Once written simply as 网 (now 冈), a pictograph of a **net** with hauling ropes (see 193). **Die** 亡 973 was added for its sound, to express **interwoven**, but any semantic role is unclear. Finally **thread** 糸 27 (in a sense of **cord**) was also added for clarity. Now also used figuratively, as **network**. Suggest taking 冂 as **cover** and 丷 as **horns**.

Mnemonic: **DEAD HORNED CREATURE COVERED BY THREADED NET**

1856

MOKU, dama*ru*
BE SILENT
15 strokes

黙殺 MOKUSATSU　ignoring
沈黙 CHINMOKU　　silence
黙り込む DAMARIKOMU fall silent

Formerly 默 . 犬 is **dog** 17. 黑/黒 is **black** 124 q.v., here acting phonetically to express **silence** but of unclear semantic role (though it may possibly lend some suggestion of being blocked, from its original meaning of soot forming on a grille/ window). 1856 originally referred to a **silent dog**, and now means **silence** in a broad sense.

Mnemonic: **BLACK DOG IS SILENT**

1857

紋

MON
CREST, PATTERN
10 strokes

紋章 MONSHŌ　heraldic crest
指紋 SHIMON　　fingerprint
波紋 HAMON　　　　ripple

Thread 糸 27 and text/ **writing** 文 68 q.v., here in its early meaning of **intricate pattern**. Thus **patterned threadwork**, a reference to a **crest**.

Mnemonic: **THREADS IN CREST FORM PATTERN LIKE WRITING**

1858

monme
MONME, WEIGHT, COIN
4 strokes

二匁 NIMONME　two monme
五匁 GOMONME　five monme
三匁 SANMONME three monme

A 'made in Japan' character formed on a phonetic basis from a stylised combination of MON 文 68 and the katakana ME メ , thus giving **MONME**. A monme was a **small weight** (3.75 grams) and a **small coin**. Suggest remembering 匁 by association with **thing** 物 387.

Mnemonic: **A MONME LOOKS LIKE AN AWKWARD THING**

1859

厄

YAKU

MISFORTUNE, DISASTER

4 strokes

厄介 YAKKAI   trouble

厄日 YAKUBI   bad day

災厄 SAIYAKU   calamity

Often felt to be associated with **dangerous** 厄 831 q.v., which is a useful mnemonic, but the overlap of elements is coincidental. 1859 was once written 厄, showing **cliff** 厂 45 and **bending figure** 乙 145, and in similar fashion to 831 later had its bending figure 乙 changed to **slumped figure** 巳 768. However, it does not refer to a figure falling down a cliff. 厂 is used phonetically to express **thrust upwards**, and almost certainly lends similar connotations of its own, combining with bending figure 乙 to give **person bent (with back) thrust upwards**. This was applied to a **hunchback**. Some scholars feel that the present meanings are borrowed, but others see them as associated, since a hunchback was generally a symbol of something unpleasant (e.g. see 997).

Mnemonic: **NOT QUITE DANGEROUS, BUT STILL A MISFORTUNE**

1860

躍

YAKU, odoru

LEAP, DANCE, RUSH

21 strokes

躍進 YAKUSHIN   rush, dash

飛躍 HIYAKU   leap

躍り込む ODORIKOMU   rush into

足 is **foot/ leg** 51. 翟 is **bird's wings** 216 q.v. (**bird** 隹 216 and **wings** 羽 812), here acting phonetically to express **leap** and probably also lending its own connotations of soaring high. Thus to **leap (with the legs)**. **Dance** and **rush** are associated meanings.

Mnemonic: **LEAP WITH FEET FLYING LIKE BIRD'S WINGS**

1861

YU

JOY, PLEASURE

12 strokes

愉快 YUKAI   pleasure

愉悦 YUETSU   joy

愉楽 YURAKU   pleasure

忄 is **heart/ feelings** 147. 俞 is **convey** 799, here acting phonetically to express **good** and possibly also lending its meaning of convey. Thus **good feelings** (conveyed to the heart?), i.e. **pleasure/ joy**. Suggest taking 俞 as **cut** 刂 181, **meat** 月 365, and **cover** 𠅃 121.

Mnemonic: **FEELINGS OF JOY ABOUT CUT MEAT BEING COVERED**

1862

YU, sato*su*
INSTRUCT, ADMONISH
16 strokes

教諭 KYŌYU — instructor
説諭 SETSUYU — admonition
諭旨 YUSHI — official advice

言 is **words/ speak** 274. 俞 is **convey** 799, here acting phonetically to express **clear/ clarify** and possibly also lending its meaning of convey. Thus **clarify verbally**, i.e. **instruct**, usually with connotations of **correcting** and/or **admonishing**. Suggest taking 俞 as **cut** 刂 181, **meat** 月 365, and **cover** 亼 121.

Mnemonic: ADMONISH VERBALLY AND INSTRUCT TO COVER CUT MEAT

1863

YU, iyasu
CURE, HEAL, VENT
18 strokes

治癒 CHIYU — cure
平癒 HEIYU — recovery
癒合 YUGŌ — knitting (wound)

Formerly 瘉 . 疒 is **sickness** 381. 俞 is **convey** 799, here acting phonetically to express **remove** and possibly also lending an idea of transport/ move (away). Thus **remove sickness**, i.e. **heal/ cure**, with **vent** being a minor associated meaning. 俞 was later replaced by 愈, a CO character combining convey 俞 with **heart/ feelings** 心 147 and meaning cure. Its etymology is unclear, just as the reason for its replacing 俞, but it contains the same elements as joy 愉 1861 and was presumably originally a variant of same. Thus its use in 1863 may have been an attempt to indicate joyful feelings following a cure. 愈 would then have acquired by association 1863's meaning of cure (i.e. in effect as a simplification of it). Suggest taking 俞 as **cut** 刂 181, **meat** 月 365, and **cover** 亼 121.

Mnemonic: FEEL ILL OVER COVERED CUT MEAT -- NEED CURE

1864

YUI, I, tada
ONLY, PROMPT (ANSWER)
11 strokes

唯一 YUIITSU — sole, unique
唯今 TADAIMA — now; I'm home
唯唯諾諾 IIDAKUDAKU — readily

口 is **mouth/ say** 20. 隹 is **bird** 216, here lending its sound (once I) to express a vocalisation indicating a **prompt response** (now E in Japanese). It is not clear whether 隹 also plays any semantic role. Thus **prompt answer (saying I)**, which could also symbolise promptness in a wider sense. It is still very occasionally found with this meaning, but is usually used to mean **only**, which is a borrowing.

Mnemonic: BIRD HAS MOUTH, ONLY DON'T EXPECT PROMPT ANSWER

1865 YŪ, kasuka

DARK, OBSCURE,

FAINT, LONELY

9 strokes

幽境 YŪKYŌ   lonely place

幽玄 YŪGEN   mystery

幽界 YŪKAI   nether world

Once written 𣎴. 𣎴 is **fire 8** (now 火), and not **mountain** 𣲆/山 24. 88/𢆶 is a doubling of **short thread** 幺 111, here acting phonetically to express **black** and possibly also lending supporting connotations of obscure (see 1227). 1865 originally referred to **something blackened by flame** and thus of **unclear appearance**, and hence came to mean **obscure** and **dark**. **Faint** is an associated meaning. It can also be used to mean **lonely**, and, as with 玄 1227, can have connotations of mysteriousness/ otherworldliness. Suggest taking 山 as **mountain**.

Mnemonic: **FOLLOW FAINT THREAD THROUGH DARK AND LONELY MOUNTAINS**

1866 YŪ

COMPOSED, DISTANT,

LONG TIME, AMPLE

11 strokes

悠然 YŪZEN   calmly

悠長 YŪCHŌ na   leisurely

悠久 YŪKYŪ   eternity

Somewhat obscure. 心 is **heart/ feelings** 147. 攸 is **strike a person with a stick** 704 q.v. (**person** 亻 39, **stick** 丨, and **striking hand** 攵 101), here acting phonetically to express **afflict** and probably lending similar connotations of attack/ beset. Thus **that which afflicts the heart**, namely **grief/ worry** (still a meaning in Chinese). **Composed/ calm** is believed by some scholars to be a borrowing, and by others to be an associated meaning, from the idea of being worried but composed. **Distant** is definitely a borrowing, with **long time** and **ample** being associated meanings with distant. Note that 攸 does exist as an independent CO character with a wide range of confusing meanings, including distant (which appears to result from its being used as a simplification of 悠 after the latter had borrowed this meaning).

Mnemonic: **STRIKE PERSON WITH STICK, BUT FEELINGS COMPOSED**

1867

YŪ, nao
MOREOVER, STILL,
HESITATE, SIMILAR
12 strokes

猶子 YŪSHI   adopted child
猶予 YŪYO   postponement
猶予期間 YŪYOKIKAN
    period of grace

犭 is dog/ **beast** 17, here indicating a **monkey** and thus to all intents and purposes a simplification of monkey 猿 1028. 酋 is chief/ liquor 927 q.v. (literally **out of** ´ 66 and **wine jar** 酉 302), here acting phonetically to express **hesitate** and presumably chosen as the phonetic partly for the association between a jar and a hesitant monkey (as in the method of using a jar as a trap). Thus **hesitant monkey**, later **hesitant/ hesitate** in general. **Delay** is an associated meaning. **Still** is also believed to be an associated meaning, from the idea of still not bringing oneself to do something (cf. mada), with **moreover** then being an associated meaning in turn from a generalised **still**. It is not clear how the minor meaning of **similar** came about. Note that there is an occasionally encountered miswritten variant 獐, which uses esteem 尊 927 instead of 酋 .

Mnemonic: **BEAST STILL HESITANT TO COME OUT OF WINE JAR**

1868

YŪ, yuta*ka*
RICH, PLENTIFUL
12 strokes

裕福 YŪFUKU   opulence
余裕 YOYŪ   margin, surplus
富裕階級 FUYŪKAIKYŪ
    wealthy classes

衤 is **clothing** 420. 谷 is **valley** 122, here acting phonetically to express **ample** and probably also lending connotations of big. Thus **ample clothes** (in the sense of loose fitting), later **ample** in general. **Rich** and **plentiful** are associated meanings, from the idea of not being constrained.

Mnemonic: **PLENTIFUL CLOTHES, ENOUGH TO FILL VALLEY**

1869

雄

YŪ, osu, o-
MALE, POWERFUL
12 strokes

雄弁 YŪBEN   eloquence
雄者 YŪSHA   hero
雄牛 OUSHI   bull

隹 is **bird** 216. 厷 is a CO character meaning **arm**. It was once written 𠂇, showing an **arm** 又 and an **elbow** ㄥ (note that the addition of flesh/ of the body 月 365 gives the NGU character arm/ elbow 肱). Here 厷 acts phonetically to express **fine/ showy**, and may also lend connotations of **strength** and hence **masculinity**. Thus **fine/ showy bird**, a reference to the **male bird** (which generally has the finer plumage) and hence **male** in general.

Mnemonic: **MALE BIRD HAS STRONG ARMS AND ELBOWS?!**

1870 YŪ, saso*u*
INVITE, TEMPT, LEAD
14 strokes

誘惑 YŪWAKU seduction
誘導 YŪDŌ induction
誘い水 SASOIMIZU
pump priming

言 is **words/ speak** 274. 秀 is **excel/ excellent** 1355, here acting phonetically to express **lead** and probably also lending similar connotations. Thus **lead with words**, i.e. **tempt**. Now used in a broad sense.

Mnemonic: **EXCELLENT WORDS LEAD TO TEMPTATION**

1871 YŪ, urei/*eru*, u*i*
GRIEF, SORROW
15 strokes

憂愁 YŪSHŪ grief, gloom
憂え顔 UREEGAO sad look
物憂い MONOUI weary, gloomy

Once written 憂, showing **head** 頁/頁/直 93 (here meaning **mind**), **heart**/ feelings ⺗ / 心 147, and **upturned foot** 夂/夊 438 q.v. (here meaning **walk slowly**). Head 直, is also believed to act phonetically to express **grief/ sadness**. Thus **walk slowly with sad heart and mind**, later **grief/ sorrow** in general. Suggest taking 夂 as **sit cross-legged**.

Mnemonic: **SIT CROSSLEGGED, HEAD AND HEART FULL OF GRIEF**

1872 YŪ, toke*ru*
DISSOLVE, MELT
16 strokes

融和 YŪWA softening
金融 KINYŪ finance
融通 YŪZŪ finance, versatility

鬲 is **large pot on stand** 1078. 虫 is **insect** 56, here onomatopoeically lending its sound CHŪ to express the sound of **steam being given off** (cf. English hiss). 1872 originally referred to **cooking something vigorously (with steam being given off with a CHŪ sound)**, and can still mean steam in Chinese. **Dissolve/ melt** is taken by some scholars to be a borrowing, and by others to be an associated meaning. Suggest remembering 鬲 by association with **round** 口 228 and **one** 一 1.

Mnemonic: **DISSOLVE INSECTS IN ONE ROUND POT ON STAND**

1873

YO, ata*eru*
GIVE, CONVEY, IMPART, INVOLVEMENT
3 strokes

与え主 ATAENUSHI giver, donor
関与 KANYO involvement
授与式 JUYOSHIKI award ceremony

Formerly 興 and earlier 𦥑. The oldest form is 𦥑. 𦥑 shows **four hands**, symbolising **many hands**. 𠫔 is a variant of fangs 㐄/牙 434 q.v., and indicates **interlocking** (fangs originally being clarified by the addition of mouth 口 20). Thus **many interlocking hands**, indicating a **joint effort** and hence by association **involvement**. The present main meaning of **give** technically stems from confusion between 与 and 与 following the dropping of mouth 口. 与 is an element combining an old variant 𠃌 of **ladle** 勺 1342 q.v. with **one** 一 1 and meant **one ladleful**, later coming to mean **give a ladleful** and eventually just **give**. However, the idea of hands together contained in itself an idea of **raising** (e.g. see 1603 and 1793), which conceptually overlaps with **offer/ give**, and thus in one sense give is an extended meaning of hands interlocking 𦥑. **Convey/ impart** is an associated meaning. See also 458 and 652.

Mnemonic: **GIVE ONE LADLEFUL**

1874

YO, homa*re*
HONOR, FAME, PRAISE
13 strokes

名誉 MEIYO honor, fame
栄誉 EIYO honor, fame
誉れ高い HOMARETAKAI renowned

Formerly 𦥯. 言 is **words/ speak** 274. 興 is **hands together** 1873, here acting phonetically to express **sing/ shout** and also lending connotations of **together**. Thus **shout out words together**, a somewhat vague reference to people **united in the singing of someone's praise**. **Honor** and **fame** are associated meanings. Suggest taking 𫩏 as a **laden table**.

Mnemonic: **FAME BRINGS WORDS OF PRAISE AND LADEN TABLE**

1875

YŌ
ORDINARY, WORK
11 strokes

中庸 CHŪYŌ middle path
凡庸 BONYŌ banality
租庸調 SOYŌCHŌ corvee, labor

Once written 𤰞, showing a combination of **hands holding pestle** 𢩙/庚 480 and **use** 甹/用 215. The latter also acts phonetically to express **work**. Thus **to work while using a pestle** (to pound rice etc.), which on the one hand came to mean **work** in a broader sense and on the other to symbolise **doing something mundane** and thus **ordinary**. Suggest taking 庸 as **building** 广 114, **hand** 彐, and **stick** I.

Mnemonic: **HAND USES STICK TO DO ORDINARY WORK IN BUILDING**

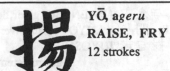

1876 YŌ, *ageru*
RAISE, FRY
12 strokes

揚水 YŌSUI pumping water
揚げ場 AGEBA landing stage
揚げ物 AGEMONO fried food

扌 is **hand** 32. 昜 is **sun rising** 144 q.v., here acting phonetically to express **raise** and also lending its own connotations of **rise/ raise**. Thus to **raise with the hand**, later just **raise**. In Japanese it has also acquired a meaning of **(deep) fry**, felt to be an associated meaning from the idea of lifting something out of a vat.

Mnemonic: HAND RAISED TO RISING SUN MAY GET FRIED

1877 YŌ, *yuru/reru/ragu/suru/suburu*
SHAKE, SWING, ROCK
12 strokes

動揺 DŌYŌ shaking
揺りいす YURIISU rocking chair
揺れ止め YUREDOME stabilizer

Formerly 搖. 扌 is **hand** 32. 𦍶 is a CO character meaning **vase/ pitcher**. Its etymology is rather unclear, though its old form 𦍌 reveals **meat** 夕/夕/月 365 and **can/ vessel** 缶/缶 (here 缶) 1095, and presumably it originally indicated a vessel for storing meat. In compounds it often appears to lend connotations of **sway/ shake/ not be straight**, but the reason for this is not clear. Here it acts phonetically to express **sway/ shake** and may possibly also lend similar connotations of its own. Thus to **shake with the hand**, later **shake/ sway/ rock** in a broad sense. Suggest taking ⺈ as **reaching hand** 303.

Mnemonic: SHAKING HANDS REACH FOR CAN

1878 YŌ, *tokeru/kasu*
MELT, DISSOLVE
13 strokes

溶液 YŌEKI solution
溶解 YŌKAI melt, dissolve
溶け合う TOKEAU melt together

氵 is **water** 40. 容 is **contain** 802, here acting phonetically to express **full** and also lending its meaning of **contain**. Thus **(a container) full of water**, which is still 1878's sole meaning in Chinese. The Japanese meaning of **dissolve** is felt by some scholars to be a borrowing, and by others to be an associated meaning from the idea of being immersed in water (with **melt** being a further association). Suggest taking 容 as **valley** 谷 122 and **roof/ house** 宀 28.

Mnemonic: HOUSE DISSOLVES IN VALLEY FULL OF WATER

1879

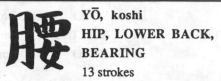

YŌ, koshi

HIP, LOWER BACK,

BEARING

13 strokes

腰痛 YŌTSŪ   lumbago

腰肉 KOSHINIKU   loin meat

物腰 MONOGOSHI   manner

Need/ vital 要 593 q.v., here in its original meaning of waist, with flesh/ of the body 月 365 added for clarity after its meaning started to change. It now means hip/ lower back rather than the waist specifically. Also used by figurative association to indicate bearing/ manner.

Mnemonic: **HIP IS VITAL PART OF BODY**

1880

YŌ, odoru

DANCE, LEAP, DOUBLE

14 strokes

踊り子 ODORIKO   dancing girl

舞踊 BUYŌ   dance, dancing

踊り字 ODORIJI   'repeat' sign

足 is foot/ leg 51. 甬 is raised/ break clear 176 q.v., here acting phonetically to express leap high and also lending similar connotations of its own. Thus to leap high (with the legs), with dance being an associated meaning. It is not clear how it also came to acquire its lesser meaning of double. Suggest taking 甬 as a simplification of pass 通 176.

Mnemonic: **DANCE, USING FEET IN PASSING**

1881

YŌ, kama

KILN, OVEN

15 strokes

窯業 YŌGYŌ   ceramics

窯業家 YŌGYŌKA   ceramist

乾燥窯 KANSŌGAMA

    drying kiln

穴 is hole 849, here meaning pit. 羔 is an NGU character meaning lamb (presumably sheep 羊 986 good for roasting [fire] ⺪ 8), here acting phonetically to express bake and possibly lending similar connotations of its own. Thus baking pit, i.e. oven, with kiln being an associated meaning.

Mnemonic: **SHEEP-ROASTING-PIT CAN BE KILN AS WELL AS OVEN**

1882 YŌ   擁護 YŌGO   protection, help
         EMBRACE, PROTECT   擁立 YŌRITSU   support
         16 strokes   抱擁 HŌYŌ   embrace

Of confused evolution and somewhat obscure as a result. Once written 𦥯, 半/扌 is **hand** 32, here meaning **arm**. 雝 comprises **bird** 隹/隹 216 and 邕/邕. The latter is a CO character meaning **union** and **harmony**. Its etymology is not fully clear, but it comprises **village** 邑 355 and **river** 川 /巛 48/ 680, and may have come to symbolise harmony through the naturalness of a village being located beside a river. The role of bird 隹 is not clear, but it should be noted that in Chinese 雝 exists as a character that can be interchanged with 邕 to mean union/ harmony. It also has an additional meaning of marsh, suggesting that it was originally an entirely separate character meaning water (near village) where birds gather before becoming confused with 邕 . To add to the confusion, 雍 also exists as a character in Chinese, interchangeable with 邕 but not 雝, despite the fact that it is obviously a simplification of 雝 rather than 邕 ! It is known that in the case of 1882 雍 acts phonetically to express **envelop/ wrap** (as well as possibly lending connotations of union and hence coming together), to give **wrap with the arms/ embrace** and by association **protect**. (Note that it is thus very similar to embrace/ envelop with the arms 抱 1794, though the latter lacks the associated meaning of protect.) Suggest taking 彡 as a variant of (short) **thread** 幺 111 and 亠 as **top**.

Mnemonic: **HAND PROTECTS BIRD WITH THREAD-LIKE CREST ON TOP**

1883 YŌ, utai, uta*u*   謡曲 YŌKYOKU   Noh chant
         NOH CHANT, SONG   民謡 MINYŌ   folk song
         16 strokes   謡本 UTAIBON   Noh text

Formerly 謠 . 言 is **words/ speak** 274. 䍃 is the somewhat unclear 'meat vessel' element seen in 1877 q.v., here acting phonetically to express **sway** and possibly also lending similar connotations of its own. **Swaying words** referred to a **modulated rendition of a noh text** or a **lilting song** (usually with little or no musical accompaniment). Suggest taking ⺈ as **reaching hand** 303 and 缶 as **can** (variant 缶 1095).

Mnemonic: **HAND REACHES FOR CAN, UTTERING WORDY CHANT**

602

1884		YOKU, osa*eru*	抑止 YOKUSHI	deterrent
		RESTRAIN, PRESS DOWN	抑圧 YOKUATSU	suppression
		7 strokes	抑制 YOKUSEI	restraint

Originally written ⿰⿱, being a mirror-image variant of **hand pressing down on bending person** ⿰/⿰ 425 q.v. (with bending person ⺃ 39 being replaced by bending/crouching person ⿱ / 巴 145). It similarly came to mean **press down** in a general sense, with **restrain** being a figurative association. A further **hand** 扌 32 was added later, and press down 印 was miscopied as raise 卬 1173 q.v. (literally bending person 卩 and a further person ⺄). Suggest taking 卩 as **bending person** and ⺄ as a reinforcing symbol of **bending**.

Mnemonic: **HAND PRESSES DOWN ON PERSON TILL DOUBLY BENT**

1885		YOKU, tsubasa	右翼 UYOKU	right wing
		WING	翼端 YOKUTAN	wingtip
		17 strokes	翼竜 YOKURYŪ	pterodactyl

羽 is **wings** 812. 異 is **differ** 807, here acting phonetically to express **wing** but of unclear semantic role. Thus **wing(s)**.

Mnemonic: **DIFFERENT WINGS, BUT WINGS NONETHELESS**

1886		RA, hadaka	裸身 RASHIN	nudity
		NAKED, BARE	赤裸裸 SEKIRARA	frankness
		13 strokes	裸馬 HADAKAUMA	bareback

衤 is **clothes** 420. 果 is **fruit**/ **result** 627, here acting phonetically to express **peel** but of unclear semantic role. Thus **to peel off clothes**/ **become naked**.

Mnemonic: **PEEL CLOTHES, LIKE FRUIT, AND BECOME NAKED**

1887	羅	RA	羅列 RARETSU	marshalling
		GAUZE, NET, INCLUDE	羅典 RATEN	Latin
		19 strokes	網羅的 MŌRATEKI	
				comprehensive

An ideograph combining the three elements of **thread** 糸 27, **net** 罒 193, and **bird** 隹 216, to give a meaning of **bird-net made of thread**. Now **net** in broad sense, including the figurative one of bring into one's fold/ **include**. **Gauze** is an associated meaning.

Mnemonic: **BIRD-NET OF THREAD, FINE AS GAUZE**

603

1888	**RAI, kaminari** **THUNDER, LIGHTNING** 13 strokes	雷雨 雷名 魚雷	**RAIU** **RAIMEI** **GYORAI**	thunderstorm renown torpedo

Once written 靐 . 雨 is **rain** 3, here in an extended sense of **atmospheric conditions**. 畾 is **three fields** 1419 (**field** 田 59), here acting phonetically to express **reverberate** and possibly also lending connotations of **quantity/ repetition**. Thus **atmospheric conditions that reverberate** (repeatedly?), a reference to **thunder**. By association it can also mean **lightning**.

Mnemonic: **RAIN FALLS ON FIELD AMID THUNDER AND LIGHTNING**

1889	**RAI, tanomu/moshii, tayoru** **REQUEST, RELY** 16 strokes	信頼 頼り無い 頼み	**SHINRAI** **TAYORINAI** **TANOMI**	trust unreliable favor, trust

Formerly 頼 and earlier 頼. A combination of shell/ **money** 貝 90 and 剌/剌/束刂. The latter is an NGU character meaning **be opposed**, but in Chinese it can also mean **cut/ slash**. It comprises **bundle** 朿/東 1535 and **sword/ cut** 力/刀/刂 181, and presumably originally meant **cut open a bundle**. Here it acts phonetically to express **profit** (but any semantic role unclear), combining with **money** 貝 to give **profit financially**. It was later borrowed to express **entreat**, giving by extension **request** and **rely**. Note that in compounds it sometimes appears to lend connotations of **divide**, probably as a result of the presence of **cut open** 束刂 in earlier forms. The modern form shows a miscopying of **sword** 刀 and **money** 貝 as **head** 頁 93.

Mnemonic: **RELY ON HEAD TO REQUEST A BUNDLE**

1890	**RAKU, karamu/maru** **ENTWINE, CONNECT** 12 strokes	連絡 絡み合う 絡み付く	**RENRAKU** **KARAMIAU** **KARAMITSUKU**	contact intertwine entwine

糸 is **thread** 27. 各 is **each** 438 q.v., here acting phonetically to express **tangle** and possibly also lending an idea of **impeded progress/ stopping** through its upturned foot element 夂. Thus **tangled threads** (which cause a halt in proceedings?), leading to **entwine** and by association **connect**.

Mnemonic: **EACH THREAD IS ENTWINED AND THUS CONNECTED**

604

1891	RAKU	酪農 RAKUNŌ	dairy farming
	CURD, DAIRY PRODUCE	酪酸 RAKUSAN	butyric acid
	13 strokes	乾酪 KANRAKU	cheese

酉 is **wine jar** 302, here indicating **fermentation**. 各 is **each** 438 q.v., here acting phonetically to express **solidify** and possibly also lending connotations of **stop moving** (freely). Thus **that which ferments and solidifies**, originally a reference to **curd** but now used of **dairy produce** in a broad sense.

Mnemonic: **EACH JAR OF DAIRY PRODUCE CONTAINS CURD**

1892	RAN	濫用 RANYŌ	abuse
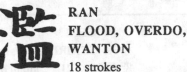	FLOOD, OVERDO,	濫費 RANPI	extravagance
	WANTON	はん濫 HANRAN	inundation
	18 strokes		

氵 is **water** 40. 監 is **supervise** 1111, here acting phonetically to express **overflow** and possibly also loosely lending connotations of **water filling a container** from its literal meaning of staring at one's reflection in a bowl of water. Thus **water overflowing**, later **overflow/ flood** and by association **overdo**. **Wanton** is also an associated meaning, from the idea of excessive.

Mnemonic: **WANTON SUPERVISION OF FLOODING WATER**

1893	RAN	欄干 RANKAN	railing
	COLUMN, RAILING,	空欄 KŪRAN	blank space
	SPACE	欄外 RANGAI	page margin
	20 strokes		

Formerly 欄. 木 is **wood/ tree** 69. 闌 is a confusing NGU character meaning **height, climax**, and **be well advanced**, while in Chinese it means rather **decline, finished, evening, overdo, wanton, fence**, and **door screen**. Its etymology is unclear, though it clearly comprises **door/ gate** 門 211 and **select/ remove from a bundle** 柬 608 q.v. In the case of 1893 it is known to have acted phonetically to express **encircle** (as well as lending a meaning of **fence?**), to give **encircling wood**, namely **fence/ railing(s)**. Encircling fence came to indicate **delineated area/ fixed space**, including by association **column** (i.e. fixed space in a text [and of late newspaper]). Suggest taking 柬 as **east** 184.

Mnemonic: **WOODEN RAILINGS ENCLOSE SPACE BY EASTERN GATE**

1894 	**RI**	吏員 RIIN	official
	OFFICIAL	能吏 NŌRI	able official
	6 strokes	吏臭 RISHŪ	'red tape'

Once written 㕛, being an early form of **thing** 事 293 q.v. and having the latter's early meaning of **work**. It came by association to mean **person at work**, and in particular to mean **official**. Note however that the addition of person 亻 39 gives use/ servant 使 287 q.v. It is not fully clear how and why 293, 287, and 1894 came to evolve along separate paths. Suggest taking 吏 as a combination of **hand** 乂, **box** 口, and **ten** 十 33.

Mnemonic: **OFFICIAL'S HAND HOLDS TEN BOXES**

1895	**RI**	下痢 GERI	diarrhoea
	DIARRHOEA	赤痢 SEKIRI	dysentery
	12 strokes	疫痢 EKIRI	infant diarrhoea

疒 is **sickness** 381. 利 is **profit** 596, here acting phonetically to express **diarrhoea** (itself phonetically associated with a term meaning **pour forth**) but of unclear semantic role. Thus the **sickness of diarrhoea** (the **'pouring forth sickness'**).

Mnemonic: **DIARRHOEA CAN BE A PROFITABLE SICKNESS?!**

1896	**RI**, ha*ku*	履歴 RIREKI	personal history
	WEAR (ON FEET), WALK,	履行 RIKŌ	performance
	FOOTWEAR, ACT	履き物 HAKIMONO	
	15 strokes		footwear, clog

Once written 㠱, showing that **again**/ return 復 782 q.v. is a miscopying of 㣽. This is a now defunct character meaning **walk slowly in clogs**. It comprises **movement (along a road)** ⼻ /彳 118, **upturned foot** ⼡ /夂 438 q.v. (here indicating **slow progress**), and **boat** 月 /舟 1354 (here indicating a type of **wooden clog** likened to a boat). **Slumped figure/ corpse** ⼫ /尸 236 was added both for its sound, to express **drag**, and for its own suggestion of **inertia/ lack of vitality**. Thus 1896 originally meant **walk slowly in clogs, dragging (the feet) lifelessly**. This gave both **walk** and **wear on the feet** (and occasionally **footwear**), with **act** being an associated meaning (originally do something slowly and reluctantly but do it nonetheless, now act in a broader sense).

Mnemonic: **CORPSE WALKS AGAIN, WEARING FOOTWEAR: SOME ACT!**

1897 RI, han*areru/su* 分離 BUNRI separation
SEPARATE, LEAVE 離陸 RIRIKU take-off
18 strokes 乳離れ CHIBANARE weaning

隹 is **bird** 216. 离 is a CO character meaning **bright/ glossy** and **oppose**. Its etymology is not fully clear but an old form 离 suggests it is a variant of scorpion 离/萬 392, presumably a type with glossy body and also associated with defiance. In the case of 1897 离 acts phonetically to express the name of a bird (a type of **oriole**) and probably also lends connotations of **bright (colored)**. Thus the **oriole bird** (a bird of bright plumage?). 1897 can still mean oriole in Chinese. Its main meaning of **separate/ leave** is generally taken to be a borrowing, but it is possible that the oriole may itself have symbolised parting through some migratory pattern (a view supported by the fact that in Chinese 1897 can also mean pass through). Suggest taking 凵 as a **box** 凵 with contents ×
(i.e. **full**) and **lid** 亠, and 内 as an 'odd' version of **insect** 虫 56.

Mnemonic: **SEPARATE BIRD FROM LIDDED BOX FULL OF ODD INSECTS**

1898 RYŪ, *yanagi* 柳糸 RYŪSHI willow branch
WILLOW, WILLOWY 花柳界 KARYŪKAI demimonde
9 strokes 川柳 SENRYŪ comic verse

木 is **tree** 69. 卯 is a variant of horse's bit 卯/卯 805 q.v., here acting phonetically to express **flow** and possibly also graphically suggesting **drooping**. Thus **tree** (whose branches) **flow** (and droop?), a reference to the **willow**. Suggest remembering 卯 as a symbol indicating **back to back**.

Mnemonic: **WILLOW TREES BACK TO BACK?!**

1899 RYŪ, RYŌ, *tatsu* 恐竜 KYŌRYŪ dinosaur
DRAGON 竜神 RYŪJIN dragon god
10 strokes 竜巻 TATSUMAKI whirlwind

Of confused graphic evolution. Formerly 龍. The earliest form 竜 shows a **four-legged creature with long tail, pointed nose, and large ears**. This then appears to have been stylised as 竜 with ⌐ felt to indicate pointed head and ears, ○ the body, 八 the legs, and 乙 the tail. A later form 龍 (the prototype of the semi-modern 龍) shows the pointed head and ears ⌐ replaced (it is not clear whether deliberately or in error) by **needle/ sharp** 辛 1432, the body and legs 八 replaced by **flesh/ of the body** 月 365, and the tail 乙 reshaped as 乚 with the addition of 彡 (**spikes/ tailplates?**). The modern form 竜 derives from the 青 part of 龍. Suggest remembering it as **stand** 立 73 and **electricity** 巳 (simplification of 電 180).

Mnemonic: **TRY TO GET DRAGON TO STAND ON ELECTRICITY**

| 1900 | RYŪ, tsubu GRAIN, PARTICLE 11 strokes | 粒子 RYŪSHI particle 一粒 HITOTSUBU one grain 粒粒 RYŪRYŪ assiduously |

米 is **rice** 201. 立 is **stand** 73, here acting phonetically to express **grain** but of unclear semantic role. Thus **grain of rice**, now **grain/ particle** in a general sense.

Mnemonic: **RICE STANDS IN GRAINS**

| 1901 | RYŪ HIGH, PEAK, PROSPER 11 strokes | 隆盛 RYŪSEI prosperity 隆起 RYŪKI upthrust 興隆 KŌRYŪ prosperity, rise |

Formerly 隆 and earlier 隆. 㞢/ 生 is **life/ growing plant** 42, here symbolising **upward growth**. 㣇 is an old form of **descend** 降 863 q.v. (later simplified to 降 and 阝夊), here acting phonetically to express **height** and also lending its own similar connotations (from its literal meaning of descend from a high hill). Thus **grow upward to a (great) height**, leading to **peak** and **high**, with **prosper** being an associated meaning. (Some scholars feel rather that its original meaning was **high hill**, with the 阝 of 㣇 being taken literally as **hill** 229 q.v.[now 阝].) Suggest taking 阝 as **hill**, and 夊 as **sit crosslegged**.

Mnemonic: **PROSPER IN LIFE AND SIT CROSSLEGGED ON PEAK OF HIGH HILL**

| 1902 | RYŪ SULFUR 12 strokes | 硫酸 RYŪSAN sulfuric acid 硫黄 IŌ* sulfur 硫化銀 RYŪKAGIN silver sulfide |

石 is **rock/ stone** 45, here meaning **mineral**. 㐬 is **newborn child** 409 q.v., here acting phonetically to express **fragile** and possibly also lending similar connotations of its own. Thus **fragile mineral**, a rather vague reference to **sulfur**. Suggest remembering 㐬 as a 'waterless' version of **flow** 流 409 (氵 being **water** 40).

Mnemonic: **SULFUR IS ROCK THAT FLOWS, WITHOUT WATER**

1903 虜	RYO, toriko CAPTIVE, CAPTURE 13 strokes	虜囚 RYOSHŪ captive 捕虜 HORYO prisoner of war ふ虜 FURYO prisoner of war

Formerly 虜 and earlier 虜, showing that the modern form 男 is not **man/ male** 男 54 -- though this may be a useful mnemonic -- but a derivative of a combination of **strength** 力 74 and 毌. The latter is a simplification of pierce 貫 1102, here symbolising **gathering/** putting together (from its literal meaning of threading items [/money] together). Thus 男 means **gather strength/ muster strength**. 虎/ 虍 is **tiger** 281, here acting phonetically to express **seize** and probably lending similar connotations of its own. 1903 originally meant to **seize something by mustering one's strength** (i.e. **by force**), and later came to mean **seize/ capture** in a broad sense. It was also used of capturing human beings (possibly partly as a result of the similarity of muster strength 男 and man 男), and by association was also used to refer to the **captive**.

Mnemonic: **MAN CAPTURES TIGER**

1904 慮	RYO THOUGHT, CONCERN 15 strokes	遠慮 ENRYO reserve 考慮 KŌRYO consideration 無慮 MURYO as many as

思 is **think** 131. 虍 is **tiger** 281, here acting phonetically to express **count** but of unclear semantic role. Thus to **think and count**, i.e. **ponder/ calculate**. This eventually came to mean **serious thought/ concern** in a broad sense, though the original association with numbers is still very occasionally encountered (see muryo above).

Mnemonic: **THINK CONCERNED THOUGHTS ABOUT TIGER**

1905 了	RYŌ FINISH, COMPLETE, UNDERSTAND 2 strokes	了解 RYŌKAI understanding 了承 RYŌSHŌ understanding 終了 SHŪRYŌ finish

Originally written , showing an **armless child** 孒 / 子 25. This was a representation of a **child unable to use its limbs due to paralysis** (presumably as a result of infantile paralysis/ poliomyelitis). The present meanings are borrowings.

Mnemonic: **UNDERSTAND THAT CHILD NEEDS ARMS TO BE COMPLETE**

1906 RYŌ, suzu*mu*/*shii*   涼味 RYŌMI   coolness
COOL   涼み台 SUZUMIDAI   bench
11 strokes   涼風 SUZUKAZE   cool breeze

氵 is **water** 40. 京 is **capital** 99, here acting phonetically to express **cool** but of unclear semantic role. Thus **cool water**, now **cool** rather of ambient temperature.

Mnemonic: **WATER IN CAPITAL IS COOL**

1907 RYŌ   猟師 RYŌSHI   hunter
HUNTING   猟銃 RYŌJŪ   hunting gun
11 strokes   渉猟 SHŌRYŌ

           extensive reading

Formerly 獵 and earlier 㦰, 犬/犭 is **dog** 17. 鼡/鼠 is a CO character of somewhat unclear etymology meaning **mane/ bristles** (conveyed in Japanese by an NGU character 鬣, which adds hair 彡 1706). 㓞 appears similar to brain and hair 惱 954, but lacks the upper stroke ノ of brain 囟 and is possibly here body and hair. 比 shows legs/ claws, and ㇂ presumably a tail. Thus 鼡 appears to have originally depicted a **hairy animal**. Here it acts phonetically to express **leap**, and almost certainly lends a meaning of **animal**. 1907 originally referred to a **hunting dog leaping on its prey**, and later came to symbolise **hunting** in general. Suggest taking 㓞 as **claws** ʼʼ and **use** 用 (variant 用 215).

Mnemonic: **DOG PUTS CLAWS TO USE IN HUNTING**

1908 RYŌ, misasagi   陵墓 RYŌBO   imperial tomb
IMPERIAL TOMB, MOUND   丘陵 KYŪRYŌ   hill, hillock
11 strokes   御陵 GORYŌ   imperial tomb

Somewhat obscure. 阝 is **hill/ mound** 229. 夌 (once written 夌) is an unclear element but is known to have once meant **high hill**. 夂/夊 is **upturned foot** 夊 438 q.v., which could mean descend from above and thus imply height (e.g. 863). 㐀 appears to combine high 儿 509 with growing plant 屮 /㞢 9/42, which could also mean upward growth and thus height (see 隆 1901, with which 1908 seems to share considerable semantic and etymological common ground). In the case of 1908 夌 lends a meaning of **high hill** and is also believed to lend its sound to express **big**. Thus **(big?) high hill/ mound**, later used in particular to refer to an **imperial burial mound**. Suggest taking 夌 as **ground** 土 60 and **out of** ノ八 66.

Mnemonic: **UPTURNED FOOT STICKS OUT OF GROUND ON MOUND OF IMPERIAL TOMB**

1909 僚	RYŌ COLLEAGUE, OFFICIAL 14 strokes	同僚 DŌRYŌ	colleague
		僚友 RYŌYŪ	colleague
		官僚 KANRYŌ	bureaucrat

亻 is **person** 39. 尞 is a CO character meaning **fuel used in sacrifices**. Its etymology is not fully clear, but an early form 尞 (later 尞) clearly shows **fire** 火 8 and **tree/ wood** 米 / 木 69. ` may possibly indicate sap/ resin (see 1334), and 呂 may possibly indicate either puffs of smoke or combustible material (see 120). In the case of 1909 its semantic role is unclear, but it is known to act phonetically to express **work**. Thus **working person**, which later came to refer in particular to an **official** as well as to a **workmate/ colleague**. Suggest taking 尞 as **big** 大 53, **away** ` ′ 66, **day** 日 62, and **little** 小 36.

Mnemonic: **PERSON AWAY ON BOTH BIG DAYS AND LITTLE DAYS IS OFFICIALLY A COLLEAGUE**

1910 寮	RYŌ HOSTEL, DORMITORY 15 strokes	寮生 RYŌSEI	boarding student
		寮歌 RYŌKA	dormitory song
		寮長 RYŌCHŌ	head of hostel

宀 is **building/ house** 28. 尞 is **fuel used in sacrifices** 1909 q.v., here acting phonetically to express **window** and possibly also lending connotations of a **(smoking) fire**. 1910 originally referred to a **window (cum smoke vent?) in a house**. Its meaning later changed rather to **house with a window**, and then to **small building**. In Chinese it now means hut, but in Japanese has come to be applied to a larger building, specifically a **dormitory/ hostel**. Suggest remembering 寮 by association with **colleague** 1909, without the **person** 亻 39 element (i.e. 'impersonal').

Mnemonic: **COLLEAGUE STAYS IN IMPERSONAL HOSTEL BUILDING**

1911 療	RYŌ CURE, HEAL 17 strokes	療法 RYŌHŌ	remedy
		療養 RYŌYŌ	recuperation
		医療班 IRYŌHAN	medical team

疒 is **sickness** 381. 尞 is **fuel used in sacrifices** 1909, here acting phonetically to express **make good** and possibly also lending connotations of supplication to the gods. Thus **make good an illness** (while praying to the gods?), i.e. **cure/ heal**. Suggest taking 尞 as an 'impersonal' variant of **colleague** 僚 1909 (i.e. without **person** 亻 39).

Mnemonic: **COLLEAGUE'S SICKNESS HEALED BY IMPERSONAL CURE**

1912		RYŌ, RŌ, kate	食糧 SHOKURYŌ provisions
		PROVISIONS, FOOD	兵糧 HYŌRŌ army provisions
		18 strokes	糧道 RYŌDŌ supplies

米 is **rice** 201, here symbolising **food** in general. 量 is **quantity** 600 q.v., here acting phonetically to express **road** and also lending its original meaning of **sack full of something**. Thus **sacks full of food for the road**, namely **provisions for a journey**. Later **provisions** in a broader sense.

Mnemonic: **QUANTITY OF RICE MAKES UP PROVISIONS**

1913		RIN	厘毛 RINMŌ a trifle
		RIN, TINY AMOUNT	二厘 NIRIN two rin
		9 strokes	一分一厘 ICHIBUICHIRIN tiny bit

Formerly written 釐. 犛 is a CO character meaning **pound wheat** (striking hand 攵 101, wheat 耒 [variant 来 217] and building 厂 [variant 广 114]). 里 is **village** 219, here acting phonetically to express **separate** but of unclear semantic role. Thus to **pound wheat and separate (wheat from chaff)**. This led on the one hand to **sort/ arrange** (still one of 1913's meanings in Chinese) and on the other to **small bit(s)**. By association with small bit, 1913 is used both in Chinese and Japanese to refer to a **small coin** (one thousandth of a yen in Japanese), and can also be used of a **small measurement** (0.3 mm. in Japanese). Suggest taking 厂 as **cliff** 45.

Mnemonic: **TINY VILLAGE BELOW CLIFF VALUED AT A MERE RIN**

1914		RIN	倫理 RINRI ethics
		PRINCIPLES, ETHICS	人倫 JINRIN morality
		10 strokes	絶倫 ZETSURIN no peerless

亻 is **person** 39. 侖 is **align neatly** 601 q.v., here acting phonetically to express **put in proper order** and also lending similar connotations of its own. Thus the **proper order which a person should observe**, a reference to **correct principles of behavior/ morality**. **Ethics** is an associated meaning.

Mnemonic: **PERSON ALIGNED ACCORDING TO ETHICAL PRINCIPLES**

1915		RIN, tonari NEIGHBOR, ADJOIN 16 strokes	隣室 RINSHITSU	next room
			隣接 RINSETSU	adjacency
			隣り合う TONARIAU *	adjoin

Of confused evolution. Correctly written 粦β, i.e. with **village** β 355 rather than **hill** β 229. Moreover, old forms such as 粦艹 show that **rice** 米 210 is a miscopying of **flame** 炎 1024 (double fire 火 8). Both 粦 and 㷠 exist as interchangeable CO characters meaning **flitting light/** will-o'-the-wisp (the correct 㷠 comprising flame/light 炎 and opposed feet 舛 1211, here believed to lend a meaning of stop and start [normally associated with the related concept of upturned feet -- see 438], and thus meaning light that stops and starts). In the case of 1915 粦 / 㷠 acts phonetically to express **row/ line**, and may possibly also lend connotations of **flickering lights**. 1915 originally referred to a **row (of houses along a road) forming a village** (their flickering lights indicating habitation?), a row of five houses or more being the legal definition of a village in ancient China. This gave rise to the present meanings of **neighbor** and **adjoin**. Suggest taking 夕 as **night** 44 and 幵 as a variant of **well** 井 1470.

Mnemonic: **NEIGHBORS WASH RICE NIGHTLY AT WELL ADJOINING HILL**

1916		RUI, namida TEAR 10 strokes	涙管 RUIKAN	tear duct
			涙雨 NAMIDAAME	light rain
			空涙 SORANAMIDA	
				crocodile tears

Formerly also written 淚. 氵 is **water** 40. 戻/戾 is **return** 1920, here acting phonetically to express **drop** but of unclear semantic role. **Drop of water** is a rather vague reference to a **tear**. Tear is sometimes conveyed by an informal character 泪, using water 氵 and eye 目 72, which is seemingly simpler and more meaningful.

Mnemonic: **WATER RETURNS AS TEARS**

1917		RUI ACCUMULATE, INVOLVE 11 strokes	累計 RUIKEI	sum total
			累積 RUISEKI	accumulation
			係累 KEIRUI	dependents

Formerly 纍. 糸 is **thread** 27. 畾 is three fields 1419 q.v. (**field** 田 59), here acting phonetically to express **bind** and probably also lending connotations of quantity/ repetition. Thus to **bind with thread** (voluminously?), leading to **bind** in a broad sense (still a meaning in Chinese). Bind led to **bring together** and hence the figurative **involve**. **Accumulate** is also felt to derive from the idea of bringing together, and may at the same time have been suggested by the accumulation of fields in 畾.

Mnemonic: **THREADS ACCUMULATE IN FIELD**

1918 RUI   土塁 DORUI   earthwork
FORT, BASEBALL BASE   敵塁 TEKIRUI   enemy fort
12 strokes   塁審 RUISHIN   base umpire

Formerly 壘. 土 is **earth** 60. 畾 is three fields 1419 q.v. (**field** 田 59), here acting phonetically to express **build up** and probably also lending its own connotations of accumulation. Thus **built up earth**, a reference to an **embankment** and by association **fort/base**. Also used nowadays of a base in baseball. Suggest taking ⅀ as a symbol of **four**.

Mnemonic: **FOUR EARTHEN BASES IN FIELD**

1919 REI, hage*mu/masu*   精励 SEIREI   diligence
ENCOURAGE, STRIVE   奨励金 SHŌREIKIN   bounty
7 strokes   励み合う HAGEMIAU   vie

Formerly 勵 and earlier 蠇. 力 is **strength/ effort** 74. 萬 is **scorpion** 392 q.v., here acting phonetically to express **strive** but of unclear semantic role (though it may possibly suggest prick/ sting/ goad). Thus **strive with effort**. **Encourage** is the causative equivalent. The later addition of **cliff** 厂 45 is believed to result from confusion with a CO character 厲, meaning whetstone (厂 being an abbreviation of stone 石 45, with scorpion 萬 acting phonetically to express grind and probably also lending connotations of sharp). The modern form uses the substitute for 萬, namely **ten thousand** 万 (see 392).

Mnemonic:**STRONGLY ENCOURAGE TO CLIMB TEN THOUSAND CLIFFS**

1920 戻 REI, modo*ru/su*   戻し税 MODOSHIZEI tax refund
RETURN, BRING BACK,   返戻 HENREI   return
REBEL, BEND, VOMIT 戻しそう MODOSHISŌ   feel sick
7 strokes

Obscure. Formerly 戾, showing **door** 尸/戸 108 and **dog** 犬 17. 1920 is believed by some authoritative Japanese scholars to have originally referred to a **dog crouching to pass under a door**. Crouching/ bending the back led to **bend** in a broader sense (now a minor meaning in Japanese). The associated idea of **crouching then returning to a normal stance** is believed to have come by further association to mean **return** in a broad sense, including return to a place. **Give back/ bring back** (including in the sense of **vomit**) is the transitive version. **Rebel** and **be perverse** (minor meanings in Japanese, but major meanings in Chinese) are seen as associated meanings with bend, from the idea of not being straight/ proper. The dog under a door theory does not seem convincing, with many of the interpretations appearing forced, and it seems equally likely that the core meaning of return stems simply from a **dog returning to its home and appearing at the door**. However, in such case it is not clear how the meaning of bend (and thus its derivatives) was acquired. Suggest taking 大 as **big** 53.

Mnemonic: **RETURN TO BIG DOOR TO VOMIT**

1921 REI, RIN, suzu   電鈴 DENREI   electric bell
          (SMALL) BELL, CHIME   風鈴 FŪRIN   wind chime
          13 strokes   鈴生り SUZUNARI*   cluster

Also written 鈴. 金 is **metal** 14, here meaning **metal item**. 令/令 is **order** 603, here acting phonetically to express **tongue** but of unclear semantic role. Thus **metal item with a tongue, a reference to a bell.**

Mnemonic: **ORDER METAL BELL TO CHIME**

1922 REI, kobo*reru*   零細 REISAI na   small
          ZERO, TINY, FALL   零下 REIKA   below zero
          13 strokes   零落 REIRAKU   downfall

Also written 零, and earlier 霝. 雨/雨 is **rain** 3, while ᴗᴗᴗ indicates **drops**. Thus **raindrops**. Note that 霝 still exists as a CO character with this meaning. **Order** 令/令 603 was later used as an alternative to ᴗᴗᴗ, lending its sound to express **fall** but of unclear semantic role. Thus **falling rain**, now **fall** in a broader sense (though it can still mean specifically falling rain in Chinese). Originally 零 could, like 霝, also mean raindrops, and this came to mean **drop** in general and by association **something tiny**. **Zero** is a further association (in Japanese only), from the idea of something being so tiny as to be to all intents and purposes non-existent.

Mnemonic: **ORDER RAINFALL TO BE ZERO**

1923 REI, RYŌ, tama   幽霊 YŪREI   ghost
          SPIRIT, SOUL   悪霊 AKURYŌ   evil spirit
          15 strokes   霊屋 TAMAYA   mausoleum

Formerly 靈. 霝 is **raindrops** 1922, here with an extended meaning of **falling/ descending from heaven**. 巫 is an NGU character meaning **sorceress/ shamaness/ temple maiden** (etymology unclear, but an old form 𤕝 suggests **people** (㇄/从 39 **at work** 工 113). 1923 originally referred to **a shamaness in a state of possession**, i.e. with the **gods/ spirits having descended upon her from heaven**. By association it came to refer to the **spirits** themselves. (Note that gods and spirits/ souls of the dead conceptually overlap as a result of ancestor worship.) Suggest taking 雨 as **rain** 3 and 巫 as a variant of **line (up)** 並 1775.

Mnemonic: **SPIRITS LINE UP IN RAIN -- HARDY SOULS**

1924 隷 **REI**
SLAVE, PRISONER
16 strokes

奴 隷 制 DOREISEI　　slavery
隷 従 REIJŪ　　slavery
隷 属 REIZOKU　　subordination

Formerly also 隸. 隶 is **seize by the tail** 1547, here meaning simply **seize/ obtain**. 柰/柰 is the rather awkward supplication to the gods/ earnest wish element seen in 1108 q.v., here acting phonetically to express **pledge** but of unclear semantic role. 1924 originally meant **obtain something pledged** (i.e. pawned). It came to refer in particular to **obtaining a pledged slave**, partly because 柰/柰 could also phonetically express bind and by association bound person/ slave, and eventually 1924 came to refer to the **slave** himself/ herself. **Prisoner** is an associated meaning with slave/ bound person. Suggest taking 柰 as **samurai** 士 494 and **show** 示 695.

Mnemonic: **SAMURAI SEIZED AND SHOWN AS SLAVE**

1925 齢 **REI**
AGE
17 strokes

年 齢 NENREI　　age, years
妙 齢 MYŌREI　　youth
高 齢 KŌREI　　great age

Formerly 齡. 齒/歯 is **teeth** 290. 令/令 is **order** 603, here acting phonetically to express **count** but of unclear semantic role. 1925 originally meant to **count teeth and thereby assess age** (believed to have been used of humans rather than animals), and later came to mean **age**.

Mnemonic: **ORDER TEETH-COUNT TO ASSESS AGE**

1926 **REI, uruwa**shii
BEAUTIFUL
19 strokes

麗 人 REIJIN　　a belle, beauty
美 麗 BIREI　　beauty
秀 麗 SHŪREI na　　beautiful

鹿 is **deer** 1204. 丽 is a now defunct character indicating **plurality** (from 丽, believed to indicate two adzes), and also acts here phonetically to express **group**. Thus **group/ herd of deer**. **Beautiful** is technically a borrowed meaning, though it should be noted that the deer was itself a symbol of grace and beauty, and thus herd of deer could be reinterpreted symbolically as **much beauty**. Suggest taking 丽 as **hoofprints**.

Mnemonic: **HOOFPRINTS LEFT BY BEAUTIFUL DEER**

616

1927		REKI, koyomi CALENDAR, ALMANAC 14 strokes	暦年 REKINEN calendar year 西暦 SEIREKI Anno Domini 花暦 HANAGOYOMI floral calendar

Formerly 暦 . 日 is **sun/ day** 62, here indicating **passage of time**. 厤/厤 is a simplification of **history/ regular path** 歷/歴 606 q.v. Thus **(that which shows) regular path of time**, a reference to a **calendar** or **almanac**. Suggest remembering 厤 as **history** 歴 minus its **foot/ stop** element 止 129.

Mnemonic: **CALENDAR RECORDS NON-STOP HISTORY OF DAYS**

1928		RETSU, oto*ru* BE INFERIOR 6 strokes	卑劣 HIRETSU baseness 劣情 RETSUJŌ lust 劣等 RETTŌ inferiority

Strength 力 74 and **few/ little** 少 143. **Little strength** indicated **inferiority**.

Mnemonic: **THOSE WITH LITTLE STRENGTH ARE INFERIOR**

1929		RETSU FIERCE, INTENSE 10 strokes	烈火 REKKA raging fire 烈女 RETSUJO heroine 烈風 REPPŪ gale

灬 is **fire** 8. 列 is **row/ line** 414, here acting phonetically to express **destroy** and possibly also lending a suggestion of **spreading**. Thus **destructive fire** (that spreads?), symbolising something **fierce/ intense**.

Mnemonic: **ROW OF FIERCE FIRES**

1930		RETSU, sa*ku/keru* SPLIT, RIP, REND 12 strokes	破裂 HARETSU bursting 分裂 BUNRETSU splitting 裂け目 SAKEME rip, crack

衣 is **clothes** 420. 列 is **row/ line** 414 q.v., here with its literal meaning of **cut up in sequence**. 1930 originally referred to the **careful cutting of cloth in order to make clothes**, but later came to mean **cut** in a destructive sense (i.e. **rip/ rend**), possibly partly because its sound could also express **destroy**.

Mnemonic: **ROW OF RIPPED CLOTHES**

1931	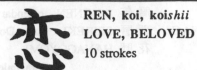	REN, koi, koi*shii* LOVE, BELOVED 10 strokes	恋愛 RENAI	love
			失恋 SHITSUREN	lost love
			恋人 KOIBITO	lover

Formerly 戀 . 心 is **heart/ feelings** 147, while 緣 is **tied together** 581. **Hearts tied together** is a reference to **love**. Some scholars believe that 緣 also acts phonetically to express **attract**. Suggest taking 亦 as a 'sort of' variant of **red** 亦 46.

Mnemonic: **LOVE SYMBOLISED BY A SORT OF RED HEART**

1932		REN HONEST, CHEAP, ANGLE 13 strokes	廉直 RENCHOKU	integrity
			廉価 RENKA	cheap price
			破廉恥 HARENCHI	impudence

Formerly 廉 . 广 is **building** 114. 兼/兼 is **combine** 850, here acting phonetically to express **steep/ sheer** but of unclear semantic role. 1932 originally referred to an **impressive building with towering steep walls**, such as a **hall** or **temple**, but this meaning has now disappeared. It came to acquire the lesser meaning of **angle/ angular** as a result of being used instead of a now defunct character 磏 , which shows **stone/ rock** 石 45 and **combine** 兼 and presumably originally meant **assemblage of rocks** or similar (with angular being an associated meaning). **Honest** and **cheap** are also borrowed meanings.

Mnemonic: **CHEAP BUILDING COMBINES ANGLES**

1933		REN, ne*ru* REFINE, TRAIN, DRILL 16 strokes	錬金術 RENKINJUTSU	alchemy
			錬成 RENSEI	training
			錬り金 NERIGANE	
				tempered steel

Formerly 鍊 . 金 is **metal** 14. 柬 is **select/ remove from bundle** 608 q.v., here acting phonetically to express **heat** and probably also lending an idea of **selecting the best/ removing impurities**. Thus to **heat metal (to remove impurities?)**, a reference to **refining** it. Now also used by association of **training/ drilling** people. Suggest taking 柬 as **east** 184.

Mnemonic: **GO EAST FOR TRAINING IN METAL REFINING**

1934 RO   炉辺 ROHEN/ ROBE   fireside
FURNACE   暖炉 DANRO   fireplace, stove
8 strokes   原子炉 GENSHIRO
                     nuclear reactor

Formerly 爐. 火 is **fire** 8. 盧 is an NGU character confusingly listed (without illustration) as meaning hut, but in Chinese it has a range of meanings centered on **receptacle/ container**. It comprises **dish/ vessel** 皿 1307, **basket** 田 399 (now usually 由 -- see also 1757), and **tiger** 虍 281. The role of tiger 虍 is not clear, but vessel 皿 and basket 田 clearly indicate **containers**. Thus **fire container**, i.e. **hearth** and later **furnace**. The modern form uses **door** 戸 108 as an essentially graphic simplification (despite wide criticism as lacking balance), though it also has some semantic relevance.

Mnemonic: **FURNACE HAS FIRE DOOR**

1935 RO, RŌ, tsuyu   露出 ROSHUTSU   exposure
DEW, REVEAL,   夜露 YOTSUYU   evening dew
SMALL, RUSSIA   露店 ROTEN   street stall
21 strokes

雨 is **rain** 3, here meaning **rain-like**. 路 is road 415, here acting phonetically to express **round/ globular** and possibly also lending an idea of tread. Thus **round rain-like things** (on which one treads?), a reference to **dew(drops)**. Since a dewdrop was a symbol of something **small** and/or **transient** 1935 is also sometimes used in these senses. It is not fully clear how it also came to mean **reveal/ make open**. This does not seem to be a borrowing, and is believed to stem from the idea of dew appearing openly for all to see. 1935 was later borrowed for its sound to refer to <u>Russia</u>.

Mnemonic: **'RAIN' ON RUSSIAN ROAD REVEALED TO BE DEW**

1936 RŌ   新郎 SHINRŌ   bridegroom
MAN, HUSBAND   郎等 RŌDŌ   retainers
9 strokes   太郎 TARŌ   male name

Formerly 郞. 阝 is **village** 355. 良/㿝 is **good** 598. 1936 was originally used as a proper noun to refer to a certain village in ancient China (literally **Good Village**). Its present meanings result from its being used as an expedient simplification of the term 良人. This combines good 良 with person 亻 39 and was used by women to address their **husband**. Hence also **man** in a broader sense, and its frequent use in **male names**.

Mnemonic: **HUSBAND IS MAN FROM GOOD VILLAGE**

| 1937 | | RŌ, nami
WAVE, DRIFT, WASTE
10 strokes | 波浪 HARŌ
浪費 RŌHI
浪人 RŌNIN | waves, surge
waste
ronin, drifter |

氵 is **water/ river** 40. 良 is **good** 598. 1937 was originally used as a proper noun to refer to a **certain river** in ancient China (literally **Good River**), and was later used instead of a complex character meaning **wave**. **Drift** and **waste** are both associated meanings (from the idea of lacking direction).

Mnemonic: **DRIFT ON WAVES ON STRETCH OF GOOD WATER**

| 1938 | | RŌ
CORRIDOR, WALKWAY
12 strokes | 廊下 RŌKA
画廊 GARŌ
回廊 KAIRŌ | corridor
picture gallery
corridor |

Formerly 廊 . 广 is (large) **roof/ building** 114, here meaning **roof**. 郎 /郎 is **man/ husband** 1936, here acting phonetically to express **space** but of unclear semantic role. 1938 originally referred to the **space under the overhang of a roof**, i.e. **veranda/ walkway**, and by association later came to mean **corridor**. Suggest remembering 郎 by association with the name **Tarō** (see 1936).

Mnemonic: **TARŌ IS IN CORRIDOR OF BUILDING**

| 1939 |  | RŌ
TOWER
13 strokes | 鐘楼 SHŌRŌ
望楼 BŌRŌ
楼閣 RŌKAKU | bell tower
watchtower
multi-storied building |

Formerly 樓 . 木 is **wood** 69. 婁/娄 is **tie/ shamaness** 151 q.v., here acting phonetically to express **build up** and possibly also lending connotations of linking/ assembling. Thus **wooden item that is built up**, a reference to a **tower**. Suggest taking 米 as **rice** 201 and 女 as **woman** 35.

Mnemonic: **WOMAN PREPARES RICE IN WOODEN TOWER**

1940 漏	RŌ, mor*u*/rer*u*/ras*u* LEAK 14 strokes	漏電 RŌDEN	short circuit
		漏出 RŌSHUTSU	leakage
		雨漏り AMAMORI	leak in roof

Once simply 屚. 尸 is **corpse** 236, here acting as a simplification of **building** 屋 236. 雨 is **rain** 3. Thus **rain on building**, a somewhat awkward reference to **rain <u>entering</u> building** and hence **leak**. **Water** 氵 40 was added later, presumably to draw attention to the rain rather than the building, but it is not clear why a more semantically relevant element such as **hole** 穴 849 or **enter** 入 63 (or some phonetic substitute) was not used.

Mnemonic: **RAINWATER LEAKS ONTO CORPSE**

1941 賄	WAI, makana*u* BRIBE, PROVIDE, BOARD 13 strokes	収賄 SHŪWAI	taking bribe
		贈賄 ZŌWAI	bribery
		賄い付き MAKANAITSUKI	
			with board

貝 is **shell**/ **money** 90. 有 is **exist**/ **have** 401 q.v., here acting phonetically to express **give** and possibly also lending an idea of **possession**. Thus **to give (someone) money** (i.e. into their possession?), meaning to **provide for someone**. **Board** and **bribe** are associated meanings.

Mnemonic: **HAVE MONEY THANKS TO BRIBE**

1942 惑	WAKU, mado*u* BE CONFUSED 12 strokes	迷惑 MEIWAKU	trouble
		惑星 WAKUSEI	planet
		戸惑い TOMADOI	bewilderment

心 is **heart**/ **feelings** 147. 或 is **a certain** 809 q.v., here acting phonetically to express **doubt** but of unclear semantic role. Confusingly, 或 normally means **delineated area**, which might be felt to suggest the opposite of **doubt**/ **uncertainty**, but since it technically means <u>roughly</u> **delineated area** (from the idea of crude markers -- see also 698) it may possibly focus on the idea of knowing something approximately but not with absolute certainty. Nevertheless, its choice as a phonetic seems very inappropriate. Thus **doubt in the heart**/ **feelings of doubt**, leading by association to **confusion**. Suggest taking 戈 as **halberd**/ **lance** 493, and 口 as a variant of **one**/ **single** 一 1 and **opening**/ **entrance** 口 20.

Mnemonic: **CONFUSED FEELINGS OVER LANCE AT SINGLE ENTRANCE**

1943 waku   枠組 WAKUGUMI framework
                    FRAME   枠無し WAKUNASHI frameless
                    8 strokes   枠内 WAKUNAI within limits

A 'made in Japan' character. 木 is **wood** 69. 卆 is usually the abbreviated form of **soldier** 卒 537, but is here an abbreviation of **rate** 率 803 q.v., here with its literal meaning of **devices for twisting threads into rope**. Thus 1943 originally meant **wooden device(s) for twisting threads into rope**, with **frame** being an associated meaning. Suggest taking 九 as **nine** 12 and 十 as **ten** 33.

Mnemonic: **FRAME MADE OF NINETEEN PIECES OF WOOD**

1944 WAN   港湾 KŌWAN   harbor
                    BAY, GULF   湾入 WANNYŪ   inlet
                    12 strokes   東京湾 TŌKYŌWAN Tokyo Bay

Formerly 灣. 氵 is **water** 40. 彎 is an NGU character meaning **bowed/ curved**, comprising **bow** 弓 836 and **tied together** 絲 581 (i.e. the shape of a strung bow). Thus **water in a bowed shape**, i.e. a **bay/ gulf**. Suggest taking 亦 as a variant of **red** 赤 46, namely **reddish**.

Mnemonic: **REDDISH WATER CHARACTERISES BOW-SHAPED BAY**

1945 腕 WAN, ude   腕章 WANSHŌ   armband
                    ARM, ABILITY   手腕 SHUWAN   ability
                    12 strokes   細腕 HOSOUDE
                                          thin arms, slender means

Formerly also written 捥, i.e. with **hand/ arm** 扌 32 instead of **meat/ (of the) body** 月 365. 宛 is an NGU character now used to mean **addressed to**, but in Chinese it can mean **bending**, **soft**, **yield**, and **obliging/ polite** (the latter clearly a figurative association with yielding, and presumably leading by further association to addressed to). It comprises **roof/ house** 宀 28 and 夗, which is a CO character meaning **turn in one's sleep** (**night** 夕 44 and **slumped/ bent body** 巳 768). 宛 may have originally been merely an embellished variant of 夗, meaning turn in one's sleep at home, but it clearly had dominant connotations of **bending the body**. Confusingly, in the case of 1945 宛 acts phonetically to express **straighten**, but also lends its meaning of **bent**. Thus 捥 means to **straighten a bent arm**, while 腕 means **straighten a bent body**. This came to symbolise a **display of strength**, either in pushing or lifting, and hence came to mean both **strong arm** and **ability**. It is now also used of **arm** in a general sense.

Mnemonic: **BODY SLUMPS NIGHTLY AT HOME, BUT ARMS STILL ABLE**

APPENDICES AND INDICES

COMMONLY OCCURRING ELEMENTS
AND THEIR PRINCIPAL MEANINGS

2 strokes

凵	container, vessel
卜	divination
亻	person
𠆢	person
人	person
入	person
儿	bending person
卩	bending person
勹	bending person
巴	slumped person
匕	fallen person
冫	ice, freeze
勹	cover, encircle, protect
冖	cover, roof, building
力	strength, effort
扌	hand
又	hand, take, help
十	ten, many, needle, cut, plant
丂	twist, flat, emerge, stop
八 丷丿	away, out of, split, oppose
𠆢 丿乚	away, out of, split, oppose
厶	nose, self, vapor, abbrev.
刀	sword, cut
刂	sword, cut
匚	container
厂	cliff, rock, stone, roof, home, building, cloth, oppose
几	table, desk, stool

3 strokes

艹	grass, plants

犭	dog, beast
山	mountain, hill, occ. fire
子	child, small
宀	roof, house, building
巾	cloth, thread
阝	(on left) hill, mound, terracing
阝	(on right) village, town
夂	upturned foot, slow progress, stop, fall, come down
工	work, measure, occ. big, dog
土	soil, earth, ground, plant, man
士	man, warrior
扌	hand, arm, manual task
女	woman, soft, yield
小 ⺍	small
忄	heart, feelings
氵	water, river, liquid
大	big, man, dog, hands, plants
巛	river
尸	corpse, slumped figure, buttocks, building
己	twist, bend, thread, rise
巳	twist, bend, serpent, embryo
廾	hands, together, raise, offer
口	mouth, say, words, opening, hole, round
弓	bow, bend, curve, pull
辶	movement, road
夂	movement
彳	road, movement
亼	lid, cover, cap
囗	enclosure

624

彡幺寸也弋夕彐/彐　hairs, delicate, pattern, attractive
short, small, thread
hand, measure, careful action
twisting, uneven
stake, measure
evening, night, upturned foot
hand

矢疒衤田石示立禾且穴生冊目罒皿

arrow, measure, speed, straight
sickness, illness, affliction
clothing
field, container
rock, stone
gods, altar, show
stand
rice plant, rice, grain, soft
pile, accumulate
hole, opening
life, birth, plant, growth, emerge
writing, recording, arranging
eye, see
eye, see, net, dish
dish

4 strokes

王日火灬艹木月犬王戈歹手少水止巴辶欠牛心爫戶礻攴

jewel, round, precious
sun, day, time, bright, speak,
　full container
fire, heat, burn, roast
fire, heat, burn, roast
grass, plants
tree, wood, plants
meat, body, moon, boat
dog, beast
king, ruler, jewel, stand
halberd, lance, weapon, cut
death, injury, cut, bones
hand, arm, manual task
few, little
water, river, liquid
foot, stop, move, occ. plant
bending person
movement
gape, open, mouth
cow, bull, horns
heart, feeling
hand, claws, reach
door, building,
altar, gods, show
stick in hand, strike, force,
　causative

6 strokes

糸㫃衣耳米羽艮虍虫竹肉豆舟羊/𦍌

thread, cord, bind, tie
fluttering flag
clothing
ear, listen
rice, grain, food
wings, flight
stop and stare, look back
tiger
insect, snake
bamboo, wood, plant
meat, body
vessel, food
boat, convey
sheep, fine

7 strokes

車　vehicle

殳斤

strike, use tool
ax, chop, cut

舛	opposed feet, firm, guard, all round
貝	shell, money, valuable item
酉	alcohol, ferment, jar
豕	pig, animal
言	word, say, speak
辛	needle, sharp, pierce, slave, prisoner
豸	clawed beast, beast
豆	vessel, food
足	foot, leg, move
臣	stare, guard

8 strokes

雨	rain, weather, atmosphere
金	metal, money, gold
隹	bird, flight
門	door, gate, building
者	person, many, various
食	food, eat

9 strokes

| 頁 | head, mind, face |

10 strokes

| 骨 | bone |
| 馬 | horse |

11 strokes

| 魚 | fish, sea creature |
| 鳥 | bird |

HIRAGANA AND KATAKANA
AND THEIR SOURCE CHARACTERS

A	あ	from	安	A	ア	from	阿
I	い	from	以	I	イ	from	伊
U	う	from	宇	U	ウ	from	宇
E	え	from	衣	E	エ	from	江
O	お	from	於	O	オ	from	於
KA	か	from	加	KA	カ	from	加
KI	き	from	幾	KI	キ	from	幾
KU	く	from	久	KU	ク	from	久
KE	け	from	計	KE	ケ	from	介
KO	こ	from	己	KO	コ	from	己
SA	さ	from	左	SA	サ	from	散
SHI	し	from	之	SHI	シ	from	之
SU	す	from	寸	SU	ス	from	須
SE	せ	from	世	SE	セ	from	世

	hiragana				katakana		
SO	そ	from	曾	SO	ソ	from	曾
TA	た	from	太	TA	タ	from	多
CHI	ち	from	知	CHI	チ	from	千
TSU	つ	from	州	TSU	ツ	from	州
TE	て	from	天	TE	テ	from	天
TO	と	from	止	TO	ト	from	止
NA	な	from	奈	NA	ナ	from	奈
NI	に	from	仁	NI	ニ	from	二
NU	ぬ	from	奴	NU	ヌ	from	奴
NE	ね	from	禰	NE	ネ	from	禰
NO	の	from	乃	NO	ノ	from	乃
HA	は	from	波	HA	ハ	from	八
HI	ひ	from	比	HI	ヒ	from	比
FU	ふ	from	不	FU	フ	from	不
HE	へ	from	部	HE	へ	from	部

hiragana				katakana			
HO	ほ	from	保	HO	ホ	from	保
MA	ま	from	末	MA	マ	from	末
MI	み	from	美	MI	ミ	from	三
MU	む	from	武	MU	ム	from	牟
ME	め	from	女	ME	メ	from	女
MO	も	from	毛	MO	モ	from	毛
YA	や	from	也	YA	ヤ	from	也
YU	ゆ	from	由	YU	ユ	from	由
YO	よ	from	与	YO	ヨ	from	与
RA	ら	from	良	RA	ラ	from	良
RI	り	from	利	RI	リ	from	利
RU	る	from	留	RU	ル	from	流
RE	れ	from	礼	RE	レ	from	礼
RO	ろ	from	呂	RO	ロ	from	呂
WA	わ	from	和	WA	ワ	from	和

hiragana			katakana		
(W)O	を	from 遠	(W)O	ヲ	from 乎
N	ん	from 无	N	ン	from 尓

<u>Other kana sounds</u> (given in hiragana only)

ga	が	gi	ぎ	gu	ぐ	ge	げ	go	ご
za	ざ	ji	じ	zu	ず	ze	ぜ	zo	ぞ
da	だ	ji	ぢ	zu	づ	de	で	do	ど
ba	ば	bi	び	bu	ぶ	be	べ	bo	ぼ
pa	ぱ	pi	ぴ	pu	ぷ	pe	ぺ	po	ぽ
kya	きゃ	kyu	きゅ	kyo	きょ				
sha	しゃ	shu	しゅ	sho	しょ				
cha	ちゃ	chu	ちゅ	cho	ちょ				
nya	にゃ	nyu	にゅ	nyo	にょ				
hya	ひゃ	hyu	ひゅ	hyo	ひょ				
mya	みゃ	myu	みゅ	myo	みょ				
rya	りゃ	ryu	りゅ	ryo	りょ				
gya	ぎゃ	gyu	ぎゅ	gyo	ぎょ				
ja	じゃ	ju	じゅ	jo	じょ				
bya	びゃ	byu	びゅ	byo	びょ				
pya	ぴゃ	pyu	ぴゅ	pyo	ぴょ				

Sounds ending in 'o' lengthened to 'ō' by adding う (rarely お).

Sounds ending in 'u' lengthened to 'ū' by adding う .

Consonants doubled by preceding with っ .

INDEX OF 'NON GENERAL USE'
AND 'CHINESE ONLY' CHARACTERS

631

邑	355	阜	229	匐	1650	酉	927

STROKE COUNT INDEX

彼	1725	風	198	飛	566	姻	1012	荘	1515
披	1726	屋	236	変	581	疫	1019	促	1536
泌	1737	界	240	便	582	卸	1042	耐	1542
苗	1740	活	244	約	591	架	1045	怠	1543
怖	1749	客	252	勇	592	悔	1063	胎	1544
附	1750	急	254	要	593	皆	1064	胆	1564
侮	1760	級	255	逆	646	垣	1073	衷	1585
沸	1767	係	268	限	665	括	1085	挑	1589
併	1774	研	272	故	668	冠	1097	勅	1600
並	1775	県	273	厚	672	軌	1125	珍	1602
奉	1793	指	289	査	678	虐	1147	亭	1614
抱	1794	持	294	祝	706	糾	1151	貞	1615
泡	1795	拾	305	政	724	峡	1164	帝	1616
房	1809	重	311	祖	736	挟	1165	訂	1617
肪	1810	昭	315	則	742	狭	1166	怒	1639
奔	1825	乗	320	退	746	契	1195	逃	1642
抹	1836	神	324	独	763	孤	1229	洞	1661
岬	1840	送	331	保	787	弧	1230	峠	1663
免	1849	待	337	迷	797	枯	1231	卑	1727
茂	1850	炭	341	映	813	恆	1251	赴	1751
盲	1852	柱	345	革	821	洪	1252	封	1762
炉	1934	直	349	巻	826	荒	1253	柄	1776
枠	1943	追	350	看	827	郊	1254	胞	1796
		度	356	皇	861	香	1255	某	1811
9 strokes		畑	369	紅	862	侯	1256	冒	1812
		発	370	砂	869	拷	1269	盆	1828
音	6	美	376	姿	877	恨	1277	幽	1865
科	81	秒	380	城	903	砕	1287	柳	1898
海	88	品	382	是	910	削	1298	厘	1913
計	105	負	383	宣	913	咲	1303	郎	1936
後	111	面	395	専	914	施	1318		
思	131	洋	404	泉	915	狩	1347	**10 strokes**	
室	136	胃	424	洗	916	臭	1356		
首	139	栄	427	染	917	柔	1363	校	21
秋	140	紀	449	奏	918	俊	1371	夏	82
春	141	軍	466	俗	925	盾	1375	家	83
食	146	型	468	段	931	叙	1384	記	95
星	154	建	473	派	955	浄	1417	帰	96
前	159	昨	486	背	957	侵	1433	原	107
草	162	信	513	肺	958	津	1434	高	119
茶	171	省	516	律	993	甚	1449	紙	132
昼	172	浅	525	哀	998	帥	1454	時	135
点	179	相	530	威	1002	牲	1474	弱	138
南	190	単	542	為	1003	窃	1488	書	142

影	1017	踏	1657	燃	765	縫	1804	謄	1658
鋭	1018	輩	1688	輸	799	膨	1817	頻	1745
謁	1022	賠	1693	憲	852	謀	1818	翼	1885
閲	1023	箱	1703	鋼	864	磨	1831	療	1911
縁	1030	範	1719	樹	888	諭	1862	齢	1925
稼	1055	盤	1723	縦	892	融	1872		
餓	1058	罷	1732	操	922	擁	1882	18 strokes	
潟	1084	賓	1744	糖	947	謡	1883		
監	1111	敷	1756	奮	966	頼	1889	顔	93
緩	1112	膚	1757	緯	1009	隣	1915	曜	216
輝	1132	賦	1758	憶	1039	隷	1924	題	340
儀	1137	舞	1761	穏	1043	錬	1933	観	445
戯	1138	噴	1770	壊	1066			験	475
窮	1152	墳	1771	懐	1067	17 strokes		類	602
緊	1179	憤	1772	獲	1079			額	635
勲	1191	幣	1778	憾	1113	講	676	織	720
慶	1204	弊	1779	還	1114	謝	701	職	721
撃	1209	舗	1786	凝	1175	績	729	簡	829
稿	1266	褒	1803	薫	1192	厳	854	難	949
撮	1305	撲	1822	憩	1205	縮	893	臨	994
暫	1311	摩	1830	激	1210	優	984	穫	1081
賜	1324	魅	1839	賢	1221	覧	991	騎	1133
趣	1350	黙	1856	衡	1267	嚇	1080	襟	1181
潤	1379	憂	1871	墾	1281	轄	1090	繭	1223
遵	1380	窯	1881	錯	1302	環	1115	顕	1224
衝	1411	履	1896	諮	1325	擬	1139	鎖	1286
縄	1420	慮	1904	儒	1352	犠	1140	瞬	1372
嘱	1429	寮	1910	獣	1366	矯	1170	繕	1504
審	1443	霊	1923	壤	1421	謹	1180	礎	1512
震	1444			嬢	1422	謙	1222	騒	1530
穂	1460	16 strokes		錠	1423	購	1268	贈	1533
請	1479			薪	1445	懇	1282	懲	1599
潜	1497	親	149	錘	1461	擦	1306	鎮	1605
遷	1498	頭	186	薦	1499	爵	1344	闘	1659
槽	1527	館	247	濁	1558	醜	1359	藩	1721
諾	1557	橋	259	壇	1571	償	1412	覆	1765
誕	1568	整	328	篤	1666	礁	1413	癖	1781
鋳	1586	薬	398	曇	1672	繊	1500	翻	1826
駐	1587	機	453	濃	1681	鮮	1501	癒	1863
澄	1597	積	521	薄	1699	燥	1528	濫	1892
墜	1606	録	611	縛	1701	霜	1529	離	1897
締	1622	衛	617	繁	1720	濯	1556	糧	1912
徹	1629	興	652	避	1733	鍛	1569		
撤	1630	築	751	壁	1780	聴	1598	19 strokes	

顧	446	驚	1172		
鏡	462	襲	1360		
識	698				
警	847	**23 strokes**			
臟	924				
韻	1015	鑑	1117		
繰	1190				
鷄	1206				
鯨	1208				
蟹	1329				
髓	1463				
瀨	1469				
藻	1531				
覇	1683				
爆	1702				
譜	1759				
簿	1790				
霧	1845				
羅	1887				
麗	1926				

20 strokes

議	454
競	463
護	670
響	1171
懸	1225
鐘	1414
讓	1424
釀	1425
籍	1486
騰	1660
欄	1893

21 strokes

艦	1116
顧	1235
魔	1832
躍	1860
露	1935

22 strokes

READINGS INDEX

Note: 1. English alphabetical order
2. Stems and endings not differentiated
3. Where ending can be varied to make more than one word, only one is given (e.g. moru but not moreru or morasu).

A	亜	997	amai	甘	1093	aru	有	401
abareru	暴	793	amaneku	普	1754	aru	在	684
abiru	浴	595	amaneku	遍	1783	aruku	歩	202
abunai	危	831	amaru	余	800	asa	朝	175
abura	油	400	amatsusae	剰	1418	asa	麻	1829
abura	脂	1319	ame	雨	3	asai	浅	525
ada	徒	554	ami	網	1855	ase	汗	1094
aete	敢	1106	amu	編	785	asebamu	汗	1094
agameru	崇	1465	AN	行	118	aseru	焦	1404
agaru	上	37	AN	安	223	ashi	足	51
ageru	挙	458	AN	暗	224	ashi	脚	1146
ageru	揚	1876	AN	案	418	asobu	遊	402
AI	愛	417	ana	穴	849	ataeru	与	1873
ai-	相	530	ana	孔	1241	atai	価	626
AI	哀	998	anadoru	侮	1760	atai	値	933
aida	間	92	ane	姉	498	atama	頭	186
aji	味	393	ani	兄	267	atarashii	新	148
ajiwau	味	393	ano	彼	1725	atari	辺	580
akagane	銅	758	aogu	仰	1173	ataru	当	183
akai	赤	46	aogu	扇	1492	atatakai	温	237
akarui	明	208	aoi	青	43	atatakai	暖	932
akatsuki	暁	1174	arai	荒	1253	ateru	充	1362
akeru	明	208	arai	粗	1508	ato	後	111
akeru	開	241	arasou	争	529	ato	跡	1485
aki	秋	140	arata	新	148	atou	能	766
akinau	商	317	aratameru	改	435	ATSU	圧	612
aku	空	15	arau	洗	916	atsui	暑	313
AKU	悪	222	arawareru	現	666	atsui	熱	560
AKU	握	999	arawareru	顕	1224	atsui	厚	672
aku	飽	1802	arawasu	表	379	atsukau	扱	1000
ama-	雨	3	arawasu	著	937	atsumaru	集	309
ama-	天	58	are	彼	1725	au	会	87
ama	尼	1674	areru	荒	1253	au	合	121

646

au	遭	1526	BAN	晩	961	BŌ	妨	1808
awa	泡	1795	BAN	伴	1712	BŌ	房	1809
awai	淡	1565	BAN	蛮	1722	BŌ	肪	1810
awaremu	哀	998	BAN	盤	1723	BŌ	某	1811
awaseru	併	1774	BATSU	末	587	BŌ	冒	1812
awateru	慌	1259	BATSU	伐	1707	BŌ	剖	1813
ayakaru	肖	1391	BATSU	抜	1708	BŌ	紡	1814
ayamachi	過	629	BATSU	罰	1709	BŌ	傍	1815
ayamaru	謝	701	BATSU	閥	1710	BŌ	帽	1816
ayamaru	誤	857	BE	部	384	BŌ	膨	1817
ayashii	怪	1061	be	辺	580	BŌ	謀	1818
ayatsuru	操	922	BEI	米	201	BŌ	矛	1843
ayaui	危	831	-beki	可	816	BŌ	妄	1851
ayumu	歩	202	BEN	勉	390	boko	凹	1032
azamuku	欺	1136	BEN	便	582	BOKU	木	69
azayaka	鮮	1501	BEN	弁	786	BOKU	目	72
aze	畔	1713	beni	紅	862	BOKU	北	205
azukaru	預	801	BETSU	別	579	BOKU	牧	586
ba	場	144	BI	美	376	BOKU	朴	1819
BA	馬	191	BI	鼻	377	BOKU	僕	1820
BA	婆	1684	BI	備	774	BOKU	墨	1821
baba	婆	1684	BI	尾	1734	BOKU	撲	1822
BACHI	罰	1709	BI	微	1735	BON	煩	1717
BAI	売	192	BIN	便	582	BON	凡	1827
BAI	買	193	BIN	貧	777	BON	盆	1828
BAI	倍	563	BIN	敏	1746	BOTSU	没	1823
BAI	梅	1689	BIN	瓶	1747	BU	分	199
BAI	培	1690	BO	母	203	BU	部	384
BAI	陪	1691	BO	墓	788	BU	不	572
BAI	媒	1692	BO	模	980	BU	武	781
BAI	賠	1693	BO	募	1787	BU	無	796
BAI	某	1811	BO	慕	1788	BU	侮	1760
bakeru	化	238	BO	暮	1789	BU	舞	1761
BAKU	麦	194	BO	簿	1790	BU	奉	1793
BAKU	博	564	BŌ	望	585	BUN	文	68
BAKU	暴	793	BŌ	防	791	BUN	分	199
BAKU	幕	977	BŌ	貿	792	BUN	聞	200
BAKU	漠	1700	BŌ	暴	793	BUN	蚊	1056
BAKU	縛	1701	BŌ	亡	973	buta	豚	1670
BAKU	爆	1702	BŌ	忘	974	BUTSU	物	387
BAN	番	196	BŌ	棒	975	BUTSU	仏	784
BAN	板	373	BŌ	乏	1805	BYŌ	秒	380
BAN	万	392	BŌ	忙	1806	BYŌ	病	381
BAN	判	769	BŌ	坊	1807	BYŌ	平	388

BYŌ	苗	1740	CHO	貯	546	CHŪ	鋳	1586
BYŌ	描	1741	CHO	著	937	CHŪ	駐	1587
BYŌ	貓	1742	CHO	緒	1382	DA	打	335
CHA	茶	171	CHŌ	町	57	DA	蛇	1341
CHAKU	着	343	CHŌ	長	173	DA	妥	1538
CHAKU	嫡	1582	CHŌ	鳥	174	DA	堕	1539
chi	千	47	CHŌ	朝	175	DA	惰	1540
CHI	地	167	CHŌ	重	311	DA	駄	1541
CHI	池	168	CHŌ	丁	346	DAI	大	53
CHI	知	169	CHŌ	帳	347	DAI	台	166
chi	血	270	CHŌ	調	348	DAI	弟	177
CHI	治	544	CHŌ	腸	547	DAI	代	338
CHI	置	545	CHŌ	張	752	DAI	第	339
CHI	質	699	CHŌ	提	753	DAI	題	340
CHI	値	933	CHŌ	庁	938	DAI	内	364
chi	乳	951	CHŌ	兆	939	DAKU	諾	1557
CHI	恥	1572	CHŌ	頂	940	DAKU	濁	1558
CHI	致	1573	CHŌ	潮	941	daku	抱	1794
CHI	遅	1574	CHŌ	弔	1588	damaru	黙	1856
CHI	痴	1575	CHŌ	挑	1589	DAN	男	54
CHI	稚	1576	CHŌ	彫	1590	DAN	談	543
chichi	父	197	CHŌ	眺	1591	DAN	団	749
chichi	乳	951	CHŌ	釣	1592	DAN	断	750
chigau	違	1006	CHŌ	脹	1593	DAN	段	931
chigiru	契	1195	CHŌ	超	1594	DAN	暖	932
chiisai	小	36	CHŌ	跳	1595	DAN	弾	1570
chijimu	縮	893	CHŌ	徴	1596	DAN	壇	1571
chikai	近	103	CHŌ	澄	1597	dasu	出	34
chikara	力	74	CHŌ	聴	1598	DATSU	脱	1560
chikau	誓	1478	CHŌ	懲	1599	DATSU	奪	1561
CHIKU	竹	170	CHŌ	塚	1607	DE	弟	177
CHIKU	築	751	CHOKU	直	349	DEI	泥	1623
CHIKU	畜	1577	CHOKU	勅	1600	deko	凸	1667
CHIKU	逐	1578	CHŪ	中	55	DEN	田	59
CHIKU	蓄	1579	CHŪ	虫	56	DEN	電	180
CHIN	賃	942	CHŪ	昼	172	DEN	伝	553
CHIN	沈	1601	CHŪ	注	344	DEN	殿	1632
CHIN	珍	1602	CHŪ	柱	345	deru	出	34
CHIN	朕	1603	CHŪ	仲	934	DO	土	60
CHIN	陳	1604	CHŪ	宙	935	DO	度	356
CHIN	鎮	1605	CHŪ	忠	936	DO	努	555
chiru	散	492	CHŪ	沖	1583	DO	奴	1638
CHITSU	秩	1580	CHŪ	抽	1584	DO	怒	1639
CHITSU	窒	1581	CHŪ	衷	1585	DŌ	同	187

DŌ	道	188	EN	園	234	FŪ	富	780
DŌ	動	362	EN	塩	428	FŪ	封	1762
DŌ	童	363	EN	演	621	fuchi	縁	1030
DŌ	堂	557	EN	延	814	fuda	札	1304
DŌ	働	558	EN	沿	815	fude	筆	569
DŌ	銅	758	EN	炎	1024	fue	笛	1624
DŌ	導	759	EN	宴	1025	fueru	増	741
DŌ	洞	1661	EN	援	1026	fueru	殖	1426
DŌ	胴	1662	EN	煙	1027	fukai	深	325
dobu	溝	1263	EN	猿	1028	fukeru	老	609
DOKU	読	189	EN	鉛	1029	fukeru	更	1248
DOKU	毒	559	EN	縁	1030	FUKU	服	385
DOKU	独	763	erabu	選	527	FUKU	福	386
DON	鈍	1671	erabu	択	1551	FUKU	副	576
DON	曇	1672	erai	偉	1005	FUKU	復	782
doro	泥	1623	eru	得	761	FUKU	複	783
E	会	87	eru	獲	1079	FUKU	腹	965
E	絵	89	ETSU	悦	1020	fuku	吹	1452
e	重	311	ETSU	越	1021	FUKU	伏	1763
E	依	1001	ETSU	謁	1022	FUKU	幅	1764
E	恵	1196	ETSU	閲	1023	FUKU	覆	1765
e	江	1244	FU	父	197	fuku	噴	1770
e	柄	1776	FU	負	383	fukumu	含	1118
eda	枝	1315	FU	不	572	fukuramu	脹	1593
egaku	描	1741	FU	夫	573	fukuramu	膨	1817
EI	泳	232	FU	付	574	fukuro	袋	1546
EI	英	426	FU	府	575	fumi	文	68
EI	栄	427	FU	布	778	fumu	践	1495
EI	永	615	FU	婦	779	fumu	踏	1657
EI	営	616	FU	富	780	FUN	分	199
EI	衛	617	FU	扶	1748	FUN	粉	577
EI	映	813	FU	怖	1749	FUN	奮	966
EI	詠	1016	FU	附	1750	FUN	紛	1768
EI	影	1017	FU	赴	1751	FUN	霧	1769
EI	鋭	1018	FU	浮	1752	FUN	噴	1770
EKI	駅	233	FU	符	1753	FUN	墳	1771
EKI	役	397	FU	普	1754	FUN	憤	1772
EKI	易	618	FU	腐	1755	funa-	船	158
EKI	益	619	FU	敷	1756	funa-	舟	1354
EKI	液	620	FU	膚	1757	fune	船	158
EKI	疫	1019	FU	賦	1758	fune	舟	1354
emu	笑	900	FU	譜	1759	fureru	触	1428
EN	円	4	FŪ	風	198	furu	降	863
EN	遠	79	FŪ	夫	573	furu	振	1437

furui	古	109	GATSU	月	16	GO	護	670
furuu	奮	966	gawa	側	535	GO	誤	857
furuu	震	1444	GE	下	7	GO	后	858
fusa	房	1809	GE	夏	82	GO	御	1158
fusegu	防	791	GE	外	91	GO	互	1236
fushi	節	523	GE	解	632	GO	呉	1237
fusu	伏	1763	GE	華	1046	GO	娯	1238
futa	二	61	GEI	芸	470	GO	悟	1239
futa-	双	1513	GEI	迎	1207	GO	碁	1240
futatabi	再	679	GEI	鯨	1208	GŌ	強	100
futoi	太	164	GEKI	劇	848	GŌ	合	121
futokoro	懐	1067	GEKI	撃	1209	GŌ	業	260
FUTSU	仏	784	GEKI	激	1210	GŌ	号	281
FUTSU	払	1766	GEN	元	106	GŌ	郷	841
FUTSU	沸	1767	GEN	原	107	GŌ	拷	1269
fuyu	冬	182	GEN	言	274	GŌ	剛	1270
GA	画	85	GEN	限	665	GŌ	豪	1271
GA	芽	434	GEN	現	666	GOKU	極	464
GA	賀	630	GEN	減	667	GOKU	獄	1274
GA	我	817	GEN	源	853	GON	言	274
GA	雅	1057	GEN	厳	854	GON	権	851
GA	餓	1058	GEN	嫌	1218	GON	厳	854
GAI	外	91	GEN	幻	1226	-goto	毎	206
GAI	害	437	GEN	玄	1227	gotoku	如	1383
GAI	街	819	GEN	弦	1228	GU	具	265
GAI	劾	1068	GETSU	月	16	GU	虞	1040
GAI	涯	1069	GI	議	454	GU	愚	1184
GAI	慨	1070	GI	技	644	GŪ	宮	256
GAI	該	1071	GI	義	645	GŪ	偶	1185
GAI	概	1072	GI	疑	835	GŪ	遇	1186
GAKU	学	10	GI	宜	1134	GŪ	隅	1187
GAKU	楽	218	GI	偽	1135	GUN	軍	466
GAKU	額	635	GI	欺	1136	GUN	郡	467
GAKU	岳	1082	GI	儀	1137	GUN	群	657
GAN	顔	93	GI	戯	1138	GYAKU	逆	646
GAN	元	106	GI	擬	1139	GYAKU	虐	1147
GAN	岸	248	GI	犠	1140	GYO	魚	98
GAN	岩	249	GIN	銀	263	GYO	漁	459
GAN	願	446	GIN	吟	1182	GYO	御	1158
GAN	眼	640	GO	五	19	GYŌ	形	104
GAN	丸	830	GO	午	110	GYŌ	行	118
GAN	含	1118	GO	後	111	GYŌ	業	260
GAN	頑	1119	GO	語	112	GYŌ	仰	1173
gara	柄	1776	GO	期	251	GYŌ	暁	1174

HŌ	崩	1801	I	意	226	imo	芋	1011
HŌ	飽	1802	I	以	419	imōto	妹	207
HŌ	褒	1803	I	衣	420	imu	忌	1122
HŌ	縫	1804	I	位	421	IN	音	6
hō	朴	1819	I	囲	422	IN	引	77
hodo	程	754	I	委	423	IN	員	228
hodokosu	施	1318	I	胃	424	IN	院	229
hogaraka	朗	995	I	移	613	IN	飲	230
hoka	外	91	I	易	618	IN	印	425
hoka	他	334	I	異	807	IN	因	614
hoko	矛	1843	I	遺	808	IN	姻	1012
hokoru	誇	1233	I	依	1001	IN	陰	1013
HOKU	北	205	I	威	1002	IN	隠	1014
homare	誉	1874	I	為	1003	IN	韻	1015
homeru	褒	1803	I	尉	1004	ina	否	962
hōmuru	葬	1523	I	偉	1005	ina	稲	1656
HON	本	70	I	違	1006	inamu	否	962
HON	奔	1825	I	維	1007	ine	稲	1656
HON	翻	1826	I	慰	1008	inochi	命	394
hone	骨	867	I	緯	1009	inoru	祈	1124
honō	炎	1024	i	井	1470	inu	犬	17
hora	洞	1661	I	唯	1864	ireru	入	63
hori	堀	1824	ICHI	一	1	ireru	容	802
horobiru	滅	1848	ichi	市	130	iro	色	145
horu	掘	1189	ICHI	壱	810	irodoru	彩	1290
horu	彫	1590	ichijirushii	著	937	iru	要	593
hoshi	星	154	idaku	抱	1794	iru	居	649
hoshii	欲	987	idomu	挑	1589	iru	射	882
hosoi	細	284	ie	家	83	iru	鋳	1586
hosu	干	825	ikaru	怒	1639	isagiyoi	潔	659
hotaru	螢	1200	ike	池	168	isamashii	勇	592
hotoke	仏	784	iki	息	332	ishi	石	45
HOTSU	発	370	IKI	域	809	ishizue	礎	1512
HYAKU	百	67	iki	粋	1455	isogashii	忙	1806
HYŌ	氷	378	ikidōru	憤	1772	isogu	急	254
HYŌ	表	379	ikioi	勢	518	ita	板	373
HYŌ	票	570	ikiru	生	42	itadaki	頂	940
HYŌ	標	571	ikou	憩	1205	itadaku	頂	940
HYŌ	兵	578	iku	行	118	itai	痛	943
HYŌ	俵	775	IKU	育	227	itamu	傷	901
HYŌ	評	776	iku-	幾	1129	itamu	悼	1648
HYŌ	拍	1695	ikusa	戦	526	itaru	至	875
HYŌ	漂	1739	ima	今	125	itaru	到	1641
I	医	225	imashimeru	戒	1060	itasu	致	1573

komaru	困	868	kowai	怖	1749	kuraberu	比	771
kome	米	201	kowareru	壊	1066	kurai	暗	224
komo	薦	1499	koyomi	暦	1927	kurai	位	421
komu	込	1275	kozotte	挙	458	kurenai	紅	862
kōmuru	被	1729	KU	九	12	kureru	呉	1237
KON	金	14	KU	口	20	kureru	暮	1789
KON	今	125	KU	工	113	kurogane	鉄	353
KON	根	282	KU	宮	256	kuroi	黒	124
KON	建	473	KU	苦	264	kuru	来	217
KON	混	677	KU	区	465	kuru	繰	1190
KON	困	868	KU	功	477	kuruma	車	31
KON	献	1219	KU	久	647	kurushii	苦	264
KON	昆	1276	KU	句	655	kuruu	狂	1161
KON	恨	1277	KU	供	839	kusa	草	162
KON	婚	1278	KU	紅	862	kusai	臭	1356
KON	紺	1279	KU	駆	1183	kusari	鎖	1286
KON	魂	1280	KU	貢	1257	kusaru	腐	1755
KON	墾	1281	KŪ	空	15	kuse	癖	1781
KON	懇	1282	kubaru	配	368	kusuri	薬	398
kona	粉	577	kubi	首	139	kutsu	靴	1052
konomu	好	859	kubiki	衡	1267	KUTSU	屈	1188
kōra	甲	1243	kubo	凹	1031	KUTSU	掘	1189
kore	是	910	kuchi	口	20	KUTSU	堀	1824
kōri	氷	378	kuchibiru	唇	1435	kutsugaeru	覆	1765
kōri	郡	467	kuchiru	朽	1150	kutsurogu	寛	1110
koriru	懲	1599	kuda	管	443	kuu	食	146
korogaru	転	354	kudaku	砕	1287	kuwa	桑	1518
koromo	衣	420	kudaru	下	7	kuwadateru	企	1120
korosu	殺	488	kudasaru	下	7	kuwaeru	加	431
koru	凝	1175	kuiru	悔	1063	kuwashii	詳	1409
kōru	凍	1643	kujira	鯨	1208	kuyamu	悔	1063
koshi	腰	1879	kuki	茎	1194	kuyashii	悔	1063
kosuru	擦	1306	kukuru	括	1085	kuzureru	崩	1801
kotaeru	答	185	kumo	雲	78	KYA	脚	1146
koto	言	274	kumoru	曇	1672	KYAKU	客	252
koto	事	293	kumu	組	160	KYAKU	却	1145
koto	琴	1178	kumu	酌	1343	KYAKU	脚	1146
koto	殊	1348	KUN	君	266	KYO	去	258
kotoba	詞	879	KUN	訓	656	KYO	挙	458
kotobuki	寿	1351	KUN	勲	1191	KYO	居	649
kotonaru	異	807	KUN	薫	1192	KYO	許	650
kotowaru	断	750	kuni	国	123	KYO	巨	1153
KOTSU	骨	867	kura	倉	531	KYO	拒	1154
kou	請	1479	kura	蔵	923	KYO	拠	1155

KYO	虚	1156	KYŪ	久	647	maku	巻	826
KYO	距	1157	KYŪ	旧	638	MAKU	幕	977
KYŌ	京	99	KYŪ	弓	836	MAKU	膜	1834
KYŌ	強	100	KYŪ	吸	837	mama-	継	1203
KYŌ	教	101	KYŪ	泣	838	mame	豆	1640
KYŌ	橋	259	KYŪ	及	1148	mamoru	守	300
KYŌ	兄	267	KYŪ	丘	1149	MAN	万	392
KYŌ	共	460	KYŪ	朽	1150	MAN	満	588
KYŌ	協	461	KYŪ	糾	1151	MAN	慢	1837
KYŌ	鏡	462	KYŪ	窮	1152	MAN	漫	1838
KYŌ	競	463	ma-	目	72	manabu	学	10
KYŌ	境	651	ma	間	92	manako	眼	640
KYŌ	興	652	ma	馬	191	maneku	招	712
KYŌ	経	658	ma	真	514	manukareru	免	1849
KYŌ	供	839	MA	麻	1829	maru	丸	830
KYŌ	胸	840	MA	摩	1830	marui	円	4
KYŌ	郷	841	MA	磨	1831	marui	丸	830
KYŌ	凶	1159	MA	魔	1832	masa	正	41
KYŌ	叫	1160	maboroshi	幻	1226	masa	将	899
KYŌ	狂	1161	machi	町	57	masaru	勝	319
KYŌ	享	1162	machi	街	819	mashite	況	1163
KYŌ	況	1163	mada	未	794	masu	益	619
KYŌ	峡	1164	mado	窓	919	masu	増	741
KYŌ	挟	1165	madou	惑	1942	masu	升	1386
KYŌ	狭	1166	mae	前	159	mata	又	1835
KYŌ	恐	1167	magaru	曲	261	matataku	瞬	1372
KYŌ	恭	1168	magireru	紛	1768	mato	的	551
KYŌ	脅	1169	mago	孫	538	matsu	待	337
KYŌ	矯	1170	MAI	米	201	MATSU	末	587
KYŌ	響	1171	MAI	毎	206	matsu	松	1394
KYŌ	驚	1172	MAI	妹	207	MATSU	抹	1836
KYOKU	曲	261	MAI	枚	976	matsuri	祭	283
KYOKU	局	262	MAI	埋	1833	matsurigoto	政	724
KYOKU	極	464	mairu	参	490	matsuru	祭	283
KYŪ	九	12	majiru	交	115	mattaku	全	330
KYŪ	休	13	majiru	混	677	mau	舞	1761
KYŪ	究	253	makanau	賄	1941	mawari	周	504
KYŪ	急	254	makaru	罷	1732	mawaru	回	86
KYŪ	級	255	makaseru	任	764	mayou	迷	797
KYŪ	宮	256	makeru	負	383	mayu	繭	1223
KYŪ	球	257	maki	牧	586	mazui	拙	1487
KYŪ	求	455	maki	巻	826	mazushii	貧	777
KYŪ	救	456	maki	薪	1445	me	女	35
KYŪ	給	457	makoto	誠	912	me	目	72

muna-	胸	840	nakunaru	亡	973	nemuru	睡	1459	
muna-	棟	1653	nama	生	42	NEN	年	64	
mune	胸	840	namakeru	怠	1543	NEN	然	528	
mune	旨	1312	namari	鉛	1029	NEN	念	561	
mune	棟	1653	nameraka	滑	1088	NEN	燃	765	
mura	村	52	nami	波	367	NEN	粘	1679	
mura	群	657	nami	並	1775	nengoro	懇	1282	
murasaki	紫	1320	nami	浪	1937	neru	練	608	
mureru	群	657	namida	涙	1916	neru	寝	1441	
muro	室	136	NAN	男	54	neru	錬	1933	
mushi	虫	56	NAN	南	190	NETSU	熱	560	
mushiro	寧	1678	NAN	難	949	NI	二	61	
musu	蒸	904	NAN	軟	1673	ni	荷	239	
musubu	結	472	nana-	七	30	NI	児	697	
musume	娘	1846	naname	斜	1337	NI	仁	906	
muzukashii	難	949	nani	何	80	NI	弐	950	
MYAKU	脈	589	nanigashi	某	1811	ni	丹	1563	
MYŌ	名	71	nao	尚	1392	NI	尼	1674	
MYŌ	明	208	nao	猶	1867	nibui	鈍	1671	
MYŌ	命	394	naoru	直	349	NICHI	日	62	
MYŌ	苗	1740	naosu	治	544	nigai	苦	264	
MYŌ	貓	1742	narabu	並	1775	nigeru	逃	1642	
MYŌ	妙	1841	narau	習	307	nigiru	握	999	
na	名	71	narau	倣	1798	nigoru	濁	1558	
na	菜	483	nareru	慣	638	NIKU	肉	365	
NA	納	953	naru	鳴	209	nikumu	憎	1532	
nado	等	361	naru	成	515	NIN	人	39	
nae	苗	1740	nasake	情	719	NIN	任	764	
nagai	長	173	nasu	為	1003	NIN	認	952	
nagai	永	615	natsu	夏	82	NIN	妊	1676	
nagameru	眺	1591	NATSU	納	953	NIN	忍	1677	
nagareru	流	409	natsukashii	懐	1067	ninau	担	929	
nageku	嘆	1566	nawa	縄	1420	niru	似	696	
nageru	投	357	nawa	苗	1740	niru	煮	1338	
nagoyaka	和	416	nayamu	悩	1680	nise	偽	1135	
naguru	殴	1035	nazumu	泥	1623	nishi	西	152	
nagusamu	慰	1008	ne	音	6	niwa	庭	352	
NAI	内	364	ne	根	282	niwatori	鶏	1206	
nai	無	796	ne	値	933	no	野	213	
naka	中	55	nebaru	粘	1679	NŌ	農	366	
naka	仲	934	negau	願	446	NŌ	能	766	
nakaba	半	195	NEI	寧	1678	NŌ	納	953	
naku	鳴	209	neko	貓	1742	NŌ	脳	954	
naku	泣	838	nemui	眠	1842	NŌ	悩	1680	

NŌ	濃	1681	Ō	王	5	okoru	起	250
noberu	述	707	Ō	黄	120	okoru	興	652
nobiru	延	814	Ō	横	235	okoru	怒	1639
nobiru	伸	1431	Ō	央	429	okotaru	怠	1543
noboru	上	37	Ō	応	622	OKU	屋	236
noboru	登	360	Ō	往	623	OKU	億	430
noboru	昇	1393	Ō	皇	861	oku	置	545
nochi	後	111	Ō	凹	1032	oku	奥	1038
nogareru	逃	1642	Ō	押	1033	OKU	憶	1039
noki	軒	1215	Ō	欧	1034	okureru	後	111
nokoru	残	493	Ō	殴	1035	okureru	遅	1574
nomu	飲	230	Ō	桜	1036	okuru	送	331
nori	典	552	Ō	翁	1037	okuru	贈	1533
nori	則	742	Ō	奥	1038	omo	主	299
noru	乗	320	obi	帯	539	omo	面	395
noru	載	1295	obiru	帯	539	omoi	重	311
nottoru	則	742	obiyakasu	脅	1169	omomuki	趣	1350
nozoku	除	711	oboeru	覚	439	omomuku	赴	1751
nozomu	望	585	ochiiru	陥	1098	omomuro	徐	1385
nozomu	臨	994	ochiru	落	408	omori	錘	1461
nugu	脱	1560	odayaka	穏	1043	omote	表	379
nuku	抜	1708	odokasu	嚇	1080	omote	面	395
numa	沼	1395	odokasu	脅	1169	omou	思	131
nuno	布	778	odoroku	驚	1172	ōmune	概	1072
nuru	塗	1637	odoru	躍	1860	ON	音	6
nushi	主	299	odoru	踊	1880	ON	温	237
nusumu	窃	1488	odosu	威	1002	ON	恩	624
nusumu	盗	1649	odosu	嚇	1080	ON	穏	1043
nuu	縫	1804	odosu	脅	1169	on-	御	1158
NYO	女	35	ogamu	拝	956	onaji	同	187
NYO	如	1383	ōgi	扇	1492	oni	鬼	1128
NYŌ	女	35	oginau	補	970	onna	女	35
NYŌ	尿	1675	ogosoka	厳	854	ono(-ono)	各	438
NYŪ	入	63	ōi	多	163	onore	己	855
NYŪ	乳	951	oiru	老	609	ori	折	522
NYŪ	柔	1363	oka	丘	1149	oriru	下	7
o-	小	36	okasu	犯	768	oriru	降	863
O	悪	222	okasu	侵	1433	oroka	愚	1184
O	和	416	okasu	冒	1812	oroshi	卸	1042
O	汚	1031	oki	沖	1583	orosu	卸	1042
o-	御	1158	ōkii	大	53	oru	折	522
o	緒	1382	okina	翁	1037	oru	居	649
o	尾	1734	okiru	起	250	oru	織	720
o-	雄	1869	okonau	行	118	osaeru	抑	1884

osameru	治	544	RAN	卵	990	RIN	鈴	1921
osameru	収	703	RAN	覧	991	RITSU	立	73
osameru	修	704	RAN	濫	1892	RITSU	率	803
osameru	納	953	RAN	欄	1893	RITSU	律	993
osanai	幼	985	REI	礼	413	RO	路	415
ōse	仰	1173	REI	令	603	RO	炉	1934
oshieru	教	101	REI	冷	604	RO	露	1935
oshimu	惜	1484	REI	例	605	RŌ	老	609
osoi	遅	1574	REI	励	1919	RŌ	労	610
osore	虞	1040	REI	戻	1920	RŌ	朗	995
osoreru	恐	1167	REI	鈴	1921	RŌ	糧	1912
osou	襲	1360	REI	零	1922	RŌ	露	1935
osu	推	908	REI	霊	1923	RŌ	郎	1936
osu	押	1033	REI	隷	1924	RŌ	浪	1937
osu	雄	1869	REI	齢	1925	RŌ	廊	1938
oto	音	6	REI	麗	1926	RŌ	楼	1939
otoko	男	54	REKI	歴	606	RŌ	漏	1940
otoroeru	衰	1456	REKI	暦	1927	ROKU	六	76
otoru	劣	1928	REN	連	607	ROKU	緑	412
otōto	弟	177	REN	練	608	ROKU	録	611
otozureru	訪	972	REN	恋	1931	RON	論	996
OTSU	乙	1041	REN	廉	1932	RU	流	409
otto	夫	573	REN	錬	1933	RU	留	805
ou	追	350	RETSU	列	414	RUI	類	602
ou	負	383	RETSU	劣	1928	RUI	涙	1916
ou	逐	1578	RETSU	烈	1929	RUI	累	1917
ou	被	1729	RETSU	裂	1930	RUI	塁	1918
ōu	覆	1765	RI	里	219	RYAKU	略	804
owaru	終	306	RI	理	220	RYO	旅	410
oya	親	149	RI	利	596	RYO	虜	1903
ōyake	公	277	RI	裏	992	RYO	慮	1904
oyobu	及	1148	RI	吏	1894	RYŌ	両	411
oyogu	泳	232	RI	痢	1895	RYŌ	漁	459
oyoso	凡	1827	RI	履	1896	RYŌ	良	598
RA	裸	1886	RI	離	1897	RYŌ	料	599
RA	羅	1887	RICHI	律	993	RYŌ	量	600
RAI	来	217	RIKI	力	74	RYŌ	令	603
RAI	雷	1888	RIKU	陸	597	RYŌ	領	806
RAI	頼	1889	RIN	林	75	RYŌ	竜	1899
RAKU	楽	218	RIN	輪	601	RYŌ	了	1905
RAKU	落	408	RIN	臨	994	RYŌ	涼	1906
RAKU	絡	1890	RIN	厘	1913	RYŌ	猟	1907
RAKU	酪	1891	RIN	倫	1914	RYŌ	陵	1908
RAN	乱	989	RIN	隣	1915	RYŌ	僚	1909

RYŌ	寮	1910	SAI	災	680	sameru	覚	439
RYŌ	療	1911	SAI	妻	681	sameru	冷	604
RYŌ	糧	1912	SAI	採	682	samui	寒	245
RYŌ	霊	1923	SAI	際	683	samurai	士	494
RYOKU	力	74	SAI	財	685	samurai	侍	1326
RYOKU	緑	412	SAI	済	871	SAN	三	23
RYŪ	立	73	SAI	裁	872	SAN	山	24
RYŪ	流	409	SAI	砕	1287	SAN	算	128
RYŪ	留	805	SAI	宰	1288	SAN	参	490
RYŪ	柳	1898	SAI	栽	1289	SAN	産	491
RYŪ	竜	1899	SAI	彩	1290	SAN	散	492
RYŪ	粒	1900	SAI	斎	1291	SAN	蚕	688
RYŪ	隆	1901	SAI	債	1292	SAN	酸	689
RYŪ	硫	1902	SAI	催	1293	SAN	賛	690
SA	左	22	SAI	歳	1294	SAN	桟	1308
SA	作	127	SAI	載	1295	SAN	惨	1309
SA	茶	171	saiwai	幸	279	SAN	傘	1310
SA	差	482	saka-	酒	302	sara	更	1248
SA	査	678	saka	坂	372	sara	皿	1307
SA	再	679	sakaeru	栄	427	saru	去	258
SA	砂	869	sakai	境	651	saru	猿	1028
SA	佐	1283	sakana	魚	98	sasaeru	支	691
SA	唆	1284	sakarau	逆	646	sasou	誘	1870
SA	詐	1285	sakaru	盛	1476	sasu	指	289
SA	鎖	1286	sakazuki	杯	1685	sasu	差	482
sabaku	裁	872	sake	酒	302	sasu	刺	1314
sabi	寂	1345	sakebu	叫	1160	sasu	挿	1517
sabishii	寂	1345	sakeru	避	1733	sato	里	219
sachi	幸	279	sakeru	裂	1930	satoru	悟	1239
sadameru	定	351	saki	先	49	satosu	諭	1862
saegiru	遮	1339	saki	崎	1297	SATSU	刷	487
sagaru	下	7	saki	岬	1840	SATSU	殺	488
sagasu	探	930	SAKU	作	127	SATSU	察	489
sagasu	捜	1516	SAKU	昨	486	SATSU	冊	874
sageru	提	753	SAKU	策	873	SATSU	札	1304
saguru	探	930	SAKU	削	1298	SATSU	撮	1305
SAI	才	126	SAKU	索	1299	SATSU	擦	1306
SAI	西	152	SAKU	酢	1300	sawa	沢	1552
SAI	切	156	SAKU	搾	1301	sawagu	騒	1530
SAI	祭	283	SAKU	錯	1302	sawaru	障	902
SAI	細	284	saku	咲	1303	sawaru	触	1428
SAI	菜	483	sakura	桜	1036	sazukeru	授	702
SAI	最	484	sama	様	407	SE	世	327
SAI	再	679	samatageru	妨	1808	se	背	957

665

SO	且	1091	SŌ	箱	1703	SŪ	数	151
SO	阻	1505	soba	側	535	SŪ	枢	1464
SO	租	1506	sodatsu	育	227	SŪ	崇	1465
SO	描	1507	soko	底	549	su	巣	1521
SO	粗	1508	sokonau	損	745	sube	術	708
SO	疎	1509	SOKU	足	51	suberu	統	757
SO	訴	1510	SOKU	息	332	suberu	滑	1088
SO	塑	1511	SOKU	速	534	subete	総	738
SO	礎	1512	SOKU	側	535	sude	既	1126
SŌ	早	50	SOKU	則	742	sue	末	587
SŌ	走	161	SOKU	測	743	sueru	据	1466
SŌ	草	162	SOKU	即	1534	sugata	姿	877
SŌ	送	331	SOKU	束	1535	sugi	杉	1467
SŌ	争	529	SOKU	促	1536	sugiru	過	629
SŌ	相	530	somaru	染	917	sugu	直	349
SŌ	倉	531	somuku	背	957	sugureru	優	984
SŌ	想	532	SON	村	52	SUI	水	40
SŌ	総	738	SON	孫	538	SUI	垂	907
SŌ	宗	889	SON	損	745	SUI	推	908
SŌ	奏	918	SON	存	926	SUI	吹	1452
SŌ	窓	919	SON	尊	927	SUI	炊	1453
SŌ	創	920	sonaeru	具	265	SUI	帥	1454
SŌ	層	921	sonaeru	備	774	SUI	粋	1455
SŌ	操	922	sonaeru	供	839	SUI	衰	1456
SŌ	双	1513	sono	園	234	SUI	酔	1457
SŌ	壮	1514	sora	空	15	SUI	遂	1458
SŌ	荘	1515	soreru	逸	1010	SUI	睡	1459
SŌ	捜	1516	sōrō	候	478	SUI	穂	1460
SŌ	挿	1517	soru	反	371	SUI	錘	1461
SŌ	桑	1518	sosogu	注	344	suji	筋	843
SŌ	掃	1519	sosonokasu	唆	1284	sukoshi	少	143
SŌ	曹	1520	sosoru	唆	1284	sukoyaka	健	474
SŌ	巣	1521	soto	外	91	suku	好	859
SŌ	喪	1522	SOTSU	卒	537	suku	透	1647
SŌ	葬	1523	SOTSU	率	803	sukunai	少	143
SŌ	装	1524	sou	沿	815	sukuu	救	456
SŌ	僧	1525	sou	添	1631	sumi	炭	341
SŌ	遭	1526	sozoro	漫	1838	sumi	隅	1187
SŌ	槽	1527	SU	子	25	sumi	墨	1821
SŌ	燥	1528	SU	数	151	sumiyaka	速	534
SŌ	霜	1529	SU	守	300	sumu	住	310
SŌ	騒	1530	su	州	304	sumu	済	871
SŌ	藻	1531	SU	素	737	sumu	澄	1597
SŌ	贈	1533	su	酢	1300	SUN	寸	909

suna	砂	869	TAI	待	337	tamawaru	賜	1324
sunawachi	即	1534	TAI	代	338	tame	為	1003
suppai	酸	689	TAI	帯	539	tameru	矯	1170
suppai	酢	1300	TAI	隊	540	tamesu	試	499
suru	刷	487	TAI	退	746	tami	民	590
suru	為	1003	TAI	貸	747	tamotsu	保	787
suru	擦	1306	TAI	態	748	TAN	炭	341
suru	摩	1830	TAI	耐	1542	TAN	短	342
surudoi	鋭	1018	TAI	怠	1543	TAN	反	371
susumeru	勧	828	TAI	胎	1544	TAN	単	542
susumeru	薦	1499	TAI	泰	1545	TAN	担	929
susumu	進	326	TAI	袋	1546	TAN	探	930
sutaru	廃	1687	TAI	逮	1547	TAN	堪	1104
suteru	捨	883	TAI	替	1548	TAN	但	1559
suteru	棄	1131	TAI	滞	1549	TAN	丹	1563
suu	吸	837	taira	平	388	TAN	胆	1564
suwaru	座	870	taka	高	119	TAN	淡	1565
suzu	鈴	1921	takai	高	119	TAN	嘆	1566
suzushii	涼	1906	takara	宝	971	TAN	端	1567
ta	田	59	take	竹	170	TAN	誕	1568
TA	多	163	take	岳	1082	TAN	鍛	1569
TA	太	164	take	丈	1415	TAN	壇	1571
TA	他	334	taki	滝	1550	tana	店	178
taba	束	1535	takigi	薪	1445	tana	棚	1562
tabaneru	束	1535	TAKU	度	356	tanagokoro	掌	1402
taberu	食	146	TAKU	宅	928	tane	種	503
tabi	度	356	taku	炊	1453	tani	谷	122
tabi	旅	410	TAKU	択	1551	tanomu	頼	1889
-tachi	達	541	TAKU	沢	1552	tanoshii	楽	218
tada	唯	1864	TAKU	卓	1553	taoreru	倒	1643
tadachi	直	349	TAKU	拓	1554	tareru	垂	907
tadashi	但	1559	TAKU	託	1555	tariru	足	51
tadashii	正	41	TAKU	濯	1556	tashika	確	634
tadayou	漂	1739	takumi	巧	1242	tasukeru	助	314
taeru	絶	733	takuwaeru	貯	546	tatakau	戦	526
taeru	堪	1104	takuwaeru	蓄	1579	tatakau	闘	1659
taeru	耐	1542	tama	玉	102	tatami	畳	1419
tagai	互	1236	tama	球	257	tatamu	畳	1419
tagayasu	耕	673	tama	魂	1280	tate	縦	892
TAI	大	53	tama	弾	1570	tate	盾	1375
TAI	太	164	tama	霊	1923	tatematsuru	奉	1793
TAI	体	165	tamago	卵	990	tateru	建	473
TAI	台	166	tamashii	魂	1280	tatoeru	例	605
TAI	対	336	tamau	給	457	tatsu	立	73

GENERAL PRINCIPLES OF STROKE ORDER

1. Top to bottom.

three 一 二 三

word 、 二 二 言 言

guest 宀 宏 客

2. Left to right.

province 、 丿 丬 州 州 州

faction 氵 汀 沠 派

example 亻 佀 佡 例

3. Horizontal strokes usually precede vertical strokes when crossing.

ten 一 十

earth 一 十 土

till 三 丰 未 耒 耕

4. However, in a few cases vertical strokes precede horizontal ones.

king 一 丁 干 王

field 冂 冂 田 田

bend 冂 曲 曲 曲

5. Center usually precedes left and right where latter do not exceed two strokes each.

small 亅 小 小

water 亅 水 水 水

receive 了 丞 承 承 承

Note that the two exceptions are the heart radical 忄 (忄 忄) and fire 火 (火 火).